Journalists and Ele...

The Chronology

Peter Jennings, ABC World News Tonight:
"THE CHRONOLOGY IS AN EXTREMELY VALU-ABLE WORK and will be immensely useful during the televised Congressional hearings on the Iran-Contra affair."

Bill Plante, White House correspondent, CBS News:
"THE ULTIMATE VIEWER'S GUIDE TO THE TELE-VISED CONGRESSIONAL HEARINGS, the Archive's chronology is an extraordinary research tool. Even an expert needs a guide through the maze, and this is it."

Stephen Engelberg, *New York Times*:
"ESSENTIAL READING.... If we're ever going to find out the truth about the Iran-Contra scandal, it will be from the sort of work the National Security Archive has put into this chronology."

Rep. Norman Y. Mineta, D-California,
Deputy Democratic Whip:
"THE NATIONAL SECURITY ARCHIVE HAS DONE A GREAT PUBLIC SERVICE. I wish I had had this chronology when I sat on the House Intelligence Committee. This is an invaluable document with information that cannot be gotten anywhere else."

***In These Times* (Chicago):**
"A much more ambitious report [than the Tower Commission Report], whose implications are much more far-reaching.... provides a never-before-seen picture of the evolution of the Iran-Contra scandal."

Please turn this page for important information on the National Security Archive.

THE NATIONAL

. . . is a nonprofit, nonpartisan research institute and library founded in 1985. It is designed to serve scholars, journalists, Congress, present and former policy makers, public interest organizations and the American public by making available the internal government documentation that is indispensable for research and informed public debate on important issues of foreign, intelligence, defense, and international economic policy.

Located at 1755 Massachusetts Avenue NW, Washington, DC 20036, the National Security Archive is operated as a division of The Fund for Peace, Inc. The Fund for Peace is a New York-based nonprofit corporation which is exempt from tax under section 501(c)(3) of the Internal Revenue Code. As an operating division of The Fund for Peace, the Archive may receive tax deductible contributions made to The Fund for Peace/National Security Archive.

Major funding for the Archive has been provided by the Ford Foundation, the John D. and Catherine T. MacArthur Foundation, the Carnegie Corporation, and The W. Alton Jones Foundation.

*   *   *   *   *   *   *   *   *   *

SCOTT ARMSTRONG, the Executive Director of the National Security Archive, is a former investigative reporter at the *Washington Post*, where he won journalism awards for his reporting on the Saudi AWACS sale, the Southwest Asia air defense system, and Korean influence peddling in the United States. He co-authored, with Bob Woodward, the bestselling book on the Supreme Court, *The Brethren* (1979); as-

SECURITY ARCHIVE

sisted Woodward and Carl Bernstein in the research and writing of *The Final Days* (1976); and served as a senior investigator for the Senate Watergate Committee. MALCOLM BYRNE, Information Analyst for the National Security Archive, is a former Assistant Editor/News Systems at the *Washington Post*, and a researcher for the *Post* Foreign Policy Project. He is a graduate of Tufts University and the Johns Hopkins School of Advanced International Studies. TOM BLANTON, Director of Planning and Research at the National Security Archive, is a former journalist, congressional aide, political campaign consultant and foundation staff member, whose articles have been published in *The New York Times*, *Atlanta Journal-Constitution* and other publications. He is a graduate of Harvard University, where he was an editor of *The Harvard Crimson* and won the Newcomer Prize in Material History.

"The National Security Archive will help journalists, scholars, public-interest groups, even policymakers themselves, find national-security and foreign-policy information that has never been compiled in usable form before. A 'Nexis' of national security. A state-of-the-art index to history."

—*Washington Journalism Review*

"Others in the intelligence community are unconcerned about any security threat posed by the archive. 'I can't do anything but applaud this project,' said former CIA director Richard Helms. 'Anything that can be done to educate people, all the better.'"

—*USA Today*

Scott Armstrong, Executive Director
Malcolm Byrne, Editor
Tom Blanton, Director of Planning and Research

Principal Editors

**Laurence Chang
Peter Kornbluh
Laura M. Markowitz
Joseph Menn
Jeff Nason
Craig Nelson**

Editors

Nicole Ball, Carolyn Bausch, Eddie Becker, Margie
Bernard, Phyllis Britt, Janet DiVincenzo, Mary Ellen
Fleck, Barry X. Freckmann, Steve Galster, Judith Henchy,
Eric Hooglund, Margaret Johnson, Kevin G. Kenety,
Paola Martino, Virginia McGee, Kenneth Mokoena, Steve
Paschke, Chris Wallace, Thomas Walsh, Bobby Williams

Contributors

Glenn Baker, William A. Davis, Jr., Sonia Jarvis, Donna
Rich, Quinlan Shea, Jr., David Sobel, Paul Wolfe

Computer Consultant

Carl Chatzky

The Chronology

The Documented Day-by-Day Account of the Secret Military Assistance to Iran and the Contras

The National Security Archive
Scott Armstrong, Executive Director
Malcolm Byrne, Editor
Tom Blanton, Director of Planning and Research
FOREWORD BY SEYMOUR HERSH

WARNER BOOKS

A Warner Communications Company

WARNER BOOKS EDITION

Photo credits: p. 1 – top: Bill Fitzpatrick—White House, bottom: Larry
Downing—Newsweek; p. 2 – top: Linda Creighton—USN&WR, bottom:
Wide World Photos; p. 3 – Thomas Sutherland—UPI/Bettmann, all others
—Wide World Photos; p. 4 – all—Wide World Photos; p. 5 – all—Wide
World Photos; p. 6 – all—Wide World Photos; p. 7 – Singlaub: Gary
Kieffer—USN&WR, Abrams: Wide World Photos, Bermudez: Reuters/
Bettmann; p. 8 – Walsh: Wide World Photos, Hamilton: Wide World
Photos, Rudman, Liman, Inouye: Linda Creighton—USN&WR, Scow-
croft, Tower, Muskie: Darryl Heikes—USN&WR.

Warner Books, Inc.
666 Fifth Avenue
New York, N.Y. 10103

 A Warner Communications Company

Printed in the United States of America

First Printing: June, 1987

10 9 8 7 6 5 4 3 2 1

Foreword

The Iran-contra affair has correctly been viewed by most Americans as a serious foreign policy gaffe, but it is more than that—it is a symptom of a government gone amok. We do a disservice to that truth by dealing with Iran-contra merely as a scandal to be resolved by traditional law-and-order methods—with an investigation and purging of the wrong-doers. That seemingly rational approach can only serve to limit the scope and significance of Iran-contra. One of the major issues that emerged this winter and spring was whether the President would be willing to admit he had "made a mistake" in authorizing his subordinates on the National Security Council staff to attempt to trade arms for hostages through Iran. Ronald Reagan's reluctance to admit a mistake was seen as another sign of a faltering President's inability to cope with a policy blunder.

This essential chronology suggests another, much more direct, reason for the President's refusal to assume blame in Iran-contra: it was just another day at the office. The evidence assembled by the National Security Archive staff tells us that secret policies and manipulation of the press, Congress and the public were not unique to Iran-contra, but systematic and endemic to the Reagan administration. This book, read carefully, shows that the Reagan manipulation began early in 1981 and remained in place. By 1985, when the White House activated its arms-for-hostage dealings with Iran, the national-security bureaucracy across the government had become involved—and corrupted—to a degree that will have to await the pending Congressional and Special Prosecutor investigations.

The Chronology tells us what happened, but not why. Its dry recital of events implicitly poses some questions that must be answered by the official investigators. Congress is shown in these pages to have had many opportunities to learn a great deal, if it had chosen, about the machinations of the White House. Why was it so slow to learn and act? How valuable are intelligence oversight committees whose function seems to be little more than to help the Administration provide a smokescreen for its real policies? Similarly, why didn't the press do more to penetrate government secrecy? Many reporters wrote first-rate stories, cited herein, about the wrong-doings, but the big picture never emerged.

Many basic facts of this government's arrogance, illegalities and abuse of power in Central America, Iran and elsewhere were repeatedly in print and in Congressional hearings and reports, but somehow there was a failure to add up the evidence. The personal popularity of the President obviously was a factor in this phenomenon but we need a more complete answer. This chronology suggests, as have other authorities in past years, that we have tilted much too far in favor of the Presidency. We have created our own Presidential nightmare: an Executive with two divine rights: the right to send our young to kill and be killed in the name of America without any recourse to Constitutionally required Congressional oversight, and the corollary right to lie to us about what has been done. In mid-1987, Congress once again has a chance, as it did in the unfulfilled hearings into illegal CIA activities in the mid-1970s, to fully investigate what has happened and try to ensure that the Executive will never have the authority to abuse power so blatantly again.

The Chronology should be a reference point for our new investigation, as well as the most thorough compendium to date of what has gone wrong. Read it and weep.

Seymour M. Hersh

Preface

In assembling and organizing material on any subject, whether contemporary or historical, the National Security Archive customarily prepares a detailed chronology of significant events and available documents. In the case of the Iran-contra affair, however, the Archive's efforts became more elaborate than usual when, in the summer of 1986, the Archive was asked by several congressional offices to assist in gathering and analyzing information regarding irregularities in the funding and arming of the contras. The resulting data base continued to grow steadily until November 1986. During November, a case study of an administration's violations of statutory authority in the conduct of a secret war in Central America suddenly blossomed into a full-scale examination of the propriety of covert programs around the globe —Iran, Israel, Lebanon, Libya, Afghanistan, Angola, South Africa.

As Senate and House committees made increasingly more regular demands for information, the Archive also began assisting the Office of the Independent Counsel to gather and organize the public record. It was out of the effort to serve all investigations on an ongoing basis that the current version of "the Chron" emerged. What provided a battle plan to government investigators soon became a road map for journalists. Each resulting investigative and journalistic addition and clarification has provided yet another detail for *The Chronology.*

This chronology is but a first step toward understanding the relationship between operating a war "off the books" in one hemisphere and secretly selling arms to an officially designated terrorist state in the other. *The Chronology* allows each new revelation of the forthcoming televised congressional hearings to be fit into the elaborately interwoven context of these previously hidden events.

It should be obvious that this book is only in small part the work of the three "authors" listed on the cover. Only the diligent efforts of every member of the Archive staff brought forth this volume, some by giving eighteen hours a day for weeks to the project, others by picking up the slack which the rest of us left unattended.

In the beginning, when the Archive was but a possibility, and later, when the need for special funds for this project arose, it was the generous fiscal and moral support of Phil Stern, the Arca Foundation, the Field Foundation, the J. Roderick MacArthur Foundation, and Congressman Jim Moody (D-Wi) that carried us forward. At a particularly difficult moment, Margery Tabankin, Mike Farrell, Shelley Fabares, Ed and Nancy Asner, Jackson Browne, David Clennon, Frederick W. Field, Jack X. Fields, Robert Foxworth, Herbert Horvitz, Stanley Sheinbaum, Wade Greene, the Libre Fund, and the Ottinger Foundation combined to keep this project on track. Cox Newspapers, the Deer Creek Foundation, the Field Foundation, the Norman Foundation, Pro Bono Publico Foundation, Time Inc. and G. Henry M. Schuler also provided crucial funds.

The boards and officers of both our parent, The Fund for Peace, and the Archive have been supportive from the beginning, particularly the generous donations of time by John Shattuck, Phil Brenner, Mort Halperin, Ed James, Joe Onek, Steve Paschke, and Walt Slocombe. Ashbel Green, friend and editor, graciously referred this project to an amiable competitor, Larry Kirshbaum, the president of Warner Books. Larry's enthusiasm and the cheerful willingness of Bob Miller and his colleagues at Warner to shorten the production gestation from nine months to a week took this book from concept to reality.

Most of all, we could not have done this without the enthusiastic support of hundreds of journalists, congressional investigators, government bureaucrats, federal prosecutors, public interest researchers, and Freedom of Information Act professionals. We remain in awe of the quality of effort put forth by the Senate Intelligence Committee staff and the staff of the Tower Commission in making public such thoroughly documented research. Our very special thanks are due to Seymour Hersh, who took time from his own work to introduce this book to the public.

Scott Armstrong—April 3, 1987

Cast of Characters

Abrams, Elliott—Assistant Secretary of State for Inter-American Affairs. Previously served as Assistant Secretary of State for Human Rights and Humanitarian Affairs. Coordinated inter-agency support for the contras. Worked closely with Lt. Col. Oliver North on the contra aid program, helping to solicit funds from third countries, including Brunei.

Abshire, David—Former Ambassador to NATO. Between December 1986 and April 1987, coordinated all White House activities related to the Iran-contra affair.

Allen, Charles—CIA National Intelligence Officer and head of the Agency's Hostage Rescue Locating Force, which was established in late 1985. Assigned by Lt. Col. North to acquire data on arms shipments to Iran.

Anderson, Terry—Chief Middle East correspondent for the Associated Press. Kidnapped on March 16, 1985, in Beirut.

Barnes, Michael—Former U.S. Representative from Maryland and chairman of the House Foreign Affairs Subcommittee on Inter-American Affairs. A leading critic of U.S. foreign policy towards Central America. Defeated in Maryland's Democratic senatorial primary in 1986.

Bermudez, Enrique—Military commander of the Nicaraguan Democratic Force (FDN), the U.S.-supported, anti-Sandinista army in Honduras. Former colonel in Anastasio Somoza's National Guard.

Boland, Edward—U.S. Representative from Massachusetts. Former chairman of the House Select Committee on Intelligence. In December 1982, sponsored an amendment, which bears his name, banning any CIA support for groups to overthrow the government of Nicaragua.

Brenneke, Richard—Oregon businessman and a freelance consultant for French and Israeli intelligence. Worked for the CIA for 13 years. In late 1985, wrote letters to several U.S. officials, including Vice President George Bush, describing the Demavand project, a large-scale private effort to sell arms to Iran.

Buckley, William—CIA station chief in Beirut, Lebanon. He was kidnapped March 16, 1984, and died in captivity in June, 1985.

Calero, Adolfo—Political director of the Nicaraguan Democratic Force (FDN), the largest contra force. On February 16, 1987, he resigned from the three-man directorate of the United Nicaraguan Opposition (UNO), an anti-Sandinista coalition organized in June 1985 at the behest of the Reagan administration.

Carlucci, Frank—President Reagan's National Security Adviser. Named on December 2, 1986, to succeed Vice Admiral John Poindexter. Former Deputy Defense Secretary and head of Sears World Trade, where he managed a defense consulting group called International Planning and Analysis Center (IPAC).

Casey, William—Former CIA Director. Resigned February 2, 1987, after entering Washington's Georgetown University Hospital for treatment of cancer on December 15, 1986. Campaign chairman for Reagan in 1980. During World War II, served with William "Wild Bill" Donovan in the London headquarters of the Office of Strategic Services (OSS), the CIA's forerunner.

Castillo, Tomas—Pseudonym for the CIA station chief in Costa Rica. Reportedly recalled to Washington for assisting the contra supply network. Said to have relayed messages between the contra groups in Costa Rica and the private air force operated by Richard Secord.

Cave, George—(a.k.a. *Sam O'neil*) CIA consultant and former official at the Agency. Started as an interpreter for secret talks with the Iranians but "became a player," according to CIA Deputy Director Clair George.

Chamorro, Edgar—Former public relations official and member of the directorate of the main contra group, the Nicaraguan Democratic Force (FDN). The CIA paid him $2,000 a month plus expenses.

Channell, Carl R. "Spitz"—Conservative activist and fundraiser. Founder of the National Endowment for the Preservation of Liberty (NEPL). Publicly lauded for his efforts on behalf of the contras by President Reagan and other administration officials. Worked closely with Lt. Col. North to raise funds for the contras and to plan and coordinate pro-contra activities. Operates a number of organizations which financed lobbying for contra aid in 1986; which paid for television commercials supporting Republican senatorial candidate and former White House aide, Linda Chavez; which ran a media campaign in Nevada in the fall of 1986 attacking a Democratic Party candidate for Senate. According to one fundraiser, some of the money raised by Channell, ostensibly for humanitarian assistance to the contras, went to provide arms for the contras.

Clarridge, Duane "Dewey Maroni"—Head of the CIA's Counterterrorism Center. Former head of covert operations for the CIA's European Division, where he was involved in the Iran arms deals and is suspected by congressional investigators of diverting weapons intended for the Afghan guerrillas to the contras. After assignments in Nepal, India, Turkey and Italy, then-CIA Director William Casey made him chief of covert operations for the Latin American Division in August 1981.

Clines, Thomas—Former CIA official in Miami and Laos. Has ties to Richard Secord and convicted arms dealer Edwin Wilson. Allegedly dispatched by Lt. Col. North for secret missions in the Middle East and Central America. As principal in Egyptian American Transport and Services Corporation (EATSCO), pled guilty on July 22, 1983, to overbillings of $8 million and agreed to pay fines totaling $110,000.

Corr, Edwin—U.S. Ambassador to El Salvador. Monitored the covert contra resupply missions, which operated out of Ilopango Air Base in San Salvador.

Corvo, Rene—Cuban exile leader. Raised money and recruited mercenaries to fight with the contras.

Coy, Craig—Lt. Col. North's aide at the NSC.

Cruz, Arturo—Former Nicaraguan Ambassador to Washington. Resigned on March 10, 1987, from the directorate of the United Nicaraguan Opposition (UNO). Paid $7,000 per month by Lt. Col. North between January and November 1986.

Daniels, Mitchell—White House political director. Member of the White House Public Diplomacy Group on Nicaragua. Resigned in January 1987 after he publicly called for Donald Regan's resignation, which eventually occurred.

Deaver, Michael—Former Deputy White House Chief of Staff, later indicted for perjury relating to his lobbying activities.

Dodd, Christopher—Democratic Senator from Connecticut and a leading congressional critic of the Reagan administration's Central America policy.

Doty, Raymond—Former CIA field supervisor for the contras in Honduras. In 1984, involved in the preparation of a psychological warfare manual for the contras, which called for "neutralizing" civilian leaders associated with the Sandinista government.

Duemling, Robert—Head of the State Department's Nicaraguan Humanitarian Assistance Office (NHAO), established in October 1984 to disburse $27 million in "non-lethal" aid to the contras.

Dutton, Robert—Retired Air Force Colonel and Richard Secord's business associate. In April 1986, took over supervision of the contra resupply operation from another retired Air Force officer, Richard Gadd, and ran it out of the Virginia offices of Stanford Technology Training Group International, the company partly owned by Secord. Also, traveled with Secord to Beirut, apparently at Lt. Col. North's request, where they debriefed hostage David Jacobsen immediately after his captors released him on November 2, 1986.

Earl, Robert—Lt. Col. North's aide at the NSC. Lieutenant Colonel in the Marine Corps.

Enders, Thomas—Former Assistant Secretary of State for Inter-American Affairs. He was replaced on May 23, 1983, a few days after he reportedly ordered a softening of a report by the CIA and the Pentagon on left-wing insurgencies in Central America, angering then-CIA director William Casey and others in the administration.

Evans, Samuel—Former lawyer for Saudi arms dealer and billionaire Adnan Khashoggi. Represented Israeli weapons dealers Guri and Israel Eisenberg of BIT Company Ltd. in secret negotiations to sell arms to Iran. In April 1986, indicted in New York along with 17 others on charges of conspiring to ship $2 billion worth of aircraft, missiles and other materiel to Iran.

Fahd bin Abd al-Aziz—King of Saudi Arabia. In February 1984, aboard a yacht off the coast of the French Riviera, CIA Director Casey reportedly asked him to provide covert funds for the contras and the rebels fighting in Angola. Subsequently, between July 1984 and March 1985 over $31 million is deposited in Cayman Islands bank accounts that belong to the contras.

Feldman, Tony (a.k.a. *Philip Mason*)—Both are pseudonyms for a CIA agent who led efforts in 1982 to create a civilian directorate for the Nicaraguan Democratic Force (FDN).

Ferch, John—Former U.S. Ambassador to Honduras. Fired by President Reagan on June 27, 1986, for his strained relations with the CIA and the contras.

Fiers, Alan—Director of the CIA's Central American Task Force since September 1984. Previously posted in Pakistan and Saudi Arabia.

Fischer, David—Former top personal aide to President Reagan. In early 1986, left the White House to work for International Business Communications (IBC), where he helped raise funds for the contras. Carl Channell's National Endowment for the Preservation of Liberty (NEPL) paid his retainer.

Fortier, Donald—The late Deputy National Security Adviser for Political-Military Affairs. Aide to National Security Adviser Robert McFarlane and his successor, John Poindexter. Lt. Col. North was his assistant. One of the architects of the administration's secret initiative toward Iran.

Fuller, Graham—CIA National Intelligence Officer for the Middle East and South Asia. In early 1985, advocated overtures to "moderates" inside Iran to prevent the possibility of serious Soviet inroads following the death of the Ayatollah Khomeini.

Furmark, Roy—A New York energy consultant. Former legal client and long-time friend of former CIA director William Casey. Acquaintance of Manuchehr Ghorbanifar. In early 1985 introduced Samuel Evans, formerly Adnan Khashoggi's lawyer, who is later indicted for conspiring to sell arms to Iran, to Cyrus Hashemi, who is an informant for the U.S. Customs Service on the case. Told Casey on October 7,

1986, that Toronto businessmen Donald Fraser and Ernest Miller were threatening to take legal action to recoup losses they have incurred in their dealings with Saudi billionaire Adnan Khashoggi, which may expose the entire secret operation with Iran.

Gadd, Richard—Retired Air Force Lieutenant Colonel and a close associate of another retired Air Force officer, Richard Secord. Started several companies in 1983 that, reportedly thanks to connections with Secord, won lucrative military contracts, many of which involved support for classified military operations. Specialized in chartering commercial aircraft for the Pentagon and the CIA in a way that cannot be traced back to the U.S. government. In January 1986, he took over direction of the contra resupply operation.

Garwood, Ellen—Leading benefactor of Carl Channell's National Endowment for the Preservation of Liberty (NEPL), contributing over $2.5 million to the organization up through October 1986.

Gates, Robert—Deputy Director of the CIA. On March 2, 1987, President Reagan withdrew Gates's nomination to succeed William Casey as CIA Director.

George, Clair—Deputy Director and Chief of Operations at the CIA. Contacted frequently by Lt. Col. North regarding covert contra aid program and efforts to free hostages in Iran, according to high administration officials.

Ghorbanifar, Manuchehr—Iranian arms dealer who served as a middleman in the U.S. arms deal with Iran in 1985 and 1986. Allegedly a former officer in SAVAK, the Shah's secret police. The CIA and intelligence agencies in Europe considered him prone to exaggeration and unreliable. Nevertheless, CIA Director Casey and the White House chose to continue using him as a channel to the Iranian government.

Gomez, Frank—Former State Department and United States Information Agency (USIA) press aide. As a partner in International Business Communications (IBC), became the public relations representative for the contras as well as a conduit for private and public aid to them.

Green, Tom—Attorney for Richard Secord and Oliver North. Told Assistant Attorney General Charles Cooper on

November 24, 1986, that in proposing the use of Iran arms proceeds for the contras, Secord and Albert Hakim "felt like they were doing the Lord's work."

Gregg, Donald—Vice President George Bush's national security adviser and former CIA official. Informed about the contra aid program by both Lt. Col. North and Felix Rodriguez, a former CIA agent who served with Gregg in Vietnam.

Hakim, Albert—Iranian expatriate and Richard Secord's business partner. Together they directed the clandestine contra resupply effort under the auspices of their company, Stanford Technology Trading Group International.

Hall, Fawn—Lt. Col. North's secretary, who allegedly helped him destroy and alter documents.

Hasenfus, Eugene—Hired in April 1986 to work as a cargo handler for covert resupply flights into Nicaragua from Ilopango Air Base in El Salvador. On October 5, 1986, his plane is shot down over southern Nicaragua and he is the sole survivor. After being tried, convicted, and sentenced to 30 years in prison, he is pardoned by President Daniel Ortega and released.

Hashemi, Cyrus—Iranian arms dealer. Informant for a U.S. Customs "sting" operation that leads to the April 1986 indictment of 18 defendants on charges of conspiring to ship $2 billion worth of aircraft, missiles and other materiel to Iran. Among them are Samuel Evans, former lawyer for Adnan Khashoggi, and Avraham Bar-Am, a retired Israeli general. In July 1986, Hashemi was found dead in New York.

Hull, John—Alleged CIA contract agent living in northern Costa Rica. His ranch, situated near the Nicaraguan border, has been used as a staging area for contra operations.

Jacobsen, David—Director of the American University Hospital in Beirut. Kidnapped on May 28, 1985, and released November 2, 1986.

Jenco, Lawrence—Roman Catholic priest and head of the Beirut office of Catholic Relief Services. Kidnapped on January 8, 1985, and released July 26, 1986.

Keel, Alton—Deputy National Security Adviser. Helped compile the Reagan administration's various chronologies of the Iran arms deals.

Kerry, John—Democratic Senator from Massachusetts and a leading congressional investigator of the contra scandal.

Khashoggi, Adnan—Saudi billionaire and arms dealer. Provided bridge financing for the sale of U.S. arms to Iran.

Kilburn, Peter—Librarian at the American University in Beirut. Kidnapped December 3, 1984, and reportedly murdered at the behest of Khaddafi in retaliation for the April 1986 U.S. bombing of Libya.

Kimche, David—Former Director General of Israel's Foreign Ministry. Got U.S. permission for arms deals with Iran as early as 1981.

Kimmitt, Robert—Former NSC Executive Secretary and General Counsel, now General Counsel at the Department of the Treasury.

Ledeen, Michael—Consultant on terrorism to the NSC. In late 1984, discussed a new Iran policy with Israeli officials and in April 1985, visited Israel with a request from President Reagan to Prime Minister Shimon Peres for help in obtaining the release of American hostages in the Middle East. Close friend of Ghorbanifar.

Martin, Ronald—President of R.M. Equipment Inc., one of the major conduits of arms to the contras.

McCoy, James—Former U.S. Military Attache in Managua, now a partner in R.M. Equipment Inc.

McLaughlin, Jane—Former fundraiser for organizations run by Carl "Spitz" Channell. Worked with Lt. Col. North to raise private funds for the contras.

McDaniel, Rodney—NSC Executive Secretary and former Navy Captain. Took notes at Vice Admiral John Poindexter's daily briefing of President Reagan.

McFarlane, Robert—President Reagan's National Security Adviser from October 17, 1983, until November 30, 1985. Initiated the review of U.S. policy towards Iran in early 1984 that led to the arms deals and supervised the early NSC efforts to support the contras. Even after departing the White

House, McFarlane continued to be involved in the Iran initiative; in May 1986 he led the unsuccessful secret mission to Tehran.

McMahon, John—Deputy Director of the CIA until he resigned March 4, 1986. After he learned that the CIA had helped Oliver North secure a plane and flight clearances for the November 1985 shipment of HAWK missiles to Iran without the legally required written authorization, or "finding," from the White House, he demanded one be drafted and signed by the President before any further CIA involvement in the operation. Allegedly to appease McMahon, a "finding" was drafted and sent to the White House, but it was never signed.

Meese, Edwin III—U.S. Attorney General. Conducted the initial probe of the National Security Council cover-up of the U.S. role in arms sales to Iran. At the request of then-National Security Adviser John Poindexter, he asked FBI Director William Webster on October 30, 1986, to delay an FBI probe into Southern Air Transport, which had been linked to the contra supply plane shot down over Nicaragua earlier that month.

Mousavi, Mir Hussein—Iranian Prime Minister. Led efforts to procure weapons for Iran, at war with neighboring Iraq. Arms dealer Manuchehr Ghorbanifar served as his intermediary with the West.

Miller, Richard—Former Reagan campaign aide and business partner, with Frank Gomez, in International Business Communications (IBC). Close associate of Carl "Spitz" Channell.

Nimrodi, Yaacov—Former Israeli Defense Attache in Tehran. Along with other Israeli arms dealers Adolph Schwimmer and Amiram Nir, proposed using weapons sales to obtain the release of U.S. hostages in Beirut and to open a dialogue with Iran.

Nir, Amiram—Beginning in September 1984, an adviser on counterterrorism to Israeli Prime Minister Shimon Peres. Reportedly suggested to North in January 1986 that the Iranians be overcharged for weapons shipped to them and the surplus funds be diverted to the contras. Told Vice President Bush in July 1986 that the U.S. and Israel were dealing with radicals in Iran, not moderates.

North, Oliver—(a.k.a. *William P. Goode, Mr. Green, Mr. White*) Lieutenant Colonel in the Marine Corps. Simultaneously managed the covert aid program for the contras and the secret initiatives toward Iran, including the diversion of funds to the rebels, from his post as Assistant Deputy Director for Political-Military Affairs at the NSC. Assisted outside fundraising efforts for the contras and oversaw a private network to supply lethal equipment to the contras.

Owen, Robert—Served as Lt. Col. North's liaison to the contras during the congressional ban on aid to the rebels. In January 1985 founded the Institute for Democracy, Education, and Assistance (IDEA) and the Council for Democracy, Education, and Assistance. In October 1985, IDEA received a $50,000 grant from the State Department's Nicaraguan Humanitarian Assistance Office (NHAO) to work with the Nicaraguan Opposition (UNO), the contra coalition. In March 1986, the Council registered as a lobbyist for contra aid.

Peres, Shimon—Israeli Foreign Minister and former Prime Minister who presided over the clandestine U.S.-Israeli arms deal with Iran. While he headed the government, Israel provided the operation with aircraft, contacts inside Iran, and a bureaucratic channel through which to funnel weapons to Iran without detection.

Perot, H. Ross—The Texas millionaire asked by Oliver North in May 1986 to put up $1–2 million in an attempt to ransom American hostages. The attempt failed and the hostage, Peter Kilburn, was eventually killed.

Poindexter, John—Navy Rear Admiral (demoted from the rank of Vice Admiral after he left the White House) and Robert McFarlane's successor as President Reagan's National Security Adviser.

Posada Carriles, Luis—(a.k.a. *Ramon Medina*) Cuban-American and former CIA agent-turned-mercenary. Worked with the contra resupply team, which operated secretly out of Ilopango Air Base and three safehouses in San Salvador. Accused of the bombing of an Air Cubana jet in 1976 that killed 73 persons.

Quintero, Rafael—Cuban-American who fought at the Bay of Pigs. Veteran of numerous covert missions under Thomas Clines at the CIA. Under the direction of Clines, Richard

Secord and Albert Hakim, helped coordinate the covert contra arms resupply effort out of El Salvador in 1986.

Rafsanjani, Hashemi—Speaker of the Iranian Parliament. In June 1985, persuaded Hezbollah, the Lebanese Shiite group, to release four hostages held aboard the hijacked TWA Flight 847. Encouraged by this development, U.S. officials struck a series of arms-for-hostages deals with Iran, believing Rafsanjani could broker the release of hostages held in Lebanon as well.

Regan, Donald—Former White House Chief of Staff. In November 1986, he characterized the arms deals with Iran as a "trade" for hostages, contradicting claims made by other administration officials. Amid widespread doubts about his ability to continue serving the President in the wake of the Iran-contra scandal, he resigned February 27, 1987, immediately after he was informed that President Reagan was replacing him with former Senator Howard Baker.

Revell, Oliver "Buck"—Executive Assistant Director of the FBI. His former associate, Oliver North, asked him in October 1986 to sidetrack the FBI's probe into Southern Air Transport's role in ferrying arms to the contras. FBI director William Webster later removed him from the Iran-contra investigation.

Robelo, Alfonso—Director of the United Nicaraguan Opposition (UNO), the contras' political coalition.

Rodriguez, Felix (a.k.a. *Max Gomez*)—Former CIA official. Visited Vice President George Bush's foreign policy adviser, former CIA official Donald Gregg, under whom he served in Vietnam. Worked for the Salvadoran air force at Ilopango Air Base, where he served as liaison with the private American crews involved in the contra resupply effort.

Sanchez, Nestor—Recently retired Deputy Assistant Secretary of Defense for Inter-American Affairs. John Singlaub's key contact. Reportedly planted a false story following the October 5, 1986, crash of the contra resupply plane in Nicaragua, saying that the aircraft was on a private mission that had nothing to do with official government activities.

Schwimmer, Adolph "Al"—In the dual role of arms dealer and special adviser to then-Israeli Prime Minister Shimon Peres, Schwimmer helped carry out the U.S.-Iran initiative. One version of events holds that Schwimmer, David

Kimche, Yaacov Nimrodi and Manuchehr Ghorbanifar first conceived the idea of an Iran weapons deal in a November 1984 meeting in Hamburg.

Secord, Richard (a.k.a. *Maj. Gen. Adams, Richard Copp*)—Retired Air Force Major General. As Deputy Assistant Secretary of Defense for the Near East and South Asia, led the Reagan administration's successful 1981 fight to win congressional approval for the $8.5 billion AWACS sale to Saudi Arabia. On that lobbying campaign, worked with Lt. Col. North, an NSC staff member. With Iranian expatriate Albert Hakim, was instrumental in the 1984–86 contra resupply effort, which they directed out of the northern Virginia offices of their company, Stanford Technology Trading Group International. The company maintained Swiss bank accounts, which have been tied to the diversion of Iran arms sales profits.

Shackley, Theodore—Ex-CIA officer and consultant for Stanford Technology. With U.S. officials, promoted Ghorbanifar as an effective channel to the Iranian government after being introduced to the Iranian arms dealer in November 1984 by General Manucher Hashemi, former head of SAVAK's counterespionage division.

Shultz, George—Secretary of State criticized by the Tower Commission for his passivity in acquiescing to a policy that he disagreed with. Also raised money overseas for the contras. Former Secretary of Labor and Secretary of the Treasury.

Singlaub, John—Retired Army Major General and chairman of the World Anti-Communist League (WACL) and its affiliate, the U.S. Council for World Freedom. Fired from his job as head of U.S. forces in South Korea after he publicly challenged former President Carter's proposal to withdraw troops from the country. With Oliver North's knowledge, Singlaub raised money worldwide for the contras. Along with Richard Secord and James McCoy, became one of the major conduits of arms to the contras, providing millions of dollars in arms while a congressional ban on such aid was in effect.

Sporkin, Stanley—General Counsel of the CIA during William Casey's tenure as director. Former enforcement chief at the Securities and Exchange Commission, which coincided with Casey's term as chairman. Now a Reagan appointee to Federal District Court of the District of Columbia.

Sutherland, Thomas—Dean of Agriculture at the American School in Beirut. Kidnapped June 10, 1985.

Tabatabai, Sadegh—Official in Iranian Prime Minister Hashemi Rafsanjani's office who negotiated portions of the Iran arms deals with Ghorbanifar, North, and Cave. An in-law of the Ayatollah Khomeini, he also opened the 1980 negotiations that ultimately led to the release of the American hostages held in Tehran.

Tambs, Lewis—U.S. Ambassador to Costa Rica from 1985 to 1987, during the period of extensive secret resupply operations to the contras. Previously served as Ambassador to Colombia. In 1980, as a professor at Arizona State University, edited the *Committee of Santa Fe* report which laid out a blueprint for President Reagan's aggressive policy in Latin America.

Tower, John—Headed President Reagan's special review board which concluded that the Iran-contra affair and the National Security Council's covert operations were an "aberration," a failure of people not process. Former Republican senator from Texas and Robert McFarlane's boss on the Senate Armed Services Committee from 1979–81.

Webster, William—Designated nominee to become William Casey's successor as CIA director. Currently Director of the Federal Bureau of Investigation. Asked by Attorney General Edwin Meese to stop an FBI probe of Southern Air Transport's involvement with contra gun running on grounds that Southern was involved with secret hostage recovery efforts. Then, allegedly agreed with Attorney General Meese that there were no criminal aspects to Meese's probe of the National Security Council cover-up of the role of U.S. arms sales to Iran.

Weinberger, Caspar—Secretary of Defense whom the Tower Commission accused of doing a "disservice" to the President for distancing himself from the Iran arms deal instead of fighting it.

Weir, Benjamin—Kidnapped May 8, 1984, in Beirut. Released on September 15, 1985, after Israel shipped 508 TOW missiles to Iran. President Reagan is not sure whether he approved the shipment.

Sources

The Chronology has been constructed from a wide variety of sources including the Report of the President's Special Review Board (the Tower Commission), the "Report on Preliminary Inquiry" of the Senate Select Committee on Intelligence, congressional documents and reports, documents obtained by the National Security Archive, and the various media organizations cited. In certain instances clearly conflicting accounts—unresolved by government investigators in the published reports—were included.

Material from reports of the Tower Commission and the Senate Select Committee on Intelligence appear in verbatim form with minor editing for clarity. Where lengthy sections of one report repeat details contained elsewhere in either report, an effort was made to strike the repetitive material. The Tower Commission and the preliminary Senate intelligence committee reports vary stylistically; these differences in spelling of names, capitalization and punctuation are reflected within the text.

The material (including documents) is presented in rough chronological order. Paragraphs referring to two separate dates may be repeated on both dates. Juxtaposition of paragraphs and cross-references among entries ("see also . . .") do not necessarily imply causal connection.

The reader should note that, unless otherwise stated, citations of court papers reflect allegations made in court proceedings and not proven facts as determined by the courts.

ABBREVIATIONS USED IN CITATIONS

AFP	-Agence France Presse
ANTEL	-Associacion Nacional Telefonico (El Salvador)
AP	-The Associated Press
BG	-The Boston Globe

CRS	-Congressional Research Service
CSM	-The Christian Science Monitor
DMN	-Dallas Morning News
DOD	-Department of Defense
DOT	-Department of Transportation
DPA	-West German Press Agency
FAA	-Federal Aviation Administration
FBIS	-Foreign Broadcast Information Service
FT	-Financial Times
HFAC	-House Foreign Affairs Committee
LAT	-Los Angeles Times
MEP	-Middle East Policy Survey
MH	-The Miami Herald
MN	-The Miami News
NYT	-The New York Times
PI	-The Philadelphia Inquirer
SFE	-San Francisco Examiner
SSIC	-Senate Select Committee on Intelligence (Entries are taken directly from the "Report on Preliminary Inquiry," January 29, 1987.)
UPI	-United Press International
VV	-The Village Voice
WP	-The Washington Post
WSJ	-The Wall Street Journal
WT	-The Washington Times

Dickey, Christopher, *With the Contras*—N.Y.: Simon and Schuster, 1985

Kornbluh, Peter, *Nicaragua: The Price of Intervention*—Washington, D.C.: IPS, 1987

Maas, Peter, *Manhunt*—N.Y.: Random House, 1986

Tower —The Tower Commission Report (Entries are taken directly from the "Report of the President's Special Review Board," February 26, 1987) Citations within the Tower Commission Report are indicated in parentheses. Where the citation is to a name, for example "(McFarlane (1) 6)," it means Robert C. McFarlane's first interview with the Commission at page 6 of the transcript. The same page in Mr. McFarlane's second interview would be designated by "(McFarlane (2) 6)."

The informing function of Congress should be preferred to its legislative function. The argument is not only that discussed and interrogated administration is the only sure and efficient administration, but more than that, that the only really self-governing people is that people which discusses and interrogates its administration.

—Woodrow Wilson,
Constitutional Government (1885)

As President, I have always operated on the belief that, given the facts, the American people will make the right decision. I believe that to be true now.

—President Reagan,
addressing the nation
on U.S. arms sales to Iran,
November 13, 1986

1980

JAN - Two foreign policy crises preoccupy the Carter Administration in 1980: the Embassy hostages seized on November 4, 1979 in Tehran and the Soviet invasion of Afghanistan on December 24, 1979. Planning has commenced both for a rescue mission to Tehran and for covert assistance to the Afghan rebels (see entries below).

JAN - CIA's first contact with [Manuchehr] Ghorbanifar was through a European intelligence service in January 1980. From the beginning, CIA found it "difficult to filter out the bravado and exaggeration from what actually happened." Other intelligence services had similar experiences with Mr. Ghorbanifar. (Tower)

MID-JAN - "In a highly secret move, we also assessed the possibility of arranging for Soviet-made weapons (which would appear to have come from the Afghan military forces) to be delivered to freedom fighters in Afghanistan and of giving them what encouragement we could to resist subjugation by the Soviet invaders," President Carter writes later. The CIA begins supplying weapons, mostly Soviet-made small arms, to the Afghan rebels across the Pakistani border. U.S. covert aid prior to the Soviet invasion had been limited to small amounts of medical supplies and communications equipment provided to the scattered rebel tribes. The rebels have been training in camps in Pakistan since the summer of

1

1978, and Saudi Arabia has provided financial aid since October 1979, despite persistent factional disputes and disunity among the rebels. (Jimmy Carter, Keeping Faith: Memoirs of a President, pp. 473, 475; WP 2/15/80; NYT 2/16/80; U.S. Embassy cable 07548 from Jidda to State Department 10/6/79)

MAR 23 - Major General Robert Schweitzer of the U.S. Army's strategy, plans and policy office has been sent to Honduras to confer with the Honduran Armed Forces about becoming a "bulwark" against communism in the region. (WP 3/23/80)

APR 25 - The Iran rescue mission aborts at Desert One as dust storms knock out three helicopters, another collides with a fuel tanker, and eight Americans die in the explosion. (Charlie A. Beckwith, Delta Force, pp. 244-260)

APR-OCT - Air Force Brigadier General Richard V. Secord serves as deputy commander of a second Iran hostage rescue mission planning team. He has previously served four tours of duty in Iran, most recently as the official in charge of all arms sales to the Iranian air force from 1975-1978. As part of the first rescue mission, Iranian expatriate businessman Albert Hakim, who knows Secord through his work representing American defense contractors in Iran, goes undercover to rent a garage in Tehran as a rendezvous point for the mission, which aborts in the desert before ever reaching Tehran. Hakim's employees over the years include former CIA agent Frank Terpil (subsequently Edwin P. Wilson's partner), and ex-CIA official Theodore Shackley. As business partners, after 1983, Hakim and Secord later become key players in the Iran-contra affair. (Official Air Force biography; WP 11/8/86; LAT 2/6/87; interviews; Maas, p.287)

MAY 20 - Retired Marine Lt. Col. Robert McFarlane, now a professional staff member of the Senate Armed Services Committee (reporting to ranking Republican member Sen. John Tower of Texas), interviews participants in the failed Iran rescue mission for the committee's inquiry. McFarlane had previously served as military assistant to Henry Kissinger and Brent Scowcroft at the National Security Council. Tower and Scowcroft later lead the Special Review Board investigation of the Iran-contra scandal. (Joint Chiefs of Staff memo 5/19/80; Congressional Staff Directory 1980)

JUL 20 - Two Afghan resistance emissaries to Cairo say that it "is no longer a secret [that] the Afghan revolution receives weapons and ammunition from Egypt." Massive U.S. military assistance to Egypt as a result of the Camp David agreements makes possible the passthrough to the Afghan rebels of Egypt's Soviet arsenal. (JPRS Near East/North Africa Report 10/8/80 p. 21; WP 12/26/80)

AUG - Lt. Col. Richard Gadd of the Air Force's special operations division in the Pentagon shares an office (4D111) with Col. Robert C. Dutton, assistant director of special plans for the Air Force. Dutton previously worked for Richard Secord in the Air Force military assistance mission in Iran. Gadd and Dutton later play key roles in the contra resupply operation set up by Oliver North and Richard Secord. (Pentagon phonebooks 8/80 & 12/81; WP 3/22/87)

SEP - By September of 1980, CIA decided to drop efforts at recruiting Ghorbanifar. It considered him neither reliable nor trustworthy. (Tower)

SEP 5 - The Special Coordinating Committee of the NSC meets to assess the policy implications of intelligence regarding a possible Soviet military intervention in Iran. (Zbigniew Brzezinski, Power and Principle, p. 451)

SEP 22 - Iraqi fighter-bombers attack Iranian airfields, marking the start of the Iran-Iraq War. The United States had adopted a policy of neutrality and refused to ship arms to either side. The result was a continuation of the arms embargo against Iran. (WP 10/23/80; NYT 10/24/80; Tower)

FALL - President Carter authorizes a CIA program to funnel approximately $1 million to anti-Sandinista labor, press and political organizations in Nicaragua. (LAT 3/3/85)

LATE 1980 - Reagan's campaign foreign policy adviser and, later, National Security Advisor, Richard V. Allen, is approached by Morris Amitay, an official with the American Israel Public Affairs Committee, who asks how the incoming Administration would view Israel's shipment to Iran of wheel and brake assemblies for F-4 fighter planes. Under U.S. law, Israel has agreed to secure prior U.S. authorization for all transfers of certain sensitive military equipment to any country and prior U.S. authorization for the transfer of any U.S. military materiel to Iran. (WP 11/29/86)

1981

- President Reagan entered office with a strong commitment to cabinet government. His principal advisors on national security affairs were to be the Secretaries of State and Defense, and to a lesser extent the Director of Central Intelligence. The position of the National Security Advisor was initially downgraded in both status and access to the President. Over the next six years, five different people held that position.

The Administration's first National Security Advisor, Richard Allen, reported to the President through the senior White House staff. Consequently, the NSC staff assumed a reduced role. Mr. Allen believed that the Secretary of State had primacy in the field of foreign policy. He viewed the job of the National Security Advisor as that of a policy coordinator.

President Reagan initially declared that the National Security Council would be the principal forum for consideration of national security issues. To support the work of the Council, President Reagan established an interagency committee system headed by three Senior Interagency Groups (or "SIGs"), one each for foreign policy, defense policy, and intelligence. They were chaired by the Secretary of State, the Secretary of Defense, and the Director of Central Intelligence, respectively.

Over time, the Administration's original conception of the role of the National Security Advisor changed. William Clark, who succeeded Richard Allen in 1982, was a longtime associate of the President and dealt directly with him. Robert McFarlane, who replaced Judge Clark in 1983, although personally less close to the President, continued to have direct access to him. The same was true for VADM John Poindexter, who was appointed to the position in December, 1985.

President Reagan appointed several additional members to his National Security Council and allowed staff attendance at meetings. The resulting size of the meetings led the President to turn increasingly to a smaller group (called the National Security Planning Group or "NSPG"). Attendance at its meetings was more restricted but included the statutory principals of the NSC. The NSPG was supported by the SIGs, and new SIGs were occasionally created to deal with particular issues. These were frequently chaired by the National Security Advisor. But generally the SIGs and many of their subsidiary groups (called Interagency Groups or "IGs") fell into disuse.

As a supplement to the normal NSC process, the Reagan Administration adopted comprehensive procedures for covert actions. These are contained in a classified document, NSDD-159, establishing the process for deciding, implementing, monitoring, and reviewing covert activities. (Tower)

- The Reagan Administration had adopted a tough line against terrorism. In particular, the United States adamantly opposed making any concessions to terrorists in exchange for the release of hostages—whether by paying ransom, releasing prisoners, changing policies, or otherwise. (Tower)

JAN - Sen. John Tower (R-TX) becomes chairman of the Senate Armed Services Committee, elevating Rhett Dawson (later director of the Tower Commission staff) to committee staff director, and Robert McFarlane to senior professional staff. Secretary of State Alexander Haig subsequently hires McFarlane as counselor to the State Department. (Congressional Directory 1981, p. 251)

JAN 19 - [M]any . . . restrictions [against Iran] were lifted, as part of the agreement that led to the release of the [U.S.] embassy staff. However, this did not extend to the embargo on arms transfers. (Tower)

JAN 20 - Ronald Reagan is inaugurated the 40th president of the United States. On the same day, the remaining U.S. hostages in Iran are released after 444 days in captivity. (WP 1/20/81, special edition)

JAN 21 - Reagan chairs the first meeting of the National Security Council, which focuses on Libya and Iran. Throughout the Reagan presidency, the Khaddafi and Khomeini regimes are reported to be subjects of urgent concern, even obsession, in the White House. (WP 2/20/87)

EARLY 1981 - The Pakistani government declares that henceforth it will recognize only the six Pakistan-based resistance organizations: the three parties in the Moderate coalition and three from the Fundamentalist coalition, to register Afghan refugees and operate schools in the refugee camps and, more importantly, to funnel arms and other material support to guerrilla groups inside Afghanistan. (Stockholm Dagens Nyheter 2/7/82 in JPRS Near East/North Africa Report 3/9/82)

- Secretary of State Alexander Haig gives permission to Israel to ship U.S.-made military spare parts for fighter planes to Iran, nearly four years before similar shipments set in motion the Iran-contra scandal. Haig's decision follows discussions between his counselor at the State Department, Robert C. McFarlane and David Kimche, the director general of Israel's foreign ministry. The first hint of the Israeli proposal for arms transfers came in late 1980 (see entry). (WP 11/29/86)

- Early in Ronald Reagan's first term, a small interagency group consisting of mid-level officials is created to manage the Administration's emerging Central America policy. Known variously as the Core Group, the Restricted Interdepartmental Group (RIG), and the Thursday Afternoon Club (although it never meets on Thursday afternoons), the group gathers on the sixth floor of the State Department as "often as necessary." The departments of State, Defense and Justice, as well as the CIA, NSC and Chairman of the Joint Chiefs of Staff are represented. The body is first headed by McFarlane, then by Thomas O. Enders, Assistant Secretary of State for Inter-American Affairs, and later by Enders's successor at State, Langhorne Motley. Other members will include National Security Council staff member Oliver L. North; Nestor D. Sanchez, the former CIA division chief for Latin America at the Directorate for Operations, then later Deputy Assistant Secretary of Defense for Inter-American Affairs (who later assists in the Iran arms shipments and in attempts to free hostages in Lebanon); and Duane "Dewey Maroni" Clarridge, Sanchez's successor at the CIA. Other officials also sit in on the meetings. (Dickey, p.102; NYT 1/15/87)

MAR - CIA Director William Casey presents proposals to the President calling for covert support of pro-U.S. forces in

Nicaragua, Afghanistan, Laos, Cambodia, Grenada, Iran, Libya and Cuba. (MH 6/5/83.)

- The September 15 Legion publishes the first volume of its "official magazine," *El Legionario*, which contains, among other essays, the writings of Sun Tzu on the "Art of War." (El Legionario 3/81)

MAR 9 - Reagan issues a formal presidential finding, authorizing the CIA to undertake "covert activities" directed against Nicaragua. More than $19 million is then allocated for the purpose. CIA Director William J. Casey brings "the Intelligence committees a presidential finding that secret operations in Central America [are] important to U.S. national security." The operation is only vaguely outlined as an effort to protect the Salvadoran government from the communist insurgency. (WP 5/8/83; Annex A, World Court Document)

MAR - Saudi Arabia has donated $15 million to the Afghan resistance. (Gulf News Agency in Bruce Amstutz, "Afghanistan: The First Five Years," p.202)

MAR 19 - Reagan formally asks Congress to repeal the 1976 "Clark Amendment," which prohibited U.S. military and paramilitary assistance to the rebels in Angola. The Administration's efforts fail in 1981 but succeed in 1985. (Reuters 3/20/81; CRS "Angola: Issues for the United States," 12/5/86)

MAY 7-20 - Deputy Assistant Secretary of Defense for Near Eastern, African, and South Asian Affairs Secord departs Andrews Air Force Base for a trip to the Middle East. He travels to Jordan, Saudi Arabia, Oman, Egypt and Israel, and returns to 8509 Cherry Valley Lane, Alexandria, VA. (DOD Travel Vouchers)

SUMMER - McFarlane prepares a report entitled "Taking the War to Nicaragua." The report, which is ordered by Haig, lists options for putting pressure on Managua and Havana. (LAT 3/3/85; Dickey, p.107)

JUL 18 - An Argentine CL-44 Turboprop cargo plane carrying military supplies from Tel Aviv to Tehran crashes in the Soviet Union after reportedly straying over the Soviet-Turkish border and being intercepted by Soviet jet fighters. The incident reveals an ongoing Israeli arrangement with the

Khomeini government to supply it with 360 tons of American-made tank spare parts and ammunition. According to Andreas Jenni, a Swiss arms dealer who is one of the principals in the deal, representatives of the Iranian regime and British middlemen working for an Israeli "cover" firm signed a $27.9 million contract in London this spring. Jenni says the deal called for twelve planeloads of supplies to be flown from Tel Aviv to Tehran via Larnaca, Cyprus. An official of the Cyprus Civil Aviation Department says later that in the months prior to the crash the Argentine plane made four stopovers there on trips between the two capitals. It is later revealed that Israel has been a consistent supplier of military equipment to Iran even after the U.S. Embassy take-over in Tehran in November 1979. Zbigniew Brzezinski, the National Security Advisor under Carter, would later write that the Administration in 1980 "learned, much to our dismay, that the Israelis had been secretly supplying American spare parts to the Iranians..." (WP 7/27/81; Brzezinski, Power and Principle, 1983, p.504)

AUG - Duane "Dewey Maroni" Clarridge becomes the CIA's division chief for Latin America at the Directorate for Operations, although he has no experience in the area. His predecessor, Nestor Sanchez, had moved to Deputy Assistant Secretary for International Security Affairs at the Pentagon, a key position in the military intelligence structure. Clarridge owes his swift rise to Casey, whom he impressed as "a real doer, a real take-charge guy" when the two met in Rome this summer at a gathering of West European station chiefs, according to Casey associates. Clarridge later assists in the shipment of arms to Iran and in abortive attempts to free hostages in Lebanon. (Dickey, pp.107-8)

AUG 6 - Max Vargas, a Nicaraguan exile in Miami, who is later identified by the Justice Department as a CIA operative, buys two AR-15 rifles at the Costa Gun Shop in Miami and sends them to contra leader Fernando "El Negro" Chamorro in Honduras. Raul Arana, Chamorro's agent in Miami, tells investigators later that he sent several large shipments of arms from Miami to Honduras in 1981 "which, if true, would violate the neutrality act." (WSJ 1/15/87)

SEP - In the first of many internal conflicts within the Nicaraguan contras over allegations of corruption, six mid-level officers of the 15th of September Legion (the core group of what later would become the Nicaraguan Democratic Force—FDN) ask for the ouster of former National Guard Col. Enrique Bermudez and his closest adviser, Col. Ricardo Lau, on grounds of "misuse of funds," "negligence of duty," "lying," and "lack of patriotic spirit." The specific charges were that Bermudez embezzled $50,000 of funds provided to the contras by the Argentines at the CIA's behest. Instead, the Argentines support their ally Bermudez and force out other Legion founders who had brought the charges. (15th of September Legion letter 9/81; interviews)

SEP 19-21 - Richard Secord flies from Andrews Air Force Base to Honolulu, returning two days later to his residence at 6502 Anna Maria Ct., McLean, VA. (DOD Travel Voucher)

SEP 28-OCT 1 - Secord travels to Jidda, Saudi Arabia. He is accompanying Assistant Secretary of State Richard Murphy on what is reported to be "almost a last-gasp effort" to overcome Saudi reluctance to compromise on the issue of control over the AWACS surveillance aircraft, which the Administration hopes to sell with congressional approval. Legislators are concerned that the Saudis not be granted too much independence in their use of the aircraft. Secord travels on to Dhahran, Saudi Arabia on October 1, returning home the following day. (DOD Travel Voucher; WP 9/30/81)

OCT - Three-day U.S./Honduran military exercises known as "Halcon Vista" begin. Their purpose is to practice maneuvers to "detect and intercept hostile coastal incursion." (SouthCom News 10/23/81)

OCT 28 - The $8.5 billion AWACS sale to Saudi Arabia is approved by the Senate in a 52-48 vote. Then-Major General Secord, Deputy Assistant Secretary of Defense for the Near East and South Asia, is point man for the Reagan Administration's successful campaign. During this effort, Secord works with several individuals later involved in the Iran-contra connection: Oliver North of the NSC, Robert H. Lilac (Air Force officer, 1982-83 NSC staffer with North, and in 1984 a business partner with Secord in selling a plane to the contras), and Paul Thompson (1981-83 in the Pentagon's legislative office, 1983-87 counsel to the NSC). It is reported in 1986 that Saudi money linked to the AWACS purchase is funding the contras and other U.S. covert operations in a "kickback" or "backchannel" operation involving the

NSC. (Hearst Newspapers 7/27/86; CBS News 7/14/86; official biographies; Pentagon phonebooks; FAA Aircraft Registry 11/21/84; WP 10/29/81)

NOV 16 - At a meeting of the NSC, the CIA presents Reagan with a 10-point program that includes political and paramilitary operations in Nicaragua. The proposal calls for the creation of a 500-man "action team" to "engage in paramilitary and political operations in Nicaragua." The CIA requested $19.95 million, although as the proposal made clear, "more funds and manpower will be needed." The proposal also stated that the CIA might "take unilateral paramilitary action—possibly using U.S. personnel—against special Cuban targets." (WP 3/10/82)

NOV 23 - Reagan issues National Security Decision Directive 17 (NSDD 17). The order authorizes $19,950,000 for the CIA to build a paramilitary force, to "work with foreign governments as appropriate" and to foster a broad opposition front against the Sandinistas. (WP 5/8/83)

NOV 30 - Weinberger and Israeli Defense Minister Ariel Sharon sign a memorandum of understanding (MOU) setting out a framework for continued bilateral consultation and cooperation in the name of the two countries' national security. The MOU cites threats emanating from the Soviet Union and Soviet-controlled forces. (CRS: "Israeli-American Relations," 12/22/86)

DEC 1 - Reagan issues his second presidential finding regarding Nicaragua, formally authorizing under the National Security Act the "covert activities" approved at the November 16 NSC meeting. The intelligence committees of both houses of Congress are informed of the finding, but are told only that the CIA will create a paramilitary force of 500 men and that this force will be used solely to interdict alleged arms traffic from Nicaragua to guerrillas in El Salvador and to strike at alleged Cuban military installations in Nicaragua. (WP 1/1/83; Annex A, World Court Document)

- In December, 1981, President Reagan signed a National Intelligence Finding establishing U.S. support for the Nicaraguan resistance forces. The policy of covert support for the Contras was controversial from the start—especially in Congress. (Tower)

- Erich von Marbod retires suddenly as head of the Defense Security Assistance Agency, the Pentagon's arms sales division (see Early 1982 entry). (Maas, p.247)

DEC 4 - Reagan signs Executive Order 12333, the main executive branch document establishing operating rules for intelligence agencies. According to the order, the CIA is in charge of covert operations unless the president orders otherwise. During the course of the Iran arms shipments in 1985-1986, Reagan fails to assign formal responsibility for the secret program to the NSC, according to Senate investigators, which places him in violation of the executive order. (WP 1/12/87)

DEC 18 - The State Department suspends the memorandum of understanding (MOU) between the U.S. and Israel (see November 30, 1981 entry) following Israel's de facto annexation of the Golan Heights on December 14. Two days after the U.S. announcement, Prime Minister Menachem Begin unilaterally cancels the MOU. A dialogue on strategic cooperation is revived in November 1983. (CRS: "Israeli-American Relations," 12/22/86)

DEC 22 - Hector Fabian, a Cuban exile leader in Miami, explains in an interview how Nicaraguan exile troops are being trained at a 79-acre training camp west of Miami. He says, "Under the Carter and Nixon administrations, what we were doing was a crime. With the Reagan administration, no one has bothered us for 10 months. Our goal is the liberation of Nicaragua . . . within 3 months the situation in Nicaragua will blow up." (NYT 12/23/81)

1982

- A series of intelligence studies [which were written in 1984 and 1985, and described Israeli interests in Iran] also reported Israeli shipments of non-U.S. arms to Iran as well as the use of Israeli middlemen as early as 1982 to arrange private deals involving U.S. arms. . . . McFarlane testified that he was never informed by CIA that Israel had been engaged in such activities during 1981-1985. In fact, McFarlane, prompted by news accounts of such activity on the part of Israel, asked the CIA—and the DCI specifically —several times whether the news reports were true. He was told they were not. McFarlane testified that if he had known that Israelis had previously shipped arms to Iran it would have made him less responsive to later Israeli proposals to resume shipments. However, in his first cable to Shultz in the matter he stated that it was obvious to him the Israeli channel into Iran had existed for some time. One of the NSC staffers who drafted the NSDD (See May 17, 1985) testified that he was aware of allegations that Israel was selling arms to Iran but discounted such reports because he believed they failed to offer conclusive evidence and because Prime Minister Peres had assured the U.S. that there was no such trade. (SSIC 1/29/87)

- A CIA psychological profile of Khaddafi written this year concludes the Libyan leader "suffer[s] from a severe personality disturbance—a 'borderline personality disorder' . . . under severe stress he is subject to episodes of bizarre behavior when his judgment may be faulty." Later intelligence estimates (see March 1985 entry) support the same conclusions, according to sources, and warn that the Administration's policy of confrontation against Khaddafi could provoke the very acts American officials hope to prevent, such as the dispatching of hit squads to the U.S. and Europe. (WP 2/2/86)

EARLY 1982 - The FBI investigates a number of alleged associates of former CIA agent Edwin P. Wilson, including then-Major General Secord, former CIA associate deputy operations director Theodore G. Shackley, former CIA Miami and Laos operative Thomas Clines, and Erich von Marbod, who had retired suddenly on December 1, 1981 as head of the Defense Security Assistance Agency (DSAA), the Pentagon's arms sales division. Maritime Administration auditors uncover massive overbillings by Egyptian American Transport and Services Corporation (EATSCO), a company set up by Clines and an influential Egyptian to collect enormous shipping commissions from the post-Camp David arms sales to Egypt. Secord and von Marbod oversaw these sales in their official capacities, and Wilson later alleges that EATSCO was a silent partnership made up of himself, Secord, von Marbod, and Shackley, with Clines as the public partner. Secord is suspended pending a polygraph test but is reinstated by then-Deputy Secretary of Defense Frank Carlucci, who overrides the Pentagon's general counsel in doing so. Secord retires in May 1983. Later, when Carlucci becomes head of Sears World Trade, he hires von Marbod as a consultant. (Maas, pp.140, 247, 279, 285, 288; WSJ 1/17/87)

JAN-SEP - Lt. Col. Richard Gadd serves as the Pentagon's liaison with the Joint Special Operations Command at Fort Bragg, N.C., and shares a secure office (2C840) with the Joint Chiefs of Staff Special Operations Division, headed by Army Col. C.L. Stearns. After Gadd retires and sets up a series of private companies to provide airplanes and other services for special operations, Stearns serves as a director of one of the companies following his own retirement. (Pentagon phonebook 8/82; WP 3/22/87)

FEB - CIA representatives reveal to the House and Senate intelligence committees that the 500-man contra paramilitary force has grown to 1,000. (WP 5/8/83)

FEB 3 & 5 - U.S. involvement with Argentina in the creation of paramilitary forces to infiltrate Nicaragua is disclosed. (ABC News 2/3/82; St. Louis Globe-Democrat 2/5/82)

LATE FEB - At the end of the month, State Department terrorism expert Michael Ledeen visits federal prosecutor Lawrence Barcella to argue that Theodore Shackley and Erich von Marbod should not be prosecuted for connections with EATSCO or Edwin Wilson, and that any questionable billing practices might have involved a covert operation. Later, in March 1985, Ledeen reportedly makes some of the first overtures to Israel for help in getting hostages released. (Maas, p.247; NYT 12/25/86; MH 12/7/86)

MAR 9 - The "Murder Board," the Administration's core Central American policy group, meets at the State Department. In attendance are: Haig; Casey; McFarlane; Chairman of the Joint Chiefs, David Jones; General Paul Gorman, head of the U.S. Central Command; Ambassador at Large

Vernon Walters; Lawrence Eagleburger; Fred Ikle; Richard Burt; Deputy Assistant Secretary of State for Inter-American Affairs Stephen W. Bosworth; Deputy Legal Adviser James H. Michel; Myles Frechette of the Bureau of Inter-American Affairs at State; Juliani; Goldberg; Montgomery. (Haig logs 3/9/82)

- Deputy Director of Central Intelligence Admiral Bobby R. Inman and Defense Intelligence Agency analyst John Hughes brief the press on reconnaissance photographs of Nicaraguan military bases, claiming that the only possible explanation for the Nicaraguan military build-up is to threaten its neighbors and support revolution elsewhere in Central America. (NYT 3/10/82 transcript of briefing; MH 3/10/82; WP 3/11/82)

MAR 12 - The State Department presents Jose Orlando Tardencillas, captured by Salvadoran security forces, as proof that the Sandinistas are exporting subversion. Tardencillas tells reporters he has been tortured and forced "to say many things about the connection between Nicaragua and El Salvador." (NYT 3/13/82; WP 3/13/82; Newsweek 3/22/82)

MAR 14 - Anti-Sandinista forces from Honduras dynamite the Rio Negro and Ocotal bridges in Nicaragua, destroying them. The Nicaraguan government declares a state of national emergency, attributing the sabotage to the Reagan administration's covert operations. CIA officials confirm in May that a CIA-trained demolition team was responsible for the operation. (NYT 3/16/82; WP 5/8/83)

MAR 23 - A former Green Beret says that he was approached by his former commanding officer and offered $50,000 for six months' work—six weeks of training in Central America followed by infiltration into Nicaragua. (CBS Morning News 3/23/82)

SPRING - From the spring of 1982 through the summer of 1984, interagency groups attempted to formulate "a security strategy" for Southwest Asia. (Teicher 6-7) (Tower)

APR - A National Security Council document written this month states that a primary U.S. goal in Central America is "not allowing the proliferation of Cuba-model states which would pose a direct military threat at or near our borders." The contents of the document become public in April 1983. (NYT 4/7/83)

APR - CIA official Duane Clarridge approaches former Sandinista leader Eden Pastora to offer U.S. support for his forces based in Costa Rica. (Dickey p. 149.)

MAY - CIA officials confirm to the House intelligence committee that key bridges in northern Nicaragua were blown up on March 14 by a CIA-trained demolition team. (WP 5/8/83)

MAY 21 - Newspaper columnists Evans & Novak report that Israel has been surreptitiously shipping arms to Iran for use in the Persian Gulf war. The column goes on to assert that Secretary of State Haig has apparently done little to stop the shipments and in fact seems ready to "reward" Israel's actions by moving toward restoring the military cooperation agreement between Tel Aviv and Washington, known as the Memorandum of Understanding. The agreement was suspended by Reagan following Israel's annexation of the Golan Heights. (WP 5/21/82)

JUN - The Reagan administration requests $5.1 million in AID funds from Congress to help the private sector and the Catholic Church in Nicaragua. Congress approves this request. (Confirmed by U.S. AID officer 5/1/83)

JUN 8 - Reagan announces Project Democracy in a speech to the British Parliament. He describes the program as a global effort "to foster the infrastructure of democracy." The basic aim is to raise money from public and private sources and make it available to organizations such as unions and newspapers in areas of the world where they might be restricted. Congress eventually turned down the administration's proposals for a $20 million FY83 and $65 million FY84 budget. (NYT 2/15/87; Project Democracy Preliminary Program Proposals 6/6/83)

JUN 15 - CSF Investments Ltd., implicated in 1986 in the Iran-contra scandal, is incorporated in Bermuda. Its first activity occurs on this date. CSF holds its bank account at the Republic National Bank in New York. Edmund Safra, known for his extensive Saudi and other Middle East ties, is the president of Republic. The majority of CSF Investments Ltd.—Bermuda stock is owned by CSF (Compagnie de Services Fiduciares) S.A. with offices in Geneva. The law firm representing CSF Investments Ltd. is Conyers Dill & Pearman—both Sir Bayard Dill and Sir James Pearman are also directors of Coastal Caribbean Oils & Minerals Ltd., $3,100 of whose stock Richard Secord owns in 1980-81. (Secord's financial disclosure forms show dealings in stock of only four small Caribbean oil exploration companies.) Representatives of Maule Air Inc. in Moultrie, Georgia, later charge that Secord purchased several airplanes from their company, one of which was was paid for with a check drawn on the account of CSF Investments Ltd. at Republic National Bank. (Hearst Newspapers 7/27/86; Secord Financial Disclosure Report 5/15/80 & 5/15/81)

MID-1982 - The Department of Defense sets up a special unit called the "Army Intelligence Support Activity" (ISA) to carry out intelligence gathering and covert operations. Its missions include one in El Salvador and another in support of anti-Sandinista forces. The ISA is probably more accurately described as a computer database of operatives with special skills who can be assigned for covert operations. (NYT 5/11/83; Interviews)

JUL - A Danish shipping company, Moensted, charters a cargo ship for the U.S. firm Western Dynamics to ship embargoed military equipment to Iran, according to a report on Danish television. The ship reportedly contains some 90,000 grenades and 2,000 detonators. However, when the ship reaches the Iranian port of Bandar Abbas, Iranian soldiers, outraged to see crates marked "Made in USA," prevent the ship from unloading the full cargo. According to the ship's captain, Tom Strheech, neither Western Dynamics nor Moensted wanted the shipment back, and he eventually sold the cargo to Iraq. Strheech claimed however that he was arrested in Dubai for arms trafficking and sentenced to six months in prison. (AFP 2/6/87)

- Some time in July of 1982, the United States became aware of evidence suggesting that Iran was supporting terrorist groups, including groups engaged in hostage-taking. (Tower)

JUL 16 - A secret Defense Intelligence Agency report dated July 16 and entitled "Insurgent Activity Increases in Nicaragua" states that the activities of various insurgent groups attempting to overthrow the government of Nicaragua include "the assassination of minor government officials and a Cuban adviser." The report characterizes one of the organizations, the 15th of September Legion, as "a terrorist group," and calls the Nicaraguan Democratic Force (FDN) "the largest, best organized and most effective of the anti-government groups." The report does not mention the fact that a number of the groups were at that time receiving money, arms and other support clandestinely from the U.S. government. An executive order on intelligence activities in effect at the time expressly bans U.S. direct or indirect involvement in assassinations. (DIA Weekly Intelligence Summary, 7/16/82; Center for National Security Studies, "From Official Files," March 1985, Kornbluh, Chapter 1)

JUL 19 - In Nicaragua, a twin-engine aircraft attempts to bomb storage facilities for petroleum products at the Pacific coast port town of Corinto, according to the Nicaraguan Foreign Ministry. (WP 8/15/83)

- A CIA briefing to House and Senate subcommittees reveals that training bases for paramilitary operations have been set up in Nicaragua. The number of troops is reported at 1500. "They were being outfitted with U.S.-financed equipment through Honduran military depots and were paid a subsistence fee of $23 a month." Later in the month, a conference of Senate and House committees amends the secret intelligence authorization bill to limit the purpose of the CIA effort. This amendment becomes public in December as the Boland Amendment. (WP 5/8/83)

AUG - Lt. Col. Richard Gadd retires from the military, where he came to know Richard Secord and Col. Robert Dutton well. All three would become deeply involved in the covert contra resupply effort. After retiring, Gadd joins Vinnell Corp., a large defense contractor, before starting companies of his own, in collaboration with Secord, in order to cash in on military contracts relating to special operations. (WSJ 2/13/87)

- Early in the month, a White House memo setting the agenda for a Cabinet-level meeting on Project Democracy declares, "we need to examine how law and executive order can be made more liberal to permit covert action on a broader scale." (NYT 2/15/87)

AUG 4 - The Nicaraguan government informs the State Department that it will not permit the disbursement of $5.1 million appropriated for private sector groups in Nicaragua on grounds that the money is intended to undermine the Sandinista regime. (WP 8/4/82)

AUG 18 - U.S. intelligence reports indicate Israel is again shipping arms to Iran. A recent deal between the two countries reportedly involved up to $50 million, possibly including arms Israel captured from the PLO in Lebanon. The Tel Aviv government acknowledges it has been selling Iran spare aircraft parts including replacement tires. (Aerospace Daily 8/18/82; WP 8/20/82)

LATE AUG - The White House cuts the CIA out of Project Democracy, fearing the Agency's affiliation might lead people to suspect a covert side to the program. (NYT 2/15/87)

SEP - Richard B. Gadd passes up possible promotion to full colonel, retiring to join briefly the Fairfax, Va. office of Vinnell Co., a large defense contractor. (WP 3/22/87)

SEP 29 - Ian Smalley, a British arms dealer living in Texas, is indicted along with two other men by a federal grand jury on charges of conspiracy to export arms. Smalley, Chris Territt, a British citizen, and David Bizzell, believed to be Irish, are accused in the indictment of preparing to export 100 M-48 tanks to Iran and 8,300 TOW antitank missiles to Iraq, in addition to other charges. Smalley, the only one of the three believed to be in the U.S., is put on trial November 29 and ultimately acquitted February 16, 1983 when the jury discounts the testimony of key prosecution witness Gary Howard (see February 16, 1983 entry). (AP 9/30/82; UPI 10/8/82; Newsweek 10/11/82; Reuters 2/16/83)

OCT 25 - Nestor Sanchez, the Pentagon's Deputy Assistant Secretary for International Security Affairs, leaves Washington on a trip to Central America. His itinerary includes Mac-Dill Air Force Base in Florida (25th-26th), Howard Air Force Base in Panama (26th-27th), San Salvador (27th-28th), Tegucigalpa (28th-29th), Golosan Air Base, Honduras (29th) and Homestead Air Base, Fla. (29th). Pentagon travel records show a wide-ranging series of trips by Sanchez throughout the region from 1981 to 1983. (DOD Travel Vouchers)

FALL - President Reagan decides to step up the quantity and quality of covert military support for the Afghan resistance. A large portion of the arms comes from old Egyptian stockpiles of Soviet weapons. The total cost of the operation is estimated to have been between $30 million and $50 million a year for the last three years with the U.S. and Saudi Arabia splitting the bills. (NYT 5/4/83)

NOV - Israel reportedly sells U.S.-made TOW antitank missiles to an Iranian arms dealer, Faroukh Azzizi, in Athens. The shipment, according to documents, goes to Amsterdam before reaching Iran, its final destination. A news report later identifies Azzizi as Israel's primary middleman with Iran. The Tel Aviv government later denies violating any agreements it has with the U.S. concerning the sale of American-made weapons to Iran. (Time 7/25/83)

NOV 2 - The Reagan administration admits supporting "small scale clandestine military operations to harass but not overthrow the Nicaraguan government." (NYT 11/2/82)

- The CIA is supporting covert efforts to overthrow the Nicaraguan government, it is reported. News accounts report that there are 4,000 active rebels, three times the number the CIA gave intelligence committees in August. (Newsweek 11/8/82; WP 5/8/83)

NOV 7 - It is reported that paramilitary forces made up of Nicaraguan exiles have improved their military performance because of increased U.S. aid. (NYT 11/7/82)

NOV 18 - Richard Secord departs National Airport at 7:40 in the evening for Tampa, Florida. He returns the following day at 3:00 pm. (DOD Travel Voucher)

NOV 28 - A newspaper item notes that many U.S. Foreign Service officers active in Central American policy played similar roles in Southeast Asia during the Vietnam war. The story mentions Thomas Enders, Craig Johnstone, Director of the Central America Affairs office, and U.S. Ambasssador to Honduras John Negroponte. (WP 11/28/82)

LATE-NOV - FDN official Edgar Chamorro meets with a man who introduces himself as Steve Davis and says, "I am speaking in the name of the government of the United States." Davis tells Chamorro that the U.S. wants to increase the size of the contras' political leadership. The two meet at the Holiday Inn in downtown Miami. At the meeting, Chamorro is introduced to Tony Feldman, whom he later describes as a CIA agent. Feldman asks Chamorro to serve on a seven-member directorate of the FDN. Feldman promises that the directorate will have the full backing of the

U.S. government and that the FDN will march into Managua by July 1983. (New Republic 8/5/85)

DEC - The CIA for the first time provides the Afghan guerrillas with bazookas, mortars, grenade launchers, mines and recoilless rifles, primarily of Soviet manufacture, according to Administration officials. One official claims that shoulder-fired anti-aircraft missiles are also being supplied. The move comes after a decision by Reagan in the Fall to bolster covert support for the rebels and raise the costs for Moscow of its commitment in Afghanistan. The U.S. and Saudi Arabia are said to be splitting the cost of aid to the Afghans of between $30 and $50 million a year. (See also May 4, 1983 entry.) (NYT 5/4/83)

DEC 3-15 - Secord leaves Washington for a trip to the Middle East. He travels to Cairo, Oman and Saudi Arabia before returning to Washington. (DOD Travel Voucher)

DEC 4 - U.S. Intelligence officials are quoted as saying that U.S. covert activities in Central America "have become the most ambitious paramilitary and political action operation mounted by the CIA in nearly a decade." The article in which they are quoted details CIA involvement in funding and organizing political opposition to the Nicaraguan government. (NYT 12/4/82)

DEC 6 - Nicaraguan exiles, who are members of the FDN, meet in Miami to discuss plans to topple the Sandinista government. The group has apparently received funding and military equipment from the CIA. They claim the FDN in Honduras commands over 5,000 armed paramilitary troops and vow to overthrow the Sandinista government by the end of 1983. (NYT 12/7/82)

- Hector Frances, an Argentine intelligence agent working with the contras, states in a videotaped confession that the Israeli ambassador to Costa Rica had offered Nicaraguan contras "Israeli passports to permit them to travel to Honduras without trouble." (Transcript of Hector Frances tape)

DEC 7 - Edgar Chamorro meets with five Nicaraguans and two Americans in an executive suite at the Four Ambassadors Hotel in downtown Miami to rehearse a press conference scheduled for the next day, at which the directors of the FDN will be introduced. According to Chamorro, the Americans are CIA agents. The American in charge is known to the group as Tony Feldman (see Late-November entry above); he is accompanied by Tomas Castillo, one of several assistants. They are there to ensure that Chamorro and other Nicaraguans say the right things when introducing the contra forces. (New Republic 8/5/85)

DEC 8 - Enrique Bermudez, commander of 3,000-6,000 troops in Honduras, says his forces are not subject to U.S. control. The commander of the FDN forces says his objective is to overthrow the Sandinistas, not to interdict the flow of arms to El Salvador as U.S. officials claim. (NYT 12/9/82)

DEC 17 - Following their defeat in the Falklands War, Argentine government officials announce that Argentine military personnel have withdrawn from Central America, where they had been training and funding the contras. (WP 12/18/82)

MID-DEC - CIA Director Casey is reported to have held closed door meetings with members of Congress in December to try to convince them that the aim of U.S. covert operations in Central America is to stop the flow of arms from Nicaragua to El Salvador, not to overthrow the Sandinistas. Casey characterizes these operations as "harassment" raids against Nicaraguan militiamen. (WP 1/1/83)

DEC 21 - Concern that [the Administration's] policy would provoke a war in the region led Congress on December 21, 1982 to pass the "Boland Amendment," barring the Central Intelligence Agency and the Department of Defense from spending funds toward "overthrowing the Government of Nicaragua or provoking a military exchange between Nicaragua and Honduras." (Tower)

DEC 22 - Congress adopts the "first" Boland Amendment in response to concern over the Administration's paramilitary support for the contras. (The Tower Commission puts the date of passage at December 21.) The amendment bars the use of FY83 funds for the purpose of overthrowing the Sandinista government or provoking fighting between Nicaragua and Honduras. (P.L. 97-377; NYT 12/23/82; CRS "U.S. Assistance to Nicaraguan Guerrillas" 12/4/86)

1983

- North Korea sells an estimated $500 million to $3 billion worth of arms to Iran in 1983. Both Koreas have reportedly been providing weapons to the Khomeini regime for the last year or two. South Korea has sold mostly small arms, ammunition and artillery shells. (WSJ 5/2/84)

- The Commerce Department this year licenses the shipment of approximately $27 million worth of equipment to Iran that can be used for military purposes. (WP 8/6/84)

- Richard B. Gadd sets up American National Management Corp. (ANMC), Eagle Aviation Services and Technology (EAST), and Airmach, naming himself as president and his wife, Sharon, secretary. Army Col. C.L. Stearns, by then retired from his post as director of the Joint Chiefs of Staff, Special Operations Division, serves as a director of ANMC until 1984. (WP 3/22/87)

JAN 13 - The FDN issues a 12-point peace initiative which essentially demands the surrender of the Sandinista government. Chamorro says this is the FDN's first public relations coup, but that it was not his doing. He claims in a 1985 interview that the initiative was drafted by the CIA. "We were told by the U.S. officials that it was 90 per cent propaganda but that we should promote it to make us look like peaceful men forced to violence." (DMN 7/14/85; New Republic 8/5/85)

JAN 14 - Reagan signs National Security Decision Directive No. 77, a classified executive order allowing the NSC to coordinate inter-agency efforts for "public diplomacy" in support of U.S. national security policy. The NSDD sets up four committees: public affairs, international information, international broadcasting, and the international political committee; the latter is authorized to "direct the concerned departments and agencies to implement political action strat-

egies in support of key policy objectives." Officials desig-
nated to manage public diplomacy include: Shultz;
Weinberger; Peter McPherson, administrator of AID;
Charles Z. Wick of USIA; David Gergen of the White
House. Staff for the effort includes Charles Hill of the State
Department's Executive Secretariat; Col. Rich Higgins, as-
sistant for interagency matters in the Office of the Secretary
of Defense; Teresa Collins, Secretariat Staff of USIA; and
Gerald Pagano, executive secretary of AID. (NSDD-77;
NSC Memo 4/18/83; NYT 2/15/87)

FEB 3 - Secord testifies as a defense witness for Edwin
Wilson in federal court in Houston, Texas. He is the only
alleged member of the EATSCO group ever to testify in a
Wilson trial. Secord admits he has had numerous personal
and professional contacts with Wilson over a 10-year period,
which included discussions of "various business opportunities." However, Wilson, apparently expecting to win his
case, refuses to implicate Secord or the others until more
than a year later. By then, he has exhausted the appeals
process and lost much of his credibility. A key witness for
the prosecution at the trial is Rafael Quintero, a Cuban-
American who fought at the Bay of Pigs and is a veteran of
numerous covert missions under Thomas Clines at the CIA.
On one occasion, Wilson recruited Quintero to assassinate a
prominent political opponent of Muammar Khaddafi. Quintero claims later to have believed that the plan, which was
never implemented, was sanctioned by the CIA. In 1986,
Quintero surfaces again to help coordinate the covert contra
resupply effort under the direction of Secord, Hakim, Clines
and others. (AP 2/5/83; WP 2/4/83; Maas, pp.65-66,
277-279, 285)

FEB 7 - A Miami-based public relations firm, Woody
Kepner Associates, begins work under a six-month contract
to promote a new, positive image for the FDN. The firm has
been retained by the CIA as part of a broad effort to win
world-wide support for the contras. (The Nation 1/17/87,
p.40)

FEB 10 - Richard Secord departs Andrews Air Force Base
for MacDill Air Force Base, Fla., arriving at 4:30 pm. On
Feb. 12, he flys to Eglin Air Force Base, Fla. He arrives at
11:25 am. Two days later, Secord returns to Washington,
D.C. (DOD Travel Voucher)

FEB 14 - The Reagan administration is reported to be working with Israel intensively to promote settlements along the border of Nicaragua and Costa Rica as part of a geopolitical strategy to isolate Nicaragua. (WP 2/14/83)

FEB 14-17 - Woody Kepner Associates, Inc., hired by the CIA as a public relations firm for the FDN, receives the first $52,000 in three checks on its contract of $300,000.00. (Kepner contract, 2/17/83)

FEB 16 - A federal jury in Dallas, Texas acquits British arms dealer Ian Smalley of conspiring to export 100 M-48 tanks to Iran and 8,300 TOW antitank missiles to Iraq. Smalley was caught with two other men, Chris Territt, a British citizen, and David Bizzell, believed to be Irish, in a federal sting operation that began in July 1981. In acquitting Smalley, the jury found the testimony of one of the prosecution's key witnesses, Gary Howard, unreliable. Howard, a former border patrol agent and a licensed arms dealer, was an informant for the U.S. Customs Service in the case, along with another ex-border patrol agent and informant, Ronald Tucker. Howard claimed that Smalley had told him he had shipped weapons out of the country using falsified documents, but defense attorneys argued that Howard lied and had stolen $1.2 million from Smalley, and that the government had tricked Smalley into believing he was part of a covert White House operation to strengthen Iran's military against a possible Soviet invasion. (Newsweek 10/11/82; Reuters 2/16/83; AP 2/17/83; NYT 2/18/83)

FEB 23 - Secord departs National Airport in Washington for a trip to the Middle East. He visits Saudi Arabia on Feb. 24, Bahrain on Feb. 25 and Oman also on Feb. 25. He returns to Dhahran from Oman on Feb. 28. (DOD Travel Vouchers)

FEB 28 - U.S. Ambassador-at-large Vernon Walters makes an unannounced visit to the Vatican to discuss the situation in Central America prior to Pope John Paul II's trip there. (National Catholic News Service 3/7/83)

MAR - Charles Z. Wick, the director of USIA, orchestrates a White House meeting with Reagan for several wealthy individuals, including Sir James Goldsmith, publisher of the French publication *L'Express*; W. Clement Stone, a Chicago businessman; and Rupert Murdoch, the Australian publishing tycoon. The aim of the session is to convince the visitors to donate money to Project Democracy, but this gathering produces no funds. According to a senior official, it is possible that other, similar meetings do succeed in raising money for the program. (NYT 2/15/87)

- The Australian government reports to Parliament the illegal activities of Nugan Hand, an Australian Bank linked to the laundering of money earned through arms sales and drug trafficking. The bank, which collapsed in 1980, conducted activities which "have the appearance of the direct involvement of the U.S. intelligence community." One of the banks co-founders, Michael Hand, who disappeared in 1980, and several of Nugan Hand's top officers are found to have extensive personal links to members of the U.S. intelligence community, including Theodore Shackley, Thomas Clines, Rafael Quintero, and Richard Secord. In a letter to the New York Times in March 1987, Shackley, however, denies being involved in any military or intelligence activities with Michael Hand and disputes reports linking him to Nugan Hand Bank.

According to the report and two subsequent investigations, Nugan Hand executives were involved in, among other things, the sale of an electronic spy ship to Iran by the U.S. Office of Naval Intelligence in early 1976, as well as shipments of arms to Angolan rebels. (NYT 3/8/87 & 3/30/87; WSJ 8/16/83 & 8/17/83)

MAR - New civilian leaders of the FDN tour European capitals accompanied by CIA agent "Tomas Castillo." (New Republic 8/5/85; Kornbluh Chapter l)

MAR 1 - Secord leaves Dhahran at 11:50 pm for the U.S., arriving the following day. (DOD Travel Voucher)

MAR 4-5 - During a symposium about low intensity conflict, Theodore Shackley, listed as President of RAI Inc., suggests that, "[a] special mechanism of government be established to control all special operations and their assets." This element he says would be " . . . dedicated to the multiple tasks of counterinsurgency, guerrilla warfare, and antiterrorist operations . . ." and that, "[t]he intelligence focus could then be applied to apparent opportunities in Mozambique, Angola, Afghanistan, Ethiopia, El Salvador, Nicaragua, and perhaps even the Western Sahara." Secretary of the Army, John O. Marsh delivers the keynote address. Oliver North is listed as a participant. The symposium is sponsored by the National Strategy Information Center, Inc., the National Defense University and the National Security Studies Program at Georgetown University. (Barnett, Frank et. al., ed. Special Operations in US Strategy; 1984.)

MAR 11 - Defense Department officials confirm reports that the U.S. Air Force has set up a radar base in Honduras. The radar system, brought into the country in January for joint U.S.-Honduras military maneuvers dubbed "Big Pine I," is to be staffed by 50 USAF personnel. Capable of monitoring a radius of 250 miles from its base near Choluteca, Honduras, it will cover most of El Salvador and Nicaragua. The $5 million expenditure for the base was made without congressional approval. (NYT 3/12/83; WP 3/12/83)

MAR 16 - Secord leaves the Pentagon at 12:15 pm for a trip to Chicago. He arrives at 2:00 pm. The next morning he returns to Washington and is back at the Pentagon by 10:00 am. (DOD Travel Voucher)

MAR 20 - The CIA is reported to have established a $50 million intelligence gathering network in Central America involving over 150 CIA operatives and technicians. These intelligence activities include infiltrating U.S. agents into Nicaragua and conducting low-altitude flights by U.S. spy planes over guerrilla-held territory in El Salvador. (NYT 3/20/83)

SPRING - Operation Staunch, a program aimed at discouraging countries from selling arms to Iran, is launched by the State Department. Over the next three years, U.S. officials file as many as "two or three" protests a month to foreign governments, including South Korea, Italy, Portugal, Spain, Argentina, China, Israel, Britain, West Germany and Switzerland, urging that they halt potential sales. In November 1986, despite disclosures the U.S. has sanctioned just such sales itself, the State Department insists that "Operation Staunch continues to be pursued vigorously." (WP 12/10/86)

APR - Pakistan expands its list of recognized Afghan resistance groups to 11, including some supported by Iran. (Le Monde Diplomatique 5/83 in JPRS Near East/South Asia Report 6/9/83, pp.52-53)

APR 3-4 - A three-tier command structure to direct Honduran-based Nicaraguan rebels is described in press reports. The tiers reportedly are: 1) the FDN command center in southern Honduras which includes participation by two or three Honduran officers; 2) the Honduran military high command, which directs the overall operation from its Tegucigalpa headquarters; and 3) U.S. participation directed out of the U.S. embassy in Tegucigalpa, with regular coordination between the CIA and the U.S. Army Southern Command. U.S. Ambassador to Honduras, John Negroponte, and the chief of the Honduran military, Gen. Gustavo Alvarez, meet daily to discuss strategy and the progress of the war. (NYT 4/3/83; Time 4/4/83)

APR 4 - For the first time, foreign reporters are allowed into the Honduran-based camps of anti-Sandinista paramilitary groups, enabling a close-up view of the rebels, their tactics and their arms. Referring to U.S. claims that CIA support for the counterrevolutionaries is intended to cut off arms supplies for insurgents in El Salvador, Commander "Suicide" of the FDN says, "We're not going to stop the transport of arms and supplies to the Salvadoran guerrillas or the Guatemalan guerrillas until we cut the head off the Sandinistas." (WP 4/3/83 & 4/4/83)

APR 7 - A highly classified NSC document from April 1982 is published. A primary U.S. goal in Central America, the document states, is "not allowing the proliferation of Cuba-model states which would . . . pose a direct military threat at or near our borders." (NYT 4/7/83)

APR 9 - Southern Air Transport of Miami carries 22 tons of small arms from Panama to a Honduran military base on a propeller-driven Hercules plane piloted by a special crew. It is reported that the flight plan is falsified. The flight plan filed with civil aviation authorities lists the destination as the Honduran capital, Tegucigalpa. Instead, the plane goes to an army base at Palmerola. (DOT Records; CBS News 7/9/84; AP 7/10/84)

APR 14 - While declining to provide specific information about U.S. activities in support of anti-Sandinista forces in Honduras, Reagan denies that the U.S. is "doing anything to try and overthrow the Nicaraguan government" and asserts that the government has not violated the terms of the Boland

Amendment. (CRS "U.S. Assistance to Nicaraguan Guerrillas" 12/4/86)

APR 18 - Stanford Technology Trading Group International, based in McLean, Virginia, is incorporated in California. Secord is listed as president and Albert Hakim as the corporation's registered agent. (Documents from the Secretary of State, Corporations Office, California)

APR 24 - A five-member delegation from the House intelligence panel travels to Honduras, Nicaragua and El Salvador to meet with top-level government officials and to investigate charges that the Reagan administration, in supporting anti-government rebels in Nicaragua, is violating the law. (WP 4/26/83; NYT 4/26/83)

APR 25 - Only five days before he is to retire, Secord leaves Dulles Airport for Europe via London. Five days later, he returns to the U.S. via Frankfurt. (DOD Travel Voucher)

APR 27 - Reagan addresses a special joint session of Congress in his first nationally televised speech on Central America. Because of Nicaragua, he contends, "the national security of all the Americas is at stake." (NYT 4/28/83)

MAY - The Khomeini regime outlaws the communist Tudeh Party, executes two hundred suspected communists and expels eighteen Soviet diplomats. At around this time, the U.S. provides authorities in Iran with a list of Soviet KGB agents and collaborators operating in the country. The question of Soviet influence in Iran is later the subject of two CIA reports, one in 1985 which emphasizes the Soviet threat and provides some of the impetus for future arms sales to Iran, and another in the spring of 1986, which concludes that the Soviet threat is minimal, particularly after the Tehran regime's suppression of communist elements this month. (See early 1985 and Spring 1986 entries.) (WP 1/13/87)

MAY - General Paul F. Gorman is appointed commander of the U.S. Army Southern Command.

MAY 1 - Secord retires from the Air Force, his record clouded by allegations surrounding his involvement with EATSCO and Edwin Wilson (see Early 1982 entry). Friends say he believes he was passed over for a promotion because of the controversy. Thirteen days before officially retiring, he joins Stanford Technology Trading Group International, Albert Hakim's northern Virginia-based company. The firm later retains Theodore Shackley as a consultant, supervises the contra re-supply operation in 1986, and maintains Swiss bank accounts tied to the diversion of Iran arms sales profits. (WP 12/9/86; Maas, pp.279, 287-88)

- Deputy Assistant Secretary of Defense for Inter-American Affairs Nestor Sanchez states: "If we didn't nickel-and-dime it, we could win this struggle. We could stop the Communist advance. Time is on their side. We can't fight a prolonged war, they can. If we feel we can live with Marxist-Communism in the area, that's fine. But I don't think we can." (NYT 5/2/83)

MAY 3 - The House intelligence committee votes along party lines, 9-5, to cut off covert funding to, and to prohibit by law any involvement with, contra forces fighting the Nicaraguan government. The legislation would instead allot $80 million over the next two years to provide overt arms interdiction assistance to "friendly" countries in Central America. Specifically, the aid would aim at halting the alleged arms flow from Cuba to leftist guerrillas in El Salvador and other countries. (NYT 5/4/83; WP 5/4/83)

MAY 4 - Reagan refers to U.S.-supported contras as "freedom fighters." He also acknowledges publicly for the first time that the U.S. is supporting the anti-Sandinista forces: "If they want to tell us that we can give money and do the same things we've been doing—money, providing subsistence and so forth—to these people directly and making it overt instead of covert, that's all right with me." (Presidential Documents 5/9/83, Vol.19, No.18)

- The Administration is reported to have stepped up its covert support for the guerrillas in Afghanistan in an effort to increase the costs for Moscow of its continued military presence in the country. Beginning last December (see entry), the U.S. has been funneling certain types of mostly Soviet-built arms into the country through Egypt and Pakistan. The new equipment includes bazookas, mortars and recoilless rifles. The U.S. and Saudi Arabia are said to be splitting the cost of the supplies, which for the last three years have been running between $30 million and $50 million a year. (NYT 5/4/83)

MAY 6 - The Senate Select Committee on Intelligence votes 13-2 to continue CIA operations in support of the contras through September 1983. The committee approves a measure requiring the President to bring a new report to the committee explaining the purpose and progress of the CIA operation in order to justify funding beyond that date. (NYT 5/7/83; WP 5/7/83)

MAY 10 - The White House announces that it is cutting Nicaragua's sugar quota by 90 percent. (White House Press Release 5/10/83; Kornbluh Chapter 2)

MAY 13 - The House Permanent Select Committee on Intelligence releases a special report, "Amendment to the Intelligence Authorization Act FY 1983" which states that the "U.S. has allied itself with insurgents who carry the taint of the last Nicaraguan dictator, Somoza" and whose activities "point not to arms interdiction but military confrontation." (Committee report)

MAY 22 - The fundamentalist Afghan coalition attempts a closer merger, transfering their resources to the unified body under Rasoul Sayaf, who is elected president for two years. (WP 5/26/83)

MAY 27 - Thomas O. Enders is replaced as Assistant Secretary of State for Inter-American Affairs. His replacement is Langhorne Motley. A few days earlier, Enders reportedly ordered a softening of a report by the CIA and Pentagon on left-wing insurgencies in Central America. The revision apparently angered CIA Director Casey and Defense Department officials and amounted to "the last straw" from the point of view of his critics within the Administration. William P. Clark, the national security adviser, Jeane Kirkpatrick, the U.N. ambassador, and others reportedly argued that Enders had let Central America "slip away" from the U.S. by not doing enough to undermine Nicaragua and bolster the military and economic positions of the governments of El Salvador, Honduras, Costa Rica and Guatemala. Motley is expected to push Reagan policy in the region more forcefully. (NYT 5/29/83; MH 6/10/83)

JUN 7 - The House Foreign Affairs Committee approves, by a vote of 20-14, the Democratic plan to end covert assistance against Nicaragua and to allot instead $80 million in arms interdiction assistance to "friendly" Central American governments. (NYT 6/8/83)

JUN - Reagan authorizes "Operation Elephant Herd," a secret, joint CIA-military plan to bypass congressional restrictions on aid to the contras. (See December 9, 1983 entry) (CBS News, 12/8/86)

JUN 13 - Reagan administration officials say that the 8,000 Honduran-based counterrevolutionaries have sufficient support within Nicaragua to continue fighting without U.S. backing. According to the analysis, the rebels will control one-third of the rural population and half of Nicaragua's territory by December 1983. (NYT 6/14/83)

SUMMER - The CIA reportedly reaches the conclusion that attacks on industrial and transportation targets would be a quicker and more effective way of hurting the Sandinistas than previous efforts. The CIA allegedly helps plan the shelling of the port city of Corinto, on October 10 of this year, as well as attacks on other economic targets. (NYT 10/16/83)

- Congressional opposition [to support for the contras] grew when reports were published that the CIA had a role in directing the mining of the Nicaraguan harbors in summer 1983. [See April 1984 entries] (Tower)

MID-1983 - CIA Latin American division chief Duane Clarridge travels secretly to South Africa to solicit aid for the contras, according to ABC News, which says Clarridge's trip was part of a "vest pocket" operation run by CIA director William Casey outside of all normal channels. The CIA denies Clarridge made the trip. Several months later, Safair Freighters (U.S.A.) Inc. is incorporated (see AUG 11, 1983 entry). Safair is owned by Safair Freighters (Pty.) Ltd. of South Africa, which passes on three Lockheed L-100 aircraft to the U.S. company, which in turn leases them to Southern Air Transport (see Aug.11 and 12, 1983 entries). (ABC World News Tonight, 2/25/87)

JUL - American National Management Corp. (ANMC) is incorporated in Delaware. Lt. Col. Richard Gadd, who later plays an important role in the covert contra resupply effort, sets up the corporation, one of many over a period of months including Eagle Aviation Services & Technology Inc., SOME Aviation and Airmach Inc. Gadd is a close associate of Richard Secord, who is listed prominently among ANMC's personnel in the company's literature. Over the next three years, ANMC wins a number of lucrative military contracts, some classified, to perform a variety of tasks from furnishing logistical assistance for military special operations to providing aircraft repair and maintenance. (WSJ 2/13/87)

JUL 3 - Secretary of State George Shultz visits Pakistan and tells Afghan refugee leaders that "they do not fight alone" and pledges continued U.S. support. (NYT 7/4/83)

JUL 6 - A National Security Council strategy paper prepared for an NSC meeting on July 8 calls for an "invigorated, long-term strategy" to obtain U.S. goals in Central America, and recommends that "the Secretary of Defense develop plans for joint exercises in the region." (NSC "Strategy for Central America" 7/6/83; Kornbluh Chapter 3)

JUL 8 - The NSC meets to discuss new strategies for Central America. The decision is made to increase the visibility of U.S. military maneuvers and the amount of aid to allies in the region. (NYT 7/17/83)

JUL 14 - It is reported that the CIA has drawn up plans to support a force of 12,000 to 15,000 anti-Sandinista guerrillas with money and material, and is seeking presidential authorization for this plan. (WP 7/14/83)

JUL 15 - The decision to send the aircraft carrier "Ranger" to Nicaragua's Pacific coast is made by Reagan "on -impulse." Even Shultz learns about the exercises only from press leaks. (Foreign Policy, Fall 1984)

JUL 17 - Concerned about the escalation of conflict in Central America, the presidents of the four Contadora countries hold a meeting on the Mexican island of Cancun. In a joint declaration, they appeal especially to Reagan and Castro to join in their effort to avert a war between Honduras and Nicaragua. The presidents also call for the removal of all foreign advisers and military bases from Central America and for international supervision of borders. (NYT 7/18/83 & 7/20/83)

JUL 18 - Reagan announces the formation of the bipartisan Presidential Commission on Central America, to be headed by Henry Kissinger. Explains Reagan: "We must not allow totalitarian Communism to win by default." (NYT 7/19/83)

JUL 19 - The House of Representatives meets in an extraordinary secret session to hear testimony on the U.S. role in aiding Honduras-based counterrevolutionaries. (WP 7/20/83)

JUL 21 - "At the request of the U.S.," Israel has agreed to give the contras military equipment captured from the PLO in Lebanon. (NYT 7/21/83)

JUL 22 - In a plea bargain with federal prosecutors, former CIA official Thomas Clines and EATSCO, the company he set up to profit from Egyptian arms sales, are allowed to plead guilty to overbillings of $8 million, and to pay fines totaling $3,110,000. As part of the deal, there will be no jail terms or further investigation into alleged silent partners in EATSCO. Reporters later speculate that heightened sensitivities in U.S.-Egypt relations following the assassination of Sadat persuaded the government not to prosecute further. (NYT 7/23/83; WP 7/23/83; Maas, pp. 279-280)

JUL 25 - "Hundreds of millions of dollars' worth of U.S.-made military equipment" is sold to Iran each year despite a State Department ban on such sales, according to dealers. The sales are made by American companies, by arms dealers operating in the U.S., and by third countries such as South Korea and Israel who are transferring arms to Tehran in violation of agreements with the U.S. One arms dealer, Balanian Hashemi, reportedly at the insistence of the Iranian government, set up various front companies to conceal his American connections in the arms business. Hashemi established R.R.C. Co., posing as a Persian rug shop, in Stamford, Connecticut; a subsidiary in London; and a company called Zoomer Fly Ltd., also in London. Hashemi's brother, Cyrus, who later becomes a figure in the Iran-contra scandal, helped finance Zoomer Fly while president of the now-defunct First Gulf Bank & Trust. Another dealer mentioned in the account is Balanian Hashemi's partner at R.R.C. Co., Carlos Vieira de Mello, a Brazilian. According to de Mello, it became so easy to export even clearly banned items such as aircraft engines and spare parts, that U.S. subcontractors who used to operate through R.R.C. began dealing directly with Iran. Ramco International Inc., for example, a major aviation-parts company in New Jersey, has negotiated large contracts during this period with the Iranian Air Force. Ramco's owner, Don Rvocco, denies any wrongdoing. (Time 7/25/83)

JUL 26 - President Reagan tells reporters that U.S. military maneuvers are "limited in purpose" and the "kind we've been holding regularly for years." (WP 7/27/83)

JUL 27 - FAA documents show the sale of a Fairchild C-123K plane from the U.S. Air Force Museum. Richard L. Uppstrom is listed as the seller representing the USAF Museum. The plane is sold to Roy Stafford of Jacksonville, Florida. It is reportedly the same plane that is later shot down on October 5, 1986 over Nicaragua while transporting arms to the contras. (See October 26, 1983 entry.) (FAA Documents)

- Reagan announces the planning of "joint training exercises" in Central America and the Caribbean, including a series of naval maneuvers and a series of ground exercises in Honduras called "Big Pine II." (CRS "War Powers Resolution: Presidential Compliance" 12/22/86)

JUL 28 - After three days of debate, the House votes 228-195 to cut off further aid to Nicaraguan rebels. (WP 7/29/83)

JUL 29 - FDN leader Edgar Chamorro criticizes the July 28 House vote against U.S. aid to his organization, saying such a move would prolong the war: "Eventually, the U.S. will have to get involved in the fighting . . . from the cost efficiency point of view, it is better for the United States to right now." (NYT 7/30/83)

AUG 3 - Casey appears before the Senate Select Committee on Intelligence to outline a proposed new finding on U.S. intelligence activities relating to Nicaragua. The committee believes the proposed activities are too broad and ambitious. A new finding is drafted, signed by Reagan, and presented to the committee on September 20 (see below). (Senate Report 98-665, 10/10/84)

- Nestor Sanchez, deputy assistant secretary for inter-American affairs at the Pentagon, testifies before the House Foreign Affairs Committee. Regarding the upcoming "Big Pine II" military maneuvers in Honduras, he is asked by

Rep. Michael Barnes (D-MD) if there will "be any coordination, contact or communication of any kind by the personnel engaged in this exercise with either U.S. intelligence personnel or the FDN fighting with Nicaragua?" He responds: "No, Sir." Barnes asks again, "None whatsoever?" Sanchez replies, "None." (Hearing 8/3/83)

AUG 8 - The first contingent of American troops arrives in Honduras for the "Big Pine II" exercises. Reagan has characterized the maneuvers as routine, however they involve several thousand ground troops, warships and fighter planes, plus the construction of airstrips, radar sites and other military facilities. Also, the Administration indicates in reports to Congress that it has tentative plans to continue the Honduran exercises through 1988. The maneuvers raise questions concerning Congress' ability to play a role in decisions that might conceivably lead to involvement in hostilities. (CRS "War Powers Resolution: Presidential Compliance" 12/22/86)

AUG 11 - Safair Freighters (U.S.A.) Inc. is incorporated in New Jersey, with two directors: Evan Augustyn of 17 Knollton Road, Allandale, New Jersey, and Anton Lombard of P. O. Box 938, Kempton Park, South Africa (the address of Safair Freighters Ltd. of South Africa). Safair's address is 28 West State Street, Trenton. The address later changes to 140 Route 17 North, Suite 202, Paramus, New Jersey (7/31/ 84). Safair lists itself as a "foreign-owned corporation organized and doing business under the laws of N.J." (Certificate of Incorporation, FAA files, 8/12/83; Aircraft Registration Application, FAA files, 12/28/83)

AUG 12 - Safair Freighters (U.S.A.) Inc. and Southern Air Transport sign a lease agreement in which SAT is to lease two Lockheed Hercules L-100's from Safair. (Lease Renewal, FAA files, 5/2/84)

AUG 16 - The Veterans of Foreign Wars establishes a fund to support counterrevolutionary groups fighting to overthrow the Nicaraguan government. The funds are to be channeled through the American Security Council. (WP 8/11/83 & 8/17/83)

AUG 31 - Safair Freighters (U.S.A.) Inc.'s president, Evan Augustyn, requests the FAA in an affidavit to assign the U.S. identification numbers N250SF and N251SF to two

Lockheed L-100's (serial numbers 4565 and 4590, respectively) which Safair intends to acquire from Safair Freighters Ltd. of South Africa. (Affidavit, FAA files 8/31/83)

SEP 8 - Eden Pastora's "new air force" sends a twin-engine Cessna 404 over Managua's Augusto Cesar Sandino Airport at dawn and drops two 150-pound bombs jerry-rigged under its belly. Little damage is done, but according to one report shock waves from the blast pitch the plane into the terminal building, killing pilot Agustin Roman and bombardier Sebastian Mueller. In Roman's wallet, investigators find what they say are the name and phone number of a CIA agent at the U.S. Embassy in Costa Rica. It is later disclosed that a Washington firm called Investair, with strong ties to the CIA, had handled the plane's export to Central America. The funds used to buy the airplanes in question are believed to have come from the money (apparently up to $660,000) that Francisco Fiallos, the Nicaraguan ex-ambassador to Washington, withdrew from his embassy's bank account when he left the embassy. (According to other reports, the plane was one of two involved in the attack. One was said to be shot down while the other escaped toward Costa Rica. According to these accounts, the planes took off from El Salvador.) (WP 9/9/83 & 9/17/83 & 2/24/85; NYT 10/6/83)

- A CIA trained force of Spanish speaking contract agents, "unilaterally controlled Latino assets" (UCLAs), attack Puerto Sandino, Nicaragua in speedboats launched from an offshore ship. News reports later say CIA operatives executed the attack. (WSJ 3/6/85; WSJ 4/18/84)

SEP 9 - Small aircraft attack the port of Corinto, causing little damage, according to the Nicaraguan Defense Ministry. Twenty homes are evacuated in the vicinity of toxic gas storage tanks which were hit by the aerial fire. (WP 9/10/83)

SEP 12 - Fred Ikle, Under Secretary of Defense for Policy, states in a speech in Baltimore, "[W]e do not seek a military defeat for our friends. We do not seek a military stalemate. We seek victory for democracy." He adds: "As long as Congress keeps crippling the president's military assistance program, we will have a policy always shy of success. We will remain locked into a protracted failure." (DOD Press Release 9/12/83)

SEP 16 - Costa Rican Minister of Public Safety, Angel Solano, expels 100 Cuban-American Vietnam veterans who had arrived in Costa Rica to take up arms against the Nicaraguan government. (Excelsior 9/17/83)

SEP 20 - A new presidential finding approved by Reagan and authorizing increased "covert activities" in Nicaragua is presented in written form by Casey and Shultz to the Senate and House intelligence committees. The finding, which is a revision of a proposal presented to the Senate committee by Casey on August 3, incorporates a new CIA plan calling for the expansion of the mercenary army to 12,000-15,000 men and emphasizing the importance of destroying vital economic installations and inflicting maximum harm on the Nicaraguan government. (Annex A, World Court Document; Senate Report 98-665, 10/10/84)

 - President Reagan signed a second Nicaragua finding authorizing "the provision of material support and guidance to the Nicaraguan resistance groups." The objective of this finding was twofold: inducing the Sandinista Government in Nicaragua to enter into negotiations with its neighbors; and putting pressure on the Sandinistas and their allies to cease provision of arms, training, command and control facilities and sanctuary to leftist guerrillas in El Salvador." (Tower)

- Deputy Secretary of Defense Paul Thayer signs a classified "program decision" memorandum ordering all military services to add funds for SouthCom activities and to plan for expanded operations in Central America, according to news reports. (NYT 9/20/83)

OCT - This month sees the peak of CIA activity in Honduras, according to Edgar Chamorro. Twenty-five to thirty Agency employees are reportedly training contras, conducting briefings, and handling paperwork and accounting. (MN 11/28/84)

 - CIA contract agent "John Kirkpatrick" drafts a "Psychological Operations in Guerrilla Warfare" manual (pseudonym "TAYACAN") for the contras. Based on a 1968 Vietnam-era, manual, it recommends "neutralizing" government officials as a means of attaining political ends. Later, it is revealed that Duane "Dewey Maroni" Clarridge, the CIA's division chief for Latin America at the Directorate for Operations, commissioned its writing. (Senate Report 98-665, 10/10/84; New Republic 8/5/85; NYT 1/21/87)

- A cargo plane with Southern Air Transport markings has crates of guns unloaded and packages of cocaine stored aboard at an airfield in Barranquilla, Colombia, according to an FBI informant. Jorge Ochoa, reputed to be the head of a Colombian cocaine smuggling ring known as "the Medellin cartel," is said to be in charge of the operation. Another Southern Air flight visits Barranquilla in October 1985, according to the witness. The informant first brings the information to the FBI's attention in July 1986, but little is done on the case until it is made known to Senator John F. Kerry (D-MA). (See September 26, 1986, entry.) (WP 1/20/87)

- Former Lt. Col. Richard Gadd retires from Vinnell Corp., a large Pentagon contractor. He has already established American National Management Corp. and Eagle Aviation Services & Technology Inc. Both concerns win lucrative contracts with the military, reportedly thanks to Gadd's background in special operations and his connections with Pentagon offices of special plans and operations. (WSJ 2/13/87; WP 3/22/87)

- Richard Gadd, under contract with the U.S. Army's Special Operations Division, arranges for the covert transfer of helicopters and pilots from a secret CIA aviation facility at Fort Eustis, Virginia, to Barbados in the Caribbean. He charters a civilian L-100 cargo plane to handle the task. Gadd, whose military career included assignments relating to special operations, reportedly earns high praise for his efforts and in coming years wins lucrative contracts with the Pentagon to provide similar services, both classified and unclassified. For example, his first classified contract, issued in 1983 by the Army's special operations division, is for $750,000 and stipulates that Gadd have on call two L-100 aircraft and pilots. In 1983-84, the same division provides companies owned by Gadd with business totaling over $1 million. (WP 3/22/87; WSJ 2/13/87)

OCT 2 - The CIA is using a Salvadoran air base and Salvadoran pilots to supply contras in Nicaragua, according to a news report. (NYT 10/2/83)

OCT 9 - North escorts the Kissinger Commission on a visit to Central America. (WP 10/10/83; WSJ 12/31/86)

OPERACIONES SICOLOGICAS EN GUERRA DE GUERRILLAS

Por **Tayacán**

OCT 10 - Using mortar and cannon fire, commandos attack fuel storage tanks in the port of Corinto, Nicaragua. The Honduras-based FDN claims responsibility for the attack. News reports later say CIA operatives executed the attack. (NYT 10/12/83; WP 10/12/83; WSJ 4/18/84)

OCT 16 - The CIA recommended and helped plan the October 10 attack on Corinto as well as other attacks on economic targets, according to news accounts. Over the summer of 1983, the CIA allegedly reached the conclusion that attacks on industrial and transportation targets would be a quicker and more effective way of harming the Sandinistas than previous efforts. Subsequent reports reveal that most of these "strategic" attacks are carried out, not by the contras themselves, but by CIA-trained and -directed teams of "unilaterally controlled Latino assets" (UCLA's) recruited from the Honduran armed forces and elsewhere. One of these UCLA's later provides television crews with details of his recruitment and training by Americans, his operations from a series of U.S. Navy vessels off the coast of Nicaragua, and a number of sabotage and demolition missions inside Nicaragua. (NYT 10/16/83; WSJ 3/6/85; Grenada Television and Insite Video, videotaped interviews, November 1985)

OCT 17 - McFarlane is sworn in as Reagan's national security adviser. (NYT 10/18/83)

OCT 18 - Reagan states: "I do believe in the right of the country when it believes that its interests are best secured to practice covert activity," but asserts that it is impossible to let the American public know about such action without "letting the wrong people know" as well. (NYT 10/23/83)

OCT 20 - The House votes for the second time in less than three months to cut all U.S. aid for paramilitary groups fighting the Nicaraguan government. The 227-194 vote provides instead for $80 million of overt arms interdiction assistance to "friendly" Central American governments. (NYT 10/21/83)

OCT 23 - The U.S Marine compound at Beirut's International Airport is bombed by terrorists; 241 servicemen are killed. The National Security Agency reportedly intercepted diplomatic messages in 1983 that showed the bombing was ordered and financed by Iran. However, it is not clear how long before the attack the White House was informed. (MH 12/7/86)

- [T]he United States determined that Iran had played a role in hijackings and bombings, notably the bombings of the American Embassy and of the Marines barracks in Beirut on October 23, 1983. Evidence of Iranian complicity in such events caused the United States to designate Iran a sponsor of international terrorism and to impose additional controls on exports to Iran on January 23, 1984. (Tower)

OCT 25 - 1,900 U.S. troops invade Grenada, less than one week after the assassination of Prime Minister Maurice Bishop and other leading members of the government by opponents within the ruling New Jewel Movement. (NYT 10/26/83)

- Lockheed Hercules L-100's with serial numbers 4565 and 4590 are deleted from the South Africa Civil Aircraft Registry, and added to the Federal Aviation Administration registry under tail numbers N250SF and N251SF, respectively, as Safair Freighters (U.S.A.) had requested on August 31. (Telex from Transport Pretoria to FAA, 10/25/83)

OCT 26 - Safair Freighters (U.S.A.) Inc. officially purchases the two L-100's 4565 and 4590 from Safair Freighters Ltd. of South Africa. (Aircraft Bill of Sale, FAA records, 10/26/83)

- FAA records show Roy Stafford of Jacksonville, Florida, selling a C-123K cargo plane to Doan Helicopter of Daytona Beach, Florida. Harry L. Doan is listed as the buyer. The tail number on the plane at the time of the sale is N4410F. This is reported to be the same plane that crashes over Nicaragua on October 5, 1986, and is believed to be the same plane used by Barry Seal in his U.S. Drug Enforcement Agency-sponsored sting operation against the government of Nicaragua. (FAA Documents; MH 10/9/86 & 10/10/86)

NOV - Congress approves funding for the National Endowment for Democracy after Casey publicly pledges that the CIA will have no role in the organization. The NED is the only activity Congress approves from a series of Project Democracy proposals made by Reagan in 1982 (see June 8, 1982 entry). A news report later suggests that the CIA was not needed in this case because officials had already decided to run Project Democracy's covert operations through the NSC. The Tower Commission disagrees with this conclusion, maintaining that Oliver North simply appropriated the name, "Project Democracy," for his private network. (NYT 2/15/87; Tower p. 550)

NOV 1 - Thomas Posey, head of Civilian Military Assistance (CMA), applies to the Bureau of Alchohol, Tobacco and Firearms for a "Ol" Federal Firearms export license "to buy weapons + ammo to send to El Salvador with that government's permission." (BATF Application for License)

NOV 3 - The Senate passes the Intelligence Authorization Act for FY84, including continued U.S. covert aid for Nicaraguan rebels. Because the House voted on October 20 to cut off such aid, the issue is referred to a conference committee. (WP 11/4/83)

- A San Francisco court orders Meese to investigate possible violations of the Neutrality Act through U.S. aid to the contras. The court upholds its decision on January 10, 1984 (see entry). (NYT 1/11/84)

NOV 8 - A network of former U.S. intelligence and military personnel is supplying aircraft, weapons, and paramilitary support to the contras, it is reported today. The CIA allegedly has helped organize the informal network. (NYT 11/8/83)

NOV 10 - Giro Aviation Corp. files the last of five annual registrations with the Florida Secretary of State. Giro's registered agent and director is Felix I. Rodriguez (a.k.a. Max Gomez, later a key link in the 1985-86 contra resupply from El Salvador). Giro Aviation's office suite is located at 444 Brickell Avenue, Suite 407, Miami, where Giro director and arms dealer Gerard Latchinian runs three other companies, including G&J Exports, Inc. Less than a year later, Latchinian would be arrested for attempting to finance a political murder with profits from a drug deal (see Nov. 1, 1984 entry). (Corporate records, Florida Secretary of State, 7/14/86; MH 11/2/84; NYT 11/3/84)

NOV 12 - The CIA has informed congressional intelligence oversight committees that the 10,000-12,000 U.S.-backed guerrillas lack the military capability, financing, training and political support needed to overthrow the Sandinistas, according to congressional sources in press reports today and on November 25. (WP 11/12/83 & 11/25/83)

- Southern Air Transport acknowledges delivery of a leased Lockheed Hercules L-100, tail number N251SF, serial number 4590, belonging to Safair Freighters (U.S.A.) Inc. (Aircraft Delivery Receipt, FAA files, 11/12/83)

NOV 16 - Pastora meets with NSC officials and speaks with 150 leaders of conservative and religious groups, businessmen, and Hispanics, at a White House gathering arranged by the Reagan administration. The Administration wants a "working agreement with a charismatic leader like him," according to a State Department official. (WP 11/18/83)

NOV 28 - In a rare public appearance, Constantine Menges, at the time senior director for Latin American affairs at the NSC, attacks Nicaragua's latest peace proposals and becomes the first senior U.S. official publicly to disparage the Contadora effort. He calls Nicaragua's peace proposals "wholly inadequate in proposing verification monitoring by virtually the same countries that were implicit guarantors of the July 1979 negotiated settlement which brought the Sandinistas and their democratic allies to power based on democratic promises." (WP 11/29/83)

NOV-DEC - After months of complaints within the contra field forces over corruption and lack of supplies, a reform group of field commanders succeeds in getting the cooperation of the contras' CIA case officers in setting up an alternative logistical supply system, bypassing Enrique Bermudez and his Tegucigalpa-based system. Former National Guard captain and September 15th Legionnaire Hugo Villagra takes over as theater commander running the alternative logistics, which reveal an enormous gap between what the CIA had been providing and what the field troops had been getting. Top FDN leaders, however, appeal to Washington and get the system and the local CIA officers overruled. Villagra resigns with a letter to Bermudez and the FDN Directorate, and a circular to his field commanders. The supply system reverts to Bermudez's control. (Villagra letter, 12/83; Villagra circular 12/83; NYT 6/21/86; National Public Radio, 6/21/86, 6/24/86)

DEC - CIA official Duane Clarridge tells the staff of the House Select Commitee on Intelligence that the contras are killing civilians. (MH 10/20/84)

- U.S. Army Colonel Ralph Mark Broman, Paris chief of the Pentagon's Office of Defense Cooperation, and Paul S. Cutter, an American diplomat and former CIA researcher and translator, join efforts to sell arms to Iran. They establish a company called European Defense Associates (EDA), with offices in Paris, California and Washington, which later attempts to supply Iran with up to $1 billion of F-4 jets, helicopters, tanks, submarines, air-to-air missiles and other materiel. An EDA telex later shows that one of the people who reviews tanks for a proposed 1984 sale to Iran is Manuchehr Ghorbanifar, an Iranian arms dealer who serves as middleman for U.S.-sanctioned weapons sales in 1985-1986 (see November 1984 entry). Cutter, who also goes by his Yugoslav name of Paul Sjeklocha, later claims "We all worked under the umbrella of Defense Department approval." Broman is also linked to French arms dealers Claude Lang and Bernard Veillot. Veillot, who is introduced to Broman by State Department official John Mowinckel, is later indicted in New York on charges of conspiring to sell arms to Iran (see April 22, 1986 entry). Disclosure in early 1987 of the activities of Broman, Cutter and their colleague, Army Colonel William H. Mott, IV (see May 1985 entry), indicates that the circle of military officers involved in arms deals with Iran is much wider, and the dates of their activities reach back far earlier than previously believed. (NYT 1/11/87)

- Richard Gadd incorporates Airmach Inc. in Delaware. Airmach is one of a number of companies Gadd sets up beginning with American National Management Corp. (ANMC) in July of this year. Gadd's companies, reportedly thanks to connections with Richard Secord, win numerous lucrative contracts with the military to perform a variety of services, mostly related to special operations. Gadd, Secord, and another associate, Robert Dutton, subsequently become deeply involved in the contra resupply effort. (WSJ 2/13/87)

DEC 4 - Sigbhatullah al-Mojaddedi, head of the Organization for Islamic Unity, a pro-Western Afghan rebel group, says "The rebels had been promised $25 million in Western arms but received only $6 million worth and still needed suface-to-air weapons such as the American-made Redeye missile." Mojaddedi also says that at least three rebel groups were dominated by Iran, which is in the fourth year of a war with Iraq and cannot provide weapons. (NYT 12/4/83)

DEC 8 - Reagan signs the Defense Appropriations Act for FY84 (P.L. 98-212) which includes the first Boland Amendment. The act limits funding to the contras to $24 million and prohibits the use of additional funds in FY84 without congressional approval. (CRS "U.S. Assistance to Nicaraguan Guerrillas" 12/4/86)

- On December 8, 1983, Congress tightened the scope of permissible CIA activities, placing a $24 million cap on funds that could be spent by DoD and CIA or any other agency "involved in intelligence activities" toward "supporting, directly or indirectly, military or paramilitary operations in Nicaragua by any nation, group, organization, movement or individual." (Tower)

DEC 9 - Reagan signs the Intelligence Authorization Act of FY84 (PL 98-215). The law reiterates provisions of the Defense Appropriations Act signed the previous day limiting funding for intelligence operations in Nicaragua to $24 million. The bill also recommends that the U.S. work with the Organization of American States and the Contadora group to seek peace in Central America. In its classified report to the intelligence committees, the Administration reportedly agrees to abide by the restrictions of the first Boland Amendment. (Senate Report 98-665 10/10/84; CRS "U.S. Assistance to Nicaraguan Guerrillas" 12/4/86)

- "Operation Elephant Herd," the covert, joint CIA-military plan authorized by Reagan in June 1983 (see entry) to avoid congressional restrictions on aid to the contras, is implemented. Under the program, the Pentagon sets aside $12 million of military equipment (the CIA originally requested $32 million) and arbitrarily declares it to be "surplus to requirements" of the military. As "surplus" materiel it is no longer considered to have any dollar value and thus can be transferred to the contras without being counted as part of the $24 million in total military aid allowed by Congress. Reagan signs legislation today setting that ceiling for FY84 (see above entry). Internal Pentagon documents show that the project, assigned the number STX-40-019, is officially run by the Joint Chiefs of Staff and coordinated by "AF/

PRPRC," the "resources and flying hours division" of the Office of the Deputy Air Force Chief of Staff for Programs and Resources. This office instructs the Air Force Logistics Command in Fairborn, Ohio, to mark as "surplus" three Cessna O-2 observation planes that can be converted to carry rockets and to "arrange movement of the aircraft." The planes are duly declared "excess to (Air National Guard) requirements" in a memorandum dated today and are flown to Andrews Air Force Base. From there they are sent to Summit Aviation Inc., a company in Middletown, Delaware, which reportedly has frequently modified airplanes such as the O-2s for military and intelligence purposes. In February 1984, Summit outfits each plane with four pods, capable of holding 28 rockets. The planes are then transferred to the Nicaraguan rebels. Oliver North is reported to have worked with the CIA on the project along with Army Col. James Longhoffer, a liaison officer between the CIA and the Pentagon who is eventually court-martialed for poor performance in supervising covert operations. Longhoffer's sentence of one year's hard labor at Leavenworth is ultimately commuted in an "unprecedented" action on November 25, 1986, the same day North is relieved of his duties at the NSC. (BG 1/3/87; CBS News 12/8/86)

DEC 19 - BATF regional regulatory administrator Robert Dougherty approves Tom Posey's November 1 application for a weapons export license. (BATF Application for License)

DEC 28 - Safair Freighters (U.S.A.) Inc. informs the Department of Transportation that "records of flight hours are available for inspection" at Southern Air Transport in Miami. The address for Safair is 1 Bankers Trust Plaza, 130 Liberty Street, Room 2205, New York, NY 10008. (Safair letter to DOT, FAA records, 12/28/83)

1983-84 - Richard B. Gadd's companies receive more than $1 million worth of business, classified and unclassified, from the small, secretive office of Army Special Operations in the basement of the Pentagon. The first contract was issued in 1983 for $750,000 and called for Gadd to have on call two L-100 transport planes and pilots. (WP 3/22/87)

1984

- Israel had a strong interest in promoting contacts with Iran and reportedly had permitted arms transfers to Iran as a means of furthering their interests. A series of intelligence studies written in 1984 and 1985 described Israeli interests in Iran. These studies also reported Israeli shipments of non-U.S. arms to Iran as well as the use of Israeli middlemen as early as 1982 to arrange private deals involving U.S. arms. (See November 21, 1986) (SSIC 1/29/87)

- At the beginning of 1984, Geoffrey Kemp, Senior Director for Near East and South Asian Affairs on the staff of the National Security Council ("NSC") and the principal NSC staff officer responsible for the Persian Gulf, (Id. at 6), wrote a memorandum to Robert C. McFarlane, Assistant to the President for National Security Affairs and head of the NSC staff, recommending that the Administration reevaluate its attitude towards Iran. He viewed the Khomeini government as a menace to American interests, and suggested a revival of covert operations against it. According to Kemp, Tehran's politics and policies enhanced Syria's standing among Arab states, and threatened western access to Persian Gulf oil. Khomeini's Iran was also believed to have engaged directly or indirectly, in terrorist acts against citizens and interests of the United States, its friends and allies. He reported that exiled Iranians, with whom he regularly communicated, hoped that, with foreign help, they might install a pro-Western government. Suggestions of divisions in the country and support from Saudi Arabia for the exiles encouraged Kemp to submit his proposal. (Kemp to McFarlane, 1/13/84)

Kemp prepared his memorandum during a period in which a number of foreign nationals living in Lebanon were kidnapped by groups known to have important ties to Iran. Further, the United States determined that Iran had played a role in hijackings and bombings, notably the bombings of the American Embassy and of the Marines barracks in Beirut on October 23, 1983. Evidence of Iranian complicity in such events caused the United States to designate Iran a sponsor of international terrorism and to impose additional controls on exports to Iran on January 23, 1984. Among those kidnapped after Kemp submitted his memorandum to McFarlane was William Buckley, CIA Chief of Station in Beirut, seized on March 16, 1984. Buckley eventually died in captivity. (Tower)

- Robert McFarlane, the National Security Advisor, and members of the NSC staff, had become concerned about future U.S. policy toward Iran. They feared that the death of Khomeini would touch off a succession struggle which would hold important consequences for U.S. interests. They believed that the United States lacked a strategy and capability for dealing with this prospect. (Tower)

- Richard Gadd begins working with Richard V. Secord out of Gadd's American National Management Corporation (ANMC) complex in Vienna, Va. (WP 3/22/87)

EARLY 1984 - CIA Deputy Director John McMahon telephones North in the middle of the night and reportedly curses and reprimands him for proposing in a classified document that Reagan authorize planning to "neutralize" terrorists. North's recommendation comes at a time when the Administration is putting together a "pro-active" policy against terrorism in the wake of the bombing of the Marine barracks in Beirut in October 1983. The outburst reflects sharp differences within the bureaucracy over the new policy. It is unclear whether North's wording is ever changed as a result of McMahon's objections, but officials report later that the final directive clearly states that the President does not condone assassination as part of the program. (WP 2/22/87)

- Sometime this year, St. Lucia Airways, later believed to be a CIA proprietary, files records with the U.S. government listing Allison Lindo of St. Lucia Island in the Caribbean as owner of 99 percent of the company's stock. In 1984 or 1985 Lindo apparently sells her interest in the company to a lawyer, Michael Gordon, although an official of the airline, Deitrich Reinhardt, a West German living in Port Charlotte, Florida, tells a reporter later that Lindo still owns the stock. The company maintains administrative headquarters in Frankfurt, West Germany, but its base of operations is the island for which it is named. At one point, both Reinhardt and Gordon are summoned before John Compton, the prime minister of St. Lucia, and asked to change the company name because "it is causing us embarrassment." Compton tells a reporter after the meeting that he believes the registered owners are "only a front," and the island base simply "a flag of convenience." In 1987, the airline is reported to own or lease at least one Hercules L-100 and two 707 cargo planes. One of the 707s is registered in the U.S., the other in St. Lucia. The latter, according to crew members, is generally used for so-called "special flights" for which logs, a former employee says, are rarely made available even to the maintenance crew. Later reports indicate that, beginning in 1985, the airline is used to ship military supplies to Angola and Iran and that McFarlane may have flown a St. Lucia plane on part of his secret trip to Tehran in May 1986. Flight records for the airline show flights to Tehran and Tel Aviv on a number of occasions that coincide with dates of U.S. sanctioned weapons deliveries to those places. (WP 2/24/87)

- Theodore Shackley relays a message from Ghorbanifar to the State Department saying that the American hostages in Lebanon are alive and the possibility exists that they can be ransomed. Shackley later claims that he received the message in a chance meeting with Ghorbanifar and that this was the extent of his involvement in the Iran arms deals. (NYT 3/30/87)

JAN-APR - A CIA document lists 19 covert operations that agency personnel conducted directly against Nicaragua during this period, including attacks from a "mother ship" in an American-piloted helicopter, and others with the guidance of a radar-equipped fixed-wing U.S. plane. (WSJ 3/5/85)

JAN 2 - Edgar Chamorro is awakened at 2 a.m. at his safe house in Tegucigalpa and handed a press release which announces that the contras are taking credit for mining several Nicaraguan harbors. He is told to rush to the FDN's clandestine radio station to read the release before the Sandinistas break the news. Chamorro knows, however, that the contras played no role in the mining. Actually, CIA contract agents known as UCLA (Unilaterally Controlled Latino Assets), working from a "mother ship" anchored off the Nicaraguan coast, had planted the small explosive devices in the harbors. Chamorro says later that the CIA often gave credit (or perhaps blame) for operations that the directorate of the FDN knew nothing about. Telegrams announcing the mining were to be sent to Lloyds of London, so that insurance rates would rise. (New Republic 8/5/85)

JAN 8 - A Piper Cherokee-Six plane, piloted by William Courtney, an Alabama National Guardsman and CMA member, and carrying Tom Posey, Dana Parker, and one other CMA member, flies from Redstone Arsenal to Honduras. (Birmingham News, 9/14/84)

JAN 10 - A San Francisco federal court upholds its original November 3, 1983 ruling ordering the Attorney General to investigate possible violations of the Neutrality Act by the U.S. government's aid to rebels opposing the Nicaraguan government. The Reagan administration had requested a reversal, arguing the Neutrality Act was meant to apply to the adventurism of private citizens and not to foreign policy decisions of the executive branch. The court argued that "the act applies to all persons, including the President." (NYT 1/11/84)

- Responding to the resignation of contra theater commander Hugo Villagra and the abolition of his reformed logistical system, forty-one contra field commanders sign a letter to FDN political chief Adolfo Calero, asking for the ouster of military commander Enrique Bermudez and six other members of his staff, alleging "mismanagement of funds" and the lack of a "strategic and tactical plan." Subsequently, the CIA conducts an investigation of the FDN, using lie detector tests, which result in the dismissal of Bermudez's chief of staff, Emilio Echeverry. Bermudez, however, manages to consolidate his power, purging some of the forty-one field commanders, paying off others, and securing retractions of charges from still others. (Letter to Calero, 1/10/84; Dickey, pp. 308-309; National Public Radio, 6/21/86, 6/24/86)

JAN 11 - Nicaraguan troops force down a U.S. helicopter with ground fire, killing a U.S. Army pilot, Warrant Officer Jeffrey Schwab. The Nicaraguan government claims the craft was violating Nicaraguan airspace; the helicopter landed in Honduras less than 100 yards from the Nicaraguan border. A Pentagon investigation later concludes that the helicopter was "in Nicaraguan airspace when shot at." The aircraft landed on a road along the border near Cifuentes, near where American journalists Dial Torgerson and Richard Cross were killed in June 1983 when their vehicle was apparently blown up by an anti-tank land mine. (NYT 1/12/84; WP 1/26/84 & 3/15/84; Dickey, p.264)

- The Kissinger Commission report is made public. It calls for over $8 billion in aid to the Central American region over a five-year period. It further states that "as part of the backdrop to diplomacy, Nicaragua must be aware that force remains an ultimate recourse. The U.S. and the countries of the region retain this option." It also declares that "the U.S. cannot use the Contadora process as a substitute for its own policies" because "the interests and attitudes of these four countries are not identical, nor do they always comport with our own." (NYT 1/1/84; Report of the Commission, January 1984)

- Rep. Michael Barnes (D-MD), responding to the Kissinger Commission report, states: "Our real objective in the region is peace, and the whole thrust of the report is that the way to achieve peace is by sending in more guns." (WP 1/12/84)

JAN 16 - Thomas Clines pleads guilty to charges of overbilling the Pentagon for millions of dollars while a visible partner in EATSCO, the company involved in shipping American arms to Egypt. Accused of taking at least two and a half million dollars from EATSCO before leaving the firm, Clines engineers a plea bargain and pays a $10,000 fine on behalf of Systems Services International, which owned 49 percent of EATSCO, and another $100,000 to settle civil claims. (AP 1/16/84; Maas, p.280)

JAN 20 - [T]he Secretary of State designated Iran a sponsor of international terrorism. (Footnote: On August 27, 1986, a new section was added to the Arms Export Control Act which prohibited the export of arms to countries which the Secretary of State has determined support acts of international terrorism. Such a determination was in effect at that time for Iran.) Thereafter, the United States actively pressured its allies not to ship arms to Iran, both because of its sponsorship of international terrorism and its continuation of the war with Iraq. (Tower)

JAN 23 - [T]he United States determined that Iran had played a role in hijackings and bombings, notably the bombings of the American Embassy and of the Marines barracks in Beirut on October 23, 1983. Evidence of Iranian complicity in such events caused the United States to designate Iran a sponsor of international terrorism and to impose additional controls on exports to Iran on January 23, 1984. (Tower)

JAN 31 - The CIA informs the House intelligence panel of its covert activities in Nicaragua, according to an "Employee Bulletin" issued by Casey on April 12 (see entry). The Senate committee is not informed until March 8, 1984. (Senate Report 98-665, 10/10/84)

JAN-FEB - National Security Advisor Robert McFarlane authorizes North to begin planning ways to funnel private aid to the contras in case Congress cuts off official U.S. assistance to the rebels. (MH 12/7/86)

FEB 2 - UCLA pilots bomb a communications center and military training camp in northern Nicaragua. (NYT 5/3/84)

FEB - Summit Aviation outfits three Cessna O-2 observation planes, transferred to the contras through Operation Elephant Herd, with four pods capable of holding 28 rockets. (See December 9, 1983 entry). (BG 1/3/87)

FEB 17 - Safair Freighters (Pty.) Ltd. of South Africa notifies the FAA that it has performed major repairs on Lockheed Hercules C-130, tail number N46965, serial number 4558, which was leased at the time by Safair Freighters (U.S.A.) to Southern Air Transport. That the repairs were done in South Africa indicates that the plane had been used for charters in Africa. (FAA Form 337, 2/17/84)

FEB 19 - CIA Director Casey ends a cruise on the French Riviera, according to a U.S. businessman. Aboard the yacht during the cruise, Casey reportedly asked Saudi Arabia's King Fahd to provide covert funds for rebels fighting in Nicaragua and Angola. (SFE 10/20/86)

MAR - Oliver North reportedly drafts a three-page memorandum for McFarlane on how to sustain the contras when official funding runs out. McFarlane subsequently transmits the proposal to Reagan who approves it. (WT 10/8/85)

MAR 7 - Nestor Sanchez, deputy assistant secretary of defense for international security affairs, testifies before the Subcommittee on Military Construction of the House Appropriations Committee. He says, "The Aguacate airfield is a Honduran facility. We have no plans for its future use, nor do we plan any additional improvements to it." However, according to a news report in September quoting "congressional sources with access to intelligence information," "U.S. aircraft had been used on ten to fifteen occasions in the past six months to ferry medical supplies, food and some military equipment to the anti-Sandinista forces . . . some of the flights carrying assistance apparently were coordinated with the CIA, since some of the aircraft landed at Aguacate, a contra base in Honduras built by the U.S. military for the CIA. . . . The sources said some of the supply flights involved aircraft that were participating in joint U.S.-Honduran war games. . . . " (MH 9/7/84)

- GAO investigators report that on at least one occasion, "DOD personnel/aircraft were used to transport ammunition for the CIA" during the Big Pine II military exercises. The GAO also reports that "U.S. Southern Command officials informed us that the austere base, 8000 foot landing strip, and the water system, constructed by the 46th combat engineers at Aguacate will be left behind for use by CIA personnel." ("GAO responses to Questions in November 14, 1983 letter"; Kornbluh Chapter 3)

- Two persistent concerns lay behind U.S. participation in arms transfers to Iran. First, the U.S. government anxiously sought the release of seven U.S. citizens abducted in Beirut, Lebanon, in seven separate incidents between March 7, 1984, and June 9, 1985. One of those abducted was William Buckley, CIA station chief in Beirut, seized on March 16, 1984. Available intelligence suggested that most, if not all, of the Americans were held hostage by members of Hizballah, a fundamentalist Shiite terrorist group with links to the regime of the Ayatollah Khomeini.

Second, the U.S. government had a latent and unresolved interest in establishing ties to Iran. Few in the U.S. government doubted Iran's strategic importance or the risk of Soviet meddling in the succession crisis that might follow the death of Khomeini. For this reason, some in the U.S. government were convinced that efforts should be made to open potential channels to Iran.

Arms transfers ultimately appeared to offer a means to achieve both the release of the hostages and a strategic opening to Iran. (Tower)

MAR 8 - The CIA informs the Senate intelligence panel of its covert activities in Nicaragua, according to an "Employee

Bulletin" released by Casey. The director claims in the bulletin to have "complied with the letter of the law in our briefings and with the spirit as well." (Senate Report 98-665, 10/10/84)

MAR 16 - CIA station chief William Buckley is kidnapped in Beirut. Soon after, North asks Texas millionaire H. Ross Perot to provide $1 million or $2 million as ransom for Buckley. Ransom efforts fail. (MH 12/7/86; LAT 1/21/87)

MAR 23 - An unmarked DC-3 slams into a mountainside in Costa Rica near the border ranch of John Hull, an American who has allowed his property to be used for airdrops of supplies to the contras. Ammunition is scattered around the area. Soon afterward, according to local residents and Costa Rican investigators, a group of unidentified men arrive at the crash site and burn the bodies of the crew. (Newsweek, 9/84)

MAR 24 - Costa Rican President Alberto Monge tells French reporters that Costa Rica has become "one of the CIA's platforms against Nicaragua." (FBIS 5/24/84)

MAR 31 - Honduran President Roberto Suazo Cordova engineers a military shake-up which results in the removal of General Gustavo Alvarez Martinez as chief of the Armed Forces, General Jose Abdenego Bueso Rosa as head of the Armed Forces Joint Command and others. Both Alvarez and Bueso are considered firm allies of the U.S. and important contributors to the Reagan Administration's efforts to aid the contras in Nicaragua. Bueso is later implicated in a plot to assassinate Suazo (see November 1, 1984 entry) and pleads guilty in a U.S. court to a related charge. He is sentenced to five years imprisonment in July 1986. That summer, North and General Paul Gorman, the former head of U.S. forces in Latin America, request leniency for Bueso from the departments of State and Justice, but their requests are denied. (NYT 2/23/87)

APR - The CIA unofficially asks Israel and Saudi Arabia to help fund the contras, according to informed sources. They say that Saudi Arabia turned down the request and that Israel has been contributing several million dollars. Press reports note that the Reagan administration is making other attempts to circumvent Congress, for example by the CIA borrowing planes from the Department of Defense and then loaning them at no cost to the rebels. (WP 5/19/84)

APR 3 - Reagan signs a National Security Decision Directive, drafted by North, establishing an anti-terrorism task force headed by Secord, according to Pentagon sources. The group reported directly to the NSC and was responsible for helping to plan a commando rescue mission to free the hostages which was considered for June, 1986 if the talks and arms deals didn't work. (MH 3/8/87)

APR 10 - Casey makes his first formal presentation to the Senate Select Committee on Intelligence on the mining of Nicaraguan harbors and the decision-making process which led to the operation. (Senate Report 98-665, 10/10/84)

- The CIA is reported to have participated in the October 1983 attacks on oil facilities at a Nicaraguan port, before it helped direct the mining of Nicaraguan harbors, according to intelligence sources. (WSJ 4/18/84)

APR 11 - Adolfo Calero of the FDN denies reports that American intelligence agents were involved in the mining. "We claim that there are no Americans involved. Not one United States citizen is involved in the mining." (NYT 4/20/84)

APR 12 - Casey issues an "Employee Bulletin" in which he asserts that the CIA "fully met all statutory requirements for notifying our Intelligence Oversight Committees of the covert action program in Nicaragua . . . and complied with the letter of the law in our briefings and with the spirit as well." The bulletin states that the House Committee was first briefed on January 31, but the Senate Committee not until March 8, 1984. (Senate Report 98-665, 10/10/84)

APR 17 - A British policewoman is shot dead outside the Libyan Embassy in London. (AFP 5/8/84)

APR 22 - Great Britain breaks off diplomatic relations with Libya following the shooting of a policewoman five days earlier. (AFP 5/8/84)

- The CIA is funneling $400,000 per month to ARDE forces operating out of Costa Rica, according to news reports. (ABC News 4/22/86)

APR 23 - FDN military commander Enrique Bermudez admits to reporters that "we received some weapons . . . that the Israeli government took from Lebanon." (NBC News 4/23/84)

<u>APR 26</u> - Casey meets with the Senate Select Committee on Intelligence and "apologizes profoundly" for not informing the members "adequately and in a timely manner" of the mining of Nicaraguan ports and harbors. (Senate Report 98-665, 10/10/84)

- Lawrence S. Eagleburger, undersecretary of state for political affairs, and Israel's David Kimche, director general of the foreign ministry, discuss increasing Israeli aid to the third world, specifically Africa and Central America. Officials speculate that the U.S. may be trying to get Israel to take over covert support for the contras, whose funding sources are nearly exhausted since CIA funding ended in March. Contra leaders say that they have been receiving Soviet-made arms from Israel, but Israel denies the charges. Intelligence sources note that the U.S. could repay Israel for its aid through defense aid and intelligence sharing, which CIA Director William Casey has greatly stepped up, for example by giving Israel reconnaissance photographs taken by U.S. spy satellites, which former Director Stansfield Turner refused to do. (WP 4/27/84 & 5/19/84)

SPRING - After a series of defeats in Congress on the contra-aid issue early in the year, Reagan authorizes McFarlane to fund the contras "in any way you can," according to an aide. North subsequently writes an internal memorandum describing the outline of future NSC efforts, including White House-led fundraising among private groups and foreign governments. Meanwhile, around this time McFarlane aide Donald Fortier, relying on raw intelligence, is beginning to build a case for a U.S. initiative toward Iran. (NYT 2/22/87)

- North suggests to McFarlane that the contras establish a provisional government as a way of increasing their credibility with Congress. McFarlane approves the idea and forwards it to the State Department, which does not respond. (WSJ 12/31/86)

MAY - North and Duane "Dewey Maroni" Clarridge, CIA division chief for Latin America at the Directorate for Operations, meet with contra leaders in Tegucigalpa, Honduras. According to Edgar Chamorro, Clarridge introduces North to the gathering saying, "If something happens in Congress, we will have an alternative way, and to assure that, here is Colonel North. You will never be abandoned." Chamorro says Clarridge also boasts of talking to Reagan twice a week and of the President's interest in contra activities. Clarridge later becomes involved in the shipment of arms to Iran and is suspected by Congressional investigators of diverting weapons from the Afghan guerrillas to the contras. (NYT 1/21/87)

- Prince Bandar bin Sultan, Saudi Arabia's ambassador to the U.S., tells McFarlane he is willing to give the contras at least $5 million of his own money, apparently in gratitude for White House support for the crucial 1981 sale of $8.8 billion in AWACS radar-equipped planes to his country. An Arab-American businessman, Suliaman Bamieh, says he declined a 1984 request from Saudi King Fahd to help channel $15 million to the contras, the report says. Bamieh says he learned from Fahd and other members of the royal family that such contributions were in response to the AWACS sale. Secord and NSC member Col. Robert Lilac reportedly worked for Congressional approval, and Secord and Lt. Col. Richard Gadd later worked for Vinnell Corp., which was under contract to train Saudi Arabia's National Guard. Lilac left the NSC in 1984 and worked as a consultant for Bandar, government investigators say. (Detroit Free Press 3/20/87)

- French President Mitterrand and Defense Minister Hernu reportedly have been briefed by this time concerning the smuggling of millions of dollars of weapons by the French firm Luchaire into Iran. Although aware of the situation, the government does not cancel Luchaire's export licenses until March 1986, by which time the firm has made around $115 million in profits (see March 1986 entry). (AFP 1/15/87; Paris Domestic Service 1/20/87)

MAY 2 - Safair Freighters (U.S.A.) Inc. and Southern Air Transport sign lease renewals for three Lockheed Hercules L-100's (tail numbers N250SF, N251SF, and N46965). The lease designates Chemical Bank, International Division, 277 Park Avenue, New York City, account number 400-321-904, as the account into which Southern Air is to deposit its payments for leasing Safair's planes. The amount cited in the leases for basic rent is $2,016,000 over two years. The leases also require, in the event of a Southern Air Transport default on the contract, that Safair notify "the Contracting Officer, Headquarters Military Airlift Command, Contract Airlift (TCRS), Scott Air Force Base, Illinois, 62225."

(Leases, FAA files, 5/2/84, pp. 4, 7, 33; Letter for amendment of lease, FAA files, 9/26/84)

MAY 8 - A commando force consisting of 15 members of a Libyan exile group attacks Khaddafi's headquarters at the El-Azziziya Barracks in an attempt to assassinate the Libyan leader. The attack is put down and Khaddafi is unhurt. Although Libya initially suspects British involvement following the April 17 shooting of a policewoman in London by someone in the Libyan Embassy, it is later reported that the Direction de la Securite Externieure, the French counterpart of the CIA, orchestrated the operation. U.S. officials reportedly were aware of the plot, one of two the French mount this year against Khaddafi. (AFP 5/8/84; NYT 2/22/87)

- The Rev. Benjamin Weir is kidnapped in Beirut. (CSM 1/2/87)

MAY 24 - The Senate Select Committee on Intelligence reports out its Intelligence Authorization Act for FY85, which includes the funds requested for the contras, but stipulates in a classified annex conditions for terminating the aid program. (Senate Report 98-665, 10/10/84)

MAY 31 - A terrorist plants a bomb at a press conference called by Eden Pastora in the Nicaraguan hamlet of La Penca, killing four people and wounding Pastora. The attack, Pastora says later, came after a CIA ultimatum, but he stressed that he had no concrete evidence to implicate any specific person or group. (WP 7/3/86)

SUMMER - Documents and testimony indicate that Adnan Khashoggi and other international arms dealers, including Manucher Ghorbanifar, were interested in bringing the U.S. into an arms relationship with Iran, and had discussed this at a series of meetings beginning in the summer of 1984 and continuing into early 1985. These discussions reportedly included the idea of an "arms for hostages" deal in part as a means of establishing each country's bona fides. Khashoggi reportedly met with various leaders in the Middle East to discuss policy toward Iran during this same period. (SSIC 1/29/87)

- By the summer of 1984, Iranian purchasing agents were approaching international arms merchants with requests for TOW missiles, the Chief of the Near East Division of the

CIA's Directorate of Operations ("C/NE") told the Board. (Tower)

"We have in the DDO probably 30 to 40 requests per year from Iranians and Iranian exiles to provide us with very fancy intelligence, very important internal political insights, if we in return can arrange for the sale of a dozen Bell helicopter gunships or 1,000 TOW missiles or something else that is on the contraband list." (C/NE (2) 98) (Tower)

- From the spring of 1982 through the summer of 1984, interagency groups attempted to formulate "a security strategy" for Southwest Asia. (Teicher 6-7) (Tower)

✳- Jonathan Jay Pollard, an employee at the U.S. Naval Security and Investigative Command in Washington, begins selling classified documents to agents of the Israeli Scientific Liaison Bureau (known as "Lekem"). By the time of his arrest on November 18, 1985, he has passed on a quantity of documents "10 feet by 6 feet by 6 feet" that includes information on the location of U.S. ships and the timing and location of U.S. training exercises. The Israeli government denies any role in the affair despite the naming of an air force officer in the indictment. (CRS: "Israeli-American Relations," 12/22/86; WP 3/5/87)

MID-1984 - Congress denies an administration request for $21 million in supplemental funding for the contras after reports in April of the CIA-directed mining of Nicaraguan harbors. Lawmakers also fear that U.S. actions may lead to a military intervention in Nicaragua. (CRS "U.S. Assistance to Nicaraguan Guerrillas" 12/4/86)

JUN 8 - Secretary of Defense Weinberger sends a memorandum to the President pledging to "provide a wide range of logistical support and manpower to assist CIA covert operations in Central America, including support of Nicaraguan rebels." (NYT 6/8/84; Kornbluh Chapter 3)

LATE JUN - The NSC meets to discuss the growing controversy over the sale of dual-purpose equipment to Iran. Since the beginning of the year, the U.S. has allowed the transfer of supplies that technically are non-military but can have military applications, such as 100 American Motors Co. jeeps and two Iranian Boeing 707 jets that have been in the

U.S. for refurbishing since before the 1979 hostage crisis. Within the Administration, the Defense Department is reported to oppose the continued sales on grounds that they may help Iran's war effort and threaten America's allies in the Gulf, as well the flow of oil from the region; the Commerce Department argues for the sales in terms of the need to promote Reagan's aggressive export policy; the State Department, meanwhile, is reportedly left in the middle, although Shultz has been pushing U.S. allies recently to comply with the arms embargo against Iran. (WP 8/6/84)

JUN 27 - An FDN bank account in Miami receives a deposit of $5,000, bringing the balance to $l7,000. This money, which Edgar Chamorro says comes from the CIA, is eventually used to pay for pro-contra advertisements. (FDN budget records; Kornbluh Chapter l)

JUL - A CIA officer using the code name "Alberto Fenton" tells contra leader Eden Pastora in a curt conversation in a Washington hotel that his support has been cut off, according to Pastora. Pastora later says what irked him most was being left with a hotel bill for nearly $5,000 that he had been told the CIA would pay. (WP 7/3/86)

- The first of a series of monthly payments, approximately $1 million each, is made to an FDN account in the name of Esther Morales at the Miami branch of the BAC International Bank of the Cayman Islands. This first payment comes from an unidentified account at the Swiss Bank Corporation, apparently in Panama. The source of the payment appears to be King Fahd of Saudi Arabia, according to banking records. The records indicate that eight installments are made to this account (#54148) from July 1984 to February 1985. The BAC account is made available to the FDN by Carlos Morales, a Nicaraguan lawyer friend of Adolfo Calero. Through March 1985, the contras would receive a total of $32 million, which news reports say comes mostly from the Saudi royal family. Other FDN accounts include three controlled by a Panamanian corporation registered in 1984, Alpha Service S.A., which Calero says was set up by the FDN, and two other FDN companies: Chester Company S.A. and Dataguard International S.A. (NYT 3/6/87; WSJ 3/6/87; LAT 3/6/87; Morales/FDN bank statements)

- Richard Gadd's main company, American National Management Corp.(ANMC), is issued a contract for $362,603.

The contracting officer's representative is listed as Lt. Col. M. Foster of the Army's Special Operations Division. (WP 3/22/87)

JUL 2 - Minor and Fraser Public Affairs, Inc. presents a "fund raising plan of action" to the FDN to raise money for contras and their families. The money is to be channelled through the Nicaraguan Development Council, the corporate arm of the FDN. (Letter from Edie Fraser to FDN director Alfonso Callejas 7/3/84)

JUL 6 - Saudi King Fahd gives 8 installments of $1 million each between July 1984 and February 1985. Esther Morales' account # 54148 at BAC in the Cayman Islands receives the first monthly deposit of $1 million from Saudi Arabia transferred from the Swiss Bank Corporation. (Morales/FDN bank statements)

JUL 9 - The CIA has been using a private cargo airline, Southern Air Transport, to ferry arms, airline parts and soldiers to U.S. military bases in Honduras where the supplies are made available to the contras. News reports say the CIA also is using Summit Aviation of Delaware and Evergreen Air of Tucson, Arizona to transport arms. (AP 7/10/84; CBS News 7/9/84)

JUL 23 - Twenty-five F-5 fighter jets are reported to be on their way from the U.S. to Iran via Turkey. According to a news report, Lloyds Insurance of London has been asked to insure the delivery which purportedly is destined for Turkey but, according to sources, is ultimately headed for Iran. (CSM 7/23/84)

JUL 26 - American Marketing & Consulting Inc. purchases Maule N5657H, a short-takeoff-and-landing plane (STOL) from Maule Air in Moultrie, Georgia. American Marketing & Consulting is located at P.O. Box 2480, Landover Hills, Maryland. On the Aircraft Registration Application also filed on July 26 with the FAA, Richard V. Secord is listed as president of American Marketing & Consulting, Karl Kaufman as vice-president, and Robert H. Lilac (also spelled Liliac in some Pentagon phone books) as secretary. Lilac worked in the Pentagon with Secord on the AWACS sale to Saudi Arabia in 1981 and later joined the National Security Council on April 9, 1982 where he worked in the Office of Political-Military Affairs with Oliver North. The Landover

Hills post office says Box 2480 is paid for by Sellers Sales and Service, which is a Chrysler Plymouth dealer in Lanham, Maryland. Sellers has recently become KTK Chrysler Plymouth of which Karl Kaufman is the owner. (FAA Documents; Unofficial White House Directories; Pentagon Phone Books; CBS News 7/14/86; Hearst Newspapers 7/27/86)

- The New York Times runs a quarter-page advertisement which states "THE VICTIMS OF COMMUNIST DOMINATED NICARAGUA NEED YOUR HELP" and asks for contributions to the Human Development Foundation, Inc. at 444 Brickell Avenue in Miami. The advertisement is paid for by a group called "Friends of the FDN" and lists the names Enrique Pereira, Octavio Sacasa, and Enrique Paguaga, New York State Representative. Similar advertisments run in the Miami Herald, and other papers across the country. Edgar Chamorro, then a member of the FDN Directorate, subsequently states that the advertisements were conceived and paid for by the CIA in order to create a cover for illicit aid from foreign countries that is flowing to the contras. According to Chamorro, the Human Development Foundation is a front account the FDN established in Panama in 1983. (NYT 7/26/84; Kornbluh, Chapter 1))

AUG - CIA had issued a notice to other government agencies warning that [Manuchehr] Ghorbanifar was a fabricator. . . . [and] instructed all its components . . . to have no dealings with Ghorbanifar. (SSIC 1/29/87)

AUG 3 - Esther Morales account at BAC receives a deposit of $1 million, apparently from Fahd. (FDN/Morales bank account statements.)

AUG 6 - The contras make their first purchase from their own accounts, several months after the last authorized covert CIA funds are expended in March. According to the FDN's Bosco Matamoros, the FDN spends $16 to $18 million of the Saudi money by May 16, 1985. After that date, the rebels claim they rely entirely on weapons purchased earlier. (WP 3/19/87)

AUG 15 - Benjamin Kashefi, an American citizen of Iranian descent, is indicted in U.S. District Court in San Diego on charges of shipping approximately $12 million worth of tank, cannon and missile parts to Iran. (Baltimore Sun 8/23/84)

AUG 31 - [McFarlane] requested an interagency study of U.S. relations with Iran after Khomeini. (See October 19, 1984 entry.) (Tower)

FALL - After meetings with top aides, Reagan gives his authorization for the establishment of a private aid network for the contras. The plan calls for fundraising events, high-profile visits by rebel leaders to the White House and other activities. Originally "fairly overt," according to one official, the program, under North's direction, began expanding in all directions in an attempt to keep pace with the rebels' needs. By the summer of 1985, it appears that North had developed a separate network that included arms deliveries to the contras. Despite rising concern about North's activities, Poindexter reportedly refuses to order North to share responsibility for the covert programs. (WSJ 1/23/87)

SEP - LtCol North's involvement in Contra support is evident as early as September 1984, before the October 1984 ban was in effect. He directed his attention to two areas: operations and fundraising. (Tower)

- In fiscal year 1984, American National Management Corp. (ANMC) holds at least three Army contracts totaling over $600,000 relating to military special operations. The company, owned by Richard Gadd and affiliated with Richard Secord, also claims to have a major part of a nearly $2.3 million classified contract this year in support of special activities. During the summer, ANMC was paid an estimated $308,900 to keep on standby a Gulfstream II and Lear jet transport for unspecified use outside the U.S. The extent of Secord's and Gadd's involvement as private citizens in sensitive and classified government operations becomes known in the wake of the disclosure of their activities in the covert contra resupply network and provokes debate over the issue of privatizing clandestine operations. (WSJ 2/13/87)

- Since September 1984, Mr. Schwimmer had . . . been a consultant to then-Prime Minister of Israel Shimon Peres. . . . Amiram Nir [was], since September 1984, an advisor to Prime Minister Peres on counterterrorism. (Tower)

SEP 1 - Dana Parker and James Powell, soldiers of fortune with ties to a private group called Civilian Military Assistance (CMA), die in a helicopter crash in Nicaragua while accompanying a group of contras on a mission there. One description of the mission says they were unarmed and meant to resupply FDN troops. Another version has them on a combat mission against a Cuban-run military training facility, possibly for Salvadoran rebels. It is noted that Powell was a former helicopter pilot in Vietnam. Parker was a veteran of the Huntsville, Alabama Police Department who served in the Alabama National Guard's elite Special Forces unit. (Dickey, p.264)

- The three Cessnas delivered to the contras as part of "Operation Elephant Herd" (see December 9, 1983 entry) carry out an air assault on a Nicaraguan military school. An accompanying helicopter carrying two American advisers is shot down, killing both. (BG 1/3/87)

- The State Department early in the month asks the U.S. Customs Service to investigate whether CMA has conformed with federal laws governing the transfer of military supplies overseas. (NYT 9/10/84)

SEP 2 - In a memorandum on September 2, 1984 LtCol North informed Mr. McFarlane of a recent air attack launched into Nicaraguan territory by the Federated Democratic Resistance ("FDN") [sic], a major Contra faction. LtCol North said that at a meeting the previous day he and a CIA official involved in Central American affairs had urged Contra leader Adolpho Calero to postpone the attack. Despite Mr. Calero's agreement, the plan was carried out and, in the course of the attack, the Contras lost "the only operating FDN helicopter on the Northern Front."

LtCol North regarded this loss as "a serious blow." He told Mr. McFarlane, "It may therefore be necessary to ask a private donor to donate a helicopter to the FDN for use in any upcoming operation against an arms delivery." Outside help was necessary since "FDN resources are not adequate to purchase a helicopter at this time." He recommended that Mr. McFarlane grant him approval to approach a private donor for "the provision of a replacement civilian helicopter."

At the bottom of the memorandum Mr. McFarlane initialed, "Disapprove," and wrote, "Let's wait a week or two." After further thought, Mr. McFarlane apparently changed his mind. He crossed out the above sentence and wrote, "I don't think this is legal." (Tower)

SEP 4 - Esther Morales' account at BAC receives a deposit of $1 million, evidently from Saudi King Fahd. (FDN/Morales bank account statements)

SEP 11 - Representatives from the CIA, State Department and Pentagon brief the Senate Select Committee on Intelligence on the September 1 helicopter crash in Nicaragua. The CIA representatives state that the Agency "had no involvement in the mission conducted in Honduras by the group of U.S. volunteers called Civilian Military Assistance" (CMA), that the CIA had no advance knowledge of the operation and no contact with any member of CMA. They go on to deny any connection with the organization. (Senate Intelligence Committee News Release 9/11/84)

LATE SEP - The Director of the CIA Central American Task Force (CATF), Alan D. Fiers, described the inter-agency process on Central America at the time he moved into his job in late September, 1984:

"There was only one point in the apparatus [sic] who was functioning and who seemed to be able and was interested and was working the process, and that was Ollie North. And it was Ollie North who then moved into that void and was the focal point for the Administration on Central American policy during that time-frame [until fall 1985.]" (Tower)

OCT 1 - The Government of Israel awards a $40.6 million contract to Recon/CAI, a division of Recon/Optical Inc., of Barrington, Ill. to produce a long range real-time aerial reconnaissance system. The contract is financed by the U.S. Department of Defense as part of the foreign military sales program. In May 1986, Recon suddenly terminates the project because delays arising from contract disputes with the Israelis threaten to jeopardize the company's financial stability, according to Recon officials. Recon subsequently files suit (see June 11, 1986 entry) against the Israeli Government after it discovers evidence that Israeli representatives at the Recon plant apparently passed confidential information about the project to an Israeli company with the aim of duplicating the project. (Chicago Tribune 8/20/86)

OCT 5 - Safair Freighters (U.S.A.) Inc. registers another Lockheed Hercules C-130, serial number 4558, tail number N46965, with the FAA, and indicates that the "records of its flight hours are available for inspection at Southern Air Transport, Inc., Miami, Florida." (FAA records 10/5/84)

OCT 12 - Congress passes an omnibus Continuing Resolution for FY85 (P.L. 98-473), which includes the suspension of aid to the contras at least until March 1, 1985. The Administration is authorized to request the release of $14 million for "military" aid to the rebels allocated by the act. The resolution also includes the "second" Boland Amendment (Section 8066(a)) (see entry below). The Amendment reflects legislators' concerns that the Administration may try to use discretionary funds to bypass congressional restrictions on support for the guerrillas. (MH 12/7/86; CRS "U.S. Assistance to Nicaraguan Guerrillas" 12/4/86)

- In October 1984, Congress cut off all U.S. funding for the Contras, unless specifically authorized by Congress. Section 8066(a) of the Fiscal Year 1985 DoD Appropriations Act provided:

During fiscal year 1985, no funds available to the Central Intelligence Agency, the Department of Defense, or any other agency or entity of the United States involved in intelligence activities may be obligated or expended for the purpose or which would have the effect of supporting, directly or indirectly, military or paramilitary operations in Nicaragua by any nation, group, organization, movement, or individual. (A narrower but substantively similar provision was incorporated the next day into the Intelligence Authorization Act for Fiscal Year 1983. A series of continuing resolutions extended the prohibition through December 19, 1985.) This legislation presented the Administration with a dilemma: how, if at all, to continue implementing a largely covert program of support for the Contras without U.S. funds and without the involvement of the CIA. As soon as the Congressional restrictions were put into effect, CIA headquarters sent instructions to its field stations to cease all contacts with resistance groups except for intelligence collection activities:

"Field stations are to cease and desist with actions which can be construed to be providing any type of support, either direct or indirect, to the various entities with whom we dealt under the program. All future contact with those entities are, until further notice, to be solely, repeat solely, for the purpose of collecting positive and counterintelligence information of interest to the United States."

From the outset, questions were raised as to whether the provision applied to the NSC staff. Some in Congress argued that the Boland Amendment applied to the NSC staff, since it is "involved in intelligence activity." Executive Order 12333 on covert action and Congressional oversight designates the NSC "as the highest Executive Branch entity that provides review of, guidance for and direction to the conduct of all national foreign intelligence, counterintelligence, and special activities, and attendant policies and programs."

But the NSC staff appears to have received different advice. A classified legal memorandum, retrieved from LtCol North's safe, apparently was prepared by the President's Intelligence Oversight Board ("IOB") between March 1 and December 19, 1985. The letterhead and transmittal information had been removed, but the document contained references to "the Board" and "the Board's Counsel" and resembled in form, style and subject matter other memoranda prepared for the NSC staff by the IOB. (Footnote: The IOB did not provide a copy of this document in response to the Board's request for all memoranda "providing legal advice to the NSC staff in 1985 and 1986." The IOB did provide two other memoranda to the Board dated May 19, 1986 and May 29, 1986, respectively, that address allegations: (a) that North and CIA employees made statements to overthrow the government in Nicaragua; and (b) that the CIA prepared an "assassination manual" contrary to law. In both cases, the IOB found the allegations unfounded. A third IOB memorandum provided in response to the Board's request is discussed infra.) The memorandum was developed in response to a letter from then Congressman Michael Barnes. It concluded: (1) "the NSC is not covered by the prohibition," (adding by footnote that "LtCol. North might be, as he evidently is on a non-reimbursed detail from the Marine Corps"); and (2) "None of LtCol North's activities during the past year constitutes a violation of the Boland Amendment."

The IOB cited three points to establish that section 8066 did not apply to the NSC and, presumably, its staff. First, the IOB looked to Congressional intent, which it asserted was demonstrated by the parallel but narrower provisions of the FY 1985 Intelligence Authorization Act. That Act, passed by Congress the day after section 8066, was narrower in two respects: (a) it omitted the reference to "any agency or entity involved in intelligence activity"; and (b) it was limited to "funds authorized to be appropriated by this Act or by the Intelligence Authorization Act for Fiscal Year 1984."

Legal intent as evinced by this narrower statute was deemed to govern interpretation of the DoD Appropriations Act.

Second, the IOB noted that E.O. 12333, which designates the NSC as the "highest Executive Branch entity" responsible for the conduct of foreign intelligence, does not include the NSC among the agencies comprising "the Intelligence Community."

Finally, the IOB argued that the exclusion of the NSC Staff was intended by Congress because the prescribed role of the NSC was to coordinate rather than implement covert action.

After October, 1984, the NSC staff—particularly Oliver North—moved to fill the void left by the Congressional restrictions. Between 1984 and 1986, LtCol North, with the acquiescence of the National Security Advisor, performed activities the CIA was unable to undertake itself, including the facilitation of outside fundraising efforts and oversight of a private network to supply lethal equipment to the Contras. (Tower)

OCT 19 - Two CIA officers and two contract employees, all Americans, are killed when their surveillance plane crashes in El Salvador. The Agency says they were monitoring arms shipments to the Salvadoran rebels from Nicaragua at night when they flew into a volcano. (Dickey, p. 264)

- [T]he State Department sent Mr. McFarlane the interagency response to his request. (See August 31, 1984 entry) It concluded that the United States had "no influential contacts" within the Iranian government or Iranian political groups. The study suggested little that the United States could do to establish such contacts. (See December 11, 1984 entry)

. . . Howard Teicher, one of the NSC staff members involved, told the Board that the interagency effort failed to identify any new ideas for significantly expanding U.S. influence in Iran. It resulted in no change in U.S. policy. The U.S. government continued aggressively to discourage arms transfers by other nations to Iran under a program called "Operation Staunch."

. . . Mr. Teicher, Donald Fortier, and perhaps other NSC staff members were unhappy with the result of the interagency effort. They placed a high priority on fashioning a strategy for acquiring influence and checking the Soviets in Iran. (Tower)

- According to the detailed interagency study completed in October 1984 (see August 31, 1984 entry), Khomeini's death was probably a precondition to changes in Iranian policies and the realistic prospect of improved Iranian-American relations. The study, which incorporated the analysis of a Special National Intelligence Estimate ("SNIE") then in preparation on Iran, concluded that the possibility of resuming arms shipments to Iran depended on Iran's willingness to restore formal relations, which itself turned on Iran's perception of the importance of such shipments and the American perception of the impact of such shipments on the regional balance of power. (Enclosure to Hill to McFarlane, 10/19/84) The study conveyed an impression of relative American powerlessness to affect events in Iran, powerlessness that would continue indefinitely. (Tower)

OCT 22 - The Senate Select Committee on Intelligence holds a closed session with CIA officials concerning the production of a Psychological Warfare Manual (pseudonym "TAYACAN") in October 1983. The manual, which the Agency provided to the contras, reportedly recommended "neutralization" as one means of attaining political ends. The CIA called the manual the work of an overzealous freelancer; however, it is revealed that Duane "Dewey Maroni" Clarridge, the CIA's division chief for Latin America in the Directorate for Operations, commissioned its writing and Ray Doty, another senior Agency official, was involved in its planning and preparation. (See November 11 and December 5, 1984 entries.) (Senate Report 98-665, 10/10/84; NYT 11/27/86 & 1/21/87; UPI 2/9/87)

NOV - Amalgamated Commercial Enterprises (ACE), a shell company, is incorporated in Panama. A year later it is purchased by Southern Air Transport and used to pass through funds for supplies to the contras. (WSJ 1/16/87)

- By November 1984, Iranians with connections to the Tehran government were indicating a connection between such weapons and the release of Americans kidnapped in Lebanon. (Tower)

- The formal reappraisal of U.S. policy toward Iran began in late 1984 when the National Security Council issued a National Security Study Directive (NSSD). An NSC official involved in the policy review testified that he was disappointed with the bureaucracy's lack of imagination in responding to this study directive and with the absence of any recommendation for change in policy. (SSIC 1/29/87)

NOV 1 - FBI agents arrest arms dealer Gerard Latchinian (a business partner of Felix Rodriguez), a former Honduran army chief of staff, and six other men on charges of smuggling $10.3 million of cocaine into the U.S. in order to finance a hit squad and coup attempt against the president of Honduras, Roberto Suazo Cordova. The plotters had approached retired Army Colonel Charles A. Beckwith, commander of the 1980 Iran rescue mission, and one of his Delta Force colleagues, retired Major Charles D. Odorizzi, who then cooperated with the FBI in setting up the sting. Among those convicted on charges relating to the assassination attempt is Honduran General Jose Bueso Rosa, who was ousted by Suazo from his post as chief of the Armed Forces Joint Command in March 1984. Bueso is considered an important contributor to U.S. policy toward Nicaragua. In the summer of 1986, North and General Paul Gorman, the former commander of American forces in Latin America, urge leniency before federal officials on Bueso's behalf (see Summer 1986 and February 23, 1987 entries). (MH 11/2/84 & 11/3/84; WSJ 11/2/84; WP 8/15/85; NYT 2/23/87)

NOV 6 - On Election Day, a senior Administration official, later identified as McFarlane, declares that top-secret intelligence information indicates that Nicaragua has received a number of Soviet-built attack helicopters in recent days, and that a Soviet freighter headed for Nicaragua is carrying crates apparently containing MIG jet fighters, a major escalation of the Sandinistas' military capacity. The Administration views their delivery as a "very serious development." This report later turns out to be false; no MIGs were on board the ship. (NYT 11/7/84 & 11/8/84; MH 11/9/84)

NOV 7 - In another memorandum to Mr. McFarlane, LtCol North sought approval to continue providing intelligence support to Mr. Calero. Mr. Calero had requested information from LtCol North to assist him in efforts to "take out" Soviet provided Hind-D helicopters recently shipped to El Bluff, Nicaragua. LtCol North told Mr. McFarlane that he earlier had forwarded Mr. Calero responsive intelligence obtained from Robert Vickers, CIA National Intelligence Officer for Latin American affairs and Gen. Paul Gorman. Mr. Calero decided to fly to Washington that day to review with LtCol North a plan to strike the Hinds and a longterm strategy for establishing a Calero-Cruz coalition. The Director of the CIA CATF contacted LtCol North when he learned of Mr. Calero's unexpected trip to Washington, but, citing the new statutory prohibitions, declined an invitation to meet with LtCol North and Mr. Calero.

Director Casey learned of LtCol North's discussions with the CIA official and expressed his concern to Mr. McFarlane that LtCol North had discussed "Calero, Guatemala, MIGs, dollars, etc." LtCol North's November 7 memorandum assured Mr. McFarlane that he had withheld much information in his conversations:

"At no time did I discuss with [name deleted] financial arrangements for the FDN. At no time did I indicate that Calero was attempting to attack the MIGs. I specifically told [the Director of the CIA CATF] that Calero was attempting to collect information on the MIGs in Corinto and would pass this information to a CIA agent in Tegucigalpa if it was available." (Tower)

NOV 9 - Vice Chairman of the Senate intelligence committee, Daniel Moynihan (D-NY), writes to Casey requesting a report on allegations by a contra leader that CIA officers gave possibly improper and illegal assistance to contra leaders in lobbying efforts on Capitol Hill. Casey responds December 7, saying "an extensive review of Agency files" and interviews with Agency personnel reveal "no record or recollection to support" the charges. (Senate Report 98-665, 10/10/84; CRS "U.S. Intelligence: Issues for Congress, 1986" 1/5/87)

NOV 11 - According to press accounts, some six mid-level CIA officials (including Tomas Castillo, later promoted to be Costa Rica station chief) have been disciplined for their role in the CIA psychological warfare manual for Nicaragua, following the recommendation of two internal investigations. However, the official who commissioned the manual, Duane "Dewey Maroni" Clarridge, division chief for Latin America in the Directorate for Operations, is promoted to head covert operations in Europe. CIA Director Casey also chooses not to discipline another Agency official, Ray Doty, who was involved in planning and approving the manual. (See October 22 and December 5, 1984 entries.) (CRS "U.S. Intelligence: Issues for Congress, 1986" 1/5/87; NYT 1/21/87; UPI 2/9/87)

NOV - At a meeting in Hamburg, West Germany, Manuchehr Ghorbanifar, an arms dealer and former officer in Savak, the shah's secret police, who is working for Iranian Prime Minister Hussein Mussavi, reportedly raises the issue of ransoming hostages with Iranian officials and former CIA agent Theodore Shackley. Shackley relays the proposal to Washington. A draft of the Senate intelligence panel's report on the Iran-contra affair, leaked in early 1987, says that Israel first introduced the idea of U.S.-Iranian contacts at a meeting between Israeli offical David Kimche, Israeli weapons dealers Al Schwimmer and Yaacov Nimrodi, and Ghorbanifar in late 1984. The report adds that the group decided the main problem in the planned opening was to convince the Americans to agree. Israeli officials later dispute this, saying the arms deal was an American idea first brought up at a meeting between Israeli Prime Minister Peres and NSC consultant Michael Ledeen (see April 1984 entry). (NYT 12/25/86; Newsweek 12/15/86; WP 1/12/87)

NOV 19-21 - Theodore Shackley, a former CIA officer, reported that, in meetings November 19-21, 1984, in Hamburg, West Germany, General Manucher Hashemi, former head of SAVAK's Department VIII (counterespionage), introduced him to Manuchehr Ghorbanifar. Hashemi said Ghorbanifar's contacts in Iran were "fantastic." ("American Hostages in Lebanon" at 2. (11/22/84)) Ghorbanifar was already known to the CIA, and the Agency did not have a favorable impression of his reliability or veracity. (Cave 3-5, 44; C/NE (2) passim) Shackley reported that Ghorbanifar had been a SAVAK agent, was known to be an international dealmaker, and, generally, an independent man, difficult to control. Ghorbanifar told Shackley that he and other Iranians wanted to help shape Iran's future policies and bring Tehran closer to the West.

"He feared that Iran would become a Soviet satellite within the near term—three to five years—if he and people like General Hashemi did not do something to stem the tide. He rhetorically asked what can we do, for despite our ability to work with the 'moderates' in Iran, we can't get a meaningful dialogue with Washington. According to Ghorbanifar, it is President Reagan who has the destiny of the Iranian people in his hand. When at this juncture Ghorbanifar was asked if he had tried to open a dialogue with the Americans, he said, 'We know the CIA in Frankfurt. They want to treat us like kleenex—use us for their purpose and then throw us out the window. We can't work with them as they are unreasonable and unprofessional. In fact, if you check on me with them, they will tell you I am unreasonable and undisciplined.'" ("American Hostages in Lebanon," supra, at 2)

To prove that he and Hashemi had influential contacts in Iran, Ghorbanifar suggested that Iran would be willing to trade some Soviet equipment captured in Iraq for TOW missiles. He further suggested the possibility of a cash ransom paid to Iran for the four Americans kidnapped in Lebanon (including Buckley), who, he said after making telephone calls, were alive. The transaction could be disguised by using Ghorbanifar as a middleman. Shackley reported that Ghorbanifar needed a response by December 7, 1984. According to Shackley, later that month, the State Department in effect replied: 'thank you but we will work this problem out via other channels.'" ("American Hostages in Lebanon" at 1 (6/7/85) (Footnote: An unattributed and undated note analysed meetings involving Hashemi, Shackley, and Iranians at about this time and in March 1985, when the same topics noted by Shackley were discussed. This note added that "[we] determined that the Iranan [sic] side was only interesed [sic] in money." See infra p. B 11.) Ledeen told the Board that Ghorbanifar had tried for some time to establish contact with the United States. "[H]aving failed to reach us at the front door, he went around to the side door." Shackley transmitted his report to General Walters. (Ledeen (1) 41-42) Ledeen and Shackley separately told the Board that, in May 1985, Shackley told Ledeen that he had no response from Walters. In June 1985, he gave the report, together with an update, to Ledeen who, without reading it, he said, passed it to North with the report "that Shackley had had a contact with an Iranian who had said he thought he could ransom Buckley." (Ledeen (1) 43; Ledeen (2) 2-6; Shackley 13-24) (Tower)

NOV 28 - Sam Nesley Hall, arrested December 1986 in Nicaragua on espionage charges, claims to visit the Pentagon at the invitation of two Navy officers, Capt. William Hamilton and Cmdr. Francis Fane, in connection with the creation of an alleged secret, paramilitary group known as the Phoenix Battalion. CBS says the two officers have acknowledged encouraging Hall. A Navy spokesman says in 1986 that the two retired many years ago. (CBS "60 Minutes" 12/21/86; WP 12/23/86))

DEC 3 - Peter Kilburn, a librarian at the American University of Beirut, is kidnapped. (NYT 12/25/86)

DEC 5 - The House Select Committee on Intelligence characterizes the CIA psychological warfare manual as illegal, and a result of negligent management. (See October 22 and November 11, 1984 entries.) (Senate Report 98-665, 10/10/84; WSJ 12/6/84; CRS "U.S. Intelligence: Issues for Congress, 1986" 1/5/87)

DEC - In a memo to North, contra supporters suggest seeking a donation for their cause from the sultan of Brunei. The sultan made a $500,000 contribution to Nancy Reagan's drug crusade in September, which apparently gave the authors of the memo the idea. On June 24, 1986, Shultz meets with the sultan for three hours; on August 19, $10 million is transferred to a Swiss bank account, the number of which was provided originally by North to Elliott Abrams of the State Department (see entries under these dates). North's apparent role in the donation request does not become known until late 1986. (MH 12/15/86)

DEC 11 - [I]n a letter . . . to Mr. McFarlane's deputy, VADM John Poindexter, the CIA professed only a limited capability to influence events in Iran over the near term.

The CIA reached a similar conclusion (see Oct 19, 1984 entry) with regard to the utility of covert action in Iran to improve the United States position. The CIA Deputy Director of Operations considered the Marxist Mujaheddin E Khalq to be well organized, influenced by the Soviets, and likely to succeed Khomeini. (DDO to Poindexter, 12/ 11/84) (Tower)

DEC 14 - The State Department distilled these views (see Dec 11, 1984 entry) into a draft National Security Decision Directive ("NSDD") at the end of 1984. This document would have directed the United States government to maintain and expand its capability to exploit opportunities that might arise in Iran, but reaffirmed, absent changes in the Iranian situation, existing policies. Thus, the draft NSDD would continue the policy of discouraging arms transfers to Iran. (Draft NSDD 5, in Hill to McFarlane, 12/14/84) Howard Teicher, Senior Director for Political-Military Affairs on the NSC staff, told the Board that these interagency efforts "produced no ideas which any of us involved considered to be of great value in terms of significantly affecting our posture in the region." (Teicher 8) (Tower)

DEC 21 - Trans World Arms, a Canadian company based in Montreal submits three end-user certificates to the Portuguese Arms Directorate requesting approval of the sale of various weapons to Guatemala. The signature on the certificates is that of Guatemalan General Cesar Augusto Caceres Rojas, who later claims it is forged. The arms are actually intended for the contras. Energy Resources International, a Vienna, Virginia company linked to Richard Secord, submits similar requests through a Lisbon weapons dealer, Defex-Portugal, which result in nine shipments of arms to the rebels totaling 800 tons and costing $5.6 million. Energy Resources, according to Panama records, was bought in 1978 by Albert Hakim's Stanford Technology Corp. It lists its address on several of the certificates as 440 Maple Ave. E, Vienna, Virginia—the same address used frequently by Secord. However, Energy Resources does not appear to occupy offices at that address, although Richard Gadd, a retired Air Force lieutenant colonel, does. Gadd plays an important role in the contra supply effort, eventually taking over direction of the operation in January 1986 (see entry). Energy Resources also occasionally uses Defex's address in Portugal. One of Defex's three partners, Jose Garnel, later identifies Thomas Clines, a former CIA official and associate of both Secord and North, as having done business with the company. Another Defex partner is Marcelino Brito, who is said by an American intelligence source to have helped facilitate shipments through Portugal. (WSJ 1/16/87; WP 1/17/87; LAT 2/13/87)

Late DEC - A meeting takes place at the home of Adolfo Calero in Miami between John Hull, an American living in Costa Rica who has allowed his property to be used for airdrops for the contras; Robert Owen, a liaison between North and the contras (see January 9, 1985 entry); Tom Posey, the head of Civilian Military Assistance (CMA); Jack Terrell, an ex-convict and member of CMA; and others at which logistics for Costa Rican missions are discussed, according to Terrell. Terrell, who sees Hull and Owen as CIA representatives, learns that they will send Posey rather than him on the first mission. (Chronology released by Sen. John Kerry 11/86; MH 6/8/86)

January - October 1985

- Testimony by several senior Administration witnesses indicates that during 1985, the Administration was occupied on a regular basis with matters relating to terrorism and the state of U.S. hostages. In particular, documents and testimony reflect a deep personal concern on the part of the President for the welfare of U.S. hostages both in the early stages of the initiative and throughout the program. The hostages included William Buckley, a U.S. official in Lebanon ...The possibility of the release of U.S. hostages was brought up repeatedly in conjunction with discussion of the program. (SSIC 1/29/87)

- Documents and testimony indicate that Adnan Khashoggi and other international arms dealers, including Manucher Ghorbanifar, were interested in bringing the U.S. into an arms relationship with Iran, and had discussed this at a series of meetings beginning in the summer of 1984 and continuing into early 1985. These discussions reportedly included the idea of an "arms for hostages" deal in part as a means of establishing each country's bona fides. Khashoggi reportedly met with various leaders in the Middle East to discuss policy toward Iran during this same period. (SSIC 1/29/87)

- At the beginning of 1985, the Administration adopted new procedures for approving and coordinating covert actions. These were meticulously set forth in elaborate detail in a National Security Decision Directive signed by the President. They included comprehensive interagency evaluation of proposed covert actions, coordinated review of actions undertaken, and notification of Congress in accordance with statute. (NSDD 159, 1/18/85) The NSDD also specified that the President would approve in writing all covert action Findings made pursuant to section 501 of the National Security Act. (Tower)

- Congressional scrutiny of LtCol North's activities increased. To varying degrees throughout 1985, Congress had pressed the NSC staff for information about LtCol North's involvement in Contra fundraising and resupply activities. (Tower)

- Early in 1985, the NSC staff undertook actions aimed at the least to improve the government's knowledge about Iran. Michael Ledeen, who, from November 1984 to December 1986, was an NSC consultant on terrorism and certain Middle East questions, including Iran, told the Board that the NSC staff regarded Iran as a strategically important place about which the United States had inadequate information. (Ledeen (1) 7-8) (Tower)

JAN - Casey tells Roy Furmark, a New York energy consultant and former legal client of his, that the U.S. "supplied and permitted the supply of arms to Iran," according to a court filing in a 1986 case involving a private attempt to ship military equipment to Iran. (NYT 1/6/87)

- Early in the year, Furmark introduces Samuel Evans, a former lawyer for Saudi arms dealer Adnan Khashoggi who is later indicted for conspiring to sell arms to Iran, to Cyrus Hashemi, who is an informant for the U.S. Customs Service on the deal. (NYT 1/6/87)

- In a series of meetings beginning in January 1985, Yaacov Nimrodi, an arms merchant and former Israeli Defense Attache in Tehran, Ghorbanifar, Amiram Nir, Advisor to Prime Minister Peres on Counterterrorism, and Adolph Schwimmer, a long-time arms merchant and, since September 1984, Special Advisor to Prime Minister Peres, considered Iran and the American hostages. Also involved was Saudi businessman Adnan Khashoggi, a man well-connected in the Middle East and enjoying a special relationship with key Israeli officials. They concluded that a plan to gain the release of the hostages and to "open up a dialogue with Iran" was realistic if they could obtain American support. Roy Furmark, a business associate of Adnan Khashoggi and participant in at least one of the meetings, told Charles Allen of the CIA that "profit was certainly a motive but that the group did see their efforts as leading toward stability in the region and the release of the hostages." Ghorbanifar and Khashoggi had a number of meetings starting in January 1985. Khashoggi reported Ghorbanifar's views on Iranian politics to McFarlane in a long memorandum on July 1.

Furmark . . . told the Board that he met Ghorbanifar in January 1985, and subsequently introduced him to Khashoggi. He recalled that Ghorbanifar and Khashoggi had a number of conversations about Middle Eastern politics (Furmark 3). (Id.; Ghorbanifar 37-38) (DCI to Poindexter, undated but after October 22, 1986). [See Late March, 1985 entry.] (Tower)

- Early in the year, Faith Ryan Whittlesey leaves her post as Reagan's assistant for public liaison. With her goes most of the impetus for the White House Outreach Working Group on Central America. North is reported to regret deeply the group's demise and, according to a high-ranking White House official at the time, "may have felt that it was up to him to keep contra aid going" until Congress resumed funding. (WP 12/7/86)

- Early in the year, a CIA memo from Graham Fuller, vice chairman of the National Intelligence Council, warns of the possibility of serious Soviet inroads in Iran following the death of Khomeini. Fuller also suggests that there are moderates within the Ayatollah's regime whom Washington might contact. The memo is a catalyst for internal discussions that eventually lead to the Iran arms deals. Casey's apparent involvement in the Iran sales dates back at least to the writing of this memo. (NYT 12/17/86; WP 12/21/86)

- Graham Fuller, then the National Intelligence Officer for the Near East and South Asia, told the Board that in early 1985 the U.S. intelligence community began to believe that serious factional fighting could break out in Iran even before Khomeini died. This change in the community's assessment provided a second opportunity for a policy review. (See October 19, 1984 and May 20, 1985 entries.) (Tower)

- Around this time, a Swiss bank account is established for the Afghan rebels. The U.S. and Saudi Arabia each promise to deposit $250 million to purchase Soviet, Chinese and other arms. In January, $50 million is taken out of an account for the rebels to pay for forty Swiss-made Oerlikon .20 millimeter automatic weapons. By January 1987, however, only eleven have reached the Afghan forces, according to Andrew Eiva, director of the Federation for American-Afghanistan Action. Eiva's disclosure comes at a time when Congress is preparing to investigate the possible misuse of CIA-run Swiss bank accounts as part of the Iran-contra controversy. (WP 1/13/87)

JAN 4 - McFarlane was prepared in January to send Ledeen to Europe on a mission of inquiry. In this connection, Rear Admiral Poindexter, McFarlane's deputy, wrote a letter of introduction saying Ledeen "has the complete confidence of Bud McFarlane and myself." (Poindexter to Schurer, 1/4/85. See also McFarlane to Grossouvre, 1/4/85) (Tower)

JAN 8 - The Rev. Lawrence Martin Jenco, head of the Beirut office of Catholic Relief Services, is kidnapped. During this period, according to Israeli Defense Minister Rabin (quoted in early 1987), the U.S. reportedly has asked Israel not to attack Iranian-backed Hezbollah guerrillas in Lebanon on grounds that they are holding American hostages. (NYT 12/25/86; State Department briefing 1/9/87)

- Reagan announces that Regan and James A. Baker III will swap official positions. Regan will become chief of staff at the White House and Baker will take over as Treasury secretary as soon as the Senate confirms Baker's appointment. Unbeknownst to Reagan, the two officials discussed the switch among themselves several weeks earlier. Presidential assistant Richard G. Darman proposed the move to the President yesterday. (WP 1/9/85)

JAN 9 - The Council for Democracy, Education and Assistance is incorporated in the District of Columbia. The council's directors are Robert W. Owen, John P. Flynn and Robert G.L. Wall. (Kenneth Reed Harrison is said later to be a director also.) The incorporators are Owen, Tina Parrish and Jeanette Tull. According to Flynn, a retired Air Force general, the council has been founded in order to help the contras. At the time of incorporation, Owen is working as a secret intermediary between North and the guerrillas while a congressional ban on aid to them is in effect. Flynn met Owen through John Hull, the American-born farmer who owns a ranch in Costa Rica and is frequently linked to contra activities. On the same day, Owen establishes the Institute for Democracy, Education and Assistance (IDEA), which, in October 1985, is given a grant of over $50,000 by the State Department's Nicaraguan Humanitarian Assistance Office (NHAO) to serve as a liaison to the contra group, United Nicaraguan Opposition (UNO), in its dealings with NHAO. The council, meanwhile, eventually receives $66,000 in donations, all of it reportedly from conservative activist Carl R. Channell (see March 1985 entry), for lobbying efforts on behalf of the rebels. (Records of the Govt. of D.C., Business Regulation Administration; testimony by Amb. Robert Duemling before HFAC, 3/5/86; MH 6/8/86 & 12/14/86; The Nation 1/17/87, p.43-44)

JAN 10 - Defex, the Lisbon weapons dealer, sends a letter to the Portuguese Arms Directorate asking permission to route one-half million rounds of 7.62 millimeter ammunition from Romania through Portugal to Guatemala. Defex is handling requests for arms intended for the contras on behalf of Energy Resources International, a company linked to Richard Secord. The requests are forged, using the letterhead of the Guatemalan military. (WP 1/17/87)

JAN 21 - Defex files papers with the Portuguese Arms Directorate requesting clearance to fly part of their December 21, 1984 weapons order to Guatemala. The arms are believed to have been shipped to the contras within the next two days. (WP 1/17/87)

JAN - Department of Transportation records show a Southern Air Transport flight carrying 23.6 tons of materials from Miami to San Salvador. (DOT Records)

JAN 22 - Bush meets with his top national security adviser, Donald P. Gregg, and Felix Rodriguez, a former CIA agent who served with Gregg in Vietnam (see also November 10, 1983 entry). (The Miami Herald puts the date of the meeting at January 24.) The purpose of the meeting is said to be to inform the Vice President of Rodriguez's desire to work in El Salvador against the insurgency. At some point in January, Gregg introduces Rodriguez to several Administration officials, including Thomas Pickering, ambassador to El Salvador; Langhorne Motley, assistant secretary of state for inter-American affairs; and DOD Latin American expert Nestor Sanchez. Rodriguez is eventually hired by the Salvadoran Air Force where he serves as liaison with private American crews involved in the contra resupply effort. Gregg denies knowing of the private network until Rodriguez informs him on August 8, 1986. (Bush Chronology in WP 12/16/86; WP 12/14/86)

JAN 28 - Defex files a request to Portuguese authorities for clearance to ship the rest of the December 1984 weapons order to Guatemala. Again, the arms are actually intended for the contras. (WP 1/17/87)

JAN 31 - R.M. Equipment, based in Miami, files two end-user certificates with the Portuguese National Defense Industry requesting approval of weapons purchases. The certificates are on stamped paper of the "Honduran Armed Forces Joint General Staff," and are signed by a Col. Julio Perez. The arms, along with others purchased in May of this year (see May 16 entry) are eventually shipped to the Honduran port of Puerto Cortez aboard the freighters Erria (see May 11, 1985 entry) and Peder Most (see June 1985), from where they are transferred to contra bases along the Nicaraguan border. (Lisbon Expresso 2/7/87; UPI 2/7/87)

FEB - Manuchehr Ghorbanifar renews the proposal to swap arms for hostages. (NYT 12/25/86)

- News accounts report that senior CIA officials drafted a plan in early 1982 to overthrow the Sandinista government by the end of 1983. One official states that the plan was never approved, but another says it was discarded in Spring 1983 only when it became apparent, as General Paul Gorman states later, that the contras were incapable of mounting a serious military challenge to the Sandinistas. (CRS "U.S. Assistance to Nicaraguan Guerrillas" 12/4/86)

FEB 6 - In 1985, LtCol North's interest in operational activities with respect to the Contras increased. In a memorandum for Mr. McFarlane on February 6, 1985 LtCol North discussed a Nicaraguan merchant ship, the MONIMBO, suspected of carrying arms via North Korea for delivery to Nicaragua. LtCol North recommended that Mr. McFarlane "*authorize Calero to be provided with the information on MONIMBO and approached on the matter of seizing or sinking the ship.*" (emphasis added). LtCol North said that Calero would be willing to finance such an operation, but would require operational support. LtCol North suggested a friendly nation's special operations unit might be asked to assist in the operation. Once the ship was seized LtCol North said:

"arrangements would have to be made for removal of the cargo for further transfer to the FDN, since it is unlikely that any of the other Central American states would allow the MONIMBO to enter their harbors once she had been pirated."

At the bottom of the memorandum VADM Poindexter indicated his agreement: "We need to take action to make sure ship does not arrive in Nicaragua." (Tower)

-On February 6, LtCol North informed Mr. McFarlane of recent efforts by Maj Gen John Singlaub, USAF Ret. to raise funds for the Contras in Asia. LtCol North said that as a result, two foreign governments offered to provide assistance. LtCol North sought Mr. McFarlane's approval to coordinate Singlaub's contacts with these governments:

"Singlaub will be here to see me tomorrow. With your permission, I will ask him to approach [X] at the [country deleted] Interests Section and [Y] at the [country deleted] Embassy urging that they proceed with their offer. Singlaub would then put Calero in direct contact with each of these officers. No White House/NSC solicitation would be made. [hand written notes:] Nor should Singlaub indicate any U.S. Government endorsement whatsoever."

We do not know if Mr. McFarlane ever approved this plan, but the Contras eventually received funds from both foreign governments. (Tower)

FEB 7 - A note from VADM Poindexter to Mr. McFarlane dated February 7 is attached to the memorandum, suggesting that the issue [of intercepting the MONIMBO] be raised at a meeting later that day of the Crisis Pre-Planning Group ("CPPG"), an interagency group established under auspices of the NSC system. VADM Poindexter wrote:

"Except for the prohibition of the intelligence community doing anything to assist the Freedom Fighters I would readily recommend I bring this up at CPPG at 2:00 today. *Of course we could discuss it from the standpoint of keeping the arms away from Nicaragua without any involvement of Calero and Freedom Fighters.* What do you think? JP" (emphasis added).

We have no record on whether this was discussed at the CPPG meeting but understand that the project was abandoned after the friendly government rejected involvement. (Tower)

FEB 14 - Defex, the Lisbon weapons dealer, submits five more end-user certificates to the Portuguese Arms Director-ate on behalf of Energy Resources International. The letter-head and signatures are identical to those used in the December 21, 1984 order, but the amount of arms requested is much larger. The list includes 10,000 rifles, 10,000 pounds of TNT, 1,500 detonators, 15,000 grenades, 250 mortars and 150 machine guns. The requests are eventually approved in part. (WP 1/17/87)

FEB 21 - Reagan in a press conference says that U.S. policy toward Nicaragua is aimed at making the Sandinistas say "uncle." Four years ago Reagan insisted that his only goal was to halt the arms flow to El Salvador insurgents. (LAT 3/3/85)

FEB 27 - A French arms dealer, Bernard Veillot, sells a contract for 39 American F-4 jet fighters to Col. Kiamars Salahshoor of the Iranian Air Force. The director general of the Societe de Conseil et de Gestion, a Paris representative for Bank Worms in Geneva, also signed the contract, which was written on the Societe's letterhead. The Societe connec-tion is indicative of the extensive contacts private arms dealers who are part of the so-called Demavand project have with major financial institutions in Europe. The Demavand project is later reported to have existed with the knowledge and tacit approval of high Pentagon officials. (NYT 2/2/87)

- Retiring head of the U.S. Southern Command, General Paul Gorman, reportedly states the contras are currently in-capable of overthrowing the Sandinista regime. (CRS "U.S. Assistance to Nicaraguan Guerrillas" 12/4/86)

MAR - Early in the month, two Cuban-Americans, who have stored crates of weapons in the homes of relatives in Miami, decide to ship the arms to the contras. The two are veterans of the Bay of Pigs invasion who have recruited other anti-communist Cubans to fight the Sandinistas. They enlist two American friends to help with the shipment: Jesus Garcia, a booking officer at the Dade County jail, and a mercenary named Steven Carr (see March 6 and June 22, 1985 entries). (New Republic 11/24/86)

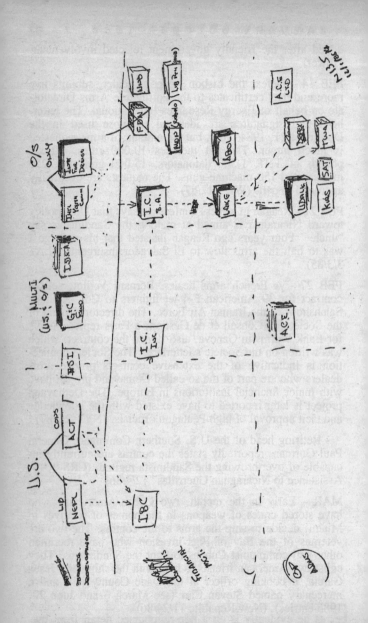

- A CIA Special National Intelligence Estimate (SNIE) entitled "Libya's Qaddafi: The Challenge to the United States and Western Interests" warns of the possibility that a U.S. policy of confrontation toward Libya could backfire. The report says that if left to himself, the Libyan leader would probably concentrate for a time on regional subversion and try to exploit diplomatic and political opportunities around the world. But the authors of the report say they believe that Khaddafi "would directly target U.S. personnel or installations if [he] ... believed the U.S. was engaging in a direct threat to his person or was actively attempting to overthrow his regime." The report adds that "[e]ssentially Qaddafi is not controllable" which, according to a press account, supports the collective view of U.S. intelligence agencies that diplomatic and economic pressure will have little or no effect on his behavior. Despite such appraisals, the Reagan administration at the end of 1985 embarks on an aggressive campaign against Libya that includes increased economic sanctions, military maneuvers and a covert CIA plan to undermine the Khaddafi regime. (WP 2/2/86)

- A memo to North from a subordinate of conservative fundraiser Carl R. Channell discusses the possibility of major donations from two individuals in return for "one quiet minute with the President." The memo links North to a nation-wide media and lobbying campaign aimed at supporting the contras and undermining their opponents in Congress. North's supervision of the effort, in possible violation of federal laws prohibiting government employees from engaging in partisan politics, is not disclosed until late 1986. (MH 12/14/86)

-As the March, 1985 Congressional vote on Contra aid approached, elements of the NSC staff focused their efforts on strategies for repackaging the Contra program to increase support on Capitol Hill. (Tower)

MAR 1 - A classified legal memorandum, retrieved from LtCol North's safe, apparently was prepared by the President's Intelligence Oversight Board ("IOB") between March 1 and December 19, 1985. The memorandum was developed in response to a letter from then Congressman Michael Barnes. It concluded: (1) "the NSC is not covered by the prohibition," (adding by footnote that "LtCol. North might be, as he evidently is on a non-reimbursed detail from the

Marine Corps"); and (2) "None of LtCol North's activities during the past year constitutes a violation of the Boland Amendment." (see also Oct. 12, 1984 entry) (Tower)

MAR 1 - Effective this date, the State Department contracts with International Business Communications (IBC) to provide $90,000 worth of "media consultant services." The services include media and congressional briefings, coordination of visits by Central Americans to the U.S. and by journalists to refugee camps in the region, and the preparation of materials (op-eds, letters to editors, briefing books, etc.) for the Office of the Coordinator for Public Diplomacy for Latin America and the Caribbean (ARA/LPD). State's contracting officer is Barbara A. Garland. News reports later describe this effort as part of the administration's public relations drive for contra aid, and IBC as a prime conduit for private funds to the contras for weapons. A second State Department contract with IBC (see SEP 2, 1986 entry) uses almost identical language for the tasks to be performed but is for $276,186 and is initially classified secret. (DOS Contract 1001-502160 3/1/85; DOS Contract 1001-602066 effective 10/1/85 but signed 9/2/86; WP 3/7/87)

MAR 3 - Vice President George Bush writes to a Guatemalan doctor and conservative political leader who had proposed, through Bush's son Jeb, an international medical brigade to help the contras. Bush's letter refers Dr. Mario Castejon to Oliver North and offers Bush's staff to set up the meeting. In a March 1 memo, Bush aide Philip Hughe had recommended this course of action, because Castejon's "proposals could materially help us out if they materialized." Castejon subsequently meets North, attends a White House briefing and a Washington meeting with Gen. John Singlaub and Adolfo Calero, and assists in preparing a medical proposal (never acted upon) for submission to the State Department's Nicaraguan Humanitarian Assistance Office. The medical proposal also circulates to TGS International Ltd., an Arlington, Virginia firm headed by Theodore G. Shackley, former CIA deputy director for operations. News reports credited Bush's letter with introducing Castejon into Oliver North's private aid network, calling it the first documentary evidence linking Bush to North. (MH 3/15/87)

- Reference is made in a newspaper article to activities of the NSC's Senior Interagency Group on Central America, known as the Core Group. The group has existed since early part of Reagan's first term and in effect manages U.S. policy toward the region. A second report says the group responsible for the management of the contra program is the "restricted interagency group"—RIG. The group is headed first by Thomas Enders and later by Langhorne Motley. Also involved are Gorman, North and Clarridge. (WSJ 3/5/85)(See undated entry near the beginning of 1981.) (LAT 3/3/85)

- Enrique Bermudez is quoted in an article as saying that when the U.S. began to take over operations in Central America in 1981, "I could feel the steps of a giant animal." The article details the escalation of the covert war against the Nicaraguan government, beginning with Robert McFarlane's November 1981 paper entitled, "Taking the War to Nicaragua"; CIA director Casey's November 1981 meeting with Argentine Gen. Leopoldo Galtieri when the future Argentine president agrees to aid the contras in Honduras. (Dickey, p.126; LAT 3/3/85)

- LtCol North had further contacts with Mr. Singlaub in March. On March 5 he sent a letter to [an ambassador of a Central American country posted in Washington] requesting "a multiple entry visa" for Mr. Singlaub. LtCol North wrote the Ambassador: "I can assure you that General Singlaub's visits to [your country] will well serve the interests of your country and mine." On March 14, Mr. Singlaub reported to North on his recent trip. He said that he had met with several FDN leaders and that he had agreed to recruit and send "a few American trainers" to provide "specific skills not available within this (sic) current resources." Mr. Singlaub specified that "these will be civilian (former military or CIA personnel) who will do training only and not participate in combat operations."

More direct NSC staff involvement in efforts to gain third country support for the Contras was evident in a memorandum LtCol North sent to Mr. McFarlane dated March 5, 1985. North described plans to ship arms to the Contras via [country deleted], to be delivered in several shipments starting on or about March 10, 1985. The transaction required certification that the arms would not be transferred out of [country deleted]. LtCol North attached copies of such end-user certificates, provided by [country deleted] for nearly "$8 million worth of munitions for the FDN." He told Mr. McFarlane that these end-user certificates are "a direct consequence of the informal liaison we have established with GEN [name deleted] and your meeting with he [sic] and President [name deleted]." (emphasis added).

LtCol North's memorandum described the need to provide increased U.S. assistance to [country deleted] to compensate them "for the extraordinary assistance they are providing to the Nicaraguan freedom fighters." LtCol North said:

"Once we have approval for at least some of what they have asked for, we can ensure that the right people in [country deleted] understand that we are able to provide results from their cooperation on the resistance issue."

An accompanying memorandum to Secretary Shultz, Secretary Weinberger, CIA Director Casey and Chairman of the Joint Chiefs of Staff Vessey requested their views on increased U.S. assistance to a Central American country, but made no reference to the Contra arms shipments or the end user certificates. (Tower)

MAR 6 - Jesus Garcia and Steven Carr (see June 22, 1985 entry) help load weapons into vans and transport them to the Fort Lauderdale airport where they are loaded onto a chartered plane and flown to Ilopango air base in El Salvador, a key base of operations for the "private aid" network supplying the contras. The weapons have been stored at the home of Frank Chanes, partner in Ocean Hunter Seafood, a shrimp importing business. Chanes later would receive money from the State Department's Nicaraguan Humanitarian Assistance Office (NHAO). Among the weapons on the plane, according to an FBI file relating to the case, are a 14-foot, .20 millimeter cannon with 150 rounds of ammunition; a crate containing between thirty and fifty G-3 automatic rifles; another crate of M-16 and M-60 machine guns; several .60 millimeter mortars with 80 to 100 rounds each; one .50 caliber machine gun, with 250 rounds; a sniper rifle and a shotgun. Once at Ilopango, the crates of weapons are unloaded by Salvadoran soldiers and stored in nearby warehouses. Within a week, the weapons are delivered to the farm of John Hull in northern Costa Rica, near the Nicaraguan border. Hull, a former CIA operative, is active in aiding the contras. Tom Posey, the head of Civilian Military Assistance (CMA), is also involved in the shipment. Some sources say Posey even donated his own shotgun and sniper rifle. Those weapons and several others from the Fort Lauderdale ship-

JANUARY-OCTOBER 1985 / 89

ment are later confiscated from a group of mercenaries by Costa Rican authorities. The serial number of the sniper rifle shows that it is registered to Posey. The plane is reportedly an American Transport charter which cost approximately $15,000. Customs Department records show that the plane was chartered by Rene Corvo, a veteran of the Bay of Pigs and leader of a Miami-based Cuban exile group, Canac (Nicaraguan Anti-Communist Aid Committee). The Justice Department says Corvo has raised funds and recruited mercenaries for the contras. An FBI file report says the plane was chartered and flown by Daniel Vasquez III, his son, Carr, Corvo, and another American mercenary, Robert Thompson. (VV 12/30/86; WSJ 1/15/87)

MAR 7 - A $4 million deposit is made to the contra account at the Miami branch of the BAC International Bank of the Cayman Islands. Previously, the monthly payments reportedly coming from the Saudi royal family to the contras averaged approximately $1 million. (WSJ 3/6/87; NYT 3/6/87)

MAR 8 - A car bomb explodes in Beirut, killing 80 people and wounding 200. It is reported later that a group of Lebanese intelligence personnel and foreigners who had been trained by the CIA under a Reagan-authorized covert action program set off the explosion. Their target, a militant Shiite leader, escaped. A congressional source later says the incident led to the closing down of the CIA's training program and the dissolution of a similar group in another country. (WP 2/22/87)

MAR 15 - A $7.5 million deposit is made to the contra account at the Miami branch of the BAC International Bank of the Cayman Islands. Previously, the monthly payments reportedly coming from the Saudi royal family to the contras averaged approximately $1 million. (WSJ 3/6/87; NYT 3/6/87)

MAR 16 - Terry A. Anderson, chief Middle East correspondent for the Associated Press, is kidnapped in Beirut. (NYT 12/4/86)

- In a memorandum to Mr. McFarlane on March 16, 1985, LtCol North outlined a fallback plan for supporting the Contras should the Congress not endorse resumption of

U.S. Government support. LtCol North recommended that the President make a public request to the American people for private funds "to support liberty and democracy in the Americas." Mr. McFarlane wrote in the margin, "Not yet." Nevertheless, he indicated his agreement to some of the accompanying elements of the proposal:

"The Nicaraguan Freedom Fund, Inc., a 501(c)3 tax exempt corporation, must be established. . . . (This process is already under way)." Mr. McFarlane wrote next to this point, "Yes."

"The name of one of several existing non-profit foundations we have established in the course of the last year will be changed to Nicaraguan Freedom Fund, Inc. Several reliable American citizens must be contacted to serve as its corporate leadership on its board of directors along with Cruz, Calero, and Robelo." (emphasis added). Mr. McFarlane wrote, "OK."

Next to the proposal that "current donors" be apprised of the plan and convinced to provide "an additional $25-30M to the resistance for the purchase of arms and munitions," Mr. McFarlane wrote, "Doubt." LtCol North recommended that Mr. McFarlane consult Secretary Shultz on the proposals, but we have no information as to whether this was done. (Tower)

-In his March 16 memorandum to Mr. McFarlane, LtCol North also reported that he had checked the legality of his proposals with private legal counsel: "Informal contacts several months ago with a lawyer sympathetic to our cause indicated that such a procedure would be within the limits of the law." He recommended that White House Counsel Fred Fielding "be asked to do conduct [sic] a very private evaluation of the President's role." Mr. McFarlane wrote, "not yet" in the margin. (Tower)

MAR 19 - The first shipment of Defex's February 14 order of arms on behalf of Energy Resources International is cleared by Portuguese authorities. The weapons are intended for the contras. (WP 1/17/87)

MAR - Department of Transportation records show a Southern Air Transport flight carrying 23.6 tons of materials from Miami to Tegucigalpa, Honduras. (DOT Records)

MAR 21 - A former top official of the Salvadoran Government charges that the senior officer in the largest U.S.-

backed Nicaraguan rebel group, the FDN, "played a key role" in organizing and training El Salvador's death squads. Col. Roberto Santivanez, who headed El Salvador's intelligence agency for several years, says the former FDN officer, Ricardo Lau, "received payment of $120,000 for arranging" the death squad execution of El Salvador's Archbishop, Oscar Arnulfo Romero, in 1980. Lau was director of intelligence for the FDN until 1984. Santivanez says he learned of Lau's involvement from documents also obtained by the U.S. Embassy in San Salvador. Lau was reportedly involved in death squad activities before joining the FDN and again in Honduras while with the FDN. (NYT 3/22/85 & 3/24/85)

MAR 25 - Another $7.5 million deposit is made to the contra account at the Miami branch of the BAC International Bank of the Grand Caymans. Before March, the monthly payments reportedly coming from the Saudi royal family to the contras averaged approximately $1 million, but this month includes payments totaling $19 million. This deposit is said to be the last installment of King Fahd's funds. (WSJ 3/6/87; NYT 3/6/87; WP 3/7/87)

LATE MAR - The Board (See JAN 1985 entry) also obtained rather cryptic evidence of a meeting in Cologne in late March involving Iranians, including probably the chief of the Iranian buying office, Dr. Shahabadi, a friend of Adnan Khashoggi. (Unsigned and undated note; Furmark 34)

"Basic thrust of the meeting is that we wanted to open discussions with Iranian officials and we also wanted the hostages freed. Shabadi said that he would discuss this with Khameni'i and [a cleric] and come back out to see us at subsequent meeting this meeting never took place. However, there were two phone conversations with someone in Tehran who according to Zaheri was [a cleric]. In this case there were requests for weapons to show our bona fides. These were turned aside. They then tried to get boeing spare karts [parts]. Finally gave us a list of ten items of spare parts for a boeing. cast of characters was Zaheri, Shoja'i, Ghorbanifar (no direct contact in his case) and Shahabadi. Zhaheri had a falling out with Shoja'i over money. Zaheri finally gave up and returned to Houston. We determined that the Iranan side was only interesed in money." (Original spelling and punctuation. Unsigned and undated note) (Tower)

APR 1 - International Business Communications Inc. (IBC), a public relations firm, signs a $90,000 contract (covering March through September) with the State Department for "media consultant services" promoting the contra cause. The same company begins work on a second contract—classified secret—with the Department on October 1 of this year (see entry) that also involves promoting the contra cause. (AP in WP 2/7/87)

APR - Michael Ledeen, a consultant at the NSC, visits Israel with a request from Reagan to Prime Minister Shimon Peres for help in obtaining the release of American hostages in the Middle East, in particular the CIA's station chief in Beirut, William Buckley. (Israel says the trip was in March.) One version of the visit states that Peres gets in touch with Al Schwimmer, a friend and weapons dealer, who suggests an "arms-for-Buckley" deal; Schwimmer enlists another Israeli arms merchant, former Mossad agent Yaacov Nimrodi; the two are then introduced by Adnan Khashoggi to Manuchehr Ghorbanifar. According to the Senate intelligence panel draft report leaked in January 1987, however, the two Israeli arms dealers first meet with Israeli official David Kimche and Ghorbanifar in late 1984 (see November 1984 entry), then later with Khashoggi, to discuss how to open U.S.-Iranian contacts. The report says Ledeen meets Ghorbanifar at Nimrodi's house in a Tel Aviv suburb and reportedly becomes convinced the Iranian has the necessary contacts in Iran. Ledeen then meets with Peres and is introduced by him to Shlomo Gazit, the former chief of Israeli military intelligence, who tells him Israel will begin a search for contacts in Iran. Gazit reportedly drops out of the operation after concluding that Schwimmer, Nimrodi and Ghorbanifar are exaggerating the extent of their influence in Iran, and after he becomes concerned that Israel's intelligence agency, Mossad, is not playing a role in the contacts. Later, friction reportedly develops between Ledeen, on the one hand, and Schwimmer and Nimrodi, on the other. (MH 12/7/86; NYT 12/25/86; WP 12/27/86 & 1/12/87; Newsweek 11/17/86)

SPRING - In the early spring of 1985, Ledeen reported to McFarlane a discussion about Iran he had had with a European intelligence official who believed the situation there was more fluid than the United States government seemed to think. Ledeen's interlocutor suggested speaking to the Israelis as the best, quick way to learn about events in Iran.

According to Ledeen, McFarlane "suggested that I talk to Peres privately and ask him whether Israel had better information about Iran than we had, whether Israel had enough information about Iran, about Iranian terrorism, about Iran's role in international terrorism, all these various subjects, so that one could evaluate a rational policy and, if so, whether they would be willing to share that information with us." (Ledeen (1) 8-9) (Footnote: Ledeen told the Board that McFarlane approved all his trips, except for his vacation in Israel in July-August 1985, and the NSC paid his expenses. Ledeen said he considered himself an employee of the United States while on these trips, and made clear to his interlocutors that he had no authority to negotiate, but would "report fully and accurately everything that transpired in these discussions and that I would, if asked, report and communicate fully and accurately back to them whatever decisions were made in Washington." (Ledeen T-15)) Documents suggest a somewhat different origin and purpose for the trip.(See April 9, 1985 entry) (Tower)

- According to Ledeen, while on a trip to Europe in April 1985, he spoke with a European intelligence official who had just returned from Iran. The official characterized the internal situation in Iran as more fluid than previously thought, and suggested it was time for the U.S. to take a new look at Iran. He said that the U.S. should discuss this with the Israelis, who the official believed were unusually well-informed about Iran. (See June 5, 1985) (SSIC 1/29/87)

APR 3 - The Administration submits a formal, classified request for funding for the contras. Reagan says the next day that the funds will not be used for military purposes if the Sandinista government accepts the March 3, 1985 offer by the "resistance to begin church-mediated negotiations." The Senate approves the request April 23, but the House rejects it the following day. (CRS "U.S. Assistance to Nicaraguan Guerrillas" 12/4/86)

APR 9 - Donald Fortier, Special Assistant to the President and Senior Director for Political-Military Affairs, reported to McFarlane on April 9, that Ledeen told him on April 8 that McFarlane was prepared to approve Ledeen's traveling to Israel (apparently a previous trip had been cancelled) if Fortier, Covey, and Teicher approved. Fortier wondered if Ledeen had accurately represented McFarlane's view. Fortier, Covey, and Teicher disapproved of using Ledeen as the government's "primary channel for working the Iran issue with foreign governments, and we think you should probably should [sic] not provide a formal letter." (Fortier PROF note to McFarlane, 4/9/85, 10:22:14) On the other hand, they thought he could usefully carry two messages to Prime Minister Peres, whom Ledeen came to know when, as Secretary of State Haig's advisor, he had responsibility for dealing with the Socialist International. (Ledeen (1) 6)

"1) the White House feels it is essential to begin to develop a more serious and coordinated strategy for dealing with the Iranian succession crisis—a crisis that is almost certain to turn on outside involvement of one kind or another; and 2) we would like his ideas on how we could cooperate more effectively. The last point is a hard one for us to ask our intelligence community to communicate, since we suspect they may be part of the problem. We don't think Mike should be the one to ask Peres for detailed operational information; he probably doesn't know, and even if he did, this should be reserved for official channels once we have arrived at ideas for restoring better cooperation." (Fortier PROF note to McFarlane, 4/9/85, 10:22:14)

On his own initiative, on April 9, Ledeen made arrangements to see Prime Minister Peres. Fortier and Teicher thought it wise for Teicher to sound out Nimrod Novik, the Prime Minister's Political Advisor, to see if Ledeen would be welcome. (Fortier PROF note to McFarlane, 4/9/85, 11:41:22) McFarlane approved the check with Novik.

"If it turns up negative, simply tell Mike that the meeting is not sponsored by us and he should not so represent." (McFarlane PROF note to Fortier, 4/9/85, 12:45:22)

He also wrote Fortier:

"Yes I think it is entirely worthwhile to cooperate closely with Iran [sic: Israel] in our planning for Iranian succession. . . . As a separate matter I want to talk to Shultz so that he is not blindsided when Sam Lewis [Ambassador to Israel] reports—as he will surely find out—about Mike's wanderings. [Apparently Ledeen thought he could make the trip without Ambassador Lewis finding out about it. McFarlane doubted it was possible. (McFarlane PROF note to Fortier, 4/9/85, 12:45:22)] So for the moment let's hold on the Ledeen aspect. I will get back to you. I do consider planning for the succession [sic] to be one of our greatest failures and

vulnerabilities so I am very glad you are turning to it."
(McFarlane PROF note to Fortier, 4/9/85, 11:22:47) (Tower)

APR 10 - Defex files another end-user certificate with Portuguese authorities on behalf of Energy Resources International. This time the latter's address is listed as the same as Defex's in Lisbon, although it is still named as the U.S. agent-addressee. (WP 1/17/87)

APR - Department of Transportation records show a Southern Air Transport flight carrying 96 tons of materials from Lajes, Portugal to Howard Air Force Base, Panama. (DOT Records)

APR 11 - During this period Lt. Col. North was well-informed about the financial and military situation of the Contras. In a memorandum to Mr. McFarlane on April 11, 1985, LtCol North detailed FDN funding received since the expiration of U.S. assistance:
"From July 1984 through February 1985, the FDN received $1M per month for a total of $8M. From February 22 to April 9, 1985, an additional $16.5M has been received for a grand total of $24.5M. Of this, $17,145,594 has been expended for arms, munitions, combat operations, and support activities."
LtCol North recommended that effort be undertaken to "seek additional funds from the current donors ($15-20M) which will allow the force to grow to 30-35,000." An attachment to this document itemized Contra arms purchases during this period. A sample entry read:
Airlift #2—March 1985:

750,000 rounds 7.62 x 39	$210,000
1,000 RPG-7 grenades	265,000
8,910 hand grenades	84,645
60-60mm mortars	66,000
1,472 kqs C-4	47,104

On May 1, 1985, a nearly identical memorandum was prepared for JCS Chairman Vessey from LtCol North. (Tower)

- In a memorandum to Mr. McFarlane dated April 11, 1985, LtCol North expressed concern that remaining Contra funds would soon be insufficient. He advised that efforts be made to seek $15 to $20 million in additional funds from the current donors which will "allow the force to grow to 30-35,000." The exact purpose to which these private funds were to be put was unambiguous. A number of memoranda from LtCol North make clear that the funds were for munitions and legal aid.

Asked by the Board about the source of such funds, Mr. McFarlane provided a written response that indicated that "without solicitation" a foreign official offered $1 million a month from what he described as "personal funds." At Mr. McFarlane's request, LtCol North provided the numbers of a Contra bank account in Miami. Mr McFarlane wrote that in 1985, the foreign official doubled his contribution to $2 million a month, a fact confirmed by two other U.S. officials. (Tower)

- As early as April 1985, LtCol North maintained detailed records of expenditures for Contra military equipment, supplies, and operations. On April 11, 1985, LtCol North sent a memorandum to Mr. McFarlane describing two sealifts and two airlifts "[a]s of April 9, 1985." The memorandum set out the kind of munitions purchased, the quantity, and in some instances the cost. LtCol North also noted that from July 1984 to April 9, 1985: "$17,145,594 has been expended for arms, munitions, combat operations and support activities." (Tower)

APR 15 - Reagan is principal speaker at a fundraising dinner for Nicaraguan refugees. Prior to the dinner, Bush and McFarlane give a White House briefing on Central America to the dinner's sponsors. This is one of many such briefings conducted by the NSC through the White House Outreach Working Group on Central America, organized by Faith Ryan Whittlesey in 1983. (WP 10/19/86)

APR 25 - Udall Research is registered by Panamanian lawyer Julio A. Quijano. The company eventually builds a 7,000-foot private airstrip in Costa Rica used for supplying the contras. Quijano is also reportedly the incorporator for two other companies linked to the contra resupply operation. One of them is Lake Resources Inc., the other is Stanford Technology Corp. (WP 12/14/86 & 12/21/86)

- Adolfo Calero writes Spitz Channell on FDN stationery that the Contras "will require at least $500,000 per month to sustain our present level of operations" and that "until a new bill is approved," "we must now rely even more on our friends in the United States." Calero's letter states, "I hereby authorize you to raise funds for our cause and to deposit them in the National Endowment for the Preservation of Liberty." Press accounts later report that NEPL raised tax-deductible funds that were passed through International Business Communications, I.C. Inc. in the Cayman Islands, and Oliver North's Lake Resources bank account in Switzerland to purchase weapons for the Contras. (Calero letter 4/25/85; ABC News 2/12/87)

APR - In the third week of April, a Danish freighter, the Erria, an integral part of the Iran-contra operation, is dispatched to a dock near Gdansk, Poland, where it takes on a load of reconditioned Soviet AK-47 rifles and East European machine guns. Half-full, the Erria steams on to Setubal harbor, Portugal, where it picks up 461 tons of additional munitions. The cargo is officially destined for Guatemala but three weeks later is delivered to the contras at a port in Honduras (see May 11, 1985 entry). The Erria reportedly has been heavily involved in arms trafficking since at least 1984 and probably well before that. At this time, it is under charter to S.A. Shipping in Copenhagen, whose agent, Thomas Parlow, describes himself as a longtime friend of Thomas Clines, the former CIA agent who plays a significant role in the Iran-contra controversy. According to Parlow, the Erria's freight charges in 1985 are paid for by the Lisbon arms dealer, Defex-Portugal, which is acting as middleman for Energy Resources International, a company with ties to Richard Secord. The Erria is bought in April 1986 by a front company in Panama, Dolmy Business Inc. Parlow claims later to be sole owner of the vessel, having used the dummy corporation to escape strict Danish laws governing ship crews, salaries and operations, but news reports quote a knowledgeable American official as saying the Erria purchase was "strictly an Ollie [North] operation." (LAT 1/21/87; WSJ 1/23/87)

APR 23 - In a series of votes on the Administration's request for $14 million for the contras, the House narrowly rejects further funding. (CRS "Assistance to the Nicaraguan Guerrillas" 12/4/86)

APR 26 - I.C. Inc. (later Intel Co-Operation Inc.) is incorporated in the Cayman Islands. The "subscribers" are listed as Cayhaven Corporate Services Ltd. of Georgetown, Grand

Cayman; David G. Bird of Georgetown; and Alastair J. N. Loudon of Georgetown. Copies obtained by reporters of bank wire transfers from International Business Communications (see Sept. 20 entry below) to I.C. and Intel include instructions to notify David Piesing or Malcolm Davies, each at the same phone number. (WP 3/7/87)

MAY - U.S. Army Colonel William H. Mott, IV, starts a company at around this time called Spearhead Atlantic, which will act as a consultant to defense firms seeking to do business with American defense manufacturers. Mott, who does not retire from active duty for another year, claims later that four senior officials at the U.S. Embassy in London where he is stationed give their approval of the enterprise. Mott and another Army colonel, Ralph Mark Broman, are later implicated in efforts to sell arms to Iran. (NYT 1/11/87)

- According to Adnan Khashoggi, the genesis of the Iran arms deal was his introduction to Manuchehr Ghorbanifar at a meeting in Hamburg, West Germany, this month arranged by New York energy consultant Roy Furmark. (See, however, April 1985 entry.) Ghorbanifar, he says, asks him at the meeting to tell the Saudi government that some Iranians are eager to put together a moderate group to take over the country after the death of Khomeini. Khashoggi says later he passed the message on to King Fahd who indicated an unwillingness to become involved in internal Iranian affairs. Khashoggi says he then went to Egypt with the idea, but after the Egyptians checked with the CIA about Ghorbanifar and received a negative report on him, they also rejected it. After that, according to Khashoggi, he had no other option but to approach Israel. The next month he met with representatives of Israel and Iran in Hamburg. (WP 2/1/87)

- In May, Shackley recalled discussing the hostage problem over lunch with Ledeen. Shackley told him about his report on his November 1984 meeting with Ghorbanifar. Shackley remembered that Ledeen asked for a copy of the report. Ledeen said people in the government were interested in investigating the hostage question, and asked if Shackley could "find out whatever that was as a channel, if it is still open." (Shackley 23) (Tower)

- Gen. John Singlaub brokers a $5.3 million arms deal for the contras, including several thousand AK-47 rifles and several million rounds of ammunition. Contra leader Adolfo

Calero later describes this deal as the "biggest and best" of the deals set up by the private suppliers of weapons to the contras. (NYT 3/6/87)

MAY 4 or 5 - Michael Ledeen, an NSC staff consultant, with the knowledge of Mr. McFarlane, went to Israel and met with Prime Minister Peres. Mr. Ledeen told the Board that he asked about the state of Israeli intelligence on Iran and whether Israel would be willing to share its intelligence with the United States. Two months later, the United States received the first of three separate requests regarding Iran from the Israeli government. (see July 3, July 13, and August 2, 1985 entries.) (Tower)

- Ledeen told the Board that, "in essence," Prime Minister Peres "said that while he thought their information was probably better than ours, he did not consider it satisfactory and he didn't feel that it was sufficient for them to base any kind of serious Iran policy, but that he agreed that it was an important matter and said that they would be happy to work with us to try to develop better information in all these areas —the internal Iranian situation, the Iran role in terror, general international terrorist questions and so forth.

"So he constituted a group of people outside the government, not government officials, to work with us to study the Iran question and the Iranian terrorist issue. The agreement was that each of us would try to find out what our respective governments knew about Iran. We would then sit down, compare notes, and see if possibly by putting them together we might be able to develop some kind of useful picture." (Ledeen (1) 10-11)

In his second interview with the Board, Ledeen added that the Prime Minister "was happy to work together to try to develop better information about Iran, but he, contrary to all these newspaper reports, which continue to drive me crazy and I don't know where they come from, there was no discussion of contacts with Iran, none. There was no discussion of hostages. And except for this one final point where he said we have received a request from the Iranian government to sell them this quantity of materiel, we will not do it without explicit American approval, will you please raise it with McFarlane when you get back to Washington and tell me shall we do it or shall we not, there was no discussion of weapons or trade or relations or anything."

"It was simply a discussion of what could be learned

about Iran and how could we better work together to understand that situation."

"[T]here was no discussion of policy at all between me and Peres. It was simply a discussion of information, and then hypothetically if there were information and they had policy recommendations to make, then okay. But we never got to them. It was purely a research trip." (Ledeen (2) 10-11)

Shlomo Gazit, President of Ben Gurion University and a former chief of Israeli intelligence, led the Israeli team. Gazit still had good relations with Israeli intelligence and could direct both the military and Mossad to provide information. Ledeen did not know the other Israelis, but assumed that David Kimche, Director General of the Israeli Foreign Ministry, worked on this matter. (Ledeen (1) 11) (Tower)

MAY 7 - Defex-Portugal, acting for Energy Resources International, receives clearance to transfer by ship an installment of arms from Portugal to Guatemala. The weapons are intended for the contras. (WP 1/17/87)

MAY 11 - The Danish freighter Erria, later tied to covert operations directed by Oliver North, steams out of Setubal harbor, Portugal, with a full load, including AK-47 rifles and machine guns picked up from Poland two weeks earlier and an additional 14,714 boxes of munitions taken on in Portugal. The ship is headed ostensibly for Puerto Barrios, Guatemala, but three weeks later appears in Puerto Cortez, Honduras, where its cargo is unloaded by contra forces. (LAT 1/21/87)

MAY 13 - When Ledeen returned to Washington [from Israel (see May 4 or 5, 1985 entry)] on May 13, he called Fortier with the news of "very positive feedback. [Ledeen] will brief me tomorrow on what that really means." (Fortier PROF note to Poindexter, 5/13/85, 18:12:20) According to Ledeen, during the May conversation (See May 4 or 5, 1985 entry), Prime Minister Peres also asked him to ask McFarlane if the United States would approve an arms shipment to Iran. Ledeen recalled that "[i]t was either ammunition for artillery pieces or some quantity of artillery pieces, but it had to do with artillery." (Ledeen (2) 13) Israel would not ship it to Iran "without explicit American approval." (Ledeen T-2) Ledeen said McFarlane subsequently authorized him to tell the Prime Minister "it's okay, but just that and nothing else." (Id.)

After Ledeen reported to McFarlane on the trip, McFarlane asked Fortier to direct the CIA to prepare a special intelligence estimate on Iran. (Ledeen (1) 1 1-12) Graham Fuller, National Intelligence Officer for Near East and South Asia, and Teicher participated in this effort. Fuller told the Board that he "regularly" saw Teicher who "shared a lot of my feelings about our strategic bind vis a vis Iran. And there were others as well in Government, but Howard was the one I was most well aware of in that regard, who felt that we should at least be working towards [sic] an expanded policy towards Iran, expanded in the broadest sense, more than a purely negative one of no arms and slap down on terrorism. It was in fact that NSDD that in the end got nowhere that was part of the rationale for the estimate that we did in '85." (Fuller 28-29).

On May 13, 1985, Fortier informed Poindexter that "[w]e have a draft [of the NSDD?]. I asked Howard and Steve [Rosen] to rework it. I will give you a copy of what we have and of the suggestions I gave them on how it could [be] improved. . . . We have also done a lot of additional work on outlining requirements for the SNIE." (Fortier PROF note to Poindexter, 5/13/85, 18:12:20) (Tower)

- Despite the criticisms of the Secretaries of State and Defense, the ideas embodied in the draft NSDD survived in action. This fact perhaps reflected the turbulent environment in which Teicher drafted the NSDD. A series of kidnappings occurred in Lebanon in 1985: on January 8, Jenco; on March 16, Anderson; on March 22, Fontaine and Carton, both French; on March 26, the British journalist Collett; on May 22, the Frenchmen Kaufmann and Seurat: on May 28, Jacobsen; on June 10, Sutherland. In the same period, meetings involving different members of the NSC staff took place with Israelis about Iran. The conversations became more systematic as time passed. Contemporaneous discussions among persons of various nationalities about Iranian-American relations also occurred. Together with violent events, especially including the hijacking of TWA Flight 847 in mid-June 1985, they formed part of the circumstances that seemed to have given life to the policies advocated by Fuller, Teicher, Fortier, McFarlane, and the Director of Central Intelligence. (Tower)

MAY 14 - Lake Resources Inc. is chartered in Panama by Julio A. Quijano. It is subsequently identified as the company into whose account Iranian and Saudi middlemen deposit funds for U.S. arms sales to Iran. (WP 12/14/86)

MID-MAY - Ledeen testified that he reported his talks [from May 4-5 with Prime Minister Peres about the situation in Iran] to McFarlane in mid-May, and that McFarlane subsequently arranged to task the Intelligence Community to produce a Special National Intelligence Estimate (SNIE) on Iran. (See June 5, 1985 entry.) (SSIC 1/29/87)

MAY 16 - R.M. Equipment of Miami, owned by Ronald Martin and James McCoy, files two end-user certificates with Portuguese authorities requesting authorization to purchase arms. Just as with two earlier purchases (see January 31, 1985 entry), the certificates are on stamped paper of the "Honduran Armed Forces Joint General Staff," and are signed by a Col. Julio Perez, "engineer, in charge of the C-4 Logistics Division." This time they are addressed to a Portuguese import-export company, Atomex. The arms are shipped aboard the freighters Erria (on May 11) and Peder Most (in June) to the Honduran port of Puerto Cortez. From there they are transferred to the contra bases. Joac Martins and Costa Corvo, the owners of Atomex, deny any part in the transaction, claiming only to have "introduced [the American] company to the National Defense Industry." (Lisbon Expresso 2/7/87; UPI 2/7/87)

MAY 17 - The CIA, concerned with the possibility of a communist takeover after Khomeini's death and reportedly desperate to free its Beirut station chief, William Buckley, suggests in a secret document that the U.S. consider easing its worldwide arms embargo against Iran. Two officials at the NSC, one of them reportedly McFarlane, incorporate the document into a six page draft National Security Decision Directive (NSDD) which argues that encouraging allied military sales to Tehran will help counter Soviet activities in the region. Defense Secretary Weinberger later writes on the proposal, "This is absurd." Regan, McFarlane and Poindexter separately acknowledge later that by June the Administration has begun to entertain the idea of an opening to Iran. (WP 12/7/86 & 12/18/86; NYT 12/25/86; Newsweek 12/15/86)

- Fuller [CIA national intelligence officer for the Middle East] submitted a five page memorandum to William Casey, Director of Central Intelligence, entitled "Toward a Policy on Iran." Fuller began his analysis as follows:

"1. The US faces a grim situation in developing a new policy toward [sic] Iran. Events are moving largely against our interests and we have few palatable alternatives. In bluntest form, the Khomeini regime is faltering and may be moving toward a moment of truth; we will soon see a struggle for succession. The US has almost no cards to play; the USSR has many. Iran has obviously concluded that whether they like Russia and Communism or not, the USSR is the country to come to terms with: the USSR can both hurt and help Iran more than the US can. Our urgent need is to develop a broad spectrum of policy moves designed to give us some leverage in the race for influence in Tehran." (Fuller to DCI/DDCI, "Toward a policy on Iran," 5/17/85)

Fuller then noted that the United States and Soviet Union both supported Iraq, but for different reasons, and this situation was inherently unstable. He wrote that both countries "lack our preferred access to Iran. Whoever gets there first is in a strong position to work towards [sic] the exclusion of the other." (Id. at 1) Fuller reported that the intelligence community monitored "Soviet progress toward developing significant leverage in Tehran," progress, which, however uneven, merited a response given the stakes. (Id.) He then analyzed American policy.

The United States had two attitudes towards Iran. First, it was prepared to respond with force if Iran was involved in a terrorist attack. Second, it strove to deny arms to Iran. Fuller believed that these "twin pillars" were no longer sensible because they were adopted to deal with a vacuum in Iran and a strong Khomeini. These conditions no longer existing, Fuller concluded, the policy pillars had become entirely negative "and may now serve to facilitate Soviet interests more than our own." (Id. at 2) While acknowledging the difficulty of formulating alternatives, he thought that

"[i]t is imperative, however, that we perhaps think in terms of a bolder—and perhaps riskier policy which will at least ensure greater US voice in the unfolding situation. Right now—unless we are very lucky indeed—we stand to gain nothing, and lose more, in the outcome of developments in Iran, which are all outside our control." (Id. at 3)

"Nobody has any brilliant ideas about how to get us back into Tehran," Fuller wrote (Id.); he then analysed a number of alternative courses, including helping Iraq to win the war and encouraging friendly states to make arms available to Iran as a means for gaining influence in Tehran. He noted that an Iraqi victory might lead to the establishment of an even more radical regime in Tehran. Attacking Iran's radical ally Libya would demonstrate our resolve and, possibly, remove Qadhafi. Iran's other radical ally, Syria, could only be pressured by Israel, which had no wish for conflict at this time. He thought demonstrating to Iranians that we were not hostile by withdrawing our fleet from the Persian Gulf and making public statements about our friendly intentions, for example, might strengthen "Iranian moderates—and opportunists"; it also might produce derision in Tehran. The best course, he concluded, was to have friendly states sell arms that would not affect the strategic balance as a means of showing Tehran that it had alternatives to the Soviet Union. (Id. at 5) Were the Soviets to gain in Iran, we would have to strengthen our commitments to Turkey and Pakistan, as they are logical next Soviet targets. (Id. at 4) The Director of Central Intelligence provided a copy of this memorandum to the Secretary of State on June 4, 1985. (Note on routing sheet) (Tower)

MAY 20 - Mr. Teicher, and to a lesser extent Mr. Fortier, worked closely with CIA officials to prepare an update of a previous "Special National Intelligence Estimate" (or "SNIE") on Iran. Dated May 20, 1985, the update portrayed the Soviets as well positioned to take advantage of chaos inside Iran. The United States, by contrast, was unlikely to be able directly to influence events. Our European and other allies could, however, provide a valuable presence to help protect Western interests. The update concluded that the degree to which these allies "can fill a military gap for Iran will be a critical measure of the West's ability to blunt Soviet influence."

- The Intelligence Community circulated a revision of its SNIE of October 1984 on Iran (SNIE 34-84, Iran.- The Post Khomeini Era) According to Fuller, "I think the [intelligence] community had very definitely felt that most of the Iranian regime perceived us as implacably hostile towards an Islamic republic in principle, and that maybe there were some gestures that could be made that would suggest that we were rather more sophisticated in our approach to it than simply that." (Id. at 11)

The first SNIE and the update tried to predict Iran's course over the next six to twelve months, and acknowledged the difficulty that effort implied. Its conclusions were consistent with Fuller's earlier memo to the DCI. The Community expected Khomeini's health to continue to decline, and predicted that Iran would soon enter a period of instability, in part the result of the regime's declining popularity, the growth of private armies, and jockeying for political advantage by competing groups. One could confidently expect "serious instability" before Khomeini's death. Already the Community saw signs of opposition to the radicals among industrial workers. The prospects for the Communist left (the Tudeh Party and Mujahedin-e Khalq) were hard to estimate, but the Soviets were discreetly keeping their options open by allowing their East European allies to sell weapons to Iran while the U.S.S.R. publicly supported Iraq. "Tehran's leadership seems to have concluded," the Community wrote, "that improvement of relations with the USSR is now essential to Iranian interests; any improvement of ties to the United States is not currently a policy option." (Iran— Prospects for Near-Term Instability at 5 (5/20/85) (to holders of SNIE 34-84)) Moscow would offer a number of incentives in return for Iran's ceasing to support the Afghan resistance. The United States currently lacked an ability to counter Soviet moves. As a whole, however, the West could take steps to improve its position.

"The United States is unlikely to be able to directly influence Iranian events, given its current lack of contact or presence in Iran. European states and other friendly states—including Turkey, Pakistan, China, Japan, and even Israel—can provide the next most valuable presence or entree in Iran to help protect Western interests. The degree to which some of these states can fill a military gap for Iran will be a critical measure of the West's ability to blunt Soviet influence. These states can also play a major role in the economic life of the country, lessening its isolation and providing alternatives to Soviet influence or that of the radical state." (Id. at 12)

According to Fuller, nothing in the May 1985 SNIE proved to be "highly controversial" in interagency deliberations. (Fuller 22)

Teicher told the Board that this estimate became the basis for a new draft NSDD on Iran. (Teicher 8-9) (Tower)
(See June 11 and June 17, 1985 entries.) (SSIC 1/29/87)

- A California businessman, Suleiman "Sam" Bamieh, holds one of several meetings with high Saudi officials that include King Fahd and the ambassador to Washington, Prince Bandar Bin Sultan. This meeting takes place at the King's residence in Jidda, Saudi Arabia. The businessman says that beginning in late 1983 and continuing through 1985, the Saudis request his help in funneling approximately $15 million to the contras through Richard Secord and Albert Hakim. He adds that Prince Bandar asks him in the course of the discussions to undertake other business dealings with Secord both to disguise the funding and to bolster Secord's business. (NYT 2/4/87; Regandie's 3/87)

MAY 22 - A high Egyptian Defense Ministry official, Col. A. A. Saleh, signs a document bearing the official Egyptian seal that authorizes Austin Aerospace of Manhattan to sell through Egypt F4-E aircraft, spare parts and related equipment to an unidentified buyer, perhaps Iran. (See also February 27, 1985 entry.) Egypt is reported later to be trying to sell F-4 equipment in order to raise money to buy more advanced F-15 jets. (NYT 2/2/87)

MAY 28 - David P. Jacobsen, director of the American University hospital in Beirut, is kidnapped. (NYT 12/25/86)

- Fortier wrote McFarlane:
"We spent the better part of the day working on the Iran NSSD [sic]. I have Dennis [?Ross, at that time an NSC consultant] here looking at the recent spate of Soviet activity and the levers we may have arising out of the war and other circumstances. I think we need about one more full day before we send up a draft for you and John [?Poindexter] to review. We also just got a bootleg copy of the draft SNIE. We worked closely with Graham Fuller on the approach, and I think it really is one of the best yet. Iran may come up in the breakfast tomorrow. If pressed for action you can credibly promise paper within the next few days. I also think the Israeli option is one we have to pursue, even though we may have to pay a certain price for the help. I'm not sure though that we have the right interlocutor. Mike has a call into me now. His message is that he needs to see me urgently to

follow up on his weekend conversation and to get a new plane ticket. Would appreciate guidance and substantive feedback. Thanks." (Fortier PROF note to McFarlane, 5/28/85 18:52:14) (Tower)

MAY 30 - Secretary Shultz . . . told the Board that, on May 30, Ambassador Lewis in Tel Aviv reported that Ledeen was on a "secret mission for the White House" and to ask if Secretary Shultz knew "what was going on."

"The answer was no. Ambassador Lewis said he had asked at the Israeli Ministry of Defense about Mr. Ledeen and had been told it was "too hot" to talk about, but that Defense Minister Rabin would tell me about it when he visited Washington." (Shultz, 12/86, 4; SRB, 9)

In his first interview, Ledeen told the Board that he made a second trip to Israel at the end of May to meet with Gazit to find out what the Israelis knew about the Iranian situation. (Ledeen (1) 13, 14-16) In his second interview, Ledeen reported that, although he thought he had made two trips to Israel in May, his passport and other records do not corroborate his memory. He concluded that he did not return to Israel until July 1985. (Ledeen (2) 15)) (Tower)

MAY-JUN - The contras make their last purchase of military supplies during this period for at least the next year and a half, according to Adolfo Calero, speaking in December 1986. The statement is in response to allegations that profits from U.S. arms sales to Iran have been diverted to the contras. ("Meet the Press" 12/14/86)

-The Board asked Mr. McFarlane whether he was aware of funds received by the FDN during this period. He provided the following written response:

"In May or June of 1984, without any solicitation on my part, a foreign official offered to make a contribution from what he described as "personal funds" in the amount of one million dollars per month for support of the FDN. He asked my help in determining how to proceed. I asked LTC North to find out where the contribution should be sent. He subsequently obtained the necessary information from the FDN leadership, and I provided it to the donor. I was told it was an FDN bank account in Miami. In early 1985 the same individual advised me that he intended to continue support in that year at approximately double the former rate. I was separately informed by the Secretary of Defense and General

Vessey that the total amount of the contribution during 1985 was 25 million dollars." (Tower)

SUMMER - Casey reportedly produces a detailed assessment on Iran contending that the circumstances there are right for talks with moderates in Tehran. He apparently releases the study to bolster McFarlane's fledgling efforts to initiate an opening through an Iranian intermediary. (NYT 12/17/86)

- North travels to Portugal on a reportedly "routine" weapons procurement mission. While there, he apparently bumps into a group of Israelis preparing a shipment of arms to Iran and in effect lays the groundwork for future White House-approved transfers of arms to Tehran. (MEP 11/21/86)

JUN - After a White House meeting, Shultz and Weinberger assume the new policy toward Iran outlined in McFarlane's May NSDD has been dropped. (Newsweek 12/15/86)

- Reagan writes a letter to Rep. Dave McCurdy (D-OK) that seems a move toward ending his quarrel with Congress over the contras' situation. In it he promises not to seek "the military overthrow of the Sandinista government or to put in its place a government based on supporters of the old Somoza regime," and commits himself to urge rebel leaders to investigate human rights abuses. (New Republic 3/31/86)

- Khashoggi, Kimche, Schwimmer, Nimrodi, Ghorbanifar and top Iranian officials meet in Hamburg, West Germany, to discuss the sale of arms to Iran, according to Khashoggi. He says the Israelis warned they would not be able to proceed without American approval. (WP 2/1/87)

- The freighter Peder Most departs Setubal harbor, Portugal, with a load of arms bound for the Honduran port of Puerto Cortez. From there the weapons are transferred to the contras. R.M. Equipment of Miami purchased the arms using end-user certificates bearing the stamp of the "Honduran Armed Forces Joint General Staff." (Lisbon Expresso 2/7/87)

- Twelve shipments of arms totaling over 400 tons are delivered to Iran by a Belgian firm, using a British cargo plane chartered by a Zairian company. Although export documents describe the shipments as "parts and machinery," they contain mainly U.S.-built spare parts for F-4 and F-14 aircraft as well as fuel used to manufacture incendiary bombs. The Belgian company is paid a total of $840,000 to deliver the cargo to the National Iranian Oil Company. The arms are flown from Brussels to the Iranian port of Bandar Abbas via Addis Abba. (AFP 12/17/86)

JUN 1 - The freighter Erria arrives at Puerto Cortez, Honduras, from Portugal (see May 11 entry). It sits at anchor for four days before being unloaded. Port officials refuse to disclose its registry, port of origin, or cargo. (Reuters 6/5/85)

- When Secretary Shultz met Defense Minister Rabin on June 1, the Defense Minister mentioned neither Ledeen nor Iran. (Id. at 5) The Secretary further testified that an NSC staff member told a member of his staff that Ledeen had asked McFarlane for permission to follow up on his earlier trip to obtain intelligence about Iran, that McFarlane "was ambivalent, refused to give Mr. Ledeen a letter to Prime Minister Peres, but reportedly agreed to allow Mr. Ledeen to pursue the matter. We were told that Mr. Ledeen went to Israel and received a positive response to this proposition." (Id. at 4-5) (Tower)

JUNE 4 - The Director of Central Intelligence provided a copy of this memorandum ["Toward a Policy on Iran"](See May 17, 1985 entry) to the Secretary of State on June 4, 1985. (Note on routing sheet) (Tower)

JUN 5 - It is reported that the option of invading Nicaragua is being discussed openly within the Administration. The disclosure prompts concern in Congress, which issues a conference report on July 29 stating the sense of Congress that no U.S. forces should be introduced into combat in or over Nicaragua. (CRS "War Powers Resolution: Presidential Compliance" 12/22/86)

- The Erria, which docked at Puerto Cortez, Honduras, on June 1, is unloaded and its cargo stored in a warehouse owned by the Honduran military. The cargo consists of weapons picked up in Poland, Portugal and possibly elsewhere, including Soviet-made AK-47 rifles, West German G-3 assault rifles, U.S. M-60 machine guns, mortars and cannons, enough to keep contra troops armed for three months, according to rebel sources. However, the weapons, one of several shipments that arrive in Honduras through early 1986, never leave the warehouse. According to a Honduran government source, the original plan calls for the weapons to be sold to the rebels by a few Honduran military officials who will then split the profits with two American arms dealers who helped broker the deal. One of the Americans is Ronald Martin, who is president of R.M. Equipment of Miami and who has an interest in the Tamiami Gun Shop in Miami. The latter concern has reportedly been involved in selling Soviet-bloc weapons to the contras since the cut-off of congressional aid to the guerrillas in 1984. Martin's attorney, Theodore Klein, later declines to reveal the name of the initial purchaser of the weapons, saying only that they were bought mostly in Western Europe by a "private foreign interest" and not a government. Federal and congressional investigators later begin looking into the history of the deal to try to determine who underwrote the multimillion dollar cost of the weapons, whether they were paid for with profits from arms sales to Iran and whether U.S. officials, including Oliver North, were involved. (Reuters 6/5/85; NYT 2/22/87)

- [Shultz] told the Senate Select Committee on Intelligence that, on June 5, 1985, while he was in Lisbon, he "sent a message to Mr. McFarlane complaining about Mr. Ledeen's contact with the Israelis, which had bypassed both Ambassador Lewis and myself. I said that Israel's record of dealings with Iran indicates that Israel's agenda is not the same as ours, and an intelligence relationship with Israel concerning Iran might not be one upon which we could fully rely. I felt that 'it could seriously skew our own perception and analysis of the Iranian scene.' I said in my message to Mr. McFarlane, 'I am mystified about the way this situation has been handled and am concerned that it contains the seeds of further embarrassment and serious error unless straightened out quickly.'" (Tower)

- McFarlane testified that if he had known that Israelis had previously shipped arms to Iran it would have made him less responsive to later Israeli proposals to resume shipments. However, in his first cable to Shultz in the matter he stated that it was obvious to him the Israeli channel into Iran had existed for some time. (SSIC 1/29/87)

JUN 6 - On June 6, 1985, Poindexter informed Robert Kimmitt, at that time Executive Secretary of the NSC, that

McFarlane had decided to cancel Ledeen's trip [to Israel] (see June 1, 1985 entry). (Tower)

JUN 7 - McFarlane responded [to Shultz] in a cable of June 7 that Ledeen had been acting "on his own hook." With regard to the Iran initiative, McFarlane stated "I am turning it off entirely," but added "I am not convinced that that is wise." (SSIC 1/29/87)

- "On June 7, 1985, in Portugal, I [Shultz] received a message from Mr. McFarlane [in response to Shultz's message to McFarlane of June 5, 1985] saying that he was 'a little disappointed in my prejudgments,' and that he had intended to tell me about the matter but had not had time to do so. He said 'I am turning it off entirely . . .' Mr. McFarlane said that it had been an Israeli initiative and that Mr. Ledeen was acting 'on his own hook.'" (Shultz, 12/86, 5-6) (Tower)

- A memorandum from Mr. Shackley dated June 7, 1985, containing a . . . suggestion by Mr. Ghorbanifar that the ransom [for the hostages in Beirut] involve items "other than money," . . . drew no response [from the State Department]. (Tower)

- On June 7, 1985, Shackley prepared a second report on "American Hostages in Lebanon." He gave it to Ledeen who passed it to LtCol Oliver North, the NSC staff officer responsible for counterterrorism. (Shackley 34; Ledeen (2) 5-6) Shackley reported that General Hashemi had taken soundings with Iranians on the possibility of arranging the freedom of Americans kidnapped in Lebanon. On June 1, Ghorbanifar told Hashemi that his Iranian friends had told him the following:

"—Iranian authorities were flooded with proposals to help obtain the release of American hostages in Lebanon. As a result, they did not know who was who.

"—Tehran was not interested in the humanitarian ploy that had been put forth by Ghorbanifar. (Footnote: Perhaps a reference to Ghorbanifar's suggestion that the hostages be ransomed for cash in a disguised transaction using himself as middleman. See supra p. B 3.)

"—Tehran wanted the following:

"(1) a dialogue with a responsible American who can identify what he represents;

"(2) a discussion of a quid pro quo that involves items other money.

"We told Ghorbanifar that we would pass on this commentary to 'friends.'" ("American Hostages in Lebanon," 6/7/85) (Tower)

- Also on June 7, North was working on various approaches to achieve the release of those Americans kidnapped in Lebanon. He submitted an action memorandum to McFarlane asking approval for two efforts aimed to secure the release of hostages. McFarlane approved both. Under the first, the United States would support efforts to find a private solution to the problem of the American and French hostages in Lebanon and the three Lebanese Da'Wa prisoners in Kuwait whose release the hostage holders demanded. "[T]he... operation will likely have produced results or failed by June 16, 1985," North wrote. The second plan involved the private ransoming of two hostages, including Buckley, for $2 million. This operation would take "considerable time (contacts inside Lebanon, financial transactions, and rental of yacht/safehouse)"; thus, it was possible to undertake it at the same time as the private efforts were underway. (North to McFarlane, 6/7/85) To implement this proposal, North asked McFarlane to contact the Attorney General to secure the services of two officers of the Drug Enforcement Agency who would work with the NSC staff on this matter. McFarlane approved and wrote "North to follow up 6/10 w/AG."

Documentary evidence suggests that the private source of these funds was H. Ross Perot. On August 6, North noted that Perot had called with the news that an NBC reporter had asked him to confirm that he had donated $2 million to obtain the release of hostages. ("6 Aug," note in North's handwriting) (Tower)

JUN 9 - Thomas M. Sutherland, dean of agriculture at the American University in Beirut, is kidnapped. (The Tower Report gives the date as June 10.) (NYT 12/25/86)

JUN 11 - Mr. Fortier and Mr. Teicher submitted to Mr. McFarlane a draft Presidential decision document (a National Security Decision Directive or "NSDD") drawing on the intelligence update (See May 20, 1985 entry). The draft set out immediate and long-term U.S. goals and listed specific steps to achieve them. First on the list was to "[e]ncourage Western allies and friends to help Iran meet its import requirements... includ[ing] provision of selected military equipment. . . . "

- Fortier and Teicher submitted to McFarlane a draft NSDD on Iran that Teicher had worked on for much of May. They described it as

"provocative. It basically calls for a vigorous policy designed to block Soviet advances in the short-term while building our leverage in Iran and trying to restore the U.S. position which existed under the Shah over the longer-term. This would require a sharp departure from ongoing . . . measures, most notably the supply of Western military hardware, U.S. initiative to dialogue with Iranian leaders . . .

"Because of the political and bureaucratic sensitivities, we believe that it would be best for you to provide a copy of the NSDD draft only to Shultz and Weinberger (eyes only) for their comments. Whether to proceed with a restricted SIG, NSPG or other forum would depend on their reactions." (Fortier and Teicher to McFarlane, 6/11/85)

Teicher's draft NSDD, which had incorporated some comments of Vincent Cannistraro, Senior Director for Intelligence and the NSC staff member principally responsible for monitoring covert operations, set forth these points at length. Mirroring the analysis by Fuller, the NSDD defined immediate United States interests as:

"(1) Preventing the disintegration of Iran, and preserving Iran as an independent buffer between the Soviet Union and the Persian Gulf;

"(2) Limiting Soviet political opportunities in Iran, while positioning the United States to adjust to changes;

"(3) Maintaining access to Persian Gulf oil and transit through the Gulf of Hormuz;

"(4) Ending Iranian sponsorship of terrorism, and policy of destabilizing neighboring states";

Longer-term goals were:

"(1) Restoration of Iran's moderate and constructive role in the non-Communist political community, the Persian Gulf region, and 'the world petroleum economy';

"(2) Continued Iranian resistance to Soviet expansion (in particular, in Afghanistan);

"(3) An early end to the Iran-Iraq war without Soviet mediation of change in the regional balance of power;

"(4) Elimination of Iranian human rights abuses;

"(5) Movement toward the normalization of Iranian-American relations;

"(6) Resolution of American legal and financial claims in the Hague tribunal;

"(7) Iranian moderation of OPEC pricing policy."

To begin the process of reaching these goals, Teicher and Fortier recommended that the United States:

"(1) Encourage Western allies and friends to help Iran meet its import requirements so as to reduce the attractiveness of Soviet assistance and trade offers, while demonstrating the value of correct relations with the West. This includes provision of selected military equipment as determined on a case-by-case basis." (Draft NSDD, U.S. Policy Toward [sic] Iran at 1-2, 5-6, in McFarlane to Secretaries of State and Defense, 6/17/85)

"(2) Cooperate with friendly intelligence services to improve ability to counter clandestine Soviet activities in Iran;

"(3) Increase contacts with allies and friends on the Iranian situation and be ready to communicate through them to Iran;

"(4) Establish links with, and provide support to, Iranian leaders who might be receptive to efforts to improve relations with the United States;

"(5) Avoid actions that could alienate Iranian groups that might respond favorably to such efforts;

"(6) Respond to Iranian supported terrorism with military action against terrorist infrastructures;

"(7) Increase our Voice of America effort to discredit Moscow's Islamic credentials;

"(8) Develop a '... plan' for supporting United States policy in various contingencies;

"(9) Continue to encourage third party efforts to seek an end to the Iran-Iraq war." (Id.) (Tower)

JUN 13 - Cuban exile leader Rene Corvo charters a plane to carry cargo from Fort Lauderdale, Fla, to Ilopango air base in El Salvador, according to Customs Department records. Corvo chartered another plane on March 6, 1985 (see entry) to ferry arms to Ilopango. (WSJ 1/15/87)

- The Central Bank of Egypt agrees to post a $5 million performance bond to guarantee delivery of F-4E fighter jets, spare parts and associated equipment to an unidentified buyer in connection with an official Egyptian document authorizing the deal. (See February 27 and May 22, 1985 entries). Egyptian officials say later they thought the equipment was going to be sold to Turkey or Greece, but documents from Michael Austin of Austin Aerospace in Manhattan, which holds the contract with Egypt, indicate that Iran was to be the final destination after a stop-over in Turkey. According to Richard Brenneke, a former CIA employee, the money is actually guaranteed by the U.S. Brenneke says a Mr. Boyle of the National Security Agency (NSA) was approached through Claude Lang, Boyle's assistant in private industry for eighteen years, about a deal to supply F-4E jets to Iran. Boyle agreed in principle in June or July of this year to provide the aircraft, according to Brenneke, contingent upon a $5 million bid/performance bond from the U.S. and a $3 million proof of funds from Iran. "The responsibility for operational aspects of the transaction," Brenneke writes in a November 30, 1985 memo to the Defense Department, "were [sic] apparently designated to Mr. H. John, an employee of the Central Intelligence Agency, stationed at the U.S. embassy in Paris, France." Brenneke says that telexes were sent on NSA machines during the course of the contract to confirm banking arrangements through Iran's Bank Melli, Bank Lambert in Brussels and City Bank, Dubai. Three months later, however, on October 15, the deal fell through, mainly because Iran refused to deal with the CIA. (Brenneke memo to Col. Richard H. Muller, USMC, 11/30/85; NYT 2/2/87)

JUN 14 - Two Lebanese men hijacked TWA flight 847 enroute from Athens to Rome, with 135 U.S. citizens aboard, and directed the pilot to land at Beirut airport. There, the hijackers removed thirteen Americans from the plane and killed an American sailor. This episode absorbed the government until the surviving hostages were released on June 29. (Tower)

- The incident precipitates a shift in U.S. policy toward both Iran and Libya. The White House comes to realize that Iran is the key player in hostage matters and is increasingly willing to use any available means for obtaining release of all captive Americans.

According to testimony by White House Chief of Staff Donald Regan, McFarlane mentioned the possibility of requesting use of the Israeli channel to Iran in briefings to the President during the crisis. Regan said that this was his first awareness of any such contacts.

At the same time, while contemplating an opening to Tehran, senior NSC and CIA officials begin a drive to toughen the Administration's stance against Libya, although there is no direct connection between Libya and the hijacking. According to an official involved in the policy-making, the idea "was to embrace the Ayatollah [Khomeini] and demolish Khaddafi.... It was not particularly rational, but [TWA] 847 had exposed the absence of both a real antiterrorist capability and policy toward the states supporting terrorism." (WP 12/7/86; Newsweek 12/15/86; SSIC 1/29/87)

- Frustration at the lack of progress in freeing the hostages in Beirut grew perceptibly within the U.S. government, especially in the face of pleas to the President for action by the families of the hostages. In the summer of 1985, a vehicle appeared that offered the prospect of progress both on the release of the hostages and a strategic opening to Iran.

Israel had long-standing interests in a relationship with Iran and in promoting its arms export industry. Arms sales to Iran could further both objectives. It also offered a means of strengthening Iran against Israel's old adversary, Iraq. Much of Israel's military equipment came originally from the United States, however. For both legal and political reasons, Israel felt a need for U.S. approval of, or at least acquiescence in, any arms sales to Iran. In addition, elements in Israel undoubtedly wanted the United States involved for its own sake so as to distance the United States from the Arab world and ultimately to establish Israel as the only real strategic partner of the United States in the region.

Iran badly wanted what Israel could provide. The United States had been the primary source of arms for the Shah, but U.S. shipments to Iran were now barred by the embargo. Iran desperately wanted U.S.-origin TOW and HAWK missiles in order to counter Iraq's chief areas of superiority— armor and air forces. Since Israel had these weapons in its inventory, it was an alternative source of supply. Israel was more than willing to provide these weapons to Iran, but only if the United States approved the transfer and would agree to replace the weapons.

Iranian interest in these weapons was widely known among those connected with the arms trade. These included Manuchehr Ghorbanifar, an Iranian businessman living in France, and Adolph Schwimmer and Yaacov Nimrodi, private Israeli arms dealers with contacts throughout the Middle East including Israel. Since September, 1984, Mr. Schwimmer had also been a consultant to then-Prime Minister of Israel Shimon Peres. In a series of meetings beginning in January, 1985, these men had discussed using arms sales to obtain the release of the U.S. citizens held hostage in Beirut and to open a strategic dialogue with Iran. Some of those meetings included Amiram Nir, since September, 1984, an advisor to Prime Minister Peres on counterterrorism. Also involved was Saudi businessman Adnan Khashoggi, a man well-connected in the Middle East and enjoying a special relationship with key Israeli officials. All these men subsequently played a role in the brokering of the arms deals that later did occur.

These men believed that the United States, Israel, and Iran, though with different interests, were susceptible to a relationship of convenience involving arms, hostages, and the opening of a channel to Iran. The catalyst that brought this relationship into being was the proffering by Israel of a channel for the United States in establishing contacts with Iran. (Tower)

JUN 17 - Mr. McFarlane circulated the draft [NSDD, which had been prepared by two members of the NSC staff] on June 17, 1985, to Secretary Shultz, Secretary Weinberger, and Director of Central Intelligence Casey. His transmittal memorandum requested that further distribution remain limited to lessen the risk of leaks. (See June 11, June 29, July 16, and July 18, 1985 entries.) (Tower) (SSIC 1/29/87)

- [T]he Director of Central Intelligence heard from his wartime friend, John Shaheen, that a Dr. Cyrus Hashemi, under indictment for attempting to sell arms to Iran, claimed to have discussed with the Iranian Foreign Ministry an exchange of hostages for the release of the Da'Wa prisoners in Kuwait, TOW missiles, and a nolle prosequi for Hashemi. (Casey to C/NE, 6/17/85) According to the CIA Inspector General, Israeli officials asked Ghorbanifar to use his influence in Tehran to obtain the release of hostages. (CIA/IG Chronology 2) (Tower)

- Iran sent the United States a message to the effect that Tehran wanted to do as much as it could to end the TWA crisis. (Teicher to McFarlane, 6/19/85) (Tower)

JUN 21 - The United States responded on June 21 that "[i]t is the view of the United States that the government of Iran cannot escape its responsibilities . . . to help secure the release of the hostages. . . ." (DT 6/21/85 1828L)

In November 1986, the NSC staff prepared a number of

chronologies. The two fullest, entitled "U.S./Iranian Contacts and the American Hostages," bear the designations "11/17/86 2000 (Maximum Version)" ("Maximum Version") and "11/20/86 2000 (Historical Chronology)" ("Historical Chronology"). The Maximum version notes that "U.S. intelligence reports indicate that Majlis speaker Rafsanjani, who was traveling in the mid-east at the time, and Iranian Foreign Minister Velayati both intervened with the captors [to secure the release]. Rafsanjani, in his speech on November 4, 1986, for the first time publicly acknowledged his role in this matter." (Tower)

JUN 29 - State Department logs and Secretary Shultz' testimony indicate that he responded in writing [to June 17 draft NSDD from McFarlane on the subject of U.S.-Iranian relations] on 29 June that the proposed policy was "perverse" and "contrary to our own interests." Weinberger made the following comment in the margin of the draft, "This is almost too absurd to comment on." According to Weinberger's testimony and that of Assistant Secretary of Defense Armitage, Weinberger responded in writing opposing such sales. (See July 16 and July 18, 1985 entries.) (SSIC 1/29/87)

- The Secretary of State responded to the draft NSDD on June 29, 1985. "The strategic importance of Iran and the value of reassessing our policy toward it are clear," he wrote. "The draft NSDD constructively and perceptively addresses a number of the key issues. I disagree, however, with one point in the analysis and one specific recommendation." (Comment on Draft NSDD, Shultz to McFarlane, 7/29/85) (Sic) In his view,

"the draft NSDD appears to exaggerate current anti-regime sentiment and Soviet advantages over us in gaining influence. Most importantly, its proposal that we permit or encourage a flow of Western arms to Iran is contrary to our interest both in containing Khomeinism and in ending the excesses of this regime. We should not alter this aspect of our policy when groups with ties to Iran are holding US hostages in Lebanon. I, therefore, disagree with the suggestion that our efforts to reduce arms flows to Iran should be ended. If the NSDD is revised to reflect this concern, I would like to see the draft again before it is put in final form." (Id.)

Secretary Shultz devoted the rest of his comments to further analysis of his reasons for opposing arms shipments to

Iran and his disagreement with the NSDD's portrayal of Iran's relations with the Soviet Union. "The inherent limits on the Iranian-Soviet relationship are underplayed in the NSDD draft. Iranians have a deep historical mistrust of the USSR. The Iranian feelers to the Soviets are for arms and for limitations on Soviet arms supplies to Iraq; the Iranians do not seek a closer relationship." Any attempt at a closer relationship with the Soviet Union would encounter resistance. His comment further reminded McFarlane that, under the Shah, "Iranian-Soviet relations were closer and more cooperative than they are now." (Id.) The Secretary had no objection to passing a message to the Speaker of the Iranian Majlis (Parliament) Rafsanjani while abroad expressing the United States interest in "correct" relations, and to encourage allies and friends to broaden their commercial relations with Iran. Such initiatives to diminish Iran's isolation should not undermine pressure to bring an end to the war and restrain arms flows. The comment concluded that this two track policy remained best. (Id.) (Tower)

JUN 30 - The hostages aboard TWA Flight 847 are released. Ali Akbar Rafsanjani, the speaker of the Iranian Parliament, reportedly played a major role in persuading Hezbollah, the Lebanese Shiite group, to release four of the hostages. (Newsweek 12/15/86)

JUN or JUL - A "National Security Agency" official attempts to arrange the sale of F-4E fighter jets to Iran, according to a November 30, 1985 memo to U.S. officials by Oregon businessman Richard J. Brenneke. Brenneke, who was a CIA employee for 13 years and a freelance consultant for French and Israeli intelligence, says the deal falls through when Iranians refuses to allow CIA involvement. (WP 11/29/86; NYT 2/2/87)

JUL - Reagan sends a secret message to Rafsanjani, who is in Tokyo for an official visit, via Japanese Prime Minister Nakasone. The message expresses Reagan's thanks for Rafsanjani's help in freeing the hostages of TWA Flight 847 and his hopes for better U.S.-Iranian relations.

JUL - When interviewed by the Board's staff . . . Ambassador [Tambs] said that prior to reporting to Costa Rica, he received instructions from the members of the Restricted Interagency Group ("RIG") to aid the Nicaraguan

Resistance Forces in setting up a "Southern Front." The members of the RIG were Mr. Abrams, LtCol North and the Director of the CIA CATF. Ambassador Tambs recounted the instructions he received in July 1985:

"Before I went (to Costa Rica) Ollie said when you get down there you should open the southern front. In the subsequent meetings and conversations (of the RIG) that was confirmed by Abrams and (name deleted—CIA official). That was sort of our mission."

When asked what this mission meant to him, Ambassador Tambs responded that "the idea was that we would encourage them to fight." He added that he never had any contacts with Contra military leaders and that he only spoke with the "political types." (Tower)

- The CIA field officer told the Board that construction of the Santa Elena airfield was a pet project of U.S. Ambassador Louis [sic] Tambs. According to the CIA officer:

"When Ambassador Tambs arrived in Costa Rica [July 1985], he called together the Deputy Chief of Mission [George Jones], the Defense Attache [either Maj. Leonard Maldonado or Col. John Lent] and myself, and said that he had really only one mission in Costa Rica, and that was to form a Nicaraguan resistance southern front.

"The [Santa Elena airstrip] was a matter which I had been monitoring, kind of as an aside, but is was essentially the Ambassador's initiative." (Tower; DOS statement 4/8/87; DOD statement 4/8/87)

- Ambassador Tambs said that he learned of the airstrip project from a CIA field officer. The officer informed him that private benefactors were behind the efforts to build the airstrip and Mr. Secord coordinated the flights.

Ambassador Tambs recalled that LtCol North asked him shortly after he arrived in Costa Rica whether the Costa Rican government would "go along" with the airstrip. He said that the Costa Rican government was interested in the airstrip primarily as a resupply station in the event of a Nicaraguan invasion of Costa Rica. As far as he knew, the airstrip was used mainly for refueling before Contra resupply planes returned to "wherever they were coming from."

According to a CIA field officer, Mr. Abrams and LtCol North were also well informed of this project. [See April 30, 1985 entry.] (Tower)

- The construction of [the airstrip] was apparently one of the operations undertaken by "Project Democracy." In a September 30, 1986, memorandum to VADM Poindexter, LtCol North described Project Democracy's role:

"The airfield at Santa Elena has been a vital element in supporting the resistance. Built by a Project Democracy proprietary (Udall Corporation S.A.—a Panamanian Company), the field was initially used for direct resupply efforts [to the Contras] (July 1985-February 1986)...the field has served as the primary abort base for aircraft damaged by Sandinista anti-aircraft fire." (President Arias learned of the existence of the airport shortly after he came to office in May 1986. He felt the airstrip compromised Costa Rican neutrality and informed Ambassador Tambs that it was not to be used.)

According to LtCol North, press reports on the existence of this airfield in September, 1986 "caused Project Democracy to permanently close Udall Corporation, and dispose of its capital assets." (A CIA field officer based in Costa Rica told the Board that Udall Corp. was closely associated with Mr. Secord.) (Tower)

- On a visit to Costa Rica shortly after he was confirmed to his new position Mr. Abrams raised the subject with the CIA officer:

"During the course of this conversation...Assistant Secretary Abrams asked me about Point West [another name for the airstrip]...I became very upset with Assistant Secretary Abrams for bringing out [sic] the question...I thought it should be closely held...I said what is this with the airstrip? Where is this known? He said well, this is known in Washington by—Colonel North told me about it and I assume that the [Director of the CIA CATF] knows about it."

Mr. Abrams testified that the Santa Elena airstrip was never used. "My understanding was nobody ever used the airstrip...that it had never quite gotten into operation." (Tower)

- In July 1985 Khashoggi sent McFarlane a lengthy paper he had written dealing with the political situation in Iran. McFarlane testified that he did not recall seeing these papers, but indicated the existence of prior "think pieces" Khashoggi had sent him on the Middle East. A staff member of the NSC testified that McFarlane gave the Khashoggi paper to another NSC staffer. Michael Ledeen, a professor at

Georgetown University, and a part-time NSC consultant beginning in February 1985, appears to have played a key role in the initial contacts between the U.S. and Israel vis-a-vis Iran. (SSIC 1/29/87)

JUL 3 - According to testimony by McFarlane, on July 3, 1985, David Kimche, Director General of Israel's Foreign Ministry and a former intelligence officer, contacted McFarlane and reported to him that Israel had succeeded in establishing a dialogue with Iran. Kimche stated that as a result of growing concerns with Soviet pressures, Iranian officials had asked Israel to determine whether the U.S. would be interested in opening up political talks with Iran. According to McFarlane, Kimche stated that the Iranians understood U.S. concerns regarding their legitimacy and therefore had proposed to use their influence with radical elements holding U.S. hostages in Lebanon. Although there was no specific Iranian request for arms, Kimche admitted to the possibility that the Iranians might raise the arms issue in the future. (SSIC 1/29/87)

- On July 3, 1985, David Kimche, the Director General of the Israeli Foreign Ministry, met at the White House with Mr. McFarlane. Mr. McFarlane told the Board that Mr. Kimche asked the position of the U.S. government toward engaging in a political discourse with Iranian officials. He recalled Mr. Kimche as saying that these Iranian officials had conveyed to Israel their interest in a discourse with the United States. Contact was to be handled through an intermediary (later disclosed to be Mr. Ghorbanifar) who was represented as having good connections to Iranian officials.

This was not the first time that Mr. Ghorbanifar had come to the attention of the U.S. government. The CIA knew of Mr. Ghorbanifar and had a history of contacts with him. CIA's first contact with Ghorbanifar was through a European intelligence service in January 1980. From the beginning, CIA found it "difficult to filter out the bravado and exaggeration from what actually happened." Other intelligence services had similar experiences with Mr. Ghorbanifar. By September of 1980, CIA decided to drop efforts at recruiting Ghorbanifar. It considered him neither reliable nor trustworthy. In addition, Theodore Shackley, a former CIA official, had met Mr. Ghorbanifar in Hamburg, West Germany, between November 19-21, 1984. Mr. Ghorbanifar at that time suggested payment of a cash ransom for the hostages in

Beirut, with himself as middleman. This proposal, contained in a memorandum prepared by Mr. Shackley dated November 22, 1984, apparently reached the State Department where it elicited no interest. A memorandum from Mr. Shackley dated June 7, 1985, containing a later suggestion by Mr. Ghorbanifar that the ransom involve items "other than money," also drew no response. At the time of his meeting with Mr. Kimche, Mr. McFarlane apparently did not know this background or even that Mr. Ghorbanifar was the intermediary Mr. Kimche had in mind. He learned this later in the month from Mr. Ledeen.

Mr. McFarlane told the Board that Mr. Kimche told him the Iranians understood that they would have to demonstrate their "bona fides" and that the Iranians believed they could influence Hizballah to release the hostages in Beirut. But Mr. McFarlane also recalled Mr. Kimche expressing the view that ultimately the Iranians would need something to show for the dialogue, and that this would "probably" be weapons.

Mr. McFarlane testified that he informed the President of his conversation with Mr. Kimche within three or four days after the meeting, shortly before the President entered the hospital for his cancer operation. . . . Mr. McFarlane told the Board that the President was interested in the proposal and said that he believed we should explore it. Mr. McFarlane said this may have occurred in the first week of July, before the President entered the hospital. (See July 13, 1985 entry.) (Tower)

- Shortly after Kimche and McFarlane meet [July 3, 1985], according to the Senate intelligence panel's draft report on the Iran-contra affair, McFarlane and Shultz exchange cables concerning the proposed U.S.-Iranian contacts. McFarlane endorses the plan in his cable, but Shultz, who is in the Far East at the time, warns of "a peril in undertaking such an initiative with Israel," although he agrees the U.S. should not ignore opportunities to obtain the release of the hostages or renew ties with a more compatible regime in Tehran. (NYT 1/11/87)

- Meanwhile, according to testimony by Ledeen, in early July he was called by Kimche who said a friend, Al Schwimmer, was coming to Washington and wanted to talk to Ledeen. Ledeen testified that he met with Schwimmer in early July. Schwimmer recounted a meeting he had attended a week or two before in Europe with Kimche, Khashoggi and Ghorbanifar. Schwimmer said Ghorbanifar had a lot of useful information about the situation in Iran and that Ledeen should meet him as soon as possible.

According to Ledeen he reported his meeting with Schwimmer to McFarlane. Ledeen told McFarlane he was going to Israel on vacation from mid-July to mid-August and would, if McFarlane thought it appropriate, meet Ghorbanifar. Ledeen testified that McFarlane agreed. (SSIC 1/29/87)

JUL - At a foreign policy meeting with Reagan in attendance, McFarlane reportedly declares the need for harsher measures to deal with Libyan support for terrorism since, he says, diplomatic and economic pressure on Khaddafi has had no effect to date. (NYT 2/22/87)

JUL 4 or 5 - [McFarlane told the Board] "Now maybe it's come to your attention that there was a meeting with the TWA 847 relatives and hostages on July 4 or 5, and the President stayed with Mrs. Reagan at Arlington Cemetery for an extra half hour or so going down and greeting each of the families there, and it was a very moving moment and it had an impact on him." (Tower)

JUL 8 - In a speech to the American Bar Association, Reagan declares Iran to be part of a "confederation of terrorist states . . . a new, international version of Murder Incorporated." He also adds, "Let me make it plain to the assassins in Beirut and their accomplices that America will never make concessions to terrorists." (WP 12/7/86; NYT 12/25/86)

JUL 11 - (Ledeen (1) 17) In his two interviews with the Board [See July 1985 entry], Ledeen recalled Schwimmer reporting that he had recently met Ghorbanifar through Schwimmer's friend, Khashoggi. Ghorbanifar's knowledge of Iranian policies impressed the Israelis.

[Ledeen said] "Ghorbanifar had for the first time given them what they considered to be a really solid picture, in detail, of the internal Iranian situation and the Iranian connection to international terrorism.

"And in addition he had various proposals that he claimed to be representing on behalf of the Iranian government, who were high individuals inside the Iranian government, and they thought it was important that I should come and meet this person.

"And I said [I] was planning to come to Israel anyway and that I would check with Bud [McFarlane] and if it was okay with Bud I would try to meet with him then. And I talked to Bud and he said fine." (Ledeen (2) 17)

Schwimmer, whom Ledeen described as one of Foreign Minister Peres' "close friends," knew about Ledeen's May conversation with the then-Prime Minister. (Id. at 19) "[A]s best as I can recall it at this point," Ledeen told the Board, "I think that what happened was that Schwimmer described Ghorbanifar and he may have talked something about hostages also, that I went to Israel and met Ghorbanifar, where all of this took on real flesh, that Kimche then came back to Washington early in August and told Bud about it, and formulated the proposition, that Bud then discussed it with the President, and by the time I came back in the middle of August the President had approved it and I then communicated that decision to the Israelis.

"And I'm quite sure that is the chronology."

General Scowcroft: "Do you have any notion how this thing got transformed from a research project into an action program over a very short period of time and who made the transformation?"

Mr. Ledeen: "It is what I wrote in the Post, General. The Iranians came forward. Ghorbanifar came forward. Ghorbanifar is really the driving force behind this whole thing. I mean, one can speculate about Americans and Israelis, but it is clear that the guy really—I mean, these ideas did not come either from the Government of the United States or the Government of Israel or arms merchants. These ideas came from Ghorbanifar. He was the person who introduced them. He was the one who put them forward, and he was the one who claimed to have the capacity to achieve them.

"So it happened because the Israelis were approached by Ghorbanifar as a way of getting to the United States, and I believe—I mean, one of the few things that I do believe that Khashoggi has said is what he said on that TV show with Barbara Walters, that he suggested to Ghorbanifar that the best way to get the Americans' attention was to go to the Israelis. That is the way he would think, and he was right, in fact, and it worked.

"So that was the channel from Iran to the United States and that is how it happened, and I was the one who found myself in a room with them, that's all. It was an accident." (Id. at 21-23) (Tower)

- A note from McFarlane's secretary, dated July 11, 1985, contained the following:

"JMP [Poindexter] talked with Michael Ledeen this morning about an urgent message from Peres for McFarlane which Al Schwimmer, a Jewish-American who provides lots of money to Peres, wants to deliver to RCM [McFarlane]."

McFarlane's secretary reported that Ledeen had lunch with Schwimmer on July 11 and left the following message for McFarlane:

"It is indeed a message from Prime Minister of Israel; it is a follow-on to the private conversation he had last week when David Kimche was here. It is extremely urgent and extremely sensitive and it regards the matter he told David he was going to raise with the President. The situation has fundamentally changed for the better and that I must explain to him because it will affect his decision. It is very important. It won't keep more than a day or two but could keep until Saturday morning. This is the real thing and it is just wonderful news." (Tower)

JUL 12-20 - Reagan is hospitalized for surgery to remove a cancerous polyp. Attorney General Edwin Meese later says that Reagan may have been ill or under sedation during a period of recovery in August and therefore may not have recalled giving oral authorization to McFarlane for arms shipments to Iran. (LAT 12/21/86)

- In his first interview, McFarlane told the Board he then reported this conversation to the President before he entered the hospital for his cancer operation in the second week of July. He informed the Secretaries of State and Defense and the Director of Central Intelligence in separate conversations. He also said he visited with the President in hospital, and the Secretary of State "to discuss it in brief." (Id.) He told the President that Kimche's question was "what is your attitude toward engaging with Iran in a political agenda, period." (Id.) According to McFarlane, the President considered the question in a broad context, including Kimche's suggestion that eventually arms transfers would become an issue.

"And while it wasn't linked to the hostages, the President said, well, it seemed to him that the Middle East experience well beyond Iran is that elements to succeed ultimately to power do need to strengthen themselves, and that the currency of doing that is usually weapons. And he said the key element is not denying history, but deciding whether or not our doing that or somebody else doing that can be distinguished as a political matter of policy between the natural perception of people that weapons are going to people portrayed as terrorists. Iran is identified as a terrorist state. He said the key element is whether or not these people are indeed devoted to change and not just simply opportunists, self-serving radicals." (Id. at 9)

In his meeting with the Board on February 11, 1987, the President said he had no recollection of a meeting in the hospital in July with McFarlane and that he had no notes that would show such a meeting. (R. Dawson & W.C. McFadden II, Memorandum for the Record, 2/9/87)

In his third interview with the Board, February 21, 1987, at the Bethesda National Naval Hospital, McFarlane recalled:

"I have felt since last November—and that is where we started—that it has been, I think, misleading, at least, and wrong, at worst, for me to overly gild the President's motives for his decision in this, to portray them as mostly directed toward political outcomes.

"The President acknowledged those and recognized that those were clearly important. However, by the tenor of his questioning, which was oriented toward the hostages and timing of the hostages, from his recurrent virtually daily questioning just about welfare and do we have anything new and so forth, it is very clear that his concerns here were for the return of the hostages. . . .

"Within a day or so of that I brought to his attention this original proposal from Mr. Kimche, and the President's reaction was quite enthusiastic and somewhat perhaps excessively enthusiastic, given the many uncertainties involved. But it was expressive of his attitude on this issue from the beginning, and from the four, five, or six meetings we had in the next thirty days on it there weren't any inhibitions as persistently as well as the Secretary of State and Defense made them, and they were very well made.

"But the President had no hesitancy about it at all, nor did he when he called me about it last week here in the hospital.

"Well, the recollection of my having briefed the President on Kimche's visit in the White House and his coming here and his reactions when here at the hospital, I briefed him on the new information received from Mr. Schwimmer, there is a vividness in my recollection that is documented datewise by the calendars that I have that the meetings were held in the image of being across the hall with Mr. Regan and the President, filling them in on this, and the President saying words to the effect that gee, that sounds pretty good.

"The weapons issue is a problem, and our discussion of that, and he says: I guess we can't do the weapons or something like that ourselves, but isn't there a way that we can get at trying to keep this channel going or something like that."

Mr. Dawson: "And that's tied in to the hostages at that point? It is clear that one of the purposes of this is not so much a strategic opening as you might have otherwise stated, but it is an attempt to get arms for hostages through the transfer from Israel to Iran?"

Mr. McFarlane: "Well, I think that was foremost in the President's mind."

Mr. Dawson: "So if he didn't state to you in so many words, Bud, go ahead and do it, he clearly led you to believe from the outset that here was a chance to bring some hostages out through a third country?"

Mr. McFarlane: "It was unambiguously clear." (McFarlane (3) 1 1-14)

On November 21, 1986, McFarlane wrote Poindexter that the President "was all for letting the Israelis do anything they wanted at the very first briefing in the hospital." (McFarlane PROF note to Poindexter, 11/21/86, 21:01) (Tower)

JUL 13 - Donald T. Regan, the President's Chief of Staff, recalled first learning of McFarlane's conversation with an Israeli about Iran while the President was in hospital, some two days after his operation. According to Regan, McFarlane wanted authority to enter discussions with the Iranians identified by the Israelis as having reasonably good connections within Iran but who were on the outside." (Regan 4) Regan told the Board:

"About the second day after the operation, I believe it was, we went out there—I can find the exact date if you don't have it—met with the President—he was in bed—and McFarlane told him that we had had a contact from Iranians whom he had reason to believe had reasonably good connections within Iran but who were on the outside, and this had come primarily as a result of Israeli connection with the Iranians.

"At that time I didn't know their names. I now know them to be Ghorbanifar, Kimche, and the like, but at that time I didn't know the names.

"And what McFarlane wanted was the President's authority to make this contact, to see if it could be developed and what it could lead to. There was a discussion of the importance of Iran as far as its strategic location . . . and the fact that it seemed worthwhile to McFarlane that this be pursued.

"The President, after asking quite a few questions—and I would say the discussion lasted for perhaps 20, 25 minutes —assented and said yes, go ahead. Open it up." (Regan 4-5)

According to McFarlane, after this meeting, he then conveyed to Kimche the President's openness to a dialogue with Iran. (McFarlane (1) 9) In his meeting with the Board on February 11, 1987, the President said he had no recollection of a meeting in the hospital in July with Mr. McFarlane and that he had no notes that would show such a meeting. (Tower)

- In his testimony, McFarlane categorically denied any discussion of Ghorbanifar with the President, recalling that it was only in December that McFarlane became aware of Ghorbanifar's identity. It should be noted, however, that McFarlane made reference to Ghorbanifar in his July 14 cable to Shultz describing the proposal. In describing his contacts with the emissary from Peres and Kimche, McFarlane stated that the Iranian officials named in the context of the proposal are an ayatollah and "an advisor to the Prime Minister named Ghorbanifar." (SSIC 1/29/87)

- Mr. McFarlane . . . stated that on July 13, 1985, he briefed Secretary Shultz, Secretary Weinberger, and Director Casey in separate conversations [about his July 3, 1985 meeting with Kimche]. (Tower)

- On July 13, 1985, Mr. McFarlane apparently received a second [Israeli government] request [regarding Iran], this time brought by an emissary directly from Israeli Prime Minister Peres. The "emissary" was Mr. Schwimmer, who delivered the request to Mr. McFarlane through Mr. Ledeen. The emissary carried word of a recent meeting with Mr. Ghorbanifar and another Iranian in which the Iranians had said that others inside Iran were interested in more extensive relations with the West, and particularly, the United States. The Iranians reportedly said that their contacts in Iran could achieve the release of the seven Americans held in Lebanon but in exchange sought 100 TOW missiles from Israel. This was to be part of a "larger purpose" of opening a "private dialogue" on U.S./Iranian relations. The emissary asked for a prompt response. (Tower)

JUL 14 - Mr. McFarlane cabled this proposal to Secretary Shultz, who was traveling in Asia. Mr. McFarlane recommended a tentative show of interest in a dialogue but with no commitment to the arms exchange. He asked for Secretary Shultz's guidance and indicated he would "abide fully" by the Secretary's decision. By return cable on the same day, Secretary Shultz agreed to "a tentative show of interest without commitment." He said this was consistent with U.S. policy of "maintaining contact with people who might eventually provide information or help in freeing hostages." Secretary Shultz advised Mr. McFarlane to "handle this probe personally" but asked that he stay in close contact. (Tower)

- The Secretary of State testified before the House Foreign Affairs Committee that he first heard of this matter while flying between Perth and Canberra, Australia, on July 14, 1985. McFarlane reported that Kimche had met him secretly the week before,

"and had asked him to confirm that the U.S was in fact uninterested in pursuing the cooperation earlier proposed to Mr. Ledeen. Mr. McFarlane wrote that he had so confirmed. He then stated that an unnamed emissary had 'today' reopened the issue on behalf of the Prime Minister. (This "emissary" apparently was Schwimmer. . . .)

McFarlane's secretary reported that Ledeen had lunch with Schwimmer on July 11 and left . . . [a] message for McFarlane.

McFarlane indicated. . . that he would see Ledeen Saturday, July 13. McFarlane's desk calendar confirms this meeting. McFarlane told the Board he supposed the "emissary" was Schwimmer, that he did not meet him and that he probably received Schwimmer's message from Ledeen. (McFarlane (2) 4) On July 13, the President underwent his cancer operation. The emissary said that in a recent meeting between Israelis and some Iranians, including Mr. Kimche, a Mr. Al Schwimmer, and Mr. Ghorbanifar, the Iranians had painted a pessimistic view of Iran. They allegedly said "their hope and that of what they portrayed as a significant cadre of the hierarchy was to develop a dialogue with the West," and emphatically with the United States. The Israelis had allegedly pressed "for some tangible show" of the Iranians' ability to deliver, and were purportedly told "that they could in the short term achieve the release of the seven Americans held in Lebanon." But, Mr. McFarlane repeated, in exchange the Iranians had said they would need to show "some gain" and sought specifically the delivery from Israel of 100 TOW missiles. "But they stated," Mr. McFarlane continued, "that the larger purpose would be the opening of the private dialogue with a high level American official and a sustained discussion of U.S.-Iranian relations."

Mr. McFarlane reviewed the "imponderable questions" raised by this proposal including "our terrorism policy against negotiating with terrorists (notwithstanding the thin veil provided by Israel as the cut out on this specific matter)." He noted that our long term interest was in maintaining the possibility of renewed ties, and the importance of doing something soon about the seven hostages. He said: "We could make a tentative show of interest without commitment and see what happened or we could walk away. On balance I tend to favor going ahead." He said the emissary was leaving soon, asked for a prompt signal, and that he would "await and abide fully by your decisions."

"I [Shultz] replied by a message to Mr. McFarlane that same day that 'I agree with you that we should make a tentative show of interest without commitment. I do not think we could justify turning our backs on the prospect of gaining the release of the other seven hostages and perhaps developing an ability to renew ties with Iran under a more sensible regime—especially when presented to us through the Prime Minister of Israel.'

"This position—indicating a willingness to talk but no commitment to pay—was consistent with Administration policy of maintaining contact with people who might eventually provide information or help in freeing hostages. I pointed out, however, 'the fraud that seems to accompany so many deals involving arms and Iran, and the complications arising from our "blessing" an Israel-Iran relationship where Israel's interest and ours are not necessarily the same.' I suggested that Mr. McFarlane should give the emissary 'a positive but passive reply.' That is, tell him that the U.S. 'is receptive to the idea of a private dialogue involving a sustained discussion of U.S.-Iranian relations. In other words, we are willing to listen and seriously consider any statement on this topic that they might wish to intitiate.' I said I thought Mr. McFarlane should manage this probe personally, but that the two of us should discuss its sensitivity and the likelihood of disclosure after my return. I told him to tell the emissary 'that you and I are in close contact and full agreement every step of the way; this is all the more important in view of the present lack of unity and full coordination on the Israeli side.'" (Shultz, 12/86, 8-10; SRB, 17-20) (Tower)

-By July 14, 1985, a specific proposal for the sale of 100 TOWs to Iran in exchange for Iranian efforts to secure the release of all the hostages had been transmitted to the White House and discussed with the President. What actually occurred, at least so far as the September shipment was concerned, involved a direct link of arms and a hostage. (Tower)

JUL 15 - According to testimony by Ledeen, the subject of Ghorbanifar's bona fides first came up in September 1985. However, Shultz testified that he saw an intelligence report on July 15, 1985, two days after he cabled McFarlane from Geneva, which indicated that Ghorbanifar was a "talented fabricator." (SSIC 1/29/87)

- Around this time, the Administration prepares various studies in connection with possible military operations against Libya. Robert Gates, then head of intelligence analysis for the CIA, writes a paper suggesting that a joint U.S.-Egyptian operation against Libya would present an opportunity "to redraw the map of North Africa." Casey orders an in-depth study of potential targets in Libya in case of a U.S. attack. Also during this period, McFarlane, Poindexter and Donald Fortier of the NSC draw up a plan for Egypt to invade Libya with U.S. air support, capture half its territory and force Khaddafi from power. The State Department and Pentagon reportedly oppose this plan because of its risks and the unlikelihood that Egyptian President Mubarak would ever agree to it. The Joint Chiefs put together a study of their own estimating that such an operation would require about 90,000 troops. Shultz, meanwhile, secretly calls his ambassador to Egypt, Nicholas Veliotes, to Washington and asks him to redraft the White House plan into a more practical policy option from the point of view of both Egypt and the United States. The State Department's version calls for "contingency planning" with Egypt in the event of a clash with Libya and other "reactive and defensive scenarios," according to a source familiar with it. (WP 2/20/87)

JUL 16 - [In a letter to McFarlane] Secretary Weinberger objected sharply to the suggestion that the United States should permit or encourage transfers of Western arms to Iran. (See June 17, 1985 entry.) (Tower)

- The Secretary of Defense submitted his reaction to the draft NSDD on July 16, 1985. He told the Board that his initial reaction was to write "absurd" in the margin. "I also added that this is roughly like inviting Qadhafi over for a cozy lunch." (Weinberger 5) While his formal comment noted his agreement

"with many of the major points in the paper, several of the proposed actions seem questionable. Moreover, it is extremely difficult to consider an explicit revision of our policy toward Iran as long as we continue to receive evidence of Iranian complicity in terrorist actions and planning against us. I do not believe, therefore, an NSDD should be issued in the proposed form." (Weinberger to McFarlane, 7/16/85) The Secretary of Defense "fully" supported the short-term goal of blocking Soviet expansion into Iran.

"Under no circumstances, however, should we now ease our restriction on arms sales to Iran. Attempting to cut off arms while remaining neutral on sales to either belligerent is one of the few ways we have to protect our longer-range interests in both Iran and Iraq. A policy reversal would be seen as inexplicably inconsistent by those nations whom we have urged to refrain from such sales, and would likely lead to increased arms sales by them and a possible alteration of the strategic balance in favor of Iran while Khomeini is still the controlling influence. It would adversely affect our newly emerging relationship with Iraq."

Secretary Weinberger then enumerated those actions— improving intelligence gathering capabilities as recommended in the SNIE, establishing contacts with "moderates," whom intelligence might identify as favoring policies favorable to U.S. and Western interests; communicating our interest in correct relations through allies and friends while remaining neutral in the Iran-Iraq war; pressing the Khomeini government in public statements to mitigate its hostile policies, while encouraging opponents of those policies; and the like—he believed best calculated to achieve United States goals in the region. He concluded by reaffirming his support for present policies in face of Iran's "international lawlessness." He emphasized that "[c]hanges in policy and in conduct, therefore, must be initiated by a new Iranian government." The United States should encourage change, and support moderation and the development in the future of amicable relations. He did not think the program outlined in the draft NSDD served these goals. (Id.) (Tower)

- On July 16, the Secretary saw an intelligence report, which indicated that Ghorbanifar, whose name McFarlane had mentioned, was "a talented fabricator." (Shultz, SRB, 20)(Tower)

In the middle of July, Ledeen went to Israel on vacation and, toward the end of the month, attended a meeting with Ghorbanifar, Kimche, Schwimmer, and Nimrodi. "[T]o the best of my recollection," Ledeen said, this conversation, "is the first time that the subject of weapons and hostages was raised. They were raised in the context of the future relationship between the United States and Iran. They were not raised separately as a deal or an entity unto themselves because what Ghorbanifar had to say, in addition to this fairly enlightening picture of Iran that he presented us with, was that there were significant and powerful people within the government of Iran who were interested in improving relations with the United States. . . . [A]s part of the evolution of this relationship in a more positive direction Iran would undertake to make gestures of good faith and to demonstrate not only their willingness but their capacity to alter their policies in a direction which we would consider positive, and that at the same time they would like to see on the part of the United States a similar demonstration of willingness and capacity and that the only such gesture by the United States that would convince them simultaneously that the President was personally involved and committed to this policy and that the United States would act and exert its power in the world to do such things would be if the United States enabled Iran to obtain weapons which were at present unobtainable because of the American arms embargo, and that the sorts of gestures that the Iranian government would make to demonstrate its good faith and capacity included weighing in to try to obtain the release of hostages in Lebanon (SSIC 1/29/87 version says Ghorbanifar referred "specifically" to William Buckley and to a cessation or moderation of Iran-sponsored terrorism), but also other things, including statements by leaders of the government which we would see clearly were moving in that direction." (Ledeen (1) 22-23)

After the meeting, Ledeen, Kimche, Schwimmer, and Nimrodi decided that someone should report the conversation to McFarlane, which Kimche offered to do. (Id. at 24) (Tower)

JUL 18 - [T]he Director of Central Intelligence wrote McFarlane on July 18, 1985, that

"I strongly endorse the thrust of the draft NSDD on U.S. Policy Toward Iran, particularly its emphasis on the need to take concrete and timely steps to enhance U.S. leverage in order to ensure that the USSR is not the primary beneficiary of change and turmoil in this critical country. While I am broadly in agreement with its assessment of the current political situation, the NSDD needs to reflect more fully on the complex of Soviet motives and recent actions towards Iran and their implications for U.S. policy initiatives . . . " (Casey to McFarlane, 7/19/85)

The Director of Central Intelligence then enumerated what he considered to be substantial weaknesses in the intelligence analysis of the draft NSDD. (Id.) (Tower)

JUL 26 - Congress, in an about-face, approves $27 million in non-lethal "humanitarian" assistance to the contras through March 31, 1986. The legislation authorizing (P.L. 99-83) and appropriating (P.L. 99-88) the aid includes prohibitions against using any funds for the rebels other than those specifically approved for the purpose. Among the legislation's other provisions is one prohibiting the CIA and Defense Department from playing a role in disbursing the funds. As a result, the Administration creates the Nicaraguan Humanitarian Assistance Office in the State Department to take over the function. (CRS "U.S. Assistance to Nicaraguan Guerrillas" 12/4/86; Time 12/22/86)

JUL 28 - Journalists Martha Honey and Tony Avirgan publish a story in the London Times revealing what they have learned about a plot to bomb the U.S. Embassy in Costa Rica and assassinate Ambassador Lewis Tambs. Honey and Avirgan have obtained their information from a carpenter named Carlos Rojas Chinchilla. A friend of his named David was working with the contras and their American supporters and learned of the bombing conspiracy. Carlos came to Honey and Avirgan with the story of his friend David in late April. One alleged motivation for the plot to assassinate Tambs was a $1-million bounty placed on him by Colombian cocaine smuggler Jorge Ochoa, who was outraged by Tambs' attempt to stifle the drug trade in Colombia when he was ambassador there. The plotters allegedly intended to pin the blame on the Sandinistas, ultimately hoping to force the U.S. into open war with Nicaragua. (VV 12/30/86)

JUL 29 - A conference report amends Section 1451 of the Department of Defense Authorization bill (P.L. 99-145, approved November 8, 1985) to state the sense of Congress that U.S. armed forces should not be introduced into combat in or over Nicaragua. (CRS "War Powers Resolution: Presidential Compliance" 12/22/86)

- Defex, the Portuguese arms dealer acting as middleman for Energy Resources International in the shipment of weapons from Portugal to the contras, files another end-user certificate with Lisbon authorities. Both companies are again listed at Defex's address in Lisbon. (WP 1/17/87)

JUL 30 - Kimche called McFarlane July 30 and saw him August 2. According to McFarlane, Kimche said that Rafsanjani, Musavi, the Prime Minister, and Khamenei, the President, had been preoccupied by domestic affairs for about a month, and, therefore, had not pursued the hostage or American issues during that period. Rafsanjani in particular had been dealing with "factional vulnerability." (McFarlane (1) 10) Now, Kimche said, they found it more difficult than they had thought to influence their friends in Lebanon. The Iranians were "more concerned about the bona fides of our side and specifically about whether or not we would provide weapons right away, not for a threat, not for expanding the war, but, as it was cast, for the expansion of and consolidation of the faction with military elements, of army elements specifically." (Id.) McFarlane informed Kimche that he did not think it "wise or likely" that the United States would transfer weapons to the Iranians, "because we had not dealt with these people.... [T]he notion of our giving weapons to people we did not know, with the track record before us, was imprudent and I thought politically silly." (Id. at 10-11) When Kimche asked what the United States reaction would be if Israel shipped weapons to Iran, McFarlane replied by asking why Israel would.

"[I]n a nutshell, [Kimche] said: Well, we in Israel have our own interests. They are basically to ensure a stalemate of the conflict with Iraq, but also to get the United States back into Iran, and that helps us if the United States' position in the Middle East is strengthened; and separately, to reduce the Iranian support for terrorism, if that is feasible, is very much in our interest, and so we might very well do this as a matter of Israeli interest.

"But he said: I pose it for us doing that, because ultimately if we provide things we're going to have to come and buy other ones, and I need to know, are we going to be able to do that or not, whether it's Hawks or TOWs or whatever else.

"And I said: Well, that really isn't the issue. Israel has bought weapons from the United States for years and always will, and so you don't need to ask whether you can buy more weapons. It is a matter of whether or not the support of the idea of providing weapons to anybody in Iran is in policy terms sensible. But I will get you our position. (Id. at 11) (Tower)

LATE JUL - Khashoggi sets up a meeting in Hamburg, West Germany, with Ghorbanifar, Kimche, other Iranians and Israelis, and two Americans, possibly from the National Security Council. According to Khashoggi, the Americans ask the Iranians at one point to deliver hostages as a sign of their influence, at which time the Iranians demand arms as a similar test. (ABC "Nightline" 12/11/86)

- At the end of July, Furmark and Ghorbanifar met Yaacov Nimrodi, an arms merchant and former Israeli Defense Attache in Tehran, Amiram Nir, Advisor to Prime Minister Peres on counterterrorism, and Adolph "Al" Schwimmer, a long-time arms merchant and, since September 1984, Special Advisor to Prime Minister Peres, at one of Nimrodi's homes in Tel Aviv. (Furmark 40; Charles Allen reported that Furmark said Nir attended this meeting. C. Allen to DCI/DDCI, 10/17/86) Furmark, who was not within earshot of the conversation, possibly because the Israelis were concerned that Furmark might be a CIA agent (Furmark at 41), provided only a sketchy account to the Board. He said that "they discussed a program to begin to open up relations between the U.S. and Iran." (Id. at 37) He heard no mention of hostages or arms, but did overhear a reference to "spare parts." (Id.) But he said,

"the U.S. had agreed, the Israelis had agreed, the Iranians had agreed to do some business, but nobody would trust each other. The Iranians would not pay for anything until they received and inspected the goods, because, I've heard on previous transactions involving even foodstuffs and stuff they would pay in advance and they opened up the crates and there were rocks in it. So they became very shell-shocked about paying in advance for anything.

"And of course the Israelis would not send anything until they were paid in advance. So now you had a stalemate. Khashoggi then said, well, I will trust the Iranians, I'll trust the Israelis, I'll trust the Americans, I'll put the money up.

"So the first transaction I understand was a million dollar transaction which he deposited into a numbered account which the Israelis told him to put the money in. The financing operates like this: He puts a million dollars into an account, and then Ghorbanifar gives him what we will call a post-dated check for a million dollars in his account at Credit Suisse. And then after the shipment is made, the Iranians inspect the goods, and they then pay Ghorbanifar's account at Credit Suisse. Ghorbanifar tells Khashoggi the check is good, deposit it.

"That is how the financing was done all throughout." (Id. at 5-6)

Furmark apparently told much the same story to Charles Allen, the CIA's National Intelligence Officer for Counter-terrorism, and George Cave, a CIA annuitant and expert on Iran, who met with Furmark on October 16, 1986. Based on Furmark's account, Allen concluded that

"[t]he idea of providing Iran with military equipment in exchange for American hostages—seen as a way of com-mencing a dialogue with Iran—also originated in the sum-mer of 1985 and he along with Ghobanifar [sic], traveled to Tel Aviv in August 1985.... Subsequently, arms were deliv-ered to Tehran in September 1985, a development that re-sulted in the release of Reverend Benjamin Weir." (C. Allen to DCI/DDCI, 10/17/86) (Tower)

EARLY AUG - McFarlane meets with Schwimmer, Nimrodi, and Kimche. The Iranians now flatly demand 500 U.S.-made TOW antitank missiles in exchange for Buck-ley's life. (Newsweek 12/15/86; NYT 1/11/87)

- When the Israelis began transferring arms to Iran in Au-gust, 1985, they were not acting on their own. U.S. officials had knowledge about the essential elements of the proposed shipments. The United States shared some common purpose in the transfers and received a benefit from them—the re-lease of a hostage. Most importantly, Mr. McFarlane com-municated prior U.S. approval to the Israelis for the shipments, including an undertaking for replenishment. But for this U.S. approval, the transactions may not have gone forward. In short, the United States was an essential participant in the arms transfers to Iran that occurred in 1985.

Whether this U.S. involvement in the arms transfers by the Israelis was lawful depends fundamentally upon whether the President approved the transactions before they occurred. In the absence of presidential approval, there does not appear to be any authority in this case for the United States to engage in the transfer of arms or consent to the transfer by another country. The arms transfers to Iran in 1985 and hence the Iran initiative itself would have proceeded contrary to U.S. law. (Tower)

- Mr. McFarlane elevated this proposition to the President at a meeting within days (see November 1985 entry) that included the Secretaries of State and Defense and the Director of Central Intelligence. The President stated that while he could understand that, assuming the legitimacy of the interlocutors, they would be quite vulnerable and ultimately might deserve our support to include tangible material, that at the time, without any first hand experience in dealing with them, he could not authorize any transfers of military material. This was conveyed to the Israelis. (Tower)

- Chairman Tower: What kind of representations did he [Ghorbanifar] make to you about the people that he was in liaison with in Iran or that he represented? Did he go into the matter of the three lines or factions with you at all in Iran? Or did he talk about one specific faction or group?

Mr. McFarlane: We had received intelligence on the political map of Tehran, so to speak, from two sources. We in the United States had received from the Israelis what they had received from the Iranians, and separately Mr. Ghorbanifar transferred to us his own product of intelligence that described, as you say, these three lines of political affiliation that were, call it, radical-center and conservative.

But that goes back to August, really, the original product. . . . (McFarlane (2) 48-53) (See December 8, 1985 entry.) (Tower)

- Felix Rodriguez makes one of a long series of telephone calls to Bush adviser Donald Gregg, expressing concern about the continuity of supplies to the contras. Shortly afterward, Gregg says later, he meets with Rodriguez and CIA officials in his office in the Old Executive Office Building. (NYT 12/13/86)

AUG 2 - Mr. McFarlane again met at the White House with Mr. Kimche. According to Mr. McFarlane, Mr. Kimche said that the Iranians had asked whether the United States would supply arms to Iran. Mr. McFarlane recalled responding that he thought not. He told the Board that Mr. Kimche then asked what the U.S. reaction would be if Israel shipped weapons to Iran, and whether the United States would sell replacements "whether it's HAWKs or TOWs or whatever else." Mr. McFarlane recalled telling Mr. Kimche he would "get you our position."

What followed is quite murky. (Tower)

AUG 6 - Reagan at a meeting with advisers gives oral approval for the shipment of U.S.-made arms to Iran via Israel, and agrees to replenish Israeli stocks, according to testimony by McFarlane. McFarlane says that Reagan fixed on three months as a rough time limit for deciding whether to continue with the operation. Present at the meeting are Shultz, Weinberger, Regan, McFarlane, Poindexter and John McMahon of the CIA. Shultz and Weinberger are strongly opposed to the idea, but the group agrees to give Israel the green light. McFarlane says the White House considered the oral approval to have the same authority as a written intelligence finding, which is required by law before covert operations can be undertaken. McFarlane also says that Meese later gave an oral opinion that Reagan's unwritten findings were legal. Chief of Staff Regan asserts later that Reagan opposed the sale and acquiesced only after the fact. (McFarlane testimony, 12/8/86; WP 12/9/86; Time 12/22/86; ABC "Nightline" 1/20/87)

AUG 8 - [A]t a meeting of the National Security Planning Group in the White House residence, McFarlane, with Poindexter, briefed the President, the Vice President, Shultz, Weinberger, Regan and Casey on the Kimche proposal to permit the sale of TOWs to Iran through Israel. There is a divergence of views as to whether approval was granted for the Israelis to ship arms to Iran either at that meeting or subsequent to it. There is also conflicting testimony on which of the participants supported the proposal, although opposition to the plan by Shultz and Weinberger is clear.

According to testimony by Regan, the President declined to authorize the sale of TOWs because of misgivings about Ghorbanifar's credentials and influence in Iran. Regan testified that the other participants agreed it was premature to get involved in arms sales to Iran. McFarlane, on the other hand, testified that Ghorbanifar's name never came up at the August meeting.

In a November 1986 interview in conjunction with the Attorney General's inquiry, Shultz "dimly recalled" a meeting at the White House residence in August on the subject of an Israeli shipment of TOWs to Iran. In his testimony before the Committee in December, however, Secretary Shultz said there was a meeting on August 6, 1985, where McFarlane briefed the President on an Israeli request for U.S. replenishment of Israeli TOW missiles proposed for shipment to Iran. In return, according to Shultz, the U.S. was to get four hostages and the entire transaction would be deniable. Shultz said he opposed the proposal, but the President did not make a decision.

According to testimony by McFarlane, the transfer was supported by Casey, Regan and Bush while Shultz and Weinberger opposed it. McFarlane testified that subsequent to the meeting President Reagan approved the Israeli request to ship arms to Iran and to purchase replacements from the U.S. Presidential approval was on the condition that the transfers would not contribute to terrorism or alter the balance of the Iran-Iraq war. Although there is no written record of a decision at this time, McFarlane testified that the President informed Shultz, Weinberger and Casey of his decision.

According to his testimony, McFarlane believed at the time that the President's decision constituted an "oral Finding" which was formally codified on January 17, in a written Finding. McFarlane testified that when he and Attorney General Meese discussed the legality of an oral Finding November 21, 1986, Meese told him that he believed an oral, informal presidential decision or determination to be no less valid than a written Finding. According to documents received by the Committee, McFarlane, when interviewed by Meese, made no mention of presidential approval of the TOW shipment of August-September 1985 or of an "oral Finding." (SSIC 1/29/87)

AUG - In his meeting with the Board on January 26, 1987, the President said that sometime in August he approved the shipment of arms by Israel to Iran. He was uncertain as to the precise date. The President also said that he approved replenishment of any arms transferred by Israel to Iran. Mr. McFarlane's testimony of January 16, 1986, before the Sen-

INTERNATIONAL BULLETIN OF THE ALIANZA REVOLUCIONARIA DEMOCRATICA "ARDE"   August, 1985

COMMUNIST GOVERNMENT OF MANAGUA PREPARES
HOLOCAUST FOR CENTRAL AMERICA

The Sandinist with their newly-acquired Soviet MI-24 death machines can in half an hour attack
the capital cities of the neighboring countries, causing thousands of deaths. They are the terror
and death of their people and of Central American Peace efforts.

ate Foreign Relations Committee, which the President embraced, takes the same position. This portion of Mr. McFarlane's testimony was specifically highlighted on the copy of testimony given by the President to the Board.

In his meeting with the Board on February 11, the President said that he and Mr. Regan had gone over the matter a number of times and that Mr. Regan had a firm recollection that the President had not authorized the August shipment in advance. The President said he did not recall authorizing the August shipment in advance. He noted that very possibly, the transfer was brought to him as already completed. He said that subsequently there were arms shipments he authorized that may have had to do with replenishment, and that this approval for replenishment could have taken place in September. The President stated that he had been "surprised" that the Israelis had shipped arms to Iran, and that this fact caused the President to conclude that he had not approved the transfer in advance.

In a subsequent letter to the Board received on February 20, 1987, the President wrote: "In trying to recall events that happened eighteen months ago I'm afraid that I let myself be influenced by others' recollections, not my own . . .

"I have no personal notes or records to help my recollection on this matter. The only honest answer is to state that try as I might, I cannot recall anything whatsoever about whether I approved an Israeli sale in advance or whether I approved replenishment of Israeli stocks around August of 1985. My answer therefore and the simple truth is, 'I don't remember—period.'"

The Board tried to resolve the question of whether the President gave prior approval to Israel's transfer of arms to Iran. We could not do so conclusively.

We believe that an Israeli request for approval of such a transfer was discussed before the President in early August. We believe that Secretary Shultz and Secretary Weinberger expressed at times vigorous opposition to the proposal. The President agreed to replenish Israeli stocks. We are persuaded that he most likely provided this approval prior to the first shipment by Israel.

In coming to this conclusion, it is of paramount importance that the President never opposed the idea of Israel transferring arms to Iran. Indeed, four months after the August shipment, the President authorized the United States government to undertake directly the very same operation that Israel had proposed. Even if Mr. McFarlane did not have the President's explicit prior approval, he clearly had his full support. (Tower)

Chairman Tower: Now, did you communicate the President's approval and inform anybody on your staff about it? Did you tell Poindexter? Who did you tell? Who did you contact to tell them the President had approved this on our side?

Mr. McFarlane: Admiral Poindexter is the short answer. In my recurring memory of how it took place—and I've asked my wife to try to recall this image—is that it occurred at home, and he called me from Camp David and that I then called Mr. Kimche and not until the next day, however, did I tell Admiral Poindexter.

There ought to be a record, although not on my record because I was at home, probably in the Camp David operators that a call took place.

General Scowcroft: Did you tell Mike Ledeen about the approval? Did you tell him to convey it?

Mr. McFarlane: I don't have any mental image of a meeting, but I expect that I did convey it to him, not for him to further carry it out but to inform him that that was the decision. [I've called that.] He came out to make a speech in Los Angeles at a moment when the Presidential party was there ... And, if not before, surely then I would have told him about it.

Chairman Tower: Understanding that this was on a pretty closely held basis, was there anybody beside Poindexter that you would have told that the President communicated to you his approval?

Mr. McFarlane: Not on the NSC staff, no, sir.

Chairman Tower: And you did not inform the other NSC principals?

Mr. McFarlane: Within a day or so I did.

Chairman Tower: Which ones?

Mr. McFarlane: It would have been the Secretary of State, Defense, Mr. Regan and the Vice President.

Chairman Tower: That the President had given you the go-ahead on this?

Mr. McFarlane: That is correct.

Mr. McFadden: How about Mr. Casey?

Mr. McFarlane: And Mr. Casey, yes.

Chairman Tower: Bud, were you aware if there was ever a

August 15, 1985

Dear Spitz:

Throughout the struggle for freedom and democracy in Nicaragua,
there are those who have carried this great burden with
dedication and a true sense of patriotism. You and the people
involved in the National Endowment for the Preservation of
Liberty are at the center of the struggle.

In the Spring when we began our campaign to help the Nicaraguan
resistance in a crucial struggle for democracy in their native
land, your resources helped carry the day. Without your fine
efforts, their situation would have gone from desperate to
hopeless. Yours was a key organization in supporting President
Reagan's legislative initiative for Congressional aid to the
Nicaraguan freedom fighters. Your paid advertising and support
of the President's program was critical to our success.

In July when you began to help educate others to the needs of the
Nicaraguan freedom fighters, their chances were greatly
increased. The special events you hosted and the generous
support your people gave carried the day and helped to save
freedom from extinction in Nicaragua. Your continuing efforts
have two very special values. The level of support you have
brought to the struggle has been nothing short of monumental.
The steadfastness and commitment you have maintained is the true
sign of patriotism. When freedom and democracy are at stake,
those who sacrifice without public acclaim it to the world are
our truest patriots.

The programs you have undertaken are crucial. Without the means
you provide, those who seek a democratic outcome in Nicaragua
will fail. As always, in the hour of critical need, we find you
and the National Endowment for the Preservation of Liberty ready
to help.

For your past efforts and your present initiatives, we salute
you.

Sincerely,

Oliver L. North
Deputy Director
Political-Military Affairs

Mr. Carl Russell Channel
National Endowment for the
  Preservation of Liberty
305 4th Street, N.E.
Washington, D.C. 20002

contingency plan to deal with this issue, a planned public diplomacy campaign of any kind to deal with it once it became public knowledge, whether by official release or by just simply being exposed?

Mr. McFarlane: I know of no such plan. (pp. 59-61) (Tower)

AUG 8 - The repeal of the Clark Amendment is signed into law (P.L. 99-83), allowing, for the first time since 1975, military aid to Jonas Savimbi's forces fighting the Angolan government. In view of the 1986 Iran-contra development, there is suspicion that covert funds from third party sources to Savimbi prior to August 1985 then began to flow towards the contras. (CRS "Angola: Issues for the U.S." 12/5/86; interviews)

AUG 15 - Congress authorized the expenditure of $27 million in humanitarian assistance [to the contras], to be administered by any agency but CIA and DOD. By its terms, the authorization would expire on March 31, 1986. (Tower)

MID-AUG - [NSC staff member] Mr. Teicher told the Board that the strong objections from Secretary Shultz and Secretary Weinberger apparently killed the draft NSDD.... Teicher sought guidance from Fortier, Poindexter, and "perhaps with McFarlane." (Id.) They asked him to see if the process had any other ideas. After discussing the matter with Richard Murphy, Assistant Secretary of State for Near East and South Asian Affairs, he concluded that

"It was clear there was no give and there really wasn't any more creativity.

"I went back to Fortier and I said the only question is to do nothing, and hope that the situation doesn't create or lead to the negative dangerous situation that we see as a possibility, or present the President with a decision memorandum which lays out, in very clear terms, the different perspectives of his advisors and asks him to make a decision.... In mid-August he was told to 'stand down' on the effort. The draft was never submitted to the President for his consideration or signature." (See June 17, June 29, and July 16, 1985 entries)

The abandonment of the draft NSDD marked the end of efforts by Mr. McFarlane and the NSC staff to use the formal interagency policy process to obtain an explicit change in U.S. policy toward Iran. From this point on, the matter moved along a different track. (Tower)

- According to testimony by Ledeen, when he returned to the U.S. in mid-August, 1985, McFarlane informed him that the program of contact with Iran would go forward and that a test of the kind Ghorbanifar had proposed would occur. Accordingly, McFarlane told Ledeen to work out arrangements with Kimche for receipt of the hostages. McFarlane said he believed at this time that the sale of TOWs would secure the release of all U.S. hostages. (SSIC 1/29/87)

AUG 20 - While Ledeen's account is not altogether satisfactory on the point, and McFarlane did not mention the episode to the Board, when Ledeen reported on his August meetings in Israel, McFarlane apparently decided to establish secure telephone communication with Kimche. Ledeen flew to London on August 20, carrying an elementary code for Kimche, which he delivered the next day. (Ledeen (1) 28) Kimche gave Ledeen documents for McFarlane obtained from Ghorbanifar. At this or another meeting, Kimche explained that "in his experience with Iranians there was no way that Iran would deliver everything that it had promised, that whatever happened would be less than what they were promising, but that he thought that even something significantly less than what they had promised would still be significant and that he was basically positive about giving it a try." (Id. at 37) (Tower)

- Congressional scrutiny of LtCol North's activities increased. To varying degrees throughout 1985, Congress had pressed the NSC staff for information about LtCol North's involvement in Contra fundraising and resupply activities. In a reply to an August 20, 1985, letter from Lee Hamilton, Chairman of the House Permanent Select Committee on Intelligence, Mr. McFarlane wrote:

"I can state with deep personal conviction that at no time did I or any member of the National Security Council staff violate the letter or spirit of the law [barring military aid to the Contras]." (Tower)

AUG 23 - Safair Freighters (U.S.A.) Inc. takes out a $7 million mortgage ("term loan") from the Banco Portugues Do Atlantico New York Agency on two of its Lockheed Hercules L-100's, tail numbers N251SF and N46965, and assigns the Southern Air Transport lease on the planes to the mortgage. (Assignment of Lease 8/23/85; Cross-Reference Recordation 9/17/85; both in FAA records)

AUG 27 - The Central Bank of Iran (Bank Markazi) deposited $1,217,410 in the account of an Iranian official at Credit Suisse. This individual, an official in the Prime Minister's office, was responsible for arms procurement in Europe. (Tower)

END AUG - According to some reports, the first planeload of Israeli-arranged U.S. arms is sent to Iran at the end of the month, including the first installment of 100 TOW antitank missiles. Other reports place the shipment in early September. (The Philadelphia Inquirer cites September 3 as the date.) Israel's defense minister reportedly refused to allow Israel to ship the weapons without written authorization from the U.S., which McFarlane provided after consulting with Reagan. (Meese claims later that the President was informed only after the fact, in late summer or early fall. He states the transaction was undertaken on the initiative of the Israelis.) Adnan Khashoggi says he put up $1 million in "bridge financing" for this shipment, then another $4 million later in the year for the rest of the 500 TOW missiles the Iranians ordered. He says he borrowed these funds, plus an additional $2.5 million whose purpose is unclear, from British industrialist Roland (Tiny) Rowland, who denies lending the money for use in arms deals. According to Khashoggi, it is Israeli weapons dealer Nimrodi who around this time comes up with the idea of overcharging Iran for the arms and funneling the excess profits back into the country to the moderate forces Ghorbanifar claims to represent. Khashoggi believes North picked up on the scheme in January 1986 when the new Israeli representative in the deal, Amiram Nir, divulged it to him. (Meese briefing 11/25/86; PI 11/26/86; ABC "20/20" 12/11/86, in WP 12/13/86; WP 12/7/86 & 2/1/87; MH 12/7/86; NYT 12/25/86 & 1/11/87)

- According to documents received by the Committee, the shipment of 508 TOWs left Israel on August 30, 1985, transited third country and arrived in Iran on September 13. North later asserted to Meese that he was totally unaware of the TOW shipment at the time it occurred. He believed he first learned of it in a November 25 or 26 conversation with Secord while in Tel Aviv. North also claimed that he did not know who had otherwise been aware of the shipment. McFarlane told Meese that he thought he learned of the shipment from Ledeen. He then informed the President, Shultz, Weinberger and Casey, but noted that the shipment had not achieved the objective of release of all the hostages. According to McFarlane, there was no official contact between the U.S. and Israeli governments regarding the shipment. (SSIC 1/29/87)

- One White House chronology prepared in November 1986 simply notes that McFarlane conveyed to Kimche a Presidential decision that a dialogue with Iran could be worthwhile. However, a second White House chronology presents conflicting accounts about whether the U.S. acquiesced in the Israeli delivery of 508 TOWs to Iran on August 30.

According to testimony by McFarlane, Israel did not feel bound to clear each specific transaction with the U.S. Israel proceeded on the basis of a general authority from the President based on a U.S. commitment to replace their stocks. Also, Israel's negotiations on hostages would not necessarily require U.S. approval. (SSIC 1/29/87)

- [McFarlane, in his final interview with the Board, amended histories previously given in three PROF notes:] ... We subsequently learned that in late August the Israelis had transferred 508 TOW missiles to Iran. (Tower)

AUG-SEP - In late August or early September, North, to whose office Ledeen was attached, (Id. at 44), was directed to prepare "contingency plans for extracting hostages—hostage or hostages—from Lebanon." (Id. at 46) (Footnote: Ledeen told the Board that he thought this episode marked the first time North heard about the program. (Ledeen (1) 46; Ledeen (2) 74)) (Tower)

- According to Ledeen, North became obviously involved in operations connected with American hostages and relations with Iran at the time of the first Israeli shipment of TOWs. "[H]e was handling all the various intelligence operations that had been started to track this thing, and it was all coming through him." (Ledeen (1) 51) On the other hand, North's office "was highly compartmentalized. [Ledeen] did not, until I was instructed by Bud to do so, I never told Ollie [North] what was going on, and Ollie never discussed what he was doing with me." (Id. at 57) (Tower)

Leeden told the Board that McFarlane did not tell him that North was to be more involved. (Ledeen (1) 51) Bernard McMahon, Staff Director of the Senate Select Committee on Intelligence, said that Ledeen testified that North told him in

September 1985 that "McFarlane has told me I'm supposed to now handle all the operational aspects of this, and McFarlane has no knowledge, A, that Ledeen is doing anything, much less that North has taken over what he is doing." (B. McMahon 10)

- In a memorandum . . . North . . . wrote that . . . an agent involved in shipping material to the Contras saw U.S. military equipment in a Lisbon warehouse, which inquiries identified as Israeli equipment being shipped to Iran by a private company.

A "high-level Israeli official" explained that the weapons were being sent to Iran in exchange for Iranian Jews, and that because private intermediaries were used, the transaction was not a technical violation of United States arms export control laws. The Israelis hoped the arms sales would enhance "the credibility of moderate elements in the Iranian army" who might become powerful enough to establish a more reasonable Iranian government than presently existed; prevent the collapse of Iran in the war with Iraq; and extricate Jews from Iran.

"In early September, in order that we not take action to terminate the arms sales, the Israelis proposed that this process be used as leverage to recover the American citizens held hostage in Lebanon. It was decided to test the validity of this proposal. . . . " ("Special Project re Iran," 12/5/85) (See September 13 and December 5, 1985 entries.) (Tower)

- In the case of the TOW shipments in August and September 1985, the price charged to Iran by Israel was far in excess of what Israel paid the U.S. Department of Defense to replenish the arms it delivered. This excess amount was roughly $3 million for the August/September TOW shipments. Nothing is known by the Board about the disposition of those funds. (Tower)

- The chronologies [prepared by Poindexter, North, McFarlane, Earl and Coy] are more confused on this [August/September, 1985] section. The November 13 Maximum Version stated "in September of 1985, the Israelis advised that they were close to achieving a breakthrough on the hostage situation and would proceed unless we objected . . . The U.S. judged that the Israelis would persist in these secret deliveries, despite our objections, because they believed it to be in their strategic interest. Shortly after Reverend Weir's release, the U.S. acquiesced in an Israeli delivery of military supplies (508 TOWs) to Tehran. U.S. acquiescence in this Israeli operation was based on a decision at the highest level to exploit the existing Israeli channels with tehran [sic] in an effort to establish an American strategic dialogue with the Iranian government." (Tower)

AUG 29-30 - The NSC staff arranged for the State Department to issue a passport in the name of "William P. Goode" for North to use on "a sensitive operation to Europe in connection with our hostages in Lebanon." (North to McFarlane, 8/30/85; Martin to Platt, n.d.; McFarlane PROF note to Martin, 8/30/85, 17:40:38; Shultz, 12/86, 12) (Tower)

AUG 30 - Israel delivered 100 TOWs to Iran. (Tower)

- Mr. Ghorbanifar told the Board that the 100 TOWs were not linked to a hostage release. They were to evidence U.S. seriousness in reestablishing relations with Iran. The next step was to be the delivery of 400 more TOWs, for which Iran was to free a hostage. The goal was to establish a new relationship between the two countries, which would include a pledge by Iran of no further terrorist acts against the United States or its citizens by those under Iran's control. (See September 13, 1985 entry.) (Tower)

AUG 31 - Poindexter established a private method of inter-office computer communication with North, preventing normal screening by the Executive Secretary of the NSC. (Poindexter PROF note, "PRIVATE BLANK CHECK" to North, 8/31/85, 13:26:58) (Tower)

AUG 31-SEP 2 - Over the Labor Day weekend, Poindexter and Fortier secretly travel to Egypt to discuss military options regarding Libya with Mubarak. The mission, authorized by Reagan, is opposed by the State Department, which succeeded earlier in watering down the White House's plans for possible joint U.S.-Egyptian operations against Khaddafi (see mid-July entry), and now is concerned that such a high-level delegation will add undue significance to the proposals it is bringing to Cairo. At the meeting with Mubarak, Poindexter reportedly discusses the current military situation regarding Libya and reiterates the Administration's pledge of support in the event of a Libyan attack. It is unclear to American officials later whether, or to what degree, Poindexter hoped to push the idea of joint military operations against Khaddafi. However, according to a U.S. report on the session, Mubarak interrupts Poindexter before he is through with his talking points and says, "Look, admiral, when we decide to attack Libya it will be our decision and our timetable." (WP 2/20/87; NYT 2/22/87)

EARLY SEP - Mr. Regan also told the Board that in early September, Mr. McFarlane informed the President that Israel had sold arms to the Iranians and hoped to get some hostages out. Mr. Regan stated that the President was "upset" at the news and that Mr. McFarlane explained that the Israelis had "simply taken it upon themselves to do this." Mr. Regan said that after some discussion, the President decided to "leave it alone." (Tower)

- CIA national intelligence officer Charles Allen is assigned by North to acquire data on the Iran arms shipments and to supply it to the chief of the Agency's European Division of the Operations Directorate. Allen subsequently becomes aware of the transfer of funds to non-American bank accounts in Switzerland (see October 1, 1985 entry). Allen, as head of the CIA's Hostage Rescue Locating Force, established late in the year, is also involved in the Administration's secret and extensive effort to free the hostages. The force analyzes technical intelligence and attempts to infiltrate terrorist groups, among other tactics. Each week the force prepares highly classified reports on the hostages' whereabouts and apparent physical condition. On at least one occasion, according to Administration officials, the CIA must withdraw an agent from a terrorist organization because of the group's requirement that new members take part in assassinations as a test of loyalty. (WSJ 12/22/86 & 1/9/87)

- By September, U.S. and Israeli Government officials became involved in this endeavor . . . to effect the release of the American hostages in Beirut in exchange for providing certain factions in Iran with U.S.-origin Israeli military materiel . . . in order to ensure that the USG would:
—not object to the Israeli transfer of embargoed material to Iran;
—sell replacement items to Israel as replenishment for like items sold to Iran by Israel. ("Terms of reference U.S.-Iran Dialogue," 4/4/86) (Tower)

- Albon Values Corp., a company with close ties to the Geneva-based financial services firm CSF, is established in Panama by Quijano & Associates. Two of Albon Values' principal officers, Roland Farina and Jacques Mossaz, are employees of CSF. Farina is an accountant and Mossaz an attorney with the Swiss concern. Panamanian records later show that Albon Values is used secretly to transfer funds to a shell corporation, Amalgamated Commercial Enterprises (ACE), which then uses the funds to finance the covert contra resupply operation. ACE is controlled by Southern Air Transport. (See November 1985 entry.) (WSJ 1/30/87)

- After the initial hostage release in September, 1985, it was over 10 months before another hostage was released. This despite recurring promises of the release of all the hostages and four intervening arms shipments. Beginning with the November shipment, the United States increasingly took over the operation of the initiative. (Tower)

- Reginald Bartholomew, the American Ambassador in Lebanon, reported on September 4 that "North was handling an operation that would lead to the release of all seven hostages. [A U.S.] team had been deployed to Beirut, we were told. Ambassador Bartholomew had been alerted directly by the NSC and would assist." (Shultz, 12/86, 12) The Director of Central Intelligence told his Deputy and Chief of Operations that "the Israelis were doing something and they believed as a part of the outcome of an affair the Israelis were in some of the hostages could be released," but that the Israelis did not want the CIA to be "notified." (George 3) . . . (Tower)

- Ledeen met Ghorbanifar, Kimche, Nimrodi, and Schwimmer in Paris on September 4. Ledeen told the Board that

"[t]he bulk of this conversation was given over to the issue of future relations and future cooperation between the United States and Iran. And from time to time Ghorbanifar, Schwimmer and Nimrod would sit down and start talking about hostages and weapons. And when this happened Kimche and I would go off and talk about the future of Iran and how we thought we were going." (Ledeen (1) 44)

According to Ledeen, Ghorbanifar predicted that Iranian leaders would soon give speeches in which they did not denounce the United States. After the speeches, Ghorbanifar called Ledeen to ask if he had seen them. Ledeen had not, but asked North to have the CIA find and translate them. Some weeks later, the CIA confirmed Ghorbanifar's account. Iranian leaders had attacked the Soviet Union. "So we were cheered by this. I was cheered by this." (Id. at 44-45) (Tower)

EARLY SEP - Ledeen provided [a senior CIA analyst] with information on Iranian-sponsored terrorism and on Ghorbanifar. According to this analyst, this was the first time Ledeen had identified Ghorbanifar by name to the CIA. According to testimony by Ledeen, the subject of Ghorbanifar's bona fides first came up in September 1985. (However, see also July 15, 1985 entry). Ledeen testified that he knew that the CIA was suspicious of Ghorbanifar, and that Ghorbanifar had raised the subject himself, in one of their meetings. According to testimony by Ledeen, it appeared to him that Ghorbanifar's credentials were well-documented.

The Committee received testimony and documents, however, indicating that the CIA had long been aware of Ghorbanifar's suspect character. In August 1984 CIA had issued a notice to other government agencies warning that Ghorbanifar was a fabricator. Documents indicate CIA was aware of one instance in which Ghorbanifar had reportedly offered to provide intelligence on Iran to a third country in return for permission from the third country to continue the drug smuggling activities of Ghorbanifar's associates with the country concerned. (SSIC 1/29/87)

SEP 9 - According to testimony from a senior CIA analyst. . . . North called him on September 9, 1985, and requested increased intelligence collection on Lebanon and Iran. North told him there was a possibility of release of American hostages. (See September 12, 1985 entry.) (SSIC 1/29/87)

SEP 10 - Maule Air Inc. of Moultrie, Georgia, sends a telegram to the FAA requesting a return telegram to confirm that a Maule M-7-235 plane has been assigned tail number N56611, serial number 4024C. Maule informs the FAA that title for the plane will pass to a foreign purchaser, NRAF Inc. of Panama, upon departure from the Maule plant on or about September 10. (FAA Documents)

SEP 12 - The International Court of Justice at the Hague begins hearings on charges brought by Nicaragua against the U.S. The U.S. refuses to participate. (CRS "Nicaragua: Conditions and Issues for U.S. Policy" 12/8/86)

- North asked Charles Allen, National Intelligence Officer for Counterterrorism, on September 12 to increase intelligence efforts against Iran and Lebanon, and informed him that Buckley might be released in the next few hours or days. (C. Allen 4-5; CIA/IG Chronology 3) (See September 13, 1985 entry.) (Tower)

- In mid-September North asked him [Charles Allen] for intelligence collection on specific individuals in Iran who were in contact with American officials. North later gave him a very restricted distribution list for the intelligence collected which specifically left out the Department of State. North said Shultz would be briefed orally by McFarlane. (See September 13, 1985 entry.) As the intelligence began to come in, this senior CIA analyst did not understand all the parties involved. However, he felt the intelligence clearly showed that hostages and some form of arms sales were involved. (SSIC 1/29/87)

- He [McFarlane] reiterated his comments (See August 20, 1985 entry) in a letter to Congressman Michael Barnes on September 12, 1985:

"I want to assure you that my actions, and those of my staff, have been in compliance with both the spirit and the letter of the law. . . . There have not been, nor will there be, any expenditures of NSC funds which would have the effect of supporting directly or indirectly military or paramilitary operations in Nicaragua by any nation, group, organization, movement or individual. . . ."

In a subsequent letter, Congressman Hamilton inquired into the nature of the NSC staff's involvement with the fundraisers. (See October 7, 1985 entry.) (Tower)

SEP 13 - A second arms shipment, consisting of 408 TOW missiles, is sent by Israel. Iran is reported to pay $5 million for the 500-plus missiles they have now received. (PI 11/26/86; MH 12/7/86; Newsweek 12/15/86; NYT 12/25/86 & 1/11/87) (The Tower Report sets the date of the second shipment at September 14, 1985, North at September 13. See below.)

- On September 13, the Israeli Government, with the endorsement of the USG, transferred 508 TOW missiles to Iran. Forty-eight hours later, Reverend Benjamin Weir was released in Beirut. Subsequent efforts by both governments to continue this process have met with frustration due to the need to communicate our intentions through an Iranian expatriate arms dealer in Europe. ("Terms of Reference U.S.-Iran Dialogue," 4/4/86) (Tower)

- When the first information [on Iran and Lebanon] was received on September 13, Allen asked

"for White House guidance on how th[is intelligence] should be disseminated. North, after consulting with National Security Advisor McFarlane, direct[ed] that dissemination be limited to Secretary Weinberger, the D[irector of] C[entral] I[ntelligence] (or Deputy Director McMahon), McFarlane, and himself. North [said] that McFarlane had directed that no copy be sent to the Secretary of State; and that he, McFarlane, would keep Secretary Shultz advised orally on the NSC project." (CIA/IG Chronology at 4; C. Allen 6) (Footnote: The original distribution list provided included Vice Admiral Moreau of the JCS staff, not Secretary Weinberger. When the Secretary saw an intelligence report pertaining to this program in the fall of 1985, he insisted that he receive all such documents. His military assistant, General Powell, reported that "the White House told [the releasing agency] that those [reports] were not to be distributed to anybody except the White House." (Weinberger 8)) (See September 12, 1985 entry.) (Tower)

- According to Furmark and Ghorbanifar, Khashoggi provided the bridge financing for the August and September shipments. (Footnote: Whereas Furmark told the Board that he introduced Ghorbanifar to Khashoggi in January 1985, (Furmark 3), George Cave, who had been stationed in Tehran before the overthrow of the Shah and who had been responsible for terminating the CIA's relationship with Ghorbanifar in 1983, told the Board that, contrary to reports he had seen, Ghorbanifar had known Khashoggi for years. (Cave 44)) The Americans and Israelis had limited faith in the Iranians, and vice versa, so that deliveries would not be made before payment was received, and payment would not be made before weapons were delivered. (Ledeen (2) 25) Khashoggi broke the impasse by providing financing. (Furmark 5; D. St. John, Memorandum of Conversation with Adnan Khashoggi, 1/29/87) In August and September 1985, Khashoggi made two separate deposits in the amounts of $1 million and $4 million into a Swiss account designated by the Israelis; Ghorbanifar gave him two post-dated drafts for $1 and $4 million, drawn on his account at Credit Suisse, which Khashoggi would negotiate when the weapons were delivered, and Ghorbanifar had received payment from Iran. "[T]hat is how the financing was done all throughout." (Furmark 6) Khashoggi was repaid later than anticipated because the first shipment of TOWs included weapons unacceptable to Iran. (Id. at 6-7) According to Furmark, Khashoggi received no money in addition to principal for these payments; for the later transactions, he expected, and received until May 1986, a return of 20% above the principal amount to cover his expenses and provide a return to financiers who invested with him. (Id. at 31, 8) (Tower)

- The United States had only a supporting role in the August and September deliveries to Iran. Israel managed the operation. The next three months saw an increasing U.S. role. (Tower)

- In the second week of September, Kimche called McFarlane with the news that a hostage would be released, and that he expected all the hostages to be released soon. McFarlane probably relayed this message to the President, Vice President, Secretaries of State and Defense, Director of Central Intelligence, and Regan. (McFarlane (1) 18-19) LtCol North, the NSC staff officer with responsibility for terrorism policy, made arrangements for receiving and debriefing Rev. Weir. . . . The Director of Central Intelligence reportedly connected this release with diplomatic efforts in Damascus and Tehran aimed at resolving the hostage problem. (CIA/IG Chronology at 4; Casey to Shultz/McFarlane, 8/16/85; Sigur to McFarlane, 9/19/85) (Tower)

Although it appears that Israel and the United States expected the release of the remaining hostages to accompany or follow the release of Rev. Weir, this did not occur. (Tower)

SEP 14 - Ghorbanifar informed the holder [an Iranian official] of the Credit Suisse account that an aircraft would arrive at Tabriz that evening, and asked that a man on the plane be given a cheque and a list of weapons desired by Iran. (See August 27 and September 18 entries.) (Tower)

- Israel shipped an additional 408 missiles. (See August 30 and September 13 entries.) There is some evidence that this shipment was returned to Israel, in whole or in part, because it contained defective or otherwise unacceptable missiles, and that Israel replaced and reshipped the weapons. (Furmark 6-7) Ghorbanifar told the Board that he accompanied the shipment of 100 TOWs to Iran and that in exchange for these weapons, the Iranians gave a "guarantee" that they would neither engage in any "wrongdoing" nor support terrorism. (Ghorbanifar 46) Israel sold Iran 400 TOWs in exchange for Weir, Gorbanifar recalled; when the plane arrived in Tabriz, eight extra TOWs were aboard. (Id. at 49; 100) [See Senate Draft Report entry for September 15, 1985, and August 30, 1985 entry] Ledeen told the Board that he did "not believe that either we or they" saw the August and September shipments as two transactions. (Ledeen (2) 27-28) (Tower)

SEP 15 - The Rev. Benjamin Weir is released. The White House delays announcement until September 18, hoping other hostages will be freed. (WP 12/7/86)

- The view that the Iranians helped to secure Weir's release appears to have been shared by McFarlane.

It should be noted that the Committee also received testimony inconsistent with this description of events. Secretary of Defense Weinberger testified in response to a specific question that he knew nothing about any connection between the release of Weir and Israeli arms sales to Iran. Regan testified that McFarlane told the President—in his presence —that the Israelis "damn them," had sold 500 TOWs to the Iranians without U.S. knowledge. Regan further testified that he, the President, McFarlane and Poindexter decided to "ignore" the incident except to "let the Israelis know of our displeasure" and "keep the channel open." According to Regan's testimony, this shipment of arms to Iran was not sanctioned by the U.S. government.

One White House Chronology states that after discussing the matter with the President, it was decided not to expose the action, thus retaining the option of "exploiting the Israeli channel to establish a strategic dialogue."

The testimony of McFarlane is inconsistent with that of Regan. McFarlane, in testimony, disputed Regan's characterization of his reaction to the TOW shipment and denied that the President had ever expressed disapproval of the Israeli action. McFarlane testified that the President was "elated" at Weir's release and denied that the President had ever instructed him to reproach the Israelis.

According to evidence received by the Committee, concurrently with the arms shipment and hostage release—and perhaps connected with both—was an airplane flight out of

Tabriz, Iran which made an emergency landing in Tel Aviv. Ghorbanifar was very interested in this event, and a CIA analyst studying the situation was convinced that there was a correlation between Ghorbanifar, the aircraft flight to Tel Aviv, and the release of Weir. The Committee has not established that there was a correlation between these events. (SSIC 1/29/87)

- At one of the President's 9:30 a.m. briefings in September (early in the month, according to Regan (Regan 8)), McFarlane reported that the Israelis had sold weapons to Iran, and a hostage had been released. McFarlane told the Board:

"[W]hile I didn't know for certain because we had not negotiated with the Iranians, the appearance was surely there that weapons were transferred and one hostage was released, and so that certainly looked causal. And you would have to be a fool not to see that, whatever our intentions were, the reality was apparently arms for hostages.

And I said so to the President in the morning meeting, and it basically kind of validated what the Secretary of Defense and State had said before, and they expressed their concerns again on that score. . . ." (McFarlane (1) 20-21)

As we have seen, Regan told the Board a somewhat different story. (Tower)

- Chairman Tower: Bud, do you remember any comment from the President after Weir was released? He made some critical comments of the Administration and of the President, characterizing Weir as being somewhat ungrateful for the efforts that were being made.

Mr. McFarlane: I don't recall that. I think it is very plausible to me that he would have been dismayed by the turn of events.

Mr. Dawson: Before we tie in this authorization to December let me not leave September for just one second and try to turn the authorization question, present it somewhat differently.

In the July, August and September time, in discussions that you had with the President did he ever exhibit any reluctance, opposition or disapproval or make any attempts to repudiate in your presence the transfer of arms by Israel to Iran?

Mr. McFarlane: No, he did not. (McFarlane (2) 34-35) (Tower)

- Regan recalled that the President had been "upset" about the September shipment. (Regan at 9) Regan explained McFarlane's belief that the President had authorized the transaction as follows: the President "hadn't raised Cain about the [first] Israeli shipment. . . ." (Id. at 14)

". . . I [McFarlane] think it would be accurate to say that the President believed in August that he was approving the Israeli sale of modest levels of arms of a certain character, filling certain criteria, but that with that approval Israel could transfer or sell modest levels without further concrete approval.

"Now as a separate but obviously related matter his concurrent expectation was that how that would be translated would be 100 TOWs. . . ." (McFarlane (2) 39-43) (Tower)

- It was from this contact [with Ghorbanifar through Kimche and Nimrodi] that the operation developed to have the Israelis at our behest deliver to Iran 500 Tow [sic] missiles and, more recently, 18 Hawk missiles in exchange for the release of all the hostages held in Lebanon. Ledeen is convinced that the release of Reverend Weir was tied directly to the first shipment of missiles. Ledeen went on to say, however, that he never really expected the Iranians to deliver all the hostages given the "Iranian's merchant mentality. . . ." (Chief, NESA, to DCI, n.d.) (Tower)

- Teicher told the Board that, although his involvement in this operation had ceased in August, after Weir was released, he became suspicious that the United States was trading arms to Iran for hostages. He queried North, who told him that he could say nothing about it, and McFarlane, who said the United States was not trading arms for hostages and that there was nothing more he could say. (Teicher 14-15) (Tower)

MID-SEP - Bernard McMahon, Staff Director of the Senate Select Committee on Intelligence, said that Ledeen testified that North told him in September 1985 that "McFarlane has told me I'm supposed to now handle all the operational aspects of this, and McFarlane has no knowledge, A, that Ledeen is doing anything, much less that North has taken over what he is doing." (B. McMahon 10) (Tower)

SEP 16 - According to the CIA Inspector General, on September 16, the Director of Central Intelligence and Charles Allen discussed recent events, including Weir's release. The

Director reported McFarlane's saying they were related to an NSC initiative. (CIA/IG Chronology at 4) (Tower)

SEP 17 - Secretary Shultz testified that, on September 17, Ambassador Bartholomew reported that

"Mr. McFarlane had said the other hostages would be released in three batches, without publicity. But Weir had no information about the others, and in fact said he had been released only to bring pressure for the release of the Da'Wa prisoners. Bartholomew was pessimistic. He said four other hostages were reportedly in the Beirut area, possibly in the same place as Weir. . . . North was not in the area, but in Washington, D.C. Bartholomew said he knew 'precious little about origins of this or who is involved. Bud has told me nothing of who else was involved.' He was pessimistic about getting any more hostages. . . . " (Shultz, 12/86, 12-13) (Tower)

SEP-NOV - "Two months then passed [from the time of Ambassador Bartholomew's September 17, 1985 report] during which, to my [Shultz's] knowledge, the Department of State heard nothing more about any aspect of an operation involving arms for Iran." (Tower)

SEP 18 - The White House announces the release of the Rev. Benjamin Weir. The announcement had been delayed in hope that other hostages would be freed. (WP 12/7/86)

- On September 18, four days after the first successful shipment of TOWs, $5 million was deposited in [an Iranian official's Credit Suisse] account. (See August 27 and September 14, 1985 entries.) (Tower)

LATE SEP - The Historical Chronology (see Nov. 26, 1986 entry) contains the following paragraph, not contained in the Maximum Version:

"In late September, we learned that the Israelis had transferred 508 Tow [sic] missiles to Iran and that this shipment had taken place in late August. [Handwritten in the margin: "30 Aug?"] The Israelis told us that they undertook the action, despite our objections, because they believed it to be in their strategic interests. The Israelis managed this entire operation, to include delivery arrangements, funding, and transportation. After discussing this matter with the President, it was decided not to expose this Israeli delivery because we wanted to retain the option of exploiting the existing Israeli channel with Tehran in our own effort to establish a strategic dialogue with the Iranian government. The total value of the 508 TOWs shipped by Israel was estimated to be less than $2 million." (Tower)

SEP 20 - Spitz Channell's National Endowment for the Preservation of Liberty pays $132,000 to International Business Communications, which passes $130,000 on the same day to North and Secord's Lake Resources bank account in Switzerland. (WP 3/7/87)

- The National Endowment for the Preservation of Liberty pays another $100,000 to International Business Communications, which passes the $100,000 on to I.C. Inc. on Sept. 26. I.C. in turn pays $100,000 to Lake Resources in Switzerland on Oct. 8. (WP 3/7/87)

SEP 26 - According to North's calendar, North had meetings on September 26 with Ledeen at 11:00 a.m. and Schwimmer at 11:30 a.m. (See October 6 and October 8 entries.) (Tower)

- International Business Communications passes $100,000 received from NEPL Sep. 20, on to I.C. Inc. I.C. in turn pays $100,000 to Lake Resources in Switzerland on Oct. 8. (WP 3/7/87)

SEP 30 - This is the last activity date in FAA records for Maule N5661J, the airplane Maule Air Inc. says Richard Secord bought. According to the FAA, however, the registered owner is Maule Air. (FAA Documents)

- Ledeen met Ghorbanifar, Kimche, Nimrodi (who was fluent in Farsi), and Schwimmer in September and October in Europe. (Ledeen (1) 46) In at least one such meeting, Ghorbanifar expressed the view that the arms and hostage matters, which engaged Schwimmer and Nimrodi particularly, should be dropped, and the prospective Iranian-American political relationship should be the focus of their energies. "[Ghorbanifar] said if we continue we shall become hostages to the hostages." (Id. at 47)

In his second interview, Ledeen told the Board that, in October, he told Schwimmer:

"if this kind of contact is going to continue it may be necessary at a certain point to have an account where there can be something for expenses for this person or persons like him. We may need an account for such things.

"And he said fine. I will do that. And he then opened an account at Credit Suisse and gave me the account number for this thing. I had no privileges on it. I couldn't sign for it. But he gave me the number. He said if at any point people want to put money in this, this is the thing which we have established for this purpose, if it would be necessary at a later date.

"I gave that number to Ollie [North]. . . .

"I have no knowledge of that account ever being used for anything. I don't know of any money that ever went into it. But I recalled this when I was reading a newspaper story the other day which suggested that Ollie had inherited a structure of bank accounts in which there was already something there, into which money could flow, or through which money could flow, or something like that, and that reminded me that, hey, I remember that day they created that account." (Ledeen (2) 41-42)

Ledeen reported these conversations to McFarlane and, in late October or early November 1985, when Ghorbanifar, Nimrodi, and Schwimmer came to Washington, he "urged that the hostage matter be dropped, and he [McFarlane] was in agreement with that." (Id at 50)

"So about a week afterwards I reported on this meeting to Bud, and I said again to him that I thought we should shut down the hostage matter and pursue the political business. He said that no, he was inclined to shut down the whole thing, that he had a bad feeling about the whole matter. He didn't like it. I appealed to him not to stop the whole thing but just to stop the hostage side of it. And he said, well, he would get back to me, and so off I went."

McFarlane told the Board in his second interview that Ledeen's memory was accurate.

"As I speculated earlier, I was surprised by the move from 100 to at least 400 and by the release of only one. The President was pleased by the release of one and/or the continuation of the relationship. But that seemed to me a very clear evidence of bad faith, and I said so to Mr. Kimche, probably because I met with Mr. Ledeen, although I don't know that but I made it very clear, and I think he's testified to the fact that I had a 'bad feeling' about this program in October. And he expressed that, too, to the Israelis.". . . (McFarlane (2) 34-35) (Tower)

FALL - McFarlane describes Administration activities in Central America since the Boland Amendment as "handholding." He says that while North has been heavily involved in the region he has not acted as a "rogue elephant," adding that whatever North has been doing he has done under instructions. (WP 10/19/86)

- By fall 1985, LtCol North was actively engaged in private efforts to resupply the Contras with lethal equipment. (Tower)

- A number of important developments regarding the Iran initiative occurred between September and December, 1985. However, it proved difficult for the Board to establish precisely what happened during this period. This is in part because the period was one of great activity for the President, the NSC principals, and Mr. McFarlane. Issues that seemed to be both more important and more urgent than the Iran initiative clearly preoccupied them.

[McFarlane speaking to the Tower Commission:] "This is not an excuse, but it is I think mitigating. Recall now that in this period from late September to November quite a number of things were happening in the government, and this was about number 12 on the agenda. I mean, you had the Soviet foreign minister in town, three other foreign heads of state, the preparation of four major Presidential speeches to lay out the agenda for the summit, bilateral, regional issues, arms control issues, human rights issues, a visit to the United Nations by the President for a couple of days, meetings with 12 or 15 heads of government up there, and in the middle of that the Achille Lauro." (McFarlane (1) 20-21) (Tower)

OCT - North meets with members of UNO, the contra umbrella group, to discuss the need for a political manifesto as part of the organization's efforts to present an improved image to the public and Congress. He tells them " 'Here is the U.S. Constitution. Read it.' " In December, UNO publishes its "Principles and Objectives for the Provisional Government of National Reconciliation." (The Nation 1/17/87, p. 41)

- A Southern Air Transport cargo plane flies to Barranquilla, Colombia, allegedly to take part in a cocaine smuggling operation, according to an FBI informant (see also October 1983 entry). Flight logs of Wallace B. Sawyer, a co-pilot on the C-123K plane that crashes in Nicaragua on October 5, 1986, show two trips to Barranquilla this month aboard a Southern Air L-382 cargo plane. (WP 1/20/87; Sawyer logs)

| AWARD/CONTRACT | 1. THIS CONTRACT IS A RATED ORDER UNDER DPAS (15 CFR 350) | RATING | PAGE OF PAGES |
| | | | 1 | 37 |

| 2. CONTRACT (Proc. Inst. Ident.) NO. | 3. EFFECTIVE DATE | 4. REQUISITION/PURCHASE REQUEST/PROJECT NO. |
| 1001-602066 | 10/1/85 | 1001-602066 |

5. ISSUED BY   CODE [ ]

U.S. DEPARTMENT OF STATE
CONTRACTS BRANCH
P.O. BOX 9115, ROSSLYN STATION
ARLINGTON, VIRGINIA 22209

6. ADMINISTERED BY (If other than Item 5)   CODE [ ]

ORIGINAL SECRET

7. NAME AND ADDRESS OF CONTRACTOR (No., street, city, county, State and ZIP Code)	8. DELIVERY
INTERNATIONAL BUSINESS COMMUNICATIONS, INC. 1912 Sunderland Place, N.W. Washington, D.C. 20036-1608 DUNS #991916230	[ ] FOB ORIGIN [X] OTHER (See below)
	9. DISCOUNT FOR PROMPT PAYMENT NET
	10. SUBMIT INVOICES (4 copies unless otherwise specified) TO THE ADDRESS SHOWN IN: ITEM SEE ITEM 11

| CODE [ ] | FACILITY CODE [ ] |

| 11. SHIP TO/MARK FOR   CODE [ ] | 12. PAYMENT WILL BE MADE BY   CODE [ ] |
| U.S.Department of State,
 ARA/LPD, Room 6253,NS,
 Washington, D.C. 20520, ATTN: Robert W. Kagan | Financial Operations
 Central Claims Division
 P.O. Box 9487, Rosslyn Station
 Arlington, Virginia 22209 |

| 13. AUTHORITY FOR USING OTHER THAN FULL AND OPEN COMPETI- TION: | 14. ACCOUNTING AND APPROPRIATION DATA |
| [ ] 10 U.S.C. 2304(c)( )   [X] 41 U.S.C. 253(c) 6 | 1960113 1001 602066 010122 2589
 OBLIGATED $276,186.00 |

| 15A. ITEM NO. | 15B. SUPPLIES/SERVICES | 15C. QUANTITY | 15D. UNIT | 15E. UNIT PRICE | 15F. AMOUNT |
| | THIS IS A COST-PLUS-FIXED-FEE CONTRACT FOR THE SERVICES SET FORTH IN SECTION C AND AT THE PRICES SHOWN IN SECTION B. | FUNDS AVAILABLE
 Sarah E. Wagner
 8/28/86 | | | NOT TO EXCEED |

| | | | | 15G. TOTAL AMOUNT OF CONTRACT ▶ | $276,186.00 |

16. TABLE OF CONTENTS

(✓)	SEC.	DESCRIPTION	PAGE(S)	(✓)	SEC.	DESCRIPTION	PAGE(S)
		PART I — THE SCHEDULE				PART II — CONTRACT CLAUSES	
X	A	SOLICITATION/CONTRACT FORM	A1	X	I	CONTRACT CLAUSES	I1-4
X	B	SUPPLIES OR SERVICES AND PRICES/COSTS	B1			PART III — LIST OF DOCUMENTS, EXHIBITS AND OTHER ATTACH.	
X	C	DESCRIPTION/SPECS./WORK STATEMENT	C1-2	X	J	LIST OF ATTACHMENTS	J1-3
X	D	PACKAGING AND MARKING	D1			PART IV — REPRESENTATIONS AND INSTRUCTIONS	
X	E	INSPECTION AND ACCEPTANCE	E1		K	REPRESENTATIONS, CERTIFICATIONS AND OTHER STATEMENTS OF OFFERORS	K1A-17
X	F	DELIVERIES OR PERFORMANCE	F1-2	X			
X	G	CONTRACT ADMINISTRATION DATA	G1		L	INSTRS., CONDS., AND NOTICES TO OFFERORS	
X	H	SPECIAL CONTRACT REQUIREMENTS	H1-3		M	EVALUATION FACTORS FOR AWARD	

CONTRACTING OFFICER WILL COMPLETE ITEM 17 OR 18 AS APPLICABLE

| 17. [X] CONTRACTOR'S NEGOTIATED AGREEMENT (Contractor is required to sign this document and return 3 copies to issuing office.) Contractor agrees to furnish and deliver all items or perform all the services set forth or otherwise identified above and on any continuation sheets for the consideration stated herein. The rights and obligations of the parties to this contract shall be subject to and governed by the following documents: (a) this award/contract, (b) the solicitation, if any, and (c) such provisions, representations, certifications, and specifications, as are attached or incorporated by reference herein. (Attachments are listed herein.) | 18. [ ] AWARD (Contractor is not required to sign this document.) Your offer on Solicitation Number _____, including the additions or changes made by you which additions or changes are set forth in full above, is hereby accepted as to the items listed above and on any continuation sheets. This award consummates the contract which consists of the following documents: (a) the Government's solicitation and your offer, and (b) this award/contract. No further contractual document is necessary. |

19A. NAME AND TITLE OF SIGNER (Type or print)	20A. NAME OF CONTRACTING OFFICER
RICHARD R. MILLER, PRESIDENT	Barbara A. Garland Contracting Officer
19B. NAME OF CONTRACTOR	19C. DATE SIGNED	20B. UNITED STATES OF AMERICA	20C. DATE SIGNED
BY _(Signature of person authorized to sign)_	9/2/86	BY _(Signature of Contracting Officer)_	SEP - 2 1986

NSN 7540-01-152-8069
PREVIOUS EDITION UNUSABLE

SECRET

STANDARD FORM 26 (REV. 4-85)
Prescribed by GSA
FAR (48 CFR) 53.214(a)

Declassified by Robert U. Kagan 1/20/08

Maule Air, Inc.

LAKE MAULE ROUTE 6 BOX 319 · MOULTRIE, GA. 31768 · PHONE 912/985-8525 ·:· TELEX (01)313 MAULE MOUL

October 7, 1985

FAA Aircraft Registry
P.O. Box 25504
Oklahoma City, OK   73125

attn: Sandi Davidson

Ms. Davidson,

This is pertaining to Registration N56611, which was exported
to Panama, RP around Sept. 10th. This aircraft was sold thru
Maule Air, Inc. to NRAF, Inc. - 52 Y el Vira Mendez, Panama, RP.

Request of Cancellation of U. S. Registration should and will
be coming from NRAF of Panama.

If you should have any further questions please let us know.

Sincerely,

Barbara Maule
Sales Secretary

cc: Dick Secord
    440 Maple Ave E
    Suite 205
    Vienna, VA 22180

- In October, 1985, the United States obtained reliable evidence that William Buckley had died the preceding June. (Tower)

- By this month, Reagan reportedly has formally approved another CIA attempt to overthrow Khaddafi. However, the House Select Committee on Intelligence, concerned over a CIA assessment in 1984 that discussed the possibility of inciting "disaffected elements" in the Libyan military to conduct "assassination attempts or to cooperate with the exiles against" Khaddafi, threatens to veto the operation. Shultz is sent before the committee to persuade members not to take that action. (NYT 2/22/87)

OCT 1 - International Business Communications Inc. (IBC), a public relations firm, begins work on a secret contract with the State Department, in cooperation with Oliver North, on behalf of the contras. The contract, worth $276,186, is not signed until eleven months later, on September 2, 1986. It covers a proposed $1 million advertising campaign for the rebels, as well as visits by contra leaders and field commanders to Washington to lobby Congress. During one such visit this month, two guerrilla commanders fight in their hotel room, leaving one commander bleeding badly on the carpet; Bosco Matamoros, the rebels' Washington representative, pays for the damages with IBC funds. Administration and contra officials say later that North meets frequently with Richard Miller and Francis Gomez of IBC for strategy sessions on the public relations campaign. (AP in WP 2/7/87)

- On October 1, 1985, Israel's air force bombed the PLO headquarters in Tunis. (Tower)

- CIA national intelligence officer Charles Allen informs Deputy Director Robert Gates that he suspects funds are being diverted to the contras. The Agency initiates a review of the matter at this point. (WSJ 12/22/86 & 1/9/87)

- Effective this date, the State Department enters into a $276,186 contract, initially classified secret, with International Business Communications (IBC) for "public diplomacy efforts" and "distribution services." This contract has almost identical specifications as the unclassified $90,000 contract of Mar. 1, 1985 (see entry of that date). It is also unusual in that the contract would not be signed until Sept.

2, 1986, and backdated to this date. IBC is later connected to private American funding of weapons for the contras. (DOS Contract 1001-602066 effective 10/1/85 but signed 9/2/86; WP 3/7/87)

OCT 4 - Islamic Jihad, a pro-Iranian terrorist group, announces it has killed CIA station chief William Buckley, but his body is not recovered. U.S. officials now think Buckley died sometime during the summer. (MH puts date of the announcement at October 14.) (MH 12/7/86; NYT 12/25/86)

- Information was received that in late 1985 the Syrians informed Ambassador Vernon Walters that Buckley's Iranian captors had tortured and killed him. The reports indicate that this information was conveyed to Vice President Bush who found it very distressing. (SSIC 1/29/87)

- [O]n October 4, according to NSC staff chronologies prepared in November 1986, the Islamic Jihad announced the execution of Buckley in retaliation for the bombing [by the Israelis of the PLO headquarters in Tunis on October 1, 1985]. The NSC staff chronologies state that "[t]his announcement led to a series of meetings in Europe among the U.S. (CIA and NSC), Israeli, and Iranian intermediaries."
According to both the Maximum Version and the Historical Chronology, this announcement was false. Iranians with whom CIA and NSC staff personnel met in the following months, and Jenco and Jacobsen, two hostages released later, reported that Buckley probably died on June 3, 1985, of "pneumonia-like symptoms." (Maximum Version 5; Historical Chronology 6)(Maximum Version 4; Historical Chronology 6) (Tower)

OCT 6 - On October 6, North asked the CIA to arrange for surveillance of Ghorbanifar and Nimrodi, whom he expected in Washington on the 7th. Such surveillance was put in place. . . . (North calendar) (See October 8, 1985 entry.) (Tower)

OCT 7 - Maule Air Inc. writes a letter to the FAA regarding the sale of Maule N56611 to NRAF Inc. in Panama. The letter states that cancellation of the U.S. registration for the aircraft will be coming from NRAF. At the bottom of the letter is "cc: Dick Secord, 440 Maple Ave. Suite 205, Vienna, Virginia." (FAA Documents, CBS News 7/14/86, Hearst Newspapers 7/27/86)

- On October 1, 1985, Mr. McFarlane replied to Congressman Hamilton (See September 12, 1985 entry):

"There is no official or unofficial relationship with any member of the NSC staff regarding fund raising for the Nicaraguan democratic opposition."

In response to the question of whether Oliver North "[sic] at any time advise[d] individuals on how they might donate money to the rebels?"

Mr. McFarlane answered, "No." (Tower)

- On October 7 the Italian ship Achille Lauro was hijacked by Palestinisn [sic] terrorists. (Tower)

OCT 8 - LtCol North's calendar indicated that he met with Mr. Ledeen, Mr. Schwimmer, Mr. Nimrodi, and Mr. Ghorbanifar (using the alias of Nicholas Kralis). . . . at 9:00 a.m. in the Old Executive Office Building. . . . Other meetings may have occurred. There is little evidence of what exactly went on in these meetings. All that is known for sure is that shortly after those meetings, David Kimche advanced a third proposal. (See November 9, 1985 entry.) (Tower)

-I.C. Inc. pays $100,000 to Lake Resources in Switzerland, money which apparently came from the National Endowment for the Preservation of Liberty and International Business Communications. (WP 3/7/87)

OCT 10 - North and Poindexter help orchestrate the interception and force-down in Sicily of an Egyptian plane carrying the five hijackers of the Achille Lauro. This is North's first prominent role in a major counter-terrorist event. At the time, he is chairman of the NSC's Terrorist Incident Working Group, established in 1984 for just such a purpose. (WP 10/12/85 & 2/17/87)

OCT 17 - President Reagan meets with Spitz Channell and a small group of donors to Channell's groups, the National Endowment for the Preservation of Liberty and the American Conservative Trust, at the White House. White House sources later tell reporters that Reagan communications director Patrick Buchanan helped set up this meeting, along with special assistant to the President for public liaison Linas J. Kojelis and Oliver North. A Channell fundraiser, Jane McLaughlin, later describes a series of meetings at the White House and the Old Executive Office Building involving Col. North, Channell, and potential donors: "the largest sums of money came in as a result" of appeals by LtCol. North. (NYT 2/26/87; WP 3/7/87)

OCT 21 - Mr. McFarlane received an inquiry from Congressman Richard Durbin. Congressman Durbin asked: "Are there any efforts currently underway in the Administration to facilitate the sending of private donations to the contras?"

McFarlane replied: "No." (Tower)

OCT 23-25 - $25,000 is transferred from the Lake Resources Swiss bank account to an FDN account in a Cayman Islands bank. This is the first of two installments. A second installment, this time of $175,000, is transferred from the Lake Resources account in Switzerland to an FDN account in the Cayman Islands. International Business Communications passes on $250,000 to I.C. Inc., which in turn pays Lake Resources $150,000 on Nov. 1. (WP 3/7/87)

OCT 30 - Spitz Channell's National Endowment for the Preservation of Liberty pays $63,000 to International Business Communications. IBC passes on $40,000 to I.C. Inc. on Nov. 8, and I.C. passes $48,000 to Lake Resources in Switzerland on Nov. 14. (WP 3/7/87)

OCT-NOV - [I]n late October or early November 1985, when Ghorbanifar, Nimrodi, and Schwimmer came to Washington, he [Ledeen] "urged that the hostage matter be dropped, and he [McFarlane] was in agreement with that."

"So about a week afterwards I reported on this meeting to Bud, and I said again to him that I thought we should shut down the hostage matter and pursue the political business. He said that no, he was inclined to shut down the whole thing, that he had a 'bad feeling' about the whole matter. He didn't like it. I appealed to him not to stop the whole thing but just to stop the hostage side of it. And he said, well, he would get back to me, and so off I went." (Ledeen 50) (Tower)

McFarlane told the Board in his second interview that Ledeen's memory was accurate.

"As I speculated earlier, I was surprised by the move from 100 to at least 400 and by the release of only one. The President was pleased by the release of one and/or the continuation of the relationship. But that seemed to me a very clear evidence of bad faith, and I said so to Mr. Kimche, probably because I met with Mr. Ledeen, although I don't know that but I made it very clear, and I think he's testified to the fact that I had a 'bad feeling' about this program in October. And he expressed that, too, to the Israelis. . . ." (McFarlane (2) 34-35) (Tower)

NOVEMBER 1985

NOV - Congress approves as part of the Intelligence Authorization Act for FY86 (P.L. 99-169) a classified amount for communications equipment and related training for the contras, and authorizes the U.S. to exchange information with them. (CRS "U.S. Assistance to Nicaraguan Guerrillas" 12/4/86)

- Around this time, Amalgamated Commercial Enterprises (ACE), a shell company incorporated in Panama last November, is bought by Southern Air Transport and used to purchase and maintain planes carrying supplies to the contras. According to one report, funds are transferred from several companies to pay for these activities. One of the companies is Albon Values Corp., a Panama-registered corporation with close ties to Geneva-based CSF. Another report states that all of ACE's officers are employed by International Management & Trust Corp., or Intertrust, a Panama incorporator. Intertrust in turn has had previous ties to Steven Samos, a Panamanian businessman who has admitted in a U.S. court to laundering millions of dollars in Colombian drug money during the late 1970s. (WSJ 1/8/87, 1/16/87 & 1/30/87)

- A front company called Dolmy Business Inc. is established in Panama. Two of Dolmy's top officers, Roland Farina and Jacques Mossaz, are employees of the Geneva-based Compagnie de Services Fiduciaires (CSF), the financial services company that has played a major role in the Iran-contra affair. Farina is an accountant and Mossaz an attorney with CSF. Dolmy later buys a freighter, the Erria (see April 28,

1986 entry), which was used in May of this year to carry arms to the contras, and becomes an integral part of Oliver North's Project Democracy program. Also known as Democracy Inc., the project is heavily involved in various undercover activities, including hostage dealings with Iran. (LAT 1/21/87; WSJ 1/22/87, 1/23/87 & 1/30/87)

- Whatever the intent, almost from the beginning the initiative became in fact a series of arms-for-hostages deals. The shipment of arms in November, 1985, was directly tied to a hostage release. Indeed, the August/September transfer may have been nothing more than an arms-for-hostages trade. (Tower)

- Mr. Secord undertook in November, 1985, to arrange landing clearance for the Israeli flight bringing the HAWK missiles into a third-country staging area. The arrangements fell apart. A CIA field officer attributed this failure to the amateurish way in which Mr. Secord and his associates approached officials in the government from which landing clearance was needed. (Tower)

- The Attorney General reached a similar judgment with respect to the activities of the CIA in facilitating the November, 1985, shipment by the Israelis of HAWK missiles. In a letter to the Board the Attorney General concluded that with respect to the CIA assistance, "a finding under the Hughes-Ryan Amendment would be required."

Apparently no determination was made at the time as to the legality of these activities even though serious concerns about legality were expressed by the Deputy Director of CIA, a Presidential finding was sought by CIA officials before any further CIA activities in support of the Iran initiative were undertaken, and the CIA counsel, Mr. Stanley Sporkin, advised that as a matter of prudence any new finding should seek to ratify the prior CIA activities. (Tower)

NOV 1 - The Lake Resources bank account in Switzerland receives $150,000 from I.C. Inc. in the Cayman Islands (see Oct. 25 entry above). (WP 3/7/87)

NOV 6 - A telegram from Maule Air, Inc. to FAA Aircraft Registry requests that Maule N56611 be removed from U.S. registry. The telegram states that the plane was exported to Honduras and purchased by NRAF Inc. of Panama. Two days later, Maule N56611 is officially deregistered. A message is transmitted to Panamanian Civil Aeronautics for re-registration of the plane. (See September 10, September 30 and October 7, 1985 entries) (FAA Documents)

NOV 8 - David Kimche has lunch with North and Michael Ledeen in Washington. He claims it is his first meeting with North and that they only discuss McFarlane's impending resignation. (NYT 12/30/86; ABC "Good Morning America" 12/31/86; CBS News 12/31/86)

- After the first shipment of TOWs, Ledeen continued to be active. He held meetings in the fall of 1985 with Kimche, Schwimmer, Ghorbanifar and Nimrodi. These meetings reportedly dealt with intelligence on the situation in Iran and who might want to cooperate with the U.S. Ghorbanifar also discussed the offer to get hostages released and the weapons that Iran needed, including HAWK missiles. Iran demanded an arms shipment before each release while the United States and Israel pushed for release in advance of any further arms shipments.

It is clear from the testimony that the Iranians believed the new channel with the U.S. would be productive. For example, they appeared to expect to receive sophisticated weaponry such as Phoenix and Harpoon missiles at some point in the future.

Ledeen testified that he briefed McFarlane on these meetings. He stated that this was a promising channel to pursue but that if it continued on an arms for hostages basis, it would be difficult to determine Iran's motives. Ledeen also suggested that if the program were to continue there was a need to bring in an intelligence service. Ledeen said McFarlane had "bad feeling" about the program and was going to stop it. (SSIC 1/29/87)

- International Business Communications passes on $40,000 to I.C. Inc. on Nov. 8, and I.C. passes $48,000 to Lake Resources in Switzerland on Nov. 14. (WP 3/7/87)

NOV 9 - Mr. Kimche met with Mr. McFarlane and LtCol North on November 9, 1985. John McMahon, the Deputy Director of Central Intelligence, told the Board that Mr. McFarlane spoke with him on November 14 (See November 14, 1985 entry). Mr. McFarlane told Mr. McMahon that Mr. Kimche had indicated that the Israelis planned to provide some arms to moderates in Iran who would oppose Khomeini. Mr. McFarlane suggested that the Israelis interpreted the Presidential authorization as an open charter for further arms shipments as long as the shipments were modest and did not alter the military balance between Iran and Iraq. Indeed, he did not recall any specific request by Israel in the late fall. He did, however, remember that early in November, Yitzhak Rabin, Israel's Defense Minister, asked whether U.S. policy would still permit Israel to buy replacements from the U.S. for arms it transferred to Iran. Mr. McFarlane confirmed that it would, although he indicated U.S. reservations about any trade of arms for hostages. They asked nothing further. (Tower)

NOV 12 - Richard Secord purchases a specially outfitted light transport airplane from a dealer in Alabama, although he does not register ownership with the FAA until November 4, 1986. The airplane is a 1973 Piper Seneca I equipped with turbocharged engines and an oxygen system that enables it to fly at altitudes of 26,000 feet, twice that of a standard Piper Seneca and high enough to evade radar detection and cross mountain ranges, according to the previous owner. (WP 12/10/86)

NOV 14 - Casey, responding to press reports (denied by Senator Durenberger) that Durenberger is dissatisfied with CIA performance under the current director, issues a public letter complaining that the process of congressional oversight of the intelligence community has gone seriously awry. (CRS "U.S. Intelligence: Issues for Congress, 1986" 1/5/87)

- [O]n November 14, McFarlane had told the Director of Central Intelligence and John McMahon, his Deputy, "that Kimche was planning or had indicated that the Israelis planned to give some arms to moderates in Iran that would oppose Khomeini." (McMahon 5) At that time, North was in London meeting Terry Waite and, separately, Ghorbanifar. (According to North's office calendar, North, McFarlane, and Kimche met on November 9, 1985.) (American Embassy, London, to North, 11/12/85; NSC Chronology of Events, dated 11/20/86) (Tower)

- [North states in a memorandum dated December 5—see entry for full text:] ". . . . We are relatively confident of information that former Beirut Chief of Station, Bill Buckley, is dead. We also know, from Waite's November 14 visit to Beirut and a separate contact through Canada, that the other five hostages, Anderson, Jacobsen, Jenco, Kilburn, and Sutherland are still alive. Waite and others credibly report that those who hold the hostages are under immense political and military pressure from the Syrians, Druze, Phalange, and Amal and that there is the distinct possibility that our hostages as well as the French and British could be killed in the near future. The Iranians, who have been in contact with the Israelis, are cognizant of the pressure being placed on the Hizballah surrogates in Lebanon and that it is entirely likely that the only leverage they will have over us (the hostages) may no longer be available in the near future. . . . " (Tower)

- The Lake Resources bank account in Switzerland receives $48,000 from I.C. Inc. in the Cayman Islands (see Oct. 30 entry above). (WP 3/7/87)

NOV 15 - Adnan Khashoggi borrows $8 million from Vertex Finances, S.A., a Cayman Islands holding company whose directors include Toronto businessmen Donald Fraser and Ernest Miller (referred to in the Los Angeles Times as Walter "Ernie" Miller). This is the first of three installments of a $21 million loan for the purpose of financing arms purchases by Iran. Later, when Khashoggi is apparently not paid back all that he is due, Roy Furmark approaches Casey and informs him of the deal. (WSJ 12/12/86; NYT 12/13/86)

NOV 16 - "[R]ight before I left for Geneva [for the Summit] with Ghorbanifar [?Gorbachev?]," Mr. [Mc]Farlane told the Board in his second interview, Israel Defense Minister Rabin saw McFarlane in Washington. "I believe that his [Rabin's] purpose in coming was simply to reconfirm that the President's authority for the original concept was still valid. We haven't changed our mind and I reconfirmed that that was the case. I don't recall that he said anything about any concrete intention in the short term to do anything else." (McFarlane (2) 36) (Tower)

- "Well, I wouldn't have reconfirmed it [the President's authorization] if I wasn't fully confident of it, and that could have been on the basis of what was a fairly routine reporting of any information that I had on this, that I would pass it on to the President and he would react to it, and his reaction was always well, cross your fingers or hope for the best, and keep me informed. But I was never to say at any point stop this or disapprove of it. . . . " (McFarlane (2) 39-43) (Tower)

NOV 17 - McFarlane testified that on November 17, while in Geneva for the Summit, he received a call from Israeli Defense Minister Rabin. Rabin requested assistance in resolving difficulties Israel was having in a shipment of military equipment through a European country onward to Iran. McFarlane told the Committee that he called Colonel North, briefed him on the President's August 1985 decision, and requested that he contact Rabin and offer assistance.

According to notes from the Attorney General's inquiry, North said he suspected that the Israeli shipment McFarlane mentioned consisted of U.S. arms. Reportedly, North told Meese that he called Rabin and was told Israel was having difficulty in getting clearance for a flight to a European country. Rabin told him the flight involved moving "things" to support a U.S. rapprochement with Iran. North said he then contacted retired Air Force Major General Richard Secord, whom he described as a close personal friend, for assistance. Secord was to try to arrange a large cargo aircraft of neither U.S. nor Israeli origin for the flight.

McFarlane testified that North called him in Geneva to explain the problem. The Israelis had failed to make proper customs arrangements for a flight to the European country. Further, the only aircraft they had available was an El Al plane which was believed unsuitable because of national markings and documentation. McFarlane testified that North told him McFarlane might have to call the Prime Minister of the European country to get the necessary approval. McFarlane stated that he did so, explaining to the Prime Minister that a transfer from Israel to Iran was in progress and the the U.S. Government would appreciate assistance. North also contacted a CIA official and obtained the CIA's support in trying to arrange the necessary flight clearances. (SSIC 1/29/87)

- In contrast to the August TOW shipment, the United States became directly involved in the November transfer of the HAWK missiles. Sometime on November 17 or 18, 1985, while Mr. McFarlane was in Geneva for the November summit, Mr. Rabin called Mr. McFarlane to say that a problem had arisen. Mr. McFarlane referred the matter to LtCol North. (See November 19-21, 1987 entry.) (Tower)

NOV 18 - Khashoggi borrows $7 million from Vertex Finances, S.A., the second of three installments of a loan used to finance the purchase of arms by Iran. (WSJ 12/12/86)

- Jonathan Jay Pollard and his wife, Anne Henderson-Pollard, are arrested on espionage charges after they try unsuccessfully to gain asylum at the Israeli embassy in Washington. Pollard is an employee of the U.S. Naval Security and Investigative Command and has been selling classified documents to the Israeli Scientific Liaison Bureau (Known as "Lekeem") since the summer of 1984. Four Israelis are named in the indictment, but the Israeli government denies any involvement in the affair. (CRS: "Israeli-American Relations," 12/22/86; WP 3/5/87)

- Secretary Shultz told the Board that Mr. McFarlane told him on November 18, 1985, about a plan that would produce the release of the hostages on Thursday, November 21. Secretary Shultz told the Board he told Mr. McFarlane that had he known of it earlier, he would have stopped it. He nonetheless expressed the hope to Mr. McFarlane that the hostages would be released. It is not clear what other NSC principals, if any, were told in advance about the plan. (Tower)

- Secretary Shultz testified before Congress and told the Board that McFarlane told him on November 18, 1985, in Geneva,

". . . that four hostages would be released on Thursday (November 21). He said that Israel would fly a plane with 100 HAWK missiles to [a third country], and transfer them to another aircraft. If the hostages were released, the airplane would fly to Iran; if not, it would fly to Israel. Israel would buy replacements for these missiles from the U.S., and would be paid by Iran. I complained to Mr. McFarlane that I had been informed so late that it was impossible to stop this operation. I nonetheless expressed my hope that the hostages would in fact be released. (Shultz, 12/86, 13; 1/87, 23-24; SRB, 27-28) (Tower)

NOV 19 - Another shipment of missiles is sent to Iran. On its way, however, the plane is apparently turned away by Portugal because American officials failed to secure landing rights. The CIA eventually arranges for another plane to go to Israel and pick up the shipment (see November 22-23 entry). Before the shipment, North tells the Israelis that Richard Secord will go to Tel Aviv to assist in the arms transfers. By this time, a congressional source says later, Secord is "already involved in the contra supply operation." (NYT 1/11/87; WP 1/14/87)

- By letter dated November 19, 1985, which North signed with his own name "for" McFarlane, Secord was asked to play a role.

"Your discrete [sic?] assistance is again required in support of our national interest. At the earliest opportunity, please proceed to [a third country transit point], and other locations as necessary in order to arrange for the transfer of sensitive materiel being shipped from Israel.

"As in the past, you should exercise great caution that this activity does not become public knowledge. You should ensure that only those whose discretion is guaranteed are involved." (McFarlane per North to Secord, 11/19/85) (Tower)

NOV 19-21 - Reagan attends the Geneva summit meeting. McFarlane says that during the course of the summit he informs the President, Shultz and Regan of the impending arms shipment to Iran by Israel for the purpose of facilitating the release of hostages. (WP 2/12/87)

- Regan said that Mr. McFarlane told the president early in the month on the margins of his briefings for the Geneva summit to expect that a shipment of missiles would come from Israel through a third country to Iran, and that the hostages would come out. (Tower)

- In his first meeting with the Board on January 16, 1987, the President said he did not remember how the November shipment came about. The President said he objected to the shipment, and that, as a result of that objection, the shipment was returned to Israel. In his second meeting with the Board on February 11, 1987, the President stated that both he and Regan agreed that they cannot remember any meeting or conversation in general about a HAWK shipment. The President said he did not remember anything about a callback of the HAWKs. (Tower)

- The President was informed "on the margins of his briefings for the Gorbachev meeting to expect that there is going to be a shipment of arms . . . missiles, transshipped through Israel into Iran, and the hostages will come out." (Regan 14) Around the time of the Geneva Summit, McFarlane told the President "that something had happened and the shipment didn't take place as originally scheduled." (Id. at 12) Regan recalled that the President had been "upset" about the September shipment. (Id. at 9) Regan explained McFarlane's belief that the President had authorized the transaction as follows: the President "hadn't raised Cain about the [first] Israeli shipment, so a second try might not be out of order. . . . Certainly there was nothing said to the President in advance, at least in my hearing, where it was said, now may we ship missiles to Iran through Israel. That was not asked of the President." (Id. at 14)

In his second interview with the Board, McFarlane expanded his first account.

"I think it would be accurate to say that the President believed in August that he was approving the Israeli sale of modest levels of arms of a certain character, filling certain criteria, but that with that approval Israel could transfer or sell modest levels without further concrete approval.

"Now as a separate but obviously related matter his concurrent expectation was that how that would be translated would be 100 TOWs. As far as the November shipment, then, I don't recall that having been a matter considered in Washington, raised to the President and decided. When I learned about it I did report it to the President and to the Secretary of State and to Mr. Regan in Geneva. I recall a conversation from Geneva with the Secretary of Defense, but I don't want to—I couldn't say beyond just the fact that it occurred because I always called him every day to debrief him on the meetings with Gorbachev, and so it might have been that.

"But, at any rate, I raised it with the President, Mr. Regan. The routine in Geneva was that each morning before the prebriefing for the Gorbachev meetings he would have just a short meeting on other Presidential matters in his residence, and for that the Secretary of State and I and Mr. Regan would go to the chateau and meet with him for 15 minutes or so on nonsummit issues, and that would have been where it would have been raised. Then we left and walked over to the motorcade and on to the summit. . . .

"Well, I wouldn't have reconfirmed it [the President's authorization] if I wasn't fully confident of it, and that could have been on the basis of what was a fairly routine reporting of any information that I had on this, that I would pass it on to the President and he would react to it, and his reaction was always well, cross your fingers or hope for the best, and keep me informed. But I was never to say at any point stop this or disapprove of it. . . ."

General Scowcroft: "But nobody talked to you about during the period from September through your learning of this shipment about the possibility of another shipment, about arrangements or anything like this before Rabin meets with you or the next day when he calls and says we're shipping something and we're in trouble?"

Mr. McFarlane: "I have no concrete recollection of anything like that. I can imagine that meetings took place, but I don't know of any idea of a number of weapons to be sent over. I remember, for example, one time Mr. Ledeen conveying a concept—it was not a hard proposal—that the United States send Phoenix and one or two other kinds of precision guided systems, and it was out of the question. I said no. But never any numerical kind of X day, Y weapons to Z place." (McFarlane (2) 39-43) (Tower)

- [McFarlane, in his final interview with the Board, amended histories previously given in three PROF notes:] Later in the fall, other transfers of equipment were made between Israel and Iran although some of the items were returned to Israel. McFarlane conveyed these reports to the President who directed that we insist on a direct meeting with the Iranian interlocutors while expressing our position against further arms transfers. (Tower)

- "The project had fallen apart during Thanksgiving week... Vice Admiral Poindexter told me [Shultz] privately ... That is thinking back to that period. He said he had recommended to the President that we disengage, but that the President did not want to...." (Shultz, SRB, 31-32) (Tower)

- North signed a letter for Mr. McFarlane dated November 19, 1985, requesting Richard Secord, a retired U.S. Air Force general officer, to proceed to a foreign country, to arrange for the transfer of "sensitive material" being shipped from Israel. That day Mr. Secord made arrangements for transshipment of the Israeli HAWKs. (Tower)

NOV 20 - North sends Poindexter a computer message saying that aircraft in Portugal scheduled to ship arms to the contras could be used to deliver arms to Iran instead. The message is described later by a congressman as "the first overlap" between North's ties to the Iran deals and the covert arms supply operation to the contras. (WP 1/14/87)

- A White House electronic message from North to Admiral Poindexter on November 20 indicates that North had a detailed understanding of the HAWK plan by that time. This message indicates that Israel would deliver 80 HAWKs to the European country November 22 for shipment to Tabriz; five U.S. hostages would then be released to the U.S. Embassy in Beirut; $18 million in payment had already been deposited in appropriate accounts; retired USAF Major General Richard Secord would make all arrangements; and replacements would be sold to Israel. According to documents received by the Committee, North continued to keep Poindexter informed on a daily basis about plans for an impending shipment of HAWK missiles to Iran and the release of American hostages.

The Committee received evidence that McFarlane contacted Secretary of State Shultz and Donald Regan and advised them that hostages were to be released and some type of arms were to be transported to Iran by Israel. This evidence indicates that McFarlane told Regan and Shultz that Israel would buy replacements for these arms from the United States. While Shultz was advised that HAWK missiles were involved, Regan said that he was informed of this fact sometime later.

Regan testified that McFarlane informed the President in Geneva that some type of arms shipment was being considered, and that if the operation were successful, hostages might be freed. Shultz expressed reservations to McFarlane, but according to Shultz, was told by McFarlane that he had cleared it with the President. (SSIC 1/29/87)

- In a message to VADM Poindexter on November 20, 1985, LtCol North described the following plan. The Israelis were to deliver 80 HAWK missiles to a staging area in a third country, at noon on Friday, November 22. These were to be loaded aboard three chartered aircraft, which would take off at two hour intervals for Tabriz, Iran. Once launch of the first aircraft had been confirmed by Mr. Ghorbanifar, directions would be given to release the five U.S. citizens held hostage in Beirut. No aircraft was to land in Tabriz until all the hostages had been delivered to the U.S. embassy in Beirut. Israel would deliver forty additional HAWKs at a later time. The Iranians would commit to seeing that there were no further hostages seized. (Tower)

- At about 9:30 p.m. on November 20, North wrote Poindexter:

"The Israelis will deliver 80 Mod[ified] HAWKS to [a third country] at noon on Friday 22 Nov. These 80 will be loaded aboard three chartered aircraft, owned by a proprietary which will take off at two hour intervals for Tabriz. . . . Appropriate arrangements have been made with the proper [country name deleted] air control personnel. Once the aircraft have been launched, their departure will be confirmed by Agshari [Ghorbanifar] who will call [his contact in Tehran] who will call Niknam (DCM in Damascus) who will direct the IRG [Iranian Revolutionary Guard] commander in Beirut to collect the five rpt [sic] five Amcits from Hizballah and deliver them to the U.S. Embassy. There is also the possibility that they will hand over the French hostage who is very ill.

"There is a requirement for 40 additional weaps of the same nomenclature for a total requirement of 120. $18M in payment for the first 80 has been deposited in the appropriate account. No acft will land in Tabriz until the AMCITS have been delivered to the embassy. The Iranians have also asked to order additional items in the future and have been told that they will be considered after this activity has succeeded. All transfer arrangements have been made by Dick Secord, who deserves a medal for his extraordinary short notice efforts.

"Replenishment arrangements are being made through MOD [Ministry of Defense] purchasing office in NYC. There is, to say the least, considerable anxiety that we will somehow delay on their plan to purchase 120 of these weapons in the next few days. IAW [In accordance with] your instructions I have told their agent that we will sell them 120 items at a price they can meet. I have further told them that we will make no effort to move on their purchase LOA request until we have all five AMCITS safely delivered. In short, the pressure is on them. . . .

"As soon as we have the release confirmed, we need to move quickly with Defense to provide the 120 missiles the Isrealis [sic] want to buy. They are very concerned that they are degrading their defence capability, and in view of the Syrian shoot-down yesterday the PM has placed considerable pressure on both Rabin and Kimche for very prompt replacement. Both called several times today.

"There is the distinct possibility that at the end of the week we will have five Americans home and the promise of no future hostage takings in exchange for selling the Israelis 120 Mod HAWKs. Despite the difficulty of making all this fit inside a 96-hour window, it isn't that bad a deal . . . Warm regards. Recommend pass to RCM [McFarlane] after review. North." (North PROF note to Poindexter, 11/20/85, 21:27:39) The remainder of the note concerned details about sending "a covert hostage debrief team to Wiesbaden." (Id.) (Tower)

NOV 21 - In the morning of November 21, North reported to Poindexter a call from Secord. The transit country's Defense Minister had assured Secord that the Prime Minister "had approved the xfer activity for Friday and that the FoMin is aware and supportive." As they were en route to Brussels, North suggested that McFarlane discreetly thank them for their help." (North PROF note to Poindexter, 11/21/85, 09:18:36. "Please pass to RCM as avail.") The operation began to unravel later that day. (Tower)

- Duane Clarridge, in 1985, Chief of the European Division of CIA's Directorate of Operations, told the Board that he first became involved during the evening of November 21. North called him for help in obtaining an over-flight clearance for an El Al 747. (Tower)

- But late in the day on November 21, these arrangements [for the transfer of "sensitive material" from Israel (see November 17 entry)] began to fall apart. The foreign government denied landing clearance to the aircraft bringing the HAWKs from Israel....A CIA field office attributed this failure to the amateurish way in which Mr. Secord and his associates approached officials in the government from which landing clearance was needed.... LtCol North contacted Duane Clarridge of the CIA for assistance in obtaining the required landing clearance. When the CIA's efforts failed, LtCol North asked Mr. Clarridge to find a reliable commercial carrier to substitute for the Israeli flight. Mr. Clarridge put Mr. Secord in contact with a carrier that was a CIA proprietary. (Tower)

- "The Secretary of State testified:
November 21—the supposed [hostage] release date—passed with no release." (Shultz, SRB, 28) (Tower)

- Adolfo Calero writes Spitz Channell on FDN stationery (the initials FDN superimposed over the initials UNO) thanking Channell for "your continued support. We are looking forward to your continued assistance in our struggle for freedom and democracy in Nicaragua." (See also Apr. 25 entry above.) (Calero letter 11/21/85)

- The White House hosts a briefing for a small group of donors to Spitz Channell's National Endowment for the Preservation of Liberty, from 6 to 7:30 p.m. The meeting begins with a welcome from Linas Kojelis (special assistant to the President for public liaison), and remarks from Linda Chavez (deputy assistant to the President for public liaison). The featured speaker is Oliver North. A Channell fundraiser, Jane McLaughlin, later describes a series of meetings at the White House and the Old Executive Office Building involving Col. North, Channell, and potential donors: "the largest sums of money came in as a result" of appeals by Col. North. (White House briefing schedule 11/21/85; NYT 2/26/87; WP 3/7/87)

NOV 22 - McFarlane telephones Pires de Miranda, the foreign minister of Portugal, requesting the assistance of the Portuguese government in shipping U.S. arms to Iran. Citing his capacity as Reagan's national security adviser, McFarlane asks that the Portuguese government authorize the transshipment through Lisbon of a cargo of two aircraft bound for Iran. Pires de Miranda asks the NSC to present this request through diplomatic channels and to explain more fully the nature of the intended operation. (Lisbon Expresso 1/31/87)

- Secretary Shultz said he told an associate on November 22 that "Bud says he's cleared with the President" on the plan. Chief of Staff Regan told the Board that the President was informed in advance of the Israeli HAWK shipment but was not asked to approve it. He said that Mr. McFarlane told the President early in the month on the margins of his briefings for the Geneva Summit to expect that a shipment of missiles would come from Israel through a third country to Iran, and that the hostages would come out.

In his first meeting with the Board on January 16, 1987, the President said he did not remember how the November shipment came about. The President said he objected to the

shipment, and that, as a result of that objection, the shipment was returned to Israel.

In his second meeting with the Board on February 11,
1987, the President stated that both he and Mr. Regan agreed
that they cannot remember any meeting or conversation in
general about a HAWK shipment. The President said he did
not remember anything about a call-back of the HAWKs.
(Tower)

- On the 22nd, Clarridge used CIA communications channels to help obtain the [overflight] clearance [for an El Al
747 that North had requested on November 21, 1985]. He
had the impression that North was already "in touch with
[the foreign] government at some level." (Clarridge 3) At
this time, Charles Allen showed Clarridge reports indicating
that the flight was part of an operation aimed at the liberation of hostages, but the CIA was permitted to reveal only
that the flight had a humanitarian purpose. Clarridge informed the U.S. official trying to obtain flight clearance that
he should be in touch with a man named "Copp," whom
Clarridge was told was an alias for Secord. Despite the
CIA's efforts, landing rights were denied. As a result, North
asked for the name of a reliable charter airline. Given the
shortage of time and the circumstances, CIA's air branch
suggested the use of a proprietary. The proprietary was told
to await a call; Clarridge suspects the caller was to be Copp.
In any event, the airline was assured that the caller would
have sufficient funds for the charter. (Id. at 2-6)

When the issue of a CIA proprietary airline was raised,
Clarridge said, he became concerned about the propriety of
CIA action. He asked Edward Juchniewicz, acting Deputy
Director of Operations, whether he would approve the oper-
ation. He did. (Id. at 4-5) According to the CIA Inspector
General, Juchniewicz remembered Clarridge alerting him
that

"North needed an aircraft to transport some unspecified
material to Israel, and that North might call him about it.
Juchniewicz remembers receiving a call at home that night
from North, who said he understood that the Agency had an
aircraft and asked whether it would be possible to charter it.
Juchniewicz says he told North that the proprietary was a
commercial venture and thus available for charter by anyone. He is certain that he did not give North the name of the

proprietary, believing North already to be in possession of that information. Juchniewicz says he did not authorize the use of the proprietary to anyone, but acknowledges that his response could have been interpreted as approval. (A CIA officer involved recalls contacting Juchniewicz on or before the morning of 25 November to confirm that the project had been approved, and being given assurances that it had.)" (CIA/IG Chronology 7)

One of North's contemporaneous messages to Poindexter supports part of Clarridge's account. In the middle of the afternoon, November 22, North wrote that landing clearance still had not been obtained. "Despite the difficulties of the past 24 hours, all continue to believe that if RCM can get thru to the PM or FOMIN, that this can be done." (North PROF note to Poindexter, 11/22/85, 19:27:15 "Status Report as of 1730") North was considering three choices for continuing the operation, (1) chartering a new airline to pick up the cargo in Tel Aviv; (2) flying the three chartered aircraft to Tel Aviv, where the cargo would be loaded and the flight resumed; or (3) flying the three chartered aircraft to Tel Aviv, loading the cargo, and proceeding directly to Iran "w/o filing until airborne. . . ." (Id.) Everybody involved (including Kimche) believed the first option to be the best. North wrote that "Kimche urges that solution be found to matter this weekend to protect hostages and those who will deliver them." (Id.)

At 6:10 p.m., North had more news for Poindexter. McFarlane had contacted the Foreign Minister at 5:30; he agreed to permit an Israeli aircraft to land. In addition, North reported on the CIA's efforts:

"Dewey [Clarridge] has arranged for a proprietary to work for Secord (Copp). Copp will charter two 707s in the name of LAKE Resources (our Swiss Co.) and have them p/u [pick up] the cargo and deliver it. . . . [T]he cargo will be xfered to the three Israeli chartered DC-8/55s for the flight to T[abriz]. Though I am sure Copp suspects, he does not know that the 707s belong to a proprietary. Clarridge deserves a medal—so does Copp."

"Kimche (DK) has been told how screwed up his people are in planning something like this on such short notice. Not only was the 747 they planned to use a national airlines a/c [aircraft], but they only had it chartered for 14hrs. We have now taken charge of that phase of the operation . . . to ensure flight clearance for the three DC-8s chartered by DK's boys. If all goes as we now hope, the cargo will be [at the staging area] by noon (local) and enroute [sic] to T shortly after dark. That means we can expect handovers (hopefully) Saturday night." (Id. ("UPDATE AS OF 1810"))

North's optimism was a hope. He wrote Poindexter at 7:00 p.m. that Schwimmer had just reported that he had released the DC-8s, despite a call from North to Kimche to keep them on call. "Schwimmer released them to save $ and now does not think that they can be re-chartered before Monday." (Id. ("UPDATE AS OF 1900")) Secord kept the operation alive. He suggested using

"one of our LAKE Resources A/C which was . . . to p/u a load of ammo for UNO. He will have the a/c repainted tonight and put into service nlt [no later than] noon Sat so that we can at least get this thing moving. So help me I have never seen anything so screwed up in my life. Will meet w/ Calero tonite to advise that the ammo will be several days late in arriving. Too bad, this was to be our first direct flight to the resistance field . . . inside Nicaragua. The ammo was already palletized w/ parachutes attached. Maybe we can do it on Weds or Thurs.

"More as it becomes available. One hell of an operation." (Id. ("UPDATE AS OF 1920")) (Footnote: On November 26, McFarlane wrote North that he was "inclined to think that we should bring this operation into the NSC and take Mike [Ledeen] out of it but will await John's [Poindexter] thoughts. No further communications to Mike on this until I have thought it through. Just tell him that I am thinking about it." (McFarlane PROF note to North, 11/26/85, 12:57:29))

Regan recalled that the President had been informed on the margins of his briefings for the Gorbachev meeting to expect that there is going to be a shipment of arms coming through [a third country] missiles, transshipped through Israel into Iran, and the hostages will come out. (Regan 14-15) (Tower)

- In a November memo, North directly links Lake Resources Inc., a Panamanian-registered company, to a plane ferrying arms to the contras. He refers to it as "our Swiss company." The company is also tied to the Iran arms sales. It has a Credit Suisse bank account into which Ghorbanifar and Khashoggi deposit funds from the sales. The company is dissolved on November 10, 1986. (WP 12/14/86 & 1/17/87; NYT 2/15/87)

- The plan went awry again on November 22, when Mr. Schwimmer allowed the lease to expire on the three aircraft they had chartered to take the HAWKs to Tabriz. Mr. Secord was able to provide an aircraft for this leg of the journey, however. The CIA arranged for overflight rights over a third country. (See November 25, 1985 entry.) (Tower)

- On November 22, 1985, LtCol North wrote VADM Poindexter that complications in an arms shipment (via a third country) to Iran required Mr. Secord to divert a plane that he planned to use for a Nicaraguan arms shipment. LtCol North told VADM Poindexter that the plane:

"was at [city deleted] to put up a load of ammo for UNO ... Too bad, this was to be our first direct flight (of ammo) to the resistance field at [x] inside Nicaragua. The ammo was already palletized w/parachutes attached. Maybe we can do it on Weds or Thurs."

LtCol North said he would meet Mr. Calero that evening to advise him "that the ammo will be several days late in arriving." (Tower)

- On November 22, I [Shultz] was told by my staff that the release had slipped again (see November 21, 1985 entry), allegedly to get airspace clearance. ... Also on that day, however, Ambassador Oakley—as these things happen, word kind of drifts around and your staff, which you don't know whether it is right or wrong—Ambassador Oakley reported to us that he had heard from various sources that the hostages would be released that afternoon, in exchange for 120 HAWKs at $250,000 each—worth $30 million in all.

By this time we were back in Washington.

At a discussion in my presence on that day, [Mr. Michael Armacost] stated: "I don't like it, it's terrible."

I indicated my own apprehension. Deputy Secretary Whitehead noted: "We all feel uncomfortable." I replied: "Bud says he's cleared with the President." I regarded it as a $30 million weapons payoff. ... (Shultz, SRB, 28) (Tower)

- Evidence suggests that at least by November 1985, LtCol North had assumed a direct operational role, coordinating logistical arrangements to ship privately purchased arms to the Contras. In a note to Poindexter on November 22, 1985, he described a prospective delivery as "our first direct flight [of ammo] to the resistance field [in] Nicaragua." This shipment was delayed when Mr. Secord was asked to use the aircraft instead to deliver the 18 HAWK missiles to Iran in November, 1985. (Tower)

NOV 22-23 - A plane loaded with eighty HAWK antitank missiles bound for Iran is refused landing clearance by Portugese authorities. According to a White House Iran chronology prepared in November 1986, Israeli officials call McFarlane at the Geneva summit to let him know of the incident. McFarlane then contacts North and tells him to secure CIA help. North in turn gets in touch with CIA official Duane "Dewey Maroni" Clarridge, at one time a member with North of the interagency Core Group on Central America (see August 1981 entry). According to one report, North tells the CIA at the time that the plane is only carrying oil drilling equipment. Clarridge calls Casey in China, then helps arrange another plane and customs clearance for the shipment. It is later reported that the CIA's station chief in Lisbon is told of the actual cargo at the time he is attempting to clear it through customs on the grounds that it is "humanitarian." According to the Senate intelligence committee draft report leaked in January 1987, the CIA sends the plane to Israel to pick up the missiles, but the plane turns out to be too small and instead delivers only eighteen missiles. The shipment is returned the following February, however; various explanations are given later. Iran says it returned the missiles because they were not the "Improved" Hawk variety that had been ordered, but an older model. Tel Aviv claims that Israeli workers "inadvertently" substituted the wrong missiles. The White House blames Israeli arms dealer Yaacov Nimrodi for the mix-up but says it is the U.S. that later demands return of the missiles because the shipment lacked the President's approval. Other sources say that some of the missiles carried the Israeli Star of David insignia, and that this further angered the Iranians. (Meese briefing 11/25/86; WP 12/7/86, 12/27/86, 1/14/87 & 2/12/87; MH 12/7/86 & 12/14/86; PI 11/26/86; WSJ 12/22/86; NYT 12/25/86; Newsweek 12/25/86)

- Subsequent to the flight, no U.S. hostages were released. The Iranians were dissatisfied with the type of HAWK missile they received and believed they had been cheated. The Secretary of State later stated that at that point he had believed the operation had collapsed and expressed relief that it was over. However, in the CIA, planning and support for future missions in support of the NSC operation continued. The CIA official who had responded to North's first request testified that he was responsible for this contingency planning and believed the direction from DDCI McMahon to cease support [see November 25 entry] did not prohibit such efforts. (SSIC 1/29/87)

- A paper entitled "Comments on Ghorbanifar's Polygraph" noted, in part, that . . .

"The test also indicated Ghorbanifar knew ahead of time that the hostages would not be released despite our providing missiles to the Iranians. He deliberately tried to deceive us on this issue both independently and with the collusion of 'B.' " (Tower)

" . . . During one of the breaks in the testing, he commented that the Israelis received $24 million as soon as the shipment was delivered and they are holding all of the funds that the Iranians are requesting be returned. He added that the Israelis told him that they had 'doubled' the cost of the shipment apparently because the Americans were involved. He said the Iranians were very upset about the last shipment and might resort to terrorist activities against U. S. interests. He remarked the Iranians have been refraining from these terrorist activities since the negotiations began." (Tower)

MID-NOV - After McFarlane gave his view of the August/ September TOW shipment to Ledeen, the arms transfers to Iran took on a new dimension. The first Ledeen said he heard of it came in what he described as a "bizarre" call from Ghorbanifar. It was related, "I [Ledeen] subsequently figured out, to the question of this shipment of additional weapons and Ghorbanifar called with a message from the Iranian Prime Minister to the President and asked me if I would transmit this.

"It was a message that said, grosso modo, we have been very patient with you people. We have behaved honorably with you people. We have done everything that we said we would have done, and now you are cheating us and making fun of us and so forth, and would you please do what you said you were going to do." (Ledeen (1) 51-53)

McFarlane being in Geneva with the President for the first Summit Meeting with General Secretary Gorbachev, Ledeen passed this message to Poindexter. It was Ledeen's "first and last" contact with Poindexter on this matter; Poindexter said "I was going to be taken off this matter, that people with more technical understanding or expertise were going to be" on it. (Id. at 53-54)

McFarlane told the Board that the episode mentioned by Ghorbanifar to Ledeen "was the first time that a U.S. government agency became involved in this matter, and it was the CIA." (McFarlane (1) 22) (Tower)

- "As an aside, Ledeen noted they had purposely overcharged the Iranians [for the HAWK missiles] and had used around $200,000 of these funds to support Subject's political contacts inside Iran. Later that same evening, Subject stated he was holding $40 million which the Iranians want returned. . . . " (Chief, NESA, to DCI, n.d.) (Tower)

NOV 23 - On Saturday, John McMahon, Deputy Director of Central Intelligence, is first informed of CIA's support role. In McMahon's view, the Agency was merely providing a secure channel of communications to assist NSC personnel seeking flight clearances for the Israeli flight. According to the evidence available to the Committee, McMahon approved provision of this support, and asked for a full briefing on the next business day. (SSIC 1/29/87)

- An official note from the U.S. Embassy is delivered to the Portuguese Foreign Ministry requesting authorization for the operation discussed by McFarlane the previous day (see entry). The note, which is signed not by Ambassador Frank Shakespeare but by a "U.S. Government official"—presumably the CIA station chief in Lisbon, according to a news report, describes the operation as the shipment of "defense equipment" to Iran on "humanitarian grounds." Pires de Miranda brings the matter to Prime Minister Cavaco Silva, who reportedly rejects the request because the explanations by the U.S. are found to be "insufficient." (Lisbon Expresso 1/31/87)

- On November 23, we heard again that no hostages were out, that the project had collapsed. I said, "It's over." (Shultz, SRB, 28) (Tower)

NOV 25 - When John McMahon, at that time Deputy Director of the CIA, heard that a CIA proprietary was involved in the November operation and that the Agency had asked foreign governments to grant overflight clearances for Israeli aircraft, he asked for a "Finding." Sending cables was one thing; shipments to Iran, whatever their character, was another. (Clarridge 9) In view of the arms embargo and other controls on trade, they smacked of an operation. (McMahon 5; Clarridge 9)

Under section 662 of the Foreign Assistance Act of 1961, as amended, 22 U.S.C. Section 2422, the CIA may not use appropriated funds to conduct operations (other than to obtain "necessary intelligence") in foreign countries "unless and until the President finds that each such operation is important to the national security of the United States. Each such operation shall be considered a significant anticipated intelligence activity [covert operation] for the purpose of section 501 of the National Security Act of 1947." Section 501(b) of the National Security Act of 1947, as amended, 50 U.S.C. Section 413, provides, in part, that, where prior notice of covert actions is not given to the House and Senate intelligence committees, the President "shall fully inform the intelligence committees in a timely fashion of intelligence operations in foreign countries, other than activities intended solely for obtaining necessary intelligence, for which prior notice was not given under subsection (a) and shall provide a statement of the reasons for not giving prior notice." NSDD 159 set forth procedures regarding implementation of these provisions, as well as for review of covert actions.

McMahon wrote on December 7, 1985, that, when he was informed about the CIA's involvement in the November shipment, he "went through the overhead pointing out that there was no way we could become involved in any implementation of this mission without a finding." (McMahon, "Memorandum for the Record," 12/7/85; J. McMahon 6) Juchniewicz first protested that "[w]e didn't do it; they came to us, and we told them we couldn't do it, so they asked us for the name of an airline, and we gave them the name of our proprietary." (J. McMahon 6) He explained that

"[w]hen General Secord visited the Agency he tried to get leads on airlines that might be available to move equipment to the Near East in a secure fashion. We told him we did not have any such airlift capability.

"However, Mr. Juchniewicz said it was pointed out to General Secord that there was a commercial airlift that might do it . . . General Secord then took it from there and made

arrangements for a flight on a strictly commercial basis."
(Memorandum for the Record, supra.)

McMahon nonetheless directed operations officers to brief
Stanley Sporkin, at that time General Counsel for the CIA,
and prepare a Finding. McMahon told Sporkin to draft it to
"cover retroactively the use of the Agency's proprietary." (J.
McMahon 6; Memorandum for the Record, supra) Sporkin
recalled thinking a Finding was prudent, but not required by
law in this instance. (Sporkin 7-8) He included language
ratifying prior acts by the CIA, and McMahon accepted it.
(Id.) (See November 26 entry.) (Tower)

- CIA General Counsel Stanley Sporkin drafts a finding
on future shipments of arms to Iran after Deputy Director
John M. McMahon expresses reservations about the legality
of the Agency's role in the latest delivery. Casey sends the
document to the White House the next day. It is later reported that the draft's intent is mainly to assuage McMahon,
and that Reagan never signs it. (Newsweek 12/25/86; WP
1/6/87)

- Apparently Kimche was given the name of a proprietary
and Israel "subsequently chartered through normal commercial contract for a flight from Tel Aviv to Tabriz, Iran on
November 25, 1985." [From chronology prepared by North,
Poindexter, McFarlane, Earl and Coy (see Nov 5-20, 1986
entry)] (Tower)

- On November 25 the aircraft [see November 22-23,
1985 entry] left a European country. Delivery was three days
late, however, and the aircraft carried only 18 HAWKs.
Contrary to LtCol North's description of this plan, the aircraft delivered the HAWKs before the release of any hostages. In fact, no hostages were ever released as a result of
this delivery.

Not only were just 18 of the initial shipment of HAWKs
delivered, the HAWKs did not meet Iranian military requirements. In addition, they bore Israeli markings. Mr. Ghorbanifar told the Board that this caused great unhappiness in
Iran and had disastrous consequences for the emerging relationship. Ultimately the Iranians returned 17 of the HAWKs
to Israel. The eighteenth had been test-fired at an Iraqi aircraft flying over Kharg Island to determine the missile's effectiveness.

When Deputy Director McMahon learned of the CIA role in the shipment some three or four days after the fact, he directed the CIA General Counsel to prepare a Covert Action Finding (Footnote: Section 662 of the Foreign Assistance Act, the so-called Hughes-Ryan Amendment, prohibits covert operations by the CIA unless and until the President "finds such operation is important to the national security of the United States.") providing Presidential authorization for the CIA's past support and any future support to the Iran initiative. A Finding was drafted and delivered to VADM Poindexter, but the evidence strongly suggests it was never signed by the President. (Tower)

- A senior Directorate of Operations official testified that while CIA had suspicions about the cargo on the November 1985 flight, it was not until . . . discussions with Ghorbanifar in early January that they knew that the aircraft carried arms. Other documentation submitted to the Committee, however, indicates that at least some CIA officials overseas were aware of the nature of the cargo much earlier, and at least one reported this back to headquarters. (SSIC 1/29/87)

NOV 25 or 26 - According to documents received by the Committee, the shipment of 508 TOWs left Israel on August 30, 1985, transited a third country and arrived in Iran on September 13. North later asserted to Meese that he was totally unaware of the TOW shipment at the time it occurred. He believed he first learned of it in a November 25 or 26 conversation with Secord while in Tel Aviv. North also claimed that he did not know who had otherwise been aware of the shipment. McFarlane told Meese that he thought he learned of the shipment from Ledeen. (SSIC 1/29/87)

NOV 26 - This draft finding [see November 25 entry and below] was prepared by Sporkin, approved by the DCI Casey and delivered to Poindexter on November 26. The draft Finding authorized CIA to provide assistance to "private parties" seeking to free American hostages. It also contained language retroactively ratifying all previous activities undertaken by U.S. officials in pursuit of this effort and directed that the Congress not be informed until directed by the President. (SSIC 1/29/87)

- The Committee received testimony that senior CIA officials made repeated calls to NSC staff in late November and early December urging that the draft November 26 Presidential Finding be signed . . . However, the Committee has received no documentary evidence that any finding of November 26 . . . was ever signed. (SSIC 1/29/87)

- Sporkin's draft Finding for the President provided:
"I have been briefed on the efforts being made by private parties to obtain the release of Americans held hostage in the Middle East, and hereby find that the following opeations [sic] in foreign countries (including all support necessary to such operations) are important to the national security of the United States. Because of the extreme sensitivity of these operations, in the exercise of the President's constitutional authorities, I direct the Director of Central Intelligence not to brief the Congress of the United States, as provided for in Section 501 of the National Security Act of 1947, as amended, until such time as I may direct otherwise.

"Description

"The provision of assistance by the Central Intelligence Agency to private parties in their attempt to obtain the release of Americans held hostage in the Middle East. Such assistance is to include the provision of transportation, communications, and other necessary support. As part of these efforts certain foreign material and munitions may be provided to the Government of Iran which is taking steps to facilitate the release of American Hostages.

"All prior actions taken by U.S. Government officials in furtherance of this effort are hereby ratified." (Draft Finding enclosed in Casey to Poindexter, 11/26/85)

After speaking to Poindexter about this draft, the Director of Central Intelligence sent it to him on November 26, confirming that it "should go to the President for his signature and should not be passed around in any hands below our level." (Casey to Poindexter, 11/26/ 85)

Despite some testimony to the contrary, the President appears not to have signed this Finding. McMahon told the Board that his records showed that someons [sic] told him on December 5 that the President had signed. (J. McMahon 7; Memorandum for the Record, supra) Sporkin remembered that "[a]nother person who worked for me told me that at one point he was with Mr. North and Mr. North said: I want to give a message to Sporkin, that I've got a piece of paper that was [s]igned, or some such thing as that." (Sporkin 8)

In November 1986, North told the Attorney General that he never saw this draft. (Meese notes of interview with North, 11/22/86) (Tower)

- "[R]ight after the summit, after I [McFarlane] got back from debriefing the Holy Father and Mitterand and Prime Minister Thatcher, we had some time to look at other things, and I didn't even come to the office. I went directly from London to Washington to California but had two days before the President got there to just kind of think through how things had gone, and they hadn't gone very well.

"The idea originally of us getting in direct communication with Iranian officials hadn't happened, and instead this imperfect demonstration of bona fides [the HAWK missile transfer] had been imperfect, rather dramatically, and had become their priority, with a very clear lack of good faith, I thought. And I said to the President after thinking about it, and I went down to Santa Barbara and we talked, both about my resignation but then about the results of this program. And I believe it occurred in the Century Plaza Hotel on a morning.

"And I said that it seems to me that we ought to try to reorient it to its original purpose, Mr. President, and that is for us to avoid dealing through intermediaries and to talk to Iranians directly, and he agreed with that. And he said convene the NSC—the Secretary of State and Defense—and let's talk it over when we get back. So that is what led me to then do two things—convene a meeting and tentatively ask Admiral Poindexter, I believe, to have a meeting with the Iranian intermediary set up in London." (See December 7 and December 8, 1985 entries.) (Tower)

NOV 27 - Rep. John LeBoutillier (R-NY) is quoted in a news report as saying convicted spy Jonathan Jay Pollard told him he had evidence that the CIA was diverting funds intended for the Afghan rebels to the contras. (NYT 11/27/85 in WP 1/13/87)

NOV 30 - Oregon businessman Richard J. Brenneke writes the first of a series of memos to Administration officials, including Bush, concerning the Demavand project, an effort by Iran to buy over $1 billion of American arms through private individuals. Brenneke, a former employee of the CIA for 13 years, discusses the project, which began in 1983, with various U.S. officials over the next several months. One of them is Lt. Col. George Alvarez of Marine Corps counterintelligence. Brenneke says in one memo that in January 1986, a top Iranian Air Force official, Col. Kiamars Salahshoor, repeated to him the essence of Brenneke's conversations with Alvarez, leading Brenneke to suspect leaks in U.S. intelligence circles. A Defense Department spokesman has suggested instead that Iran may have tapped the unsecured phone lines Brenneke and Alvarez reportedly used. The Brenneke documents come to light in late November 1986 as part of an investigation in New York into the smuggling of arms to Iran by international businessmen (see April 22, 1986 entry). They demonstrate that high U.S. officials were aware as early as December 1985 of large-scale private efforts to sell sophisticated weapons to Iran and, along with evidence compiled by newspaper investigations, point to the willingness of these officials to allow the sales to continue. The officials are reported to have believed that valuable intelligence benefits could accrue from the project, as well as access to advanced Soviet T-80 tanks captured by Iran in the Persian Gulf war and promised by Brenneke. In return, Brenneke insists in this first memo, but drops the demand later, that he and his associate, John DeLaocque [sic], have exclusive rights to act as third party in any upcoming arms deals with Tehran. The memos discuss, among other things, Iranian willingness to intercede with terrorists, to allow renewed U.S. monitoring of Soviet military movements from within Iran and to permit the U.S. to inspect captured Soviet weapons, in exchange for arms. One official response to Brenneke comes in a February 6, 1986, letter from Bush aide LtCol. E. Douglas Menarchik, which states the government's firm stance against the provision of military supplies to Iran. (Brenneke memo to Col. Richard H. Muller, USMC (Reserve), 11/30/85; WP 11/29/86; MH 11/30/86; NYT 2/2/87)

LATE 1985 - Before his departure from the NSC, McFarlane learns of a $20 million Saudi donation to the contras. (NYT 1/13/87)

- On November 30, 1985, Mr. McFarlane resigned as National Security Advisor. VADM Poindexter was named National Security Advisor on December 4. (Tower)

- At the end of November, according to McFarlane's testimony, he obtained the President's approval to go to London on December 8 to meet with Iranian intermediaries. A meeting of principals in the White House was scheduled for December 7 to discuss Iran. (SSIC 1/29/87)

- [Assistant Secretary of Defense Richard] Armitage had lunch with North in late November, after seeing reports that someone in the White House was meeting with Iranians. North acknowledged meeting Iranians in Europe, and Armitage

"said to him, I don't think my boss knows anything about this. I doubt that Secretary of State Shultz knows anything about [this]. I think your ass is way out on a limb and you best get all the elephants together to discuss the issue.

"Ollie was, I think, a little shocked that I was so strong about the necessity of getting everybody together." (Armitage 4-5) (Footnote in Tower Report)

Ambassador Oakley, the Near East and South Asia bureau at the State Department, told the Board that he and Under Secretary of State for Political Affairs Michael Armacost forced an NSPG meeting to be held at this time. (Oakley 4) (Tower)

DECEMBER 1985

DEC - Carl "Spitz" Channell's National Endowment for the Preservation of Liberty transfers $400,000 this month to International Business Communications (IBC), a public affairs and political counseling organization that has signed contracts with the State Department to provide "media consultant services" and to build support for the contras in the U.S. (See April 1 and October 1, 1985 entries). (AP in WP 2/7/87; NYT 2/26/87)

- North meets with contra leader Arturo Cruz and offers to arrange a $7,000 monthly stipend. The payments begin the following January and end suddenly in November, Cruz says, when North is fired from the NSC. (See January listing.) (NYT 2/21/87)

- While the United States was seeking the release of the hostages in this way, it was vigorously pursuing policies that were dramatically opposed to such efforts. The Reagan Administration in particular had come into office declaring a firm stand against terrorism, which it continued to maintain. In December of 1985, the Administration completed a major study under the chairmanship of the Vice President. It resulted in a vigorous reaffirmation of U.S. opposition to terrorism in all its forms and a vow of total war on terrorism whatever its source. The Administration continued to pressure U.S. allies not to sell arms to Iran and not to make concessions to terrorists.

No serious effort was made to reconcile the inconsistency between these policies and the Iran initiative. No effort was made systematically to address the consequences of this inconsistency—the effect on U.S. policy when, as it inevitably would, the Iran initiative became known. The January 7 meeting had earmarks of a meeting held after a decision had already been made. Indeed, a draft Covert Action Finding authorizing the initiative had been signed by the President, though perhaps inadvertently, the previous day. (Tower)

- Southern Air Transport carries out the first of five flights (through May 1986) carrying explosives to Guatemala, Honduras, and El Salvador. News reports describe these flights as part of the contra supply operation. (WSJ 3/6/87)

DEC 1 - McFarlane suggests to the President on December 1 that the negotiations with the Iranians "seemed to be getting skewed towards arms going that way and hostages coming this way. . . . I thought we ought to seek a meeting directly with the Iranians and discontinue any kind of sponsorship of arms transfers." (McFarlane (1) 25) (Tower)

DEC 3 - Samuel Evans, an American citizen resident in London at the firm of Evans and van Merkensteijn, and former general counsel to Saudi billionaire Adnan Khashoggi, acts as broker for the first of a series of meetings among international businessmen discussing the sale of U.S.

military equipment to agents of Iran. French businessman Bernard Veillot makes a specific offer during this week to Iranian arms merchant Cyrus Hashemi, a cousin of the speaker of the Iranian parliament (Hashemi Rafsanjani). Unknown to Evans, Veillot and the other businessmen involved, Hashemi has become a U.S. Customs Service informant and begins a "sting" operation that culminates in April 1986 with the arrests in Bermuda and New York of more than a dozen participants in the deal. Details of the chronology of the sting through April 22, 1986 are listed below. During this week in December 1985, Hashemi claims to be the buying agent for Iran; and Veillot distributes to the group pro forma invoices for 10 new Bell helicopters, 10 reconditioned Bell helicopters, 39 F-4E aircraft, 50 F-104 aircraft, and 10,000 BGM 71A TOW missiles. Also in attendance this week are Bihn, Schneider, Kourentis, Thanos and Kopka. (Court papers, U.S. District Court, New York; WP 1/6/87)

DEC 4 - Reagan announces McFarlane's resignation and names Vice Admiral John M. Poindexter as his successor, effective January. North, the NSC staff member dealing with terrorism, is designated to replace McFarlane on the Iran initiative. It is later disclosed that McFarlane keeps a computer link-up to the NSC at his home for ten months after resigning. (WP 12/7/86 & 1/14/87; NYT 12/25/86 & 2/14/87)

- That same day, LtCol North raised with VADM Poindexter a new proposal for an arms-for-hostages deal. It involved the transfer of 3,300 Israeli TOWs and 50 Israeli HAWKs in exchange for release of all the hostages. The arms were to be delivered in five installments, spread over a 24-hour period. Each installment was to result in the release of one or two hostages, so that in the end all five U.S. citizens held in Beirut and a French hostage would be freed (Footnote: In October, 1985, the United States obtained reliable evidence that William Buckley had died the preceding June.). If any installment did not result in a hostage release, all deliveries would stop. (Tower)

- In an electronic message of December 4, North provided Poindexter with a status report on the [Iran arms] situation. North's message stated that it was based on discussions held in Geneva between Kimche, Secord, Ghorbanifar and the

Iranian contact. The message recounted Iranian unhappiness with the HAWK shipment in late November. It indicated that release of the hostages is tied to a series of arms shipments beginning later in December and that North, Secord, Kimche and Schwimmer were to meet in London on December 7 to go over arrangements for the next shipments. It stated that North had gone over all the plans with the CIA official who had assisted in the November 25 flight. He indicated that the only officials fully informed about the long term goals are McFarlane, Poindexter and North. (SSIC 1/29/87)

- "Given the relatively low level of competence on the part of the Iranians in Europe, and the fact that any supplies delivered will undoubtedly have to be examined by an Army or Air Force officer, it is very doubtful that a 'single transaction' arrangement can be worked out with the parties in Tehran, no matter what is agreed to in Europe. In short, they have been 'scammed' so many times in the past that the attitude of distrust is very high on their part. At the same time, in all discussions (including today's phone calls) they are desperate to conclude some kind of arrangement in the next 10 days and have even asked that the meeting scheduled for Saturday in London be advanced. Based on what we can conclude from intelligence in Beirut, we believe that they are very concerned that the hostages (the only Iranian leverage point besides the Jews in Iran) may be killed or captured/released by the Syrians, Druze, Phalange or Amal in the near future. Waite's contacts with the captors seems [sic] to corroborate this assessment. In short, time is very short for all parties concerned.

"—The total 'package' from the Israelis wd consist of 50 HAWKs w/ PIP (product improvement package) and 3300 basic TOWs.

"—Deliveries wd commence on or about 12 December as follows:

"H-hr: 1 707 w/300 TOWs = 1 AMCIT

"H + 10hrs: 1 707 (same A/C) w/300 TOWs = 1 AMCIT

"H + 16hrs: 1 747 w/50 HAWKs & 400 TOWs = 2 AMCITs

"H + 20hrs: 1 707 w/300 TOWs = 1 AMCIT

"H + 24hrs: 1 747 w/2000 TOWs = French Hostage

"OpSEC concerns are threefold: communications, deliveries enroute to Iran and replenishment of Israeli stocks. To solve the first problem an OPs Code is now in use by all parties. *This code is similar to the one used to oversee deliveries to the Nicaraguan Resistance and has never been compromised.* [emphasis added] The delivery/flight planning security problem has been solved by a much more deliberate selection of aircraft and aircrews as well as a series of transient airfields which can be used enroute to the field controlled by the Iranian Army at Tabriz. Appropriate arrangements have also been made to ensure that the overflight . . . is not challenged. All A/C will be inspected by one of the Iranians at a transient location between Tel Aviv and Tabriz. Before the A/C actually crosses into Iranian airspace, the appropriate release(s) must occur. The last OPSEC concern, that of replenishing Israeli stocks is probably the most delicate issue. The quantity of TOWs requested represents [a significant proportion of] the Israeli PWR [prepositioned war reserves]. Meron and I are working w/ the Israeli purchasing office in NYC to ensure that the replenishment can be accomplished [as] quickly after December 12 as possible. All recognize that quantities such as those being discussed degrade Israeli readiness and that the items will need to be dispatched quickly in order to preclude disaffection and leaks. Meron has solved at least one of the problems in this regard by identifying a means of transferring the required cash to an IDF account which will allow cash (rather than FMS credit) purchases from the U.S.

"In order to put this plan into action, Kimche, Copp, Schwimmer and Goode [North] plan to meet in London on Saturday morning to review all arrangements. If we are satisfied that all our assets (money, aircraft, aircrews, transit facilities, overflight arrangements and military equipment) are prepared, Copp and Kimche will meet at another hotel with Gorba and [an Iranian diplomat] to finalize the plan.

"Once in hand, the hostages will be flown to Larnaca on our Navy HH-53 where they will be picked up by a EUCOM C-141 and flown to Wiesbaden for debriefing. The debrief team will be staged at Wiesbaden 12 hours in advance, just as we did two weeks ago without notariety [sic]. Dewey [Clarridge] is the only other person fully witting of this. . . . The Israelis are in the same position. Dewey and I have been through the whole concept twice looking for holes and can find little that can be done to improve it given the "trust factor" with the Iranians. In that all parties involved have great interest in keeping this as quiet as possible, . . . we beleive [sic] it to be worth the risk. I have not confided in Dewey re the longer term goals we could/ should hope to achieve. Thus, the only parties fully aware of all dimensions of what we are about are you and RCM [McFarlane].

"I have given careful consideration to what you suggested re an RCM meeting with the Iranians in an effort to obtain release of the hostages before starting on an effort to undo the present regieme [sic] in Tehran. Like you and Bud, I find the idea of bartering over the lives of these poor men repugnant. Nonetheless, I believe that we are, at this point, barring unforseen [sic] developments in London or Tel Aviv, too far along with the Iranians to risk turning back now. If we do not at least make one more try at this point, we stand a good chance of condemning some or all to death and a renewed wave of Islamic Jihad terrorism. While the risks of proceeding are significant, the risks of not trying one last time are even greater." (North PROF note to Poindexter, 12/04/85, 02:02:55) (Tower)

- In December, 1985, Congress passed two measures. The first, contained in section 8050 of the Fiscal Year 1986 Defense Appropriation Act, reenacted the Boland prohibition. (Footnote: Section 8050 of P.L. 99-190 provided: None of the funds available to the Central Intelligence Agency, the Department of Defense, or any other agency or entity of the United States involved in intelligence activities may be obligated or expended during fiscal year 1986 to provide funds, material, or other assistance to the Nicaraguan democratic resistance unless in accordance with the terms and conditions specified by section 105 of the Intelligence Authorization Act (Public Law 99-169) for fiscal year 1986.) The second, set out in section 105(a) of the Fiscal Year 1986 Intelligence Authorization Act, authorized classified amounts for communications, communications equipment training and "advice" for the Contras.

The communications and advice provisions introduced substantial uncertainty as to whether any US officials—CIA, DOD or the NSC staff—could advise the Contras on the delivery or distribution of lethal supplies. First, the provisions were so ambiguous that even the drafters debated their meaning. Second, applicable statutory provisions were contained in an annex classified top secret, and developed pursuant to a legislative history likewise classified. Whether such secrecy was warranted, it did not enhance common understanding of the statute.

- In December 1985 Congress approved classified amounts of funds to the contras for "communications" and "advice." The authorization was subject, however, to a classified annex negotiated by the Senate and House Intelligence committees. An exchange of letters, initiated the day the law passed, evidences the extreme difficulty even the chairmen of the two committees had in deciding what the annex permitted or proscribed.

On December 4, 1985, the date the provision passed, Lee Hamilton, Chairman of the House Permanent Select Committee on Intelligence, wrote to CIA Director Casey on the statute:

"[I]ntelligence personnel are not to act as military advisors to the contras. This certainly includes advising them on logistical operations upon which military or paramilitary operations depend for their effectiveness."

David Durenberger, then Chairman of the Senate Select Committee on Intelligence, offered a different view, forwarding CIA Director Casey a copy of his letter to Congressman Hamilton of December 3:

"[A]dvice on logistics activities integral to the effectiveness of particular military and paramilitary operations is precluded if it would amount to participation in such activities, even if there is no physical participation. At the same time . . . the conferees did not mean to place the entire subject of logistics off limits. We certainly would, for example, want to encourage advice on logistics related to the effective distribution of humanitarian and communications assistance."

Congressman Hamilton countered by letter of December 9:

"[T]he Act makes clear direct CIA logistical advice on the effective distribution of humanitarian assistance is not appropriate." (See December 1985 entry.) [Footnote in the Tower Report]

DEC 5 - The NSC reportedly begins a six-week debate on whether to seek a new relationship with Iran. It says limited arms sales to "moderate" Iranians are proposed. (PI 11/26/86)

- Senior CIA officials made repeated calls to NSC staff in late November and early December urging that the draft November 26 Presidential Finding be signed. According to a memorandum for the record prepared by McMahon on December 7, CIA was informed on December 5 that the President had signed the finding and had directed the CIA not to inform Congress for reasons of safety of the hostages. Sporkin testified that one of his assistants had been informed by North that the finding had been signed and was in Poindexter's safe. CIA believed the December 5 finding contained the provision retroactively ratifying previous actions. However, the Committee has received no documentary evidence that any finding of November 26 or December 5 was ever signed. (SSIC 1/29/87)

- In a memorandum, dated December 5, 1985, North provided . . . a different account of the origins of Iran arms transactions. He wrote that "[s]everal months ago" an agent involved in shipping material to the Contras saw U.S. military equipment in a Lisbon warehouse, which inquiries identified as Israeli equipment being shipped to Iran by a private company.

A "high-level Israeli official" explained that the weapons were being sent to Iran in exchange for Iranian Jews, and that because private intermediaries were used, the transaction was not a technical violation of United States arms export control laws. The Israelis hoped the arms sales would enhance "the credibility of moderate elements in the Iranian army" who might become powerful enough to establish a more reasonable Iranian government than presently existed; prevent the collapse of Iran in the war with Iraq; and extricate Jews from Iran.

"In early September, in order that we not take action to terminate the arms sales, the Israelis proposed that this process be used as leverage to recover the American citizens held hostage in Lebanon. It was decided to test the validity of this proposal and on September 14, the Israelis, using chartered aircraft, delivered 500 Tow missiles to Tabriz, Iran. Prior to commencing this operation, we committed to the Israelis that we would sell them replacements for the items they sold and delivered to Iran. Two days later Reverend Benjamin Weir was released." ("Special Project re Iran," 12/5/85) (Tower)

- Poindexter told Secretary Shultz the operation was at a decision point, and that he had set up a meeting for Saturday, December 7. (See entry.) (Shultz, SRB, 29) (Tower)

- North's memorandum briefly summarized the history of the transactions with Iran through Weir's release and then described the current situation.

"(T)ime is running out for the hostages. We are relatively confident of information that former Beirut Chief of Station, Bill Buckley, is dead. These Iranians, the same that arranged the release of Weir, have now proposed that in exchange for an immediate delivery of 3,300 TOW missiles and 50 Improved HAWK Surface-to-Air missiles from Israel, they will guarantee:

"—The release of the five Americans and one of the French hostages still being held.

"—No further acts [of] Shia fundamentalist terrorism (hijackings; bombings, kidnappings) directed against U.S. property or personnel."

"Next Steps: The Iranians, the Israelis, and our U.S. businessman plan to meet in London on Saturday, December 6 to discuss whether or not to proceed with the sale of the TOWs and HAWKs. The Israeli government has informally told us that if they can be assured of 'prompt' resupply, they will sell the quantities requested from their prepositioned war reserve. 3,300 TOWs represents [sic] [a significant proportion] their available supplies.

"The greatest operational security concern is that of replenishing Israeli stocks. The Israelis have identified a means of transferring the Iranian provided funds to an Israeli Defense Force (IDF) account, which will be used for purchasing items not necessarily covered by FMS. They will have to purchase the replenishment items from the U.S. in FMS transaction from U.S. stocks. [sic] Both the number of weapons and the size of the cash transfer could draw attention. If a single transaction is more than $14.9 M, we would normally have to notify Congress. The Israelis are prepared to justify the large quantity and urgency based on damage caused to the equipment in storage.

"If this process achieves the release of the hostages and proves the credibility of the Iranian contacts in Europe, Bud McFarlane would then step in to supervise achieving the longer range goals. Additional meetings with the Iranians would be arranged to further our objectives without requiring such large scale sales/deliveries by the Israelis.

"Approval is now required for us to take the next steps on Saturday. After carefully considering the liabilities inherent in this plan, it would appear that we must make one last try or we will risk condemning some or all of the hostages to death and undergoing a renewed wave of Islamic Jihad terrorism. While the risks of proceeding are significant, the risks of not trying are even greater. ([North], "Special Project Re Iran," 12/5/85) (Tower)

DEC 6 - A full-scale White House meeting on the Iran sales is called at Shultz's insistence. State Department officials have prevailed on him to take advantage of the bungled November missile shipment and McFarlane's resignation to register his objection to the program. It is reported that many officials are discouraged that after three shipments of arms to Iran only one hostage, Benjamin Weir, has been released. There are also reports that both Washington and Jerusalem have lost faith in Schwimmer and Nimrodi. At the meeting, McFarlane, an initiator of the deals, now apparently joins Shultz and Weinberger in recommending an end to them, while Poindexter reportedly remains neutral for the time being. As a result of Shultz's and Weinberger's criticisms, Reagan agrees to halt the arms sales but proposes that efforts to find an opening to Iran continue. McFarlane is then sent to London to relay the message to a high-ranking Iranian whom Israeli middlemen have promised will see him. (See December 7, December 8, 1985 and early 1986 entries.) (Meese briefing 11/25/86; WP 12/7/86 & 1/14/87; Newsweek 12/25/86)

- North had traveled on December 6 to meet Kimche, Secord, and Schwimmer "to review all the arrangements" in connection with the plan North set forth in his note to Poindexter of December 4. (North PROF note to Poindexter, 12/4/85, 02:02:55) (See December 4, 1985 entry.) (Tower)

- Gorbanifahr noted that nine Hizballah leaders had been summoned to Tehran on Friday [December 6] and that, given the pressures inside Lebanon, all it would take for the hostages to be killed would be for Tehran to "stop saying no." . . . (North to McFarlane/Poindexter, 12/9/85) (Tower)

- Spitz Channell's National Endowment for the Preservation of Liberty pays $400,000 to International Business Communications. IBC passes on $300,000 directly to Lake Resources in Switzerland on Dec. 16. (WP 3/7/87)

DEC 7 - North, Secord, Kimche and Schwimmer were to meet in London on December 7 to go over arrangements for the next shipments. (SSIC 1/29/87)

- The premise of the McFarlane December 7 trip had been to try to break the arms/hostage link. (Tower)

- The President met his principal national security advisors on December 7 in his residence. The President, Secretaries of State and Defense, Deputy Director of the CIA (McMahon), McFarlane, Poindexter, and the President's Chief of Staff attended. (Ellen M. Jones, Presidential Diarist, to Jay M. Stephens, 1/24/87 (information from the Presidential Calendar, which apparently is called a Diary) (Tower)

- Most participants who testified before the Committee believed there was a consensus at this discussion that McFarlane would inform the Iranians in London that the U.S. would not trade arms for hostages. Shultz and Weinberger both testified that they left the meeting believing that the arms component of the contacts with elements in Iran was over.

- Reagan meets with Shultz, McFarlane, Poindexter, Weinberger and Deputy CIA Director McMahon. The November arms shipment to Iran is discussed in detail. (WP 2/12/87)

- Poindexter told Secretary Shultz "the operation was at a decision point, and that he had set up a meeting for Saturday, December 7." . . . (Shultz, SRB, 29)
According to notes of the Secretary's side of the conversation taken by the Secretary's Executive Assistant, Poindexter said there would be "[n]o calendar to show it." The Secretary of State "said the operation should be stopped; that I had been informed that Iran was playing a big role in Lebanon which even Syria could not influence. I told him: "We are signalling to Iran that they can kidnap people for profit." (Id.) In the course of this "long phone call," (Id. at 30), in which, according to notes by the Secretary's Executive Assistant, Poindexter gave Secretary Shultz more information

than McFarlane ever had, Poindexter may have made use of a memorandum, dated December 5, 1985, apparently by North (see entry). Poindexter told the Secretary of State "that 3,300 TOWs and 60 HAWKs were being discussed." (Id.) (Tower)

- However, at least one participant, DDCI McMahon, testified that there was no decision or consensus. He testified that the meeting was divided over whether to proceed with the Iran initiative, with White House staff supporting continuation and all others disagreeing. There also is disagreement in the Committee's record about whether McFarlane's meeting with the Iranians in London was discussed at the December 7 meeting, or what specific guidance was approved. Two participants did not recall any discussion of instructions Mcfarlane claimed to have received—to make clear that the U.S. remained open to a political dialogue, but would not exchange arms for hostages. (SSIC 1/29/87)

- Recollections of the meeting vary. In his meeting with the Board on January 26, 1987, the President said he recalled discussing a complex Iranian proposal for weapons delivered by the Israelis in installments prior to the release of the hostages. The President said that Secretary Shultz and Secretary Weinberger objected to the plan, and that this was the first time he "noted down" their opposition. The President said that the discussion at the meeting produced a stalemate.

The Attorney General remembered attending; he did not think McFarlane was present, and thought that Fortier probably attended. (Meese 4) The subject of the meeting—the Iran transactions—was announced in advance, and the principals had time to prepare. (Shultz, SRB, 31; Armitage, 5) According to the Secretary of State,

"Poindexter suggested that Mr. McFarlane could contact the Iranians in London to ask them to release the hostages without getting equipment. If they would do so, we, then, would be prepared for a better relationship with them.

"I fully supported this proposal.

"Vice Admiral Poindexter suggested that Mr. McFarlane should be authorized to ask the British to sell arms to Israel [?Iran] if the Iranians rejected his first proposal. I opposed this idea. I said it was still U.S. arms, that it was a more complicated deal that would make us even more vulnerable. Other views were expressed.

"No decision was made, however, at that meeting, as far as I could see. . . .

". . . I felt in the meeting that there were views opposed, some in favor, and the President didn't really take a position, but he seemed to, he was in favor of this project somehow or other. And, of course, by now he has said publicly that he was in favor of working at the Iranian operation and being willing to sell arms as a signal, as he has now put it." (Shultz, SRB, 31-32)

When the Secretary of State returned to his office, he told his staff that Secretary Weinberger and Regan also strongly opposed the initiative. The Secretary of Defense spoke for thirty minutes. The Secretary told his staff he felt that he perhaps should have barged in earlier and confronted the President. The problem, he felt, was that McFarland [sic] did not tell him the whole story.

The Secretary of Defense had a different recollection of the meeting, which he remembered as taking place in the Oval Office.

"[T]here was a quite specific, more detailed proposal that there had indeed been negotiations and discussions between somebody representing McFarlane's office and some Iranians who were reported to be moderates. I think at that meeting John McMahon was there. I'm not sure. Bill Casey may have been, or they both may have been. But there were some adverse comments passed about the veracity of the Iranians involved, I think Ghorbanifar or some such name, but a more formal presentation was now made by McFarlane about what could be accomplished with this and points with respect to getting a better relationship with Iran as well as hopes that they might have a favorable effect on the release of the hostages.

"Again, I opposed it very strongly and said I thought really it was a terrible idea and that the transfer of arms which was part of the plan which was to be done to establish the good faith of the negotiators—I think I made some comment about what about the good faith of the Iranian negotiators, and why—went through a whole catalogue of things which didn't require any gift of prophecy as to what would happen if this became public. . . . [T]he advice I gave in this case was as firm as I could do it, obviously not persuasive enough but as persuasive as I could do it, that all kinds of very unfortunate effects would result if this took place, that we were pleading with a large number of countries not to do this, that Jordan and Egypt regarded Iran as at least as much of a great Satan as they regarded us, and that it would be a very bad thing in every way to do, and that it wouldn't accomplish anything, and that they would undoubtedly continue to milk us.

"At this time again, the Israeli connection—or the Israeli support of such a transaction I guess is the better way to put it, was advanced by McFarlane. And I said that another of the problems that I thought with it was that doing anything of this kind and attempting to keep it on a clandestine basis would leave us open to blackmail of the very most elementary kind by the people who knew about it, that is, the Israelis and also Iranians, and that any time they weren't getting what they wanted, they could in one way or another, in Mideast fashion, go public with it and cause all kinds of problems with it, that there was no way that I ever felt I could talk with [moderate Arab States] again if we were supplying arms to [a] bitter enemy when we wouldn't supply arms to him et cetera, et cetera, just a whole series of arguments.

"George Shultz made some very strong arguments along the same line . . . A very strong, very persuasive argument. And again, my impression pretty clearly was that the President agreed that this couldn't be done, that it might be a good thing to achieve these objectives but it wouldn't work, and that this was not a good way to do it." (Weinberger 9-12)

Armitage remembered the Secretary of Defense saying that he and Secretary Shultz "thought they had 'strangled the baby in the cradle.'" (Armitage 6)

. . . [McFarlane told the Board in his first interview that at] the meeting "we went through the record of what had occurred since August in terms of Israeli transfers and the absence of meetings, and at consensus, the unanimous view of all of his advisors, the President decided: All right, you go to London, McFarlane, and you meet with the Iranians and make clear that we remain open to the political discourse, and here it is. And there were about four generic areas that we wanted to talk to Iran about, our disagreements and so forth.

"And the second point is that we will not transfer nor encourage any other government to transfer weapons to them." (Id. at 26)

"[McFarlane told the Board at his second interview] a

meeting was convened on December 7 of the NSC, and I would, I believe, have presided because I was still sitting in the chair. What I am saying now is based upon routine and not notes from it. But I always started off by briefing the issue. Here we are today convened to talk about the Iranian program. Here is what has happened since the beginning and here is the return, the benefits and the liabilities of it, and the decision is what should we do or what should we do henceforth—continue as we have, change, or something else.

"And then invite the comments of everybody around the table, usually start with the Secretary of State, then the Secretary of Defense, and around the table, and that would have led to the Director of the CIA, and any one of the other ad hoc members that happened to be present. Usually it was Mr. Regan.

"And it was unanimous in the meeting that this really had gone badly off course and that we should yes, still be open to talking to Iranian officials, authorities, and have a concrete political agenda to describe. And we talked a little bit about that—our view of our interests in the area, how they were threatened by Iran, disagreements we had with them over terrorism and fundamentalists' crusade in the Middle East, and ultimately perhaps even some common interest—Afghanistan and elsewhere.

"But because of how things had gone up until then we ought to also tell them that we were not going to transfer U.S. weapons, sell U.S. weapons. We were not going to allow or encourage anybody else to do so. And I don't recall anybody disagreeing with that at all.

"The President wasn't terribly—didn't intervene in the meeting, as I recall, very much on one side or the other, but at the end said well, okay. That's what you should say. And I left that evening and was in London the next morning, and we took off from there." (McFarlane (2) 45-47) (Tower)

Regan's recollection is somewhat different. He recalled that, although McMahan [sic], for example, was informally dressed,

"[T]he December meeting got to be more formal because McMahon, among others, raised the question of, you know, what the hell are we doing here? Arms are being sent. Where is the formal authority? You know, what are we doing here? Is this going to be policy?

"And as a result of that meeting and people expressing

views which now are commonly known, such as State Department and Defense was opposed to this. CIA was in favor. NSC was in favor. And I must say that I favored it. I won't deny that I favored keeping the channel open, if necessary selling a modest amount of arms, in order to make certain that we were having contacts with Iran and at the same time, if as a result of this they could influence the Hizballah, as they had in the case of Benjamin Weir, why not.

"So I am not certain, but I think I probably also reflect for the most part the President's view on that." (Regan 14-15)

John McMahon, who represented the CIA, recalled that ["][t]here was no decision. We didn't walk away with any marching orders or any decision at that moment." The President asked questions about strengthening moderates in Iran by selling weapons. McMahon "pointed out that we had no knowledge of any moderates in Iran, that most of the moderates had been slaughtered when Khomeini took over." (J. McMahon 11-12) He noted that any weapons sold "would end up in the front, and that would be to the detriment of the Iran-Iraq balance." (Id. at 12) He did not know that McFarlane was about to leave for London. (Id.) (Tower)

DEC 8 - McFarlane testified that prior to meeting the Iranians in London, he and North met Kimche, who urged the U.S. to be more patient and permit the Iranians to demonstrate their bona fides. According to McFarlane, he told Kimche his mission was "to close down" the operation. He and North then met with Kimche, Nimrodi and Ghorbanifar. (See December 8 entry.) (SSIC 1/29/87)

- On December 8, before meeting with Ghorbanifar, and Nimrodi, McFarlane privately reported his instructions to Kimche. Kimche

"was upset and he said: I think you're missing a big opportunity; that you have to have some patience; that these movements take time to consolidate; and these people are delivering to us important items, information basically; and that we see signs from our intelligence that they're making headway and beginning to lock up and arrest radical elements and put their own people in more responsible positions, and the gradual evidence of their growing influence and ability to act.

"And I said: Well, we don't see that; and further, we think

it is being skewed off in the wrong direction. So he said: Well, we disagree.

"And we went ahead and met with this Mr. Ghorbanifar, and in the course of about three hours I covered my instructions. And he said: Well, I understand the political dialogue, and our people in Iran are very much open to that; and so, the point is that you are misunderstanding how much turmoil there is in Iran. There is quite a lot of conflict between the radical and centrist and traditionalist elements there, and it is just not going to succeed in getting my superiors to take much in the way of risk if they don't see that the United States is truly willing to demonstrate the political capital investment to do it.

"And I said: I understand what you say; my instructions are these, and we are not going to transfer any more arms. Well, we had not and did not, but Israel had." The Maximum Version's account of this part of the conversation reads: "Mr. McFarlane made clear that a Western dialogue with Iran would be precluded unless Iran was willing to use its influence to achieve the release of western hostages in Beirut. He also made clear that we could not and would not engage in trading arms for hostages." (Maximum Version at 5)

The Historical Chronology account reads: "At this meeting, Mr. McFarlane, as instructed by the President, stated that:...

"—the U.S. could under no circumstances transfer arms to Iran in exchange for hostages." (Historical Chronology at 7)

On November 23, 1986, North told the Attorney General, W. Bradford Reynolds, Charles J. Cooper, and John Richardson, that McFarlane told Kimche during these meetings that the transaction could not be seen to be an exchange of arms for hostages. (Reynolds notes) (McFarlane (1) 27-28))

In his second interview with the Board, McFarlane provided more detail than in his first:

"Colonel North was already there, and I went alone, and I may have had—I think I was alone, and was met on arrival by Colonel North at Heathrow and we went in to the Hilton Hotel and I asked to get together with Mr. Kimche. And he said well, we will set that up right away, and we did, I believe, within an hour or so in the Hilton that morning.

"And I had known him for a long time and then got right to the point and said that this was well-meaning, well-intentioned, but it hasn't turned out and the President has decided that it has to be reoriented very substantially and my instructions are to say that if they are open to dialogue, we are too, and if not so be it, but under no circumstances are we prepared to sell arms nor to allow anybody else to either.

"And he rejoindered and said he thought that we should have more patience and try to keep this going."

Chairman Tower: So this was in effect going back to the August approval on our part, or the termination of the August approval?

Mr. McFarlane: Yes, sir.

Chairman Tower: I'm sorry to interrupt. Go ahead.

Mr. McFarlane: And Mr. Kimche said that while he could understand why we were disappointed that this was the nature of things in the Middle East and they couldn't always go as hoped, and we ought to keep going with it. And it was irreconcilable, really, and I said I'm sorry, we just—I have my instructions. And he told me the meeting, I think the meeting was for 3:00, I think, 2:00 or 3:00 in the afternoon, and we went on separately to the meeting.

"And at the meeting, which was in a West End London apartment—and I don't know. I've seen reports that it was Mr. Schwimmer's apartment. I don't know that first hand. But at the meeting I met with, from the Israeli side, again Mr. Kimche and Mr. Nimrodi. The only Iranian present, to my knowledge, was Mr. Ghorbanifar. And from the American side myself and Colonel North.

"And it was about a three-hour meeting, as I recall. Colonel North was the notetaker. And I began my brief saying here is our experience or our view of the experience of the past three months or so, and our purposes are these, and they haven't been met, and we think that there has been bad faith on the Iranian side, and it calls into question two fundamentals from our point of view. Number one, is there good faith at all and whether or not there is, is there competence, is there real authority. Can you take decisions and change things?'

"Our conclusions are that we are open to a political dialogue, and I have developed that, to his great dismay, for about an hour. And I said that the President has decided that there can be no sale of U.S. weapons nor will we approve the sale by others of weapons.

"And he replied in a kind of a cursory fashion, accepting that his superiors in Tehran were in fact interested in changing Iranian policy and forming a government with better relations with the West, but that I had to understand that their vulnerability was quite high and that they needed badly to maintain their own support from within the military and that the coin of that relationship and support and strength within Iran was the weapons.

"And I listened to him talk for a half hour or so, and just in observing, as any human being does, to evaluate what kind of person this was, and by this time I had also after the Summit gotten a lot more information about him, but it was mostly from that meeting where it was very apparent that his agenda was buying weapons and his interest in our political agenda very superficial.

"And though he purported or represented that his seniors were interested in that he personally obviously was not conversant with those things and had only a passing interest in them. And after hearing him out I said, well, I understand what you have said. I delivered my instructions. Please convey that to your government. And that's the end of it.

"And I left and went back briefly to the Hilton to pick up some things and went on out to the airplane and took off."

Senator Muskie: Did Ghorbanifar express any concern about the quality of the arms shipment, the HAWKs?

Mr. McFarlane: That seems likely, Mr. Secretary. I think he complained about a lot of things that were foreign to me, but I think probably he did.

Chairman Tower: What kind of representations did he make to you about the people that he was in liaison with in Iran or that he represented? Did he go into the matter of the three lines or factions with you at all in Iran? Or did he talk about one specific faction or group?

Mr. McFarlane: We had received intelligence on the political map of Tehran, so to speak, from two sources. We in the United States had received from the Israelis what they had received from the Iranians, and separately Mr. Ghorbanifar transferred to us his own product of intelligence that described, as you say, these three lines of political affiliation that were, call it, radical-center and conservative.

"But that goes back to August, really, the original product, and in this meeting he did describe that the people with whom he was associated included basically those who were oriented toward a less extreme return to kind of a nonaligned position but normal trade and discourse with the

West and retrenchment on this fundamentalist crusade, and recognized the isolation that it was producing, and did however have within it mullahs, some bazaaris and a substantial number of military leaders and people from outside the government like the bazaaris." (McFarlane (2) 48-53)

Ghorbanifar provided the Board with his version of the December meeting. He said the meeting took place at Nimrodi's London home, with Kimche, Schwimmer, McFarlane, North, and Secord. Ghorbanifar described the meeting as an exchange of "tough" lectures.

"McFarlane gave a lecture that we want to know the importance, strategic point of Iran, we know the people, we know we had bitter relations before, and so on and so on, and we want a better one.

"I said what are you talking about? You just left a mess behind and you want something else? I was tough. I explained, I explained to him that what is the situation inside Iran between the rival groups, between the politicians, what is this mess, what the hell a problem has brought this one, this issue has presented to this big policy. . . .

"I told him what the hell is this, what is the problem, you leave a mess behind, and if you want to continue this way, I said, just is better you cut off and don't put us, the blame on us, and by the fire on your side because then there will be fire back on your interests." (Ghorbanifar 122-123)

Ghorbanifar also remembered Nir saying that Ledeen, Schwimmer, Nimrodi, and Kimche no longer would participate in the negotiations or the transaction. (Id. at 120) (Tower)

- McFarlane meets in London with Kimche and later with Ghorbanifar to pass on Reagan's decision of December 6. He is reportedly disappointed that the high-ranking Iranian he has been promised he will meet is not there. His meeting with Ghorbanifar lasts three hours, McFarlane says. Ghorbanifar tells him "we haven't succeeded" in obtaining release of the hostages. (WP 12/7/86 & 12/27/86; ABC "Nightline" 1/20/87)

- [McFarlane] and North then met with Kimche, Nimrodi and Ghorbanifar, to whom McFarlane made "emphatically" clear that the U.S. would engage in no more arms transfers. According to McFarlane, Ghorbanifar argued strongly for continued U.S. arms transfers, and McFarlane came away convinced the U.S. should not "do business" with Ghorbanifar. (SSIC 1/29/87)

- Mr. McFarlane's message at the London meeting was that, while the United States wanted the U.S. hostages released, and would be interested in better relations with Iran, it was making no offer of arms. According to a memorandum written by LtCol North, Mr. Ghorbanifar refused to transmit this message to his Iranian contacts, reportedly stating that to do so would endanger the lives of the hostages. There appears to be no formal record of the London meeting. (Tower)

- McFarlane testified that when he and Attorney General Meese discussed the legality of an oral Finding November 21, 1986 . . . [he told] Meese that he told Kimche at a December 1985 meeting in London that the U.S. was disturbed about the shipment of TOWs, and could not approve it.
One White House Chronology prepared in November 1986 simply notes that McFarlane conveyed to Kimche a Presidential decision that a dialogue with Iran could be worthwhile. However, a second White House chronology presents conflicting accounts about whether the U.S. acquiesced in the Israeli delivery of 508 TOWs to Iran on August 30. (SSIC 1/29/87)

- Kimche meets North, he claims, for the second and final time. He declares that "at no time . . . was there any discussion about diverting funds to the contras." North has related to congressional investigators that Kimche first introduced the notion to him. (NYT 12/30/86; CBS News 12/31/86)

- McFarlane conveyed these reports [of Israeli arms transfers to Iran in late August and in November, 1985] to the President who directed that we insist on a direct meeting with the Iranian interlocutors while expressing our position against further arms transfers. A meeting was arranged to take place in London in early December. The President instructed McFarlane to represent the US at the meeting and to make two basic points: 1. That the US was open to a political dialogue with Iran; but that no such dialogue could make progress for as long as groups seen as dominated by Iran held US hostages, and 2. That we could under no circumstances transfer arms to Iran in exchange for hostages. These points were made to the Iranian interlocutor. He replied that unless his circle of associates were strengthened they could not risk going ahead with the exchanges. Mr. McFarlane acknowledged the position but stated we could not change our position and returned to Washington. He debriefed the President and appropriate Cabinet officers, recommending that no further action be pursued. He then left the government. (Tower)

- The President also noted on December 9 that Mr. McFarlane had returned from London. He had met with an Iranian agent described as "a devious character." The President noted that the Iranian agent had said that Mr. McFarlane's message would kill the hostages. (Tower)

- Sam Nesley Hall, later arrested for espionage in Nicaragua, claims he is "told" he has been "chosen" to head a covert paramilitary group named the Phoenix Battalion, and is given $12,500 to start. (WP 12/23/86)

- North returns from London on December 8. (Tower)

DEC 9 - In a memorandum of December 9, 1985 the day before McFarlane reported on his trip, North summarized the options on the Iran program to Poindexter. North wrote that Ghorbanifar was a reliable interlocutor. He noted that the U.S. should gain operational control to avoid past problems experienced with Schwimmer. He then posed five options: (1) allow the Israeli shipment of TOWs to go forward, with U.S. replenishment; (2) attempt to rescue the hostages; (3) allow Israel to make only a token shipment of TOWs as a sign of good faith; (4) do nothing; (5) issue a covert action finding and make arms deliveries ourselves through Secord. North indicated that there was little to lose by allowing Israel to go ahead with the delivery of TOWs. (See entry below for text.) (SSIC 1/29/87) The December 9 memorandum raises at least a question as to whether LtCol North, who accompanied Mr. McFarlane to the London meeting, fully supported the thrust of McFarlane's instructions in his own conversations in London with Mr. Ghorbanifar and others. (Tower)

- Phone monitoring of the Evans/Veillot/Hashemi group begins, pursuant to Hashemi's informing the Customs Service of the impending deal. Evans, Veillot, and John Delaroque (mentioned as a partner by Richard Brenneke in a November 30, 1985 memo, see entry) discuss potential sales of F-104 aircraft, F-4 aircraft, TOW missiles, and Bell helicopters to Hashemi and Iran for $900 million. (Court papers, U.S. District Court, New York)

DEC 10 - Mr. McFarlane reported the results of his trip directly to the President at a meeting held in the Oval Office on December 10. Once again, no analytical paper was distributed in advance, no minutes were kept, and no formal Presidential decision resulted. The President, Secretary Weinberger, Director Casey, Chief of Staff Regan, and VADM Poindexter were present. Secretary Weinberger has no recollection of the meeting though Mr. McFarlane recalled that the Secretary asserted his opposition to the operation. Secretary Shultz was in Europe, but his staff reported to him on the meeting apparently after talking to VADM Poindexter.
Mr. McFarlane reported that an impasse in the talks developed when he refused to discuss the transfer of arms to Iran. Mr. McFarlane also told the Board he recommended against any further dealings with Mr. Ghorbanifar or these arms transfers and left government thinking the initiative had been discontinued. (Tower)

- According to Casey's written account of that meeting, McFarlane recommended that the U.S. not pursue a relationship with the Iranians through Ghorbanifar, of whom he did not have a good impression, but that we should work through others. Casey's memo said that "everyone" supported this idea, though it stated that the President "argued mildly" for letting the Israelis go ahead without any U.S. commitment except to replace arms they might ship. The memo indicated the President was concerned for the fate of the hostages if we stopped the discussions, and stated that Casey told the President that the contacts could be justified later as trying to influence events in Iran. (SSIC 1/29/87)

- Mr. Regan told the Board that at the meeting the President said the United States should try something else or abandon the whole project. Mr. Regan also said that the President noted that it would be another Christmas with hostages still in Beirut, and that he [the President] was looking powerless and inept because he was unable to do anything to get the hostages out. (Tower)

- On his way to the NATO Ministerial Meeting in Brussels, the Secretary of State received a report of the meeting:

"White House meeting this morning. The turn-off is complete (we think). McFarlane turned down in London. Ollie did paper saying this means hostages will die." (Shultz, SRB, 34)

The President told the Board on January 26, 1987, that McFarlane expressed no confidence in the Iranian intermediary he met in London (Ghorbanifar). The President said McFarlane recommended rejection of the latest Iranian plan. (This appears to be the plan discussed at the meeting on December 7, 1985.) The President said he agreed. "I had to." In a memorandum, dated December 10, 1985, the Director of Central Intelligence noted that McFarlane

"did not have a good impression of Gorbanifehr [sic] and recommended that we not pursue the proposed relationship with him. He recommended that we pursue the relationship with others representing the moderate forces in the Iranian government, talking and listening to them on a purely intelligence basis but being alert to any action that might influence events in Iran.

"2. Everybody supported this in our roundtable discussion. Other options which Bud had suggested were to let the Israelis go ahead doing what they would probably do anyway, and hope we get some benefit, or to mount a rescue effort. The President argued mildly for letting the operation go ahead without any commitments from us except that we should ultimately fill up the Israeli pipeline in any event, or the Congress will do it for us. He was afraid that terminating the ongoing discussions, as Bud had speculated they might, could lead to early action against the hostages. The trend of the succession of this was that it was a little disingenuous and would still bear the onus of having traded with the captors and provide an incentive for them to do some more kidnapping, which was the main burden of the argument against going forward on the program. The President felt that any ongoing contact would be justified and any charges that might be made later could be met and justified as an effort to influence future events in Iran. I did point out that there was historical precedent for this and that was always the rationale the Israelis had given us for their providing arms to Iran. . . .

"4. As the meeting broke up, I had the idea that the President had not entirely given up on encouraging the Israelis to carry on with the Iranians. I suspect he would be willing to run the risk and take the heat in the future if this will lead to

springing the hostages. It appears that Bud has the action."
(Casey to DDCI, 12/10/85)

In his first interview with the Board, McFarlane remembered that the meeting occurred on December 11, and that the Vice President and John McMahon (for the Director of Central Intelligence) attended.

"I debriefed that I had carried out my instructions and came home. But I added, I said: Whatever may be the case in Iran, this fellow is a person of no integrity and I would not do any more business with him, the Iranian Ghorbanifar. And I left the government believing that it was discontinued." (McFarlane (1) 28)

In his second interview, McFarlane added:

"I believe, unlike the preparatory meeting on the seventh, this time Mr. Casey was there but the Secretary of State was not. And Mr. Regan and the Secretary of Defense I recall specifically sitting opposite me in the Oval Office. And it was a short meeting, I think probably fifteen or twenty minutes, and I stated basically that I had carried out the instructions, that I had made the two points, and went through the specific content of our political agenda that we were prepared to talk about, and the second point on the unwillingness from our side to sell arms or authorize anybody else to do so, and that they acknowledged that they were prepared for this political dialogue but that it was unrealistic to assume that it could occur or make any headway without weapons, and that at that impasse the talks were broken off.

"And then separately I provided kind of a commentary on my evaluation of Mr. Ghorbanifar, which was that he was not a trustworthy person and had a very different agenda from our own and was an unsatisfactory intermediary. And finally I believe I also said that it is conceivable some day that our original point, the political dialogue, they may come back to you on. I doubt it, but I recommend that you have nothing further to do with this person nor with these arms transfers.

"And the President was rather pensive. At that point the Secretary of Defense kind of assertively made the point. He said, I agree with Bud that this program is a very ill-advised program and that we should have nothing further to do with it, and the President was still kind of reflective, nodding but not saying anything, as I recall it. I think Mr. Casey was essentially passive but listening and said well, so be it or something accepting that kind of emerging consensus. And that was the end of it. . . . "

General Scowcroft: In other words, you think what you said is let's stop this program and if the dialogue is going to come maybe they will get back to us, but clear termination of the program?

Mr. McFarlane: Yes, it is, General, and I say that not only because I believe that was my reaction to the three months' experience of it but because as a practical matter I was leaving the government and I had real misgivings about this thing going on at all afterwards.

General Scowcroft: Do you remember Ollie North saying to you or writing a memo or anything saying this means the hostages will die?

Mr. McFarlane: No, I don't.

Senator Muskie: Or Ghorbanifar?

Mr. McFarlane: I hadn't thought about that, Mr. Secretary, although he was given to extravagant kinds of things. It wouldn't surprise me if he said that. . . .

"[The President] was, however, of a mood that was not uncommon when he was uncomfortable with the situation, when in this case everyone else in the room seemed to be of one view and he didn't want to oppose that view. I don't recall his having been emphatic about an opposing point of view.

"The President was always very hopeful, optimistic and on almost every issue, and I think on this one on that day, was disappointed that he hadn't turned out so far, but always looking for the bright side or the possibility that it could be salvaged. But concretely did he say anything by way of decision? I don't believe so.

"And I drew my conclusion that well, Mr. Regan did say he agreed that it ought to be closed out, as I recall. . . .

"I would characterize it as a recommendation on my part that there should be nothing more to do with this person, Ghorbanifar, that there be no further arms shipped whatsoever by anyone, that in my judgment that would lead to a complete discontinuation of any exchanges, finally that I could imagine someday they might come back and say all right, without any arms involved we are open to your political agenda, but that concretely don't do business with that person and don't sell any arms."

Chairman Tower: Well, was the suggestion that if there

was to be a reopening of this that it would come from them?

Mr. McFarlane: "That's right." (McFarlane (2) 55-58)

Regan recalled that,

"right after [McFarlane's] return there was a meeting with the President, and I believe Shultz, Weinberger and Casey were present, to discuss what further should be done. Bud led me to believe that this contact, while it wasn't as good as they had hoped and that it wasn't as productive a contact as they had hoped, and we weren't getting any hostages out, we weren't really meeting with the top side of the Iranian government. And, accordingly, something different had to be tried. . . .

"The NSC were trying to make contacts through Ghorbanifar directly to a higher level within Iran. They were trying to establish better relations than just the people with whom they were meeting in Europe. This is one of the things that McFarlane brought back from his meeting. . . . [Despite his negative impression of Ghorbanifar, McFarlane stated] that we could and should make contacts at a different level, at a better level than Ghorbanifar. . . .

"[T]he President urged that, as a matter of fact, that we try something else or abandon the whole project, because he wanted to keep it open not only for geopolitical reasons but also the fact that we weren't getting anywhere in getting more hostages out. And we were going to spend another Christmas with hostages there, and he is looking powerless and inept as President because he's unable to do anything to get the hostages out." (Regan 15, 31-32, 17)

Weinberger did not remember this meeting. (Weinberger 14) (Tower)

- Casey describes military sales to Iran as a trade of arms for hostages in a memo written around this time. According to a high ranking government official, Casey declares that, should the arms sale become public, Reagan is prepared to portray it as a political opening to Iran. (NYT 12/24/86)

DEC 15 - Defex-Portugal receives clearance to ship another installment of arms from Portugal to Guatemala. The weapons are intended for the contras. Defex is the middleman for Energy Resources International, a company with links to Richard Secord. (WP 1/17/87)

DEC 16 - The Lake Resources bank account in Switzerland receives $300,000 from International Business Communications. (WP 3/7/87)

MID-DEC - Until mid-December, a series of messages relating to possible future missions [to transfer arms to Iran] was exchanged between CIA headquarters and U.S. posts in various European and Middle Eastern countries. Documents received by the Committee indicate that a variety of government officials, liaisons and other sources were involved during this time. (SSIC 1/29/87)

- Udall Research turns over to the Costa Rican government the 7,000-foot airstrip it built in that country in mid-month. The strip has been part of an air supply network for the contras under the supervision of Corporate Air Services, the company for whom Eugene Hasenfus claims to be working when his C-123K cargo plane is shot down over Nicaragua on October 5, 1986. The CIA station chief in Costa Rica apparently played a role in the building of the strip. Working closely with Ambassador Lewis Tambs, the CIA officer pressured the Costa Rican government to allow the facility to be built, and was deeply involved in overseeing its use. Tambs and other embassy officials reportedly maintained close contact with the private supply network set up by North. Tambs unexpectedly announces his retirement, effective January 1987, shortly after the Iran-contra affair becomes public. Udall Research is reported closely tied to other companies that held secret Swiss bank accounts funneling profits from the Iran arms sales in the covert contra supply operation. A man calling himself Gadd reportedly supervised construction of the strip. A retired U.S. Air Force lieutenant colonel, Richard Gadd, later assumes direction of the covert supply operation (see January 1986 entry), and reportedly has links to Corporate Air's president, Edward de Garay. (CBS News 12/11/86; MH 12/13/86; WP 12/14/86; WSJ 1/15/87; NYT 12/26/86)

DEC - Reagan holds a series of meetings with the families of American hostages, attended by North and other White House aides, to tell them that attempts to free the hostages by Christmas have failed. After the emotional meetings, the President orders Regan and Poindexter to redouble efforts to gain their release. Poindexter, with Regan's and Casey's support, directs North to contact Amiram Nir, an Israeli counterterrorism expert who earlier assisted Bush's task force on terrorism. Israeli officials say Nir persuades Prime Minister Peres to assign him to the task, replacing other Israeli middlemen including Yaacov Nimrodi. Then, in

Nimrodi's words: "The starling Nir went to the raven North and told him, in the American phrase, 'Whatever they can do we can do better.'" (WSJ 12/22/86; NYT 1/12/87)

- A computer printout labeled "NEPL Contributions 1985" shows that one wealthy widow provided more than half of the total budget for the National Endowment for the Preservation of Liberty in 1985. Barbara Newington of Greenwich, Connecticut gave NEPL $1,735,578 (in a total budget of $3,360,990) in this year; the next largest contributor, Fred Sacher, gave $305,750. (NEPL Contributions 1985 printout)

DEC 18 - Richard J. Brenneke, a former CIA employee, is contacted by an agent from the CIA's Los Angeles office concerning the large-scale private effort to sell arms to Iran known as the Demavand project. Beginning in November, Brenneke writes a series of memos to Administration officials about the project, which the Pentagon allows to proceed in hopes of gaining intelligence on Iran and Soviet weapons from the Gulf war. (NYT 2/2/87)

DEC 19 - The Director of Central Intelligence meets Ledeen on December 19. (Tower)

LATE DEC - [A]s a result of Ledeen's activities, the question of Ghorbanifar's bona fides as an intermediary arose again. Ledeen testified that, at Ghorbanifar's request, they met during a private trip by Ledeen to Europe. At this time, Ghorbanifar again provided information on developments in Iran and complained about his treatment by the CIA.

According to Ledeen, when he returned to the United States in late December 1985, he briefed DCI Casey and other CIA officials about his conversations with Ghorbanifar. He said he stressed to them that Ghorbanifar was a useful channel in gaining a political opening to elements in Iran, and that with proper precautions we should keep working with him. Subsequent to this discussion, Casey asked him to arrange for Ghorbanifar to submit to a CIA polygraph. Ledeen contacted Ghorbanifar abroad and obtained his agreement to the polygraph which was administered in mid January. (SSIC 1/29/87)

- Poindexter orally approves the sale of 10,000 TOW missiles to Iran by a private company, according to a memo by Oregon businessman Richard Brenneke dated January 1, 1986. The figure is five times that given by the Administration. (Brenneke memo to Col. Richard H. Muller, USMC (Reserve), 1/1/86; WP 11/29/86)

- Poindexter tells two key aides, Ken deGraffenried, director of intelligence programs, and NSC senior director Rodney B. McDaniel that he and North would be handling the "Iran account." He directs deGraffenried not to become involved in anything North might be doing in the Middle East. Such freezing out of key officials later hampers the investigation of the Iran arms deals. (WP 2/16/87)

- Amiram Nir visits Washington after being contacted by North on Poindexter's instructions. He tells U.S. officials the Iranians have promised to free all hostages in exchange for more arms. (The Wall Street Journal says Nir's visit comes in January.) It is reported later that, after a meeting with Israeli officials in December, Poindexter briefs Reagan on the necessity of arms sales to Iran. He apparently persuades the President in January to resume the shipments. (WSJ 12/22/86; NYT 12/25/86 & 1/12/87)

DEC 22 - Allen gave the NSC staff a copy of an August 1984 CIA "burn notice" on Ghorbanifar to the effect that he was a fabricator whose information should not be trusted. (CIA/IG Report 19) (Tower)

- According to the CIA's report of the meeting Ledeen met this official [the Chief of the CIA's Iran desk] alone, and reviewed his relationship with Ghorbanifar.

"He said about a year ago, he (Ledeen) had gone to the former National Security Advisor Robert McFarlane to discuss the need for an Iran policy. Ledeen suggested to McFarlane that he be authorized to contact the Israeli Government to see what could be done in conjunction with them. McFarlane authorized this contact and shortly thereafter Ledeen met Prime Minister Peres. Ledeen added that Peres was very enthusiastic about working with Ledeen and the U.S. Government on the Iranian problem and told him about their contact with Subject [Ghorbanifar]. Two Israeli officials, David Kimche and Jacob Nimradi [sic], introduced Ledeen to Subject. Since then, he has seen Subject 20-30 times, often in conjunction with Kimche and Nimrodi. It was from this contact that the operation developed to have the Israelis at our behest deliver to Iran 500 Tow [sic] missiles and, more recently, 18 Hawk missiles in exchange for the release of all the hostages held in Lebanon. Ledeen is convinced that the release of Reverend Weir was tied directly to the first shipment of missiles. Ledeen went on to say, however, that he never really expected the Iranians to deliver all the hostages given the "Iranian's merchant mentality."

"—The delivery of the Hawk missiles has been an operational nightmare. There was a misunderstanding about the type of missiles the Iranians were seeking. They wanted a missile that could hit a target at seventy-thousand feet and already had Hawk missiles in their arsenal. What they thought they were going to get was a modified and advanced version of the Hawk. They are quite angry about the delivery of the missiles and have asked that they be removed from Iran as soon as possible. Their presence in Iran is politically troublesome to the Iranian hierarchy. They are now asking for Hercules or Phoenix missiles.

"—Ledeen stated that at a recent high-level meeting which included the President, Secretary of State Shultz [sic] and Defense Secretary Weinberger a decision was made not to proceed with Ghorbanifar in an effort to release the hostages. Shultz and Weinberger reportedly were quite unhappy about this operation.

"—As an aside, Ledeen noted they had purposely overcharged the Iranians and had used around $200,000 of these funds to support Subject's political contacts inside Iran. Later that same evening, Subject stated he was holding $40 million which the Iranians want returned.

"—Ledeen is a fan of Subject and describes him as a 'wonderful man. . . . [sic] almost too good to be true.' He had asked Subject to come to the U.S. to meet with us in order to straighten out his credibility and to find a way to keep the relationship going with him. The number one item in this latter area is his proposed Libyan operation. Ledeen said that when he learned of our Burn Notice on Subject, he contacted him in an effort to have him explain situation (see Attachment A). He commented that Subject admitted lying to us, saying he could not reveal his source nor explain his relationship with senior Iranian officials. He felt we would not understand his relationship with the Iranian government. We suggested that perhaps a new polygraph would be useful given these latest revelations. He agreed to a polygraph to be conducted in the Hqs area on 6 January.

"—In closing out this session, Ledeen made the point that any serious covert action operations directed against Iran using Ghorbanifar should be run out of the White House not CIA because it will leak from Congress." (Chief, NESA, to DCI, n.d.)

The meeting continued at 9 p.m. at Ledeen's house, with Ghorbanifar. Ghorbanifar discussed a three-man "Iranian hit team," operating in Europe with instructions to assassinate a number of Iranian ex-patriots. [sic] (Tower)

- According to the NSC "Chronology of Events: U.S.-Iran Dialogue," dated 11/20/86, Ghorbanifar came to the United States on December 22 for meetings with American officials. This date is consistent with a suggestion in a memorandum from the Chief of the CIA's Near East Directorate to the Director of Central Intelligence. Ghorbanifar told the Board only that he visited Washington in December 1985. (Ghorbanifar 127) (Tower) Ghorbanifar's visit was one of a number of meetings and conversations in December 1985 about which little is known. Early in the month, Ledeen told Clarridge and Charles Allen that he had important intelligence about Iranian-backed terrorism in Western Europe. He provided Ghorbanifar's name and telephone numbers to Allen, and said he had McFarlane's approval to pursue the matter. He told Allen Kimche was involved. (C. Allen 10; CIA/IG Chronology 11) (Tower)

DEC 23 - Ghorbanifar again met the CIA official [The Chief of the Iran desk], and named his source about the assassins. This name provoked the comment:

"This is the same source who provided the false information last March concerning an alleged Iranian plan to assassinate Presidential candidates which did not hold up during subject's polygraph. . . .

"(Comment: Subject's reporting on this team [Iranian hit team] is very reminiscent of his previous terrorist reporting which, after investigation and polygraph, turned out to be fabricated. It is our feeling there are bits of valid information in Subject's reporting but he has embellished and projected his own feelings in presenting this information as hard fact. This has been a presistant [sic] problem throughout the four years we have known him. His reporting has sometimes been useful but it is extremely difficult to separate the good from the bad information. It is hard to find in the file any instance where his reporting in fact resulted in a solid development.)" (Id.)

The Chief of the Near East Division in CIA's Operations

Directorate later said of him: "This is a guy who lies with zest." (C/NE (1) 48)

Ghorbanifar used the rest of the interview to discuss Iranian politics—he described political groupings as "Lines." He also provided information on Islamic Jihad, which preliminarily did not appear useful to the CIA, and his relations with Iranian leaders, especially an official in the Prime Minister's office.

"—Subject said that because of the negotiations concerning the exchange of the hostages for missiles, there has not been a terrorist act directed against the USG since July. He implied that this might change now that the negotiations have broken off."

Ghorbanifar, supported by Ledeen, then proposed a "sting" operation against Qadhafi—accepting $10 million to stage the disappearance of the Libyan opposition leader, al Mugarief.

Ghorbanifar planned to travel to London on December 24; he agreed to return for a polygraph test on January 5 or 6. The interview ended when, at 11 p.m., North "dropped by to say hello to Subject and to talk with him about the problem of retrieving the missiles from Iran. We departed at 2400 hours and it was arranged to get together on the afternoon of 23 December to discuss further some of his ideas." (Chief, NESA, to DCI, n.d.)

On December 23, North met Ledeen at the Madison Hotel at 2:30 p.m. (North calendar), where Ghorbanifar was staying under the alias Nicholas Kralis. (Chief, NESA, to DCI, n.d.)

At 3:45 p.m. on the 23rd, North met Secord at the Hay Adams Hotel. (North calendar)

Also on December 23, the Director of Central Intelligence sent the President a memorandum, including as the fifth paragraph:

"The Iranian Gorbanifar [sic], who the NSC staff believes arranged to release Weir, turned up in Washington over the weekend. Ollie North put him in touch with us. He has 3 or 4 scenarios he would like to play out. He gave us information about 3 Iranians going into Hamburg as a hit team. We have verified their movement but not their purpose. It could be a deception to impress us. It is necessary to be careful in talking with Gorbanifar. Still, when our man talked to him on Saturday and asked him if he would take another polygraph he said he would. We think this is worth doing for what we might learn. We want to prepare thoroughly for polygraphing him and because he is going to Switzerland for Christmas, it is understood that he will return here in a week or so for further discussions and for a polygraph." (Casey to President, 12/23/86) (See January 11, 1986 entry.)

Finally, Charles Allen told the Board that he understood that Nir came to Washington in December, and North briefed him on December 23 "on this initiative"—that is, on the program in light of McFarlane's meetings in London. (C. Allen 53) (See December 8, 1985 entry.) (Tower)

DEC 24 - Ghorbanifar planned to travel to London on December 24. . . . (Chief, NESA, to DCI, n.d.) (Tower)

- On December 24, North met Gen. Uri Simhoni and Col. Moshe Zur (North calendar), whom his secretary described to Allen and Bernard Makowka as "Israeli intelligence." (CIA/IG Chronology 12) (Tower)

DEC 26 - A press report links the contras to drug trafficking. The article states that according to U.S. law enforcement officials and volunteers in Nicaragua, "the smuggling operation included refueling planes at clandestine airstrips and helping transport cocaine to other Costa Rican points for shipment to the U.S." The article also makes reference to a CIA intelligence estimate prepared on drug trafficking which alleges that one of the top commanders of the contra group "ARDE," loyal to ARDE leader Pastora, used cocaine profits to finance a $250,000 arms shipment and a helicopter. (WP 12/26/85)

DEC 27 - Terrorists bomb airports in Rome and Vienna, killing 20 people, five of them Americans. The NSC's Crisis Pre-planning Group immediately puts together contingency plans to retaliate against Libya, which some U.S. officials assert played a major role in the attacks. It is later reported that the only connection is that three Tunisian passports used by the terrorists in Vienna were traced to Libya. A news report later says that a CIA analysis concludes, as does Israel, that the attacks appeared to be the work of a Palestinian faction led by Abu Nidal. The same report says that plans for military operations against Libya are set aside following Defense Department objections. Planning for strikes against Khaddafi continues, however. (WP 2/20/87; NYT 2/22/87)

DEC 31 - Exiled Iranian Cyrus Hashemi, participant in a U.S. Customs Service sting operation, tells French business-man Bernard Veillot that official U.S. approval for the pri-vate $2 billion sale of arms to Iran is "going to be signed by Mr. Bush and [U.S. Marine Corps Commandant] Gen. Kelly on Friday." (MH 11/30/86)

- By the end of 1985, American National Management Corp. (ANMC), the company owned by Richard Gadd and affiliated with Richard Secord, reports gross assets of over $1 million. Much of its work involves support for classified military special operations. (WSJ 2/13/87)

JANUARY 1986

- North is reported to have kept large amounts of cash in an office safe at the NSC on behalf of the contras at a time when Congress had banned aid to the rebels. He apparently boasted at one time that he had $1 million on hand, adding fuel to reports that as a specialist in covert operations he routinely handled large sums, sometimes without clear ac-counting. (LAT in MH 1/8/87)

- The U.S. is reported to have provided both Iran and Iraq with disinformation in recent years. Intelligence sources say that the disinformation included distorted data given to Iran concerning the size of Soviet troop buildups on their border, and altered or incomplete satellite photographs to Iraq. The officials say the motive for the Administration's actions, which often conflicted with each other and with U.S. diplo-matic goals in the region, was to prevent either side in the Iran-Iraq war from prevailing in that conflict. The officials added that the Administration's actions reflected the thinking of Casey, Poindexter and the late Donald R. Fortier, who was a senior NSC deputy until last year, and that planning took place largely without consultation with government regional experts. (NYT 1/12/87)

- Casey sends Ben Wickham Jr., the former CIA station chief in Managua from 1982-84, to assist in directing the private contra aid network. (WSJ 4/2/87; LAT 4/3/87)

JAN - Contra leader Arturo Cruz receives his first $7,000 monthly allowance from North, electronically transferred to one of his three private bank accounts. North told him at a meeting last December that it would come from "a private foreign source." The payments end in November when North is fired from the NSC. Federal investigators and the independent counsel, Lawrence Walsh, eventually take up the issue of where the funds originated. It is reported that the true source may have been a Swiss bank account used by North for profits from the Iran arms sales. (NYT 2/21/87)

- Spitz Channell's National Endowment for the Preservation of Liberty budgets $2 million for January through March 15, 1986, for an advertising campaign and media/speaking tours under its Central American Freedom Program. The budget and project description explicitly describes its objective as winning the Congressional vote on aid to the Contras: "Target democrat swing votes in the house (63 total, 36 are in just eight states)." The budget and project description also states, "We have hired two democrat lobbyists, PRODEMCA and Bruce Cameron, formally [sic] of Americans for Democratic Action who was fired due to his support for the Freedom Fighters." (Central American Freedom Program Budget, NEPL, undated but references "January through March 15")

- Richard Gadd, a retired U.S. Air Force lieutenant colonel, and his assistant, John Cupp, take charge of the covert resupply program, according to sources who participate in the operation. Gadd heads a firm named Airmach Inc. (military sources say he runs a small company called American National Management Corp.), which receives more than $100,000 in State Department contracts, reportedly to transport nonlethal aid to Central America. However, Gadd's specialty is chartering commercial aircraft for the Pentagon and CIA in a way that cannot be traced to the U.S. government. He reportedly used this so-called "black" airlift method to transfer helicopters to Barbados before the invasion of Grenada, and appears now to be engaged in identical activities relating to the contras. Gadd's company hires Southern Air Transport, apparently to ship the nonlethal aid. But the company is also involved in the covert resupply operation. Department of Transportation records show Southern Air making one trip to Ilopango air base in El Salvador this month. (DOT Records; NYT 12/4/86; WP 12/7/86; CBS News 12/11/86)

- The intergovernmental "Operations Sub-Group" (OSG) is established to provide a regular forum within the Administration to coordinate counterterrorist activities. Oliver North and Robert Oakley of the State Department initially cochair the group. Oakley is eventually replaced by L. Paul Bremer, also from State. In addition, members include representatives of the Joint Chiefs, Pentagon, FBI and CIA. Richard Armitage of the Defense Department and the FBI's Oliver B. (Buck) Revell serve for a time. The OSG, among other things, develops the Administration's escalating response to Libyan terrorism, beginning with economic sanctions and culminating with the April 14 bombing raid. Of the several classified actions the group takes in the coming months, a number reportedly involve the Pentagon's covert Intelligence Support Activity (ISA) which was created in 1980 to take part in the Iran hostage rescue attempt. Despite bad publicity in 1982 over lack of oversight and mishandling of some of its $10 million budget, the ISA continues to function throughout 1986. (WP 2/17/87 & 2/20/87)

JAN 1 - Richard Brenneke, an ex-CIA employee, writes a second memo to the Pentagon regarding the Demavand project to sell large amounts of arms to Iran. The document repeats his request for legal authorization to pursue arms sales to Iran for himself and his associate, John DeLaocque (sic). He also updates the Iranians' requests for weapons and their offers to release hostages and deliver a Soviet T-80 tank as part of the exchange. He says that the Iranian government has deposited $1 billion with Chemical Bank in New York under the account of Galaxie Trade Co. (he is unsure of the spelling), account #009089985. He asks on behalf of DeLaocque for verification that Marine Corps Commandant P.X. Kelley has been informed of his communications; as proof, DeLaocque asks "that the General supply him with the first name of Mrs. West who used to live in St. Thomas." Brenneke also requests a meeting in person with Pentagon officials and says the Iranians would like to meet in Paris on January 3. He also writes that Poindexter, "approximately one week ago," orally authorized the sale of 10,000 TOW missiles to Iran. (Brenneke memo to Col. Richard H. Muller, USMC (Reserve), 1/1/86)

JAN 2 - Nir meets with North and Poindexter. According to the draft Senate intelligence panel report leaked in early 1987, Nir proposes a fresh start to the Iran initiative, minus Nimrodi and Schwimmer. He also reportedly suggests at a January meeting with North that the Iranians be overcharged for the weapons shipped to them, and that the surplus funds be diverted to the contras. Today's session sparks a series of events, including preparation of a draft intelligence finding dated January 6, and a full-scale NSC meeting January 7. Ghorbanifar also reportedly meets with Administration officials in the first week of the new year. He is said to be supported by Casey who presses for acceptance of his proposals despite the Iranian's failure of a CIA-administered lie-detector test of his credibility. (WP 12/16/86 & 12/27/86 & 1/10/87 & 1/12/87)

- A direct connection between the arms sales to Iran and aid to the Nicaraguan resistance was made in January 1986 in discussions between North and Amiram Nir, terrorism advisor to Israeli Prime Minister Peres. Notes taken at the interview of North by Meese on November 23, 1986 quote North as saying that he had discussed support for the Nicaraguan resistance with Nir in January 1986 and that Nir proposed using funds from arms sales to Iran for that support. [According to some notes, North believed Nir made the suggestion on his own.] The Attorney General testified that he was uncertain as to whether North or Nir brought up the subject of Nicaraguan resistance. North also recalled turning down other Nir suggestions that U.S. funds to Israel or Israel's own funds could be used to support the Nicaraguan resistance.

Other notes of that interview reflect only that Nir told North in January that the Israelis would take funds from a residual account and transfer them to a Nicaraguan account.

Notes of the Meese-North interview further reflect that

APR 11 1986

PUBLIC VOUCHER FOR PURCHASES AND SERVICES OTHER THAN PERSONAL	VOUCHER NO. 010254

DEPARTMENT, BUREAU, OR ESTABLISHMENT AND LOCATION	DATE VOUCHER PREPARED
Department of State	January 30, 1986
Nicaraguan Humanitarian Assistance Office	CONTRACT NUMBER AND DATE
Room 228, SA-6	NHAO 603-028 01/03/86
Washington, DC 20520	REQUISITION NUMBER AND DATE

SCHEDULE NO.
PAID BY

PAYEE'S NAME AND ADDRESS	Wire transfer of funds to: ABA #056 004 241, First American Bank of Virginia, for the Account of AIRMACH, INC., Account #0684-8818

DATE INVOICE RECEIVED

DISCOUNT TERMS

PAYEE'S ACCOUNT NUMBER

SHIPPED FROM	TO	WEIGHT	GOVERNMENT B-L NUMBER

NUMBER AND DATE OF ORDER	DATE OF DELIVERY OR SERVICE	ARTICLES OR SERVICES	QUAN-TITY	UNIT PRICE COST	PER	AMOUNT
603-028 1/3/86		Air charter services				
		Invoice No. 561087				$26,900
		Invoice No. 561086				$26,900

(Payee must NOT use the space below)		TOTAL	$53,800.00

PAYMENT	APPROVED FOR	EXCHANGE RATE	DIFFERENCES
PROVISIONAL	$ 53,800.00	= $1.00	
COMPLETE	BY		
PARTIAL 1st X	P. J. Buechler [signature] P.J. Buechler R.E. Vis		Amount verified, correct for
FINAL			(Signature or initials)
PROGRESS	TITLE		
ADVANCE	Operations Coordinator, NHAO		

Pursuant to authority vested in me, I certify that this voucher is correct and proper for payment.

(Date)	(Authorized Certifying Officer)	(Title)

ACCOUNTING CLASSIFICATION

$53,800.00 - 115/60062 - 2017 - 603028 - 010400 - 0000 - 2202 - 600000

CHECK NUMBER	ON ACCOUNT OF U.S. TREASURY	CHECK NUMBER	ON (Name of bank)
CASH	DATE	PAYEE	
$			

PER
TITLE

North commented that he had discussed Israeli help in general with Defense Minister Rabin, but could not recall asking specifically for help from the Israelis. (SSIC 1/29/87)

- By the time of the North-Nir discussion in January, the Israelis may have been holding funds from the November 1985 HAWK transfer available to use for the Nicaraguan resistance. A CIA document reflects that during one of the breaks in a CIA polygraph examination of Ghorbanifar in January 1986, he commented that Israelis received $24 million as soon as the HAWK shipment was delivered and that they were holding all of the funds. The Iranians were requesting the funds be returned. Ghorbanifar reportedly stated that the Israelis told him they had "doubled" the cost of the shipment apparently because these Americans were involved. Ghorbanifar reportedly stressed how upset the Iranians were at not getting the $24 million back. (SSIC 1/29/87)

- North said after the meeting with Nir in January 1986, he had contacted Adolfo Calero and as a result of that contact three accounts were opened in Switzerland. The notes quote North as saying he gave the account numbers to the Israelis, and money was deposited in those accounts. North guessed the money got to the contras; they knew money came and were appreciative.

Notes taken at the meeting further reflect that North identified two transactions from which money may have been diverted . . . to the contras: 1) the transfer of 1000 TOWs in February [1986], from which $3-4 million may have gone to the contras; and 2) the transaction [in May 1986] involving payment for HAWK parts and payment for replenishment of the 508 TOWs.

Notes taken at the meeting indicated North said there was no money for the contras in the October shipment of 500 TOWs to avoid a perception of private profit and because the resumption of U.S. funding made it unnecessary. According to North, Nir was upset because the October price was not the same as charged earlier.

Meese testified that North did not explain how he reported the arms sale matter to Poindexter. Meese testified that he got the impression that there was very little real communication about it between North and Poindexter and that North was not acting on orders from anyone. (SSIC 1/29/87)

- It is not clear who took the lead in developing the arms-for-hostages proposal that was soon presented by the Israelis. It is clear, however, that on January 2, 1986, Mr. Nir advanced a proposal just when the initiative seemed to be dying.

Mr. Nir met with VADM Poindexter in his office on January 2. Secretary Shultz recalls being told by VADM Poindexter that Mr. Nir proposed an exchange of certain Hizballah prisoners held by Israeli-supported Lebanese Christian forces, together with 3000 Israeli TOWs, for the release of the U.S. citizens held hostage in Beirut. (Tower)

- "I felt that one of the things Israel wanted was to get itself into a position where it's [sic] arms sales to Iran could not be criticized by us because we were conducting this Operation Staunch and we were trying to persuade everybody not to sell arms. That is what all that is about." (Shultz, SRB, 37) (Tower)

JAN 3 - North and Poindexter meet with Casey at his home to discuss the Nir meeting and the Iran initiative. (WP 1/15/87)

- North's first draft finding was dated January 3, 1986.

- CIA General Counsel Stanley Sporkin continued working on a draft Finding, and on January 3, he carried a copy to North. (CIA/IG Chronology 13) His draft offered a choice between notifying Congressional intelligence committees or postponing such notification until the President determined it would be appropriate. (Sporkin 26) North then prepared the necessary documents for Poindexter to submit to the President with the proposed Finding. North's draft Finding did not refer to hostage rescue until Sporkin insisted that it do so. (Id. at 22-23; CIA/IG Chronology 13) The draft Finding did not include the option of notifying Congress. (Tower)

- The State Department's Nicaraguan Humanitarian Assistance Office contracts with Richard Gadd's company, Airmach, to fly nonlethal aid to the contras. Between January 17 and April 11, Airmach flies fifteen times to Central America. (MH 3/22/87; NHAO program summary.)

JAN 4 - Richard Brenneke writes a cover memo outlining Iranian terms concerning the exchange of U.S. arms for hostages, captured Soviet military equipment and other items. It is addressed "To Whom It May Concern" and is included in a letter to the State Department on January 6 (see entry). (Brenneke memo, 1/4/86)

- North submitted the package [containing a draft Finding and supporting documents, to be submitted to the President] to Poindexter by memorandum dated January 4. North wrote that the Finding was

"based on our discussions with Nir and my subsequent meeting with CIA General Counsel Stanley Sporkin.

"At Sporkin's request, I talked to Bill Casey on [telephone] re the Finding and the overall approach. He indicated that he thought the finding was good and that this is probably the only approach that will work. He shares our goal of achieving a more moderate government in Iran through this process." (North to Poindexter, Action Memorandum, 1/4/86.)

The package included a memorandum from Poindexter to the President and a Finding, dated January 6.

North's first draft Finding was dated January 3, 1986. The accompanying memorandum is undated. The changes from the first drafts are indicated below by square brackets. When the changes were material, the original language is reproduced in footnotes.

The following Finding was attached:

"I hereby find that the following operation in a foreign country (including all support necessary to such operation) is important to the national security of the United States, and due to its extreme sensitivity and security risks, I determine it is essential to limit prior notice, and direct the Director of Central Intelligence to refrain from reporting this Finding to the Congress as provided in Section 501 of the National Security Act of 1947, as amended, until I otherwise direct.

"SCOPE Iran

"DESCRIPTION [Assist selected friendly foreign liaison services, third countries, which have established relationships with Iranian elements, groups, and individuals] sympathetic to U.S. Government interests and which do not conduct or support terrorist actions directed against U.S. persons, property or interests, for the purpose of: (1) establishing a more moderate government in Iran, and (2) obtaining from them significant intelligence not otherwise obtainable, to determine the current Iranian Government's intentions with respect to its neighbors and with respect to terrorist acts, [and (3) furthering the release of the American hostages held in Beirut and preventing additional terrorist acts by these groups.] Provide funds, intelligence, counter-intelligence, training, guidance and communications, and other necessary assistance to these elements, groups, individuals, liaison services and third countries in support of these activities. The USG will act to facilitate efforts by third parties and third countries to establish contact with moderate elements within and outside the Government of Iran by providing these elements with arms, equipment and related material in order to enhance the credibility of these elements in their effort to achieve a more pro-U.S. government in Iran by demonstrating their ability to obtain requisite resources to defend their country against Iraq and intervention by the Soviet Union. This support will be discontinued if the U.S. Government learns that these elements have abandoned their goals of moderating their government and appropriated the material for purposes other than that [sic] provided by this Finding." (Tower)

JAN 5 - According to Sporkin, this language ["... and (3) furthering the release of the American hostages held in Beirut and preventing additional terrorist acts by these groups..."] was added [to the draft finding] after a meeting on January 5 between Sporkin, North, and Director Casey at the Director's house. (Sporkin 22-23) (Tower)

- Khashoggi borrows $6 million from Vertex Finances, S.A., the last of three installments of a $21 million loan to finance Iran's purchase of arms. At around this time, Khashoggi also receives a $9 million loan from a Cayman Island-based bank, Euro Commercial Finances, controlled by Canadian businessmen Donald Fraser and Walter Miller, in exchange for 75% of the stock of Edgington Oil Co., a subsidiary of Khashoggi's Triad America Corp. Fraser is a director and president of Triad America; Miller is a director. (WSJ 12/12/86 & 1/15/87; NYT 12/13/86)

JAN 6 - Reagan meets with Bush, Regan, McFarlane and Poindexter. A background paper for the meeting is prepared for the President. The group discusses North's draft intelligence finding on the Iran arms sales. Reagan eventually signs it, but officials say later they do not know exactly when. Apparently, only Casey and Poindexter are aware of the signature. The finding is unusual in that it has been drafted without interagency participation. It is also not clear why the President would sign a draft document in the first place. (WP 1/10/87 & 1/15/87)

- [Regan remembered] "it was discussed with the President, the Vice President and myself on January 6 as, '[h]ere's something.'" "You know how you brief the President 24 hours in advance of this next meeting so when [he] is doing his homework he is familiar with the subject."

"He was given that piece of paper by John Poindexter at a regular Monday morning meeting, a 9:30 meeting, saying '[t]his is what we're going to discuss tomorrow,' and the President signing it for some reason. I don't know. I think it was in error." (Regan 17-18; 22-23)

After the President signed this draft, Sporkin reviewed it and, by hand, added the words "and third parties" after "third countries" in the second line of the "Description." (Sporkin 24-25) The Finding was retyped before the President signed it on January 17; Sporkin's addition was the only change.

In response to a question, Regan said that he, the President, the Vice President, Poindexter, and Rodney McDaniel, Executive Secretary of the NSC, attended this briefing. According to the Presidential Diary, Fortier, not McDaniel, attended. (Jones to Stephens, 1/24/87) Regan remembered this fact, and subsequently corrected himself. (Regan 42)) (Tower)

- Administration officials believe this undated Poindexter memo was falsified in November 1986 to match the false chronology prepared at the time. Walsh and FBI are investigating whether memos and other documents in Poindexter's office are missing or falsified. (WSJ 2/24/87)

- Members of the National Security Planning Group, including Reagan, Shultz, Weinberger, Casey, Poindexter and other officials, meet to discuss retaliation against Libya following the December 27 airport bombings in Rome and Vienna. A decision is reached to deploy U.S. Navy ships and aircraft to the Gulf of Sidra. According to an NSC aide who attends the meeting, the purpose of the exercise is to try to provoke a response from Khaddafi which could then be used to justify a bombing strike against Libya. Reagan is reported to insist that a raid be seen as a just response. The

Joint Chiefs of Staff, who are said to be wary of using force to combat terrorism, are also reported to be resisting efforts by the White House staff to have a third aircraft carrier moved into the Mediterranean. (NYT 2/22/87)

- Richard Brenneke speaks with Col. Alvarez (see November 30, 1985 entry) who tells him the government has no interest in his information concerning Iran. The same day, Brenneke writes a letter to Ralph Johnson and addressed to the State Department's European Bureau, Room 6519. The letter begins, "Many thanks for your help." He writes that his Iranian contacts want to meet in Paris on January 7, but adds that his "partner in Europe will inform them" that that is not possible. He asks Johnson's help with his situation. (Brenneke letter to Johnson, 1/6/86)

JAN 7 - Reagan meets with the NSC at mid-day to discuss new proposals brought by Nir and Ghorbanifar to swap arms for hostages. Bush, Regan, Shultz, Weinberger, Meese, Casey, Poindexter and McFarlane are present. One part of the plan suggested by Nir is to ship 2,000 more TOW missiles to Iran. In all, two U.S. shipments are apparently called for, one in February and another in May, each to result in the release of hostages. Ultimately, the plan evolves to include one shipment in February as a signal that the operation is underway, a second on McFarlane's late May flight to Tehran, and two more to follow McFarlane's departure. No notes or minutes are taken at this meeting. Casey, Regan and Poindexter reportedly favor the proposal, but Shultz and Weinberger again oppose sending weapons to Tehran. Reagan is reportedly persuaded by Poindexter to proceed, although North says later that he decides to leave the issue of sending arms open at this point, pending the release of all the hostages. During the next ten days, Poindexter, Regan, Casey and North reportedly discuss ways to bypass Shultz and Weinberger, as well as other members of the National Security Planning Group. (WP 11/26/86 & 12/16/86 & 12/27/86 & 1/15/87; Meese briefing 11/25/86; NYT 12/25/86; CSM 1/2/87)

- On January 7, 1986, this proposal [presented by Nir on January 2] was discussed with the President at a meeting, probably held in the Oval Office, attended by the Vice President, Secretary Shultz, Secretary Weinberger, Attorney General Meese, Director Casey, Mr. Regan, and VADM Poindexter. Although the President apparently did not make a decision at this meeting, several of the participants recall leaving the meeting persuaded that he supported the proposal. Secretary Shultz told the Board that the President, the Vice-President, Mr. Casey, Mr. Meese, Mr. Regan, and VADM Poindexter "all had one opinion and I had a different one and Cap shared it." (Tower)

- On January 7, 1986, the President and his principal advisors met, apparently after an NSPG meeting that morning, to consider the Iranian project. As the Attorney General described it:

"After an NSC meeting or an NSC-type meeting in the Situation Room, a few of us were asked to gather in the Oval Office.

"Now, if you have any information that would vary from or amplify on what I know, do not hesitate to bring up the questions. I am trying to recall from memory.

"One of the difficulties that I have, and that I suspect others may have, is that I considered this so highly sensitive and classified that I took almost no notes at any time during the thing because I didn't want to reduce anything to paper. I talked with no one about it, up until a certain point, which I will relate.

"So, therefore, the memory even a year later, is fairly hazy.

"Anyway, on the seventh, I joined with the President, the Vice President, Cap Weinberger, George Shultz, Don Regan, Bill Casey, John Poindexter, and I was there, and there may have been an assistant to John Poindexter. It may have been Don Fortier. I am not sure.... It was not North, to the best of my recollection.... Bud wasn't there.... At that time, the topic was brought up about an initiative to Iran. It was discussed in some detail, largely by John Poindexter, with some participation by Bill Casey.

"It dealt with some overtures to be made to what were described as more moderate elements within the Iranian Government, and it was related to establishing a relationship so that we would have some influence in the future at whatever time it was possible for the Iranian Government to change, either with the death of the Ayatollah, or what.

"There was also, as I remember, some discussion that

these moderate, these more moderate forces, thought that they might change in the government even sooner than that event happening.

"They also talked about this being helpful in terms of ending the Iraq-Iran War, trying to get a more reasonable policy where the Iranian Government would be less inclined to participate or support subversion and terrorism in other countries; and it was also talked about these people using their influence to try to help us get our hostages back.

"All of these were factors that went into this strategic initiative in regard to Iran." (Meese 3-5)

The Attorney General noted that prior events, such as the arms shipments, were President [sic] had signed a Finding the previous day.

"As the discussion ensued, it was the idea that these people wanted a showing of our good faith and that that involved the shipment of some limited quantities of arms. They particularly talked about TOW missiles, I believe, and that they, in turn, would show their good faith by using their influence to get the prisoners, the hostages, back.

"Again, this is not a precise recollection; but my general recollection is that this was anticipated: that it would take place over a fairly short period of time—30 to 60 days—and that that was kind of the general framework of which everybody was thinking, because they talked about us making available limited quantities of arms, then they would produce hostages as showing that they were really able to do something for us, and that we would then ship more arms if their good faith had been shown by helping us get the hostages.

"It was kind of a sequence that these events would follow, along with each other.

"There was also a discussion that, because of the extreme sensitivity, it was recommended that the President not inform Congress until we had gotten the hostages back. I vaguely remember there was discussion that as soon as we got the hostages, even on our planes en route to Wiesbaden, that we would notify Congress then, before it became public generally.

"So, the subjects and the discussion of a finding was made at that time, that a finding would be necessary because of the way in which this was to be done, with CIA being involved in the transfer of the weapons.

"This was discussed for about an hour and twenty minutes

or so. I remember because I consulted back on my calendar, and I had a group waiting for me in the White House Mess that day, and I was late to that luncheon by more than an hour.

"Cap and George were opposed to the idea.

"I don't remember what the Vice President or Don Regan might have said. Bill Casey was very much in favor of the idea.

"My own views were that it was a very close decision. I have called it since a '51-49 decision.' But I felt, in the long run, that the risks that were attendant to this probably were worth the potential benefit, and the potential benefits to me were both the opening into Iran and also the assistance that would be provided in getting the hostages back. . . . It was my independent judgment because nobody had talked to me about it beforehand. But it was also as a result of the discussion back and forth, and particularly Poindexter and Casey were the principal protagonists of going ahead and doing this. . . . There was a relatively thorough—I mean, it was very clear that their [Shultz's and Weinberger's] positions were that they were opposed to it, that George felt this was at odds with our policy in regard to terrorism, that it could hurt us with our allies or with friends around the world.

"Cap was concerned primarily about the the terrorism policy.

"The rejoinder, I think by Poindexter, was that this was a special situation and that this was not at odds with our overall policy; it was an exception to the general situation.

"I think what most influenced me was the idea that we would be taking—that the risks would be fairly short-term because if it did not work, we would be able to stop it; if this didn't produce results after, say, the first foray, that the thing would be stopped. There was quite a bit of discussion about that, that this would be in stages so that it could be stopped.

"We knew, in retrospect, that it did not work out that way.

"But that was one of the things that made it, while a close call, acceptable, as far as I was concerned." (Id. at 6-10)

The Attorney General believed that the President had an adequate understanding of the arguments for and against the project. Nobody described the operational details, apart from the arms transfers from the Defense Department to the CIA. Ghorbanifar's name was mentioned, but not Khashoggi's or other middlemen's and financiers'. The 'thinness' of operational security was not raised.

"The feeling was that this would not be revealed, or at least not be revealed while the hostages were still in jeopardy, and the risks to the people involved was also discussed, so it was felt that they would not be revealing this." (Id. at 11)

The Attorney General had the impression "that the channel would be, sort of, simply from DOD to the CIA to the Israelis." (Id. at 12) The President was confident that the Israelis constituted "a relatively secure channel." (Id.) Nevertheless, the Attorney General remembered,

"there were always, I won't say questions, but I think that the Iranians were the sort of a sticking point, that we had to try this out carefully and be cautious as we implemented this thing, to be sure that these Iranians would be able to or were sincere and would be willing to show good faith.

"In other words, I think there was a question mark left about the Iranians that could only be tested by going through with this thing." (Id. at 13)

At his meeting with the Board on January 26, 1987, the President said he approved a convoluted plan whereby Israel would free 20 Hizballah prisoners, Israel would sell TOW missiles to Iran, the five U.S. citizens in Beirut would be freed, and the kidnappings would stop. A draft Covert Action Finding had already been signed by the President the day before the meeting on January 6, 1986. Mr. Regan told the Board that the draft Finding may have been signed in error. The President did not recall signing the January 6 draft.

The President told the Board that he had several times asked Secretary Weinberger for assurances that shipments to Iran would not alter the military balance with Iraq. He did not indicate when this occurred but stated that he received such assurances. The President also said he was warned by Secretary Shultz that the arms sales would undercut U.S. efforts to discourage arms sales by its allies to Iran.

The President did not amplify those remarks in his meeting with the Board on February 11. [He did add, however, that no one ever discussed with him the provision of intelligence to Iran.]

The Secretary of State also remembered the meeting as occurring in the Oval Office:

"I again stated my views in full. I recall no discussion about a finding then or at any time thereafter, until it was revealed by Vice Admiral Poindexter in a meeting at the White House on November 10, 1986.

"I might say that when he read out that finding, I said that's the first I heard of that. Cap, who was sitting across the room from me, said, 'I have never heard of it either.'

"I recall no specific decision being made in my presence, though I was well aware of the President's preferred course, and his strong desire to establish better relations with Iran and to save the hostages.

"So I felt at that meeting that Cap was against it and I was against it and everybody else in the room was in favor. . . . "

"Well, I stated all of the reasons why I felt it was a bad idea, and nobody, in retrospect, has thought of a reason that I didn't think of. I mean, I think this is all very predictable, including the argument against those who said well, this is all going to be secret or it is all going to be deniable; that that is nonsense.

"So, all of that was said. And in that January 7 meeting, I know that I not only stated these things, but I was very concerned about it, and I expressed myself as forcefully as I could. That is, I didn't just sort of rattle these arguments off. I was intense. The President knew that.

"The President was well aware of my views. I think everybody was well aware of my views.

"It wasn't just saying oh, Mr. President, this is terrible, don't do it. There were reasons given that were spelled out and which are the reasons that you would expect. . . . "

"[N]obody said very much. As I made these arguments, Cap basically agreed with them. He didn't restate them. But I took the initiative as the person in the room who was opposed to what was being proposed. I cannot give you a full accounting, but it was clear to me by the time we went out that the President, the Vice President, the Director of Central Intelligence, the Attorney General, the Chief of Staff, the National Security Advisor all had one opinion and I had a different one and Cap shared it. . . . "

"The nature of the players the risks when—I would say "when," not "if"—it came foward publicly—the description always was that Israel was going to be the conduit, and, therefore, it would be deniable, and we'd just say well, we don't know anything about it, and it's something Israel is doing, and so on. All of this was argued with, that it wouldn't work." (Shultz, SRB, 38, 42-44)

Regan's recollection differed. He recalled discussion of Congressional notification at the NSPG meeting.

"I remember Casey speaking on it and Ed Meese speaking

on it at the NSPG on December 7 [sic: January 7], that this should be on a close hold basis . . . and notification given later to the Congress because there were lives involved where we would be dealing here with hostages and because of the sensitivity of the new contacts we were attempting to establish within Iran being blown if there was premature disclosure, that the notification should come later rather than now. . . .

"Now why did the President do it? There are two things, I think. First of all, he does have this feeling, still has this feeling, that we cannot allow Iran to fall into the Soviet camp. Khomeini is 86. He's been reported and reported in ill health and on the verge of death. We have no contacts there. We are alone. Well, not alone, but we are one of six nations that doesn't have an ambassador or some type of relationship with that country.

"We are in the position of not being able to be ballplayers there if any type of situation erupts as a result of the Ayatollah and we should have contacts.

"Secondly, there is no doubt in our minds that they have an enormous amount of influence on various religious factions within the Lebanon-Syria area. Some of these factions probably have our hostages and they can be instrumental in getting those out, and he wants to keep that avenue open.

"I think [that] is what led him to do it." (Regan 24, 29)

In response to a question about the degree of discussion of the risks, Regan noted:

"The President was told, but by no means was it really teed up for him of what the downside risk would be here as far as American public opinion was concerned. There was no sampling. No one attempted to do this. The NSC certainly didn't in any paper or any discussion say that.

"I don't believe the State Department in its presentation arguing against this really brought out the sensitivity of this. None of us was aware of that, I regret to say." (Id. at 30)

Nor was the President warned that "all hell would break loose" with Congress. (Id. at 31) Regan heard, but disagreed with, the opponents of the program.

"I recognized the validity of what [Secretaries Shultz and Weinberger] were saying, you know, that we didn't want to be in a position of trading one for one. Give me a hostage, and to get 100 rifles or whatever the price would be. No, we couldn't be in that.

"But I have to be a little bit personal here. In my other

capacity as head of Merrill, Lynch, I opened an office in Tehran for Merrill, Lynch and have very close connections in Tehran in the era of the Shah during the '70s. I believed in that country and I thought that that country had quite a future. And I recognized that for us, the United States, to have no connections whatsoever with Iran was a foolish thing to do from an international political point of view as well as an economic point of view.

"And, accordingly, I was all for keeping a line open to whoever was the constituted government of Iran in an effort to sometime be a player in that country's future." (Id. at 36-37)

The Secretary of Defense had an imprecise recollection of the meeting, except with regard to one point:

"The only time that I got the impression the President was for this thing was in January, which was January 6 or 7, and at that time it became very apparent to me that the cause I was supporting was lost and that the President was for it. And shortly after that, we got a call, I didn't, but Colin Powell did, I believe, from John Poindexter who by that time had succeeded, saying there had been such a decision and the President wanted us to proceed with the transfer of this initial set of arms. The numbers changed. I think initially it was 2,000, and went up to 4,000, but they were to be transferred in amounts sort of as drawn.

"But we were to transfer them to the CIA and to nobody else. And I made clear that that was the only way that we would operate, that it had to be transferred to the CIA, not directly by us to anyone else because we couldn't do that, and that it had to be an Economy Act transfer, which as you know, means we've got to be paid value for it.

"I said we would carry out the Commander-in-Chief's orders to do this, and obviously we would hold it as closely as possible because that was not only the direction but the obvious thing to do." (Weinberger 14-15) (Tower)

- Subsequent to the January 7 meeting, legal analysis of the finding and various means to implement the program continued. The Department of Defense insisted that the sale of arms by the Defense Department to a foreign country, be it Iran or Israel, could not be hidden from Congress under the law. This argument applied not only to future direct or indirect sales to Iran, but also to the replenishment of Israel's TOW stocks, which had to be done under this program because Israel could not afford the replacement cost for the TOWs. The solution was to have DoD sell the Arms to the CIA under the Economy Act, an approach that CIA General Sporkin had urged on legal grounds despite the Agency's desire not to be involved. The CIA could then resell the arms, as part of a covert action operation, to a private company that in turn would sell them to Iran and (for the 508 TOWs) Israel. A small change in the January 6 Finding, adding the words "and third parties," sufficed to authorize this new approach. (SSIC 1/29/87)

- The January 7 meeting [of the NSC] had earmarks of a meeting held after a decision had already been made. Indeed, a draft Covert Action Finding authorizing the initiative had been signed by the President, though perhaps inadvertently, the previous day. (Tower)

- Reagan, citing "irrefutable" evidence of Khaddafi's complicity in the Rome and Vienna airport bombings, announces economic sanctions against Libya, including a ban on direct import and export trade. According to a White House aide, the NSC staff, particularly Donald Fortier, support the policy because they want "to get economic sanctions out of the way so the next time they could do more." Reagan may have been unaware of his staff's plans, the aide notes, saying "We were making an end run on the president." (NYT 2/22/87)

- An undercover U.S. Customs agent attends meetings with Veillot, Hashemi, Bihn, Schneider, Kourentis, and Thanos. Hashemi phones Delaroque, described as Veillot's partner, and agrees to give Delaroque more time to obtain official approval from the U.S. The Customs agent tells the group of the need for viable documents on the deal. (Court papers, U.S. District Court, New York)

JAN 8 - Cyrus Hashemi is told by a suspect in the U.S. Customs Service sting operation that documents which will provide official U.S. approval for the private sale of arms to Iran "are on the desk of the . . . vice president." (MH 11/30/86)

- A press report quoting Pentagon and NSC sources notes a $10-12 million arms transfer to Iran through Israel. The story is denied by the White House and receives little attention elsewhere. (John Wallach, Hearst Newspapers, USA Today 12/11/86)

- Spitz Channell's National Endowment for the Preservation of Liberty pays $400,000 to International Business Communications. IBC passes on $360,000 to I.C. Inc. on Jan. 13; and on Jan. 21, the Lake Resources bank account in Switzerland receives $360,000. (WP 3/7/87)

JAN 9 - Reagan signs a finding authorizing the CIA to provide intelligence advice, training and communications equipment to the contras. Under the order, the Agency spends $13 million during 1986 ($10 million on stepped-up intelligence gathering, $3 million for communications equipment and training), and as a result succeeds in keeping the guerrilla effort alive until congressional military funding resumes in the fall. Although the finding is reported to the intelligence panels, committee members reportedly disagree over the legality of the activities the CIA conducts under the order. (WP 1/14/87)

JAN 10 - Delaroque indicates to Hashemi that it would be better to get official approval and do the arms deal to Iran legally, since to do it illegally would be much more expensive. (Court papers, U.S. District Court, New York)

- $450,000 of the $27 million provided by Congress for Nicaraguan humanitarian assistance is paid "to the commander in chief" or high command of a Central American country's armed forces. A GAO report on contra wrongdoings which later discloses this information does not identify the country, but Rep. Michael D. Barnes (D-MD), chairman of the House Foreign Affairs subcommittee on Latin America, says it is Honduras. News accounts suggest later that this and additional payments to the Honduran armed forces are the result of the military's control of the primary stores and warehouses provisioning the contras, and amount to payoffs for allowing the rebels to operate in Honduras. (NBC News 6/11/86; MH 6/12/86; LAT 6/12/86; NYT 6/12/86)

- NHAO awards a contract to Vortex, an aircraft and leasing firm in Miami owned by Alberto Herreros, to ferry humanitarian supplies to the contras. (NHAO program summary; MH 3/22/87)

JAN 11 - Veillot tells his colleagues that if he cannot obtain authority from the U.S. for the sale to Iran, he has contacts in South America who might be able to provide end-user certificates. He also states that he can get only 10 to 13 F-4 aircraft, instead of the 39 previously anticipated. (Court papers, U.S. District Court, New York)

- Because of an NSC request for clearance of Mr. Ghorbanifar, on January 11, 1986, the CIA had administered a polygraph test to Mr. Ghorbanifar during a visit to Washington. Although he failed the test, and despite the unsatisfactory results of the program to date, Mr. Ghorbanifar continued to serve as intermediary. A CIA official recalls Director Casey concurring in this decision. [See also Mid-January entry.] (Tower)

JAN 11 - Neither Mr. Ghorbanifar nor the second channel seem to have been subjected to a systematic intelligence vetting before they were engaged as intermediaries. Mr. Ghorbanifar had been known to the CIA for some time and the agency had substantial doubts as to his reliability and truthfulness. Yet the agency did not volunteer that information or inquire about the identity of the intermediary if his name was unknown. Conversely, no early request for a name check was made of the CIA, and it was not until January 11, 1986, that the agency gave Mr. Ghorbanifar a new polygraph, which he failed. George Cave prepared the questions for the examination. (Cave 3-5; C/NE (2) 76)) Ghorbanifar took a polygraph test in the afternoon and evening, January 11, 1986 and showed deception on almost all of the questions. (Memorandum for the Record, "Ghorbanifar Polygraph Examination")

. . . On January 11, 1986, Ghorbanifar was tested in "a local hotel" in Washington. "The english [sic] language was used." ("Polygraph" Division to C/NE/IRAN, 1/13/86)

The polygraph examiner reported, on January 13, 1986, to the effect that Ghorbanifar was indeed a fabricator of evidence. He noted, moreover, that polygraph examinations in March and June 1984 had produced the same conclusion.

"He showed deception on virtually all of the relevant questions. He has lied/fabricated his information on terrorist activities and tried to mislead us concerning his relationship with the Farsi line inside Iran. He also has distorted [name deleted] role in Islamic Jihad. Moreover, Ghorbanifar was tested on his involvement in the deal to release the hostages. The test indicated that he knew ahead of time that the hostages would not be released and deliberately tried to deceive [sic] us both independently and with 'B.'

"Ghorbanifar provided new information concerning an alleged terrorist plan to attack U. S. interests in Saudi Arabia. He was also tested on this information and was shown to be lying.

"It seemed clear from Ghorbanifar's behavior that he realized that the polygraph test indicated deception. While he commented during the test that he was comfortable with all of the test questions, he said that perhaps the machine might indicate some problems on a series of questions concerning Farsi and the rightists inside Iran. He said he had been told by 'White House representatives' not to discuss this topic with CIA because the operation was 'too far advanced' and if CIA were involved 'it would require Congressional briefings.' He went on to add that he supposedly expended $800,000 of his own funds for this purpose and has been assured by these 'White House representatives' that he will be reimbursed for these expenditures. (Comment: The polygraph operator stated that Ghorbanifar's explanation/rationalization would not influence the test results on the questions being asked in connection with Farsi and his supporters.)

"In discussing the hostage deal, Ghorbanifar stated he was very comfortable with the questions asked. During one of the breaks in the testing, he commented that the Israelis received $24 million as soon as the shipment was delivered and they are holding all of the funds that the Iranians are requesting be returned. He added that the Israelis told him that they had 'doubled' the cost of the shipment apparently because the Americans were involved. He said the Iranians were very upset about the last shipment and might resort to terrorist activities against U. S. interests. He remarked the Iranians have been refraining from these terrorist activities since the negotiations began.

"Ghorbanifar is clearly a fabricator and wheeler-dealer who has undertaken activities prejudicial to U. S. interests.

"Neither Ghorbanifar nor Ledeen have [sic] been advised about the results of the test. Michael Ledeen asked that he be informed about the results of the test as soon as possible. He was called on the morning of 12 January and told that the polygraph operator will be reviewing the results on Sunday January 12 and we should have feedback about the test on 13 January."

A paper entitled "Comments on Ghorbanifar's Polygraph" noted, in part, that he "(a) Lied/fabricated his information on terrorist activities;

"(b) Tried to mislead us concerning his relationship with the 'rightist line inside Iran';

"(c) He distorted the leadership role of Seyyed Mohammad Khatemi inside Islamic Jihad;

"(d) He showed deception on the question of whether he was under the control of the Iranian Government.

"The test also indicated Ghorbanifar knew ahead of time that the hostages would not be released despite our providing missiles to the Iranians. He deliberately tried to deceive us on this issue both independently and with the collusion of 'B.' ("Comments on Ghorbanifar's Polygraph")

"Deception indicated to thirteen of the fifteen relevant questions. Inconclusive to the remaining two." Some "relevant" questions, answers, and tracings by the polygraph were:

"A. Has IDEN C . . . personally told you he is willing to cooperate with 'US' intelligence? ANSWER: Yes.

"B. Are you trying to deceive us about IDEN C's actual degree of influence with IDEN E [Islamic Jihad]? ANSWER: No."

Testing showed deception to question B. Question A is inconclusive due to inconsistent reactions.

Ghorbanifar was questioned about his knowledge of Iranian terrorist activities. "Relevant" questions and answers were:

"C. Are you trying to deceive [sic] us in any way about the source of the information regarding the three-man team (the IDEN G [Hamad Hassani] three-man hit team)? ANSWER: No.

"D. Regarding European-based IDEN B [Iran/Iranian] terrorist, have you deliberately fabricated any of the information you have provided? ANSWER: No.

"E. Did IDEN F . . . tell you the Hamburg Team (The IDEN G three-man hit team) killed IDEN L [Aziz Muradi]? ANSWER: Yes.

"F. Other than what you have told us, are you aware of ongoing plans targeting 'US' persons or interests for acts of terrorism you are not telling us about? ANSWER: No.

Testing showed deception to questions C, D, E, and F.

The test produced similar results when Ghorbanifar was questioned about "new" information about terrorists' current plans targeted against "USG." While discussing this topic, "G" was occasionally evasive and often reluctant to answer questions. He also contradicted himself, although he did outline a meeting, during which IDEN C asked an Iranian for 300 kilograms of plastic explosive to use against United States facilities in Saudi Arabia, and a Lebanese Palestinian Shiite terrorist asked for more efficient Iranian logistical support in delivering $6,000,000 worth of terrorist armaments. ("Polygraph" Division to C/NE/IRAN, 1/13/86) (Tower)

- At the request of the Director of Central Intelligence, Charles Allen interviewed Ghorbanifar for five hours. This conversation generated a nine-page report. Director Casey wanted, Allen reported, "to obtain a general overview of the information he possesses, not to conduct a detailed debriefing." Ghorbanifar sought a "more principled" relationship with the CIA, based on his usefulness as "a turn-key project man," rather than an employee. He explained that, when, in 1980-82 the CIA had communicated its mistrust of him to other intelligence agencies, he had retaliated. Ghorbanifar had persuaded individuals whom he could influence not to cooperate with the CIA.

Ghorbanifar explained his present goal was the modification of the Khomeini regime and the alignment of Iran with the West.

"Subject [Ghorbanifar] stated that he wished to work with the US Government and CIA in a number of areas. Clearly, the US hostages held in Lebanon were a high priority. He would continue to work with the White House on this issue; this effort would be kept separate. A second area would be to assist the West in blunting Iranian terrorism. A third area would be working with the Agency to thwart Libyan and Syrian-sponsored terrorism and to assist in the overthrow of Libyan leader Qadhafi."

With regard to the hostages, Ghorbanifar made three points. High Iranian officials were interested in a new relationship with the United States. They could release, or kill, the hostages. Whether the United States pursued a relationship with Iran would decide the hostages' fate. If the United States missed the opportunity, the hostages would be killed and new terrorist acts would occur.

Ghorbanifar's Tehran contact, Prime Minister Mir Hosein Musavi-Khamenei, and Minister of Oil Gholam Reza Aqazadeh "'will lose face' soon," unless the United States went forward with arms supplies through Israel. These men told

President Ali Khameini that the United States was willing to provide advanced weapons "in return for Tehran's promise to secure the release of US hostages held in Lebanon. They had assured other senior officials that a longterm relationship with the United States was possible and in negotiation; as a result, Iranian terrorist attacks against the United States had ceased for seven months. "Subject stated that the 'Islamic Jihad Organization (IJO)' would strike soon unless a new understanding was reached, perhaps as early as 24 January."

Characterizing Ghorbanifar, Allen wrote that he "is a highly energetic, excitable individual who possesses an extraordinarily strong ego that must be carefully fed. Intelligent and clearly an individual who has made a considerable amount of money in procurement of arms and in provision of 'other services,' he is relatively straight forward about what he hopes to get out of any arrangement with the United States. He deeply resents 'his treatment' by the Agency in the 1980-82 timeframe and frequently speaks scornfully of a woman with the name 'Lucy' from the US Embassy in London who met with him at that time. A personable individual, he also consistently speaks of his love of Iran and the need to change the composition of the current government there. It is difficult to gauge just what Subject's 'organization' consist [sic] of but he appears to have influence over or business arrangements with a substantial number of individuals in the Middle East and Europe and inside Iran itself. We have hard evidence that he is close to the Prime Minister, the Minister of Oil, and other senior officials like an official in the Prime Minister's office. There is no question, however, that he exaggerates and inflates for his own reasons some [?of these?] relationships. He is impatient if one tries to pin him down on the specifics of some of the complex plots that he describes. For this reason, the best strategy is to go back over details in a series of meetings so that all aspects of the plot can be determined. This indirect approach takes time but builds rapport with Subject. The worst approach to Subject would be to attempt to lecture him." (C. Allen, "Interview with Subject [Ghorbanifar]," 1/29/86. Copies to: DCI, DDCI, DDO, DDI, DC/NE, O/DDO (Clarridge)) (Tower)

JAN 13 - Veillot says he cannot get U.S. authorization for the Iran deal. It becomes more difficult for Delaroque to make arrangements to proceed illegally since he is an American citizen. Nevertheless, Delaroque obtains an end user certificate for the F-104 aircraft, and Veillot is assigned to get the end-user certificate for the F-4s. (Court papers, U.S. District Court, New York)

- Ghorbanifar . . . argued . . . in Washington on January 13, that his Iranian contacts could be of great use to the United States. (SSIC 1/29/87)

- International Business Communications pays $360,000 to I.C. Inc., which then passes the money on to the Lake Resources bank account in Switzerland. (WP 3/7/87)

JAN 14 - Invoice from International Procurement & Sales Inc, signed by Hermann Moll, to Galaxy Trade Inc. (a Bermuda corporation), care of Samuel M. Evans Esq. Listed are 15 F-4 aircraft, 10 spare engines for the F-4s, spare parts, ammunition and other related items, amounting to $253.6 million. Included is a schedule of model numbers, serial numbers and details of 13 F-4 aircraft. The prices include shipping costs from a Mediterranean port with a $3 million buyers' deposit. (Court papers, U.S. District Court, New York)

- Before the President signed the Finding of January 17, 1986, North began to lash together the CIA and Department of Defense to implement the plan he had outlined to Poindexter in December and incorporated in Poindexter's memoranda to the President in January. Before January 17, he encountered resistance. Poindexter asked him to discuss the matter with the Director of Central Intelligence. North did so on January 14. He reported that

"I[n] A[ccordance] W[ith] yr direction, met w/Casey last night after W'bgr speech at Ft. McNair. Casey then tried to contact Cap but he had already departed. Casey has called urging that you convene a mtg w/ he and Cap ASAP so that we can move on. Casey's view is that Cap will continue to create roadblocks until he is told by you that the President wants this to move NOW and that Cap will have to make it work. Casey points out that we have now gone through three different methodologies in an effort to satisfy Cap's concerns and that no matter what we do there is always a new objection. As far as Casey is concerned our earlier method of having Copp deal directly with the DoD as a purchasing agent was fine. He did not see any particular problem w/ making Copp an agent for the CIA in this endeavor but he is concerned that Cap will find some new objection unless he is told to proceed. Colin Powell, who sat next to me during Cap's speech asked the following questions (my answers are indicated):

"Q. Does Copp deal w/ Iranians or Israelis?

"A. With the Israelis.

"Q. Is the intelligence a prerequisite?

"A. It is probably something that can be negotiated but in any event it is not a DoD matter. It is covered in the [January 6] finding and is in fact one of the few means we have to make a long term penetration in Iran. Our ulterior motive of changing/moderating the govt. is served by this. (Tower)

JAN 15 - In a speech to the National Defense University, Shultz states that under international law, "a nation attacked by terrorists is permitted to use force to prevent or pre-empt future attacks, to seize terrorists or to rescue its citizens, when no other means is available." The remark is reported to be part of a carefully constructed scenario regarding possible U.S. actions against Libya. According to a White House official, the State Department in coming weeks begins to put together a legal argument asserting, in part, that "in the context of military action what normally would be considered murder is not." (NYT 2/22/87)

- Richard Brenneke writes to Bush summarizing his contacts with the U.S. government to date and the general lack of interest in his information concerning the sale of arms to Iran. He mentions that his partner's name is John Hortrich DeLaocque (sic), who "is known to Gen. Kelly (sic) of the United States Marine Corps." (Brenneke letter 1/15/86)

- While coordinating with the Defense Department and the Director of Central Intelligence, North also spoke to Nir about the Israeli-Ghorbanifar side of the transaction. Nir, who had just spent thirty-six hours in Lebanon, "believes that Gorba does indeed have at least $10,000 per Tow [sic] available," North reported to Poindexter on January 15, "and that Gorba probably lied to Schwimmer and that Schwimmer probably lied to Nir re how much there was available. Nir is fully prepared to proceed any way we wish but noted that time is rapidly running out." (North PROF note to Poindexter, 1/15/86, 15:41:44)

JAN 16 - A final meeting was held in Poindexter's office on January 16 to review a final draft of the finding. Attending were Poindexter, Casey, Meese, Sporkin and Weinberger.

Weinberger again voiced opposition to the program. There was also discussion of the question of notification of Congress.

The Attorney General testified that he gave his opinion that withholding notification was legal, on the basis of the President's constitutional powers and justifiable because of jeopardy to the hostages. Meese testified that it was his recollection that Congress was to be notified as soon as the hostages were freed. Sporkin testified that his recollection was that the participants agreed to defer notification of Congress until the release of the hostages, even though they understood this might mean a lengthy delay. (SSIC 1/29/87)

At the same time, the Director of Central Intelligence, Poindexter, and North expressed concern about Ledeen's role.

"Have told this to Ami [?Nir]. You [Poindexter] should be aware, however, that it is my opinion, based on my meeting w/ Gorba on Monday night [January 13], that Gorba tells Ledeen everything. Ami suspects that there is probably a secret business arrangement among Schwimmer, Ledeen and Gorba that is being conducted w/o the knowledge of any of the three respective governments and that this will result in at least some cross-fertilization of information. This may not be altogether bad if we can keep in touch w/Ledeen enough to get a feel for what is really going on. I have no problem w/someone making an honest profit on honest business. I do have a problem if it means the compromise of sensitive political or operational details. We might consider making Mike a contract employee of the CIA and requiring him to take a periodic polygraph. Yes? No?"(North PROF note to Poindexter, 1/16/86, 13:50:49) (Tower)

JAN 17 - Prior to this date, Samuel Evans locates and contacts prospective Israeli sellers of military hardware, Guri and Israel Eisenberg of B.I.T. Company Ltd. (later described as the Bazelet International Trading Company), who can supply U.S. equipment and end-user certificates. (Court papers, U.S. District Court, New York)

- It [The proposal to shift to direct U.S. arms sales to Iran] was considered by the President at a meeting on January 17 which only the Vice President, Mr. Regan, Mr. Fortier, and VADM Poindexter attended. Thereafter, the only senior-level review the Iran initiative received was during one or another of the President's daily national security briefings.

These were routinely attended only by the President, the Vice President, Mr. Regan, and VADM Poindexter. There was no subsequent collective consideration of the Iran initiative by the NSC principals before it became public 11 months later. (Tower)

- Because of the obsession with secrecy, interagency consideration of the initiative was limited to the cabinet level. With the exception of the NSC staff and, after January 17, 1986, a handful of CIA officials, the rest of the executive departments and agencies were largely excluded. (Tower)

- With the signing of the January 17 Finding, the Iran initiative became a U.S. operation run by the NSC staff. LtCol North made most of the significant operational decisions. He conducted the operation through Mr. Secord and his associates, a network of private individuals already involved in the Contra resupply operation. To this was added a handful of selected individuals from the CIA. (Tower)

- The National Security Act also requires notification of Congress of covert intelligence activities. If not done in advance, notification must be "in a timely fashion." The Presidential finding of January 17 directed that Congressional notification be withheld, and this decision appears to have never been reconsidered. (Tower)

- Invoices from International Procurement & Sales Inc., signed by Hermann Moll, to Galaxy Trade Inc., care of Samuel M. Evans Esq., for (1) 15 VA-145 Pulsed Twystr Amplifiers for $1,725,000; and (2) 200 M-48 tank engines for $38 million. The phone conversation between Moll and Evans is monitored by Customs. (Court papers, U.S. District Court, New York)

- Reagan meets with Bush, Regan and Poindexter's deputy, Donald R. Fortier. The session lasts only 20 minutes. Poindexter arrives late with a three-page background paper, from which he orally briefs the group. Reagan signs the secret presidential finding drafted the day before authorizing U.S. arms shipments to Iran. It is identical to the January 6 draft finding, except that it mentions "third parties" in the deals and omits any reference to Israel. Meese says later that the finding allows the CIA to be the agent for transferring money from Iran through intermediaries, described as representatives of Israel. He says the only legal opinion that is given or asked for during this process is a routine concurrence with the finding. The finding also directs Casey not to disclose the Iran operation to congressional oversight committees, an idea that reportedly originated with CIA General Counsel Sporkin. Despite a 1982 National Security Decision Directive (NSDD) requiring that findings be circulated among the eight senior members of the National Security Planning Group, only half of the members, Bush, Casey, Meese and Regan know of the document. The other four, Shultz, Weinberger, Treasury Secretary James A. Baker III and Adm. William J. Crowe, chairman of the Joint Chiefs of Staff, reportedly are not informed either that the final version exists or that Reagan has signed it. A memorandum from Poindexter to the President attached to the finding notes that Shultz and Weinberger oppose the plan, while Meese and Casey approve it. A hand-written note at the end of the memorandum, initialed "JP," reads: "President was briefed verbally from this paper" and "VP, Don Regan and Don Fortier were present." The document is placed in Poindexter's safe. (Memorandum from Poindexter to the President & Attachment Tab A: "Covert Action Finding" 1/17/86; Meese briefing 11/25/86; WP 12/7/86, 12/11/86, 12/28/86, 1/10/87 & 1/15/87; PI 11/26/86)

- On January 17, a second draft Finding was submitted to the President. It was identical to the January 6 Finding but with the addition of the words "and third parties" to the first sentence.

The President told the Board that he signed the Finding on January 17. It was presented to him under cover of a memorandum from VADM Poindexter of the same date. The President said he was briefed on the contents of the memorandum but stated that he did not read it. This is reflected in VADM Poindexter's handwritten note on the memorandum. That note also indicates that the Vice President, Mr. Regan, and Donald Fortier were present for the briefing.

Although the draft Finding was virtually identical to that signed by the President on January 6, the cover memorandum signaled a major change in the Iran initiative. Rather than accepting the arrangement suggested by Mr. Nir, the memorandum proposed that the CIA purchase 4000 TOWs from DoD and, after receiving payment, transfer them directly to Iran. Israel would still "make the necessary arrangements" for the transaction....This was an important change. The United States became a direct supplier of arms to Iran. The President told the Board that he understood the plan in this way. That day, President Reagan wrote in his diary: "I agreed to sell TOWs to Iran." (Tower)

- Administration officials believe this Poindexter memo and others were falsified in November 1986 to match the false chronology prepared at the time. Lawrence Walsh and the FBI are investigating whether memos and other documents in Poindexter's office are missing or falsified. (WSJ 2/24/87)

- Regan did not recall the event. He wondered if Poindexter had not simply placed the document in the President's daily briefing book for signature during the morning intelligence briefing. (Regan 20, 41-42) (Tower)

- Full-scale implementation of the January 17 Finding began immediately. LTC North flew to London to brief and negotiate with Ghorbanifar, who was told what the United States was prepared to do as a sign of good faith and interest in a long-term relationship. He was told particularly that the United States would provide intelligence of Iraqi positions in the war zone. Ghorbanifar also was told that more TOW missiles would be sold to Iran and that the unwanted HAWK missiles would be picked up and removed from Iran in connection with the first delivery of 1,000 TOWs. (SSIC 1/29/87)

- Weinberger testified before the Committee that later that day he received a call from Poindexter informing him of the President's action. Weinberger testified that he instructed military aide, Major General Colin Powell, to arrange for transfer of the weapons under the Economy Act to the CIA, and that the matter was to be closely held at the direction of the President.

General Powell had had previous discussions with North about the program and about Israel's problems in getting replacement TOWs. Assistant Secretary Armitage testified that Weinberger gave his aide authority to inform Armitage, which was done at a later date. Armitage testified that Deputy Secretary Taft later told him that in April Taft had seen the finding in Poindexter's office, where it was kept. According to Armitage and a CIA official, Powell worked with Major General Vincent Russo, of the Defense Logistics Agency to provide the material securely and without any loss of funds for the Army.

CIA's Deputy Director for Operations testified that he was informed by the DDCI or the DCI that the CIA was going to provide support to a White House initiative which had two aims: (1) strategic dialogue with Iran; and (2) the release of the hostages. (SSIC 1/29/87)

- "Some time ago Attorney General William French Smith determined that under an appropriate finding you could authorize the CIA to sell arms to countries outside of the provisions of the laws and reporting requirements for foreign military sales. The objectives of the Israeli plan could be met if the CIA, using an authorized agent as necessary, purchased arms from the Department of Defense under the Economy Act and then transferred them to Iran directly after receiving appropriate payment from Iran.

"The Covert Action Finding attached at Tab A provides the latitude for the transactions indicated above to proceed. The Iranians have indicated an immediate requirement for 4,000 basic TOW weapons for use in the launchers they already hold. The Israeli's [sic] are also sensitive to a strong U.S. desire to free our Beirut hostages and have insisted that the Iranians demonstrate both influence and good intent by an early release of the five Americans. Both sides have agreed that the hostages will be immediately released upon commencement of this action. Prime Minister Peres had his emissary pointedly note that they well understand our position on not making concessions to terrorists. They also point out, however, that terrorist groups, movements, and organizations are significantly easier to influence through governments than they are by direct approach. In that we have been unable to exercise any suasion over Hezballah during the course of nearly two years of kidnappings, this approach through the government of Iran may well be our only way to achieve the release of the Americans held in Beirut. It must again be noted that since this dialogue with the Iranians began in September, Reverend Weir has been released and there have been no Shia terrorist attacks against American or Israeli persons, property, or interests.

"Therefore it is proposed that Israel make the necessary arrangements for the sale of 4,000 TOW weapons to Iran. Sufficient funds to cover the sale would be transferred to an agent of the CIA. (Footnote: Probably a reference to General Secord) The CIA would then purchase the weapons from the Department of Defense and deliver the weapons to

Iran through the agent. If all of the hostages are not released after the first shipment of 1,000 weapons, further transfers would cease.

"On the other hand, since hostage release is in some respects a byproduct of a larger effort to develop ties to potentially moderate forces in Iran, you may wish to redirect such transfers to other groups within the government at a later time.

"The Israelis have asked for our urgent response to this proposal so that they can plan accordingly. They note that conditions inside both Iran and Lebanon are highly volatile. The Israelis are cognizant that this entire operation will be terminated if the Iranians abandon their goal of moderating their government or allow further acts of terrorism. You have discussed the general outlines of the Israeli plan with Secretaries Shultz and Weinberger, Attorney General Meese and Director Casey. The Secretaries do not recommend you proceed with this plan. Attorney General Meese and Director Casey believe the short-term and long-term objectives of the plan warrant the policy risks involved and recommend you approve the attached Finding. Because of the extreme sensitivity of this project, it is recommended that you exercise your statutory prerogative to withhold notification of the Finding to the Congressional oversight committees until such time that you deem it to be appropriate."

At the bottom of this page appeared:

"Recommendation

"OK NO

"RR per JMP" That you sign the attached Finding.

"Prepared by:

"Oliver L. North

"Attachment

"Tab A - Covert Action Finding "1000 17 Jan 1986

"President was briefed verbally from this paper. VP, Don Regan and Don Fortier were present. JP" (Tower)

- In the months that followed the signing of the January 17th Finding, LtCol North forwarded to VADM Poindexter a number of operational plans for achieving the release of all the hostages. Each plan involved a direct link between the release of hostages and the sale of arms. LtCol North, with the knowledge of VADM Poindexter and the support of selected individuals at CIA, directly managed a network of private individuals in carrying out these plans. None of the plans, however, achieved their common objective—the release of all the hostages. (Tower)

JAN 18 - The day after the President signed the Finding, the CIA formally joined the program. Clair George, Director of Operations, Sporkin, and Chief of the Near East Division (C/NE), met Poindexter, North, and Secord and read the Finding. (C/NE (1) 4; George 9) C/NE and North then discussed logistics and financing. "At the meeting on that Saturday [January 18]," C/NE recalled, "it was clear that what was needed was 4,508 TOW missiles, which were to be sold to the Iranians as a portion of a larger strategic effort which would get all the American hostages back out, but would also move to changing the nature of the relationship with the U.S. and the Iranians." (C/NE (1) 4) C/NE thought the program had been "an NSC operation" since November; nothing that subsequently happened changed his mind. (Id. at 43, 44)

North instructed C/NE to contact General Powell about arranging for the CIA to purchase the missiles from the Defense Department; C/NE found Powell already working on the problem. Powell directed C/NE to consult Major General Russo, Assistant Deputy Chief of Staff for [Army] Logistics, about pricing. When informed that the TOWs would cost some $6,000 each, North told C/NE that old TOWs, useless to the American Army and in less than optimal condition, would suffice. These cost about $3,407 apiece. (Id. at 4-6) The Defense Department insisted on being paid value for the missiles; the CIA insisted that its treasury not provide a float; and the Iranians would pay only on delivery. North needed a Swiss bank account to hold the money. C/NE provided an already existing account as the quickest solution to North's problem. Setting up a new account for the sums in question would take time. (Id. at 6)

The structure made Ghorbanifar important to success; he raised the necessary "venture capital." (Id. at 7) As a result of the polygraph, George decided not to use Ghorbanifar for intelligence or covert actions and, moreover, to terminate CIA relations with Ledeen. (CIA/IG Chronology 14 (1/12 or 13/86)) The Director of Central Intelligence took a more flexible position, and C/NE followed his lead.

"The Director's position when this started up, late January-early February, was Ghorbanifar is a rascal. They had a lot of experience with this guy. He's unreliable. But the channel, there's something in this channel that's working and it's worth a try, and nothing else is working, so let's see where it goes."

"And if it doesn't go, we'll turn it off." (C/NE (1) 23-24) (Tower)

- Weinberger receives an "urgent" telephone call from the White House directing him to make arrangements for the transfer of up to 4,000 TOW antitank missiles from the Pentagon to the CIA for a covert action. Bypassing normal channels used for covert shipments, he instructs his senior military assistant, Lieutenant General Colin L. Powell, to handle the transfer. Weinberger is informed by the White House of the finding signed by Reagan the previous day. (WP 1/10/87 & 1/15/87)

- The Army's involvement began on January 18 when it received a request to deliver 3,504 (later increased to 4,509) TOW missiles to "the receiver" at Redstone Airfield, for an unknown purpose and destination. Transfer depended on receipt of funds by the receiving agency. It was delayed. (See February 10 & 11 entry.) (Tower)

JAN 19-21 - Bush's deputy national security adviser, Colonel Samuel Watson, meets with Felix Rodriguez in El Salvador "to discuss counterinsurgency operations," according to a chronology released by Bush's office in December 1986. Among those Watson also contacts is the chief U.S. military adviser in that country, Colonel James Steele, who is reported later to be in constant touch at this time with the covert arms resupply operation to the contras. (WP 12/16/86)

JAN 21 - Delaroque says he now has the F-104 end-user certificate, obtained from Pakistan, and will shortly have the necessary F-4 end-user certificate from Greece. Evans now represents the B.I.T Company and the Eisenbergs. Phone conversation between Evans and Moll is monitored. (Court papers, U.S. District Court, New York)

- North asks the CIA to set up a Swiss bank account to handle the Iran arms sales. When his request is not handled fast enough, he instructs the Agency to deposit the first funds from the Iran deal into the joint U.S.-Saudi account for the Afghan rebels. (WP 1/13/87 & 1/15/87)

- North's "notional timeline" for the Iran arms sale program [see January 24 entry] provided for a funding mechanism in which Iranian funds would be put into an account in the same bank that was controlled by Secord. Secord's account manager, in turn, would transfer enough funds to the CIA to cover the actual cost of the arms and transportation. Those funds would be transferred by the CIA to a Defense Department account, at which point DOD could begin to move the material to the staging area. According to testimony received by the Committee, on January 21 North asked the CIA to open a Swiss bank account for their part of the funding chain. According to testimony by CIA officials, CIA personnel decided that the fastest and most secure mechanism would be to use an existing account that also contained funds for an unrelated operation. A CIA official gave the number of that account to North; it was used for several months, until a separate account was created in a routine manner. CIA testimony indicates that there was no commingling of funds between the two projects that used the same bank account for these months. Testimony and documents also indicate that, in practice, DoD needed only an assurance that CIA had the requisite funds in its possession. Actual payment occurred months later, after DoD had formally billed the CIA for the arms. (SSIC 1/29/87)

- On January 21, the CIA was asked to assist LTC North in preparing for a meeting in Europe with Ghorbanifar. They did so later that day. (SSIC 1/29/87)

- The Lake Resources bank account in Switzerland receives $360,000 passed on from I.C. Inc. and IBC. (WP 3/7/87)

LATE JAN - Late in the month, Nir meets in Washington with North who gives him the price of the weapons to be shipped to Iran as well as the number of a Swiss bank account into which to deposit payments. (WP 11/23/86 & 12/7/86)

JAN 22 - Evans receives invoices for the deal on B.I.T. letterhead from the Eisenbergs. Customs monitors another phone conversation between Moll and Evans. (Court papers, U.S. District Court, New York)

- The Secretary of State recalled that "[o]n January 22, my staff noted reports received about Lieutenant Colonel North. They speculated that perhaps the operation was alive again. But the reports seemed implausible, namely a proposal by Lieutenant Colonel North to seek the help of the Pope and

Cardinal O'Connor, and to trade some Shia prisoners held by General Lahad in South Lebanon as Nir had earlier suggested. (Tower)

JAN 23 - Sam Evans and Guri Eisenberg discuss the possibility of getting needed end user certificates from Turkey. (Court papers, U.S. District Court, New York)

- At Ghorbanifar's request, on January 23, Allen met a follower of Ayatollah Shirazi, who was visiting the United States. He confirmed Ghorbanifar's connections "in key areas" of the Middle East. (C. Allen, "Meeting with Hojjat ol-Eslam Seyyed Mohsen Khatami," 1/31/86) (Tower)

JAN 24 - North writes a long-term plan in connection with the Iran initiative that envisions an arms-for-hostages exchange as a sign of good faith with Iran, the involvement of religious leaders regarding the plight of the hostages, and ultimately an end to Khomeini's rule. Said to be typical of the contingency plans North frequently draws up, the paper illustrates, according to a White House official, that "Ollie North lived in a Peter Pan world." (WP 1/15/87)

- On January 24, LtCol North sent to VADM Poindexter a lengthy memorandum containing a notional timeline for "Operation Recovery." The complex plan was to commence January 24 and conclude February 25. It called for the United States to provide intelligence data to Iran. Thereafter, Mr. Ghorbanifar was to transfer funds for the purchase of 1000 TOWs to an Israeli account at Credit Suisse Bank in Geneva, Switzerland. It provided that these funds would be transferred to an account in the same bank controlled by Mr. Secord; that $6 million of that amount would be transferred to a CIA account in that bank; and that the CIA would then wire the $6 million to a U.S. Department of Defense account in the United States. The 1000 TOWs would then be transferred from the DoD to the CIA.

Mr. Secord and his associates, rather than the CIA, had the more substantial operational role. He would arrange for the shipment of the TOWs to Eilat, Israel. From there, an Israeli 707, flown by a crew provided by Mr. Secord, would deliver the TOWs to Bandar Abbas, Iran. On the return flight, the aircraft would stop in Tehran to pick up the HAWK missiles delivered in November of 1985 but later rejected by Iran. The plan anticipated that the next day (February 9) all U.S. citizens held hostage in Beirut would be released to the U.S. embassy there. Thereafter, 3000 more TOWS would be delivered . . . (Tower)

- When North returned from a late January meeting with Ghorbanifar in London, he prepared "a notional timeline for major events in Operation Recovery." (North to Poindexter, draft Action Memorandum, 1/24/86.) "[T]he only persons completely cognizant of this schedule," North wrote, "are: John Poindexter, Don Fortier, Oliver North, John McMahon, Clair George, C/NE, Dewey Clarridge, Richard Secord, Amiram Nir, Prime Minister Shimon Peres." The timeline was attached:

Notional Timeline for Operation Recovery
Friday, January 24
—CIA provide cube and weight data to Copp for a/c loading.
—CIA prepare intel sample for pass to Gorba.
—Copp provide a/c tail # to CIA for pickup. . . .
Saturday, January 25
—Dispatch intel sample to Gorba via Charlie Allen.
Sunday, January 26
—C. Allen deliver intel sample to Gorba at Churchill Hotel, London.
—Copp finalize a/c requirements w/ air carrier in Oklahoma.
Monday, January 27
—Gorba place intel sample on 1300 GMT flight to Tehran fm Frankfurt, Germany.
Wednesday, January 29
—Gorba transfer funds for purchase/transport of 1000 basic TOWs to Israeli account at Credit Suisse Bank, Geneva.
—Israeli account manager automatically transfers deposit fm Israeli account to Copp account in same bank (bank record keeping transaction).
—Copp's account manager automatically transfers $6M to CIA account in same bank (bank record keeping transaction).
Thursday, January 30
—CIA transfers $6M to DoD account by wire service transaction.
—CIA orders movement of 1000 TOW missiles fm DoD storage facility Anniston, Alabama. . .
—CIA bills Copp account $26K for cost of moving 1000 TOW missiles fm Anniston, Alabama. . .

Sunday, February 2

—Copp travels to Israel for site survey of transfer point (Eliat [sic], Israel).

—Copp proceeds to rendezvous w/ Clarridge to establish command post.

Monday, February 3

—Lahad responds to papal ltr that he will release 50 Hezballah prisoners in 2 groups of 25.

Tuesday, February 4

—1000 TOWs sanitized and prepared for shipping....

—Copp a/c packers arrive... and arrange for Copp a/c to lift TOWs fm Kelly AF Base San Antonio, TX, on CIA contract.

Wednesday, February 5

—Copp a/c arrives Kelly AF Base for loading.

—CIA provides remainder of first intel sample to Gorba at Iranian Embassy in Bonn, Germany.

Thursday, February 6

—Copp a/c commence lifting TOWs fm Kelly AF Base to transfer point at Eliat, Israel.

—Israeli AF "sterilized" 707 a/c arrives at transfer point for loading.

—Copp aircrew arrives Eliat, Israel, to pilot Israeli a/c.

—Remainder of first intel sample flown fm Germany to Tehran in diplomatic pouch on scheduled Iran Airways flight.

Friday, February 7

—Israeli "sterile" a/c piloted by Copp crew commences movement of TOWs fm Eliat to Bandar Abbas, Iran, via Red Sea route.

Saturday, February 8

—Delivery of 1000 TOWs completed.

—25 Hezballah released by Lahad,

—Returning Israeli a/c pickup 18 HAWK at Tehran airport for return to Israel.

Sunday, February 9

—All U.S. hostages released to U.S./ British or Swiss Embassy.

—Second group of 25 Hezballah released by Lahad

—Israelis return $5.4M to Gorba when HAWKs land in Israel.

Monday, February 10

—Gorba transfers funds to Israel account for purchase/ transportation of 3000 TOWs (amount transferred is sufficient to cover purchase of 508 additional TOWs owed to Israel for Weir release and all transportation costs).

—Israelis transfer funds to Copp account at Credit Suisse Bank, Geneva.

—Copp transfers funds to CIA account for purchase/transportation of 3508 TOWs ($21.048M).

—Four (4) remaining Lebanese-Jews released by Hezballah.

Tuesday, February 11 (Anniversary of Iranian-Islamic Revolution)

—Khomheini steps down.

—CIA transfers $21.048M to DoD account for purchase of 3508 TOWs at $6K each.

—CIA starts moving TOWs... fm Anniston, Alabama, in lots of 1000.

Thursday, February 13

—Copp packers return...

Tuesday, February 18

—Copp a/c pickup 1000 TOWs at Kelly AF Base, Texas; deliver to transfer point (Eliat).

—Israeli "sterilized" 707 a/c w/Copp crew commences delivery of 1000 TOWs to Iran.

Thursday, February 20

—Copp a/c pickup 1000 TOWs at Kelly AF Base, Texas; deliver to transfer point (Eliat).

—Israeli "sterilized" 707 a/c w/Copp crew commences delivery of 1000 TOWs to Iran.

Saturday, February 22

—Copp a/c pickup 1000 TOWs at Kelly AF Base, Texas; deliver to transfer point (Eliat).

—Israeli "sterilized" 707 a/c w/Copp crew commences delivery of 1000 TOW's to Iran.

Monday, February 24

—Copp a/c returns ... pickup 508 TOWs for delivery to Israel.

—Collett (British hostage) and Italian hostages released and Buckley remains returned.

Tuesday, February 25

—Second sample of intel provided to Gorba at Iranian Embassy in Bonn, Germany....

Mr. Ghorbanifar's recollection of the terms of the arrangements are radically different. Mr. Ghorbanifar stated adamantly that the 1000 TOWs were to reestablish U.S. good faith after the disastrous November shipment of HAWK missiles. Mr. Ghorbanifar said there was no agreement that the U.S. hostages would be released as a result of the sale. (Tower)

- [North writes Poindexter to express again his concern about Ledeen's role:]

"Casey shares our concerns. More recent information tends to indicate that there is even further grounds for concern given what may well be/have been a financial arrangement among Schwimmer, Nimrod[i], Gorba and our friend." (North PROF note to Poindexter, 1/24/86, 10:40:36) Perhaps because of these doubts, Ledeen ceased to be an official American contact with Ghorbanifar (See January 14 entry) (Tower)

- Deputy Director John McMahon, who had opposed arms transfers to Iran from the beginning, read the January 17 Finding on January 24. "[G]iving TOW missiles was one thing," he remembered telling Poindexter. "[G]iving them intelligence gave them a definite offensive edge, and I said that can have cataclysmic results." (J. McMahon 14) He was unimpressed with Poindexter's description of the plan:

"[G]ive some intelligence to the Iranians on the Iraqi front, . . . to establish bona fides that the U.S. really was intent on moving in this direction, and then give them 1,000 TOW missiles and then see what the Iranians did, like release a hostage."

"I objected to that. Poindexter didn't take me on. He didn't challenge that at all, but he said: 'We have an opportunity here that we should not miss, and we ought to proceed to explore it; and if it doesn't work, all we've lost is a little intelligence and 1,000 TOW missiles; and if it does work, then maybe we can change a lot of things in the Mideast.'

"So I came back to the building. Bill Casey was [abroad] at the time. I sent him a cable laying out what was happening, saying we have a directive from the President, a finding to do this, Poindexter said that the Attorney General had checked off on it, and that we were so directed to proceed to support the mission.

"And I said, I am so proceeding. I asked for confirmation from Bill to make sure that he was aware of what was happening, and I didn't receive any. Casey had moved on to [country name deleted], so I sent it again to [country name deleted]. And it came back saying: Yes, he has read it and confirmed, and he had seen it.

"Then we proceeded to have DoD transfer weapons to us, and we would arrange for the flights over there. All throughout this, I must insist that even at its peak the Agency was only in a supportive role. We took directions, we followed directions." (Id. at 14-16) (Tower)

JAN 25 - According to testimony of Robert Gates, who was Deputy Director for Intelligence at the time, a meeting was held on January 25 at CIA to discuss preparation of intelligence material which was to be passed to the Iranians. Participants testified that the meeting was attended by officials from CIA and LTC North from the NSC. Gates testified that he objected to the release of some specific intelligence relating to Iraq but that he was overruled by the NSC, and CIA was directed to prepare the intelligence material. A CIA official was directed to take the intelligence sample to Ghorbanifar. (SSIC 1/29/87)

JAN 26 - North's plan called for intelligence samples to be given to Ghorbanifar in Europe on January 26, 1986. According to testimony and a cable from Deputy Director McMahon to Director Casey, McMahon argued strongly with Poindexter that this should not be done, both because Ghorbanifar could not be trusted and because intelligence could give Iran an advantage in the war; but, McMahon testified, Poindexter insisted, and he obeyed. (SSIC 1/29/87)

- The intelligence material was given to Ghorbanifar in a meeting held in Europe in late January, according to testimony and documents received by the Committee. Ghorbanifar complained bitterly about his polygraph and argued as he had done in Washington on January 13, that his Iranian contacts could be of great use to the United States. (SSIC 1/29/87)

JAN 27 - Evans says in monitored phone call that a Mr. Northrop could obtain for Hashemi and Iran some 13 items made by "his company and 30 spare engines." (Court papers, U.S. District Court, New York)

JAN 29 - St. Lucia Airways, which is linked to CIA missions to Angola and later to U.S.-sanctioned arms deliveries to Iran and Israel, travels from Kelly Air Force Base in San

Antonio, Texas to Cape Verde off the coast of Africa, according to flight records. Cape Verde is reported to be a refueling site on the way to Zaire. According to press reports, the airline makes several trips to Zaire this year with military supplies that are eventually turned over to U.S.-backed rebels in Angola. (See March 20 - April 20 entry, for example.) (WP 2/24/87)

JAN 30 - Honduran Armed Forces head Walter Lopez Reyes resigns. Honduran military and foreign diplomatic sources claim that the CIA backed a group of right-wing officers who pressured Reyes into resigning, and sought to isolate a group of progressive junior officers. Honduran military sources say Lopez Reyes quit because of a dispute over the contra presence in Honduras. (WP 2/9/86)

- President Reagan meets with Spitz Channell and a small group of donors to Channell's groups, the National Endowment for the Preservation of Liberty and the American Conservative Trust, in the Roosevelt Room of the White House. The meeting begins at 2:30 p.m. with a welcome from Linas Kojelis (Special Assistant to the President for Public Liaison), remarks from Linda Chavez (Deputy Assistant to the President for Public Liaison), and a "Central American Overview" by Elliott Abrams (Assistant Secretary of State for Inter-American Affairs). At 3:15 p.m. President Reagan addresses the group, followed by a "Report on Nicaragua" by Oliver North. A Channell fundraiser, Jane McLaughlin, later tells reporters that the price for inclusion in this session with the President was a $30,000 or more contribution to Channell's groups. Two of the donors in attendance, Inman Brandon of Atlanta and John Ramsey of Wichita Falls, Texas, later confirm to reporters that they each gave $100,000 or more. Ramsey says, "If they could have given the money for weapons legally, that would have suited me fine." (White House briefing agenda 1/30/86; ABC News 2/12/87; WP 3/7/87; NYT 2/26/87)

JAN - After a meeting with Oliver North and Spitz Channell in the Old Executive Office Building, retired mining executive E. Thomas Clagett makes a $20,000 contribution to the National Endowment for the Preservation of Liberty with the understanding that the money would pay for Contra weapons to "kill the commies—direct military support for the troops —guns and ammunition." The money goes into a special

NEPL account called "Toys," which former Channell employees describe as "for weapons only." North played a central role in Channell's efforts to raise money from conservative donors for the contras. Jane E. McLaughlin, a fund-raiser working for Carl "Spitz" Channell, does not believe "the money we raised ever directly helped the Nicaraguan freedom fighters." She also believes some of the contributions, ostensibly intended for humanitarian assistance, were used to provide military aid to the rebels. McLaughlin says North's role in the operations was supposed to be kept secret. "I was told by Spitz that you must never refer to Colonel North as Colonel North over the phone," she says. "It was crucial to keep these things quiet." She says workers in her office referred to North instead by the code name "Green." McLaughlin says one of Channell's operations was known in the office as Project Toys. Money donated for the program, according to McLaughlin, was deposited into bank accounts of Channell's National Endowment for the Preservation of Liberty (NEPL), which then transferred large sums to International Business Communications (IBC). According to photocopies of bank statements and ledger books in McLaughlin's possession, NEPL paid a total of over $3 million to IBC from December 1985 through May 1986. (NYT 2/26/87; NEPL "Top 25 Contributors" list 10/3/86; WP 3/12/87; ABC News 2/12/87)

JAN 30-FEB 10 - Evans and Moll discuss with others in a series of monitored phone calls the sale of military equipment to Hashemi and Iran. (Court papers, U.S. District Court, New York)

JAN 31 - Moll claims in a monitored phone call that he can get an end-user certificate from a NATO country for five to six percent of the price of the goods, but that the dealers needed to avoid the U.S. (Court papers, U.S. District Court, New York)

- Cyrus Hashemi is told by a French businessman hoping to sell arms to Iran that "[a]n assistant of the vice president's going to be in Germany . . . and the indication is very clear that the transaction can go forward . . ." referring to Bush's alleged approval of the private sale. (MH 11/30/86)

THE WHITE HOUSE

WASHINGTON

CENTRAL AMERICA BRIEFING

FOR THE AMERICAN CONSERVATIVE TRUST AND THE

NATIONAL ENDOWMENT FOR THE PRESERVATION OF LIBERTY

January 30, 1986, 2:30 p.m. -- The Roosevelt Room

*   *   *

2:30 p.m.	Welcome -- Linas Kojelis, Special Assistant to the President for Public Liaison
	Remarks -- Linda Chavez, Deputy Assistant to the President for Public Liaison
	"Central American Overview: An Update" -- Elliott Abrams, Assistant Secretary of State for Latin America
3:15 p.m.	Remarks -- The President
	"Report on Nicaragua" -- Oliver North, Deputy Director, Political-Military Affairs, National Security Council

*   *   *

FEBRUARY 1986

FEB - The initial CIA action officer on the Iran project met with North on several occasions in 1986. The CIA officer described Secord and Hakim as "almost co-equal lieutenants" of North. The CIA action officer testified that on a trip in February he learned from North that Secord and Hakim were the principal aids to North in his contra activities. North did not describe those activities to the CIA officer other than saying that Hakim was responsible for the effort in Europe to help the contras . . . It seemed to the CIA officer as if North was splitting his time between the contras and the Iran project and that he was having trouble keeping up with both. North was visiting Honduras and going to meetings and otherwise working hard on support for the fighters. The CIA officer testified that North's activities were widely known in the CIA and the NSC. (SSIC 1/29/87)

- Casey testifies that two payments for deliveries of weapons to Iran are made to a U.S.-managed Swiss bank account early this month. (WP 12/16/86)

- According to New York businessman Roy Furmark, Khashoggi advances $10 million this month to finance a third shipment of arms to Iran. Khashoggi says Ghorbanifar tells him to deposit the money into the account of Lake Resources at the Credit Suisse Bank in Geneva. Furmark says the Saudi arms dealer "got back $12 million" at the end of April, including $2 million for financing and "other costs." Earlier, Khashoggi reportedly provided funds of $1 million and $4 million to pay for the two initial arms shipments through Israel in 1985. He deposited those funds, he says, into a Swiss account belonging to Yaacov Nimrodi. He is later reimbursed by the Iranians through Ghorbanifar. (WP 12/24/86 & 2/1/87)

- Poindexter specifically tells NSC Director of Political-Military Affairs Howard J. Teicher that North will not be under his command. He also informs Teicher that North will remain responsible for contra-related matters and that Teicher should not involve himself in those issues. (NYT 1/12/87)

- Lt. Gen. Dale A. Vesser, chief of plans and policy for the Joint Chiefs of Staff, travels to Egypt to work on military "contingency planning" regarding Libya. The State Department reportedly believes such planning falls within existing guidelines of "defensive" activities between the two countries, but other sources report that joint attacks on Libya are part of the ongoing discussions. (WP 2/20/87)

- By early February, CIA had put in motion the acquisition of the weapons, designated a Swiss bank account, and arranged for two Boeing 707s to be at the disposal of General Secord at Kelly Air Force Base. (CIA/IG Chronology 18)

FEB 1 - St. Lucia Airways flight SX 501 leaves Ostend, Belgium for North Yemen. Its cargo and purpose are unknown. The airline is later disclosed to be a proprietary of the CIA and is believed to have taken part in arms deliveries to Angola and Iran, and may have carried McFarlane on part of his journey to Iran in May 1986. The company is run by Deitrich Reinhardt, a West German living in Port Charlotte, Florida who denies any link to the CIA. The chairman of the board is Michael Gordon, a lawyer, who bought a 99 percent interest in the company "two or three years ago" from Allison Lindo of St. Lucia island in the Caribbean. (WP 2/24/87)

FEB 2 - A recently declassified CIA report defends the contras against reports that they engaged in atrocities in Nicaragua. (CRS "U.S. Intelligence: Issues for Congress, 1986" 1/5/87)

FEB 3 - Evans, the Eisenbergs, and Hashemi discuss the financing of the Iran transaction, including the need for Hashemi's bank to confirm to the sellers' bank the existence of sufficient funds to cover the deal. These discussions started as early as January 23. (Court papers, U.S. District Court, New York)

FEB 5 - North is in London for a meeting in connection with the Iran arms sales. Casey's prepared testimony, delivered to Congress on November 21, 1986, refers only to an NSC official at the meeting; he and his aides deny knowing who the official was. According to North's own chronology of events, he is accompanied by a CIA representative. (WP 1/20/87)

- On February 5, North traveled to London. (North calendar) According to the NSC chronologies, he met Ghorbanifar, Nir, and Ghorbanifar's Tehran contact.

According to the Maximum version and the Historical Chronology, 149 C/NE attended this meeting. (Maximum Version at 5, Historical Chronology at 9) The CIA Inspector General notes that a meeting occurred, but does not mention C/NE. (CIA/IG Chronology 18) C/NE denied that there was a meeting with the Tehran contact on February 15. (C/NE (1) 14) The Maximum Version states that the meeting was in Germany; the Historical Chronology places the meeting in London. The accounts of what was discussed are similar:

—The Iranian intermediary (Ghorbanifar) would deposit funds in an Israeli account.

—The Israelis would transfer funds to a sterile U.S.-controlled account in an overseas bank.

—Using these funds, the CIA would covertly obtain materiel authorized for transfer from U.S. military stocks and transport this to Israel for onward movement to Iran.

Using the procedures stipulated above, funds were deposited in the CIA account in Geneva on February 11, 1986 and on February 14 1,000 Tows were transported to Israel for prepositioning. The Tows were off-loaded and placed in a covert Israeli facility. (Maximum Version 6. Cf. Historical Chronology 9)

Ghorbanifar told the Board

"Let's say this meeting is somewhere around between first of February till fifth of February. It took place in Frankfurt ... The Iranian delegation stayed also in Hotel Intercontinental, in Frankfurt—a mixture of Iranian authorities, from Prime Minister's [office] and Iranian officers from intelligence department.

"This is a historical meeting, after seven years of break, that the two top officials of the two countries, they come together for such an important meeting, such an important mission, to work out against the intelligence against the Russians, against the Iraqis, and also to clean the mess [the November 1985 shipment of HAWKs]." (Ghorbanifar 131-32)

On the American side, Ghorbanifar said, were North, Secord, and someone identified to Ghorbanifar as "one of the top senior officers from the CIA. His hair was all white, white hair, good looking—baby face. (Footnote: This description might fit C/NE.) . . . No[t] Cave. Cave came later on for making the total disaster." (Id. at 134) Nir, who was always identified as an American in meetings with Iranian officials, (Id. at 135-36), also attended. Ghorbanifar described a "happy" scene, with Americans kissing Iranians. (Id. at 136) The military men talked, and

"Mr. North told him [Ghorbanifar's Tehran contact] that if you want to know that we were good feeling, good gesture, we were not going to cheat you now. We take out what we brought back in mistake [the 18 HAWKs] and we give you 1,000 TOWs. And then the Iranian kissed them and they made again dinner party." (Id. at 137) (Tower)

- Whether or not this meeting took place as described by Ghorbanifar—his description does not resemble C/NE's of the Frankfurt meeting, February 24-25 (C/NE (1) 18-20)—North returned from London on February 7 (North calendar), with the operation in full swing. (Tower)

FEB 6 - The next day, Khashoggi lent Ghorbanifar $10 million to pay for the missiles; Khashoggi insisted on a 15-20% return to pay finance costs. (Tower)

- Bush aide Lt. Col. E. Douglas Menarchik writes to Richard Brenneke in response to the latter's January 15 request to Bush for assistance in brokering arms deals with Iran. The letter states: "The U.S. government will not permit or participate in the provision of war materiel to Iran and will prosecute any such efforts by U.S. citizens to the fullest extent of the law." (Menarchik letter to Brenneke, 2/6/86)

- The treasurer of B.I.T., later reported to be Rabbi Yitzhak Hebroni, meets in New York with Hashemi and his banker to discuss financing. (Court papers, U.S. District Court, New York)

FEB 7 - On February 7, the Army began to consider whether a provision of the Intelligence Authorization Act for FY 1986 required Congressional notification of this transfer of arms to CIA. (See January 18 entry.) (SSIC 1/29/87)

- On February 7, Ghorbanifar said, he [Khashoggi] deposited the money in Lake Resources' Swiss account. North "told us that this time no Israeli deal. Off. This is ourself we directly will dealing." (Id. [Ghorbanifar] at 138)

"The money was paid to Lake Resources directly, and then they delivered the stuff. There was no talk of release of hostage. There was no hostage. So it is proof to you that there is no deal on hostage. There is no deal for hostage, tit for tat—give me, take this. You understand clearly it was a policy. It was a very big policy, very important strategic policy to go into water. No question about who is going." (Id. at 142) (Tower)

- North returned from London on February 7 (North calendar), with the operation in full swing. (Tower)

- The day after Menarchik writes to Brenneke, Cyrus Hashemi is informed by Evans, a suspect in the Customs Service sting operation, that "[t]he green light now finally has been given [for the private sale of arms to Iran], that Bush is in favor, Shultz against, but nevertheless they are willing to proceed." (MH 11/30/86)

FEB 8-9 - The next day or the day after [following North's return from London February 7, according to North's calendar], he [North] met Charles Allen, C/NE, Noel Koch from the office of Assistant Secretary of Defense Armitage, and Secord to review the schedule. TOW missiles would be delivered, hostages released, and Buckley's body returned by early March 1986. (C. Allen 14) At North's request, C/NE made flight arrangements for Southern Air Transport, a former CIA proprietary, to fly into Kelly Air Force base. (CIA/IG Chronology 19)

The United States Army made a record of its role in the TOW transfer because of Congressional reporting requirements. Under the Intelligence Authorization Act for Fiscal Year 1986, transfers of defense articles or services by an intelligence agency worth $1 million had to be reported to Congressional intelligence committees. Once apprised of this statute, the Army General Counsel advised Russo that where the Army "support[s] another agency, it is responsible to make the necessary notification." (Russo, note, 2/13/86, on Crawford to Marsh, 2/13/86) "During the course of coordination with OSD (M[ajor] G[eneral] Powell) and O[ffice of the] S[ecretary of the] A[rmy] G[eneral] C[ounsel], questions were asked as to the responsibility for end item usage. This was identified as a responsibility of the receiver."

(Russo, "Support for Intelligence Activities," 2/25/86.) The "receiver" was Southern Air Transport, operating under the direction of General Secord and Colonel North. (Tower)

FEB 9 - The plan ["Operation Recovery"] anticipated that the next day (February 9) all U.S. citizens held hostage in Beirut would be released to the U.S. embassy there. Thereafter, 3000 more TOWS would be delivered. (Tower)

FEB 10 - North introduces himself at a meeting of United Methodist Church leaders as a veteran of two wars—Vietnam and Angola. The incident adds to suspicion inside the government that North violated prohibitions on aid to Angolan rebels. (PI 3/15/87)

- Evans tells Minardos of B.I.T. in a monitored phone call that the letter Evans sent to Moll concerning the proof of Hashemi's financing was unacceptable to Moll. (Court papers, U.S. District Court, New York)

- UNO leaders Adolfo Calero, Arturo Cruz, and Alfonso Robelo attend a two-day conference in Madrid, Spain to discuss a "short and long term strategy" to build European support for the contras. (The Nation 1/17/87)

- Udall Corp. buys a two-seat Maule M-7 plane, FAA records show. An American mechanic working on the resupply operation says the plane is used in El Salvador and Honduras. (PI 2/6/87)

FEB 10 & 11 - [A] total of $3.7 million was deposited (by Ghorbanifar) in the CIA account used to pay for 1,000 TOW missiles. (CIA/IG Chronology 19) (Tower)

FEB 11 - Hebroni meets with Hashemi in New York to confirm the availability of funds and the availability of the items of Guri Eisenberg's invoice (except for one Skyhawk aircraft possibly unavailable), and that the letter of credit was not made through the U.S. The letter of credit is supposed to be divisible, with one portion for the merchandise and one portion for the end-user certificates, which Eisenberg is to obtain. (Court papers, U.S. District Court, New York)

- The plan ["Operation Recovery"] anticipated that Khomeini would step down on February 11, 1985, the fifth anniversary of the founding of the Islamic Republic. The Board has found no evidence that would give any credence to this assumption. (Tower)

FEB 12 - On February 12 the CIA notified the Army that funds were available [for the transfer of TOW missiles]. (SSIC 1/29/87)

FEB 13 - . . . the TOWs were turned over to the CIA [by the Army]. (SSIC 1/29/87)

- On the 13th of February, the Army's Office of the General Counsel determined that congressional notification [of arms sales to Iran] was the responsibility of the CIA rather than the Army. (SSIC 1/29/87)

- North wrote Poindexter that
"Operation RESCUE is now under way. 1000 items are currently enroute [sic] . . . from Anniston[,] Alabama. Copp is enroute to Ben Gurion Apt [airport] to conduct final briefing for his flight crews who arrived today and commenced fam flights on the two Israeli 707s. All 1000 items will lift off from Kelly AFB at 1400 on Saturday. 500 will be delivered to Bandar Abbas to arrive at dawn on Monday [February 17]. The meeting we had wanted has now been slipped to Weds [February 19] by Gorba. We will explore a second mtg/agenda/location/participants w/ him at this mtg per yr dir. Second 500 will go to Bandar Abbas on Friday vice Thurs. Copp, North plan to meet in Frankfurt on Tues. [February 18] along w/ one of Dewey's people to wire my hotel room for mtg. Carrying the luggage C/NE gave me for this purpose is too much of a hassle going thru customs/airport security in Europe. [possibly a reference to video and recording devices requested by C/NE on January 21. (CIA/IG Chronology 16] If all goes according to plan, Lahad will release 25 Hizballah . . . , hopefully on Friday. This wd keep our schedule for releasing the Americans on for Sunday, Feb. 23. Something to pray for at church that day." (North PROF note to Poindexter, 2/13/86, 21:39:47) (Tower)

FEB 13-14 - Having received certification that the money was available, the Army delivered the first 1,000 missiles on February 13-14. North's and Secord's reports complete the story of the delivery. (See February 13 entry, above.) North's notional timeline had to change. (Tower)

FEB 14 - The terms of payment and delivery for the Hashemi deal are agreed on, including a $3 million deposit from Hashemi. (Court papers, U.S. District Court, New York)

- Press reports citing U.S. and Honduran sources claim that the CIA continued in 1981-1984 to provide training to Honduran security forces that the CIA knew were responsible for killing civilian detainees. According to U.S. Embassy officials, "The CIA had nothing to do with picking people up. But they knew about it and when some people disappeared, they looked the other way." (NYT 2/14/86; CRS "U.S. Intelligence: Issues for Congress, 1986" 1/5/87)

- Richard Brenneke, in Europe on "an extended business trip," delivers to the U.S. Embassy in Paris photocopies of data to back up his earlier memoranda to various U.S. government officials. Once inside the Embassy, he seals the copies inside an envelope and mails it to Lt. Col. Alvarez of the Marine Corps in Washington. He later claims that "The information I sent was given me by [a] European national. At no time did I talk with any Iranian or Middle-East nationals. I can assure you that the documents have been authenticated by at least one European intelligence service." (Brenneke letter to Menarchik, 2/25/86)

- Southern Air Transport this month makes one flight from Dulles Airport to Ilopango air base in El Salvador, and two flights from Kelly Air Force Base, Texas to Tel Aviv. Administration sources say the company is providing the planes used in the Iran arms deliveries. One account of this month's U.S. shipment to Iran relates that the CIA, after receiving 500 TOW antitank missiles from the Pentagon, flies them to Israel. From there they are flown to Tehran. (DOT Records; WP 11/23/86 & 12/7/86 & 12/16/86)

FEB 15-16 - The 1,000 TOWs [priced at $3,515,000] were shipped to Israel on February 15-16 . . . (SSIC 1/29/87)

FEB 17 - . . . half of them [the 1,000 TOW missiles sent to Israel February 15-16] were flown to Iran on February 17. (SSIC 1/29/87)

- North wrote Poindexter that "500 [items] will be delivered to Bandar Abbas to arrive at dawn on Monday [February 17] . . . (North PROF note to Poindexter, 2/13/86, 21:39:47) [See February 18 entry.] (Tower)

FEB - The first of two shipments of U.S. arms is sent to Iran as part of a new plan adopted by Reagan in January to gain release of the hostages. The delivery includes 1,000 TOW

TRANSACTION FOUR: FEBRUARY 1986 SALE OF 1,000 U.S. TOW MISSILES

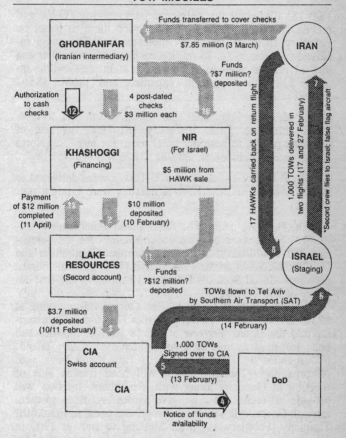

antitank missiles. The second shipment is scheduled for May. (WP 12/16/86 & 1/10/87)

- Iran returns the November 1985 delivery of arms to Israel. (NYT 12/25/86)

FEB 18 - The plane that delivered the remaining TOWs, and picked up the 18 HAWKs and returned them to Israel on February 18. [sic] Testimony indicates that Khashoggi received four checks for $3 million each from Ghorbanifar and that $1 million went to the investors as interest, while another $1 million covered expenses and profit. (SSIC 1/29/87)

- North wrote Poindexter that "Copp, North plan to meet in Frankfurt on Tues. [February 18] along w/ one of Dewey's people to wire my hotel room for mtg" . . . (North PROF note to Poindexter, 2/13/86, 21:39:47) (Tower)

- On February 18, the first 500 TOWs were delivered to Bandar Abbas, and the HAWK missiles were brought out. (Tower)

- On February 18, 1986, North asked Poindexter to authorize the issuance of alias documentation for the delegation that would travel to Germany to meet Ghorbanifar and his Tehran contact on the 19th. (C/NE (1) 14) His memorandum reproduced Secord's February 18 report of the first delivery of 500 TOWs.

"Aircraft returned safely to Ben Gurion this morning at 0730 EST. Seventeen HAWK missiles (Footnote: Ghorbanifar told the Board that one of the 18 HAWK missiles had been test-fired against an Iraqi fighter over Kharg Island. (Ghorbanifar 143)) aboard. Gorba called one hour ago. [Ghorbanifar's Tehran contact] will head Iranian side of meeting in Germany along with five others. Iranians will provide all names after we give names and titles to them through Gorba. All will arrive via private plane in Frankfurt, Thursday [February 19] p.m. Meeting to start at 1700 in Iranian Embassy (sic) for two hours. Iranians have asked for second delivery of 500 TOWs on Friday a.m. They say they will release all hostages, if, repeat, if [intelligence is good]. They say we will get hostages Friday or Saturday. They envision a future meeting in Iran with us to consider next steps while we are delivering balance of TOWs (3,000). We have already rejected embassy as meeting site. Suggested following names from our side:

Nir (Office of Israeli Prime Minister)

MGEN Adams (Director, Current Intelligence—DIA) (AKA—Secord)

William Goode (Office of President)

Albert Hakim (Support Assistant to Director DIA) (Secord to North, 2/18/86, [?received at] 8:30 a.m., in North. to Poindexter, 2/18/86)

North identified Hakim for Poindexter as "VP of one of the European companies set up to handle aid to resistance movement. He is fluent in farsi [sic] and would need one time alias documentation as a DIA official." (Footnote: In discussing what he insisted was a meeting in Frankfurt in the first week of February, but which he may have confused with the meeting February 20, Ghorbanifar told the Board that when he heard that Hakim was to attend the meeting, he successfully persuaded the Americans to change the delegation. "I said are you crazy? The Albert Hakim is known to all Iranian intelligence agencies and Iranian authorities, that he works, is operating for CIA. He was acting against Islamic Republic by CIA in 1980 and 1981, in Turkey, in the form of companies performing for making trouble for them in the Turkish border, and so on. They know him. If he comes in, they call this again another trick. So, I don't accept that such a man comes. They call me back in two days and say you are right." (Ghorbanifar 133)) Secord, using the alias Major General Adams wrote, "we appear to be much closer to a solution than earlier believed. [The attendance by an official from the Prime Minister's office] at the Frankfurt meeting tends to support our hope that this whole endeavor can succeed this week, if we appear to be forthcoming." (See February 20 entry.) (Tower)

FEB 19 - North wrote Poindexter that "The meeting we had wanted has now been slipped to Weds [February 19] by Gorba. We will explore a second mtg/ agenda/location/participants w/ him at this mtg per yr dir" . . . (North PROF note to Poindexter, 2/13/86, 21:39:47) (Tower)

- The CIA Inspector General's chronology states:. . . . C/ NE, North, Secord, and Nir meet with Ghorbanifar in

Frankfurt. Iranian officials are expected, but do not show. (Tower)

- Barry Seal, drug smuggler and later Reagan Administration informant on drug ties to the Sandinistas is brutally murdered in a Baton Rouge, Louisiana parking lot. Three men armed with Ingram Mac 10 and Uzi weapons fired more than fifty rounds through the passenger window of Seal's car. From 1977 to 1982 Seal was a smuggler, first running marijuana then cocaine from Ecuador and Colombia to Louisiana. He became a federal informant in March 1984, flying dope missions for the Drug Enforcement Administration and setting up former associates in the U.S. and Latin America for prosecution. His undercover activities took him to Managua where he met with Colombian drug traffickers allegedly working with a Sandinista official. Federal officials were quick to blame Seal's murder on Colombian cocaine lords, against whom Seal was expected to testify in February 1986. There is some evidence that Seal may have set up the Sandinista cocaine smuggling operation as a sting on orders from and with the cooperation of top Administration officials. (VV 7/1/86; Barry Seal testimony to President's Commission on Organized Crime 10/5/85; MH 10/12-14/86; ABC 20/20 7/24/86)

FEB 20 - Evans receives the second and revised pro forma invoice from B.I.T. and Iran. Phone conversation between Evans and Minardos of B.I.T. is monitored. (Court papers, U.S. District Court, New York)

- On February 20, North, Nir, C/NE, and Secord met Ghorbanifar in Frankfurt. (North calendar) They expected the official from the Prime Minister's office, but he did not appear. C/NE remembered that: "we told Ghorbanifar to let us know when his Iranian friend came, that we were going home, and that we wouldn't be back until we had a confirmation that the Iranian had come off from Tehran and was waiting." That happened within a week. (C/NE (1)13)

C/NE remembered who attended and that the meeting took place February 19. (C/NE (1) 14) According to the Maximum version, the meeting occurred February 19-21.

("U.S. and Iranian officials (NSC and CIA) met again in Germany to discuss problems in arranging a meeting among higher-level officials. At this meeting, the U.S. side agreed to provide 1,000 Tows to Iran as a clear signal of U.S. sincerity. This delivery was commenced on the morning of February 20 and completed in two transits to Tehran on February 21. (Maximum Version 6)

(The Historical Chronology states:

(On February 19-21, U.S. (NSC and CIA), Israel; and Iranian officials met in Germany to discuss problems in arranging a meeting among higher-level officials. After coded authorization was received from Washington, the U.S. side agreed to provide 1,000 Tows to Iran as a clear signal of U.S. sincerity. This delivery was commenced on the morning of February 20 and completed in two transits to Tehran on February 21. Transportation from Israel to Iran was aboard a false flag Israeli aircraft. On the return flight from Iran, these aircraft carried the 18 HAWK [sic] missiles which Israel had sent to Tehran in November 1985 with USG aforeknowledge. [sic] (Historical Chronology 10)

(The CIA Inspector General's chronology states:

19 February 1986: C/NE, North, Secord, and Nir meet with Ghorbanifar in Frankfurt. Iranian officials are expected, but do not show.

20 or 21 February 1986: The delivery of 1,000 TOW's from Israel to Iran begins, using a false flag aircraft. (The backload on the return flight from Tehran was the HAWK missiles which had been shipped in November 1985. The Iranians returned them because they were outdated models. The delivery is completed 27 February.) (CIA/IG Chronology))

(CIA/IG Chronology 19) On February 20, a deposit of $7.85 million was made to an Iranian account at Credit Suisse in connection with the delivery of the TOWs. (Tower)

- The U.S. side agreed to provide 1,000 Tows to Iran as a clear signal of U.S. sincerity. This delivery was commenced on the morning of February 20 (Maximum Version 6) (Tower)

- [O]n February 20, 1986, after Ghorbanifar passed him information on preparations for a number of terrorist attacks, Charles Allen wrote that: "I believe we should move quickly to consolidate our relations with Subject [Ghorbanifar]. Although he exaggerates and manufactures some of his information, he has excellent contacts with Iranian officials in Tehran. He also has interesting contacts with Iranian nationals in western Europe. I believe we would be remiss unless we begin to work with Subject and evaluate the potential of some of his associates, particularly [names deleted]. I have met [name deleted] and believe that he has excellent potential." (C. Allen, "Discussions with Subject," 2/20/86) (Tower)

FEB 20 or 21 - The CIA Inspector General's chronology states: . . . . The delivery of 1,000 TOW's from Israel to Iran begins, using a false flag aircraft. (The backload on the return flight from Tehran was the HAWK missiles which had been shipped in November 1985. The Iranians returned them because they were outdated models. The delivery is completed 27 February.) (CIA/IG Chronology 19) (Tower)

FEB 21 - North wrote Poindexter that "Second 500 will go to Bandar Abbas on Friday vice Thurs" . . . (North PROF note to Poindexter, 2/13/86, 21:39:47) (Tower)

- "[The] delivery [of 1,000 TOWs that] commenced on the morning of February 20 [was] completed in two transits to Tehran on February 21." (Maximum Version 6) (Tower)

- Internal UNO memoranda cite the possibility of creating a $1.2 million lobbying program in Europe "to change European public opinion, particularly in Spain, France and Germany . . . in relation to the U.S. government's granting of aid to the contras." (UNO documents; The Nation 1/17/87)

- Reagan writes a letter to conservative lobbyist Carl "Spitz" Channell lauding the "unique and vital role" Channell's National Endowment for the Preservation of Liberty (NEPL) is playing in support of the contras. The President writes that NEPL's efforts put the organization on "America's Front Line" against the "Sandinista propaganda barrage" which attempts "to directly influence members of Congress in their home districts to confuse the issue." One of NEPL's major activities is launching a $1.3 million television lobbying campaign this month aimed at winning congressional votes for the Administration's $100 million aid package to the rebels (see March 31, 1986 entry). (Reagan letter 2/21/86; Adam Goodman letter 3/31/86; AP 12/17/86)

FEB 23 - Evans receives a copy of a letter from C. Robert Gates of Northrop Corporation, to Mr. Northrop, outlining types and quantities for military equipment available to Mr. Northrop's customer. Northrop indicates to Evans that Gates wrote the letter on a personal basis, and that there was no official channel from the corporation itself. The list includes

13 F-4 aircraft. Northrop says that all the goods listed in Gates's letter are available for delivery and that he has end user certificates for them. Northrop invites Hashemi or Evans to come to Israel to inspect the goods. (Court papers, U.S. District Court, New York)

FEB 24 - In monitored calls, Evans says he met with Flearmoy, Kopka and Bihn to supply hardware to Hashemi. Evans mails pro forma invoice on B.I.T. Company Ltd. letterhead to Galaxy Trade Inc. Apparently invoice included F-4 aircraft, C-130E Hercules aircraft (model 382-4B), Skyhawk aircraft (A4E, A4H, A4E x 30mm, A4E x 20 mm), TOW missiles (anti-tank, surface-to-surface, and air-to-surface), Sparrow AIM 7E guided missiles, AIM 9-0/G A/A guided missiles (Sidewinders), AIM 72A "Chapparal" missiles, Maverick Electric-Optic guided bombs, Hawk missile batteries, and other items from the U.S. munitions lists, from Israel and other foreign countries. (Court papers, U.S. District Court, New York)

- Reagan in an Oval Office interview with Jack Anderson refers to what the columnist describes as a "hush-hush, barely perceptible tilt toward Iran." Anderson also hints in his column at arms sales to Tehran. However, he does not reveal another statement Reagan apparently has made to him, having pledged to keep it secret until the hostages are freed. (USA Today 12/11/86)

- This is the last activity date with the FAA for Maule N56632, another plane that Maule contends Richard Secord bought. FAA documents show no registration for the aircraft. (FAA Documents, Hearst Newspapers 7/27/86)

- On February 24, North went to Frankfurt to meet the official from the Iranian Prime Minister's office. He returned through London. In Frankfurt, he, Secord, Hakim, Nir, Ghorbanifar, and Iranian officials held the meeting the Americans thought was going to occur the 20th. North returned to Washington on February 26 and reported on the meeting the next day to the Director of Central Intelligence, Poindexter, and McFarlane. He wrote McFarlane:

"Just returned last night from mtg w/ [official from the Iranian Prime Minister's office] in Frankfurt. If nothing else the meeting serves to emphasize the need for direct contact with these people rather than continue the process by which we deal through intermediaries like Gorbanifahr [sic]. Because CIA wd not provide a translator for the sessions, we used Albert Hakim, an AMCIT who runs the European operation for our Nicaraguan support activity. [C/NE] accompanied so that I wd have someone along who wd provide "objective" account.

"Throughout the session, Gorbanifahr intentionally distorted much of the translation and had to be corrected by our man on occasions so numerous that [the Iranian official] finally had Albert translate both ways. Assessment of mtg & agreement we reached as follows:——[the Iranian official] has authority to make his own decisions on matters of great import.——He does not have to check back w/ Tehran on decisions take [sic].——The govt. of Iran is terrified of a new Soviet threat.——They are seeking a rapprochement but are filled w/ fear & mistrust.—— All hostages will be released during rpt during the next meeting.——They want next mtg urgently and have suggested Qeshm Is. [sic] off Bandar Abbas.——They are less interested in Iran/Iraq war than we originally believed.——They want technical advice more than arms or intelligence.——Tech advice shd be on commercial & military maintenance [sic]—not mil tactics—they committed to end anti-U.S. terrorism.——They noted the problems of working thru intermediaries & prefer dir. contact—noted that this was first USG/GOI contact in more than 5 yrs. [sic] Vy important—recognizes risks to both sides—noted need for secrecy.—stressed that there were new Sov. moves/ threats that we were unaware of. While all of this could be so much smoke, I believe that we may well be on the verge of a major breakthrough—not only on the hostages/terrorism but on the relationship as a whole. We need only to go to this meeting which has no agenda other than to listen to each other to release the hostages and start the process. Have briefed both JMP and Casey—neither very enthusiastic despite [C/NE]/North summary along lines above. Believe you shd be chartered to go early next wf [sic]—or maybe this weekend—but don't know how to make this happen. Have not told JMP that this note is being sent. Help. Pls call on secure yr earliest convenience. Warm, but fatigued regards, North." (North PROF note to McFarlane, 2/27/86, 8:54:13)

C/NE recalled:

"This is the second meeting. This is the first meeting with [the official from the Prime Minister's office], the second February meeting. This is the first time we've had somebody like this out. It should be a very interesting experience. This is a man who ... is on the low end of the scale in intelligence for [his former profession], and he's an even dumber member of the Iranian Prime Minister's office, but he's full of a little fear and a little trepidation and a lot of distrust of the U.S., for we truly are the great Satan in his eyes.

"But he has been promised hundreds of Phoenix missiles, howitzers, TOWs; just about anything else he wants, he's going to get in this channel. He's promised that by Ghorbanifar in order to get him to this meeting. And we are promised that all the hostages will come out after the first two transactions, and that we are going to have a meeting with Rafsanjani and President Khamenehi within the first two months of this procedure, and one of the things in the scenario was that sometime in April there was a precise date given that Khomeini was going to step down and that he was going to resign all powers.

"This is extraordinary nonsense. Essentially Ghorbanifar, as a negotiating technique, lied to both sides to get them to the table, and then sat back and watched us fight it out. It was a real slugging match. It was awful.

"At the end of the first meeting, which was at 3:00 a.m. on the 25th, we agreed to nothing except that we would have another meeting the next day." (See February 25 entry.) (C/NE (1) 18-20) (Tower)

FEB 25 - Reagan formally requests congressional approval for the transfer of $100 million from the FY86 Department of Defense Appropriations to aid the contras through September 30, 1987, in accordance with P.L. 99-83 and P.L. 99-88. $70 million of this would be used for military equipment. The request is denied on March 20. After much further deliberation, including the attachment of numerous restrictions on the use of the funds, final legislation on the matter is incorporated as part of the FY87 Continuing Appropriations bill and passed by Congress on October 17, 1986. (CRS "U.S. Assistance to Nicaraguan Guerrillas" 12/4/86)

- Richard Brenneke writes to Bush aide Douglas Menarchik concerning new information on arms sales to Iran that he has gathered while on an "extended business trip" to Europe this month. He identifies a "project known as Condor/Demavand, purportedly run by the U.S. government since 1984, [and] is still, I am told, a real operation which is still going" (see November 30, 1985 entry). He also mentions data he collected which "purports to show that the U.S. has supplied chemical warfare materiel to Iraq." (Brenneke letter to Menarchik, 2/25/86)

- NHAO negotiates a $96,961 contract with Vortex (a Miami air leasing firm) official Michael B. Palmer (see also June 19, 1986 entry) to pay for transportation of supplies to the contras. (MH 3/22/87)

- C/NE recalled:

". . . . The next day's meeting [February 25] was an agreement that we would proceed immediately to ship in 1,000 TOWs as a sign of our good faith and that [the Iranian official] would immediately arrange for one or two hostages to be released as a sign of their good faith. We left the meeting; nothing happened. No hostages.

"The communications were still going through Ghorbanifar. We had several hints at this meeting with [the Iranian official] that he wasn't happy with Ghorbanifar. Ghorbanifar was clearly very concerned that this Farsi speaker, Hakim, would in some way arrange to cut him out and have direct contacts with [the Iranian official].

"There was enormous distrust all the way around. Nir was insistent that we keep Ghorbanifar in it. They had a relationship that went back with him prior to the revolution. So they know him well, and they recognize his limitations. They recognize that he's a congenital liar, but they know how to deal with it and they know how to use him." (C/NE (1) 18-20) (Tower)

FEB 26 - Evans and Hashemi meet in New York and discuss Hashemi and B.I.T. agreement, including that all equipment was U.S. made, that the letter of credit was to be payable to a single beneficiary (B.I.T.), and that the cost of the end user certificate for the Hawk missile battery was much higher than originally anticipated. They also discuss Northrop's deal for U.S.-manufactured equipment. (Court papers, U.S. District Court, New York)

-UNO records show a transfer of $70,000 from BAC International Bank (Bahamas) Ltd.—bank account #16-305-8 of the Tuira Corporation—to the Banco Anglo Costarricense de San Jose, Costa Rica bank—account #88929-5 of Commercial Tulin S.A. The transfer is requested by UNO administrator Evenor Valdivia. (UNO memoranda)

Muammar Kaddafi has plans for America.

He's already threatened to strike at "American citizens in their own streets". Kaddafi used to be far away...

...but now he sits on our doorstep — supplying arms and terrorist experts

to the communists in Nicaragua, only two hours away from our borders,

where training also comes from the P.L.O. terrorists of Yassir Arafat.

Here is terrorism we *can* do something about. If...we support the President on Nicaragua.

Dear Spitz:

The National Endowment for the Preservation of Liberty
is serving a unique and vital role in its Central American
Freedom Program.

Your efforts to educate the American public on the true nature
of the Communist regime in Nicaragua are critically important.
I am confident that your work will make clear to all that we
face a choice between Communism on the North American continent and support for the Nicaraguan freedom fighters. There
is no doubt that we must champion the cause of freedom.

Your Central American Freedom Program is a vital link in
the effort to forge a democratic outcome in Nicaragua. The
Sandinistas have gone to New York not just to buy designer
glasses, they have also gone to Madison Avenue to hire a
public relations firm. The Sandinistas have retained teams of
lawyers and public relations experts, who are registered with
our Justice Department as foreign agents, to spread their
propaganda across the United States. They hope to directly
influence members of Congress in their home districts to confuse the issue. The Sandinista propaganda barrage, which
cynically uses our freedoms while denying the same free
expression to the Nicaraguan people, cannot go unanswered.

In the next few weeks we will initiate an historic effort to
achieve Congressional support for the cause of the freedom
fighters in Nicaragua. If this effort is successful, it will
herald the first light of a new dawn of freedom in Nicaragua.
Your Central American Freedom Program puts you on "America's

Front Line" in the battle for democracy. Courageous Americans
have saved this nation countless times in the past by holding
truth as our shield against the distortions of dictators.

Best wishes and may God bless you.

Sincerely,

Ronald Reagan

Mr. Carl Russell Channell
President
National Endowment for the
   Preservation of Liberty
305 Fourth Street, N.E.
Washington, D.C. 20002

- Preparations for the next meeting with Iranians, in which McFarlane was to participate, immediately began when North returned from Frankfurt. Clair George, with C/NE's support, urged that George Cave join the team as interpreter. C/NE recalled that he had told North on the way home from Frankfurt at the end of February that the government should provide an interpreter. Secord and Hakim, who is of Iranian origin, had appeared at the first and second Frankfurt meetings, respectively, without prior notice to C/NE. (C/NE (1) 11; C/NE (2) 76) C/NE not only believed that the government could perform the roles assigned to Secord and Hakim, but also thought Hakim had a potential conflict of interest arising from his own business relationships. (See C/NE (1) 11-12, 40) C/NE recalled that Hakim was involved in arms transactions "that might or might not be legal. There wasn't any prosecution going against him, but there was a little suspicion . . . And North, to his credit, accepted that advice and we introduced George Cave." [See March 5 entry for more on Cave. (Tower)

FEB 26 & 27 - [T]he official from the Prime Minister's office remained in Frankfurt to coordinate the shipment to Bandar Abbas with his colleagues in Tehran. (Tower)

FEB 27 - On February 27, the second 500 TOWs were delivered to Bandar Abbas. Although a hostage release and a later meeting between senior U.S. and Iranian officials had been agreed upon at the Frankfurt meeting, the plan fell through. No hostages were released and the meeting failed to materialize until much later.

Although the cover memorandum to the January 17 Finding stated that further arms transfers would cease if all the hostages were not released after delivery of the first 1000 TOWs, the United States continued to pursue the initiative and arranged for another delivery of arms two months later. (Tower)

C/NE asked the CIA for alias passports for C/NE, Cave, Secord, and Hakim. On March 3, the passports were provided. Hakim never used his passport, which was returned on May 22. Secord's passport was returned on November 20, 1986. (CIA/IG Chronology 20).) (Tower)

- The morning of February 27, North heard from Secord. The second 500 of the 1,000 TOWs had been delivered to Iran.

"707 has signaled success and due to land at Ben Gurion in a few minutes.

"Met with Nir and Gorba this a.m. for one hour. Nir continues to agonize over the two soldiers, while Gorba worries about money matters and how he can stay in the center as the indispensable man. Nir then left for Tel Aviv. Subsequently, Gorba, Abe [Albert Hakim], and I met with [the Iranian official] for about one hour. Abe did beautiful job of rug merchanting with [the Iranian official] and also helped Gorba's ego a lot. He was extremely interested in Russian intentions. He propagandized a lot about Iranian fighting spirit and we assured him Americans respected Iranian people. He emphasized need for quick meeting at Kish, an "old SAVAK-maintained island off the coast of Iran," (C. Allen 15), and said he would possibly, repeat, possibly surprise us by getting some hostages released before meeting. [S]uggest you make contingency plan to accommodate early release (i.e., as early as Sunday). So, bottom line is on to Kish ASAP to seize the potential opening now created." ("Copp 2/27/86 1020. 161455Z Feb. 86")

North wrote the following note on this message:

"1120 EST—707 Back at B.G. Apt.

"Gorba got 13,200/missile Gets $260/missile Gives $50/ missile to Ledeen." (Handwritten note on id.)

The Board has seen no evidence supporting the implication contained in this Document, and Ledeen "flatly" denied receiving any commissions in connection with the arms transfers to Iran. (Ledeen (1) 63) (Tower) (See also Jan 16, 1986 entry for North's speculation on Ledeen)

- North reported his later activities of February 27 to McFarlane:

"Since the missive of this morning, met w/ Casey, JMP, [C/NE], Clair George and all have now agreed to press on. Believe we are indeed headed in the right direction. Just finished lengthy session w/ JMP he indicated that he has passed substance to you and has given me dates that you are not avail. Will endeavor to sched. mtg so that these do not conflict but noted to JMP that it was their call as to date of mtg. Just rec'd msg fm Secord via secure device we are using. [The Iranian official] has again reaffirmed that once we have set a date we shall have a very pleasant surprise. Dick & I believe that they may be preparing to release one of the hostages early. Dick also indicated that yr counterpart at the mtg wd be Rafsanjani. Nice crowd you run with! God willing Shultz will buy onto [sic] this tomorrow when JMP [briefs] him. With the grace of the good Lord and a little more hard work we will very soon have five AMCITS home and be on our way to a much more positive relationship than one which barters TOWs for lives.

"I value your friendship and confidence very highly and did not mean to infer that you had revealed these exchanges. By asking that you not indicate same to JMP I was only informing that I had not told him anything of it so as not to compromise myself at a point in time when he needs to be absolutely certain that this can work. He is, as only you can know, under tremendous pressure on this matter and very concerned that it go according to plan. My part in this was easy compared to his. I only had to deal with our enemies. He has to deal with the cabinet. Many thanks for yr. trust. Warm regards, North." (North PROF note to McFarlane, 2/27/86, 20:11:51)

Meanwhile, McFarlane had written North that afternoon:

"Roger Ollie. Well done—if the world only knew how many times you have kept a semblance of integrity and gumption to US policy, they would make you Secretary of State. But they can't know and would complain if they did—such is the state of democracy in the late 20th century. But the mission was terribly promising. As you know I do not hold Gorbanifar [sic] in high regard and so am particularly glad to hear of [the official in the Prime Minister's office] apparent authority.

"I have just gotten a note from John asking whether or not I could go some time next week and the President is on board. I agreed. So hunker down and get some rest; let this word come to you in channels, but pack your bags to be ready to go in the next week or so. Incidentally, I have had periodic requests from Mike [?Ledeen?] to assist in getting visas for [sic] Gorbanifar to come to Switzerland. . . . I have refused. Surely if they have any real bona fides they can get a visa in Tehran from the Swiss embassy or somewhere else. I do not intend to tell Mike any of this new info. Recommend against your doing so. Bravo Zulu." (McFarlane PROF note to North, 2/27/86, 16:02:23)

North replied in the evening.

"Am reading things out of sequence due to fatigue. Many

thanks for yr note. Have responded to most of this in my reply re exchanges—before I read this one. Yr concerns re Mike are shared here. WILCO re the passing of info. He means well but poses a significant problem. Nir says he has info that Mike has a financial relationship w/ Gorba, Nimrodi and perhaps Schwimmer. If true, this is not good. We also know that Gorba tells Mike everything and that is an additional reason to get Gorba out of the long range picture ASAP. We will still need to have him involved in the TOWs transactions since he manages the financial end for the Iraniansin [sic] Europe. We ought to sit quietly and think about how we handle Mike so that he does not start talking out of disgruntlement (if that's a word). Have asked JMP for a session w/ you and Dick Secord as soon as possible after Dick returns tomorrow night fm Eur where he is setting up an arms delivery for the Nic resistance. A man of many talents ol' Secord is. Must be off. Am supposed to make a speech on aiding the Nic resistance to a group of supporters. Best regards. North." (North PROF notes to McFarlane, 2/27/86, 20:22:22) (Tower)

- On February 27, the Director of Central Intelligence met with Poindexter, George, and C/ NE, (DCI Telephone Calls and Meetings, 1-9/ 30/86); talking points were prepared on the same day for the Director, possibly for use in that meeting.

"Continued discussions on a very serious and important matter and I would like to suggest some guidelines:

"(1) The initial meeting should be exploratory only.

"(2) We should provide information about the Soviet Union threat to the northern border, about the level and quality of Soviet arms going to Iraq, about the Soviet thrust in Afghanistan.... That seems like another reason for emphasizing the Soviet aspect. If the fact of the talks leak, that would be the best way to get public and Arab understanding of the discussions.

"(3) The contact should be direct. Israel and Gorbanifar [sic] should not be involved in these discussions. We can't afford any more telephone conversations which the Soviets and others can listen in on.

"(4) The first indispensable step is to set up a secure commo channel from the point where the talks are held or some point in that country to Western Europe where further secure conversations can be passed through to Washington.

We should have this before discussions begin, and for this purpose we should fly Secord into Teheran as soon as possible.

"(5) The group at the meetings should be as small as possible. I recommend that it consist of McFarlane, North, [C/NE], a staffer for McFarlane, and George Cave. George Cave is an ideal interpreter. He speaks not only Farsi, but also Mullah and understands all dialects. He is a known and proven quantity. In contemplation of where these discussions could possibly go, we should avoid having a foreign interpreter, even though the man in Switzerland is accepted and trusted. (Probably a reference to Hakim. Ghorbanifar told the Board that Cave's Farsi was "very, very poor," probably due to disuse. (Ghorbanifar 159)) He should be our man.

"(6) These discussions ought to go forward. The president should call Prime Minister Peres, thank him, tell him we are not going to take his man to the meeting because we think it is in the best interest of the two countries not to involve them directly at this time, assure him that we have Israel's interests in mind, and will protect them and report to Peres after the meeting.

"(7) We need to continuously plan in case the discussions leak. The fact of discussions between the United States and Iran could change the whole universe. Iraqi resistance could weaken. The Arab world could go mad unless the discussions are carefully and adequately explained. Some element of the explanation could be:

—The Soviets have been talking to both parties for years;

—The Arabs would cheer if Iran could be moderated; and

—Of course, we will do almost anything to get our hostages back.

"We should remember that leaking the fact of this meeting could be viewed as working to the advantage of Israel. Only four men in Israel know of the discussions—the Prime Minister, his military secretary (Neer [sic]) who attended the Frankfurt meeting and who is the Prime Minister's terrorism advisor, and Neer's boss in the Prime Minister's office." (DCI, Talking Points, 2/27/86) Attached to the copy of these talking points in North's file was the following note in North's handwriting:

"—Probing for foothold

—access before transition

—fear of Soviets—left inside

—Anti western terrorism

—Tactical success in near-term could be to our advantage in that it offers opportunity for settlement.
—People who know
—Shultz
—Weinberger
—Powell
—Koch
—Casey
*[C/NE]
*McMahon
*Allen
*Gates
—RR
—JMP
—Don R[egan].
—Don F[ortier]
—VP
—Peter [Rodman]
—Howard [Teicher]."
(Hand written note. Feb. 1986) (Tower)

- Evans and Minardos meet with others to discuss the sale of the items listed above (see February 24 entry), as well as 155mm howitzers long-range artillery, a Cobra helicopter engine, TOW missiles (BGM-71AK, improved I-TOW), Huey helicopter engines, turboprop engines for the C-130E Hercules aircraft, and F-5 "Tiger" aircraft. (Court papers, U.S. District Court, New York)

FEB 28 - On February 28, Poindexter told the Secretary of State that the hostages would be released the following week. According to the Secretary of State:

"Poindexter reported nothing about arms. Rather, he said that the Iranians wanted a high-level dialogue, covering issues other than hostages. He said the White House had chosen McFarlane for the mission, and that he would go to Frankfurt, West Germany, to meet with a deputy of Rafsanjani.

"I [Shultz] said fine, but asked that Mr. McFarlane be given instructions to govern his negotiations. I was shown these instructions, and I was satisfied with them.

"Wholly independent of the hostage issue, Vice Admiral Poindexter said the Iranians had asked for help on intelligence as to what the Soviets were doing on the Iranian border and in Afghanistan. He saw a path to reemerging relations.

"Vice Admiral Poindexter said that the hostages would be released at the time Mr. McFarlane was meeting with the Iranians in Frankfurt.

"[T]he presumption was that, after the meeting, they were pursuing this matter, and that, as a result of pursuing it, the Iranians wanted the meeting, and the meeting itself, having it with a high-level person like Mr. McFarlane, the President's former advisor, was a mark of a high-level interest; and the other side of that coin was the release of the hostages. It's sort of like the London proposition returning again, I thought.

"It seemed very unlikely to me, but I said well, if you've got that arrangement, that's great." (Shultz, SRB, 51-52) (Tower)

LATE FEB - Reagan sends a secret memo to Shultz and Weinberger summarizing U.S. contacts with Iran. (PI 11/26/86)

- In a memo describing a meeting between Bush and Amiram Nir in July 1986 (see July 29 entry), Bush aide Craig Fuller quotes Nir as saying a meeting took place in February with "the prime minister on the other side," apparently referring to Iranian Prime Minister Mir Hussein Mousavi. According to the memo, "Nir did not make it clear who else attended the meeting. He said the meeting was 'dramatic and interesting.' He said 'an agreement was made on 4,000 units—1,000 first and then 3,000. The agreement was made on the basis that we would get the group'" apparently referring to American hostages, "'[t]he whole package for a fixed price,' he said." In January, Poindexter mentioned the same figures—the units in question being TOW missiles—in a briefing paper on the Iran initiative prepared for Reagan, Bush and Donald Regan. (Fuller memo 7/29/86 in WP 2/8/87; WP 2/8/87)

- By the end of February 1986, the representatives of the United States were disappointed by the results of negotiations with Ghorbanifar and Iranian officials. But disappointment was gilded in hope, and the effort was pursued.

At this time, American policy changed with regard to terrorism. Since the terrorist bombings at the Rome and Vienna airports in December 1985, the United States was prepared to use military force to affirm its rights. In March 1986, units of the Sixth Fleet undertook what was described as a routine assertion of the right of passage through the international waters of the Gulf of Sidra. In the course of that exercise, ships crossed what Qadhafi had designated a "line of death," and Libyan forces attacked them. In April, Libya directed the bombing of a West Berlin discotheque frequented by Americans, and, in response, American aircraft attacked Libyan targets on April 14. (Tower)

- At the end of February, Israeli Prime Minister Peres wrote to President Reagan encouraging him to continue his efforts to gain a strategic opening in Iran and pledging to assist in this effort. Director Casey proposed that the President call Peres to reassure him that the program would continue and to thank him for Israel's assistance. His talking points also argued, however, that the next meeting should be U.S.-Iranian, without a direct Israeli role. (SSIC 1/29/87)

SPRING - Casey is said to be aware by at least this time of the diversion of funds from the Iran arms sales. According to an intelligence source: "Casey knew from the beginning that the Iranians were being overcharged. . . . And he knew that some money was being siphoned off." Sources say that top-secret communications disclosing overcharges to Iran came over the CIA's "privacy channel" and were automatically delivered to the CIA director's desk, as well as to other offices in the CIA, White House and Pentagon. Two Agency communicators accompany McFarlane the presence of these three officials, according to an Administration source, would make it easy for Casey to know every detail of the Iranian side of the sales. (NYT 12/17/86; WSJ 12/11/86)

- Casey provides the White House with a revised assessment of the Soviet threat to Iran that substantially downplays the danger of a Soviet intervention or increased influence after the passing of Khomeini. The 25-page analysis, called a Special National Intelligence Estimate (SNIE), alters the conclusions of a similar report drafted a year ago by the CIA's Graham Fuller (see January 1985 entry). Fuller's paper, which warned of serious threats to Iran from Moscow, became a catalyst for the Iran initiative. (WP 1/13/87)

- The U.S. ambassador to Britain, Charles H. Price II, cables the State Department with an inquiry from British businessman Tiny Rowland who has recently been approached by Khashoggi and Ghorbanifar about the possibility of financing arms sales to Iran. The cable makes its way to Under Secretary of State Michael H. Armacost and from him to Shultz. According to Shultz's later testimony to a Congressional panel, this is one of many hints he receives that the U.S. has engaged in arms deals with Tehran. He testifies that he approached Poindexter and Regan on the matter at the Tokyo economic meeting (see May 4-6, 1986 entry). (NYT 1/24/87)

MARCH 1986

MAR - In 1986, North established a private secure communications network. North received 15 encryption devices from the National Security Agency from January to March, 1986, provided in support of his counter-terrorist activities. One was provided to Mr. Secord and another, through a private citizen, to a CIA field officer posted in Central America. Through this mechanism, North coordinated the resupply of the Contras with military equipment apparently purchased with funds provided by the network of private benefactors. The messages to LtCol North from Mr. Secord and the CIA officer: (a) asked him to direct where and when to make Contra munitions drops; (b) informed him of arms requirements; and (c) apprised him of payments, balances and deficits. (Tower)

- In the period of March through May, 1986, all efforts in the Iran arms sale program were directed at arranging a high-level meeting between U.S. and Iranian officials. These efforts led to the McFarlane mission to Tehran in late May and the associated transfer of HAWK missile parts to Iran. Throughout this period, no hostages were released. (SSIC 1/29/87)

- At least nine arms shipments were coordinated through [North's private secure communications network] from March through June, 1986. The CIA field officer in Costa Rica outlined his involvement in the resupply network and described the shipments: "This was all lethal. Benefactors only sent lethal stuff." The CIA officer added that the private benefactor operation was, according to his understanding, controlled by LtCol North.

Mr. Secord was in charge of arranging the actual deliveries, using at least in part Southern Air Transport ("SAT"). Assistant Commissioner William Rosenblatt told the Board that LtCol North contacted him after a SAT C-123 aircraft crashed in Nicaragua, prompting a customs investigation. North told him that the Customs investigation was focused on "good guys" who committed "no crimes." The Customs Service then narrowed the investigation to the specific aircraft involved in the crash rather than on the activities of the whole company. U.S. Customs Commissioner William von Rabb[sic] said that LtCol North had previously contacted him to complain that Customs' agents were conducting an investigation involving a Maule aircraft. A former CIA officer in Central America said that at least one Maule aircraft was used in support of the Contra forces. Mr. Rosenblatt and Mr. von Raab told the Board that LtCol North never asked them to close out their investigations. The Board obtained evidence that at least one Maule aircraft was used in Contra military operations. This evidence was referred to the Independent Counsel. (Tower)

- Early in the month, North meets with Nir, Ghorbanifar, George Cave and others in Europe. Cave reports to Casey afterward in the last line of a long cable that Ghorbanifar has suggested overcharging the Iranians and funneling the profits to Nicaraguan and Afghan rebels. This is reportedly the first hint of a possible diversion of funds. Casey does not respond. (WP 1/10/87)

- In early March, Ghorbanifar asked for another meeting with U.S. and Israeli officials in Europe. Ghorbanifar was demanding that the U.S. sell Harpoons and 200 PHOENIX missiles to Iran, which the U.S. Government was not prepared to do. One CIA official noted that North was planning to take a hard line with Ghorbanifar, while Israel was possibly providing additional non-U.S. arms on the side to move the process along. (SSIC 1/29/87)

- The initial CIA action officer on the Iran project met with North on several occasions in 1986 . . . In March 1986, the CIA officer knew that North was very active in the contra program. It seemed to the CIA officer as if North was splitting his time between the contras and the Iran project and that he was having trouble keeping up with both. North was visiting Honduras and going to meetings and otherwise working hard on support for the fighters. The CIA officer testified that North's activities were widely known in the CIA and the NSC. (SSIC 1/29/87)

- CIA Director Casey makes a secret visit to South Africa to discuss, among other things, the routing of weapons to the Angolan rebels, UNITA. During the same time period, according to news reports, South African aid to the contras is being discussed. (ABC World News Tonight 2/25/87)

- Air Force Lt. Col. David H. Rankin Jr., deputy commander of the U.S. military forces in El Salvador, arranges and vouches for about six purchases of fuel and oil from the Salvadoran Air Force for planes being used to airlift weapons to the contras, according to a mechanic in the resupply operation. Crew members in the effort say Rankin meets with the pilots and is the only active-duty U.S. military officer on a list of contacts provided them on their arrival. (PI 1/18/87)

- Col. Robert C. Dutton goes to work for Richard V. Secord at Stanford Technology Group International as staff director. In that position, Dutton directed the day-to-day operations of the contra supply effort out of El Salvador. (WP 3/22/87)

- Iain Crawford, claiming that he flew on a dozēn air drops to arm the Contras, states that North and Secord bought five airplanes for the air drops and participated in a meeting regarding the planes, which took place at El Salvador's Ilopango air base with Contra leaders and Salvadoran officials. (Reuters 2/5/87)

- In March, FDN task force commanders and founders of the 15th of September Legion (including Hugo Villagra and others) meet in Miami with retired Maj. Gen. John Singlaub to present him with their extensive critique of the contra status quo and corruption, along with a military battle plan for invading Nicaragua. The group, known as the CONDOR

(Nicaraguan Coalition of Opposition to the Regime) group, seeks to bypass the chain of command and the CIA by appealing to Singlaub, whom they saw as directly in touch with President Reagan. The CONDOR memorandum alleges "abuse of power," "croneyism and nepotism rampant," and "inept, improvised quackery in conducting the war" by the FDN leadership. Instead of presenting the memo to President Reagan, however, Singlaub takes it back to Bermudez and no reform is forthcoming. (CONDOR memorandum, 3/86; MH 6/25/86)

- The first of two C-123K cargo planes is purchased for use in the covert resupply program for the contras. The purchase is made with a check drawn on a Southern Air Transport account. (WP 12/7/86)

- Southern Air Transport this month makes eight flights to Ilopango air base in El Salvador. Six of the flights are from Dulles Airport carrying a total of 135 tons of cargo, the other two flights are from Portugal with a total of 45 tons on board. (DOT Records)

- During the first or second week of March, Gates asked analysts to prepare briefing materials on the Soviet military threat to Iran for use by McFarlane in briefing the Iranians. A week later, other CIA analysts met with Gates and some of the participants in the early March meeting with Ghorbanifar. They were provided a list of Iranian intelligence requirements regarding Iraq and they discussed how to respond to it. The tasking and discussions in early March eventually led to the materials that CIA would hand over in mid-May and that would be used in Tehran in late May. (SSIC 1/29/87)

- The French government cancels the export license of the firm Luchaire for illegally selling arms to Iran. However, President Mitterrand and Defense Minister Hernu reportedly have been aware of Luchaire's dealings with Tehran since May 1984, yet wait until now to act. For his part, Hernu denies repeatedly that the French government sold arms to Iran and claims that if French arms reached Iran it was because "the government's instructions were contravened." (AFP 1/15/87; Paris Domestic Service 1/20/87)

MAR 1 - A White House "public diplomacy group" on Nicaragua meets in the morning to discuss strategy for the upcoming House vote on $100 million aid to the contras. The group gathers on the next two Saturday mornings as well to plan "the most aggressive legislative and public relations drive of Reagan's second term," according to one report. The meetings are chaired by Dennis Thomas, deputy to Regan. Participants include Patrick Buchanan; legislative liaison Will Ball; political director Mitchell E. Daniels Jr.; deputy national security adviser Donald R. Fortier; Cabinet secretary Alfred H. Kingon; presidential advance chief William Henckel; scheduling director Frederick J. Ryan Jr.; Bush's deputy chief of staff, Frederick N. Khedouri; and press office deputies, either Peter H. Roussel or Edward P. Djerejian, among others. (WP 3/20/86)

- It is reported that Vice President George Bush wrote to a Guatemalan doctor and conservative political leader who had proposed, through Bush's son Jeb, an international medical brigade to help the contras. Bush's letter referred Dr. Mario Castejon to Oliver North and offered Bush's staff to set up the meeting. In a Mar. 1 memo, Bush aide Philip Hughes had recommended this course of action, because Castejon's "proposals could materially help us out if they materialized." Castejon subsequently meets North, attends a White House briefing and a Washington meeting with Gen. John Singlaub and Adolfo Calero, and assists in preparing a medical proposal (never acted upon) for submission to the State Department's Nicaraguan Humanitarian Assistance Office. News reports credited Bush's letter with introducing Castejon into Oliver North's private aid network, calling it the first documentary evidence linking Bush to North. (MH 3/15/87; NYT 3/16/87)

MAR 2 - Defex-Portugal, acting as middleman for Energy Resources International, receives clearance to transport by ship another installment of arms from Portugal to Guatemala. According to Lisbon airport records, they are loaded onto a Southern Air Transport plane the following day with a flight plan for Guatemala via Santa Maria in the Azores. However, the arms never arrive in Guatemala, according to authorities there. Southern Air logs show only one flight this month from Portugal, and that is to Lajes in the Azores. The same logs show two flights in March from Lajes to Ilopango Air Base in El Salvador, a main supply point for the contras. (DOT Records; WP 1/17/87)

MAR 3 - John Hull, alleged CIA contract operative whose ranch in Costa Rica has been used as a delivery point for weapons and supplies for the contras, is scheduled to be interviewed by FBI and Justice Department officials, but cancels the meeting after the U.S. consul general in Costa Rica, Kirk Kotula, advises him not to go without a lawyer. (VV 12/30/86; WSJ 1/15/87)

- On March 3, the [alias] passports . . . for C/NE, Cave, Secord, and Hakim . . . were provided [by the CIA]. Hakim never used his passport, which was returned on May 22. Secord's passport was returned on November 20, 1986. (CIA/IG Chronology 20). (Tower)

MAR 4 - John McMahon resigns as deputy director of the CIA. He denies press reports linking his departure to his opposition to the Agency's increased covert assistance to anti-government guerrillas abroad. (CRS "U.S. Intelligence: Issues for Congress, 1986," 1/5/87)

- At 4 a.m., Khashoggi calls Emmanuel Floor, then president of Khashoggi's Triad America Corp., and has him fly to the Cayman Islands, where the two of them meet with Donald Fraser and Walter Miller, controllers of EuroCommercial Finances, D.B., Floor says in an interview. Khashoggi borrows $10 million from the two Canadians, telling them he will generate $40 million in revenues and up to $8 million in profits from an arms deal with Iran, Floor says. Khashoggi denies that he sought a profit, and the Canadians deny knowing the money was to finance the arms deal. Eventually, Khashoggi uses Fraser and Miller in an attempt to collect from the U.S. government. (PI 2/22/87)

MAR 5 - . . . [Cave] joined the team on March 5. When C/NE introduced him to North, (North calendar; Cave 3), he recalled being "a little bit horrified when I found out that [Ghorbanifar] was involved in this." (Cave 5) . . Cave had served in Tehran and was widely respected for his knowledge of Iran and Farsi. At this time, although retired, he was a consultant to the CIA. (CIA/IG Chronology 20; George 11; C/NE (1) 12; Cave 3) He had been responsible for terminating the CIA's relationship with Ghorbanifar in 1983, and had helped craft Ghorbanifar's polygraph examination in January 1986. (C/NE (2) 76) . . . (Tower)

- A note of March 5 from MG Russo to MG Powell conveyed Russo's belief that CIA had this responsibility [to notify Congress of the Iran arms sales] and said that CIA was fully aware of this. In the meantime, the Army had given CIA a price of $3,515,000 for 1,000 TOWs. (SSIC 1/29/87)

- Ambassador Robert Duemling, head of the State Department's Nicaraguan Humanitarian Assistance Office (NHAO), testifies before the House Subcommittee on Western Hemisphere Affairs that his office, after first refusing, gave a $50,675 grant to the Institute for Democracy, Education and Assistance, Inc. to help the contra umbrella organization, the United Nicaraguan Opposition (UNO), in its dealings with NHAO. One of the Institute's directors is Robert Owen, who served as a liaison between North and the contras during a congressional ban on aid to the rebels. Duemling says that he initially declined to hire Owen as a consultant but changed his mind after receiving a letter from the leaders of UNO requesting that Owen be taken on. As a State Department consultant in Costa Rica, Owen allegedly diverted thousands of dollars in U.S. humanitarian aid to buy arms for the rebels. Officials of Kisan-South, a faction of an Indian rebel group, and other sources say Owen and Felipe Vidal —a Cuban exile they believe works for the CIA—controlled the $231,000 received by the group in late 1985 and 1986, keeping it in the Miami account of Moises Nunez and spent $25,000 freed up by a false receipt for clothing at a store, Creaciones Fancy, on military supplies. Rebel leaders Jenelee Hodgson and Franklin Reed say they struggled with Vidal over his management of the funds. (MH 2/16/87; Internal UNO accounting records; Duemling testimony; MH 6/8/86)

- White House Communications Director Pat Buchanan writes in the Washington Post about the impending House vote on $100 million in assistance to the Nicaraguan rebels, "With the vote on contra aid, the Democratic Party will reveal whether it stands with Ronald Reagan and the resistance—or Daniel Ortega and the communists." (WP 3/5/86)

MAR 7 - North, C/NE, and Cave travelled to Paris on March 7 to meet Ghorbanifar the next day. (Footnote: Cave said the meeting took place on March 7. (Cave 5) According to North's calendar, travel forms, and subsequent report to McFarlane, it took place on March 8.) (Tower)

MAR 7-8 - In a memorandum of a meeting with Mr. Ghorbanifar in Paris on March 7-8, George Cave reported that Mr. Ghorbanifar, in an aside, "proposed that we use profits from these deals and others to fund support for the rebels in Afghanistan. We could do the same with Nicaragua."

Before the Board, Mr. Cave said that neither he nor Mr. Ghorbanifar made any mention of diversion. (Tower)

MAR 8 - LtCol North, Mr. Cave, and a CIA official met with Mr. Ghorbanifar in Paris on March 8, 1986. LtCol North reported on this conversation to Mr. McFarlane on March 10. He said he told Mr. Ghorbanifar that the United States remained interested in a meeting with senior Iranian officials as long as the hostages were released during or before the meeting. He said he briefed Mr. Ghorbanifar on the Soviet threat to Iran using intelligence supplied by Mr. Robert Gates, then the CIA Deputy Director for Intelligence. Mr. Ghorbanifar responded by presenting a list of 240 different types of spare parts, in various quantities, needed by Iran for its HAWK missile units. He also emphasized the importance of an advance meeting in Tehran to prepare for the meeting with Mr. McFarlane. This advance meeting would establish the agenda and who should participate from the Iranian side.

While further discussion occurred over the next month, it resulted in little progress. (Tower)

- C/NE recalled frustration after the Paris meeting. "We had delivered our missiles and the shoe was on their foot, but they were acting like the shoe was still on our foot. Ghorbanifar came to that meeting and said, well, they've decided they didn't want TOWs after all. So the TOWs don't count. What we need now are HAWK spare parts; we don't need any more TOWs. We want HAWK spare parts.

"And he presented us a list of HAWK spare parts he needed. So, you know, it's a bag of worms. I was present when North briefed Poindexter after that meeting, and Poindexter at that point was fed up and wanted to just cut it off entirely, forget it. It wasn't going anywhere." (C/NE (1) 20)

"There was a lot of discussion essentially to try to figure out a way to get Ghorbanifar out of it and, North, who you must have sensed by now is a man of a lot of energy and a lot of determination, essentially kept it alive because of the President's personal and emotional interest in getting the hostages out—in my view." (Tower)

- The White House "public diplomacy group" on Nicaragua meets a second time (see March 1 entry) to discuss strategy concerning the upcoming House vote on $100 million in aid to the contras. Pollster Richard Wirthlin attends. (WP 3/20/86)

MAR 9 - Ghorbanifar called Charles Allen, reporting, among other things, that the Paris meetings had been successful, although additional effort remained. Allen thought Ghorbanifar "seemed unusually subdued and less sanguine than in previous conversations." (C. Allen, "Conversation with Subject," 3/1 1/86. CIA Docs.) (Tower)

MAR 9-30 - There was no further effort undertaken on our behalf to contact the Iranian Government or the intermediary. ("Terms of Reference U.S.-Iran Dialogue," 4/4/86) (Tower)

MAR 10 - LtCol North reported on this conversation [with Ghorbanifar on March 8] to Mr. McFarlane. (Tower)

- McFarlane was concerned by North's reports about the meeting in Frankfurt. He wrote late on March 10:

"I guess I'm a little puzzled about the Iranian wiring diagram. From whom are we getting the word concerning a meeting in the Gulf? Is Gorba involved in that dialogue or is that info coming through the Israelis? It strikes me that it is probably OK to keep Gorba in the dark—to the extent that is possible to do if there is another channel. Gorba is basically a self-serving mischief maker. Of course the trouble is that as far as we know, so is the entire lot of those we are dealing with. The Soviet threat is the strategic menace and I would guess that they would like to avoid having the Russians in Iran. But it is going to take some time to get a feel for just who the players are on the contemporary scene in Teheran [sic]. So the sooner we get started the better." (McFarlane PROF note to North, 3/10/86, 22:14:24) (Tower)

- Evans and Minardos travel to Israel and discuss the B.I.T. contracts with the Eisenbergs and others. Evans and Minardos report that the goods are in Israel, that the end user certificate from the Philippines was withdrawn, and that the sellers want an advance of funds for an end user certificate. (Court papers, U.S. District Court, New York)

MAR 11 - North answered McFarlane:

"[Ghorbanifar] is aware of the Kish mtg and is basically carrying our water on the mtg since he is still the only access we have to the Iranian political leadership. It wd be useful, I believe, for you to talk w/George Cave, the Agency's Iran expert. He shares our concern that we may be dealing only w/ those who have an interest in arms sales and their own personal financial gain. . . . Will advise. If you wd like to meet w/ George, pls let me know and I will arrange." (North PROF note to McFarlane, 3/11/86, 07:23:34) (Tower)

- Poindexter told the Secretary of State "that this arrangement [a McFarlane-Iranian meeting in Frankfurt] had fallen through, apparently because Mr. McFarlane objected to the idea." (Shultz, SRB, 52) (Tower)

MAR 12 - A House intelligence committee report is quoted as saying that the CIA expects the contras to hold territory and administer it. The committee report states that the goal of this new plan is not to overthrow the Sandinistas, but to pressure them to negotiate with the contras. (Knight-Ridder 3/12/86)

MAR 13 - Ghorbanifar went to Tehran on March 13, "at some personal risk," returning to France on the 17th. (C. Allen, "Conversation with Subject," 3/12/86 CIA Docs.) [See March 20 entry] (Tower)

MAR 14 - Assistant U.S. Attorney Jeffrey Feldman allegedly tells a federal public defender, John Mattes, to stop investigating reports of an illegal arms shipment from Florida to the contras that purportedly originated in the NSC. (See December 12, 1986 entry.) (NYT 12/13/86)

- Evans returns from Israel and receives pro forma invoice from Northrop on letterhead of Dergo Establishment, "a Lichtenstein establishment," giving a total purchase price of $250 million for goods, end user certificates, and commissions. (Court papers, U.S. District Court, New York)

MAR 15 - The White House "public diplomacy group" on Nicaragua meets for a third time (see March 1 entry) to discuss strategy concerning the upcoming House vote on aid to the contras. (WP 3/20/86)

- The U.S. sends a third aircraft carrier into the Mediterranean. The three carriers and their 30-ship escort head toward the Gulf of Sidra, ostensibly to begin "exercises." In fact, they are being sent to provoke a reaction from Khaddafi that will justify a bombing raid against Libya (see January 6, 1986 entry). While the task force is en route, an argument of tactics takes place at a meeting of the Crisis Pre-planning Group, according to an NSC aide. Poindexter's assistant, Donald Fortier, reportedly asks the Joint Chiefs' representative to the group, General Moellering, to discuss the Navy's rules of engagement regarding a possible Libyan assault on the task force. When Moellering responds, "Proportionality," according to the aide who is present at the meeting, Fortier sharply insists, "They should be disproportionate." Fortier and Poindexter reportedly agree that the U.S. should bomb five targets in Libya if there is any loss of American life during the operation. (NYT 2/22/87)

MAR 17 - On or prior to this date, discussions between Hashemi and Veillot/Delaroque end when the latter fail to obtain hardware. (Court papers, U.S. District Court, New York)

- International Business Communications receives the first of three large payments this month from Spitz Channell's National Endowment for the Preservation of Liberty: $263,000 from check 1055 from NEPL's Palmer National Bank account 40000494. News reports later link this payment to further payments by IBC that end up in the Lake Resources bank account in Switzerland used by Richard Secord and Oliver North for aid to the Contras and the Iran arms sales. Adolfo Calero later says that $200,000 given to contras from the Swiss bank account of Lake Resources Inc. controlled by North was not used to purchase weapons. Calero says he has "no way of knowing" where the funds came from, but he says it is unlikely it was from the Iran arms sales. (See also Mar. 31 entry.) (NEPL Bank Statement 3/31/86; WP 3/7/87)

MAR 20 - The House rejects by a vote of 222-210 Reagan's February 25 request for $100 million in aid to the contras, despite a compromise offer from the president yesterday. (CRS "U.S. Assistance to Nicaraguan Guerrillas" 12/4/86)

- Khashoggi, through a subsidiary of his U.S. corporation, Triad America Corp., puts up several lots of Utah land development as collateral for three promissory notes in late 1985 and early 1986 from Vertex Finances, S.A. He used the loans to finance Iran's purchase of arms. (WSJ 12/12/86)

- On March 20, Ghorbanifar "returned with a proposed meeting scenario that is being communicated to us thru the Israeli, Nir, fm Peres' office. Still don't have details yet since his secure comms down, but should have necessary info tomorrow." (North PROF note to McFarlane, 3/20/86, 07:21:03. 1986 PROF notes) (Footnote: Ghorbanifar went to Tehran on March 13, "at some personal risk," returning to France on the 17th. (C. Allen, "Conversation with Subject," 3/12/86. CIA Docs.) On March 20, Ghorbanifar told Allen he had briefed Nir ("Adam") on his meetings with the Iranian Prime Minister, Rafsanjani, and Ahmad Khomeini (the Ayatollah's son). He reported that the Ayatollah remained "very ill"; that the Prime Minister had uncovered Soviet penetration of his office; that he was sending a report to North, which would include some requirements from the Iranian military; and that he hoped a meeting of principals could take place soon. (C. Allen, "Conversation with Subject," 3/21/86)) (Tower)

MAR 20-APR 20 - The CIA reportedly makes the first of three series of arms deliveries to the guerrillas in Angola via an air base in Zaire. Using C-130 and Boeing 707 cargo jets with the markings "Santa Lucia Airways," (other reports refer to "St. Lucia Airways") diplomatic and business sources say, the arms operation is supervised by "a black American everyone called Colonel" who is "in charge of about 20 men. Very few Zairois were involved." On two other occasions, in the last half of May and during one night in mid-October, the planes make several more deliveries. U.S. officials have refused to reveal how American aid to Angola, set at $15 million in 1986, makes its way there. (NYT 2/1/87)

MAR 21 - According to flight records from the government of the Caribbean island of St. Lucia, a St. Lucia Airways flight stops over on its way from Kelly Air Force Base in Texas to Cape Verde, which is reported to be a refueling site en route to Zaire. (WP 2/24/87)

SPRING - CIA personnel provide military training and assistance to contra units at bases in Yamales and Aguacate, Honduras, according to contras and former U.S. officials. At Yamales, basic and advanced military training is taught; at Aguacate, a CIA officer trains contras in parachute jumps. In addition, American agents supervise the transport and distribution of weapons delivered by the NSC network. (LAT 3/28/87)

MAR 22 - Nicaraguan troops stage an armed raid across the border into Honduras. Although it is later reported that similar incursions have occurred fifty to sixty times over the last six months with little concern expressed publicly by either Honduras or the U.S., the Reagan Administration uses this opportunity to press its case for congressional approval of $100 million in aid to the contras. A senior Honduran official later asserts that his country never felt its security was threatened by the attack. (See March 25, April 1 and April 9 entries.) (NYT 4/3/86; WP 4/6/86 & 4/30/86)

MAR 24 - [An excerpt] from the messages received by LtCol North on this channel [using encryption devices from the National Security Agency] follow[s]:

(1) On March 24, 1986, Mr. Secord sent LtCol North a secure message in which he discussed plans for an upcoming "drop" to Contra troops along the Costa Rican border (the so-called southern front):

"[X] should have held discussions with [Y] by now re. L-100 drop to . . . Blackies troops. If you have lined up [Z] to go to [location deleted] on the L-100, suggest you call [Y] secure and ensure he does all possible get load released from [location deleted]—also emphasize we ought to drop something besides 7.62; e.g., grenades, medical supplies, etc."

LtCol North's handwritten notes on this document enumerate quantities of various ammunition types. (Tower)

MAR 24-25 - It was reportedly well-known in the Administration that deploying the fleet in the Gulf would probably provoke Khaddafi. Libya fires missiles at ships of the U.S. Sixth Fleet, engaged in exercise Prairie Fire in the Gulf of Sidra. U.S. forces retaliate, attacking four Libyan ships, destroying two of them. Navy aircraft also attack a radar site on the Libyan coast. Khaddafi is warned that any of his forces venturing beyond the 12-mile limit recognized by the

U.S. will be subject to attack. There is no direct response from Libya which, according to a news report later, frustrates the NSC staff. A senior State Department official is quoted in the report as saying, "Everybody wanted to beat the hell out of Libya." Instead, the U.S. task force leaves the Gulf after only three days, two days earlier than planned. (WP 2/20/87; NYT 2/22/87)

MAR 24-28 - Documents captured by the Nicaraguan government from a C-123K cargo plane shot down in southern Nicaragua on October 5, 1986, indicate that around this period a small force of supply planes is regularly landing at contra bases or dropping supplies from the air. A log book kept by Wallace B. Sawyer, an American pilot who later dies in the October crash, shows a DHC-4 listed as "23" using El Salvador's Ilopango military airfield and another field designated as "AGU," apparently Aguacate, a U.S.-built airstrip used by the contras in eastern Honduras. Between March 24-28, the plane, flying out of Aguacate, takes part in 10 missions marked "ops," common shorthand for military operations. During this period, Nicaraguan government troops cross into Honduras to attack contra camps. According to records at Canada's Ministry of Transport, Propair, a company based in the city of Rouyn in western Quebec, sold a DHC-4 with the serial number 23 in February 1986. The licensing for the plane was then shifted to El Salvador, where the contra supply network was reportedly based. Propair President Jean Pronovost said that the plane was one of two DHC-C "Caribou" cargo planes that he sold to a "numbered" Panamanian firm—known to him only by a set of numbers. He said the buyer paid the "market rate" for the planes, which he estimated at between $400,000 and $525,000 each. Pronovost said the purchase was a "cash transaction," with the money transferred by wire into his bank account. He said that the second plane, sold a month after the first (March 1986), has Canadian markings CGJLP. (See April 9, 1986 entry.) (AP 10/21/86)

MAR 24-APR 2 - In a series of telephone conversations with Ghorbanifar and Nir, March 24-April 2, Charles Allen learned that Ghorbanifar was under pressure in Tehran; that he was passing through a difficult period financially, but that the Israelis were helping him; that an important meeting would occur on March 29, at which Khomeini himself would be informed of the state of play with the United

States; and that, after that meeting, Ghorbanifar had "excellent news" for North. An NSC consultant reported to Allen that Ghorbanifar was upset in part because his California girlfriend's house had been entered, as had Furmark's office in New York. Ghorbanifar blamed the CIA. (C. Allen, Memoranda for the Record, 3/27, 3/28, 3/28, 3/31, 4/2/86) (Tower)

MAR 25 - Reagan notifies Congress that he is requesting $20 million in emergency aid for Honduras after Nicaraguan forces launched a raid across the border on March 22. The President's request comes a day after Honduran President Jose Azcona Hoyo asked for U.S. help to repel the incursion. However, it is reported later that the U.S. deliberately exaggerated the danger of the attack and pressured the Honduran government to make its plea in order to influence Congress on the contra aid issue. According to Rep. Edward J. Markey (D-MA), of the $20 million package, only $410,000 worth of air transport and C-rations arrived during the week-long fighting. The remaining $19.6 million either arrived after the Nicaraguans withdrew or was still on its way more than a month later. Markey charges afterwards that the aid was in fact "an end run around Congress" designed "to circumvent established procedures for funding military aid to foreign countries." The State Department later confirms that North and the Department's top Latin American official, Elliott Abrams, worked closely to orchestrate the granting of the "emergency" aid. (NYT 4/4/86; WP 4/30/86; MH 1/8/87)

 - Khaddafi declares "It is a time for confrontation—for war" against the U.S., following military clashes in the Gulf of Sidra. The same day, U.S. agencies reportedly intercept coded messages from Libya to diplomatic posts in eight countries, including East Germany, ordering attacks against U.S. targets. (WP 2/20/87)

MAR 26 - Fourteen unarmed military helicopters with fifty American crewmen aboard transport a battalion of Honduran troops to the Nicaraguan border area to engage invading Nicaraguan forces. The action raises again the question of the applicability of the War Powers Resolution. (CRS "War Powers Resolution: Presidential Compliance" 12/22/86)

 - In Spring 1986 LtCol North also was involved in other efforts to help facilitate Contra military purchases through third countries. On March 26, 1986, three months after Mr. McFarlane left Government service, LtCol North informed Mr. McFarlane of his efforts (again, with Secord's assistance) to obtain Blowpipe launchers and missiles for the Contras:

"[W]e are trying to find a way to get 10 BLOWPIPE launchers and 20 missiles from [a South American country] thru the Short Bros. Rep. . . . Short Bros., the mfgr. of the BLOWPIPE, is willing to arrange the deal, conduct the training and even send U.K. 'tech. reps' fwd if we can close the arrangement. Dick Secord has already paid 10% down on the delivery and we have a [country deleted] EUC [end user certificates] which is acceptable to [that South American country]. (Tower)

MAR 27 - The Senate in a 53-47 vote adopts S.J. Res. 283, approving Reagan's request for $100 million in contra aid. The resolution attaches a number of conditions and restrictions along the lines of the President's proposed compromise to the House last week. (CRS "U.S. Assistance to Nicaraguan Guerrillas" 12/4/86; CRS "War Powers Resolution: Presidential Compliance" 12/22/86)

- The Senate passes an amendment proposed by Alan Dixon (D-Ill.) declaring that "No member of the United States armed forces, or employee of any department, agency, or other component of the United States government may enter Nicaragua to provide military advice, training, or logistical support to paramilitary groups operating inside that country." (CRS "War Powers Resolution: Presidential Compliance" 12/22/86)

- Greek authorities detain in Ashdod a ship owned by a Haifa company and registered in the Cayman Islands on its way to Portugal and Guatemala from Israel. The ship is carrying a helicopter, 24 submachine guns, and 280 tons of explosives and ammunition. All of the arms were purchased legally, and the ship is allowed to continue. It is reported that the ship is leased by a Latin American company through the Israeli company. An Israeli news report reveals that arms sale was approved by a ministerial committee, the defense minister, and the director general of the Defense Ministry. (FBIS 3/28/86 & 3/31/86 & Tel Aviv Hadashot 3/28/86 & 3/30/86)

- The U.S. ends the Prairie Fire exercise in the Gulf of Sidra after only three days, two days earlier than planned. (WP 2/20/87; NYT 2/22/87)

MAR - North pages Casey at a golf course to relay information on U.S. naval maneuvers off the coast of Libya. Casey is reported to be North's only remaining mentor in the Administration after the departure of McFarlane. (WSJ 12/31/86; WP 1/10/87)

MAR 28 - Retired Maj. Gen. John K. Singlaub and members of the staff of GeoMiliTech Consultants Corporation, a Washington-based military consulting firm, visit General Juan Rafael Bustillo, commander of El Salvador's Air Force at his Ilopango Air Force Base office. Along with Singlaub is Barbara Studley, whom he had encouraged to found GeoMiliTech in 1983. Studley, a former radio show host in Miami and later in Washington had supported the contras and other conservative causes on the air. She is listed as president of GeoMiliTech. Singlaub and Studley discuss with Bustillo the possible sale of T-28 and BAC 1-11 jets, as well as the EL/M-2106H (Point Defense Alert Radar capable of detecting hovering helicopters), according to a letter allegedly written by Studley following the March 28 meeting. Studley says that the letter is a forgery. Singlaub later claims he served GMT as an unpaid adviser. The company also has listed as advisers, at one time or another, retired major general George J. Keegan Jr., a former chief of U.S. Air Force Intelligence; John E. Carbaugh, a former top foreign policy aid to Sen. Jesse Helms and retired Army lieutenant general Robert L. Schweitzer, who worked for the NSC and was chairman of the Inter-American Defense Board before joining GMT. It is reported that in the summer of 1985 Studley would help Singlaub arrange a $5 million shipment of AK-47 and RPG grenade launchers from Europe to Honduras for the contras aboard a 15,000-ton Greek-flag freighter. The money for the shipment was transferred from the contras' bank account in Panama to a Panamanian corporation created to handle the transaction. The money then went to an arms dealer's Swiss bank account. (Letter from GeoMiliTech/Studley to Bustillo; WP 3/26/87)

- A cashiers check for $475,000 signed by "Udall Research Corporation (Southern Air)" and drawn from account number 473636801 at the Sun Bank in Daytona Beach, Florida, is made payable to Harry Doan of Doan Helicopter. The payment is for a C123k plane later used in resupply efforts for the contras. (Interviews)

MAR 31 - Adam Goodman, media/political director of The Robert Goodman Agency, Inc. (a Republican advertising agency), writes a letter to Carl "Spitz" Channell of the National Endowment for the Preservation of Liberty (NEPL) to praise a recent series of television spots in support of the contras that the agency produced for NEPL. NEPL's participation in the effort to lobby Congress appears to have been in violation of its status as a tax exempt organization. The letter begins, "Dear Spitz: Congratulations. . . . The National Endowment's television campaign in support of the Nicaraguan 'freedom fighters' not only has all of official Washington talking, but has broken new ground in the area of public policy advocacy." The letter continues, "As you recall, we began with one clear objective: winning Congressional approval of the President's $100 million aid request . . ." Goodman notes that the four-week national campaign, launched in February, was designed to reach "all 435 Members of the House (and 100 United States Senators)" and included "spot commercials in 23 additional television markets. . . . covering the home Districts of nearly thirty Congressmen experts considered to be at the core of the key 'swing vote' on Contra funding . . ." Goodman goes on to say, "We are very optimistic about our chances of winning the next House vote scheduled for April 15th . . ." On its 1985 tax forms, NEPL responded "n/a" to the question "Did the organization spend any amounts in attempts to influence public opinion about legislative matters or referendums?" The same forms indicate that NEPL had a balance of over $1 million at the end of 1985. Just two months later, NEPL ran the contra television campaign at a cost of $1.3 million. It is reported later that International Business Communications Inc. (IBC), a public relations firm, took part in "media consultant services" and a Goodman-produced ad campaign on behalf of the contras under two contracts with the State Department totaling over $360,000 (see April 1 and October 1, 1985 entries). (IRS Form 990, 1985; letter dated 3/31/86; AP 12/17/86)

- International Business Communications receives two large payments on the same day from the same bank account of the National Endowment for the Preservation of Liberty, Palmer National Bank account 40000494. The amounts are $500,000 (check 1066) and $225,000 (check 1073). News reports later link these payments to a further IBC payment of $740,000 on Apr. 9 to a Cayman Islands corporation, I.C. Inc., later renamed Intel Co-Operation Inc. I.C. Inc. in turn pays $650,000 to the Lake Resources bank account in Switzerland on Apr. 11. The Tower Commission report notes that on Apr. 3 North scribbled himself a reminder to tell Secord to send "650K to LAKE." On Apr. 16, Secord reported "650K received today as reported by the banker." (NEPL Bank Statement 3/31/86; WP 3/7/87)

APRIL 1986

APR - Richard Secord, his deputy Richard Gadd, and "a man described by others present as Lt. Col. Oliver North" meet with Southern Air Transport pilots at a safe house in San Salvador. The pilots are told that third country nationals will fly weapons into Nicaragua—some of those nationals are South African, according to American officials. (ABC World News Tonight, 2/25/87)

- Another set of U.S.-Honduran exercises in Central America comes to an end. Over the past four years such maneuvers have brought at least 30,000 American troops to Central America and involved the construction of "temporary facilities" including nine airfields and two radar stations. Some officials have remarked that Honduras is becoming a permanent U.S. military staging area. It is reported later that a new U.S.-Honduras security pact provides for American defense of Honduras in case of Nicaraguan attack. (CRS "War Powers Resolution: Presidential Compliance" 12/22/86)

- North orchestrates an abortive "sting" operation to free American hostage Peter Kilburn, according to intelligence sources. Duane "Dewey Maroni" Clarridge, head of the CIA's Counterterrorism Center and at one time a member with North of the interagency Core Group on Central American policy, is detailed by Casey to work with North and agents of the FBI in elaborating the plan. Basically, the plan involves paying a ransom for Kilburn and seizing the kidnappers after luring them onto a boat off the Lebanese shore. The plan fails when an intermediary the Americans have set up with the necessary funds never closes the deal with the captors. (Another version of the same plan pays the ransom for Peter Kilburn with chemically treated bills that would disintegrate after several days.) The plan to rescue Kilburn began in 1985 when a Canadian citizen of Armenian extraction contacted U.S. officials and announced that he represented the kidnappers. Administration officials began negotiating with the man after he delivered Kilburn's identification card as proof of his bona fides. After initially being set at $500,000, the ransom was increased to more than $3 million, payable in small denominations. The FBI and CIA then organized the sting under the coordination of the interdepartmental group on terrorism headed by Oliver North. Before the operation could be carried out, however, the U.S. attacked Libya and Khaddafi paid Kilburn's captors to kill him. The failure of the plan, which North attributed to footdragging by the CIA, contributes to North's decision to rely on private individuals rather than official channels for secret missions. (NYT 3/2/87; WSJ 12/26/86)

- Poindexter asks McFarlane to fly to Tehran to meet with top Iranian officials. He tells McFarlane a deal is in the works to free all U.S. hostages before the American delegation arrives in Iran. (CSM 1/2/87)

- One report says Reagan hopes to re-establish electronic "eavesdropping posts" dismantled after the 1978 Iranian revolution to listen in on Soviet missile facilities in Iran. (WP 11/14/86)

- Reagan signs a presidential finding authorizing a more active counter-terrorism policy. It is reviewed by Congress. The Administration's new Operations Sub-Group (OSG), formed in January, is responsible for laying down strategies and tactics to go along with the order. It envisions such unorthodox measures as providing terrorists with faulty weapons. (WP 2/17/87)

- Retired Air Force Colonel Robert C. Dutton assumes direction of the covert program to ship arms to the contras, according to sources who participated in the operation. He takes over from Richard Gadd. Dutton works for Stanford Technology Trading Group International Inc., the company partly owned by Richard Secord. (NYT 12/4/86; WP 12/7/86)

- William Cooper, pilot of the C-123K that crashes in Nicaragua on October 5, 1986, calls John McRainey, a former colleague from the days of the CIA's Air America operations in Indochina, and asks if he wants to fly "123s" again, this time in Central America. Several other veterans of Air America and Vietnam are recruited, nine pilots in all by the fall, to take part in the high-risk, covert air-drops of supplies to the contras inside Nicaragua. In addition to Cooper and McRainey, the pilots are: Frank Hines, Jerry Stemwedel, Jake Wehrell, Wallace B. Sawyer Jr., John Piowaty, Elmo Baker and David Johnson. McRainey calls the group the "over-the-hill gang" because all except Johnson (31) are over 50 years of age. Seven mechanics and three "kickers," cargo handlers such as Eugene Hasenfus, round out the operation. Cooper is in charge of the group, although the main liaison with the contras is Rafael (Ralph or Chichi) Quintero, a Cuban-American veteran of the Bay of Pigs and protege of former CIA official Thomas Clines. The team is nominally employed by Corporate Air Services of Quarryville, Pennsylvania, but the pilots believe the orders are coming from Stanford Technology Trading Group International Inc., Secord's company. They are paid in cash, in envelopes stuffed with $100 bills, usually $10,000 at a time. Over the six-month course of the operation, they each pick up four or five such envelopes at a Southern Air Transport office in Miami. None of the pilots is sure where the money comes from. Quintero, who works from the offices of his Coral Gables, Florida, firm, Orca Supply Co., is reportedly paid $4,000 a month for his efforts by a network consisting of Secord, his partner Albert Hakim, and Clines. The funding for many of the supply missions reportedly comes from Saudi Arabia. (SFE 12/7/86; Newsweek 2/9/87)

- Southern Air Transport this month makes two flights to Ilopango air base in El Salvador. One flight is from New

Orleans, carrying 23 tons of cargo, the other is from Lisbon, Portugal, with 45 tons on board. (DOT Records)

- Two of the riskiest of the Southern Air Transport flights into Nicaragua take place this month, according to sources who participated in the supply program. Col. James Steele, former chief American military officer in El Salvador, is reported to watch one of the flights take off from the main Salvadoran air base at Ilopango. An American Embassy official denies, however, that Steele did anything more than "observe" the flight. (NYT 12/4/86)

- During April, other activities, including the strike against Libya, occupied the attention of those responsible for the Iran operation. Progress toward the long-promised high-level meeting with representatives of the Iranian government was slow. (Tower)

APR 1 - A senior Honduran official declares that the U.S. deliberately exaggerated the threat posed to his country by the March 22-25 raid by Nicaraguan forces. The official also asserts that President Jose Azcona Hoyo's subsequent request for $20 million in emergency American aid was made under heavy U.S. pressure. (NYT 4/3/86 & 4/4/86)

APR 3-4 - U.S. officials North, Allen, Cave, C/NE met with Ghorbanifar in Washington on April 3 and, less formally, on April 4. Discussions of the proposed visit to Iran covered a wide range of detailed issues: where the meetings would be held; how the U.S. delegation would fly in, and with what passports; what communications they would have; what arms or material they would bring to sell to Iran; and how the delivery of the arms and the release of hostages would be orchestrated. In addition to the 240 types of HAWK parts, Iran wanted HAWK radars and mobile I-HAWK missile batteries, as well as more TOW missiles. The Soviet threat to Iran and Afghanistan was an area of agreement and Ghorbanifar said that Ayatollah Khomeini was going to issue a "fatwa" against hostage-taking. The United States insisted that all the hostages be released before the 240 HAWK parts were delivered, and only then would discuss further arms deals.

It was unclear whether the subject of devoting some profits to the contras arose at this meeting. One memorandum indicated the support for the mujahedin in Afghanistan was mentioned. Another memo indicated that Ghorbanifar discussed using the profits to support "Afghan rebels, etc."

The Officials

top: President Reagan *(back to camera)* and his national security advisers *(from left clockwise around the table)* Secretary of State George Shultz, Attorney General Edwin Meese, CIA Director William Casey, Chief of Staff Donald Regan, National Security Adviser Vice Admiral John Poindexter, Arms Control and Disarmament Agency Director Kenneth Adelman, Chairman of the Joint Chiefs of Staff William Crowe and Secretary of Defense Caspar Weinberger.

bottom: President Reagan *(back to camera)* with his staff *(from left to right)* Vice Admiral John Poindexter, Robert McFarlane and Donald Regan.

The President, North and the Contras

top: President Reagan with contra leaders *(from left to right)* Adolfo Calero, Alfonso Robelo and Arturo Cruz.

bottom: Lt. Col. Oliver North taking the Fifth Amendment before the House Foreign Affairs Committee.

The Hostages

Still Held:

Thomas Sutherland

Terry Anderson

Killed:

William Buckley

Peter Kilburn

Released:

Reverend Lawrence Jenco

David Jacobsen

The Weapons

top: TOW (Tube-launched, Optically-tracked, Wire-guided) anti-tank missiles.

bottom: HAWK (Homing-All-the-Way Killer) anti-aircraft missiles.

The Iranians and the Israelis

top: Iran middleman Manuchehr Ghorbanifar *(on left)*.
Speaker of the Iranian Parliament Hashemi Rafsanjani *(on right)*.

bottom: Adolph "Al" Schwimmer, Israeli arms dealer and special adviser to Prime Minister Shimon Peres. He and Yaacov Nimrodi were instrumental in arranging the secret transfer of arms to Iran *(on left)*.
Former Director General of the Israeli Foreign Ministry David Kimche. He got U.S. permission for arms deals with Iran as early as 1981 *(on right)*.

The Players

Retired Air Force Major General
Richard Secord

Saudi billionaire Adnan Khashoggi

Secord's business partner
Albert Hakim

Terrorism expert Michael Ledeen

New York businessman Roy Furmark

The Central American Connection

top left: Retired Air Force Major General John Singlaub.
top right: Assistant Secretary of State for Inter-American Affairs Elliott Abrams
bottom: The contras' top military commander and former Somoza National Guardsman Enrique Bermudez.

The Investigators

clockwise from upper left: Chairman of the House Iran-contra Investigating Committee Lee Hamilton; Tower Commission members Brent Scowcroft, John Tower and Edmund Muskie; Vice Chairman of the Senate Investigating Committee Warren Rudman, Chief Counsel Arthur Liman and Senate Committee Chairman Daniel Inouye; Special Prosecutor Lawrence Walsh.

A third, undated memorandum apparently referring to this April meeting indicated that Ghorbanifar said the United States could do the same with Nicaragua. (SSIC 1/29/87)

APR 4 - Shortly before 8:00 pm Eastern Standard Time, a terrorist bomb destroys the La Belle discotheque in West Berlin, killing one American serviceman, wounding at least 50 others, and causing almost 200 civilian casualties. The National Security Agency (NSA) intercepts Libyan communications before and after the attack which White House officials say provide "irrefutable" evidence of Libyan involvement. However, West Berlin police officials declare repeatedly in the days following the incident that they know of no evidence to suggest such a claim. (NYT 2/22/87)

- North's [undated and unsigned] memorandum for Poindexter to forward to the President reviewed the negotiations and specified how the profits on the sale of weapons to Iran could be spent [including $12 million to be diverted to the Nicaraguan contras]. The Board has obtained no evidence that Poindexter showed this memorandum to the President:

"Background.—In June 1985, private American and Israeli citizens commenced an operation to effect the release of the American hostages in Beirut in exchange for providing certain factions in Iran with U.S.-origin Israeli military materiel. By September, U.S. and Israeli Government officials became involved in this endeavor in order to ensure that the USG would:

"—not object to the Israeli transfer of embargoed material to Iran;

"—sell replacement items to Israel as replenishment for like items sold to Iran by Israel.

"On September 13, the Israeli Government, with the endorsement of the USG, transferred 508 TOW missiles to Iran. Forty-eight hours later, Reverend Benjamin Weir was released in Beirut.

"Subsequent efforts by both governments to continue this process have met with frustration due to the need to communicate our intentions through an Iranian expatriate arms dealer in Europe. In January 1986, under the provisions of a new Covert Action Finding, the USG demanded a meeting with responsible Iranian government officials.

"On February 20, a U.S. Government official met with an official in the Iranian Prime Minister's office—the first direct U.S.-Iranian contact in over five years. At this meeting, the U.S. side made an effort to refocus Iranian attention on the threat posed by the Soviet Union and the need to establish a longer term relationship between our two countries based on more than arms transactions. It was emphasized that the hostage issue was a 'hurdle' which must be crossed before this improved relationship could prosper. During the meeting, it also became apparent that our conditions/demand had not been accurately transmitted to the Iranian government by the intermediary and it was agreed that:

"—The USG would establish its good faith and bona fides by immediately providing 1,000 TOW missiles for sale to Iran. This transaction was covertly completed on February 21, using a private U.S. firm and the Israelis as intermediaries.

"—A subsequent meeting would be held in Iran with senior U.S. and Iranian officials during which the U.S. hostages would be released.

"—Immediately after the hostages were safely in our hands, the U.S. would sell an additional 3,000 TOW missiles to Iran using the same procedures employed during the September 1985 transfer.

"In early March, the Iranian expatriate intermediary demanded that Iranian conditions for release of the hostages now included the prior sale of 200 PHOENIX missiles and an unspecified number of HARPOON missiles, in addition to the 3,000 TOWs which would be delivered after the hostages were released. A subsequent meeting was held with the intermediary in Paris on March 8, wherein it was explained that the requirement for prior deliveries violated the understanding reached in Frankfurt on February 20, and were [sic] therefore unacceptable. It was further noted that the Iranian aircraft and ship launchers for these missiles were in such disrepair that the missiles could not be launched even if provided.

"From March 9 until March 30, there was no further effort undertaken on our behalf to contact the Iranian Government or the intermediary. On March 26, [the official in the Prime Minister's office] made an unsolicited call to the phone-drop in Maryland which we had established for this purpose. [He] asked why we had not been in contact and urged that we proceed expeditiously since the situation in Beirut was deteriorating rapidly. He was informed by our Farsi-speaking interpreter that the conditions requiring additional materiel beyond the 3,000 TOWs were unacceptable and that we could in no case provide anything else prior to the release of our hostages. [The Iranian official] observed that we were correct in our assessment of their inability to use PHOENIX and HARPOON missiles and that the most urgent requirement that Iran had was to place their current HAWK missile inventory in working condition. In a subsequent phone call, we agreed to discuss this matter with him and he indicated that he would prepare an inventory of parts required to make their HAWK systems operational. This parts list was received on March 28, and verified by CIA.

"Current Situation.—On April 3, Ari Gorbanifahr [sic], the Iranian intermediary, arrived in Washington, D.C. with instructions from [his Tehran contact] to consummate final arrangements for the return of the hostages. Gorbanifahr was reportedly enfranchised to negotiate the types, quantities, and delivery procedures for materiel the U.S. would sell to Iran through Israel. The meeting lasted nearly all night on April 3-4, and involved numerous calls to Tehran. A Farsi-speaking CIA officer in attendance was able to verify the substance of his calls to Tehran during the meeting. Subject to Presidential approval, it was agreed to proceed as follows:

"—By Monday, April 7, the Iranian Government will transfer $17 million to an Israeli account in Switzerland. The Israelis will, in turn, transfer to a private U.S. corporation account in Switzerland the sum of $15 million.

"—On Tuesday, April 8 (or as soon as the transactions are verified), the private U.S. corporation will transfer $3.651 million to a CIA account in Switzerland. CIA will then transfer this sum to a covert Department of the Army account in the U.S.

"—On Wednesday, April 9, the CIA will commence procuring $3.61 million worth of HAWK missile parts (240 separate line items) and transferring these parts to . . . This process is estimated to take seven working days.

"—On Friday, April 18, a private U.S. aircraft (707B) will pick-up the HAWK missile parts at . . . and fly them to a covert Israeli airfield for prepositioning (this field was used for the earlier delivery of the 1000 TOWs). At this field, the parts will be transferred to an Israeli Defense Forces' (IDF) aircraft with false markings. A SATCOM capability will be positioned at this location.

"—On Saturday, April 19, McFarlane, North, Teicher,

Cave, [C/NE], and a SATCOM communicator will board an aircraft in Frankfurt, Germany, enroute [sic] to Tehran.

"—On Sunday, April 20, the following series of events will occur:

"—U.S. party arrives Tehran (A-hour)—met by Rafsanjani, as head of the Iranian delegation.

"—At A+7 hours, the U.S. hostages will be released in Beirut.—At A+15 hours, the IDF aircraft with the HAWK missile parts aboard will land at Bandar Abbas, Iran.

"Discussion.—The following points are relevant to this transaction, the discussions in Iran, and the establishment of a broader relationship between the United States and Iran:

"—The Iranians have been told that our presence in Iran is a 'holy commitment' on the part of the USG that we are sincere and can be trusted. There is great distrust of the U.S. among the various Iranian parties involved. Without our presence on the ground in Iran, they will not believe that we will fulfill our end of the bargain after the hostages are released.

"—The Iranians know, probably better than we, that both Arafat and Qhadhaffi are trying hard to have the hostages turned over to them. Gorbanifahr specifically mentioned that Qhadhaffi's efforts to 'buy' the hostages could succeed in the near future. Further, the Iranians are well aware that the situation in Beirut is deteriorating rapidly and that the abilitiy [sic] of the IRGC [Iranian Revolutionary Guard Corps] to effect the release of the hostages will become increasingly more difficult over time.

"—We have convinced the Iranians of a significant near term and long range threat from the Soviet Union. We have real and deceptive intelligence to demonstrate this threat during the visit. They have expressed considerable interest in this matter as part of the longer term relationship.

"—We have told the Iranians that we are interested in assistance they may be willing to provide to the Afghan resistance and that we wish to discuss this matter in Tehran.

"—The Iranians have been told that their provision of assistance to Nicaragua is unacceptable to us and they have agreed to discuss this matter in Tehran.

"—We have further indicated to the Iranians that we wish to discuss steps leading to a cessation of hostilities between Iran and Iraq. . . .

"—The Iranians are well aware that their most immediate needs are for technical assistance in maintaining their air force and navy. We should expect that they will raise this issue during the discussions in Tehran. Further conversation with Gorbanifahr on April 4, indicates that they will want to raise the matter of the original 3,000 TOWs as a significant deterrent to a potential Soviet move against Iran. They have also suggested that, if agreement is reached to TOWs, they will make 200 out of each 1,000 available to the Afghan resistance and train the resistance forces in how to use them against the Soviets. We have agreed to discuss this matter.

"—The Iranians have been told and agreed that they will receive neither blame nor credit for the seizure/release of the hostages.

"—The residual funds from this transaction are allocated as follows:

"—$2 million will be used to purchase replacement TOWs for the original 508 sold by Israel to Iran for the release of Benjamin Weir. This is the only way that we have found to meet our commitment to replenish these stocks.

"—*$12 million will be used to purchase critically needed supplies for the Nicaraguan Democratic Resistance Forces. This materiel is essential to cover shortages in resistance inventories resulting from their current offensives and Sandinista counter-attacks and to 'bridge' the period between now and when Congressionally-approved lethal assistance (beyond the $25 million in 'defensive' arms) can be delivered.* [emphasis added]

"The ultimate objective in the trip to Tehran is to commence the process of improving U.S.-Iranian relations. Both sides are aware that the Iran-Iraq War is a major factor that must be discussed. We should not, however, view this meeting as a session which will result in immediate Iranian agreement to proceed with a settlement with Iraq. Rather, this meeting, the first high-level U.S.-Iranian contact in five years, should be seen as a chance to move in this direction. These discussions, as well as follow-on talks, should be governed by the Terms of Reference (TOR) (Tab A) with the recognition that this is, hopefully, the first of many meetings and that the hostage issue, once behind us, improves the opportunities for this relationship. Finally, we should recognize that the Iranians will undoubtedly want to discuss additional arms and commercial transactions as 'quids' for accommodating our points on Afghanistan, Nicaragua, and Iraq. Our emphasis on the Soviet military and subversive threat, a useful mechanism in bringing them to agreement on the hostage issue, has also served to increase their desire for means to protect themselves against/deter the Soviets.

"RECOMMENDATION

"That the President approve the structure depicted above under 'Current Situation' and the Terms of Reference at Tab A.

Approve——Disapprove——"

(Unsigned, undated memorandum, "Release of American Hostages in Beirut.")

The following "Terms of Reference" for a "U.S.-Iran Dialogue" were attached:

"I. BASIC PILLARS OF U.S. FOREIGN POLICY

"—President Reagan came into office at a time when Iran had had a certain impact on the American political process —perhaps not what you intended.

"—The President represented and embodied America's recovery from a period of weakness. He has rebuilt American military and economic strength.

"—Most important, he has restored American will and self-confidence. The U.S. is not afraid to use its power in defense of its interests. We are not intimidated by Soviet pressures, whether on arms control or Angola or Central America or Afghanistan.

"—At the same time, we are prepared to resolve political problems on the basis of reciprocity.

"—We see many international trends—economic, technological, and political—working in our favor.

"II. U.S. POLICY TOWARD IRAN: BASIC PRINCIPLES

"A. U.S. Assessment of Iranian Policy

"—We view the Iranian revolution as a fact. The U.S. is not trying to turn the clock back.

"—Our present attitude to Iran is not a product of prejudice or emotion, but a clear-eyed assessment of Iran's present policies.

"—Iran has used 'revolutionary Islam' as a weapon to undermine pro-Western governments and American interests throughout the Middle East. As long as this is Iran's policy, we are bound to be strategic adversaries.

"—Support for terrorism and hostage-taking is part of this strategic pattern. We see it used not only against us, but against our friends. We cannot accept either. Your influence in achieving the release of all hostages/return of those killed (over time) is essential.

"—We see your activity in many parts of the world, including even Central America.

"—The U.S. knows how Iran views the Soviet Union. But subversion of Western interests and friends objectively serves Soviet interests on a global scale.

"—Thus, our assessment is that a decisive Iranian victory in the war with Iraq would only unleash greater regional instability, a further erosion of the Western position, and enhanced opportunities for Soviet trouble-making.

"—The U.S. will therefore do what it can to prevent such a development. We regard the war as dangerous in many respects and would like to see an end to it.

"B. Possible Intersection of U.S.-Iranian Interests

"—Despite fundamental conflicts, we perceive several possible intersections of U.S. and Iranian interests. I propose to explore these areas.

"—First, the U.S. has had a traditional interest in seeing Iran preserve its territorial integrity and independence. This has not changed. The U.S. opposes Soviet designs on Iran.

"—Second, we have no interest in an Iraqi victory over Iran. [Discussion of US-Iraq Relationship] We are seeking an end to this conflict and want to use an improved relationship with Iran to further that end.

"—Third, we have parallel views on Afghanistan. Soviet policy there is naked aggression, a threat to all in the region. Our mutual friends—China and Pakistan—are threatened. We have ties with different elements of the Mujahideen. But our objective is the same: the Soviets must get out and let the Afghan people choose their own course.

"C. U.S. Objective Today

"—We have no illusions about what is possible in our bilateral relations. Perhaps this meeting will reveal only a limited, momentary, tactical coincidence of interests. Perhaps more. We are prepared either way.

"—In essence, we are prepared to have whatever kind of relationship with Iran that Iran is prepared to have with us.

"III. SOVIET MILITARY POSTURE

"—[Discussion of Soviet interests in Iran]

"—Afghanistan illustrates the price the Soviets are ready to pay to expand areas under their direct control.

"—Summarize Soviet capabilities along border and inside Afghanistan which could threaten Tehran.

"—U.S. is aware of Soviet activity in Baluchistan, air strikes.

"—Iranian support to Sandinista regime in Nicaragua aids and abets Soviet designs—makes U.S.-Iranian relationship more difficult ($100 million in oil last year, plus arms).

"—U.S. can help Iran cope with Soviet threat.

"IV. AFGHANISTAN

"—[Discussion of situation in Afghanistan]

"V. HARDWARE

"—We may be prepared to resume a limited supply relationship.

"—However, its evolution and ultimate scope will depend on whether our convergent or our divergent interests come to loom larger in the overall picture.

"—What does Iran want?" ("Terms of Reference U.S.-Iran Dialogue," 4/4/86) (Footnote: Teicher prepared the draft terms of reference and submitted it to North and Rodman, "and they worked on it." (Teicher 18) (Tower; see also LAT 12/20/86; WSJ 12/22/86; NYT 12/25/86 & 1/19/87; WP 1/10/87)

-On April 4, Mr. McFarlane replied (See March 26, 1986 entry) to LtCol North, "I've been thinking about the blow-pipe problem and the Contras. Could you ask the CIA to identify which countries the Brits have sold them to. I ought to have a contact in at least one of them."

In the same message, Mr. McFarlane also asked: "How are you coming on the loose ends for the material transfer? Anything I can do? If for any reason, you need some mortars or other artillery—which I doubt—please let me know."

When shown the aforementioned message, Mr. McFarlane submitted the following written response:

"Since the area of mortars and artillery is one in which I have expertise, gained through 20 years of experience as an artillery officer, I was prepared to assist LTC North by furnishing information and advice. I did not offer to assist LTC North in negotiating, purchasing, or obtaining mortars or other artillery for the Contras, nor did I ever take any such action." (Tower)

APR 5 - Libyan communications intercepted by the NSA immediately before and after the La Belle discotheque bombing are decoded, translated and rushed to the California White House where Reagan is spending Easter. White House officials claim they prove Libyan involvement in the attack. Reagan, who has reportedly opposed a bombing raid against Khaddafi up till now, is apparently convinced by the evidence. That afternoon, the decision to launch a strike is made (see April 14 entry). NSA officials are reported later to have doubts about whether the Administration should have relied on the intercepts as proof of Libyan complicity in the April 5 discotheque bombing. Earlier in the year, White House officials apparently set up special procedures and clearances for the handling of Libyan communications which bypassed many of the usual NSA channels and sent the intelligence immediately to the White House. (NYT 2/22/87)

- St. Lucia Airways, linked to CIA missions to Angola, stops over in the Caribbean island of St. Lucia on its way from Kelly Air Force Base in Texas to Cape Verde off the African coast. Cape Verde is said to be a refueling point on the way to Zaire where the airline reportedly is dropping off military supplies that are then to be transported overland to the U.S.-backed rebels in Angola. (WP 2/24/87)

- From this date through April 18, Veillot and Delaroque discuss in monitored phone calls the sale of hardware to Hashemi for Iran. Veillot says he has in Europe 400 AM-90 Sparrow missiles, two years old, for $27,000 each with end user certificates, and F-104 aircraft with end user certificates. The buyer would have to provide shipping. Veillot says he cannot get TOW missiles. (Court papers, U.S. District Court, New York)

APR 7 - By this time, NSC official Howard Teicher has prepared a discussion paper for the proposed bombing strike against Libya. According to a source, the document includes the suggestion that intercepted Libyan communications allegedly proving a connection between Khaddafi and the recent discotheque bombing in West Berlin be made public. The point, according to the source, is to prevent the President from having second thoughts about going ahead with the raid. (NYT 2/22/87)

- U.S. Ambassador to West Germany Richard Burt publicly ties Libya to the discotheque bombing. (NYT 2/22/87)

-On April 7, North reported the meeting (with Ghorbanifar, see APR 3, 1986 entry) to McFarlane.

"Met last week w/ Gorba to finalize arrangements for a mtg in Iran and release of hostages on or about 19 Apr. This was based on word that he had to deposit not less than $15M in appropriate acct. by close of banking tomorrow. Have talked at length w/ Nir who is handling him on thie [sic] bank xfer and Nir believes that Gorba may be having trouble closing the final arrangements back home. Per request of JMP have prepared a paper for our boss which lays out arrangements. Gorba indicated that yr counterpart in the T[ehran] mtg wd be Rafsanjani. If all this comes to pass it shd be one hell of a show. Meanwhile we have some evidence that Col Q [Qadhafi] is attempting to buy the hostages in order to stage a propaganda extravaganza. As far fetched as this may seem, CIA believes it is a distinct possibility. Bottom line: believe you shd avail yrself of this paper @ yr earliest convenience. Wd like to see you anyway. Am going home—if I remember the way." (North PROF note to McFarlane, 4/7/86, 23:18:58) (Tower)

APR 8 - Assistant Secretary of State Elliott Abrams testifies before the House Western Hemisphere Affairs Subcommittee, defending the Administration's handling of the March 22-25 Nicaraguan raid into Honduras. The hearing is convened after a senior Honduran official charged that the U.S. deliberately exaggerated the danger of the incursion in order to influence congressional debate on aid to the contras. In a heated exchange during the hearing, Abrams insists that the Administration "underplayed the event," to which Rep. Peter Kostmayer (D-Pa.) responds, "Frankly, Mr. Secretary, I am not surprised at anything you say to this committee anymore. . . . I am not surprised at the level of your audacity. . . . An increasingly large number of people are beginning to regard Administration statements as simply untruthful." (MH 4/9/86)

- Ghorbanifar conveyed the Iranian response to Allen on April 8. He said "he had 'good news,' asserting that an agreement had been reached in accordance with Washington's wishes." (C. Allen, "Conversation with [Ghorbanifar]," 4/8/86) He claimed to be "working the problem through Line One adherents, i.e. those conservative elements within the Iranian Government that are concerned over the Soviets and who do not believe that the clerics should necessarily be in charge of all government activities." (Id.) (Tower)

- Within the Executive Branch, interpretations [of section 8050 of the Fiscal Year 1986 Defense Appropriation Act, and section 105(a) of the Fiscal Year 1986 Intelligence

Authorization Act] differed. The CIA, in a "Question for the Record re 28 January Covert Action Update Briefing," concluded that it was not authorized to provide "specialized logistics training" needed by the Contras. The IOB, by memorandum of April 8, 1986, provided VADM Poindexter a classified legal analysis that concluded that under the "communications" and "advice" provision, any U.S. agency may lawfully provide basic military training to the Contras, "so long as such training does not amount to the participation in the planning or execution of military or paramilitary operations in Nicaragua . . . " (Footnote: The IOB memorandum addressed the question, "Can the Central Intelligence Agency or any other agency of the U.S. Government legally provide generic military training to the Nicaraguan democratic resistance?" It concluded:

"[T]he Intelligence Authorization Act for FY 1986 does authorize the obligation or expenditure of funds by the Central Intelligence Agency, the Department of Defense or other intelligence-related agencies of the U.S. Government to provide basic military training for the Nicaraguan democratic resistance so long as such training does not amount to the participation in the planning or execution of military or paramilitary operations in Nicaragua.") (Tower)

APR 9 - The flight log book of Wallace B. Sawyer, the American killed in the October 5, 1986, crash of a cargo plane delivering arms to the contras, shows him flying to the Rouyn, Quebec Airport via Detroit and Montreal today and then out of Rouyn on April 11 aboard a DHC-4, with Canadian markings CGJLP. These are the same markings that were on the plane sold by Propair to a numbered Panamanian corporation in March (see March 24-28, 1986 entry). After several stops at American airports, the plane flies to Ilopango on April 30. (AP 10/21/86)

- Richard Gadd's company, Airmach, using a Southern Air Transport plane, carries a load of NHAO nonlethal supplies from New Orleans to El Salvador. The supplies are offloaded and the plane is reloaded with weapons. (MH 3/22/87)

-From January to March, 1986, LtCol North received fifteen encryption devices from the National Security Agency for use in transmitting classified messages in support of his counterterrorist activities. These devices enabled LtCol

North to establish a private communications network. He used them to communicate, outside of the purview of other government agencies, with members of the private Contra support effort. . . . On April 9, 1986, LtCol North received another (see March 24, 1986 entry) secure message from Secord about preparations for a special shipment. North's notations on this message read: "Apr 9-1900. Confirmed arrival [city, country deleted] of L-100 w/load of [specified quantities of] ammo. . . . Confirming drop, Friday 11 April 0030." (Tower)

- After receiving large payments in March from the National Endowment for the Preservation of Liberty, International Business Communications pays $740,000 to a Cayman Islands corporation, I.C. Inc. (later Intel Co-Operation Inc.), which passes on $650,000 to Lake Resources in Switzerland. (WP 3/7/87)

APR 10 - Evans says Northrop and his partner Bar-Am want to meet with Hashemi to finalize the deal. The partner is described as a retired Israeli general who had served 30 years and is currently in the reserve officer corps as an adviser to the Northern Army Command in Israel. (Court papers, U.S. District Court, New York)

APR 11 - Special Envoy Philip Habib states in a letter to Rep. Dan Slattery (D-Kan.) that the U.S. will cease aid to the contras if Nicaragua signs the Contadora agreement. Says Habib, "We interpret these provisions as requiring a cessation of support to irregular and/or insurrectional movements from the date of the signature. We do not believe these provisions would prohibit financial or other humanitarian aid for the purpose of relocating or repatriating such forces." (CAHI 4/28/86)

- According to the Canadian Propair executives, the planes were sold to Southern Air Transport president William G. Langton who uses money from Amalgamated Commercial Enterprises and also arranges for the purchase of two C-123K cargo planes, one of which is later downed in Nicaragua. (PI 2/6/87)

- After receiving $740,000 from International Business Communications, I.C. Inc. of the Cayman Islands pays $650,000 to the Lake Resources account in Switzerland. (WP 3/7/87)

- An Airmach/Southern Air plane, loaded with seven tons of weapons, flies an airdrop to contras in Nicaragua. (MH 3/22/87)

APR 11-SEP 20 - Tomas Castillo (pseudonym), the CIA station chief in Costa Rica, his deputy, and two or three junior officers arrange seven air drops of arms and equipment to the rebels' southern front during this period, according to a top rebel official. Other contra sources put the number of shipments at about 10. A crew member aboard the first flight the night of April 11 says Army Col. James Steele, commander of the U.S. military forces in El Salvador, helps guide the flight. Salvadoran phone company records show that calls are placed from the San Salvador safehouse used by crewmen and organizers of the Ilopango resupply operation to the home and office of the man described as the San Jose station chief. Also during this time, CIA operatives known as Mick and Moe help orchestrate airdrops from a warehouse and airstrip at Aguacate, crewmen who work there say. According to crew member Iain Crawford, Mick and Moe directed three or four helicopter supply missions weekly from Aguacate into Nicaragua from April to June. Contra leaders say Castillo gave at least six field commanders $5,000 bonuses to leave Pastora for Chamorro, whose forces grew dramatically during this period. Pastora was also not provided with any of the arms drops to the southern front. (MH 3/1/87 & PI 1/18/87 & 2/5/87)

APR 12 - Defex-Portugal, acting on behalf of Energy Resources International, receives clearance to ship another installment of arms from Portugal to Guatemala. According to Lisbon airport records, the weapons are loaded onto a Southern Air Transport aircraft. They are intended for the contras. Guatemalan authorities say they never received any Portuguese arms. (WP 1/17/87)

- On April 12, 1986, LtCol North received a secure message from the CIA field officer confirming a successful drop to the UNO South Force and outlining plans for the next two to three weeks:

"[A]ir drop at sea for UNO/KISAN indigenous force area . . . lethal drop to UNO South . . . transfer of 80 UNO/FARN recruits . . . carrying all remaining cached lethal materiel to join UNO South Force. *My objective is creation of 2,500 man force which can strike northwest and link-up with quiche to form solid southern force.* Likewise, envisage formidable opposition on Atlantic Coast resupplied at or by sea. Realize this may be overly ambitious planning but with your help, believe we can pull it off." (emphasis added). (Tower)

APR 13 - Evans and Guri Eisenberg meet with others including Hashemi, Northrop and Bar-Am to discuss the sale. Evans is to be the intermediary. Northrop and Bar-Am through Dergo Establishment (a Lichtenstein company) would obtain the latter part of the hardware list and sell to Galaxy Trade Inc. (the buyer for Iran), with fraudulent end user certificates. An undercover U.S. Customs agent attends the meeting. During the meeting, Evans produces a draft of three separate written contracts agreeable to both buyer and seller, except for the price which was to be adjusted as the parties agreed at the meeting. The three contracts are as follows: (1) 3750 TOW missiles for FOB Israel at $61,875,000 plus shipping and insurance. (2) 18 F-4 fighter planes for FOB Israel at $360 million plus shipping and insurance. (3) 5 C-130E Hercules aircraft, 2 Hawk missile batteries, 4 Radr Set Am/TPS, 46 Skyhawk aircraft fighter/bombers, 30 Sparrow guided missiles, 200 tires and tubes for F-4 fighter planes, 8 F-4 anti-skid test equipment, 200 AIM guided missiles, 200 Maverick guided bombs, 600 Chapparal missiles, 90 SUU-21/A bomb dispensers, 22 SUU-44 flare dispensers, 70 camera KB-18—for a total price FOB Israel of $415,130,880 plus shipping and insurance.

Evans also produces another contract for $343 million as a model for the final contract between Galaxy Trade Inc. and Dergo Establishment, including among other items the following: 50 long-range artillery howitzers, 1 Cobra helicopter engine, 5000 TOW missiles, 13 F-5 aircraft, 4 Huey helicopter engines, and 2 turboprop engines for C-130 Hercules aircraft. The contract states that the seller is to provide "currently effective end user certificates applicable to said goods and approved by relevant U.S. authorities and confirmed by relevant Israeli authorities which in turn will have issued all appropriate export licenses." At the meeting the undercover agent is asked by Northrop whether he worked for the U.S. government, and Northrop advises them all not to go to the U.S. because the deal is illegal. (Court papers, U.S. District Court, New York)

MID-APR - . . . further difficulties arose. Although Ghorbanifar assured the United States that Iranian officials were prepared to meet with McFarlane, he also reported that Iran was insisting upon not releasing all the hostages before the HAWK parts were delivered; Iranian intransigence was increased, he said, by the realization that McFarlane could not possibly carry all the parts on the plane that would take him to Iran. Iran also continued to insist upon HAWK radars, as well as the other parts. (SSIC 1/29/87)

- The Board found evidence that LtCol North, Mr. Cave, Mr. Allen, and another CIA official knew as early as mid-April that if all the HAWK spare parts were not delivered with the delegation, then only one U.S. hostage would be released. Mr. McFarlane may not have been advised of this. (Tower)

APR 14 - It is reported that the CIA spent several million dollars refurbishing the image of the United Nicaraguan Opposition (UNO), the contra umbrella organization despite a congressional ban on aid to the rebels. (AP 4/14/86; CRS "U.S. Intelligence: Issues for Congress, 1986" 1/5/87)

- Reagan announces that U.S. Air Force and Navy planes have conducted bombing strikes against targets in Libya. (The raid occurs early on April 15, Libyan time.) He describes the attack as an act of self-defense under Article 51 of the U.N. Charter, and as a pre-emptive strike designed to deter Libya from future acts of terrorism. One news report in early 1987, based on interviews with over 70 current and former Administration officials, concludes that the primary aim of the operation is to assassinate Khaddafi. "The mission," according to the report, "authorized by the White House, was to be the culmination of a five-year clandestine effort by the Reagan Administration to eliminate" Khaddafi.

The raid is planned by "a small group of military and civilian officials in the National Security Council," the same people involved in the secret arms deals with Iran that are being negotiated at this time, and utilizes many of the same methods, including a back channel of communication to further limit access to information about the operation.

Members of the ad hoc Crisis Pre-planning Group that put together the plan include Army Lt. Gen. John H. Moellering of the Joint Chiefs of Staff; Michael H. Armacost, undersecretary of state for political affairs; Richard L. Armitage, assistant secretary of defense for international security affairs;

Oliver North; Howard Teicher, a Near East specialist on the NSC; Capt. James R. Stark of the Navy, assigned to the office of political-military affairs at the NSC; and NSC Executive Secretary Rodney B. McDaniel, a former Navy captain in whose office the group met, shunning the Situation Room where their presence would draw undue attention from other staffers. CIA Director Casey is also involved generally as the intelligence officer for a secret task force on Libya established in mid-1981. As such he reportedly provides intelligence over a period of time, some of it fabricated, according to other members of his secret group, linking Khaddafi to alleged "hit squads" targeting American officials and other terrorist activities around the world. According to the article, Israeli intelligence assists in the operation by providing continuous updates on Khaddafi's whereabouts, the last fix coming at 11:15 pm, Libyan time, two hours and 45 minutes before the attack begins.

Early in the year, the National Reconnaissance Office (NRO), which is responsible for procuring and deploying intelligence satellites, takes a signals intelligence satellite (SIGINT) out of its stationary orbit over Poland and moves it over North Africa so that Libyan communications could be monitored more closely. Ever mindful of the need to cover tracks, according to the report, the planners are careful to conceal the real aim of the raid, going so far as to omit explicit references to Khaddafi's tent as a target in the official bombing orders, and denying after the fact that the U.S. had specific knowledge of where the Libyan leader was that night. As it turns out, the bombers fail to kill Khaddafi, which senior Air Force officers later call a fluke, despite the fact that four of the nine F-111's charged with targeting Khaddafi (a total of 18 aircraft are initially involved in the raid) experience mechanical problems with their guidance systems and a fifth F-111 bombs a residential area through human error, killing more than 100 people. Citing the involvement in the operation of a number of White House officials who "believed in force, stealth and operations behind the back of the citizenry and the Congress," the article concludes that North, who is later perceived as an "aberration" because of his activities while at the NSC, is actually only "part of a White House team" of people possessing similar convictions and aims. (WP 4/17/86; CRS "War Powers Resolution: Presidential Compliance" 12/22/86; NYT 2/22/87)

APR 15 - The [CIA] field officer sent another secure message (see March 24, 1986 entry) to confirm a delivery to an airbase in a Central American country; he tells LtCol North the delivery is loaded with ammunition "for your friends." He asks LtCol North: "When and where do you want this stuff? We are prepared to deliver as soon as you call for it."

The field officer testified before the Board: "[T]his private benefactor operation . . . was, according to my understanding, controlled by Colonel North." He also informed the Board that all the shipments he was involved in were arms deliveries: "This was all lethal. Benefactors only sent lethal stuff."

Even before the CIA field officer made his disclosures to the Board, his activities had triggered a legal debate within the CIA. In a memorandum dated December 5, 1986, to the Deputy Director for operations, CIA Associate General Counsel Jameson stated that "contacts with the benefactors, although contrary to policy, were not contrary to law." Flight vectors, Sandanista antiaircraft positions, and other similar information needed to carry out safe aerial deliveries fell within the terms of the "advice" authorized in December, 1983, by the Intelligence Authorization Act. By memorandum to the CIA General Counsel of January 22, 1987, the CIA Inspector General's office questioned Jameson's interpretation. The Inspector General maintained, among other things, that the field officer's activities could be characterized as planning for a paramilitary operation, expressly barred in the joint Explanatory Statement accompanying the Conference Committee Report to H.R. 2419.)

The CIA field officer explained the legal regime under which he was operating:

"I could not plan or engage in any military operation inside Nicaragua . . . But I could provide information that would allow the safe delivery of material to the people inside; I could pass information concerning potential deliveries to supply them, but not for any specific military operation. In other words, I could be the conduit for information; passing of information was legal or permissible under the agreement reached between the House and the Senate with the Agency under the Boland Amendment . . . "

Asked if LtCol North ever discussed the legality of actions with him, the field officer answered,

"I asked him, 'are you sure this is all right—you know, that sort of thing. Are you sure this is okay?' He said, 'yes, yes, all you're doing is passing information.'"

The field officer was a member of a group that met for three minutes with President Reagan in the Oval Office in 1986. [photo session] The group comprised the Minister of Public Security from a Central American country and his wife, Chief of Staff Regan, VADM Poindexter and LtCol North. (Tower)

APR 16 - LtCol North wrote VADM Poindexter seeking approval for a meeting with Mr. Ghorbanifar in Frankfurt on April 18. In his reply of the same date, VADM Poindexter approved the trip but insisted that there be no delivery of parts until all the hostages had been freed. He expressly ruled out half shipments before release. "It is either all or nothing." He authorized LtCol North to tell Mr. Ghorbanifar: "The President is getting very annoyed at their continual stalling." On April 21, VADM Poindexter sent a message to Mr. McFarlane informing him of this position. (Tower)

- On April 16, North wrote Poindexter that:
"Recognize that all are very busy. Have been unable to get thru to you or Don [Fortier] via phone/appointment. [C/NE] and Gates have urged that Cave and North proceed tomorrow to meet with [the Iranian official] and Gorba in Frankfurt on Friday, and return to Washington on Saturday. All this based on a series of phone calls btwn Gorba/[the Iranian official]; North/Nir; Nir/Gorba; Allen/Gorba over the last 72 hours. [The NSC staff and CIA officers involved in the initiative learned at this time that the Iranian official's instructions to Ghorbanifar were that, if the U.S. did not deliver all the HAWK spares with the arrival of the U.S. delegation, only one hostage would be released. It was presented to Ghorbanifar as a "take it or leave it" proposition to the U.S.] In order to arrive for a Friday mtg Cave/North wd fly out tomorrow night to arrive Friday a.m. No deposit has been made yet because Nir does not want to risk losing the money if the operation is not going to go to closing.

"He doesn't need the 240 parts. We have a problem on our side in that over 50 of the parts now do not appear to be in stock or are no longer made for our version of the system. Nir is checking in their older inventories to see if they have them on hand. Please advise soonest, must make reservations." (North PROF note to Poindexter, 4/16/86, 16:40:45)

Poindexter replied:
"You may go ahead and go, but I want several points made clear to them. There are not be be any parts delivered

until all the hostages are free in accordance with the plan that you layed [sic] out for me before. None of this half shipment before all are released crap. It is either all or nothing. Also you may tell them that the President is getting very annoyed at their continual stalling. He will not agree to any more changes in the plan. Either they agree finally on the arrangements that have been discussed or we are going to permanently cut off all contact. If they really want to save their asses from the Soviets, they should get on board. I am beginning to suspect that [the official in the PM's office] doesn't have much authority." (Poindexter PROF note to North, copy to Thompson, 4/16/86, 21:08:42) (Tower)

- In the aftermath of that action [the U.S. attack on Libyan targets], hostage Peter Kilburn was killed by his captors, reportedly at the behest of Libyan leader Muammar Qadhafai [sic]. Some press stories have suggested that the U.S. attack resulted in delays in the mission to Iran. A White House chronology indicates that instead Iran wanted to accelerate planning for the mission, so that it would not be accused of involvement in the Kilburn death. The Committee has found no other documentation or testimony indicating that these events had an impact on the arms sale program. (SSIC 1/29/87; WSJ 12/24/86)

- The Defense Department, meanwhile, continued to track down the HAWK spare parts. CIA formally requested 234 types of HAWK parts in mid-April, and 2 HAWK radars later in the month. By the end of April, the cost of the HAWK spare parts that the Army had located was fixed at $4.4 million, including transportation. (SSIC 1/29/87)

- The Reagan administration responds to charges that contras are involved in drug dealing, saying that some rebels "may have engaged in such activity" but that they were not acting on the orders of their leaders. The Administration's comments are contained in a three-page document delivered by Assistant Secretary of State Elliott Abrams to Rep. Charles W. Stenholm (D-Tex.) who has expressed concern to the president over the contra allegations. (WP 4/17/86)

- The Eisenbergs of B.I.T. arrange to meet Hashemi in Bermuda to sign and finalize the contract. Israel Eisenberg confirms that end user certificates from various countries have been obtained for all the equipment except 46 Skyhawk aircraft. (Court papers, U.S. District Court, New York)

APR 18 - Delaroque says he cannot meet with the buyer or discuss the deal in New York because of the illegality in the U.S. (Court papers, U.S. District Court, New York)

- A St. Lucia Airways cargo plane makes a stop in the Caribbean island of the same name on its way from Kelly Air Force Base in Texas to Cape Verde off the African coast. The aircraft is reportedly on another of several CIA-backed missions to Zaire to deliver arms for the Angolan rebels. (WP 2/24/87)

- North flies with Gadd to El Salvador to "solve some problems" of the resupply network. (PI 2/4/87)

APR 20 - Iain Crawford, a parachute rigger on apparent CIA-directed contra resupply missions, briefs North regarding the April 11, seven-ton arms airdrop, Crawford says in a later interview. The briefing, which Crawford says takes place on an El Salvador to Washington flight, is three days before North meets with Reagan, other high administration officials, and the CIA's Costa Rican station chief, Tomas Castillo, to discuss the Central America situation. According to press reports, reliable contra sources have said the station chief helped plan the resupply missions. Five other crewmen and radio operators confirmed Crawford's role in the operation. (PI 2/4/87)

- At a closed budget hearing, Weinberger is asked by Rep. Norman D. Dicks (D-WA) about the Air Force's targeting of Khaddafi at the El-Azziziya Barracks in Tripoli, Libya. "Mr. Secretary, you are a lawyer," Dicks says. "Can you characterize this in any other way than an attempt to eliminate a foreign leader?" "Oh, yes, Mr. Dicks, we sure can," Weinberger answers. "His living quarters is a loose term. This is a command-and-control building. His living quarters vary from night to night. He never spends two nights in the same place. His actual living quarters are a big Bedouin sort of tent. We are not targeting him individually." It is reported later that Israeli intelligence provided the U.S. with continuous updates on Khaddafi's whereabouts until two hours and 45 minutes before the actual bombing began. At the time of the last update, Khaddafi reportedly was still at work in his tent inside the grounds of the El-Azziziya Barracks. Other Administration officials, including Shultz and Chairman of the Joint Chiefs Adm. William J. Crowe Jr., also deny later that the raid amounted to an attempt to assassinate the Libyan leader. (NYT 2/22/87)

APR 21 - Delaroque and Veillot arrange travel to Bermuda to sign the contract and receive the letter of credit. Flearmoy and Kopka meet unidentified individual in New York to discuss proposed M-48 tank sale. Moll and an unidentified individual meet in New York to discuss F-4 sales. (Court papers, U.S. District Court, New York)

- Senator Patrick Leahy (D-Vt.) says the Administration's use of covert paramilitary operations as a normal instrument of foreign policy has strained relations between the CIA and the two congressional intelligence committees. (CRS "U.S. Intelligence: Issues for Congress, 1986" 1/5/87)

- North reported the last days' activities to McFarlane on April 21.

"Both Charlie Allen and Nir have been in touch w/ Gorba in an effort to set up a meeting with [the Iranian official] in Europe. We know that [the Iranian official] is apparently trying to extract additional concessions from us prior to releasing the Americans. George Cave, our resident expert believes that [the Iranian official] had probably received some kind of authority to cause the release of the hostages prior to our Libyan action and that the current delays and efforts to force new concessions are a consequence of internal disputes over what the Iranians shd do about this matter in the wake of the U.S. action in Libya. Gorba has been out of touch all day and Cave/North cancelled the trip to Frankfurt for a second time because we do not want to meet again w/ only Gorba. The Kilburn tragedy has us very concerned because there appears to be some possibility of Syrian complicity in Kilburn's death and the same could happen to our other hostages if the Syrians are able to put their hands on them. If the mtg takes place this week it would still be a minimum of eight and a maximum of 10 days from deposit of funds before we can assemble the requisite parts. We do not believe they will make this deposit until after the mtg. We also need to make it known that we simply do not have some of the parts requested since we have modernized our HAWK systems. I have sent Nir a coded msg asking him to determine whether or not they have in stock the items which we lack. If it is determined that they do not have them we will have to determine the effect this will have on the understanding we reached last week w/ Gorba. Nir believes that the Israelis will be able to give us an answer in the next 2 days. Cave and North are prepared to lunch again tomorrow if Gorba surfaces and has set up a mtg w/ [his Tehran contact]. Bottom line: earliest timeframe for RCM/Cave/North trip to Iran is 30 April and this will slip a day for every day of delay in the Frankfurt mtg & its complementary financial transaction." (North PROF note to McFarlane, 4/21/86, 20:31:28)

Poindexter transmitted North's note to McFarlane and added the following cover:

"[The Iranian official] wants all of the HAWK parts delivered before the hostages are released. I have told Ollie that we can not do that. The sequence has to be 1) meeting; 2) release of hostages; 3) delivery of HAWK parts. The President is getting quite discouraged by this effort. This will be our last attempt to make a deal with the Iranians. Next step is a Frankfurt meeting with Gorba, [the Iranian official], North and Cave. Sorry for the inconvenience." (Poindexter PROF note to McFarlane, 4/21/86, 20:31) (Tower)

APR 22 - Law enforcement officials working with the cooperation of the Bermuda government arrest all the principals of the Hashemi deal in Bermuda, with the exception of Veillot and Delaroque, who remain at large. 18 defendants are indicted in New York on charges of conspiring to ship $2 billion worth of aircraft, missiles and other military materiel to Iran. Among them is retired Israeli general Avraham Bar-Am and Samuel Evans, chief counsel for Khashoggi. Bar-Am, is described at length in the press as having been the number two officer in the Northern Army Command in Israel in 1982, when the command was responsible for the invasion of Lebanon. He was chief of staff of the Israeli Defense Forces manpower branch before he was forced to resign in 1984 amid allegations of improper conduct relating to promotion practices and distribution of weapons to personal friends. All accounts note that Bar-Am had a routine Israeli Defense Ministry document authorizing him to prospect abroad for sales of Israeli arms but banning him from the actual negotiations.

The Israeli daily Davar quotes Bar-Am as saying, "I didn't act in a purely private capacity. Many people in the military establishment knew about the activities of the group of which I was an adviser. If the government doesn't intercede on my behalf, if I'm extradited to the United States, I'll make embarrassing disclosures. I'm only a cog in the works." Bar-Am says that after his arrest the first thing he did was call the Israeli military and defense attache, Uri

Simhony. Simhony is quoted by Time magazine as telling Bar-Am curtly, "Buddy, you better get yourself the best legal advice available." Bar-Am also claims that the day after his arrest, Mossad checked with the CIA on the Customs agents in the case. Ghorbanifår, who was in Switzerland, was jailed for a day. According to testimony of the CIA consultant, officials surmised that he had been held because he was an investor in the failed scheme. This development seemed likely to make Ghorbanifar (and Iran) more eager to do business through the one reliable channel to the United States, but it also made Iran ever more insistent upon not giving Ghorbanifar the money in advance. (NYT 11/30/86; Iran Times 9/19/86; Court Papers, U.S. District Court, New York; SSIC 1/29/87)

- McFarlane agreed with Poindexter's outline (see April 21, 1986 entry). "Your firmness against the recurrent attempts to up the ante is correct," McFarlane responded. "Wait them out; they will come round. I will be flexible." (McFarlane PROF note to Poindexter, 4/22/86, 20:35:17) (Tower)

- [LtCol North] wrote Mr. Fortier: "[T]he picture is dismal unless a new source of 'bridge' funding can be identified . . . We need to explore this problem urgently or there won't be a [contra] force to help when Congress finally acts." (Tower)

APR 23 - During the same general time period, the President had two meetings which appeared to relate to Central American policy at which North was present. The exact topic of discussion cannot be determined from records available to the Committee. Both meetings occurred on April 23. White House documents list as the general topic of one meeting a discussion of a recent trip by Elliott Abrams to El Salvador, Honduras, and Costa Rica. The meeting was attended by the President, the Vice-President, Deputy Secretary of State John Whitehead, Abrams, Regan, Poindexter, and Fortier in addition to North. The other meeting for which no topic is listed was attended by the President, North, Regan, Poindexter, a Central American security official and his wife, and the senior CIA officer in that country. The CIA officer was later the subject of an internal CIA investigation initiated in the fall of 1986 concerning unauthorized contacts with private supporters of the Nicaraguan resistance. [The

CIA official is later identified as the CIA's station chief in Costa Rica. The station chief used the pseudonym Tomas Castillo. (See February 1, 1987 entry) (BG 2/22/87)](SSIC 1/29/87)

APR 24 - In North's view, the situation (see April 21 and 22, 1986 entries) warranted continued pursuit of the meeting and consummation of the transaction. He received support from Major Julius Christensen, a member of the Director of Central Intelligence/Hostage Location Task Force. On April 24, Christensen sent North an analysis of options to secure the release of the hostages. On balance, he concluded that "the back channel initiative" could succeed. But he noted that arms shipments could affect the balance in the Iran-Iraq war and that the longer the operation lasted the greater the risk of exposure. He attached a fuller analysis of the options—doing nothing, diplomatic efforts, Waite, paying ransom, and using force, unilaterally or multilaterally. He looked to the NSC for guidance. (Christensen to North, 4/24/86) (Tower)

APR 25 - Charles Allen set forth his own views as to the parties' desiderata. He thought the Iranians urgently needed weapons; wanted a source of continuing supply; a favorable end to the Iraq war; and "re-establishment of their 'rightful place' and spread of fundamentalism," in that order. He noted that the United States refused to supply HAWK radars, which Iran has demanded, and had imposed a termination date 2-3 weeks hence if the operation had not succeeded. He thought that, unless the United States were "willing to sweeten the pot, we can only stand fast and present to them the appearance that time is on our side and not on theirs. This would require resolve on our part in the face of possible damage to one or more hostages." The Israelis could solve the problem of continuing supply to Iran by the United States committing a sin of omission. (C. Allen, Working Paper, 4/25/86) (Tower)

APR 28 - Compagnie de Services Fiduciaires (CSF) buys the Danish freighter Erria through its agents Albert Hakim and Willard Zucker, the company's attorney. The ship is purchased from its Danish captain, Arne Herup, for $312,500. Herup is forwarded the money from an account at the Credit Suisse bank in Geneva, according to Tom Parlow, the Danish businessman who cooperates in subsequent clandestine operations involving the Erria ordered by Oliver North. The new legal owner of the ship is Dolmy Business Inc., a front company registered in Panama. The purchase is said to be "strictly an Ollie operation." (LAT 1/21/87)

APR 29 - North wrote Poindexter on April 29:

"We are seeing increasing evidence of Libyan efforts to buy the hostages and other signs of increasing disarray inside Lebanon. Further, there is increasing indication of seepage around the edge of our hostage project. Bottom line: [the Iranian official] knows this and wants to proceed quickly with a release. [Available information indicates that [the Iranian official] does indeed have the requisite authorities to bring this all to a conclusion.... In any event—all here agree that Cave, North and Nir ought to go to meet w/ [the Iranian official]. Agency has prepared foreign Documents as necessary. If you approve, we wd depart Thurs p.m. [May 1], commercial to Frankfurt then to Tehran Friday via private jet over Turkey. If you do not believe that we can proceed with the radars I will try to convince them to take what we have in terms of parts and if necessary some of the TOWs as acceptable alternatives. We know . . . that Gorba has tried, unsuccessfully to date, to convince [the Iranian official] that this is the preferred course of action." (North PROF note to Poindexter, 4/29/86, 19:46:06)

According to the CIA Inspector General, the NSC staff and CIA received word that Iran would welcome a high-level American delegation to Tehran. (CIA/IG Chronology 22) (Tower)

APR 30 - Wallace Sawyer, pilot of the C-123K plane shot down in Nicaragua, flies a DHC-4 "Caribou" with Canadian markings CGJLP to Ilopango military airfield in El Salvador. The plane was purchased from Propair by a numbered Panamanian company in March of this year. (See March 24-28, 1986 and April 9, 1986 entries). (AP 10/21/86)

- Felix Rodriguez and Col. Sam Watson meet to discuss the progress of the insurgency in El Salvador and the need for helicopter parts. (WP 12/16/86)

- North to Poindexter, (see May 5 entry) Bottom line: earliest timeframe for RCM/Cave/North trip to Iran is 30 April and this will slip a day for every day of delay in the Frankfurt mtg & its complementary financial transaction. (Tower)

LATE APR - By late April, the lack of progress in arranging the high-level visit to Iran had led the U.S. officials to decide that the operation would be shut down unless there was movement within 2-3 weeks. A CIA official wrote that the differences between the United States and Iran appeared intractable. He suggested the sale of two HAWK radars to Iran and renewed emphasis upon a long-term military supply relationship with Iran. The CIA official noted that Israel was eager for such a relationship and might already be quietly supplementing U.S. sales. Then Ghorbanifar and/or Nir apparently proposed that the mission to Iran be only a preliminary meeting. U.S. officials rejected this idea, noting that if Iran understood and abided by what had been agreed to in February, there would be no need for any preliminary meeting. (SSIC 1/29/87)

APR - Nir reportedly meets with Khashoggi, Ghorbanifar and British businessman Roland W. (Tiny) Rowland in an unsuccessful bid to get Rowland to provide $15 million to finance an arms deal with Iran. Rowland has already reportedly lent Khashoggi $7.5 million which the Saudi weapons dealer used to help finance the first shipments to Iran (see August 1985 entry). (WP 12/27/86 & 2/1/87)

END APR - [D]ocuments indicate that the U.S. Embassy in London became aware of the fact that Ghorbanifar and Khashoggi had approached a major British arms dealer in hopes of getting a $50 million line of credit for arms sales to Iran with U.S. approval. The British dealer had been assured by Israeli officials that this was a White House operation and did indeed have U.S. approval. (SSIC 1/29/87)

MAY 1986

MAY - By May, 1986 VADM Poindexter became concerned that LtCol North's operational activities were becoming too apparent. He informed LtCol North that he had been notified by an NSC staffer that LtCol North had offered a Danish-registered ship under his control to the CIA—apparently for use in an unrelated operation. (Tower)

- The United States directly managed four arms deliveries in 1986. In each case the purchase money was deposited in Swiss bank accounts held in the name of Lake Resources and under the control of Richard Secord. Again, the price charged to Iran was far in excess of what was paid to the Department of Defense for the arms. The excess amounts totaled almost $20 million for the four deliveries: $6.3 million for the February shipment of TOWs, $8.5 million for the May and August shipments of HAWK parts, and $5 million for the October shipment of TOWs. (Tower)

- Khashoggi and two Canadian investors arrange a new $15 million loan for a fourth shipment of arms to Iran. According to Roy Furmark, Khashoggi intends to charge Iran $18 million, including $3 million for financing and "other costs." Khashoggi then makes a deposit in a Swiss bank account, possibly as high as $15.7 million. Casey testifies to Congress that the deposit is the second of two totaling only $12.2 million. Furmark later says Khashoggi is reimbursed $3 million in July and $5 million in August. The remaining $10 million (investigators later give a figure of at least $8 million) reportedly is never repaid, resulting in Furmark's meeting with Casey on October 7, 1986 on behalf of the Saudi arms dealer. (NYT 12/4/86 & 12/25/86; WP 12/24/86; LAT 1/15/87)

- In addition to the above, several key financial transactions take place this month involving the Swiss bank accounts in which funds from the Iran arms sales are held. Some money is transferred to the contras, who apparently receive $8.5 million in all from weapons sales this month. Also, $6.5 million is paid to the Pentagon for the weapons later sent to Iran. (LAT 1/15/87)

- Notes taken at the [November 23 Meese-North] meeting ... reflect that North identified two transactions from which money may have been diverted ... to the contras: 1) the transfer of 1000 TOWs in February [1986], from which $3-4 million may have gone to the contras; and 2) the transaction [in May 1986] involving payment for HAWK parts and payment for replenishment of the 508 TOWs. (SSIC 1/29/87)

- The NSC suggests that Reagan ask Saudi Arabia to contribute money to the contras. During the summer, McFarlane calls Shultz to inform him the Saudis have donated $31 million to a contra group. It is not clear whether this includes an earlier $20 million donation received before McFarlane left office late last year. (NYT 1/13/87)

- Assistant Secretary of Defense Richard Armitage replaces Noel Koch, a deputy assistant secretary, as the Pentagon's representative on the Administration's informal intergovernmental counterterrorism group headed by North. (WP 2/22/87)

- [Tom Green, an attorney, tells Assistant Attorney General Charles Cooper (see November 24, 1986 entry), that] "at a meeting on the arms sales in Europe in early 1986, where Hakim served as interpreter for the Americans, Hakim told the Iranians that in order to foster the relationship and show their bona fides, the Iranians should make a contribution over the purchase price for use of the contras or "of us." Green added that Hakim probably said the U.S. government was desirous of this. Green said that was the basis upon which the February shipment of TOWs was priced.

According to Cooper's notes, Green said the money from that sale was routed through Israelis into Hakim's financial network ... The same thing happened again in May. Green reportedly said none of this violated the law because no U.S. money was involved—only Iranians making a contribution. (SSIC 1/29/87)

MAY 1 - Bush meets with Rodriguez and Edwin Corr, the new ambassador to El Salvador. Bush's national security adviser Donald Gregg insists that the discussion is solely about Rodriguez' helicopter operations against Salvadoran insurgents. North and former Senator Nicholas Brady (R-NJ) join the meeting after a short time. Bush is quoted in newspaper reports as saying he "never, ever had a discussion with [Rodriguez] about the contras and contra support of any kind." (WP 12/14/86; WP 12/7/86; Bush Chronology in WP 12/16/86)

- Stanford Technology Trading Group International of McLean, Virginia is officially suspended by the California Franchise Tax Board for failing to file tax returns for financial years 1985 and 1986. The corporation, as of this date, is not allowed to do business. (California Franchise Tax Board Documents)

- North writes Bruce Hooper, a wealthy Pennsylvanian, on National Security Council Stationery: "I hope you will remain steadfast with the President as he leads this effort. . . . Please maintain your invaluable, strong support." Hooper responds with $100,000 for Spitz's National Endowment for the Preservation of Liberty and notes, "Please have Ollie contact me to let me know what he is going to do with it." (North letter 5/2/86; NEPL records; Hooper letter 5/27/86)

MAY 2 - LtCol North informed VADM Poindexter that he believed the Contras were readying to launch a major offensive to capture a "principal coastal population center" in Nicaragua and proclaim independence. North warned that if this occurred "the rest of the world will wait to see what we do—recognize the new territory—and UNO as the govt—or evacuate them as in a Bay of Pigs." He suggested that the U.S. should be prepared to come to the Contras' aid.

Assistant Secretary of State for Inter-American Affairs Elliot Abrams testified that he could recall "a time when Ollie was pushing for the Contras to grab a piece of Nicaraguan territory and proclaim independence." Mr. Abrams said that he might have indicated to LtCol North his support for the plan, but never took the idea seriously: "It was totally implausible and not do-able." (Tower)

MAY 3 - At this time, the Secretary of State again heard that the operation had not died. While at the Tokyo economic summit, Under Secretary Armacost cabled a report from Ambassador Price in London about Khashoggi's efforts to interest Tiny Rowlands, a British entrepreneur, in the transactions with Iran. Rowlands met with Khashoggi, Nir, and Ghorbanifar. Nir outlined the plan, indicating that the shipment of spare parts and weapons to Iran . . . Nir and Khashoggi told Rowlands

"[t]he scheme, moreover, was okay with the Americans. It had been cleared with the White House. Poindexter allegedly is the point man. Only four people in the U.S. government are knowledgeable about the plan. The State Department has been cut out. (Armacost to Shultz (State cable), 5/3/86)

The Secretary of State recalled that:

"That same day, I sought out Vice Admiral Poindexter with the President's party, but found Mr. Regan. That is, I got this in the morning. We were in the midst of these meetings. You know how they are. And I read this thing.

"So I am in one part of the hotel; the President and his staff—Regan, Poindexter, and so on—are in another part. So I just marched over to their wing of the hotel to find whoever I could find, and I wound up finding Don Regan. Everybody else I could not get to.

"I told Mr. Regan and I showed him this—I said that he should go to the President and get him to end this matter once and for all. I opposed dealing with people such as those identified in the message and said it would harm the President if the activity continued.

"Mr. Regan, I felt, shared my concern, said he was alarmed and would talk to the President.

"I later learned that Vice Admiral Poindexter reportedly told Ambassador Price that there was no more than a smidgen of reality to the story. 'Smidgen' is his word.

"When I got to him, I told Vice Admiral Poindexter my feelings, but he did not share my concerns.

"He claimed that we were not dealing with these people; that that was not our deal.

"I told him the president was very exposed.

"Soon thereafter I recall being told by both Vice Admiral Poindexter and Mr. Casey that the operation had ended and the people involved had been told to 'stand down.'

"During this period [May 1986], I heard from time to time

of reports that the operation may have resumed—that is, through the things that roll around on the grapevine. I heard nothing official to this effect, however." (Shultz, SRB, 53-55)

Ambassador Price also called Poindexter with the same news. Poindexter wrote North a summary of the tale.

"I told Charlie [Price] that there was only a shred of truth in this and the US connection was highly distorted. Tiny told [Bob] Frasure [on Price's staff] that he didn't like the deal and did not want to get involved unless it was an American operation. I told Charlie to advise him not to get involved.

"What in the hell is Nir doing? We really can't trust those sob's." (Poindexter PROF note to North, 5/3/86) (Tower)

MAY 4-6 - At the Tokyo economic conference, Shultz confronts Poindexter about hints he has been hearing concerning the shipment of arms to Iran. The secretary testifies later that Poindexter explicitly affirms that the deliveries have stopped when in fact they are continuing. Shultz also informs Regan of his concerns and says that Regan replied he was "alarmed" and would talk to the president. It is unclear even at the time of Shultz's testimony on January 21, 1987 whether Regan knew of the shipments. Some House Foreign Affairs Committee members believe Shultz was implying Regan had misled him. According to Secretary Shultz, he was later told by both Admiral Poindexter and Director Casey that the operation had ended. (SSIC 1/29/87; NYT 1/24/87)

MAY 5 - [A] CIA official warned Director Casey and the Deputy Director that "the White House initiative to secure release of American hostages in Lebanon remains dead in the water." (SSIC 1/29/87)

- North replied at length, seeming to inform Poindexter of the way the operation was financed.

"I agree that we cannot trust anyone in this game. You may recall that nearly a month ago I briefed you to the effect that Tiny Roland [sic] had been approached and we went back through Casey to tell these guys that the whole thing smelled very badly. We know that Khashoggi is the principal fund raiser for Gorba and that only after Gorba delivers a cargo does he get paid by the Iranians. We do not believe that Tiny is still engaged in this effort. Nir has been told to stay off the skyline on the issue. The story you had relayed to you by Price was the one made up by Nir to cover the transaction and Clair George reported it to us when the issue first came up several weeks ago. At the bottom line, this typifies the need to proceed urgently to conclude this phase of the operation before there are further revelations. We all know that this has gone on too long and we do not seem to have any means of expediting the process short of going to Iran. In that regard, George [Cave] and I are leaving tomorrow at 0700 to meet with Gorba in London. We intend to tell him that unless a deposit is made by the end of the week, the whole operation is off. We wd then have Gorba call [his contact in the PM's office] in our presence and have George reinforce the criteria for proceeding: We go to Tehran; within 24 hrs all hostages released; 8hrs [sic] later we deliver the 240 parts; within 10 days we provide those parts which cannot fit on the a/c. In return we get to raise the issues of Nicaragua, no more terrorism and help for the Afghan resistance. This SEEMS to be what [the Iranian official] has already said he has gotten the 'authorities' at his end to accept, but we want to be sure before we proceed. Lord willing, Gorba will then make the requisite deposit on Thursday, we will start to assemble the cargo by Friday, and the following weekend we will go to Tehran. We all hope." (North PROF note to Poindexter, ?5/5/86, 22:34:44) (Tower)

- Spitz Channell's National Endowment for the Preservation of Liberty pays $9,000 (check 1106, Palmer National Bank account 40000494) to PRODEMCA, which had been described in a January memo as a "democrat lobbyist" hired by Channell to work for aid to the Contras. Further payments to PRODEMCA occurred on May 15 ($8,000, check 1109) and May 29 ($9,000, check 1113), during a period of intense Congressional activity leading up the eventual June vote in the House of Representatives for aid to the Contras. (NEPL Bank Statement 5/31/86)

MAY 6 - LtCol North and Mr. Cave met with Mr. Ghorbanifar in London. Mr. Ghorbanifar promised a meeting with senior Iranian officials but asked that the U.S. delegation bring all the HAWK spare parts with them. Mr. Cave recalls the Americans agreeing that one-quarter of the spare parts would accompany the delegation. Notwithstanding, LtCol North informed VADM Poindexter on May 8: "I believe we have succeeded . . . Release of hostages set for week of 19 May in sequence you have specified." (Tower)

- [J]ust a few days after the incident just recounted [see May 4-6 entry], U.S. officials again met with Ghorbanifar in Europe. Ghorbanifar assured them that financing for the arms sale would be no problem. Testimony and documents indicate that Ghorbanifar frequently left the talks to call Tehran. On one occasion, according to later testimony, the CIA officer who was serving as interpreter joined in the talks with Tehran to explain that the United States could not or would not bring all the HAWK spare parts at the same time that the McFarlane delegation arrived. The Iranian at first was unwilling to agree to the release of all the hostages before all of the parts arrived, but it was agreed that McFarlane's plane would bring as many of the parts as possible, with the rest to arrive after release of the hostages. A White House chronology indicates that at this meeting, Israel privately indicated to the United States that it wanted the replacement TOWS that the April 4 memo indicated would be funded by this sale. The price for the HAWK spares that was discussed at this meeting was roughly $22.5 million, plus over $20 million for the HAWK radars, but the CIA officer who attended the talks later testified that he was not present when such matters were discussed. However, testimony indicates that LTC North discussed the overpricing problem with another CIA official. And the CIA officer who attended the talks wrote that the dispute over how many HAWK parts to deliver before the release of hostages remained a problem. A CIA official has testified that reporting on these matters was available to the McFarlane delegation. (SSIC 1/29/87)

- The State Department issues a lengthy policy statement on terrorism, three weeks before North's attempt to ransom American hostages with the help of H. Ross Perot. In part, the statement says: "The U.S. Government will make no concessions to terrorists. It will not pay ransoms, release prisoners, change its policies or agree to other acts that might encourage additional terrorism. . . . The policy of the U.S. Government is, therefore, to reject categorically demands for ransom, prisoner exchanges and deals with terrorists in exchange for hostage release." (NYT 12/3/86)

- North went to London on May 6. The evening before, Poindexter instructed him: "Do not let anybody know you are in London or that you are going there. Do not have any contact with Embassy . . ." (Poindexter PROF note to North, 5/5/86)

Cave remembered that the first May meeting set the stage for the trip to Tehran. Cave spoke to the Iranian Prime Minister's office to fix the arrangements. They haggled over what the Americans would bring with them, the Iranians asking for all the HAWK spare parts. Agreement was reached on one-quarter—one pallet. Ghorbanifar said

"We would be meeting with the Prime Minister, the President, Khameini, possibly Hashemi Rafsanjani, and another well-known conservative Ayatollah, named Ayatollah Farsi. He was one of the original candidates for president in the election when Bani Sadr was elected President. (Cave 8)

Ghorbanifar informed the Americans that financing had been arranged, and that he would deposit funds "in an account controlled by Mr. Nir. We eventually got the money in our account on the 16th of May, and that was a deposit from General Secord into the account we had in Switzerland, in Geneva." (Footnote: The transaction involving HAWK spare parts in May 1986 covered some 299 items worth $6.5 million. Iran was to have paid $15 million. The financial arrangements followed the pattern established for the February shipment of 1,000 TOWs. Khashoggi raised $15 million from various financiers and deposited the funds in the Lake Resources account on 14 May. CIA's Swiss account was credited with $6.5 million on 16 May to repay the Defense Department. The transaction was not completed. The United States failed to deliver all the spare parts because Iran failed to secure the release of all American hostages being held in Lebanon. In reviewing price lists for what had been provided, Iran discovered a substantial overcharge. By August, Tehran had provided Ghorbanifar with only $8 million to repay Khashoggi, leaving the Saudi $16 million in debt (the balance of the $15 million advanced plus a 20 per cent "costs and financing" markup—in this case $3 million). When the United States decided not to use Ghorbanifar as an intermediary, Khashoggi had little prospect to recover the rest of his money. All he held were unfunded drafts from Ghorbanifar. When Khashoggi attempted, through Roy Furmark, to obtain his money from Lake Resources, he discovered that only $30,000 remained in the Lake account. Another $8.5 million was unaccounted for, leaving the amount for diversion at somewhat just short of $15 million (including $6.3 million unaccounted for from the February transaction). An additional $2 million was unaccounted for after the November 1986 shipment of 500 TOWs.)

Cave told the Board that the CIA had no idea where the money went after Ghorbanifar made the deposit into Nir's account, "nor do we have any idea of how much was deposited." (Id. at 9) (Tower)

- Amalgamated Commercial Enterprises, a company described by North as a key part of the operation to fund the Nicaraguan insurgents, is listed on a foreign banking form as a subsidiary of Energy Resources International, a company owned by Richard Secord. At the bottom of the form, dated May 6, 1986, is a phone number next to a blacked out signature. The phone number belongs to the Defense Department Security Division. According to the document, Energy Resources International controlled six overseas bank accounts which were held in a Detroit agency of Banco de Iberoamerica, a Panamanian bank owned by Banco Atlantico. The Arab Banking Corp., a consortium run by Kuwait, Abu Dhabi, and Libya, owns 70% of Banco Atlantico. (WT 3/27/87)

MAY 7 - Carl "Spitz" Channell's National Endowment for the Preservation of Liberty (NEPL) transfers $1.25 million to International Business Communications (IBC), which has already received $800,000 from NEPL since December 1985. (See January 1986 entry). (AP in WP 2/7/87; NYT 2/26/87)

- Spitz Channell's National Endowment for the Preservation of Liberty pays $1,250,000 (check 1011 from Palmer National Bank account 2007576) to International Business Communications. IBC's Feb. 16, 1987 report to Channell lists the date as May 8. IBC in turn passes the $1,250,000 on to Intel Co-Operation Inc. in the Cayman Islands, which was the renamed I.C. Inc. This was the largest single payment of dozens of such transactions in 1985 and 1986. (NEPL Bank Statement 5/31/86; WP 3/7/87)

EARLY MAY - Immediately after the Europe meeting in early May, U.S. officials moved to get ready for a trip to Tehran. The Defense Department was told to be ready to transfer the HAWK spare parts. Prices were quoted as $4.4 million for the HAWK parts and transportation; $1.8 million for the 508 TOWs; and $6.2 million for the two radars. (SSIC 1/29/87)

MAY 8 - When North returned to Washington, he wrote Poindexter that "I believe we have succeeded. Deposit being made tomorrow (today is a bank holiday in Switzerland [May 8]). Release of hostages set for week of 19 May in sequence you have specified. Specific date to be determined by how quickly we can assemble requisite parts. Thank God —He answers prayers." (North PROF note to Poindexter, 5/8/86, 8:07:46) (Tower)

- In a May 8 message, LtCol North also informed VADM Poindexter of an Israeli offer to assist in Central America:

"DefMin Rabin sent his MilAide to see me with the following offer: The Israelis wd be willing to put 20-50 Spanish speaking military trainers/advisors into the DRF if we want this to happen. They wd do this in concert with an Israeli plan to sell the KFIR fighter to Honduras as a replacement for the 28 yr old [Super Mystere] which the Hondurans want to replace. . . . Rabin want to meet w/me privately in N.Y. to discuss details. My impression is that they are prepared to move quickly on this if we so desire. Abrams likes the idea."

Mr. Abrams told the Board that he did not recall ever discussing any offer of Israeli assistance to the Contras with LtCol North. Former U.S. Ambassador to Costa Rica Louis Tambs and a senior CIA official stationed in Central America said that to their knowledge Israel never shipped any arms to the Contras. (Tower)

MAY 9 - Director of Central Intelligence William Casey reportedly visits South Africa to appeal for funds to aid the contras. (BG 3/1/87)

- Israeli Defense Minister Yitzhak Rabin later denies that he offered to send Spanish-speaking military instructors to train the contras. Rabin insists that North approached him in May 1986 with the suggestion, saying he had first proposed the idea to Reagan. This is the first indication from an Israeli official that Reagan may have been aware of attempts to solicit Israeli help for the contras at a time when Congress had banned such requests. (WP 2/28/87)

MAY 12 - Rodney McDaniel noted that during the national security briefing on May 12, 1986, VADM Poindexter discussed with the President the hostages and Mr. McFarlane's forthcoming trip. (Footnote: Mr. McDaniel became Executive Secretary of the NSC in February, 1986. Though unin-

volved in both the policy and implementation of the Iran
initiative, Mr. McDaniel accompanied VADM Poindexter to
his morning briefings of the President as a note taker.) The
notes indicate that the President directed that the press not be
told about the trip.

- Notes made by the NSC Executive Secretary indicate
that at the daily national security briefing on May 12, 1986,
VADM Poindexter discussed with the President the hostages
and Mr. McFarlane's forthcoming trip. The notes indicate
that the President directed that the press not be told about the
trip. (Tower)

MAY 13 - The way was now clear for McFarlane to visit
Tehran. While planning the trip, other issues continued to
occupy the NSC staff. The United States received information about Iranian terrorist operations to be conducted
against the United States. Poindexter wondered if Ghorbanifar should be reminded "that we thought we had a commitment [sic] from them on future terrorist activity against US."
(Poindexter PROF note to North, 5/13/86, 19:08) (Tower)

MAY 15 - Reagan authorizes a secret visit to Iran by U.S.
officials and approves a three-and-a-half page document outlining the "pillars and principles" of American policy toward
Iran that is to be delivered to officials in Tehran during the
visit. The trip takes place May 28-31. (LAT 1/15/87)

- Mr. McDaniel's notes indicate that the President authorized Mr. McFarlane's secret mission to Iran and the Terms of
Reference for that trip. Those notes indicate that the trip was
discussed again with the President on May 21. (Tower)

- Director Casey has testified that on May 15, the President approved the McFarlane mission to Tehran. (SSIC
1/29/87)

- According to documents and testimony received by the
Committee, it is possible that the following two events occurred on the same day, May 15, 1986. First, according to a
chronology of the Iran program prepared at the White House
in November 1986, the Terms of Reference for Mr. McFarlane's trip to Tehran were approved on May 15, 1986. These
Terms of Reference appear to be identical to the Terms of
Reference dated April 4 which were found in NSC files attached to the Undated Memorandum discussing diversion of
funds to the contras. Second, Poindexter gave the President

a status report on the Nicaraguan resistance in preparation for an NSPG meeting on Central America scheduled for the next day. According to Poindexter's memorandum, Poindexter included in his status report a note that outside support for the Nicaraguan resistance would be consumed by mid-July and no further significant support appeared readily available. The memorandum stated that the $100 million aid request was stalled in Congress. Poindexter identified as options: reprogramming Presidential appeal for private donations; and direct and very private Presidential overture to certain heads of state. (SSIC 1/29/87)

- [O]n May 15, according to a later CIA letter to the Committee, the Hyde Park Square Corporation deposited $6.5 million in the CIA's account in Switzerland, to cover both the HAWK parts and the 508 TOWs. (A White House chronology lists the date as May 16, and a different CIA memo cites May 20 as the date. Director Casey's testimony follows the White House chronology. The May 20 date may reflect a second deposit that was expected for the HAWK radars.) On May 16, the CIA notified the Army of the availability of funds for both the HAWK parts and the TOWs. The TOWs were transferred to the CIA on May 19 and shipped to Israel on May 23. According to testimony, the HAWK parts were also supposed to be shipped to Israel during this period. On May 20, the CIA certified the availability of funds to test, inspect and service the old HAWK radars; the next day, it received more detailed cost information on the radars. (SSIC 1/29/87)

- The evidence before the Board contained no record that LtCol North's role to support the Contras was formally authorized. It appears, however, that LtCol North did keep the National Security Advisor informed, first Mr. McFarlane and then VADM Poindexter. It is not clear to what extent other NSC principals or their departments were informed. On May 15, 1986, VADM Poindexter cautioned North: "From now on, I don't want you to talk to anybody else, including Casey, except me about any of your operational roles." (Tower)

- On May 15, according to testimony, Adnan Khashoggi paid $15 million into the account of Lake Resources. CIA officials were later told that Khashoggi had obtained this money from an Arab investor and two Canadians. Testimony indicates that Khashoggi was given post-dated checks totaling $18 million, which included 20 percent interest for a one-month loan. Testimony and documents indicate that CIA officials were told in October 1986 that at the May meeting of Khashoggi and Ghorbanifar, Ghorbanifar stated that the high price was because the money was being used to support the contras. (SSIC 1/29/87)

- On May 15, North replied in two parts. First, he noted that everybody shared Poindexter's concern. Some members of the team thought the Syrians had recruited important members of Hizballah. Others, like Cave, blamed factionalism within Iran's ruling group.

"Nir is already aware of this and intends to note to Gorba that his $15M is at great risk if one of these events does indeed happen. Gorba is probably not the best interlocutor on this matter and we wd stand a far better chance talking directly to [the official in the Prime Minister's office]. It wd be worthy of some consideration to do just that before we go all the way through with the execution of what is now in motion. Cave and North are still prepared to go if you think it wd help. I do. So does George. (North PROF note to Poindexter, 5/13/86) (Tower)

North's second note informed Poindexter that his wish had been carried out, and warned of Ghorbanifar's having "penetrated" the CIA.

"Nir and Copp are with Gorba. Both have made points as you urged. In response, Gorba has promised that every effort will be made to stop unauthorized actions being undertaken by Hizballah or Iranian activists in the field. He has also provided the following which was transmitted a few minutes ago via Dick's secure device: "As you remember fm London, Gorba suggested we get together with Howaldi Al Homadi (or Hamadi) of Libya whom Gorba claimed to be the head of internal security and de facto number 2 man in the country. Nir checked this in his records and indeed Homadi is head of internal security and in key govt position plus connection to terrorists abroad. . . . Homadi does not believe that this is an effective channel since FoMin is not well connected. Homadi is willing to come to any point in Europe to meet with North or other appropriate official without preconditions. Homadi willing to deliver three things—no more attacks against U.S.; work out schedule to get terrorists out of Libya; to transfer business contracts from EastBloc [sic] to West. In return, Homadi wants to settle misunderstandings btwn Libya and U.S. to include some kind of mutual public expressions. Willing to come anywhere in Europe given one week's notice. Gorba says Homadi sees himself as heir apparent to Qadhafi, knows about USG plans to use exiles for new Libyan govt; says it will not work." END OF NIR MESSAGE FROM GORBA.

"There may or may not be anything to what Gorba has said of Homadi wanting to meet w/ North or other USG official. . . . I have not passed any of this to any but you. Nir has asked that we protect him and not reveal his involvement in this to CIA. Nir is, as you know, operating w/o Mossad back-up and has considerable concern about the CIA becoming more knowledgeable about his activities. Based on what Gorba has just told us, Nir has reason to be concerned." (North PROF note to Poindexter, 5/15/86, 21:36:09)

"The CIA are really bunglers," Poindexter replied. "You had better pass most of this to Casey directly. I would not pass it to anybody else. Leave me out of it. We need to think about a message to pass back to Homadi thru Gorba next week." (Poindexter PROF note to North, 5/16/86) (Footnote: At this time, Poindexter became concerned that North's "operational role" was becoming "too public." [See next paragraph for text of memo.] (Tower)

- On May 15, 1986, in an internal NSC message to LtCol North, entitled "Be Cautious," VADM Poindexter warned:

"I am afraid you are letting your operational role become too public. From now on, I don't want you to talk to anybody else, *including Casey, except me about any of your operational roles. In fact, you need to quietly generate a cover story that I have insisted that you stop.*" (emphasis added). (Poindexter PROF note to North, 5/15/86, 21:21:58) North replied on May 15: "Done." (North PROF note to Poindexter, 5/15/86, 21:39:23) (Tower)

- Notes made by the Executive Secretary on May 15, 1986, indicate that the President authorized Mr. McFarlane's secret mission to Iran and the Terms of Reference for that trip. Those notes indicate that the trip was discussed again with the President on May 21.

After the President approved the trip, (Footnote: According to both the Maximum Version and Historical Chronology, the President approved the trip on May 15. (Maximum

Version 7; Historical Chronology 11) McFarlane told the Board that, in his view, "the President was very moved by the hostage captivity, and that is purely speculation. But I know that that was terribly important to him."

[The President met with the hostages' families] almost every time he took a trip. I remember one to Dallas, Indianapolis, Chicago, on separate occasions. And there would be a family or two, and they would come in and he'd meet with them, and it would be a very anguishing kind of a thing.) Poindexter relied on North to make arrangements. At the same time, he kept informed and made his views known. North's first plan required that the delegation stay in Israel for most of the weekend, May 23-25, and that Poindexter approve a request for aircraft. (North PROF note to Poindexter, 5/19/86, 12:03) Poindexter had

"problems with this plan. An a/c request is too closely linked to what is happening. I don't see how we can use a military a/c. Why do you have to stay so long in Israel? I had in mind you would travel separately, RDVU [rendezvous] in Israel at a covert location, and proceed to Iran." (McFarlane (1) 30) (Poindexter PROF note to North, 5/19/86) (Tower)

MAY 15-30 - The CIA reportedly makes the second of three series of arms deliveries to the guerrillas in Angola via an air base in Zaire. Using C-130 and Boeing 707 cargo jets with the markings "Santa Lucia Airways," diplomatic and business sources say, the arms operation is supervised by "a black American everyone called Colonel" who is "in charge of about 20 men. Very few Zairois were involved." On two other occasions, from March 20 to April 20 and during one night in mid-October, the planes make several more deliveries. U.S. officials have refused to reveal how American aid to Angola, set at $15 million in 1986, makes its way there. (NYT 2/1/87)

LATE SPRING - In the late spring, 1986, the Administration directed its energy to persuade Congress to fund the Nicaraguan resistance. Absent Congressional appropriations, the Administration looked to third countries to help the resistance pay its bills. The Assistant Secretary of State for Inter-American Affairs told the Board:

"By spring [1986], we were running out of money. The $27 million was running out. It ran out about in June or July, and at that point, it was also clear to us that though both Houses [of Congress] had voted the hundred million, we weren't going to get it that fast.

" knew we'd get it before or believed we'd get it before the adjournment. But, in any event, we were out of money.

" was at that point that we made a solicitation to another government for a kind of bridge to extend the $27 million until we had the $100 million.

" had discussed in the department [of State] on several occasions whether we should utilize the authority which we believe we had to go to a third government. I don't remember the dates of those discussions, but the Secretary's staff has those dates. I mean, there are notes of those discussions. It was in the spring—March, April, May, starting— as authority to obligate the $27 million ran out March 31. After that, we were dealing with the pipeline, which we knew would last about two months, ten weeks, something like that. (Tower)

MAY 16 - According to documents received by the Committee, on May 16, 1986, the President held an NSPG meeting where solicitation of third-country humanitarian support for the Nicaraguan resistance was discussed. Those present included the President, Vice President, Craig Fuller, Secretary Shultz, Ambassador Habib, Assistant Secretary Abrams, Secretary Baker, Secretary Weinberger, Under Secretary Ikle, Director Casey, the CIA task force chief, General Wickham, Lt. Gen. Moellering, Don Regan, Admiral Poindexter, William Ball, Djerejian, McDaniel, Burghardt, and North.

White House documents reflect that the issues discussed at this meeting included the negotiation process and the status of Contadora, and the $100 million aid package before Congress for the Nicaraguan resistance. The document states that the situation with the resistance was good but could reverse abruptly as they were running out of money. Two options to get the money were considered—seek to get reprogramming through Congress or go to other countries. The final decision was to look at both approaches. According to the documents, Secretary Shultz was to provide a list of countries which could be approached.

Abrams testified that the State Department had legal authority from Congress to solicit humanitarian assistance from third countries. According to Abrams, Secretary Shultz agreed it was a good idea to do so.

Regan recalled such an NSPG discussion, although not the precise date of May 16, and testified that there was absolutely no mention of the possible use of funds from the Iran arms sale including sales by third parties or countries, to provide humanitarian or military assistance to the Nicaraguan resistance. (SSIC 1/29/87)

- Ghorbanifar informed the Americans that financing had been arranged, and that he would deposit funds "in an account controlled by Mr. Nir. We eventually got the money in our account on the 16th of May, and that was a deposit from General Secord into the account we had in Switzerland, in Geneva." (See May 6, 1986 entry) (Tower)

- In the course of informing Poindexter that he had passed Ghorbanifar's information to the Director of Central Intelligence and Clarridge, North told Poindexter that the Nicaraguan resistance now has more than $6M available for immediate disbursement. "This reduces the need to go to third countries for help. It does not, however, reduce the urgent need to get CIA back into the management of this program. We can only do this by going forward with the reprogramming proposal and getting the requisite authorities for CIA involvement. Unless we do this, we run increasing risks of trying to manage this program from here with the attendant physical and political liabilities. I am not complaining, and you know that I love the work, but we have to lift some of this onto the CIA so that I can get more than 2-3 hrs of sleep at night. The more money there is (and we will have a considerable amount in a few more days) the more visible the program becomes (airplanes, pilots, weapons, deliveries, etc.) and the more inquisitive will become people like Kerry, Barnes, Harkins, et al. While I care not a whit what they say about me, it could well become a political embarrassment for the President and you. Much of this risk can be avoided simply by covering it with an authorized CIA program undertaken with the $15M. This is what I was about to say in the meeting today and a point that I believe Shultz does not understand in his advocacy of Third [sic] country solicitation. *I have no idea what Don Regan does or does not know re my private U.S. operation but the President obviously knows why he has been meeting with several select people to thank them for their 'support for Democracy' in CentAM.* [emphasis added] In short, we need to proceed with the $15M. Shall I work this up?" (North PROF note to Poindexter, 5/16/86) [The Tower Report notes elsewhere that this message is in response to a Poindexter message of the same day.] (Tower)

MAY 17 - Carl "Spitz" Channell's National Endowment for the Preservation of Liberty (NEPL) transfers $263,000 to International Business Communications (IBC). NEPL has already paid IBC over $2 million since December 1985. (NYT 2/26/87)

- Poindexter authorized North to prepare a paper "for the $15M reprogramming." (Poindexter PROF note to North, 5/17/86) He added: "I understand your concern and agree. I just didn't want you to bring it up at NSPG. I guessed at what you were going to say. Don Regan knows very little of your operation and that is just as well." (Id.) (Tower)

MAY 18 - A CIA official spoke with Ghorbanifar on May 18 and was assured that the hostages would be available when the Americans arrived in Tehran. He was also assured that McFarlane would meet the top three political officials in Iran (i.e. President Khamenei, Prime Minister Musavi and Majlis Speaker Rafsanjani). (SSIC 1/29/87)

MAY 19 - The TOWs were transferred to the CIA. (SSIC 1/29/87)

- McFarlane has testified that he received pre-trip briefings during the week of May 19. He indicated that he was assured by Admiral Poindexter that Secretary Shultz was involved in the planning for the trip and that Secretary Weinberger had been apprised. His terms of reference emphasized long-term U.S. and Iranian common interests in opposing the Soviet threat. They accept the Iranian revolution as a fact, but note the need for Iran to end its support of terrorism and hostage-taking and its efforts to undermine American interests. They indicate that the United States wants neither an Iraqi victory or an overwhelming Iranian victory in the Iran-Iraq war. McFarlane's terms of reference show him to offer the prospect of a limited military supply relationship, but say that this depended upon whether Iran and America's convergent or divergent interests come to loom larger in the overall picture. (SSIC 1/29/87)

- Constantine Menges, who alerted conservatives to a letter Philip Habib wrote to a Democratic congressman pledging the "disbanding of the contras" and supporting the Contadora process, is dismissed from his position on the NSC. The letter in question was dated April 11, 1986 (see entry). (Evans & Novak WP 5/21/86)

-Late on May 19, North prepared a detailed plan

"We will endeavor to do it any way you want but we are experiencing significant logs [logistics] problems which are considerably eased by the use of a military a/c which can deliver the people, communications equipment (classified SATCOM, beacons, etc.) and still provide a modicum of rest. The present plan includes the A/C as a part of the OPSEC in that RCM has reason to use such an A/C. . . . The same applies to a lesser extent to RCM. The following sched is what is driving us:

Weds; May 21

1000—Copp dep for final sched mtg w/ Gorba 1000—240 Items arrive for final packing/sanitizing by CIA.

Thursday; May 22

1000—240 items + 508 TOWs moved fm to Kelly AFB by CIA 1400—Commercial 707 (#1) arrives Kelly to load most of 240 items 30—Copp arr. Geneva 1700—Commercial 707 (#1) Dep Kelly for Israel w/ bulk of 240 items aboard 45—North Dep Wash. for London 2000—Copp Dep Geneva for Israel w/ 707 Special Crew for IAF 707 via LearJet.

Friday; May 23

0100—G-3 Dep Andrews w/ Cave, Teicher, CIA communicators (2) plus equipmt 0200—G-3 P/U RCM at Laguardia [sic] (speech that evening in NYC) 0230—Copp arr. Israel w/ 707 Spec Crew 1400—G-3 w/ RCM arrive Gatwick; P/U North 1400—Commercial 707 (#2) Dep Kelly AFB w/ 508 TOWs for IDF enr Israel 1400—Commercial 707 (#1) Arr Israel w/bulk of 240 items; commence xfr to IAF 707s prior to commencement of Sabbath.

Saturday; May 24

0800—G-3 w/ RCM; communicators & party arrive Israel—start rest period 1700—Commercial 707 (#2) Arrives w/ 508 TOWs & remainder of 240 items; complete xfr of 240 items to IAF 707s after sunset (end of Sabbath)

2200—IAF 707 (#A) w/ Copp special crew & RCM

party dep Israel enr T. 2200—bulk of 240 items transloaded fm Commercial 707 (#2) to IAF 707 (#B). Sunday;

May 25

0830—RCM & party on IAF 707 (#A) arrive T. prepared for mtgs.

Monday; May 26

0800(?)—U.S. parties turned over to CRS or ICRC in Brt. [Beirut] 1000—IAF 707 (#A) Arrive T. w/ bulk of 240 items.

"In the plan above all times are local. As indicated in earlier discussions we have had on this matter every effort is being made to preserve OPSEC. Because of real world constraints on what can fit in the a/c we will load part of the 240 on 707 #2 and they will be handled separately when they arrive in Israel w/ 508 IDF TOWs. We have tried to compartment the whole effort at . . . Kelly AFB so that no two work shifts at either location has a clear picture of what is being loaded out via the two commercial 707s. The same thing applies to the 707 aircrews (3 of them) which we are providing for this mission. No one crew knows about the other, nor will they see each other. For example, the crew that is going out with Copp to fly the IAF 707 (#A) w/ RCM & party does not know about the two 707s arriving frm Kelly. The only part of this operation that we are not doing ourselves is the CIA comms, beacons and documentation for the party. ALL other arrangements have been made through Copp or affiliates and if we have to, I suppose we can arrange to fly RCM and the communicators out on their own.

Quite frankly, however, I do not see the vulnerability of using a military G-3 which will considerably ease our clearance problems given the hour of the day/night in which we are moving. We now have, I believe, a G-3 (or two) available which do (does) not have the usual USA marking on the side. Finally, the length of stay in Israel is not, in my opinion excessive, given the rather reigorous [sic] schedule we are attempting to accommodate. We are being driven by Sabbath requirements in Israel, Ramadan in T. and an awareness that the situation for our four in Beirut looks more desperate by the day. In an effort to address all of these competing and conflicting concerns (to include the availability of commercial 707s, cleared special mission crews, and the peculiar demands of low profile work schedules at . . . Kelly AFB and in the IAF) we have had one hell of a circus. In short, the use of a military G-3 would provide a much needed respite from the havoc of trying to answer all of these issues all over again without further risking OPSEC. It can be done, but it would be much better if we did not have to." (North PROF note to Poindexter, 5/19/86, 23:00:07)

Poindexter then wondered about using a CIA aircraft: what did the Director of Central Intelligence use when he travelled. (Poindexter PROF note to North, 5/20/86) North replied that CIA aircraft in the United States lacked the necessary range, and available CIA proprietary aircraft were overseas and lacked certificates necessary to fly in the United States. The Director of Central Intelligence used military aircraft, but that option, North wrote, "is in the realm of too hard." He proposed "to make other arrangements." (North PROF note to Poindexter, 5/20/86, 10:38:12) Poindexter noted that

"It is not that it is too hard; I just don't think it is a good idea. Leaks at this point could be disastrous. This is different from other secret missions in that anybody that knows anything (or thinks they know something) connected with this mission will be sorely tempted to talk about it afterwards if it is successful. Let me know what you work out." (Poindexter PROF note to North, 5/20/86, 14:10:03) (Tower)

MAY 20 - CIA certified the availability of funds to test, inspect and service the old HAWK radars. (SSIC 1/29/87)

- Bush speaks briefly with Felix Rodriguez and Salvadoran Air Force commander Juan Rafael Bustillo at a large reception in Miami on Cuban Independence Day. (Bush Chronology in WP 12/16/86)

- Later on May 20, North sent Poindexter another schedule and itinerary for the delegation:

"This further re transportation arrangements for RCM & party: Cave + Teicher + Communicators will depart IAD aboard Private (Democracy INC.) G-3, stops in NYC to p/u RCM. G-3 proceeds direct to Rhein Main military airfield, cleared thru customs by CIA . . . North . . . picked up in London by Lear 35 owned by Democracy INC. European subsidiary. Lear 35 drops North at commercial side of Rhein Main, North passes thru customs/immigration as Goode, proceeds to military side to rvs [rendez-vous] w/ RCM party. RCM party on arrival at FM offloads from G-3, transloads to CIA 707 (if available) or to chartered Swiss Challenger a/c for direct flight to Tel Aviv. Still having local point clearance problems for bringing G-3 into RM w/o customs/immigrations clearances. We are going to have to bring . . . Frankfurt into this to work out clearances. Will talk to him tonight via PRT-250 @ approx 0300. Shd have answer shortly thereafter . . . today provided recommended turnover points for hostages. We have sent one of our Democracy INC couriers to deliver flight schedule and turnover info to Gorba in London. Gorba scheduled to go to Tehran on Thursday [May 22]. Copp departure for Geneva/Tel Aviv postponed 24 hrs fm original schedule in order to complete coordination of RCM flight planning. Norta [sic] still on schedule to depart Thurs pm for . . . London. Complete ops plan and annexes being prepared for yr use during op. Will prepare in advance necessary paperwork and cables for dispatch of Hostage debrief team, Nightengale Medevac support and hospitalization alert for Wiesbaden—all of which wd be dispatched only when hostages are released. Will also have required checklist for alerting State to notify families, move same to Europe for reunion. OPLAN includes three sets of press guidance—appropriate to various circumstances which could occur on mission. (Footnote: Press guidance prepared covered the release of the hostages, the discovery of the mission to Tehran, and the holding of the delegation hostage. (North to Poindexter, "Hostage Recovery Plan," 5/22/86) Finally, need guidance as to whether or not you want to predeploy. . . . It wd be good insurance if things get screwed up during/after turnover of hostages—particularly if turnover does not result in hostages being brought all the way to our embassy. All involved believe it is unlikely that Iranians can get them this far with or without help from Hizballah. Most likely is release at one of the few Western Embassies remaining in W. Beirut or at AUB Hospital. We also suggested the Military Hospital crossing on the green line as a possibility. At the afternoon planning mtg [C/NE] suggested that we look at the Finding again to determine whether we can sell certain items of hardware to IRAQ in concert w/ what we are doing in Iran. He believes that such a step wd add considerably to our leverage in the area if this activity is uncovered by the Sovs. I share his concern. Far too much is being said over the open telephone by Gorba for them to be completely ignorant. Finally, we have several policy issues which need to be addressed.

—RCM should be able to suggest to the Iranians that we are willing to put a permanent Comms unit (2 CIA) into

Tehran to facilitate future exchanges of information—w/o a middle man/ [sic]

—What do we do if they can only spring one two or three of the hostages after making a good faith effort?—What do we do if, after 72 hrs, nothing happens?

These are the kinds of things I had envisioned for discussion in the private mtg w/ RR. At the very least, you shd talk to RCM about these things, preferably face to face. While we all expect this thing to go peachy smooth, it may not. RCM is taking no small risk in this endeavor—just flying around the way we will have to. He doesn't have to take this kind of chance. I know that everyone is very busy, but it wd, in my humble opinion, be thoughtful if you can find a few minutes to discuss the issues above w/ him and say good by. While I'm confident he'll be back next week, I could be wrong and it might be a very long time before anyone sees him again. (North PROF note to Poindexter, 5/20/86, 15:37:49) (Tower)

MAY 21 - Mr. McDaniel's notes indicate that the President authorized Mr. McFarlane's secret mission to Iran and the Terms of Reference for that trip. Those notes indicate that the trip was discussed again with the President on May 21. (Tower)

- Regan testified that the President met with McFarlane prior to his trip to Tehran and discussed the objectives for McFarlane's talks with the Iranians. Regan testified that he did not recall seeing a document entitled "Terms of Reference" similar to the Updated Memorandum nor did he recall approval ever being given for such a document. Regan testified, however, that the President's approval should have been required if those instructions were given to McFarlane for his visit to Tehran. A copy of Terms of Reference identical to those attached to the Undated Memorandum and bearing the date May 21, 1986 has been located in White House files. (SSIC 1/29/87)

- Ghorbanifar thanked the [CIA] official (see May 18 entry) for information relayed to him by Richard Secord and described the greeting and accommodations that the U.S. team could expect. (SSIC 1/29/87)

MAY 22 - LtCol North submitted the final operating plan for the trip to VADM Poindexter. It provided that the McFarlane delegation would arrive in Tehran on May 25, 1986. The next day (but no later than May 28), the hostages would be released. One hour later, an Israeli 707 carrying the balance of the spare parts would leave Tel Aviv for Tehran. (Tower)

- North asks Texas millionaire H. Ross Perot to have $1 million or $2 million in cash flown to Cyprus by today in an attempt to ransom American hostages. It is unclear whether this operation is the same as the earlier, unsuccessful "sting operation" to free hostage Peter Kilburn (see April 1986 entry). A description of the plan involving Perot's funds indicates that Thomas Clines, a former CIA official and associate of Secord and Edwin Wilson, helps North obtain a ship (the Erria) for the mission using funds from the account of Democracy Inc., a corporation tied to the Iran initiative and contra supply network. But the effort fails once again when Lebanese intermediaries working with North do not show up with the hostages or the money. McFarlane testifies later that Perot's money was not ransom but payment to a "source" assisting in the release. (WP 12/10/86; WSJ 1/2/87 & 1/16/87; LAT 1/21/87)

- In the afternoon of May 22, North submitted to Poindexter an updated schedule for the trip. It did not materially differ from the versions prepared on the 19th and 20th.

The updated schedule was part of a package of materials North prepared. It included an "Operations Plan," which defined the objective as: "To secure the return of four American hostages [Jenco, Anderson Jacobsen, and Sutherland] who continue to be held by Hizballah elements in Lebanon." (North to Poindexter, "Hostage Recovery Plan," 5/22/86, Tab I, "Operations Plan") The "Concept" was: "Provide incentives for the Government of Iran to intervene with those who hold the American hostages and secure their safe release." (Id.) The CIA was responsible for delivering "supplies" to Kelly Air Force Base; providing an interpreter, communicators and their equipment, and travel documents; providing an intelligence briefing package, with photographs; "[f]und maintenance and test/calibration of two Phase I radars at Letterkenney, PA. Investigate availability of two Phase II radars from DOD/FMS channels"; provide a communications schedule, including frequencies; recommend site and conditions for the release of the hostages in Beirut. "Democracy Inc. Charter" was to provide two Boeing 707s to transport "supplies" from Kelly to Tel Aviv. "Democracy, Inc." would provide two vetted crews for the Israeli aircraft; a Swiss Air Learjet to transport Secord from Geneva to Tel Aviv on May 22; a "CANAIR Challenger for delegation airlift from Dulles to Ramstein AFB on Friday, May 23"; and six Blackhawk .357 magnums in presentation boxes. Secord would act as liaison by secure communications between the CIA/NSC and the delegation. The Israelis were to provide funds for 508 TOWs (to replenish Israeli stocks after the August/September 1985 transfers, (CIA/IG Chronology 24); two black 707 aircraft for transport to Tehran; and a "liaison officer" to the American delegation.

NSC responsibilities constituted the longest list. They included the senior emissary; liaison with the White House; contingency press guidance; and arranging for the debriefing of hostages and the reunion of families, among other details. The Defense Department's role consisted of providing equipment and supplies "through intermediaries," transport for the hostage reception team and transportation in connection with the release of the hostages. The delegation would carry alias passports. There would be no rehearsal. (Id.) The schedule noted that McFarlane would board a CIA proprietary 707 at Ramstein for the trip to Tel Aviv.

The day North submitted his package, Ledeen saw Peter Rodman, Deputy Assistant to the President for National Security Affairs (Foreign Policy). Rodman wrote Poindexter that Ledeen

"urge[d] that we use our Iranian channels as a vehicle for stirring up dissidence within Iran, rather than for (as he puts it) cutting deals involving arms for hostages.

"Mike says his contac Gorbanifahr [sic] has access and influence with a dissident Ayatollah . . . as well as with disloyal elements spread throughout the military and the bazaars. There is great potential here, Mike feels, for a U.S. covert program to undermine the regime. He claims that both Bill Casey and Bud agree with this, and that it's a perfect program for Dewey Clarridge's operation.

"The obstacle, he says, is that we are following an alternative approach that is too much hostage to the hostage problem.

"I said nothing to Mike, but I have to say that I have long had a similar concern that we might be gearing our policy too much to the hostage issue rather than to the strategic menace that the regime represents. The special one-page finding of a few months ago put the hostages in a properly subordinate place among our objectives—but in practice our approach seems to require a hostage release as an early token of good faith. . . .

"Perhaps this is something for you to discuss with Casey, with Bud, and with Ledeen." (Rodman to Poindexter, 5/22/86)

McFarlane recalled that Poindexter asked him to attend a briefing on the trip in the last week of May.

"I was asked by the Admiral to come by and get my instructions that he said had been approved by the President— these were about four pages—the political agenda. Here are the political issues that you should develop and they dealt basically with our view of our interests in the Middle East, our view of Iranian conflicts with us and disagreements, basically—terrorism, the continuity of the war, the expansion of fundamentalist influence in other moderate regimes in the area, and, separately, our view of their vulnerabilities to the Soviet Union and our sense of milestones for dealing with specific issues that might over time get us toward a more stable relationship.

"And I asked again. I said, is the Secretary of State and Defense, DCI, the President all on board with this. He said, well, they are involved in the preparation of these instructions. He said that, and they are involved in this decision, yes. The President has approved it. And then these instructions. The positions haven't changed. The Secretary of State is against the arms component of it, as is the Secretary of Defense." (McFarlane (1)33-34)

McFarlane had the sense the instructions represented an NSPG "product." He was not aware that his aircraft would carry military equipment to Iran until he arrived in Tel Aviv. (Id.) at 34) (Tower)

MAY - The CIA rejects a proposal by North to broadcast anti-Khaddafi propaganda from the Erria off the Libyan coast. (WSJ 2/13/87)

MAY 23 - The TOWs were . . . shipped to Israel on May 23. According to testimony, the HAWK parts were also supposed to be shipped to Israel during this period. (SSIC 1/29/87)

- At 6:05 pm, a St. Lucia Airways 707 cargo plane with tail number J6SLF (apparently the same plane that travels to Tehran on November 25, 1985—see entry), flies from Ostend, Belgium to Tel Aviv via a U.S. Air Force base in Ramstein, West Germany. The plane continues from there to Tel Aviv, according to Belgian flight records. The aircraft's cargo is unknown, but the flight coincides with the U.S. sanctioned delivery of TOW missiles to Israel and McFarlane's mission to Iran. (WP 2/24/87)

- Spitz Channell's fundraisers meet for a training session on raising money for TV ads to support the Strategic Defense Initiative. A memo on how to approach potential donors states, "We are going to give them an opportunity to give a $30,000.00 tax deductible political contribution. . . . So when these people give us $30,000.00 and our ads cost $35,000.00 a day around the country they are in many districts literally giving a political contribution to support President Reagan's congressional candidates." Such political campaign activity raises questions about violations of the Internal Revenue Code's prohibitions regarding tax-exempt charities. (Fundraisers Meeting memorandum 5/23/86)

- Mr. McFarlane, along with LtCol North, Mr. Cave, and a CIA official, left the United States on May 23. Mr. Nir had pressed to be included in the delegation. The Chief of the Near East Division in the CIA operations directorate told the Board that this request was initially rejected, and that position was transmitted by the White House to Israeli Prime Minister Peres who appealed it. He said that ultimately, the decision was left to Mr. McFarlane, who decided to let Mr. Nir join the group. Mr. Ghorbanifar recalls that in meetings with Iranian officials, Mr. Nir was always presented as an American. (Tower)

MAY 23-25 - The McFarlane delegation traveled from the United States to Iran via Europe and Israel on May 23-25. In Israel they took on a single pallet of the HAWK missile parts that Iran had requested. McFarlane later testified that Secord met the plane in Israel, but that McFarlane identified his role primarily in connection with the aircraft (possibly a St. Lucia Airways aircraft). Also on the flight are Howard J. Teicher, the NSC's Near East area specialist; Amiram Nir; George Cave, who will serve as interpreter; and two CIA communicators (McFarlane says only one). The presence of Cave and the two Agency officials, according to an Administration source, put Casey in a good position to know the details of the Iranian side of the operation. Cave will later testify that the group arrives with 10 falsified passports, believed to be Irish, a Bible signed by Reagan and a key-shaped cake to symbolize the hoped-for "opening" to Iran. McFarlane says these are North's ideas. He has been told earlier by Poindexter to expect that all hostages, as well as William Buckley's remains, will be released before he lands. (McFarlane says later two are to be released upon his arrival, two shortly thereafter, and Buckley's remains within hours after that.) However, upon arrival he learns by telephone from Poindexter that none have been freed. After several days of waiting in the former Hilton Hotel, and fruitless talks with Iranian officials McFarlane leaves Iran. He says later that he is unable to prevent the Iranians from getting the spare parts he says were brought on his plane, but he cancels the scheduled delivery of two additional planeloads of arms, rejecting new Iranian promises of help in exchange for the two shipments. En route to the United States, North tells McFarlane not to view the trip as a "total lost cause," because some funds from the sale have been applied to Central America. McFarlane claims later he was concerned enough about the statement to talk to certain individuals in the White House about it, but not to the President. Upon his return, he advises Reagan to scuttle the entire operation because he believes the Iranians are not ready for a new relationship. Nevertheless, the Iranian offer of help in exchange for the two cancelled shipments continues to be considered, ultimately bringing about renewed negotiations, further deliveries of weapons and the concurrent release of Lawrence Jenco, David Jacobsen, and Robert McFarlane. (Meese Briefing 11/25/86; McFarlane testimony 12/8/86; WP 12/7/86, 12/10/86, 12/16/86 & 2/24/87; NYT 12/3/86, 12/17/86, 1/11/87; CBS "Face the Nation" 12/14/86; ABC "Nightline" 1/21/87; SSIC 1/29/87)

MAY 24 - Defex-Portugal, acting on behalf of Energy Resources International, receives clearance to ship more arms from Portugal to Guatemala. The shipment is loaded onto a Southern Air Transport plane which has a flight plan to Guatemala via Santa Maria in the Azores. Guatemalan authorities say the plane never arrived in their country. Southern Air logs list only two flights originating in Lisbon in May, both to Ilopango Air Base in El Salvador, a main transfer point for supplies to the contras. The flights carry a total cargo of 90 tons on board. (WP 1/17/87)

US Department of Transportation
Research and Special Programs Administration

REPORT OF CIVIL AIRCRAFT CHARTERS PERFORMED BY U.S. CERTIFICATED AND FOREIGN AIR CARRIERS
(Pursuant to 14 CFR Part 217)

Date: [8][6][0][5][1] (1-4) Carrier: [S][A][Q] (5-7) Page: [0][0][1] (8-10)

Quarter Ended __JUNE 30__ 19 __86__

Air Carrier __SOUTHERN AIR TRANSPORT, INC.__

Line No. (1)(1-12)	Type of aircraft (OAG Code) (15-20)	Number of Flights (21-27)	Type of charter (28-29)	Flight leg 1 2	Point of enplanement of each group (OAG Code) (31-33)	Point of deplanement of each group (OAG Code) (34-36)	(37-40)	(41-46)	(47-52)	Passengers each group enplaned (53-57)	Tons of property enplaned (58-62)
1	L-100	5	EC	1	FTL	PTY	R	R	R		115.0
2	L-100	1	EC	2	MIA	HAV	R	R	R		23.0
3	L-100	1	EC	4	HAV	MIA					8.0
4	L-100	1	EC	1	PHANI-MIA	YSV - ILOPANG-E	E	E	E		23.0
5	L-100	1	EC	2	MIA	MIA					23.0
6	L-100	1	EC	4	LGO	LGO	S	S	S		13.0
7	L-100	1	EC	2	MIA	MIA					23.0
8	L-100	1	EC	1	LSP	LSP	E	E	E		13.0
9	L-100	1	EC	1	MSE	LAD					15.0
10	L-100	1	EC	1	PTY	GIH	R	R	R		23.0
11	B-707	2	EC KELLY ALF.G, TX-SKF		TLV - TEL AVIV						90.0
12	B-707	2	EC	LISBON-LIS	YSV - ILOPANG	V	V	V		90.0
13	B-707	1	EC	1	FQT	BRO	E	E	E		40.0
							D	D	D		

I, the undersigned, (Title) __Mgr. Rate & Anal__ of the above named carrier certify that the above report has been examined by me and to the best of my knowledge and belief it is a true, correct and complete report for the period stated.

Signature: _Bria Doggett_

Date: __8/4/86__

DOT Form 217 (5-68)
Formerly CAB Form 217

- Assistant U.S. Attorney Jeffrey Feldman sends U.S. Attorney Leon Kellner a memo saying that there is enough evidence to indict several individuals for arms smuggling to the contras and requesting permission to empanel a grand jury. Kellner does not grant permission. (VV 3/31/87)

- (From Memorandum of Conversation Subject: U.S.-Iran Dialogue, see May 27 entry) The United States Government will cause a 707 aircraft to launch from a neutral site at 0100 in the morning to arrive in Tehran, Iran at 1000 on the morning of May 28, the seventh day of Khordad. This aircraft will contain the remainder of the HAWK missile parts purchased and paid for by the Government of Iran, a portion of which was delivered on May 24. (Tower)

MAY - In addition to the two flights from Portugal noted above (May 24), Southern Air Transport logs lists a third trip to Ilopango air base in El Salvador, from New Orleans with a 23-ton load. The company also flies 90 tons of cargo this month from Kelly Air Force Base in Texas to Tel Aviv. That cargo is believed to be military equipment bound for Iran. (DOT Records; WP 12/7/86)

- A congressional official speculates during the course of the Iran-contra investigation that the diversion of funds from the Iran arms sales to the rebels begins after the shipment in late May. He cites Iranian complaints that the price of weapons in the May shipment are significantly higher than those in the first shipment in late February. During the summer, CIA agents report increases in supplies to the contras in El Salvador, Honduras and Costa Rica. (WSJ 12/11/86; NYT 12/25/86)

- (Memorandum Conversation Subject: U.S.-Iran Dialogue): Post Mortem
Most American accounts of the meetings conform more or less faithfully to the contemporaneous written record. Ghorbanifar's account is different.
According to Ghorbanifar, the meetings started badly because they were inadequately prepared. Ghorbanifar proposed that North and he go to Tehran first to prepare the way. The Americans refused. (Ghorbanifar 161) Ghorbanifar's Iranian interlocutors were incredulous at the notion that McFarlane would arrive without preparation, but agreed to welcome him "if he comes with the whole of what he has

promised to come here, the spare parts, okay." (Id. at 162. See also 168)

The American delegation arrived two hours earlier than Ghorbanifar thought they would; as a result, they waited an hour and a half at the airport until the Iranian officials arrived. (Id. at 163-64) From the beginning, the Iranians were disappointed that the Americans had brought less than all the spare parts alleged to have been promised. Ghorbanifar recalled that the Americans raised the hostage question as something to be resolved before progress could be made on other subjects, and that this condition was mentioned for the first time since February. (Id. at 165-66) Ghorbanifar stressed that McFarlane's arrival and treatment were remarkable in light of the recent history of Iranian-American relations and the fate of Iranian officials such as Barzagan who met with American officials. They discussed cooperation against the Soviet Union, which also was remarkable. This fact contradicts, Ghorbanifar said, the image of the meetings conveyed in the press as negotiations about an arms-for-hostages trade, facilitated by self-interested arms traders. (Id. at 166-68)

Ghorbanifar remembered that Ayatollah Khomeini approved the meetings, and that he, Ghorbanifar, arranged for the head of the Majlis foreign relations committee to meet McFarlane. According to Ghorbanifar, "the Parliament is everything in Iran, the Majlis, and he is the number one for foreign affairs." (Id. at 169) This man urged McFarlane not to press the Iranians, but to give them time

"that we cook the way we want the Ayatollah Khomeini to pave the ground for this, to make it ready, prepare for him. Don't push him. From the first place, Mr. McFarlane was insisting on we have nothing to discuss and nothing is going on to get to this agenda if the whole four American hostages are not released. . . . He waited one day. I pushed the Iranian side every day. Do something. He is here. You will have to save his face.

"After three days the man came to him and said, Mr. McFarlane, I have good news for you. We accepted the whole agenda, approved that we go and we coordinate. And the good news to that is this; we prepared the old man. Everything is ready right now. It was seven in the evening, and I have six witnesses—Mr. Nir, Mr. North, Cave, and the other gentleman and myself." (Id. at 170-71)

The Iranian said the Lebanese were proving difficult, but

that it was possible to arrange the immediate release of two hostages.

Ghorbanifar remembered that McFarlane stormed out of the room in response to this message. Nir and North eventually persuaded him to return. Despite the pleadings of the Iranians and what Ghorbanifar described as the "panic" of Nir and North at McFarlane's behavior, McFarlane behaved as if he were giving an ultimatum, Russian-style. (Id. at 171-73) The Iranians continued to plead; the Majlis foreign affairs expert said Khomeini had agreed to release the hostages first, but McFarlane

"said no, if by six o'clock all the hostages are not out, I leave. He says, okay, take two now and give us another day. No. And he left at six o'clock. And, believe me, I saw the tears in the eyes of North, Nir, and everybody.

"Why he did so? I know why. I tell you why. Number one, he had $15 million in his pocket. We were a hostage to him. Number two, the Iranians, they are not real politicians. The people came to him. They were so soft and they were so open to him; they explained to him deeply how they are in disaster. They need the help of the United States financially —I mean the support-wise, logistic-wise, military-wise. And he is a smart guy.

"He found out that in such a catastrophe and that situation they are. They are really in need of it. And, besides that, he says what the hell is this. I know now all the big shots. I have their telephone number. We have relation. We go out. We have the money. We have them. We know their need. They will follow. Who needs this man, middle man? Who is he?

"So he checked out and he left. And they left the poor guys alone in Tehran. I stayed one day, two days in Tehran. I told them this issue is so big that nobody can leave it on the air. Let me go and talk to them and finalize what I can do. But there is no way I can do unless you do something. First we have to do something." (Id. at 173-74)

McFarlane's recollection corresponded to his contemporaneous record. In addition, he noted that the Iranians confiscated the pallet of spare parts, but that no additional delivery was made because no hostage was released. In Israel on the trip home, McFarlane was disappointed. North said well, don't be too downhearted, that the one bright spot is that the government is availing itself of part of the money for application to Central America, as I recall, although I took it to be Nicaragua. (Footnote: According to the CIA Inspector General, during the meetings Ghorbanifar told Cave the price of the weapons quoted to the Iranians was $24.5 million, and asked Cave to say "the price is right" if the Iranians asked. Cave informed North, and together they asked Nir about it. Nir told them "Don't worry, it involves other deals, and that there are enormous expenses in this operation...." Cave had the impression that McFarlane could "care less about the pricing discrepancy." (CIA/IG Chronology 26) (McFarlane (1) 42) C/NE recalled that the spare parts cost the Americans $6.5 million, but that the Iranians were charged between $21 and $24 million (C/NE (1) 10-11)

After returning to the United States, Cave remembered evaluating the situation. "It was quite clear that Ghorbanifar was lying to both sides in order to blow this deal up as big as he could." (Cave 24) Cave learned from the Tehran trip that the Iranians had less control over the holders of the hostages than the Intelligence Community believed. He also concluded that the Kuwaitis held the key to the hostage problem. American hostages would not be released until Kuwait released the Dawa prisoners. (Id. at 41-42) (Tower)

- McFarlane's first cable reported:

"Delegation arrived Tehran Sunday morning. Absence of anyone to receive us for over an hour and recurrent evidence anxiety ineptitude in even the most straightforward discourse makes it clear that we must take a step back from the history of the past 8 years and put our task in a different light.

"It may be best for us to try to picture what it would be like if after nuclear attack, a surviving Tatar became Vice President; a recent grad student became Secretary of State; and a bookie became the interlocutor for all discourse with foreign countries. While the principals are a cut above this level of qualification the incompetence of the Iranian government to do business requires a rethinking on our part of why there have been so many frustrating failures to deliver on their part. The other reason for the several snafus has been the extreme paranoia that dominates the thinking of the political leadership here. More about this later. First let me debrief the meetings that have been held before giving you a sense of where and how fast matters can progress." (Tower)

MAY 26 - On the 26th, there were, again, no discussions until late in the afternoon. The interpreter later noted that the

Moslem holy period of Ramadan, during which one fasts during daylight hours may have interfered with normal schedules. McFarlane began the discussions by presenting the U.S. position, emphasizing the long-term interests as stated in the terms of reference. This was reasonably well received, but the Iranians then presented a list of demands from the captors of the U.S. hostages. They also accused the United States of going back on its commitments, because McFarlane had not brought half of the HAWK missile parts. Members of the U.S. delegation were surprised at this allegation, but they subsequently learned that Ghorbanifar had given the Iranians the impression that they would bring half of the HAWKS with them. The U.S. delegation continued to insist that the hostages must first be freed before any further deliveries of arms.

When no progress could be made, McFarlane threatened to end the discussion and leave. The Iranians protested that this was not proper behavior; McFarlane then retired from the negotiations, indicating that he would return if there were an agreement. The Iranians then emphasized how risky it was for them to have this set of discussions, and the American team came to the conclusion that top-ranking officials—particularly Khomeini himself—had not been informed of the meeting.

MAY 27 - [I]t appeared to the U.S. team that the Iranians were stalling, although the Iranians did drop nearly all of the Lebanese demands that had been raised the previous day. The American team drafted an agreement that became the topic for discussion that evening. At midnight the Iranians broke to caucus among themselves. (SSIC 1/29/87)

- Notes made by Mr. McDaniel indicate that on May 27 the President received a report on the McFarlane trip. Those notes also indicate that Mr. McFarlane reported on his trip in person to the President on May 29. The notes indicate that the Vice President, Mr. Regan, VADM Poindexter, Mr. Teicher, and LtCol North also attended. Mr. McFarlane told the Board, and the notes confirm, that he told the President that the program ought to be discontinued. It was his view that while political meetings might be considered, there should be no weapons transfers. (Tower)

MAY 28 - At about 2 a.m. on the 28th the chief Iranian official asked to see McFarlane. They asked for more time to gain control of the hostage situation and obtained assurances that the remainder of the HAWK parts would arrive within a few hours of the release of the hostages. McFarlane gave them until early the next morning, claiming that he had instructions to leave on the evening of the 27th. In a second message to Admiral Poindexter, McFarlane indicated that his discussions had been low-key and that the common interests between the two countries had been understood. The Iranian official had clearly been told, however, that the balance of the HAWK parts would be forwarded only after the hostages were released. McFarlane recommended that, despite the vastly improved tone in the discussions, the President authorize him to leave on the 28th unless there were clear evidence on an impending hostage release. McFarlane added that he had told the Iranian that further discussions could be arranged after the visit.

On the morning of May 28, one of the Iranians asked whether the United States would settle for two of the hostages to be released before the delivery. McFarlane replied that although the U.S. team was departing, the delivery would not be called until 9:30. There was no sign of an impending release, however, and the President gave McFarlane authority to decide when to leave. The U.S. team left at 9. (sic) A later White House chronology drawing upon McFarlane's messages, stated that despite Iran's unwillingness or inability to obtain the release of the hostages, the visit "established the basis for a continuing relationship" and the CIA officer later noted that the U.S. team did meet senior Iranians. One NSC staff member later testified, however, that McFarlane was not pleased with the results.

The CIA officer who served as interpreter later testified that Ghorbanifar had told him at one of the sessions that other Iranians might protest the price of $24 million for the HAWK spare parts. Ghorbanifar, according to this testimony, asked the CIA officer to uphold that price. The CIA officer says that he then spoke to LTC North who could not explain it, and both approached another delegation member about the matter, again without obtaining a satisfactory explanation. (SSIC 1/29/87)

- While McFarlane's delegation was negotiating in Tehran, the President heard discussion about using force to free the hostages. (McDaniel log, 5/28/86) Once North returned, Poindexter sought his views on the subject. He wrote North:

I am beginning to think that we need to seriously think about a rescue effort for the hostages. Is there any way we can get a spy into the Hayy Assallum area? See Charlie's [Allen] weekly report [on hostage locations]. Over a period of time we could probably move covertly some . . . people into Yarze. (Poindexter PROF note to [?North], 5/31/86) (Tower)

- Richard J. Brenneke and two associates meet in Room 2B-869 of the Pentagon with three representatives of the Joint Chiefs of Staff. The meeting concerns the Demavand project, a private effort to sell high-tech American weapons to Iran. Brenneke, a former CIA employee and freelance consultant with Israeli and French intelligence, has been in contact with the Pentagon about the project since December (see November 30, 1985 entry). The officials he meets with are attached to the Joint Special Operations Agency, a counterterrorist unit formed in 1984, which he says took over dealings on the Demavand project from the CIA (see December 18, 1985 entry). (NYT 2/2/87)

MAY 28-JUN 5 - While McFarlane and North are completing their talks in Tehran, the freighter Erria appears at the Cyprus port of Larnaca. North's associate, Thomas Clines, apparently boards the ship there on May 28 and sets off toward Lebanon. The Erria has been outfitted with four cots in the expectation that American hostages will soon be released using ransom money donated by H. Ross Perot. For the next several days, the Erria makes repeated approaches to the Lebanese coast, staying in constant radio contact with Israeli navy ships. But the expected release never takes place and the Erria finally leaves Cyprus on June 5. Four months later the vessel would return to make another futile attempt to pick up hostages. (LAT 1/21/87)

MAY 29 - On May 29, McFarlane, North, and Teicher reported on the Tehran trip to the President, accompanied by Poindexter, Regan, and the Vice President. They informed the President that the Iranians had asked for the delivery of all HAWK spare parts before hostages would be freed. The United States delegation had rejected this proposal, but agreed with the Iranians to establish a secure communications network. Contact would continue. McFarlane argued that no new meeting should take place until all hostages were freed. (McDaniel log) McFarlane recalled this report to the President.

"I told him that I had talked to people and that while I thought that there were people legitimately oriented toward change that they had not yet gotten to a position of confident ability to act. I had not met with Rafsanjani. He must have felt vulnerable, as Mr. Brzezinski's meeting with Barzagan had led to certain consequences, and he probably was fearful about it. But that ought to tell us something and that I thought it was unwise to continue anything further.

"If they wanted to have political meetings that is a judgment we could make, but that there ought not be any weapons transfers.

"The President didn't comment really, but that was not untypical. He would often hear reports, say that he would think about it, and that was—and he didn't react to me and I left, and that's the last I heard about it."

Chairman Tower: "And that ended your involvement in the matter?"

McFarlane: "Yes, sir." (McFarlane (1) 45) (Tower)

- The McFarlane mission to Tehran marked the high-water mark of U.S. efforts to deal with Iran through Mr. Ghorbanifar. For a year he had been at the center of the relationship. That year had been marked by great confusion, broken promises, and increasing frustration on the U.S. side. LtCol North and other U.S. officials apparently blamed these problems more on Mr. Ghorbanifar than on Iran. The release of Rev. Jenco did little to mitigate their unhappiness. (Tower)

- The initiative continued to be described in terms of its broader strategic relationship. But those elements never really materialized. While a high-level meeting among senior U.S. and Iranian officials continued to be a subject of discussion, it never occurred. Although Mr. McFarlane went to Tehran in May of 1986, the promised high-level Iranians never appeared. In discussions among U.S. officials, the focus seemed to be on the prospects for obtaining release of the hostages, not on a strategic relationship. Even if one accepts the explanation that arms and hostages represented only "bona fides" of seriousness of purpose for each side, that had clearly been established, one way or another, by the September exchange. (Tower)

- Two American journalists bring a $23.8 million dollar civil suit against 30 persons said to be linked to Nicaraguan contras, alleging that they have smuggled weapons and drugs and planned to assassinate Eden Pastora. Among the defendants: Adolfo Calero, John Singlaub, CMA leader Tom Posey, Theodore Shackley and Richard Secord. Singlaub blasts the suit as "transparently scurrilous, cynical and duplicitous." Andy Messing, head of the National Defense Council, also named in the suit, calls the charges "laughable." The journalists are Tony Avirgan and his wife Martha Honey, who are represented by Daniel Sheehan of the Christic Institute. The suit centers on allegations about the activities of John Hull. It charges that Hull joined forces with Cuban-American contra supporters Rene Corvo and Felipe Vidal to organize an anti-Sandinista guerrilla force in Costa Rica, in violation of the U.S. Neutrality Act. The suit also charges that Hull and others were paid fees by Colombian drug dealers who refueled their planes on Hull's farm. Hull and others are said to have used drug money to purchase weapons illegally in Miami for the contras. Hull's libel suit against Avigan and Honey in Costa Rica was dismissed earlier in the month.(WP 5/30/86)

- Mr. McFarlane testified that while standing on the tarmac at Tel Aviv airport after the trip to Tehran in May of 1986, LtCol North told him not to be too downhearted because "this government is availing itself of part of the money [from the Iranian initiative] for application to Central America." Assistant Secretary of Defense Richard Armitage told the Board that North told him some time in November of 1986 that: "it's going to be just fine . . . as soon as everyone knows that . . . the Ayatollah is helping us with the Contras." (Tower)

MAY 31 - Carl "Spitz" Channell's National Endowment for the Preservation of Liberty (NEPL) transfers separate payments of $500,000 and $225,000 to International Business Communications (IBC). NEPL payments to IBC since December 1985 total $3,038,000, including today's transactions. (NYT 2/26/87)

SUMMER - CIA agents report increases in supplies to the contras in El Salvador, Honduras and Costa Rica. (WSJ 12/11/86)

- The Danish freighter "Ilse TH" makes four 900-ton shipments of arms from Eliat, Israel, to the Iranian port of Bandar Abbas between May and August, according to members of the Danish Sailors Union. Sailors on board the ship are "certain" the arms inside the 64 containers carried on each trip are American-made, although there are no markings and the Iranian military officer who meets the ship each time believes the weapons are from Yugoslavia. (Iran Times 9/19/86)

- Glenn Robinette, a former CIA employee, installed a 2,000 electronic security gate at the home of Oliver North in Great Falls, Virginia in the summer of 1986, at the behest of retired Gen. Richard Secord. Robinette picked up the tab for the gate as "an advance from me, I guess a business venture...hoping I would get some more business." Robinette tells reporters he met Gen. Secord through former CIA officer Thomas G. Clines, another actor in the contra aid network. (CBS Evening News 3/16/87; WP 3/17/87)

JUNE 1986

JUN - In a June, 1986 note to VADM Poindexter regarding the third country issue, LtCol North discussed previous solicitations from [two countries deleted]. He told VADM Poindexter:

"I have no idea what Schultz knows or doesn't know, but he could prove to be very unhappy if he learns of the [two countries deleted] aid that has been given in the past from someone other than you. Did RCM (McFarlane) ever tell Schultz?" (Tower)

JUN 2 - the CIA instructed the Army "to put the radar transfer action on 'hold,' a status which continued until 30 July 1986." (Army/IG Report 9) (Tower)

JUN 3 - North was not prepared to replace the program [of negotiations aimed at freeing hostages in Iran] with force. He

[fully agree[d] that if the current effort fails to achieve release then such a mission should be considered. You will recall that we have not had much success with this kind of endeavor in the past, however. After CIA took so long to organize and then botched the Kilburn effort, Copp undertook to see what could be done thru one of the earlier DEA [Drug Enforcement Agency] developed Druze contacts. [Diplomatic sources say that LtCol North worked with Israeli intelligence in 1986 in order to develop a plan for American commandos to rescue hostages in Lebanon. Because the Israelis could not determine the precise location of the hostages, no plan was ever attempted. (Reuters 1/14/87)] Dick has been working with Nir on this and now has three people in Beirut and a 40 man Druze force working "for" us. Dick rates the possibility of success on this operation as 30%, but that's better than nothing.

In regard to U.S. military rescue ops, JCS has steadfastly refused to go beyond the initial thinking stage unless we can develop some hard intelligence on their whereabouts. We already have . . . one ISA officer in Beirut but no effort has been made to insert personnel since we withdrew the military mission to the LAF. If we really are serious, we should start by getting CIA to put a full time analyst on the HLTF [Hostage Location Task Force] and then organizing a planning cell-preferably not in the pentagon [sic], but at CIA, to put the operation together. Dick, who has been in Beirut, and who organized the second Iran mission, is convinced that such an operation could indeed be conducted. My concern in this regard is that JCS wd insist on using most of the tier 2 and 3 forces in such an undertaking. If you want me to task this thru the OSG we will do so, but [I] urge that we start by you having Casey staff the HLTF as there has been a certain amount of planning undertaken on this matter already. It might be useful to sit down w/ Dewey and Moellering on this after next week's OSG meeting (Thursday 1500-1600 [June 12]) if you have the time. We can probably brief you in about 20 min max. (North PROF note to Poindexter, 6/3/86, 11:42:43) (Tower)

JUN 6 - At his morning national security briefing on June 6, the President is said to have approved military planning to rescue the hostages as well as reviving [previously planned efforts]. (McDaniel log) (See June 19 and July entries)

Meanwhile, the United States knew that at least Ghorbanifar refused to treat the Tehran meeting as the end. On June 6, he pressed [his contact in the Prime Minister's office] for another meeting with the United States. He promised that the United States would deliver the remaining HAWK spare parts and, if Iran paid in advance, the radars. [The Iranian official] seems to have treated Ghorbanifar's advocacy as nothing new, to have been unimpressed with his idea, and inclined to drop the initiative. (Tower)

JUN 8 - Afghan rebels admit to harvesting opium to finance their war. (NYT 6/8/86)

JUN 10 - A November 1986 chronology of the program prepared by the NSC staff indicates that on June 10, 1986 Majlis Speaker Rafsanjani made a speech that guardedly mentioned Iranian interest in improved relations with the United States. The Committee does not know whether that speech was seen as a signal at the time, but CIA personnel were soon told that there might be another meeting, and Iranian officials were made aware that a meeting in Europe was possible. (SSIC 1/29/87)

- On June 10, 1986, early in the process thus described to the Board, North wrote Poindexter:

Hopefully you have by now been informed that UNO/FDN safely released the eight West Germans this evening just before dark at the religious commune at Presillas.

Franklin is headed North in attempt to get across the Rama Rd before the Sandinistas can close in on him. At this point the only liability we still have is one of DEMOCRACY INC.'s airplanes is mired in the mud (it is the rainy season down there) on the secret field in Costa Rica. They hope to have it out by dawn. On a separate but related matter: The reason why I asked to speak to you urgently earlier today is that Ray [?Burghardt] called Elliott Abrams regarding the third country issue. Elliott has talked to Shultz and had prepared a paper re going to [other third countries] for contributions. Elliott called me and asked "where to send the money." I told Elliott to do nothing, to send no papers and to [sic] talk to no one further about this until he talks to you. He is seeing you privately tomorrow. At this point I need your help. As you know, I have the accounts and the means by which this thing needs to be accomplished. I have no idea what Shultz knows or doesn't know, but he could prove to be very unhappy if he learns of these others countries aid that has been given in the past from someone other than you. Did RCM [McFarlane] ever tell Shultz?

I am very concerned that we are bifurcating an effort that has, up to now, worked relatively well. An extraordinary amount of good has been done and money truly is not the thing which is most needed at this point. What we most need is to get the CIA reengaged in this effort so that it can be better managed than it now is by one slightly confused Marine LtCol. Money will again become an issue in July, but probably not until mid-month. There are several million rounds of most types of ammo on hand and more ($3M) worth on the way by ship . . . Critically needed items are being flown in from Europe to the expanded warehouse facility at Ilopango. Boots, uniforms, ponchos, etc. are being [sic] purchased locally and Calero will receive $500K for food purchases by the end of the week. Somehow we will mollify the wounded egos of the triple A with not being able to see RR. We should look to going back to a head of an allied government on the blowpipes if we are going to do anything at all about outside support in the next few days, and I wd love to carry the letter from RR . . . if we are going to move on something. Meanwhile, I we recommend that you and RCM have a talk about how much Sec Shultz does or does not know abt [third country assistance approaches] so that we don't make any mistakes. I don't know [one of those governments] knows since Fred never told me. At this point I'm not sure who on our side knows what. Help.(North PROF note to Poindexter, 6/10/86, 23:21:54) (Tower)

- In June, the pressures on North worried McFarlane. He wrote Poindexter that

[i]t seems increasingly clear that the Democratic left is coming after him [North] with a vengeance in the election year and that eventually they will get him—too many people are talking to reporters from the donor community and within the administration. I don't [know] what you do about it but in Ollie's interest I would get him transfered or sent to Bethesda for disability review board (appartwently [sic] the Marine Corps has already tried to survey him once[)], That wuld [sic] represent a major loss to the staff and contra effort but I think we can probably find a way to continue to do

those things. In the end it may be better anyway. (McFarlane PROF note to Poindexter, 6/10/86) (Tower)

JUN 11 - Recon/Optical Inc. of Barrington, Ill. files suit against the Government of Israel charging theft of technology relating to sophisticated aerial reconnaissance cameras the company was under contract to produce for the Israeli Air Force. Recon officials say Israeli representatives assisting on the project tried to remove technical drawings and 50,000 pages of handwritten notes from the company's plant in May this year after Recon shut down the program, apparently over cost disputes. A possible target of inquiry in the case is Shlomo Nir, the former chief of the Israeli Air Force's Air Intelligence Systems Branch and current employee of Recon. Nir made two trips to Israel in the Spring of 1986 where he met with representatives of American subsidiaries and Israeli companies including El Op (Israel Electric Optical Industry), which Recon charges was the intended recipient of the confidential technology. (WP 8/20/86)

- "(Elliot Abrams) is seeing you privately tomorrow . . . I told Elliot to do nothing, to send no papers and to [sic] talk to no one further about this until he talks to you." (North PROF note to Poindexter, 6/10/86, 23:21:54)

- Poindexter indicated he would think about McFarlane's concern [about pressures on North]. (Poindexter PROF note to McFarlane, 6/11/86) (Tower)

- Poindexter replied [to North note dated June 10]: Out of the last NSPG on Central America Shultz agreed that he would think about third country sources. I wanted to get an answer from him so we could get out of the business. As I understand the law there is nothing that prevents State from getting involved in this now. To my knowledge Shultz knows nothing about the prior financing. I think it should stay that way. My concern was to find out what they were thinking so there would not be a screw up. I asked Elliot at lunch. (footnote: Burghardt wrote [Poindexter] at this time [?]: I understand that Elliott [Abrams] briefed you today on where this stands ["aid for freedom fighters"]. If we do not get a positive response fairly soon from the Saudis or Brunei, I would advocate moving right away. . . . I can understand the reluctance to incur a debt, but it would be almost a sure thing and we will definately [sic] need the $10 M bridge money. With the House scheduled to take up the issue on the 24th, Senate approval would be after the July 4 recess and the date of delivery keeps fading into the distance. (Burghardt PROF note to [?Poindexter], reply to note of 6/9/86)) He said he had recommended Brunei where Shultz is going to visit. They have lots of money and very little to spend it on. It seems like a good prospect. Shultz agrees. I asked Elliot how the money could be transferred. He said he thought Shultz could just hand them an account number. I said that was a bad idea not at all letting on that we had access to accounts. I told Elliot that the best way was for Brunei to direct their embassy here to receive a person that we would designate and the funds could be transferred through him. Don't you think that is best? I still want to reduce your visibility. Let me know what you think and I will talk to George. I agree about CIA but we have got to get the legislation past. (Poindexter PROF note to North, 6/11/86.)

In another message, Poindexter added: "We should not mention Brunei to anybody, Elliot said only Shultz and hill are aware." [sic] (Poindexter PROF note to [?Burghardt])

"With respect to private solicitations," Abrams told the Board,

we never did any of that. As a matter of fact, the state of our knowledge of that was limited. We had intelligence reporting, which improved over time as the restrictions on what the Agency could do with the Contras were reduced. We had better information on what was being received, better in 1986 than in 1985.

We in the department never made any other solicitation for anything from anybody. One time, this summer, I would say, General Singlaub called me from Asia . . . and said I can get some aid for the Contras, through me, if you will just sort of let this foreign government know, just tell their ambassador—I don't remember who I was supposed to tell —this is official.

I said I can't do that. It's just not right; I can't do that.

He said well, then, I'm going to blow it. But I just couldn't do that.

So that was the only other time when I was asked, in a sense indirectly, to solicit, and said no.

We had virtually no, we had no information on who was

paying for it. CIA people have testified that they were able to trace money back to secret bank accounts but couldn't get behind the bank secrecy laws; and they have testified that they knew the arms were coming from [a foreign country]; that is to say, the last stop before Central America . . . but they could not go beyond that and find out who was paying.

Well, I have to say that we did not think it was our job to find out who was paying, since it seemed to us, as long as it didn't violate the Neutrality Act or the Arms Export Control Act that it was legal and proper.

Once or twice we, in particular, actually CIA and not State, came up with some facts that indicated a violation of the Neutrality Act, a shipment of arms from the U.S., and we reported that to the Department of Justice.

But we did not engage in nor did we really know anything about this private network. We knew that it existed. We knew it in part because somebody was giving the Contras guns.

We knew it also because you couldn't be in Central America and not know it.

We have significant military assistance through El Salvador via Ilopango Airport, which is the Salvadoran Airport.

Also, we ran a good proportion of the $27 million in humanitarian aid through Ilopango Airport. (Abrams 11-13) (Tower)

JUN 12 - Spitz Channell's National Endowment for the Preservation of Liberty pays $5,000 to former Congressman Dan Kuykendall (R-Tenn.) with check 1116 from NEPL's Palmer National Bank account 40000494. Kuykendall is head of the Gulf & Caribbean Foundation, which later shows up on a hand-drawn chart found by the Tower Commission in Oliver North's safe, apparently outlining the private aid network. (NEPL Bank Statement 6/30/86)

- "It might be useful to sit down w/ Dewey and Moellering (to discuss possible military rescues) on this after next week's OSG meeting (Thursday 1500-1600 [June 12] if you have the time. We can probably brief you in about 20 min max." (North PROF note to Poindexter, 6/3/86, 11:42:43)

JUN 13 - Claiming that Ghorbanifar told him that [the Iranian official] wanted to talk, George Cave, using his alias "O'neil," called [the Iranian] on June 13.

[The official in the PM's office] said that this was not true, but "our friend" [Ghorbanifar] had been pressing him to go through with the deal.

O'neil then asked what we should do about the situation. B replied that he did not know why we didn't complete the deal when in Dubai [sic] [?Tehran]. O'neil interupted to state that he had a suggestion. We should first meet in Europe to make sure there were no misunderstandings as happened before. Then our gorup [sic] would go to Dubai [coverterm for Tehran] at an agreed upon date. Upon arrival in Dubai the four boxes [hostages] would be turned over, then the rest of the spares would arrive and later dependeing [sic] on timeing [sic] the two Quties [coverterm for HAWK radars] would arrive. We would stay until everything was delivered. B said that the meeting in Germany was not neccessary and that deal was unacceptable to them. He proposed that we arrive with the remaining 240 spares, then two hostages would be truned over [sic]. When the two radars arrive, the two other hostages would be turned over.

We haggled abit [sic] O'neil insisting on our deal and he insisting on his. O'neil suggested that meeting in Germany was necessary and B finally agreed that if really necessary he would come. He parrried [sic] the request that the H [?] also attend. He added that it would be very difficult to get away at this time.

When discussing the possible trip to Dubai, B suggested that it was not necessary for the chief to accompany group that comes.

Since discussion was getting nowhere, O'neil suggested that he was in [a] position to decide on B insistance [sic], and there for it best [sic] that O'neil confer with his superiors and B with his and O'neil will get back to him in one or two days. At the end B stated that it should not be that we give such importance to who does what first, once this deal is completed there are many important issues that we must discuss. He again insisted on the need of the US to demonstrate good faith.

O'neil asked if the hostages were now under their control because at one point B said that he did not know if their delegation was still in Lebanon. B hesitated to answer k—this [sic] one but said that they could get them. O'neil said "then they are in your hands" and B said they were (note O'neil doubts this is true). (Tower)

JUN 14 - The Danish ship Pia Vesta is seized by Panamanian authorities at the request of Peruvian President Alan Garcia and found to be carrying a secret cargo of Soviet-made weapons. Many details of the shipment are unclear. Its point of origin is said to be East Germany, its destination either Peru or El Salvador. Adding to the mystery are rumors of CIA involvement, to which Garcia is reported to object, and which result in his request to Panamanian authorities. The Wall Street Journal, in its editions of July 18, 1986, reports that Oliver North established a network by which arms were purchased in Eastern Europe and shipped to the contras. (Latin American Database chronology)

- The next day, the Iranian official told Ghorbanifar that Iranian officials were prepared to meet American representatives in Europe if the remaining HAWK spares and radars were delivered first. If all equipment were delivered, all hostages would be freed; if half the equipment, half the hostages. Ghorbanifar and his Tehran contact discussed the matter for the rest of June. (Tower)

MID-JUN - Two French hostages who have been held in Beirut, Philippe Rochet and Georges Hansen, are released after a $2.2 million ransom is paid to their kidnappers. The ransom allegedly was negotiated by a senior aide to Prime Minister Chirac with the help of Lebanese business executives and was transferred to the kidnappers through an Arab bank in Switzerland. French officials deny the report. (NYT 12/13/86)

JUN 16 - A Swedish newspaper, Dagens Nyheter, reports that Israel served as a mediator for $500 million worth of mortar shell material and other arms supplied by Swedish companies to Iran through Israel and Argentina over the past 6 years. (FBIS 6/16/86)

JUN 18 - Several former officers of the Nicaraguan rebel forces assert that the top military leaders are siphoning off large amounts of money received from the United States, enriching themselves at the expense of their troops. Interviewed in the Miami area, the former officers of the contras say their allegations are based mostly on their experiences in the field. They describe the use of phony receipts, black market currency deals, the substitution of inferior goods and other techniques. Gerardo Martinez says he commanded an

800-member group known as Task Force Jeane Kirkpatrick until he was dismissed in January 1986 for complaining about corruption. "I think the entire leadership is corrupt," says Martinez, who goes by the nom de guerre "Chaco." Other contra leaders and field commanders say the corruption is widespread and that military commander Enrique Bermudez was notorious for pilfering funds while the CIA protected him and stifled complaints against him. Bermudez at one point allegedly told field commanders that the CIA had cut funds, but when some of them went to a "Colonel Raymond," an American officer coordinating contra activities for the CIA in Honduras, they were told that funds had actually been increased. "The CIA told us that the general staff was taking the money that belonged to us," said Marlon Blandon Osorno, a field commander known as Gorrion. As a result, a separate command with a separate supply system was set up for the contra units in the Honduran-Nicaraguan border area. Bermudez and his staff complained about the separate command, as did local CIA operatives, and after about two months the CIA dissolved it. (NYT 6/21/86)

JUN 19 - Poindexter asked the Director of Central Intelligence to intensify efforts to locate the hostages. (Poindexter to DCI, 6/19/86. CIA/IG Chronology 19) (Tower)

- Vortex official, Michael Palmer, is charged with conspiracy and drug possession for allegedly importing more than 1000 lbs of marijuana from Colombia to the United States between 1977 and 1986. (MH 3/22/87)

JUN 20 - Mr. McDaniel's notes indicate that on June 20, 1986, the President decided that no further meeting with the Iranians would be held until the release of the hostages. (Tower)

- Ghorbanifar provided the Iranian official with a detailed analysis of the price and availability of the remaining HAWK spare parts. According to Ghorbanifar, 177 units would cost $3,781,600 in addition to the $24,173,200 Iran already had paid. He reported that, as a gift, the United States would add ten diesel generators essential to operating the HAWK system, and had offered to provide test and calibration equipment and technicians to operate it.

At his morning national security briefing the same day, the President discussed both [our] ability to rescue hostages and next steps with Iran. The President is said to have decided that there would be no meetings with Iranian officials until the hostages were released. (McDaniel log)

JUN 21 - The next day, Ghorbanifar and the Iranian official argued pricing, using an oil transaction as cover. (Tower)

Late JUN - In late June, all the parties were apparently trying to patch together a new schedule of arms deliveries and hostage releases. According to one report, Iran was considering whether to release a hostage before any further deliveries of arms. Another report suggests that Israel offered to "sweeten the pot" by adding some free equipment to the proposed arms sale package.

According to testimony received by the Committee, the Iranians were upset by the high prices being charged, especially for spare parts for HAWK missile systems and by the fact that the U.S. had not upheld its part of the deal in shipping one half of the HAWK missile spare parts to Tehran with the U.S. delegation in May of 1986. A CIA official who participated on the trip contends that no such promise had been made. At the same time according to the testimony of a CIA official it became clear that Iran was unable to control the captors of U.S. hostages. (SSIC 1/29/87)

JUN - According to testimony by Shultz, in June 1986 Abrams came to Shultz with a proposal to seek such aid [humanitarian assistance from third countries] and said there was a Swiss account that could receive the money and Shultz approved. Shultz testified that apart from a request for communications equipment, which was not honored, only one country was asked for a contribution pursuant to this policy. (SSIC 1/29/87)

- Shultz testified that in June, McFarlane telephoned him to report that a third country had previously contributed $31 million to the Nicaraguan resistance. McFarlane, in his testimony, recalled a similar phone call to Shultz informing him of a $30 million third country contribution to the FDN. (SSIC 1/29/87)

SUMMER - FBI Director William Webster learns of the covert arms deals to Iran from an FBI official [presumably Oliver "Buck" Revell] who is a member of an interagency counterterrorism team. Webster meets with Attorney General

Meese at this time to make sure Reagan has authorized the sales with a formal finding. Meese tells Webster that he has personally checked the legality of the finding. (WP 4/2/87)

JUN 22 - "[P]er instructions" from the official in the Prime Minister's office, who had unsuccessfully tried to reach him, Cave called the Iranian, June 22.

2. Although there was a lot of talk one thing emerged and that is that the B's people want to somehow go through with the deal. The difficulties that dealing with us was causing them [sic]. The B emphasized that there are many people that oppose dealing with us. When O'neil asked if this was causing his group political difficulties, he confirmed that this was the case. His problem is that they must appear to have made a good deal. He pointed out that the previous release of the one person in return for the 1,000 had not left them in good oder [sic] as the 1,000 were not that important, and they had to return the other materials.

3. O'neil stated that we were very much interested in the deal and a long term relationship between the two companies, but the chief of our company was insisting on the release of our embargoed 4,000,000 dollars [coverterm for hostages] before we delivered the remainder of 240 [HAWKs] spares and then the two large boxes [radars]. What was interesting at this point is that the B did not say there could be no deal on this basis. He said that some fromula [sic] must be worked out whereby we can deliver what we promised at much the same time as they deliver the 4,000,000. For the first time he said that they needed political currency to deliver on their end. He stated that they have a serious problem with the 4 million in explaining why it is that they need it. This has been a serious problem in their negotiations with those that control the 4 million. When O'neil asked the direct question can they gain control of the 4 million, the B hesitated but said that this was within their capabilities. He said that if we had stayed in Dubai [Tehran] a few days longer they could have delivered 2 million immediately. He emphasized in answer to an O'neil question that they could not specifically say exactly when the 4 million would be transfered, but this was still in their power, despite the fact that the situation where the 4 million are held was continually deteriorating. The B urged that we try to do this deal as soon as possible, so that our two companies could

have a meaningful future relationship. O'neil said that he would call back at approximately the same time on 23 June.

4. The B continually spoke of the serious problems that trying to consumate [sic] this deal was causing him and his colleagues. He urged O'neil to contact the merchant [Ghorbanifar] to get all the details. He would try to contact the merchant immediately to provide as much background as possible. The B on several occasions said that there was [sic] considerable forces arrayed against this deal and he considered himself in some danger. Most interesting note is that during this conversation the B insisted that they want to go through with deal. Although he bordered on the inarticulate at times, long pauses and some relapses into his old song and dance, he did not reject our position outright. O'neil's recommendation [sic] is that we sit down and talk it out with him in [sic] person, we may get more out of this than the transaction we are interested in. (Tower)

JUN 24 - Shultz pays an unusual three-hour visit to the Sultan of Brunei. The sultan later deposits approximately $10 million into a Swiss bank account, reportedly intended for the contras. The amount is significantly more than congressional investigators are initially led to believe. Senator Durenberger later says that Assistant Secretary of State Elliott Abrams provided the number of the account to Brunei officials, having gotten it from North. Sources say later that Shultz, although aware of the contribution, did not personally solicit it. (LAT 12/6/86; WP 12/7/86 & 12/25/86; MH 1/8/87)

- Two days later, North reported to Poindexter that the Iranian official was trying to reach Cave again.

As of this minute they have not yet connected. We are trying to have him call back. Nir advises that [the Iranian official] called Gorba about an hour ago in a state of great agitation to say that he was trying to get Sam [O'neil] to arrange for the release of one U.S. hostage. Nir believes it to be sincere and that we may really be close. I am not so sure but [C/NE] Sam and Charlie [Allen] all think it may be real. We'll see. Sam will call me later tonight and I'll come back into here or CIA to receive the report. Wd be nice to have some kind of secure voice to save these middle of the night trips. Will advise in a.m. of any developments. (North PROF note to Poindexter, 6/24/86, 21:28:15) (Tower)

- On June 24, 1986, H.Res. 485 was introduced, directing the President to provide to the House of Representatives "certain information concerning activities of Lieutenant Colonel North or any other member of the staff of the National Security Council in support of the resistance."

JUN 25 - The House approves $100 million in aid to the contras through September 1987, in legislation similar to that approved by the Senate on March 27. It is passed as an amendment to the military construction appropriations bill (H.R. 5052), and allows the aid to be handled by any U.S. agency, including the CIA. The bill includes another amendment that prohibits American personnel from providing assistance in Honduras and Costa Rica within twenty miles of the Nicaraguan border. That measure is incorporated into the continuing appropriations resolution (P.L. 99-591, approved October 30, 1986). (CRS "U.S. Assistance to Nicaraguan Guerrillas" 12/4/86; CRS "War Powers Resolution: Presidential Compliance" 12/22/86)

- Fernando "El Negro" Chamorro, commander of an anti-Sandinista group fighting in southern Nicaragua, confirms that two Cuban exiles captured in Nicaragua were recruited in Miami for his contra forces. Chamorro says Ubaldo Hernandez Perez and Mario Eugenio Rejas Lavas joined the Nicaraguan Revolutionary Armed Forces (FARN) about a year ago. He adds, "We have had total cooperation from the Cuban exile community. They have spilled their blood on Nicaraguan soil." At a press conference in Managua, the Cuban prisoners say they were recruited in Miami by Bay of Pigs veteran Rene Corvo. (MH 6/26/86)

JUN 25 - At about the same time, a successful rescue began to look possible. North wrote in late June:

You should also be aware that CIA believes that they have made a major breakthrough on the location of at least two of the hostages. The info is being carefully analized [sic] before passing to JSOC, but there hasn't been this much enthusiasm on the issue in a long time. Our other effort seems to be at a standstill w/ Ashgari [sic] [Ghorbanifar] and [his Tehran contact] screaming at each other about prices and Geo. Cave telling [the Iranian official] that we are fed up w/ the whole thing and are tired of being insulted by people who "pretend to be able to do things they cannot." (North PROF note to [?Poindexter], reply to note of 6/25/86)

Ghorbanifar told the Board that Cave's telephone calls "every night" created a problem in Tehran. He recalled Cave saying the President said this, McFarlane said this, Poindexter said this, and making a lot of confuse [sic] for Iranians. Because he doesn't know there are three groups that must come together to make a decision.

General Scowcroft: Who was Cave talking to when he called?

Mr. Ghorbanifar: To the man who is the head of this operation, the special aide to the Prime Minister, the number one in his office. (Ghorbanifar 175) (Tower)

JUN 27 - The International Court of Justice at the Hague rules the U.S. has breached several of its obligations under international law by its actions against Nicaragua. (CRS "Nicaragua: Conditions and Issues for U.S. Policy" 12/8/86)

- According to North's desk calendar, North met "Tabatabaie," (probably refers to Tabatabai, who, North reports, is "allegedly well-connected to Rafsanjani"; see July 21 entry) possibly with Senator Helms, on June 27. (Tower)

- On June 29, 1986, a column by Jack Anderson and Dale Van Atta in the Washington Post stated: "We can reveal that the secret negotiations over arms supply and release of American hostages have involved members of the National Security Council and a former official of the CIA.'" (See July 10 entry.) (Tower)

JUN 30 - Reagan fires Ambassador to Honduras John Ferch. The State Department claims that Ferch's relations with the CIA and the contras were strained. Ferch was criticized for his lack of pressure on the Honduran government to reverse itself when it allegedly blocked shipments to the contras in late 1985. (WP 7/1/86, NYT 7/1/86, FBIS 7/2/86)

- North urges leniency from the departments of State and Justice in the case of a Honduran general convicted of plotting to assassinate the Honduran president in 1984. General Jose Bueso Rosa pleaded guilty in June to two counts of traveling in furtherance of a conspiracy to plan an assassination and is now serving five years in a minimum-security Federal prison at Eglin Air Force Base in Florida. Among those convicted in the plot was Gerard Latchinian, a former business partner of Felix Rodriguez, also known as Max Gomez. Latchinian was sentenced to 30 years on charges of murder-for-hire and cocaine smuggling. The assassination was to have been financed by selling more than $10 million of cocaine in the U.S. According to an Administration official familiar with the case, both North and former chief of U.S. forces in Latin America General Paul Gorman made requests for leniency on behalf of Bueso, but their requests were turned down by Justice. Bueso, who was head of the Honduran army before a military shake-up in March 1984, was considered a firm supporter of the U.S. and reportedly gave valuable assistance to Reagan Administration efforts to aid the contras. (NYT 2/23/87)

- The official in the Prime Minister's office and Ghorbanifar held a number of discussions at this time. The Iranian official complained that the United States charged six times the 1985 price for the weapons at issue. Ghorbanifar tried to explain the pricing, while complaining that his financial problems had forced him into hiding. He needed $5 million to avoid ruin. On June 30, Ghorbanifar told his Tehran contact that the Americans again explained the high prices, and had suggested that, once the matter was resolved and relations were improved, the United States would assist Iran to obtain loans from international banks and American agencies. Ghorbanifar then proposed, without indicating who may have originated the idea, that Iran obtain the release of one hostage to coincide with the July 4 celebrations and the centennial of the Statue of Liberty. He added that, within twenty-four hours of such release, the United States would ship the rest of the HAWK spare parts. The radars would follow, and Iran would effect the release of the last two hostages. The Iranian official doubted a hostage could be released by July 4; for one thing, there had to be agreement on the price of the materiel. Ghorbanifar agreed they had to solve the price problem before the timing of the hostage releases could be fixed.

Cave also spoke to the official in the Prime Minister's office about the price of HAWK spare parts on June 30. Cave reported that:

1. This was fairly lengthy call during which B [the official in the Iranian Prime Minister's office] continued to harp on the Price [sic] of the 240 items. Sam [O'neil] told him that we had sent a copy of the prices to the mercahnt [sic] [Ghorbanifar], These constituted the prices that the middlemen paid for the goods. B wanted to know [sic] if Sam had a

copy so he could relate some of them to B. Sam said that he did not have a copy of the prices. During the course of the conversation, B would inisist [sic] on discussing pricing [sic]. He refused to be stonewalled and said that he was under enormous pressure to get some adjustment in the pricing. When Sam asked about the Micro [sic] fiche list. He confessed that he had not sent it but would on the morrow. Th;is [sic] is some kind of indicator that such a list might not exisit [sic]. However, he does have something and suspect it might be an old invoice. He said that his superiors are shocked that the USG would sell [sic] them parts at black market prices. Sam -pointed [sic] out that he was buying from the merchant. B was insistant that something [sic] must be done on pricing as they were not prepared to pay six times pricing [sic].

2. Sam told him that something must break soon as the Chief of our cómp[any] is fed up with the whole deal. He was must [sic] disturbed at the way our delegation was handled in Dubai [Tehran] and is on the verge of corking off the while [sic] deal. This did not seem to make a great impression on B. Sam also said that he and Goode [North] are in deep trouble for having recomended [sic] the deal in the first place. B said that we were in no more trouble than he was on his end. Sam said that we were then all in the same trench together.

3. At one point in the pricing argument, Sam pointed out that we do not cheat on prices, were they displeased with the [?HAWKs]? when [sic] B kept insisting on some kind of break in the price, Sam told him that as far as we were concerned they could buy the parts elsewhere. This deal was set and it would have to go through [sic] the merchant [sic].

4. Toward the end of the conversation, B made a plea to Sam to do something about the end of the price if at all possible. He also extracted a promise from Sam to call him back tomorrow. (Tower)

JULY 1986

JUL - The second of two C-123K cargo planes is bought for use in the secret air resupply network to the contras. The purchase is handled by William J. Cooper, a former pilot for CIA-owned Air America, who ultimately is killed in the October 5 downing of a C-123K in Nicaragua. (WP 12/7/86)

- By July, the United States had asked Israel to help [rescue hostages; see June 6 and June 19 entries]. (See North PROF note to Poindexter, 07/11/86, 07:27:44) (Tower)

- I [Assistant Secretary of State for Inter-American Affairs Elliott Abrams] got actual authority to go ahead and make a particular solicitation [to another government for a kind of bridge to extend the $27 million until we had the $100 million] in July, as I recall it. There is cable traffic on this. It was from the Secretary, and we sent a cable—this was done through the embassy in that country—saying do you think they'll give, and there was a sort of back and forth with the Ambassador. The Secretary decided that we should go ahead and make the request, which I then did.

The actual solicitation was made by me, not by the Ambassador, in London, meeting with an official of that government.

They ultimately said yes.

Let me back up a step.

Before I went off and made the solicitation, it was clear that they might say yes. They, after all, agreed to meet us on a matter of highest importance. I don't know whether they knew what it was going to be, but it was certainly plausible. . . . (Abrams 3-7) (Tower). (See Early Aug, 1986 entry and Jun 24, 1986 entry)

JUL 2 - The Secretary of State told the Board that on July 2, Mr. Armacost wrote me a memo, informing me "that there is renewed" conjecture, that the NSC-sponsored search for a U.S.- Iran deal for hostages will produce an early result. The story is that one hostage may be released tomorrow in Lebanon.

Arms were not mentioned. I do not recall having seen this memo, but this reported "conjecture" would have added nothing to my knowledge of the matter. You heard this from time to time. (Shultz, SRB, 56) (Tower)

- On July 2, Ghorbanifar told his contact in the Prime Minister's office that the United States thought Iran used the pricing problem as an excuse to cover Iran's inability to obtain the release of another hostage. He said that United States suggested that, if another hostage were released, then the United States immediately would ship the remaining HAWK spare parts. (See Early July entry.) (Tower)

JUL 3-4 - 23 tons of arms are shipped to Iran, via Spain and Yugoslavia, on a Boeing 707 belonging to Race Aviation. Race Aviation is a small cargo company with operations in Madrid. It has connections with now-defunct Global International, which often transported arms to Egypt from 1981-1983 under contract with Egyptian American Transport and Services Corp. (EATSCO), the company operated by Thomas Clines, Richard Secord, Edwin Wilson and others (see "Early 1982" entry). Global's chief stockholder before it failed was Farhad (or Farhat) Azima, an Iranian emigre, who with Linda Azima currently owns Race Aviation. His two brothers, Farzin and Fariborz, supervise the operations of Race's single Boeing 707. Later, it is reported that since Race has no company markings or colors, a second plane with forged tail numbers could have delivered the weapons to Iran. Israel has used this method of disguising shipments in the past, and there is evidence it is being used elsewhere in the Iran arms operation as well. (MH 12/7/86; LAT 11/9/86; WP 11/20/86; PI 11/26/86; CSM 1/2/87; WSJ 1/2/87; CBS News 1/2/87)

EARLY JUL - Early in July, LtCol North called Charles Allen, a CIA official, and asked him to take over the day-to-day contact with Mr. Nir. LtCol North wrote in a memorandum to VADM Poindexter about this same time that he believed he had "lost face" because of his failure to obtain the release of an American hostage. Mr. Allen recalled that Mr. Nir was alarmed at losing direct contact with LtCol North. Mr. Allen told the Board that as a result, Mr. Nir worked closely with Mr. Ghorbanifar to obtain the release of an American hostage. (Tower)

- "In June and July," Charles Allen told the Board, "there seemed to be sort of a stalemate. In early July, Colonel North called me out of a meeting—I was lecturing to a group at the Office of Personnel Management—and stated that he had been assured by Amiram Nir, special assistant to the Prime Minister, Peres at that time, of Israel that another American would be released very shortly. He at that stage briefed some of the senior people in the government. We sent a hostage briefing team to Wiesbaden and no release occurred, and we brought the team back. [On July 2, Ghorbanifar told his contact in the Prime Minister's office that the United States thought Iran used the pricing problem as an excuse to cover Iran's inability to obtain the release of another hostage. He said that the United States suggested that, if another hostage was released, then the United States immediately would ship the remaining HAWK spare parts.] Colonel North was deeply disappointed and he said that he had been admonished by Admiral Poindexter on this, and he cut off all contact with Amiram Nir at that stage and asked that I talk to Amiram Nir for a period of two or three weeks. According to the CIA Inspector General: "[July 7-26]: Allen remains in almost daily contact with Nir by telephone. (According to Allen, Nir is clearly alarmed at losing direct contact with North and appears to be working feverishly with Ghorbanifar and others to free an American hostage.) Nir tells Allen that, according to Ghorbanifar, I/1 is making an effort to secure the release of a hostage. He asks Allen to refrain from informing North since he does not want to raise North's 'hopes too high.' When Father Jenco is released, North again resumes direct contact with Nir." (CIA/IG Chronology 27) (C. Allen 21) (Tower)

- By early July, two CIA officers were comparing notes on whether the [Iran arms] program was in danger; one has testified that he also made LTC North aware of Iranian anger over the high prices. Through early July, various schedules were floated without success. Iran had price lists for HAWK parts, and the gross discrepancies between that list and the prices being charged to Iran were too large to explain away or to ignore.

During this same period, Iranian officials privately told officials of two other countries that they desired better relations with the United States; in one case they noted the possibility of hostage releases. LTC North noticed both these approaches and by July 17 had secured approval for positive responses to Iran through those countries. (SSIC 1/29/87)

JUL 7 - Telephone records from the Salvadoran phone company, ANTEL, show a phone call on this date to Southern Air Transport in Miami, (305)871-5171, from the San Salvador safehouse where Luis Posada (aka Ramon Medina), Felix Rodriguez (Max Gomez) and other Cuban-Americans involved in the contra resupply operation stayed. This house, one of three such safehouses, is located at Number 1, Avenida El Mirador Norte, in the Escalon section of San Salvador, and the telephone was registered to Comercial San Jorge. ANTEL records made available to reporters cover the Posada/Medina safehouse for the end of June 1986 and the full month of July 1986. In addition to the specific phone calls listed below from this safehouse, the records also show 31 calls during this period to private numbers in Florida, and 12 calls to Costa Rica, most to the same number, 506-283-037. (ANTEL phone records, 8/8/86)

JUL 8 - It is reported that the contras, through currency conversions in two Miami bank accounts, sold dollars provided under the U.S. nonlethal aid package for profit and put cnthe extra money into their "general funds." (AP 7/8/86)

- U.S. Customs Service agents serve subpoenas and search warrants on employees of the Israeli Ministry of Defense Procurement Mission in New York City and three U.S. companies. The focus of the investigation, at least the third in the last fourteen months involving possible illegal exports to Israel, is the alleged sale of cluster bomb technology to representatives of Israel. The U.S. has banned such exports since Israel reportedly used the weapons, which are intended for defensive purposes only, in the 1982 invasion of Lebanon. The companies under investigation are Vector Corp. in Marion, Iowa; Bexco International in Cedar Rapids, Iowa; and Assembly Machines Inc. in Erie, PA. U.S. Ambassador to Tel Aviv Thomas Pickering meets with Prime Minister

Shimon Peres and gives him a letter outlining the Customs Service allegations and a list of questions for him to answer concerning the affair. In early August, the subpoenas of Israeli citizens are dropped in return for Israeli government cooperation in the matter. (WP 7/9/86 & 8/6/86)

- According to the CIA/IG report, Cave obtained the following letter, purportedly written by Ghorbanifar to his Iranian contact, on 8 July 1986. (CIA/IG Chronology 27) Clair George told the Board that, while Cave began his involvement as an interpreter, he "became a player. . . . I'm afraid he got way out there somewhere and we didn't have a string on him every step of the way." (George 49-50) (Tower)

"My dear and esteemed brother [B]:

"After greetings, I feel it is necessary to state the following points with respect to the American issue, which for a year has taken up everyone's time and has become very unpleasant:

"If you remember, we had some very lengthy telephone conversations Monday and Tuesday [30 June and 1 July]. I stressed the fact that the essence of a [good] policy is to identify the moment, exploit the occasion, and recognize the proper and appropriate time in order to take advantage of them and to get concessions. I said that Friday was the 4th of July and the celebration of the 210th anniversary of the American Independence as well as the 100th anniversary celebration of the Statue of Liberty in New York. For this reason, there was going to be a very elaborate and majestic celebration titled 'Liberty Day' in New York at the foot of the Statue of Liberty. The Americans were calling it the Celebration of the Century; and the US President and the President of France will be hosting the celebration; for it is the day of liberty and celebration of freedom. [I said] that if we could mediate for the release of the American hostage clergyman on Thursday, 3 July, and he could attend these celebrations—as he is clergy—we could exploit it and benefit from it a great deal; we could get the Americans to accept many of our demands. Naturally, as usual, nobody paid any attention to my suggestions. The Americans were expecting us to take at least these steps for them. Anyway, the Americans are saying that last year after the Iranians mediated the release of an American clergy, M. Mier [sic] who was kept hostage in Beirut, they [the Americans]—as a goodwill gesture and as a first step—made available to Iranians 504 [sic]

TOW missiles. Also, during the year since then, they [the Americans] have taken the following positive and constructive steps as a sign of goodwill and utmost respect toward the Islamic Republic. However, in return, the Iranians have not made the slightest attempt nor shown the smallest sign —even discreetly—to improve relations:

"1. After the clergyman's release, whenever and wherever American officials talked about countries supporting and nurturing terrorism, they did not include Iran; also, the Chief Justice of the Supreme Court [translator believes he means Attorney General of the United States] in an official interview, mentioned Libya, Syria, South Yemen, and Cuba as the countries supporting, protecting, and strengthening terrorism.

"2. With regard to the Iran-Iraq war, the US Department of State, in an official note, strongly condemned the use of chemical weapons.

"3. The American Ambassador at the United Nations was the first person to vote for official condemnation of Iraq for the use of chemical weapons.

"4. [Issuance] of an official announcement terming the Mojahedin-e Khalq Organization terrorist and Marxist; the [issuance] of a circular to the Congress and to all American firms and institutions, and banning of any and all types of assistance to the opponents of the regime of the Islamic Republic of Iran.

"5. Opposition to the decrease in oil prices; so much so that Mr. George Bush, the Vice President, on two occasions during speeches and interviews announced that the reduction in oil prices would ultimately be harmful for the United States and that oil prices should increase.

"6. Dispatch of two US planes with more than 1,000 TOW missiles on two separate occasions, at cost price.

"7. Dispatch of a high-ranking 5-man team from the White House and the Defense Department for a meeting with B and his accompanying team, and the provision of certain preliminary military data on Iraq with an agreement that more complete and comprehensive data should be made available in subsequent meetings and after the final agreement.

"8. Arrival of a very high-ranking delegation from the White House headed by Robert McFarlane, Mr. Reagan's special assistant and advisor, together with five high-ranking civilian and military officials for a 4-day stay in Tehran; they brought more than one-fifth of the requested spare parts for missile systems; further, some complete military, technical, and intelligence information and data with regard to Soviet threats against Iran, and the military and political—[sic] of that government [USSR] with full details on [plan for] invasion of Iran; Soviet activities in Kurdestan, Baluchestan, and Iraq; [Soviet] cooperation with opponents of the Islamic regime; and above all, a clear and explicit announcement by the US Government that it considers the regime of the Islamic Republic stable and it respects that regime. Also, that the USG does not in any way oppose that regime; and promises that it has no intentions or plans to bring it under its [sphere of] influence, create changes, or interfere in its internal affairs. Later, Minutes [sic] of the meeting and agreement were submitted, reflecting the goodwill and total cooperation of the United States with the Islamic Republic; specifically with respect to the war and other problems threatening this regime. [You may read these Minutes again.]

"The Americans are saying: 'We were treated in an insulting and unfriendly fashion; they made us return empty-handed while we were ambassadors of friendship and assistance.'

"The gentlemen themselves know the details of the events better than anyone else.

"As you know, the US officials in Tehran reiterated over and over that in exchange for what they proposed, they only expected that our [Iranian] authorities should mediate and use their religious and spiritual influence for the release of the four American hostages who have been kept in Beirut for more than two years; that by this humanitarian deed, they could bring happiness to the families and children waiting to see their fathers; and that they could further be free in every respect to provide us [Iranians] with secret and necessary support.

"They made it very clear that they are fully prepared and willing to provide [Iran] with all types of political, economic, and weapons cooperation and accord, on the condition that such assistance should not be considered part of [a bargain for the release of] hostages; but rather it should be considered a goodwill and better relations and friendship gesture by the United States.

"Prior to the arrival of the US team and myself in Tehran

on 25 May 1986, there was full agreement that upon arrival of the high-ranking US delegation in Tehran, bringing some of the requested items, the Iranian authorities would begin immediately mediating for the release of all American hostages in Beirut all, together and collectively. And that after this, the remaining items requested by Iran would arrive in Tehran. The US team would stay in Tehran until the rest of equipment [items]—among them the large HP radars—also arrived in Tehran. Further, there was supposed to be official agreement and commitment for providing the rest of Iran's weapon needs, as well as secret agreements in some political and economic areas. The Americans were to leave Iran only after all of these stages had been completed.

"However, although the 10-man US team and their giant special aircraft was in Tehran for four days, unfortunately nothing was accomplished. You well remember that on the last day of the stay, His Excellency [redacted] in the presence of you and another gentleman, insisted several times that everyone should agree for the time being about the mediation for the release of two hostages. But Mr. McFarlane did not accept this and stated that they were there [in Tehran] and were prepared to discuss and solve some basic and strategically important issues and to stand by you [Iranians]; all of these must be solved together, so that no problem remain and the way could thus be paved for everything once and for all.

"I must [at this point] remind you that in 1985 there were 45,703 deaths on US highways, and that during the same year, 1,301 Americans died as a result of choking on their food [gluttons]. Thus, we must not put the Americans under such pressure that they end up including these four [hostages] as part of the above statistics, and we end up losing this historic opportunity which has combined one whole year of hardship and difficulties with some heavy expenses for me.

"You know that this matter has been tangled for 45 days. I can assure you that the Americans neither can nor will be able to take another step along this path unless we should at least carry out as a preliminary and beginning step that which was [redacted] was insisting upon. I also believe that whatever we want to do and whatever decision you make, must be carried out within the next 2-3 days.

"Now, there are only three solutions; I have totally convinced them [Americans] and they are in total agreement with all of the three solutions. I believe and strongly recommend that the first solution be chosen:

"1. You should immediately pay in cash the amount for the items that have already arrived, including the remaining 177 items. The money for the 240 items, as well as the money for the two HP's, should be paid through the London branch of Bank Melli Iran on 30 July, that is, in 21 days.

"2. That same evening, you should mediate and release two of the hostages.

"3. Within a maximum of 24 hours after this, the Americans would deliver all of the 240 items, that is approximately 4,000 spare parts and two giant HP's at Bandar Abbas.

"4. Immediately after receiving all of the above items and their full inspection, you should take immediate steps for the release of the remaining two hostages. Also, for humanitarian and religious reasons, you should mediate for identification of the burial place of the hostage who died last year [W. Buckley] so that his body can be transferred to the United States to be buried next to his mother as was his wish.

"5. Seventy-two hours after the delivery and receipt of all the 240 items of [HAWKs] and the two HP's and the release of all hostages, a high-ranking US team will be present in Geneva, Frankfurt, or Tehran—as you wish—and will take careful steps with respect to providing the proposed Minutes of the meeting and will make a commitment. Further, the team will study the matter of the remaining HP's and helicopter spare parts and all other needs and requirements of the Iranian army. In this regard, agreement as to the date for their delivery could be specified. Meanwhile, they [Americans] are ready to send immediately technical experts and equipment for testing and repairing them.

"Second solution, which would require more time and would entail more headaches:

"1. You should pay in cash the amount for the items that have already arrived, including the remaining 177 items. The money for the 240 items should be paid through issuance of a check via London branch of Bank Melli Iran on 20 July, that is in 11 days.

"2. That same evening, you should mediate and release one of the hostages.

"3. Within 12 hours after this, they will deliver all of the 240 items in Tehran.

"4. Immediately after receiving fully and accurately all of.

the 240 items in Tehran, you must mediate and release the same day two more hostages and must pay the money for the two HP's.

"5. Within a maximum of 24 hours after the release of these two hostages and the payment of the amount for the HP's, the radar equipment will be delivered at Bandar Abbas.

"6. After the complete and correct delivery of the two HP's, you will mediate and take steps for the release of the last [fourth] hostage as well as the body of William Buckley.

"7. Seventy-two hours after receiving all of the 240 items of [HAWKs] and the two HP's and the release of American hostages, a high-ranking US team will be present in Geneva, Frankfurt, or Tehran—as you wish—and will take careful steps with respect to providing the proposed minutes of the meeting and will make a commitment. Further, it will study the matter of the remaining HP's and helicopter spare parts and all other needs and requirements of the Iranian army. And in this regard, agreement can be made as to the specific date for their delivery. Meanwhile, they [Americans] are ready to immediately send technical experts and equipment for testing and repairing them.

"8. I personally and on my honor—whatever way you deem it proper—would guarantee and make commitment that immediately after carrying out the last phase—that is, after the delivery of the 240 items and the two HP's and after the release of all American hostages, within a maximum of one month—I shall deliver in Tehran 3,000 TOW missiles at a cost of $38.5 million which is the cost to the Americans themselves, plus 200 Sidewinder missiles mounted on F-4 and F-5 planes, again at cost. Naturally, [only] if you make the money available to me—not like this [last] time when you did not leave anything for me.

"Third solution:

"Since I have tried to be a mediator for good, I do not wish to be a cause of misdeeds. I have tried to bring [the two sides] together and create friendship, and not to cause further division, hostility, and alienation. Thus, if you do not find either of the above-mentioned solutions advisable, return immediately the exact items that they brought so that the whole case can be closed and we can pretend nothing happened, as if 'no camel arrived and no camel left' [old Persian saying]. Everyone can thus go his own way. Hopefully, in the future, [when] conditions and circumstances are once again suitable, steps can be taken. I mean we should not 'put a bone inside a wound' [another old Persian saying, meaning not to make things worse]. There is no reason for it. If I have encountered great difficulties and many material, spiritual, and prestige problems solely due to friendship, good intentions, honesty, belief, and trust, it was simply for the love of [my] country and my friendship with you and it does not matter. I hope good and generous God will compensate me for it, as my intentions were all good.

"I beg you to take a speedy and decisive step and make a quick decision on this issue, for the good and the welfare of the Islamic Republic.

"Thanking you and with highest respect,

"Manuchehr Qorbanifar

"signed 9 July 1986" (Tower)

JUL 10 - In the middle of July, two senior foreign government officials visited Tehran. One of them reported a feeler by Rafsanjani to the effect that the Americans knew what had to be done to improve relations. North wrote Poindexter on July 10 that:

"[y]ou will recall that several months ago the [name deleted] initiated direct discussions with the Iranians on the matter of our hostages. This is the third such overture they have made on our behalf. In addition to the information in the cable. . . . [of the [country deleted] Embassy in Washington] made the following comments:

"—The perception of a Soviet threat to Iran is a concern that has reached the highest levels of the Revolutionary Government.

"—There are obviously members of the Iranian Government who foresee the possibility that 'given the right conditions' Iran could 'cause the release' of the American hostages.

"—Although none of the Iranian officials responded positively to [Director General of the [country deleted] Foreign Ministry's] suggestion that direct secret discussions be initiated between the U.S. and Iran, it was not rejected. Rafsanjani noted that "the U.S. Government knows what it should do."

"—The [country deleted] have clearly explained to the Iranians that they are reporting directly back to the American Government on these contacts.

"From this and earlier meetings, it is apparent that the

[country deleted] have been able to establish and maintain a direct link at the highest levels of the Iranian Government. Given the stalemate on other initiatives and our inability to ensure that we are in direct contact with responsible Iranian officials we may be able to use this most recent [country deleted] visit to Tehran as an opportunity to establish such a contact. [Name deleted], who has acted as our conduit for these matters, has suggested that they have the ability to pass a secure communication directly to Rafsanjani through their ambassador in Tehran.

"It is important to note that, during the meeting, [name deleted] pointedly asked whether we had conveyed our willingness to eventually normalize U.S.-Iranian relations when our "officials were in Tehran." A direct response was avoided and [name deleted] was advised that our willingness to talk with the Iranians is "common knowledge." It is disturbing that the visit may also be common knowledge. [On June 29, 1986, a column by Jack Anderson and Dale Van Atta in the Washington Post stated: "We can reveal that the secret negotiations over arms supply and release of American hostages have involved members of the National Security Council and a former official of the CIA."]

North proposed sending the following message:

"We have reported the results of the June 27-29 discussions to the American Government and they have asked us to relay the following message in highest confidence. The highest levels of the American Government are prepared to open direct and private discussions with responsible officials who are empowered to speak on behalf of the Iranian Government. They have asked us to tell you that under the right conditions, the American Government is prepared to take steps leading to a normalization of relations between your Government and theirs. If you are agreeable, a senior American official is prepared to meet with responsible representatives of your government at the time and place of your choosing. They are prepared, as you have suggested, to make an appropriate gesture of goodwill. (North to Poindexter, 7/10/86, "Non-Log") (Tower)

JUL 10-11 - The freighter Erria docks in Szczecin (Stettin), Poland, where it takes on 158 tons of AK-47 rifles. Tom Parlow, who is assisting in North-directed operations involving the Erria, says the purchaser is Energy Resources International. Eight days later, the ship arrives in Setubal,

Portugal, where it picks up another load of weapons. It announces its destination from there as Yemen. (LAT 1/21/87 & 2/13/87; AFP 1/24/87)

JUL 11 - The U.S. Attorney's office in Miami discloses that it believes supporters of the contras illegally shipped at least one load of weapons to the rebels from Fort Lauderdale-Hollywood airport in 1985. (MH 7/12/86)

- Three phone calls are placed from the Posada/Medina safehouse in San Salvador to Stanford Technology Trading Group International (Richard Secord's office) in Virginia, (703)356-4801. (ANTEL phone records, 8/8/86)

JUL 13 - A new contra program will be run by the CIA, according to a news report. Army Colonel William C. Comee Jr., who has just finished a year as commander of the U.S.-Honduran military exercises, will reportedly act as program coordinator. (WP 7/13/86)

- Two phone calls are placed from the Posada/Medina safehouse in San Salvador to Richard Secord's home number in Virginia, (703)560-4931. (ANTEL phone records, 8/8/86)

- Fred C. Ikle, under secretary of defense for policy and a central decision-maker on Nicaragua-related matters, says in an interview that U.S. military spending against Nicaragua will be handled largely by the CIA and will go beyond the $70 million voted by the House. The money, he asserts, will go toward training, primarily in guerrilla tactics, and military hardware ranging from surface-to-air missiles to bullets. (WP 7/13/86)

- It is reported that joint U.S.-Latin American exercises in Central America that came to an end in April 1986 were designed to include at least 30,000 American troops and involved the construction of "temporary facilities," including nine airfields and two radar stations. The report also said that a U.S.-Honduras security pact provided for American defense of Honduras in case of Nicaraguan attack. (CRS "War Powers Resolution: Presidential Compliance" 12/22/86)

JUL 15 - Contributions appear to have been channeled through a series of non-profit organizations that LtCol North apparently had a hand in organizing. A diagram found in LtCol North's bank safe links some of these organizations to

bank accounts controlled by Richard Secord and others
known to be involved in purchasing and shipping arms to the
Contras.

Other documents and evidence suggest that private contributions for the Contras were eventually funneled into
"Project Democracy," a term apparently used by LtCol
North to describe a network of secret bank accounts and
individuals involved in Contra resupply and other activities.
In a message to VADM Poindexter dated July 15, 1986,
LtCol North described "Project Democracy" assets as worth
over $4.5 million. They included six aircraft, warehouses,
supplies, maintenance facilities, ships, boats, leased houses,
vehicles, ordinance, munitions, communications equipment,
and a 6520-foot runway. The runway was in fact a secret
airfield in Costa Rica. We have no information linking the
activities described herein as "Project Democracy" with the
National Endowment for Democracy (NED). The latter was
created in 1983 by Congressional act and is funded by legislation. Its purpose is to strengthen Democratic institutions
around the world through private, non-governmental efforts.
NED grew out of an earlier Administration public initiative
to promote democracy around the world, which came to be
known as "Project Democracy." It appears that North later
adopted the term to refer to his own covert operations network. We believe this to be the only link between the NED
and North's activity. (Tower)

MID-JUL - According to the head of CIA's Central American Task Force, the Nicaraguan resistance started to incur
debt after they used up the $27 million; by the middle
of July 1986, that debt amounted to over $2.5 million.
(H/CATF 38) (Tower)

JUL 15 - A phone call is placed from the Posada/Medina
safehouse in San Salvador to Stanford Technology in Virginia. (ANTEL phone records, 8/8/86)

- According to a lobbying registration form filed with the
Clerk of the U.S. House of Representatives on this date, the
Council on Democracy, Education, and Assistance, Inc., a
501(c)(4) tax-exempt organization, is paying Bruce Cam-
eron $6,000 per month to lobby for contra aid. The docu-
ment shows that the lobbying is financed with $40,000 from
Sentinel, a Carl "Spitz" Channell organization. (Report Pursuant to Federal Regulation of Lobbying Act, 7/15/86)

- North's tour of duty at the NSC ends. Poindexter tries first to relieve North of his duties, then to put contra matters under the control of NSC staff members Kenneth deGraffenreid, Raymond Burghardt and Vince Cannistraro, a report says. After concerned calls from conservative lawmakers and a story by columnists Rowland Evans and Robert Novak which describes North's loss as "a symbol of the degradation of the once-mighty NSC staff," Poindexter accedes to North's requests to stay on and continue his work on contra issues. NSC sources speculate that Poindexter didn't fire North either at this opportunity or when he reportedly offered to resign in December 1985 (see entry), when Poindexter succeeded McFarlane, in part because the two were linked by the Iran arms sales and profit diversions. (WP 2/25/87)

- In the middle of July, Poindexter asked to see North. After the meeting, North wrote:

"The opportunity to discuss the Central America issue with you was welcome and at the same time, disturbing. In view of last night's CBS piece and this morning's appalling Washington TIMES item, I can understand why you may well have reservations about both my involvement in Nicaragua policy and even my continued tenure here. Since returning a few minutes ago I have been told that even my luncheon engagement with my sister yesterday is in question. Under these circumstances, and given your intention that I extricate myself entirely from the Nicaragua issue, it probably wd be best if I were to move on as quietly, but expeditiously as possible. I want you to know that it is, for me deeply disappointing to have lost your confidence, for I respect you, what you have tried to do and have enjoyed working with you on a number of issues important to our nation. On the plus side of the ledger we have had a close relationship on several initiatives that could not have been accomplished without absolute trust between two professionals. At the same time you should not be expected to retain on your staff someone who you suspect could be talking to the media or whom you believe to be too emotionally involved in an issue to be objective in the development of policy options and recommendations. I know in my heart that this is not the case, but as I said in our discussion yesterday, we live in a world of perceptions, not realities. I have taken the liberty of forwarding to you a memo transmitted two weeks ago which I wd like to be sure you have had a chance to see—mostly because it predates the current controversy, I want to be sure that you do indeed know that I have and will continue to tell you the truth as I see it—for I deeply believe that this is the only honorable thing to do. That this, and the relationships established in the region over the past five years are no longer enough to enable me to serve in the various policy fora on Nicaragua is, for me, unfortunate. Nonetheless, I consider myself to have been blessed to have had the chance to so serve for as long as I did. Finally, to end on a substantive note, you should be aware that Gen Galvin will be here for DRB sessions on Mon & Tues next week and wd vy much like to have the chance to meet privately with you. He has suggested any time after 1630 on Tues, but is amenable to yr schedule as long as he will not have to absent himself from DRB sessions. Given the controversy that rages over the CINC SOUTHCOM role in the project, I strongly recommend that you see him if at all possible. (North PROF note to Poindexter, 7/15/86, 12:21:30)

Poindexter replied:

"Now you are getting emotional again. It would help if you would call Roger Fontaine and Jerry O'Leary and tell them to call off the dogs. Tell them on deep background, off the record, not to be published that I just wanted to lower your visibility so you wouldn't be such a good target for the Libs. As it has worked out both you and Vince will represent NSC on Elliot's group. Don't go intodetail [sic]. I do not want you to leave and to be honest cannot afford to let you go. By the way they are making a big mistake by calling Rod a soft liner. He disagrees with Stan Turner and Bernie as much as I do.

"NEW SUBJECT: I can see Jack Galvin this afternoon. Let me know how the calls go." (Poindexter PROF notes to North, 7/15/86, 14:06; 14:07:02; 14:09:02) The matter was straightened out as far as concerned North's relationship with Poindexter later in the month. (See North PROF note to Poindexter, 7/23/86, 15:05:39; Poindexter PROF note to North, [7/23/86])

Afterward, North wrote Poindexter about the need to turn over certain material in Central America to the CIA.

"We are rapidly approaching the point where the PROJECT DEMOCRACY assets in CentAm need to be turned over to CIA for use in the new program. The toal (sic or sp) value of the assets (six aircraft, warehouses, supplies, maintenance facilities, ships, boats, leased houses, vehicles, ordnance, munitions, communications equipment, and a 6520' runway on property owned by a PRODEM proprietary) is over $4.5M.

"All of the assets—and the personnel—are owned/paid by overseas companies with no U.S. connection. All of the equipment is in first rate condition and is already in place. It wd be ludicrous for this to simply disappear just because CIA does not want to be "tainted" with picking up the assets and then have them spend $8M-10M of the $100M to replace it weeks or months later. Yet, that seems to be the direction they are heading, apparently based on NSC guidance.

"If you have already given Casey instructions to this effect, I wd vy much like to talk to you about it in hopes that we can reclama [sic] the issue. All seriously believe that immediately after the Senate vote the DRF will be subjected to a major Sandinista effort to break them before the U.S. aid can become effective.

PRODEM currently has the only assets available to support the DRF and the CIA's most ambitious estimate is 30 days after a bill is signed before their own assets will be available. This will be a disaster for the DRF if they have to wait that long. Given our lack of movement on other funding options, and Elliot [sic]/Allen's plea for PRODEM to get food to the resistance ASAP, PRODEM will have to borrow at least $2M to pay for the food.

That's O.K., and Dick is willing to do so tomorrow—but only if there is reasonable assurance that the lenders can be repaid. The only way that the $2M in food money can be repaid is if CIA purchases the $4.5M+ worth of PRODEM equipment for about $2.25M when the law passes. You should be aware that CIA has already approached PRODEM's chief pilot to ask him where they (CIA) can purchase more of the C-135K A/C. The chief pilot told them where they can get them commercially from the USAF as excess— the same way PRODEM bought them under proprietary arrangements. It is just unbelievable. If you wish I can send you a copy of the PROJECT DEMOCRACY status report which includes a breakdown of assets. It is useful, nonattributable reading." (North PROF note to Poindexter, reply to note of 7/15/86, 14:07) (Tower)

JUL 17 - Telephone records from the Salvadoran phone company, ANTEL, show a phone call on this date to Southern Air Transport in Miami, (305)871-5171, from the San Salvador safehouse where contra resupply pilot William Cooper and other crewmembers were based. This house, one of three such safehouses, is located at Number B-1, Calle San Rafael, in the Escalon section of San Salvador, and the telephone was registered to Raul Salvador Rodriguez Porth. ANTEL records made available to reporters cover the Cooper safehouse for the end of July 1986 and the full month of August 1986. In addition to the specific phone calls listed below from this safehouse, the records also show 10 calls in August to a Pennsylvania number apparently that of Corporate Air Services, (717)786-1039, 5 calls to Costa Rican numbers, and 9 calls to private numbers in Florida. (ANTEL phone records, 9/8/86, p. 4834)

- During this . . . period, Iranian officials privately told officials of two other countries that they desired better relations with the United States; in one case they noted the possibility of hostage releases. LTC North noticed both these approaches and by July 17 had secured approval for positive responses to Iran through those countries.

In mid-July, there was some progress. It was made clear to Iran through multiple channels that there would be no further movement by the United States unless a hostage was released. According to documents received by the Committee, the Iranians accepted this and took steps to arrange for the release of a hostage. Iran also agreed to pay $4 million for the HAWK parts that had been delivered on McFarlane's plane.

During the same period, according to documents received by the Committee, the United States was developing an alternative channel of communications with Iranian officials. In mid-July, Albert Hakim and a U.S. Government employee met with an acquaintance of Hakim's who was interested in putting together arms deals. The acquaintance knew of an Iranian official who wanted to contact the U.S. Government and talk about arms sales. Hakim had things arranged so that the Iranian would be steered toward him, rather than toward participants in the existing channel.

By late July, LTC North reported to Admiral Poindexter that there had been meetings with some people to see whether they could become intermediaries; it is not clear whether he was referring to the mid-July meeting or to a later one. Hakim was pleased because his acquaintance was willing also to consider deals for non-lethal items; Hakim reportedly stated that he wanted to pursue that avenue irrespective of whether the U.S. Government used the channel. One proposal that later bore fruit was for some medical supplies to be sold at cost. (SSIC 1/29/87)

- In his memorandum to Poindexter, dated July 17, North indicated that Poindexter approved sending this message. (Regarding U.S. support for "normalization of relations" between an unnamed government and the government of Iran, see July 10 entries) (Tower)

JUL - Cyrus Hashemi, Iranian arms merchant and Customs Service sting agent in the Bar-Am/Evans case, is found dead in New York. (WP 1/6/87)

JUL 18 - Contra suppliers and pilots John McRainey and William J. Cooper buy a C-123K plane for $250,000 in two cashier's checks drawn from the Eaux-Vives branch of Credit Suisse, according to the seller, Ascher Ward of Sepulveda, Calif. The plane is eventually used for resupply missions. (PI 2/6/87 & 3/6/87)

- Notes made by the NSC Executive Secretary indicate that on July 18, VADM Poindexter informed the President of the latest communications with the Iranian interlocutors. (Tower)

JUL 19 - The freighter Erria docks at Setubal harbor, Portugal. There it takes on 6,916 boxes of munitions weighing 210 tons, paid for by Energy Resources International. Its ultimate destination with these weapons is listed in one set of port documents as Yemen, but the ship's cargo manifest lists Puerto Barrios, Guatemala. In 1985, the Erria claimed Puerto Barrios as its destination on one trip, but instead the ship went to Honduras where weapons it was carrying were delivered to contra forces (see May 11, 1985 entry). On this occasion, the Erria does not actually get underway for two months, twice setting out from Setubal only to return claiming mechanical problems. Port authorities are later skeptical of these excuses since the ship does not even approach a dock the second time. Some Portuguese officials suspect the crew of purposely delaying its departure, perhaps even sabotaging their own ship for the purpose. Tom Parlow says later that this explanation "could be possible, yes . . . I won't deny that." In mid-September (see September 13 entry), the ship docks in Cherbourg, France, where its cargo is unloaded and apparently transferred to another freighter, the Iceland Saga. (LAT 1/21/87 & 2/13/87; AFP 1/24/87)

- On or around this date, Amiram Nir informs the Iranians that he will cancel the arms-for-hostages deal if they do not produce evidence that hostages will be released. Nir's statement, made "about 10 days" before a meeting he has with Bush in Jerusalem on July 29 (see entry), comes at a time when the Israelis believe the deal "would just die if we didn't push forward to see what could be delivered." (Fuller memo 7/29/86 in WP 2/8/87)

JUL 20 - Iranian Prime Minister Mousavi calls Nir or others participating in the arms-for-hostages deal to announce that Iran is taking steps to release one American, "the priest," Nir tells Bush at their July 29 meeting. After the priest, Mousavi says, another hostage will be freed, "Jacobsen," at which time he says that Iran should be given "some equipment." Nir says later that no denial or approval of the deal is given and that the Iranians are told there will be no discussion of an agreement until a release is made. (Fuller memo 7/29/86 in WP 2/8/87)

JUL 21 - LtCol North, Mr. Cave, and Mr. Nir met with Mr. Ghorbanifar in London. They discussed the release of the hostages in exchange for the HAWK spare parts that remained undelivered from the May mission to Tehran. (Tower)

"[Available information] indicate[s] that the decision to release Father Jenco was made in Tehran on or about July 21. (North to Poindexter 7/26/86) (Tower)

- [T]he United States obtained a clear indication that a hostage might be freed soon. North reported that:
"We have just been told by Nir that 'the Iranians claim to have taken action this morning to release one hostage.' . . . I have asked CIA to alert [appropriate personnel in] Beirut and no others to the possibility in order to preclude a repeat of Jul[y] 4. We have not put any other USG assets on alert. RELATED SUBJECT. Absent further developments on this approach, George Cave will proceed to Frankfurt to meet w/ Tabatabai [According to North's desk calendar, North met

"Tabatabaie," possibly with Senator Helms, on June 27] the cousin of the man I met w/ here. T is allegedly well connected to Rafsanjani and several other of the so called "pragmatists." Purpose of the meeting is to determine T's real access and willingness to act as an interlocutor. If bona fides prove out he could also be used to pass the same message we sent back via [a third country]. In that regard, who was [that country's emissary] to give our message to on the Iranian side? (North PROF note to Poindexter, 7/21/86, 18:04:38) Poindexter informed North the same day that [the emissary] was to pass the message to "the Iranian FM [Foreign Minister]. Don't tell anybody including Cave about this." (Poindexter PROF note to North, 7/21/86, 20:10:14) North in turn replied:

"Roger, WILCO. Am concerned, however that if tonight's [information] does indeed bear the fruit promised, that we may be confusing an already difficult situation. Maybe that's not as bad as it might otherwise be since those guys will all get the message eventually if anything develops. (North PROF note to Poindexter, 7/21/86, 20:20:23) (Tower)

- [North wrote in a memorandum for Poindexter to give to the President on July 26] [Available information] indicate[s] that the decision to release Father Jenco was made in Tehran on or about July 21. [Tab I to North to Poindexter] [see July 26 entry]

"[We received information on 21 July that the Iranian official] had taken action with other Iranian authorities to release one hostage. To reinforce this commitment, he transferred $4M to a West European bank to pay his European intermediary for the HAWK spare parts removed from our mission aircraft in May. [A memorandum from the Director of Central Intelligence, attached by North to a memorandum for Poindexter and the President; see July 26 entry] (Tower)

JUL 22-23 - According to Nir, a message is intercepted on either of these two dates between Tehran and those guarding American hostages. He says that movement of three captives takes place on July 25 (see entry). (Fuller memo 7/29/86 in WP 2/8/87)

JUL 23 - "Our Israeli point of contact advised us that 'if, as we hope, a hostage is released, it will be Jenco.'" It was also on this date that the Israeli point of contact (Amiram Nir) told the Iranian intermediary in Europe that the USG was breaking off all contact on this matter. [Tab I to North to Poindexter] (see July 26 entry) (Tower)

- On Wednesday, July 23, when no hostage had been released, Ghorbanifar was instructed to inform [the Iranian official] that "the deal was off." [A memorandum from the Director of Central Intelligence, attached by North to a memorandum for Poindexter and the President; see July 26 entry] (Tower)

JUL 24 - The House Armed Services Committee votes 26-6 against legislation that would force Reagan to release all documents and information relating to secret contacts between North and the contras. The legislation was prompted by press reports suggesting North may have violated a congressional ban on aiding the rebels that was in effect between October 1984 and August 1985. (MH 7/25/86)

- "We have also learned that July 24 was a key date in the most recent release:
"—The Iranian Government paid their European intermediary $4M on Thursday, July 24, as partial payment for HAWK missile parts which were removed from our mission aircraft at the end of May. (It is important to note that in order to pay the Israelis for the HAWK missile parts, the Iranian intermediary in Europe borrowed more than $15M and has been under threat of death from his creditors. The Israelis regard this payment as further proof that the Iranians wish to continue the contact with the U.S. on the hostage issue.)
"—Father Jenco has told Ambassador Eagleton . . . in Damascus that it was on Thursday, July 24, that he was separated from the other American hostages in Beirut and delivered to a location in the Bekka Valley. It was from this location in western Lebanon that he was subsequently released to Lebanese authorities, who in turn delivered him to a Syrian military checkpoint. [Tab I to North to Poindexter] (see July 26 entry) (Tower)

- "On Thursday, July 24, the Israelis [obtained information] indicating Jenco would be released. [A memorandum from the Director of Central Intelligence, attached by North to a memorandum for Poindexter and the President; see July 26 entry] (Tower)

- Adolfo Calero writes Spitz Channell "because of our critical situation." The letter says, "Our 22,000 men are in difficult conditions. We need to provide them their basic needs for food in the next 72 days. For that, $100,000 is necessary before the Congressional aid is available. As you understand, your support is urgently needed. I hope you can help us." (Calero letter 7/24/86)

JUL 25 - The White House and State Department strongly deny charges made by recently dismissed ambassador to Honduras John Ferch, that the administration wants a military solution in Nicaragua. (MH 7/26/86)

- Three American hostages are moved from their places of captivity following a message from Tehran to the captors a few days earlier (see Jul 22-23 entry). (Fuller memo 7/29/86 in WP 2/8/87)

- Sometime in July, 1986, an Iranian living in London proposed to Mr. Hakim a second Iranian channel—the relative of a powerful Iranian official. On July 25, Mr. Cave went to London to discuss this possibility. (Tower)

- On July 25, Poindexter wrote North:
Bob Oakley must have told Shultz about a discussion that took place in OSG. Shultz called me about a Cave meeting in the next few days. I vaguely remember that you told me something about this. George just wanted to be sure that we did not have any disconnect between what [the emissary] will be telling them and what Cave tells them. (Poindexter PROF note to North, 7/25/86, 11:33:17) In his reply, North reminded Poindexter where the various communications stood.

"Cave is meeting w/ [a relation of a powerful Iranian official] and Tabatabai to determine level of access and current political sentiments toward the present regieme [sic]. He was prepared to pass a message identical to the one we sent thru [a friendly foreign official] but I held it back when you advised that the FoMin, not Rafsanjani was to be the recipient. We have likewise sent no message back thru [the other friendly government]. At the present, the only active courier is [the emissary of the first country] and the only recipient is the FM. Cave will report his findings when he returns from Frankfurt and we can then determine whether we wish to use any of these new contacts as interlocutors. Also related: Nir and [the official in the Iranian PM's office] are both out of their respective pockets. Charlie agrees that it is entirely possible that they are meeting in Europe. (North PROF note to Poindexter, 7/25/86, 18:43:42) (Tower)

- Workers at Sekman Aviation Corp., located at Miami International Airport near the headquarters of Southern Air Transport, are asked to weigh the C-123K that would later be shot down over Nicaragua. The fees for the weighing are paid by Southern Air, according to Sarino Costanzo, Sekman Aviation's secretary and director. Southern Air would later have "no comment" regarding the landing and weighing fees and would stick to its story that it had serviced the C-123K, but did not own it. (MH 10/10/86)

JUL 26 - The Rev. Lawrence Jenco is taken from his place of captivity, placed into a trunk and driven to a village in the Bekka Valley where he is released. The White House is again disappointed that additional hostages are not freed. (WP 12/7/86; Fuller memo 7/29/86 in WP 2/8/87)

- VADM Poindexter briefed the President on the Jenco release that same day over a secure telephone. He used a memorandum prepared by LtCol North that claimed the release was "undoubtedly" a result of Mr. McFarlane's trip in May and the continuing contacts thereafter. A July 26, 1986 memorandum to VADM Poindexter from Director Casey reached the same conclusion. (Tower)

- On July 26, Father Lawrence Jenco was released. McFarlane wrote Poindexter: "Bravo Zulu on Jenco's release. Do you correlate this to the anxious calls that have come since the trip to Iran and our insistence that they move first? Or is it really a Syrian effort?" (McFarlane PROF note to Poindexter, 7/26/86)

North apparently received a copy of this message. He wrote McFarlane: "[t]he bottom line is that this is the direct result of your mission and neither the Syrians nor a nonexistent Casey trip had anything to do with it." (North PROF note to McFarlane, 7/29/86, 20:36:04 (reply to note of 7/26/86, 13:51)

Poindexter explained how it had come about in his reply:

"Thank you. It is directly related to your trip out there. The Syrians only entered at the last minute. Gorba finally convinced [his Tehran contact] after numerous telephone calls that they should come forward with a humanitarian gesture. Gorba either on his own or as Nir's agent is out a lot of money that he put up front for the parts. [The Tehran contact] has been unwilling to pay him since all of the material has not been delivered. Gorga [sic] has cooked up a story that if Iran could make a humanitarian gesture then the US would deliver the rest of the parts and then Iran would release the rest of the hostages. Of course we have not agreed to any such plan. Nir and Gorba are in London. [The Iranian official] is enroute [sic]. I am trying to decide whether to send Ollie and George Cave. The problem is that if parts aren't delivered, Gorba will convince [his Tehran contact] that we welched on the deal. Although through several conversations Cave has repeated to [the Tehran contact] what our position has been—all of the hostages out before anything else moves[,] I have aboutdecided [sic] to send Ollie to make certain our position is clear. It seems to me that we may have some leverage over [the official in the PM's office] now since he is out on a limb in Tehran and may fear for his own safety." (Poindexter PROF note to McFarlane, 7/26/86, 14:58:07) (Tower)

- McFarlane agreed with Poindexter's approach.

"I agree with your strategy; to send Ollie and to reaffirm our position. Of course the unknowables are: 1. Do they— as they have said—no longer have control over the others (Itend [sic] to believe they do still have control over all; Jenco ought to be able to throw some light on that). 2. Will [the Iranian official] have the courage and influence in Tehran to be able to recommend the release of allwithout [sic] something coming from us. I tend to doubt it. He is a simple [person] way over his head and afraid of his own shadow; not the kind to take risks or to trust foreigners he cannot begin to understand. But it is likely that the higher ups—[a senior foreign policy advisor] (the most senior guy we met) will understand and respect that we are sticking to our original position. Over time, constancy is respected. 3. Finally however, there is the risk that even the higher ups will see no great downside in killing one of the remaining hostages. I'm afraid that's just a risk we will have to run for to do otherwise will lead to a thousand reoccurences [sic] of this scenario in the months ahead as they see that we really can be strung out." (McFarlane PROF note to Poindexter, 7/26/86, 21:53:58) (Tower)

- On July 26, the day of Jenco's release, Poindexter "[b]riefed [the] President on secure phone," (Poindexter, handwritten note on North to Poindexter 7/26/86), from a paper by North on "what we know of the Jenco release," for Poindexter to give the President. (North to Poindexter 7/26/86)

"The release of Father Lawrence Jenco is a second positive step in our protracted and difficult dialogue with the Iranians. Father Jenco's release undoubtedly comes about as a result of Bud McFarlane's trip at the end of May and the continuing direct and indirect contacts we have had with Iranian officials. Our Israeli contacts and the Iranian intermediary in Europe advise that the Iranian Government now expects some reciprocal move on our part—though exactly what, we are uncertain.

"[Available information] indicate[s] that the decision to release Father Jenco was made in Tehran on or about July 21. On Wednesday, July 23, our Israeli point of contact advised us that "if, as we hope, a hostage is released, it will be Jenco." It was also on this date that the Israeli point of contact (Amiram Nir) told the Iranian intermediary in Europe that the USG was breaking off all contact on this matter. We have also learned that July 24 was a key date in the most recent release:

Our next step will be to have two USG representatives meet with the Israeli and Iranians in Europe, if possible, tomorrow in an effort to determine Iranian expectations, This is not a negotiating session, but rather an attempt to maintain contact and, if possible, assess how we should now proceed. To our knowledge, no new Israeli deliveries have occurred and all remaining HAWK missile repair parts are still in a covert depot in Israel. (Tab I to North to Poindexter, 7/26/86) (Tower)

With this memorandum, North attached a memorandum from the Director of Central Intelligence on the "American Hostages." [According to the CIA Inspector General, Charles Allen prepared this memorandum. (CIA/IG Chronology 28]

"After discussing the release of Father Lawrence Jenco with Charlie Allen and Dewey Clarridge, I believe it is important that you have our assessment of this development and prospects for release of additional hostages.

"First, it is indisputable that the Iranian connection actually worked this time, after a series of failures. You will recall that the [Iranian official]-Ghorbanifar connection also resulted in the release of Reverend Weir in September 1985.

Syria played no role either in the release of Weir or Jenco. After the impasse in Tehran over in late May, [the Iranian official] continued to initiate direct contact with one of my officers, George Cave, even though the Iranians had been told that we were no longer interested in pursuing the matter. The fact that [this official] persisted in contacting us indicates his desire to arrange a "deal" with Washington either through Ghorbanifar or, if necessary, with Cave. He also clearly wanted to keep a channel open. Amiram Nir, Special Assistant to the Prime Minister of Israel on Counter-Terrorism, has also played a critical role in a determined effort to force Iran to begin the release of American hostages. He has been supported by Prime Minister Peres and Defense Minister Rabin in this endeavor. In order to make the terms of the arrangements more palatable, Israel, on its own, offered additional arms 'to sweeten the deal.' . . .

"[We received information on 21 July that the Iranian official] had taken action with other Iranian authorities to release one hostage. To reinforce this commitment, he transferred $4M to a West European bank to pay his European intermediary for the HAWK spare parts removed from our mission aircraft in May. On Wednesday, July 23, when no hostage had been released, Ghorbanifar was instructed to inform [the Iranian official] that "the deal was off." On Thursday, July 24, the Israelis [obtained information] indicating Jenco would be released.

"In return for the release, [the Iranian official] probably expects to receive most of the HAWK spare parts not yet delivered, along with additional military equipment that Israel unilaterally has added to the arrangement. Once this equipment is delivered, [the Iranian official] stated that Iran would take action to obtain the release of one more hostage and would pay the remainder of the money owed to the Iranian intermediary for the HAWK spare parts. According to [our information, the Iranian official] apparently expects to then receive the two HAWK radars and the remainder of the HAWK spare parts, although it is unclear as to the timing of these additional deliveries. [The Iranian official], moreover, indicated a willingness to meet with U.S. officials again on these matters, either in Tehran or "somewhere else"—presumably Western Europe.

"This is how we see the current situation:

"—The Ghorbanifar-[Iranian official] connection has

worked for the second time—and another American has been released.

"—Ghorbanifar is an uncontrollable factor, but appears to respond generally to Nir's direction.

"—Nir has every reason to work for further releases of our hostages. Peres and Rabin have put their reputation on the Ghorbanifar-[Iranian official] connection and support Nir fully in his endeavors. There would be a considerable loss of face for Nir and his superiors if the link were broken. This connection appears to be the only hope they have for recovering their own missing soldiers.

"—[The Iranian official] has now acted and likely expects the United States to respond quickly in turn by delivering most of the remaining HAWK spare parts. He probably believes the United States is also supplying the additional military equipment that has been promised.

"—If the deliveries do not occur, [the Iranian official] will lose badly with his superiors in Tehran and matters could turn ugly, especially since the Lebanese Hizballah captors probably are not pleased with the Jenco release.

"—If there is not USG contact as a result of Jenco's release, it is entirely possible that Iran and/or Hizballah could resort to the murder of one or more of the remaining hostages.

"In summary, based on the intelligence at my disposal, I believe that we should continue to maintain the Ghorbanifar-[Iranian official] contact and consider what we may be prepared to do to meet [the Iranian official's] minimum requirements that would lead to release of the rest of the hostages. Although I am not pleased by segmented releases of the American hostages, I am convinced that this may be the only way to proceed, given the delicate factional balance in Iran. I also see resolution of the hostage issue as potentially leading to contacts with moderate factions in Iran that we may be able to deal with in the longer term. (Casey to Poindexter, 7/26/86)

The Maximum Version and the Historical Chronology both state: "On June 10, Majlis speaker Rafsanjani, in a speech in Tehran made guarded reference to Iranian interest in improved relations with the U.S. On July 26, Father Lawrence Jenco was released in the Bekka Valley and found his way to a Syrian military checkpoint." (Maximum Version 8; Historical Chronology 13)

On July 26, North wrote to Poindexter that "Cave is departing Geneva tonight to meet North/Secord in Frankfurt tomorrow (Sunday) morning. Nir and Ghorbanifar depart London tomorrow and have called [Ghorbanifar's Tehran contact] to meet them in Frankfurt, GE, Sunday morning. The purpose of the meeting is to assess Iranian expectations and ability to release the remaining Iranian hostages." (North to Poindexter, 7/26/86) North prepared talking points for the meeting, which Poindexter approved on July 26. (North to Poindexter, 7/26/86)

"— You have seen the President's statement regarding the release of Father Jenco. This is very much in line with what your people had suggested.

"—Our government remains prepared to open direct and private discussions with your government leading to a normalization of relations.

"—We recognize the important role played by your government in the release of Father Jenco and regard this to be a very positive step.

"—It is important that there not be any misunderstandings or false expectations regarding the release of Father Jenco.

"—On every occasion, including our meetings in Tehran, we made it clear that we were not going to barter over the lives of human beings.

"—While we are not empowered to negotiate with you regarding any further deliveries of materiel, it is important that you recognize that the understanding we proposed in Tehran is still operative. We have been instructed to report back to our government any changes to this proposal.

"—We continue to believe that a direct channel of communication, which will prevent misunderstandings is important. As we indicated in Tehran, we are prepared to dispatch a secure satellite communications team to Tehran to facilitate this communication." ("North/Cave Talking Points," Tab II to North to Poindexter, 7/26/86) (Tower)

JUL 27 - A phone call is placed from the Cooper safehouse in San Salvador to Richard Secord's home number in Virginia, (703)560-4931. (ANTEL phone records, 9/8/86, p. 4834)

- North and Cave met with Nir and Ghorbanifar the afternoon of July 27, North reported:

"Lengthy meeting this afternoon with Gorba and Nir followed by discussion with [the official in the Prime Minister's office] via phone. Following are salient points. [The Iranian official] believes he has demonstrated his ability to perform and has expectations we are now prepared to deal. Despite our earlier and current protestations that we want all hostages before we deliver anything, this is clearly not the way they want to proceed. They see clearly that the ball is now in our court. In discussion with [the Iranian official] he repeatedly asked quote—"When are you going to deliver?" While [the official] made no specific threat, he noted that he was under intense pressure and could not totally control events. We will call him back 28 July at 1100 Frankfurt time and urge that he come to Europe for a meeting and to do nothing rash in the meantime. We are trying to make this idea attractive—using [his interest in the U.S. establishing] a 'special account' for him as an incentive. Jenco has expressed a desire to thank the three world leaders responsible for his release. The Pope, The Archbishop of Canterbury and RR. The first two intend to oblige. Can we deliver on the last? Unodir [unless otherwise directed] we will call [the Iranian official] in A.M. and urge him to meet us in Europe ASAP. Since it will take him several days to get authorization to come, we plan to return to D.C. via Pan Am 061 on 28 July and report to JMP in evening. Please advise via this channel if other instructions obtain. Warm regards. North/Cave.

"Bottom line, is that if we want to prevent the death of one of the three remaining hostages, we are going to have to do something."

[Handwritten at bottom: "Put this in a sealed envelope and have Ollie pick it up." JP]

(Document misdated 6/27/86) Another version of this message contained the following:

"P.S. Please call Dewey and tell him George will send hard copy to he [sic] and [C/NE, CIA DO] in A.M. via NIACT." (Id.) Yet another version, bearing the word "done" with a tick mark next to the P.S., has the following handwritten note: "Read all to JMP, except P.S. 7/27 1830." (Id.) (Tower)

LATE JUL - Col. James Steele, commander of U.S. military forces in El Salvador, convenes a meeting with about 10 of the crew members involved in the contra resupply effort.

According to three of those present, Steele asked to hear about problems in the operation and is told about difficulties in security and in getting fuel, spare parts and transportation to Ilopango air force base. He promises to help, and crewmen recall that he terms the effort a "delicate situation" that could be squelched if anyone gets shot down or the operation is found out. To avoid risks of identification, Steele urges them to "leave your billfold at home when you go out," one crewman says. (PI 1/18/87)

- It is reported that Casey secretly traveled to Syria in an attempt to obtain the release of American hostages held in Lebanon. Syria later denies the visit. (CRS "U.S. Intelligence: Issues for Congress, 1986" 1/5/87)

- He [North] wrote McFarlane: "[t]he bottom line is that this [the release of Jenco] is the direct result of your mission and neither the Syrians nor a nonexistent Casey trip had anything to do with it." (North PROF note to McFarlane, 7/29/86, 20:36:04 (reply to note of 7/26/86, 13:51) (See July 26 entry) (Tower)

- In a memorandum to VADM Poindexter dated July 29, 1986, LtCol North recommended that the President approve the immediate shipment of the rest of the HAWK spare parts and a follow-up meeting with the Iranians in Europe. Notes of the NSC Executive Secretary indicate that the President approved this proposal on July 30. Additional spare parts were delivered to Tehran on August 3. (Tower)

- According to North's calendar, North met Jenco in Germany on July 29. On the same day, he set forth his views on the next steps regarding hostages in a memorandum to Poindexter.

"The debrief of Father Jenco has proceeded well and he continues to cooperate fully with our team. Though Jenco's geographic knowledge is understandably limited by the brief time he was in Beirut before he was seized and the conditions of his captivity, he has made every effort to answer our questions.

"[Terry] Waite is accompanying Father Jenco to meetings with the Pope and the Archbishop of Canterbury on Wednesday and Thursday. Father Jenco is sched meet with the President on Friday, August 1, at 2:00 p.m.

"Based on information derived from the Jenco debrief,

our discussions with Ghorbanifar, Nir, and [the Iranian official]; and the videotaped and private messages delivered by Jenco, we have drawn the following conclusions:

"—Jenco was released as a direct result of action taken by [the official in the Iranian PM's office] on or about July 21.

"—Though Iranian influence over the hostage holders is still considerable, the captors themselves are increasingly disenchanted with the Iranian relationship:

"—The delay between [the Iranian official's] 'instruction' to the captors on July 21 and the actual release on July 24 was likely occasioned by the hostage holders need to find a new prison site, arrange for the videotape by Jacobsen, place their story in An Nahar.

"—The Iranians have been unable to deter the Syrians from moving in strength against Hizballah strongholds in Lebanon.

"—The continued reluctance of the Hizballah itself to follow precise Iranian instructions on how to release the hostages is seen as an indication of efforts by Hizballah to demonstrate at least partial independence.

"—[The Iranian official] believed that he had consummated an arrangement with the Americans through Ghorbanifar on the terms for release of the hostages.

"—[The Iranian official's] expectations regarding the immediate delivery of the 240 HAWK missile parts were apparently transmitted to higher authority in Iran. Discussions with [him] in Europe (Sunday, July 27) and calls from him today indicate that [he] is in considerable personal jeopardy as a consequence of not having received what he believed we promised.

"—It is entirely possible that if nothing is received [the Iranian official] will be killed by his opponents in Tehran, Ghorbanifar will be killed by his creditors (they are the beneficiaries of a $22M life insurance policy), and one American hostage will probably be killed in order to demonstrate displeasure.

"—Although the Dawa 17 in Kuwait continue to be mentioned as the ultimate demand on the part of the hostage holders, Jenco himself does not believe this and we have not seen reference to this issue since our meeting in Tehran (Tab B).

"It is obvious that the conditions for the release of the hostages arranged between Ghorbanifar and [the Iranian official] are unacceptable. Nonetheless, we believe that Ghorbanifar acted on what he considered to be the following arrangement:

"Step 1: One hostage released and $4M to Ghorbanifar for items removed from the aircraft in Tehran during the May visit (Ghorbanifar received the $4M on July 28).

"Step 2: Remainder of 240 parts plus full quota of electron tubes (Item 24 on Iranian parts list) and 500 TOWs delivered to Iran.

"Step 3: Second hostage released and Ghorbanifar paid for remainder of 240 parts.

"Step 4: 500 TOWs and 1 HIPAR radar delivered.

"Step 5: Third hostage released and Ghorbanifar paid for one radar.

"Step 6: Meeting in Tehran to discuss future followed by release of the last hostage and delivery of second HIPAR radar.

"We believe that the mixture of HAWK parts and TOWs is designed to satisfy both the military and the revolutionary guards in Iran. At this point, [the Iranian official] will probably be able to retain his credibility if just the 240 parts are delivered from Israel. We believe that he can be convinced to follow-up this delivery with a meeting in Europe to discuss next steps.

"At such a meeting, we should endeavor to produce a concrete schedule that is agreeable to both parties and which allows all remaining hostages to be released simultaneously. The Jenco release . . . indicate[s] that this is clearly within the power of the Iranians, if they are so inclined. While they will continue to haggle over prices, timing, and sequence, the delivery of the 240 should help to assure the Iranians that we will keep our word. It is important that a face-to-face meeting occur so that we can establish the terms rather than having Ghorbanifar negotiate for us. Finally, even after the parts are delivered, we still retain some leverage over [the Iranian official]:

"—He has been told that we have video tapes and photographs of him meeting with us in Tehran and he is concerned that we could make these public.

"—He also wants assurance of asylum in the U.S. should "things go wrong." He has been told that we are prepared to offer such and need to meet with him to arrange exfiltration procedures. We intend to use this ploy as a further reason for establishing a direct communications link in Tehran.

"RECOMMENDATION

"That you brief the President regarding our conclusions on the Jenco release as indicated above and obtain his approval for having the 240 HAWK missile parts shipped from Israel to Iran as soon as possible, followed by a meeting with the Iranians in Europe. (North to Poindexter, 7/29/86)

Poindexter initialed "Approve" and wrote: "7/30/86. President approved. JP." (Tower)

- The Vice President was in Israel on July 29. While there, he met with Nir. The Vice President told the Board that, before the meeting, he had been uneasy, and tried to call Poindexter.

Failing to contact Poindexter, Mr. Bush spoke to North who indicated that the Israeli Prime Minister thought the meeting with Mr. Nir was important for the Vice President to meet with Nir. According to the Vice President, North had originally requested that the Vice President meet with Nir on the basis that the Israeli Prime Minister thought the meeting was important. North's position was apparently confirmed when after the meeting with Nir, the Israeli Prime Minister asked Mr. Bush how the meeting had gone. The Vice President indicated that there had been no discussion of the Nir meeting between himself and the Israeli Prime Minister. (W. Clark McFadden II, "Discussion with the Vice President," 12/29/86) The Vice President expressed concern to the Board about what he perceived as the extent to which the interests of the United States "were in the grip of the Israelis." Now, according to the Vice President, the Israelis themselves may be in some sense seeking cover. Vice President Bush related that his discussion with Mr. Nir was generally about counterterrorism. There was no discussion of specifics relating to arms going to the Iranians, e.g., the price of TOW missiles was never raised. (Tower)

The Vice President's Chief of Staff, Craig Fuller, attended the meeting and memorialized it:

"THE VICE PRESIDENT'S MEETING WITH MR. NIR - 7/29/86 0735-0805

"PARTICIPANTS: The Vice President, Mr. Nir, Craig Fuller

"DATE/TIME: 7/29/86 0735—0805

"LOCATION: Vice President's suite/King David Hotel, Jerusalem

"1. SUMMARY. Mr. Nir indicated that he had briefed

Prime Minister Peres and had been asked to brief the VP by his White House contacts. He described the details of the efforts from last year through the current period to gain the release of the U.S. hostages. He reviewed what had been learned which was essentially that the radical group was the group that could deliver. He reviewed the issues to be considered—namely that there needed to be ad [sic] decision as to whether the items requested would be delivered in separate shipments or whether we would continue to press for the release of the hostages prior to delivering the items in an amount agreed to previously.

"2. The VP's 25 minute meeting was arranged after Mr. Nir called Craig Fuller and requested the meeting and after it was discussed with the VP by Fuller and North. Only Fuller was aware of the meeting and no other member of the VP's staff or traveling party has been advised about the meeting. No cables were generated nor was there other reporting except a brief phone call between Fuller and North to advise that "no requests were made."

"3. Nir began by indicating that Peres had asked him to brief the VP. In addition, Nir's White House contacts with whom he had recent discussions asked him to brief the VP.

"4. Nir began by providing an historical perspective from his vantage point. He stated that the effort began last summer. This early phase he said "didn't work well." There were more discussions in November and in January "we thought we had a better approach with the Iranian side," said Nir. He said, "Poindexter accepted the decision."

"5. He characterized the decision as "having two layers—tactical and strategic." The tactical layer was described as an effort "to get the hostages out." The strategic layer was designed "to build better contact with Iran and to insure we are better prepared when a change (in leadership) occurs." "Working through our Iranian contact, we used the hostage problem and efforts there as a test," suggested Nir. He seemed to suggest the test was to determine how best to establish relationships that worked with various Iranian factions.

"6. Nir described Israel's role in the effort by saying, "we activated the channel; we gave a front to the operation; provided a physical base; provided aircraft." All this to "make sure the U.S. will not be involved in logistical aspects." Nir indicated that in the early phase they "began moving things over there."

[Charles Allen told the Board that he remembered the memorandum as reporting Nir to have talked about "the Israelis initiating, taking the initiative, proposing this, sort of directing this. I think probably overstated my understanding of the situation. Indeed, I think they were proposing it and pressing it on the United States, but based on my understanding and all the memoranda that I have put together is that Mr. McFarlane saw a real strategic need to pursue this effort. And also, an ancillary aspect was to solve the hostage problem in order to move to broader relationships." (C.Allen (2) 13-14)]

"7. Before a second phase a meeting was desired. Nir indicated a February meeting took place with "the Prime Minister on the other side." Nir did not make it clear who else attended the meeting. He said the meeting was "dramatic and interesting." He said "an agreement was made on 4,000 units—1,000 first and then 3,000." The agreement was made on the basis that we would get the group," Nir said. "The whole package for a fixed price," he said.

"8. Although there was agreement the other side changed their minds and "then they asked for the other items," according to Nir. "We were pleased because these were defensive items and we got to work with the military," said Nir. He continued, "there were 240 items on the list we were provided and we agreed to it."

"9. A meeting was organized for mid May in Tehran to finalize the operation. The VP asked Nir if he attended the meeting and Nir indicated he did attend. Nir said, "Two mistakes were made during this phase." "Two people were to be sent to prepare for the meeting but the U.S. had concerns about McFarlane," according to Nir. He described the meetings as "more difficult—total frustration because we didn't prepare." And he said, "Their top level was not prepared adequately." During the meeting in Tehran the other side kept reminding the group that "in 1982 there was a meeting which leaked and the Prime Minister was thrown out of office." Nir said that at the end of the May meeting, "they began to see the light." "McFarlane was making it clear that we wanted all hostages released," Nir reported and, "at the last moment the other side suggested two would be released if those at the meeting stayed six more hours." According to Nir, "the Deputy Prime Minister delivered the request (to delay departure) and when the group said 'no,' they all departed without anything."

"10. According to Nir, "the reason for delay is to squeeze as much as possible as long as they have assets. They don't believe that we want overall strategic cooperation to be better in the future. If they believed us they would have not bothered so much with the price right now." Further, according to Nir, "there are serious struggles now within the Iran power groups. Three leaders share the view that we should go ahead but each wants to prove his own toughness."

"11. Turning to what Nir said was the final or most recent phase, he reported, "We felt things would just die if we didn't push forward to see what could be delivered. They asked for four sequences, but we said no to talks until they showed something."

"12. According to Nir, he told them about 10 days ago he would cancel the deal. Then nine days ago their Prime Minister called saying that they were taking steps to release one —the Priest. The second one to be released would be Jacobsen. The Prime Minister also said that one would be released and then "we should give some equipment." Nir indicated to the VP that the bottom line on the items to be delivered was understood to be the same or even less but it was not the way the deal was originally made. The items involved spares for Hawks and TOWs. No denial or approval was given according to Nir. Nir said he made it clear that no deal would be discussed unless evidence is seen of a release.

"13. On Tuesday or Wednesday a message was intercepted between Tehran and the guards according to Nir. On Friday, three hostages were taken out and on Saturday Janco [sic] was taken out, put into a trunk and driven to a village in the Bakka [sic] Valley. Nir then described what Janco reported with regard to the conditions under which he was held and what he knew of the other hostages including Buckley. (I assume we have detailed briefing already.) The VP asked Nir if he had briefed Peres on all of this and he indicated that he had.

"14. Nir described some of the lessons learned: "We are dealing with the most radical elements. The Deputy Prime Minister is an emissary. They can deliver . . . that's for sure. They were called yesterday and thanked and today more phone calls. This is good because we've learned they can deliver and the moderates can't. We should think about diversity and establish other contacts with other factions. We have started to establish contact with some success and now more success is expected since if these groups feel if the extremes are in contact with us then it is less risky for the other groups—nothing operational is being done . . . this is contact only."

"15. Nir described some of the problems and choices: 'Should we accept sequencing? What are the alternatives to sequencing? They fear if they give all hostages they won't get anything from us. If we do want to move along these lines we'd have to move quickly. It would be a matter still of several weeks not several days, in part because they have to move the hostages every time one is released.'

"16. Nir concluded with the following points: 'The bottom line is that we won't give them more than previously agreed to. It is important that we have assets there 2 to 3 years out when change occurs. We have no real choice than to proceed.'

"17. The VP made no commitments nor did he give any direction to Nir. The VP expressed his appreciation for the briefing and thanked Nir for having pursued this effort despite doubts and reservations throughout the process."

"BY: CRAIG L. FULLER [initialed:] "CF 8/6/86" (Tower)

- That arms deals are being made with radicals and not moderates, a fact not disclosed until Fuller's memo is leaked to the press in February 1987, contradicts virtually every statement the Administration has made regarding its purpose in dealing with Iran. (NYT 2/9/87; WP 2/8/87)

JUL 30 - Reagan authorizes delivery of Hawk antiaircraft missile parts to Iran. According to a source, the shipment consists of about a half planeload of electronic parts for the weapons on three pallets. They apparently arrive on August 3. (WP 2/8/87)

- A member of the Hostage Location Task Force reported, on July 30, that "Charlie Allen advises that the President today approved further shipments of arms to Iran in response to the release of Rev. Jenco. Apparently, internal White House disagreements over who was responsible, the Syrians or the Iranians and, ultimately, the [Ghorbanifar-Iranian official] connection. (Tower)

AUGUST 1986

EARLY AUG - According to documents and testimony received by the Committee, in early August, efforts were resumed in the old channel to arrange for possible shipment of the two HAWK radars that Iran wanted. (SSIC 1/29/87)

- Elliott Abrams, the Assistant Secretary of State for Inter-American Affairs told the Board) . . . "So we needed a place to put the money. When [sic. what] I did was go to [the] head of the Central American Task Force at CIA and say—and I must say that I am relying on his memory of this as I don't remember this conversation. But I asked him about it a couple of weeks ago, and so, this is his account of it.

"It was so how do I do this? I mean, can UNO, the Nicaraguans, the Contras, can they set up an account? How do we do this?

"He said yes, he would pass a message to them to set up an account, which would receive any money, the number of which I would give to the foreign official, and then that would be the place they would receive the money.

Chairman Tower: Set up an account where?

Mr. Abrams: It didn't matter to me, and I think—I don't actually know the answer to that any more, but there are records that the CIA has—I believe the answer is Panama. Actually, they dispatched, a message was passed to an official of UNO, "Go open an account," because there may be some money being put in it.

"So they did that.

"I asked the same question more or less the same day, probably even the same hour, of Ollie North—What do I do here? I think there may be some money coming in for the contras, can we set up an account?

"Again, I don't have much memory of that conversation

either, and I haven't asked Ollie for obvious reasons. So I don't know what his memory, if any, is of that.

"At any event, at some point later, like a week later, probably both of these guys gave the index cards with an account number and the name of a bank on it.

"I then went to Charlie Hill who is the Executive Assistant to Secretary Shultz (sic) . . . Well, for the account number which was given to me by Ollie North, [the bank] was Credit Suisse, in Geneva . . . To continue, I went to Charlie Hill, who is Executive Assistant to the Secretary and said now what do I do? I asked both these guys and they both came up with accounts.

"So Charlie and I kicked it around. This was the first week in August, as I recall. We decided to use the account number that had been provided by Ollie, on the grounds that it looked, oddly enough in retrospect, kind of cleaner because we were unsure, first of all, whether this account had any relationship to any other agency account. We wanted a separate account. And, I would have to say there was probably some institutional rivalry there; that is, this is something State was doing, why should we get the CIA involved in the distribution of funds, because I don't know who was a signatory for that. I still don't—for that account.

"I then gave the account number that Ollie had given me to this foreign official." (Abrams 3-7)

According to the head of CIA's Central American Task Force [Alan Fiers], the Nicaraguan resistance started to incur debt after they used up the $27 million; by the middle of July 1986, that debt amounted to over $2.5 million. (H/ CATF 38) This CIA official told the Board:

"In early August of 1986, when we were seeing this debt problem, which had been a focal point of discussion, saying my God, the resistance is going to run out of money and they are going to start starving to death; we ought to get this law passed. We knew we weren't. We were running into summer recess, even though both chambers had passed the bill. And we had a number of discussions about how are they going to survive for the next three months.

"The obvious answer was solicit some money from someplace. So State Department, who had the writ and the charter to do that, went out and looked at the possibilities and came up with Brunei, obviously. One day I got a phone call on Thursday from Elliott [Abrams] saying we have a possibility to solicit some money from the Sultan of Brunei. Only the Secretary and I are aware of it. I am going to be making a trip. How should we deposit this money? How should we handle it?

"And I said, well, the best way, the mechanisms that I would prefer to use, which are an Agency-controlled bank account and so on and so forth, are not—the other mechanisms are too hard to start up. The best way to do it is to get the resistance forces, one person in particular in whom we have complete trust and confidence, to open a bank account, and you put the money in a bank account and make him accountable to you for how it's used.

"And he said that sounds like a good idea. I'll open a bank account. So I got hold of this particular individual and asked him to open a bank account in the Bahamas. I wanted to stay away from Cayman Islands and Panama. And he did open up a bank account and had it co-signed with his financial officer. And I gave Elliott the account number. And that's all.

"I subsequently asked the individual if any money had been deposited and asked Elliott if he thought the mission had been successful, and the answers to both were, Elliott, I don't know, and to the individual, he said no, no money has been deposited. We subsequently checked and no money was deposited in that account.

"And that's the last I thought or heard of it until . . . I received a phone call [from the Deputy Director for Operations] saying, God, did you give Elliott a bank account in Geneva. And do you have a private bank account in Geneva? And I said no, who are you talking about? Well, the FBI says that you gave Elliott a bank account in Geneva, to which Elliott deposited $10 million from the Sultan of Brunei, which is missing.

"And I said, wait a minute, something's badly wrong here. That was the first time I knew that Elliott—then we got it sorted out after about a few hours of almost frantic phone calls, and it was the first I knew that Elliott apparently had gotten another, allegedly had gotten another bank account from Ollie North in Geneva.

General Scowcroft: He didn't tell you he was not going to use your account?

[Head of Central America Task Force (Alan Fiers)]: No, he never told me that. That probably left me as speechless as anything in this whole endeavor, that that $10 million which we sorely needed and still do need—I mean, it would be the margin of comfort even in today's operation—went into a bank account in Geneva and disappeared. It just left me dumstruck [sic] and still does. I still find it hard to believe." (H/CATF 44-47) (Tower)

- According to testimony by Roy Furmark, a New York businessman and a lawyer for Adnan Khashoggi, Ghorbanifar told him in a meeting in August in Paris, that proceeds from the inflated Iran arms sale prices may have gone to Afghanistan or Nicaragua. (SSIC 1/29/87)

AUG - Felipe Vidal and an American CIA official reclaim six launches, some outboard motors and a Nissan van when they disbanded the Costa Rican Kisan-South rebel organization. Five current and former rebel officials say Vidal continues as the CIA liaison to the contras' southern front through February 1987. (MH 2/16/87)

AUG-SEP - [The Senior CIA analyst on the Iran Project] testified that he had conversations with Ghorbanifar and with Nir in August and September about funding problems with the Iran arms transfers [see Mid-September entry]. (SSIC 1/29/87)

AUG-OCT - Through August, September, and October 1986, numerous additional meetings were held in Europe between U.S. representatives and the new and Iranian contacts [sic] (Maximum Version 9; Historical Chronology 13-14)

AUG 2 - An unmarked helicopter carrying two U.S. personnel and two Miskito Indians crashes in Tegucigalpa. The bodies are removed quickly to a secret location. The helicopter is known to have been used by CIA pilots to ferry contras in Honduras. (WP 8/10/86)

On August 2, Secord reported:
"I. Planning to operate 707 TAIL No. EIptm fm Ben Gurion to Bandar Abbas. Cargo Wt. 48000 lbs. 12 Pallets. ETD 2400L-2100Z and ETA is 0730L-0400Z. Rt of flt is down red sea, East btwn S. YEMEN and Socotra to vic Char Bahar, Direct to Bandar Abbas. Expect EI-PTM to contact Bandar Abbas approach control, circa 0700L-0330Z on VHF

124.2 Pt. 2. Pls ensure authorities in Bandar Abbas know we are coming and are ready to off load and refuel the 707. Fuel is expected to be free as in the past. Past experience shows that the authorities at Bandar Abbas are not in the picture and much confusion results. pls get Sam [O'Neil] to emphasize this to the Australian [coverterm for official in Iranian Prime Minister's office]. We wd like to get out of Bandar Abbas and return here in Daylight hours. Pt. 3. 707 will transmit ops normal position reports in blind to IAF command post on HF/SSB Freqs Night: 8739 or 5605 or 10475 or 3115; Day; 8858 or 11290 or 12600. Reports will be given abeam jidda, socotra and approaching B. Abbas. Pt. 4. It is now 7 hrs til planned takeoff. If coord w/ Tehran cannot be accomplished, we plan 24 hr delay." ("Adams" [Secord] to [?North], 8/2/86) (Tower)

- Apparently in response to the approval of President Reagan, the HAWK parts reached Iran on August 3. (SSIC 1/29/87)

AUG - Another shipment of arms is sent to Iran via Israel. The White House issues an "alert" that more hostages are expected to be released. As of late November 1986, this is reported in the press as the third such delivery; later reports indicate it is the fifth. When this shipment does not produce more freed hostages, North drops Ghorbanifar and initiates contact with an unnamed Iranian, known as the "doctor," with whom he collaborates until news of the secret arms deals leaks out. (WP 11/26/86 & 12/21/86)

AUG 3 - Pursuant to the President's decision of July 30, 1986, on August 3, the United States delivered twelve pallets of HAWK spare parts to Iran. ("Adams" [Secord] to [?North], 8/2/86) Israel provided logistical assistance. (CIA/IG Chronology 28; Maximum Version 8; Historical Chronology 13)

On August 3, the remaining three pallets (less than 1/2 planeload) of electronic parts for Iranian anti-aircraft defenses (HAWK missile sub-components) arrived in Tehran. As in all flights to/from Iran this delivery was made with an Israeli Air Force aircraft (707) using false flag markings. Timing of the delivery was based on coordination among U.S., Israeli and Iranian officials. (Historical Chronology, Tower)

In early August 1986, the contact with the Iranian expatriate [Ghorbanifar] began to focus exclusively on the willingness of the USG to provide military assistance to Iran in exchange for hostages and we sought to establish different channels of communication which would lead us more directly to pragmatic and moderate elements in the Iranian hierarchy. In mid August, a private American citizen (MGEN Richard Secord, USAF [Ret.]) acting within the purview of the January Covert Action Finding, made contact in Europe with . . . a relative . . . of a senior Iranian official . . . with the assistance of the CIA, this Iranian was brought covertly to Washington for detailed discussions. We judged this effort to be useful in establishing contact with a close confidant of the man judged to be the most influential and pragmatic political figure in Iran . . .). These discussions reaffirmed the basic objectives of the U.S. in seeking a political dialogue with Tehran. We also provided assessments designed to discourage an Iranian offensive and contribute to an Iranian decision to negotiate an end to the war. (Historical Chronology 13, Tower)

The Maximum Version of the delivery of spare parts omits the last two sentences in the first paragraph quoted above. (Maximum Version 8) The Historical Chronology added the following sentence to the second paragraph quoted above, from the Maximum Version (id. at 8-0): "The assessments also detailed the Soviet threat to Iran." (Historical Chronology 13, Tower)

Cave told the Board that "the decision to get rid of Ghorbanifar was on our part to clean this up operationally, so that we had better control." (Cave 25, Tower)

Furmark told the Board that, when he and Ghorbanifar discussed "the inflated pricing in August, Ghorbanifar said the money may have gone to the Contras, or the Afghans, or someplace. And he even said—and he said that North told him that now they've passed this bill, if we don't complete this transaction we'll pay you the money back, the $10 million; they passed the Aid to the Contras bill—so Ghorbanifar said, if they never complete the deal we'll still get our money back because now they can, you know.

So that's an inference that the money was used and they'll repay it back." (Furmark 17) (Tower)

AUG 4 - A phone call is placed from the Cooper safehouse in San Salvador to Southern Air Transport in Miami. (ANTEL phone records, 9/8/86, p. 4834)

AUG 5 - The Justice Department withdraws Customs Service subpoenas against eight Israeli citizens in connection with an investigation into the alleged export of cluster bomb technology to Israel. The move follows requests by Israel and is agreed to by the Administration "in return for pledges of cooperation by the government of Israel," according to Associate Attorney General Steven Trott. (WP 8/6/86)

AUG 6 - LtCol North was interviewed by members of the House Permanent Select Committee on Intelligence on August 6, 1986. An internal NSC staff account made the following points:

Contact with FDN and UNO aimed to foster viable, democratic, political strategy for Nicaraguan opposition, gave no military advice, knew of no specific military operations. ·

Singlaub—gave no advice, has had no contact in 20 months; Owen—never worked from OLN office, OLN had casual contact, never provided Owen guidance.

Shortly thereafter, VADM Poindexter forwarded the above to LtCol North with the message: "Well Done." (Tower)

- North receives a copy of Craig Fuller's memo describing the Bush-Nir meeting in Jerusalem. (WP 2/8/87)

AUG 7 - North went to London on August 7. (North calendar) North requested travel orders to go to Frankfurt on August 6. According to the NSC staff Chronology of Events, dated 11/20/86, the first American contact with [the] relative occurred in London and Madrid on August 10. North wrote McFarlane on October 3 that [the] relative came into contact with us through Dick Secord who met him in Brussels while arranging a pick-up for our friends in a certain resistance movement." (North PROF note to McFarlane, 10/03/86, 22:08:16) North was on leave when the Director of Central Intelligence briefed Poindexter on Cave's meeting, July 25, with Tabatabai in London. Vincent M. Cannistraro of the NSC staff wrote Poindexter that Tabatabai "claims to be a channel to Rasfanjani [sic] and has passed the usual message via Cave that the Iranian government wishes to establish a regular channel to the U.S. but is constrained until after the end of the war with Iraq. (We also know that Tabatabai has made contact with some of the Iranian exile groups in Paris —particularly the Ali Amini crowd. His bonafides [sic] as an authentic channel to Rasfanjani, however, have yet to be proven.)" (Cannistraro to Poindexter, 8/13/86) (Tower)

AUG 8 - In August pursuant to the policy approved by the President in May, Abrams approached a third country and asked it to contribute $10 million for humanitarian assistance to UNO. Abrams reportedly met with a representative of that country on August 8; he pointed out that Congress had approved $100 million but it had not been appropriated yet and money was needed to bridge this gap between the previous $27 million [in humanitarian aid] and passage of the appropriation by Congress, which the contras had not yet received. When the third country agreed, Abrams asked the CIA task force chief and North for advice on handling the contribution.

According to testimony received by the Committee, the task force chief (Alan Fiers) recommended having UNO open a bank account in its name and then having NHAO or the State Department monitor the expenses and authorize them from that account. Abrams agreed, and the task force contacted UNO Secretary General Naio Sommariba and asked him to open an offshore bank account for use to deposit the funds. According to testimony received by the Committee, this was done at a bank in the Bahamas, with signatures of Sommariba and his accountant on the bank account. According to testimony received by the Committee, Abrams needed the account number urgently and the number was obtained and passed on to Abrams at a meeting in the NSC situation room. The task force chief said he provided this assistance on his own authority after consulting with the task force lawyer to make sure it was legal. He testified that he informed CIA Deputy Director for Operations and the Latin America Division Chief after the fact, and they raised no questions as to legality. The task force chief went on to testify that this was the way he handled 95 percent of his activities. CIA officials considered that the State Department was legally within its bounds to solicit the money and did not consider CIA's assistance to be in any way circumventing the law.

Abrams testified that he asked *both* the CIA task force chief and North to provide accounts for the donation from the third country. He testified that the account opened by North was with Credit Suisse. Abrams testified that he discussed the situation with Charles Hill, Executive Assistant to Secretary Shultz, and they decided to use the account opened by North without procedures for monitoring expenditures from the account. (SSIC 1/29/87)

- Bush aide Donald Gregg and his deputy, Samuel Watson, meet with Felix Rodriguez. Rodriguez reveals for the first time to anyone from the vice president's office (according to Bush aides), his concern that the unofficial contra supply program will not survive until the delivery of congressionally approved funds and equipment to the contras. (Bush Chronology in WP 12/16/86)

- A phone call is placed from the Cooper safehouse in San Salvador to Southern Air Transport in Miami. (ANTEL phone records, 9/8/86, p. 4834)

AUG 9 - A U.S. engineer working for an American firm in Iran, Jon Pattis, is arrested and accused of spying by the Iranian government. Pattis had been given a non-American passport in order to be granted a visa by Iranian immigrations. Pattis worked in a telecommunications center, and came under suspicion when he left the center shortly before an Iraqi air raid on the region. (AFP 8/9/86)

AUG 12 - Around this date, Bush adviser Gregg sets up a meeting between Rodriguez and officials of the CIA, State and Defense departments to discuss Rodriguez's concerns about the adequacy of aid to the contras. Gregg says he does not recall whether he informed Bush of the meeting, nor what actions resulted from the meeting. (WP 12/14/86)

- The U.S. Army Audit Agency circulates a draft report on "Exercise Blazing Trails 86," an "engineering training" exercise to build a road in Panama (from Boca del Rio Indio to Miguel de la Borda) and 20 kilometers of road in Honduras (from Puentecita to Jocon). The report concludes that Blazing Trails 86 cost $38.3 million and involved 10,000 Reserve and active soldiers. Later reports (see October 23, 1986 entry) conclude that at least 47 of these soldiers were Reservists on illegally extended tours. (U.S. Army Audit Agency, "Draft Report of Exercise Blazing Trails 86, Republics of Panama and Honduras," 8/12/86)

AUG 13 - The Senate passes the House version of legislation on $100 million in aid to the contras by a 53-47 vote. The

CIA is allowed to disburse the money, which is divided into $70 million of military aid and $30 million of humanitarian aid. The House bill (H.R. 5052), is incorporated into H.J.Res. 738 (Continuing Appropriations for FY87). (CRS "U.S. Assistance to Nicaraguan Guerrillas" 12/4/86; CSM 2/1/87).

- Spitz Channell notifies "all staff" that they should "not call IBC [International Business Communications] for any requests" after this date. Channell says, "Mr. Steve Schwartz of IBC indicated on the 12th of August that the only work IBC would be doing for our organizations beginning the 13th of August would be activities and projects pertaining to Western Goals Radio." This memo represents a marked change from the preceding nine months, in which Channell's groups funneled millions of dollars to IBC—money which news reports later cite as direct aid to the Contras in addition to public relations work for Channell. The memo also raises questions about subsequent payments to IBC as a retainer for a former Reagan White House aide, David C. Fischer (see Sept. 5 entry below) and the catalyst for any breakdown in the relationship between the two organizations. (Memorandum 8/13/86)

AUG 14 - The White House adopts a plan to convince Khaddafi that he will once again be the target of American bombers and perhaps a coup, according to later press reports. Citing Administration planning papers and informed sources, the reports detail an elaborate disinformation campaign which resulted in a series of articles in major newspapers depicting a resurgence of Libyan-sponsored terrorism and hinted at a new military strike against Libya. Senior U.S. intelligence officials in September did discover new plans for terrorist activities by Khaddafi and feared they were in response to the previous month's media offensive. (WSJ 8/25/86; Reuters 8/20/86; WP 10/2/86)

MID-AUG - Secord begins to cultivate a new Iranian contact after a shipment of arms to Iran this month fails to result in the release of more hostages. Ghorbanifar is dropped as an intermediary. (WP 12/31/86)

- . . . In mid-August, Amiram Nir told CIA personnel that he had authorized most of what Ghorbanifar had offered in the way of price cuts and alternative schedules, although

Ghorbanifar had offered at least one item that was not authorized. Nir also conceded that Ghorbanifar was probably no longer trusted by the Iranians. The latest proposal involved the HAWK radars, some electron tubes for the HAWK systems, 1,000 TOWs, another trip to Tehran, and an Israeli sale, along with the staggered release of the three remaining hostages. (SSIC 1/29/87)

- Later in August, at a meeting of Ghorbanifar, Nir and North, a new schedule was proposed that added still another 1,000 TOWs, instead of the Israeli sale, and added the requirement that William Buckley's body be returned for proper burial. By late August, preparations for a shipment of 500 TOWs had begun. (SSIC 1/29/87)

AUG 19 - The Sultan of Brunei transfers $10 million to a Swiss bank account, the number of which has been provided by U.S. officials. The donation, reportedly intended for the contras, follows a June 24 three-hour meeting between the Sultan and Secretary of State Shultz. (WP 12/7/86 & 12/25/86; State Department briefing 1/8/87)

- According to a document submitted by the Justice Department to the Swiss government in December 1986, the Credit Suisse account number that North gave Abrams is the same as the number of the account suspected of being used by North, Hakim, and Secord for proceeds from Iran arms sales. (SSIC 1/29/87)

LATE AUG - Toward the end of August, after returning from vacation, North reported to Poindexter the latest Iranian and Nicaraguan information:
"We have had an intensive series of discussions w/ Nir, Gorba and [Ghorbanifar's Tehran contact] over the past 48 hrs. It is not clear whether Nir/Gorba are aware that we are talking directly to. . . . Basic proposal as outlined to you over phone remains unchanged; i.e., sequential release for sequential deliveries. We must, however resolve the problem of how to provide the parts which we promised but do not have in stock. [C/NE] has assigned an officer to work w/ Army logistics in an effort to find (or manufacture, if necessary) the missing/wrong items. Both Gorba and [his Tehran contact] have been told not to ship the 63 defective/wrong parts back and that we will backhaul them on the next deliv-

ery. Copp has been told to keep a crew in readiness for a further mission and has been apprised of the general parameters of the arrangement. He notes that from a logistics perspective, the sequential arrangement is preferable in that it requires only one crew and one A/C throughout thus reducing visibility and enhancing OPSEC. We should have a better fix on availability of parts early in the week and meanwhile have told Gorba and [the official in the Prime Minister's office] that both sides should bring a technical expert familiar w/ the appropriate system to the meeting. [The Iranian official] told Geo. [Cave] this morning that it wd be best to bring an expert w/ us to Tehran for the meeting and he could see for himself what the problems are. Having discussed this proposal this a.m. w/ both Clarridge and Cave we all believe this to be the best course of action, especially if we can leave our 'technical expert' and a communicator behind in Tehran. CIA is now looking for a good Ops officer who is familiar w/ the system. Dick already has one identified but CIA wd prefer to use its own officer if they can find one. We should get back to [the Iranian official] w/ an answer by Monday [August 25]. All of us rate the risk to be relatively low, particularly given the experience we had in May. If you approve, we wd use [false] documents (as we did in May) and go in via the Iran Air flight to/ from Frankfurt. Estimated time on mission wd be two days. We wd plan to go over a weekend to reduce visible absence fm D.C. NEW SUBJECTS: . . .

"On the hostages—I just don't know. One of the things that has concerned me for some time was the report that you got from Copp [Secord] about how the parts really help their problem for lack of test equipment, not ordering all of the right parts and the lack of knowledge of the system. If we get into a sequential arrangement, we really have to be prepared to deliver a lot more material and arrange a rather continuing technical agreement. Of course that could all be done, but after the hostages are released. I just don't see how we can have such a continuing relationship until that happens. . . . Before we agree to a sequential arrangement I think we ought to straighten out our commitment on the 240 —that alone will help establish our good faith that we aren't trying to cheat them. Then we should wait a bit and see what [a friendly country approach] delivers." (Poindexter PROF note to North reply to note of 8/23/86, 5:52) (Tower)

AUG 22 - Defex-Portugal is cleared by Portuguese authorities to transport more arms to Guatemala. The delivery, made on behalf of Energy Resources International, is actually to be sent to the contras by ship. As with previous weapons requests made by these companies, the original end-user certificate for this order used forged signatures from the Guatemalan military. (WP 1/17/87)

- A phone call is placed from the Cooper safehouse in San Salvador to Stanford Technology in Virginia, and one call to Richard Secord's home number in Virginia. (ANTEL phone records, 9/8/86, p. 4834)

AUG 25 - Secord met with the Relative of a powerful Iranian official (the "Relative").

Secord reported to North:

"1. Following is summary report of three long meetings —total circa eight hours—with Iranian gp visiting Brussels. Meetings took place August 25 in three segments. Iranian side was [the Relative], and [a] former Iranian Navy officer —20 years—and alleged London businessman now—definitely an important agent for Rafsanjani gp and possibly Savama. Our side included me—true name—Abe [Hakim] in true name, and [another Iranian expatriate], our agent. Meetings constituted comprehensive tour de force regarding Iran/Iraq War, Iranian views of U.S. and other western policies, Soviet activities, activities of nearly all important Iran government figures, hostage matters, activities in the Hague, and Iranian forces equipment and material shortages.

"2. Special interest items included claim that an "Al Haig gp" and "a Senator Kennedy gp" have recently tried to meet with [the Relative]—he has declined—he wants to deal with the Presidents [sic] representatives. [The Relative] is very sharp, well educated youngman [sic]—speaks no English. [He] is well-known favorite of [Majlis speaker] Rafsanjani . . . They badly need air defense items, armor spares, TOWs, gun barrels, helo spares, and tactical intelligence. I told them all things negotiable if we can clear the hostage matter quickly. [The Relative] knew great deal about McFarlane msn to Thn. He also knows all about [the official in the Prime Minister's office], Gorba, Israeli connection, and this gps financial greed. Gorba was nastly [sic] classified as a crook. [The Relative's] wealth of current information but also volunteers to discuss hostage matter and USG connection with Rafsanjani in next 10 days. He will then return to Brussels for meeting with us. [The Relative] said categorically he would not screw up [official in Prime Minister's office, Cave] efforts but would carefully examine them for feasibility. [The relative] will recommend two courses to Rafsanjani:

a. Assist in current . . . effort [by official in Prime Minister's office] to release hostages or start new effort.

b. Provide us with current intelligence on their location, etc., . . . [The relative] says there are many specific things USG can do in the Hague and on Voice of America programming to help start USG/GOI talks—he will give us documents on these subjects at next meeting.

"3. Numerous military supply problems were discussed and I will detail these for you later this week in Washington. FYI: They need oil barter deals.

"4. My judgement[sic] is that we have opened up new and probably much better channel into Iran. This connection has been effectively recruited and he wants to start dealing. Recommend you plan on bringing George to next meeting in two weeks or less." (Secord ("Copp") to North, 8/26/86, Tower)

An undated, unsigned note, adds a grace note to Secord's message:

"[The Relative] claims he can be of great assistance in establishing the right relation. The Hague, he claims, is the best avenue.)

NOTE: The report goes into detail regarding the above 3 items.

"5. ([S]ecord's Iranian expatriate agent's] recommendations: Try everything not to lose this man if he can not be a representative of [Rafsanjani] he definitely is trainable to be an excellent source in country. P.S. [Rafsanjani] participated with Hafezalasad for release of Hostages. The release of the rest is possible." (Tower)

AUG 25-OCT 5 - Flight logs show that 19 shipments of military supplies to the contras occurred between these dates. (WP 12/7/86)

AUG 26 - Mr. Secord and Mr. Hakim met with the second channel and other Iranians in London. The Iranians said they were aware of the McFarlane visit, the Israeli connection, and Mr. Ghorbanifar's role. They referred to Mr. Ghorbanifar as a "crook." Notes taken by Mr. McDaniel indicate that the President was briefed about the second channel on September 9, 1986. (Tower)

- During the last six months China has become the largest arms supplier to Iran, delivering at least $300 million worth of missiles and other military equipment, in spite of U.S. efforts to stop the shipments. The introduction of new arms to Iran is considered to be a setback to U.S. efforts over several years to create an embargo against Iran. U.S. officials are concerned that the balance of power will be upset by the Chinese military shipment of heavy tanks, aircraft and rocket launchers. The Chinese have consistently denied any arms shipment to Iran, however, Chinese officials informally told a U.S. official that the sale was justified because Iran will use the arms to aid the anti-Soviet forces in Afghanistan. However, given the type of weapons, U.S. officials say that this is not likely. A State Department official claims that "it does appear" as if China will be supplying Iran with J-6 fighters. The International Institute for Strategic Studies (IISS) reported last fall that China and Iran signed a $1.6 billion agreement in March, 1985 covering the supply of J-6 fighters, T-59 tanks, heavy artillery, multiple rocket launchers and surface-to-air missiles. (WP 8/26/86)

AUG 27 - [A] new section was added to the Arms Export Control Act which prohibited the export of arms to countries which the Secretary of State has determined support acts of international terrorism. Such a determination was in effect at that time for Iran. (Tower) (See January 20, 1984 entry.)

- On August 27, the Relative informed Secord that the Iranians were trying to buy TOWs in Madrid at a cost of $13,000 each. Secord thought it was "a big steal." The United States was not involved, and the Relative reportedly worried that the transaction could upset the effort to establish a new relationship with the United States. (Secord to [?North], 8/27/86; North to Poindexter 9/2/86) (Footnote: At North's request, on September 2, Charles Allen tipped law enforcement officials of another possible arms transfer to Iran from Houston. Ghorbanifar and Khashoggi were thought to be involved. (C. Allen, Memorandum for the Record, 9/2/86; Earl PROF note to North, 8/28/86, 19:09)) (Tower)

AUG 29 - Telephone records from the Salvadoran phone company, ANTEL, show a phone call on this date to Southern Air Transport in Miami, (305)871-5171, from the San Salvador safehouse where Eugene Hasenfus and other contra resupply crew members were staying. This safehouse, the third used by the resupply operation, is located across from the Cristo Redentor church in the Escalon section, and the telephone was registered to Jose Figueroa Cordero. ANTEL records made available to reporters cover the Hasenfus safehouse for the end of August and the full month of September 1986. (ANTEL phone records, 10/8/86, p. 4752)

LATE AUG - Republican Senate candidate Linda Chavez calls North to ask him to help take a pro-Chavez television commercial off the air, according to Ed Rollins who managed her Maryland campaign. The commercial runs from Aug. 29 to Sep. 8. It has been independently paid for by the Anti-Terrorism American Committee, a conservative political action committee run by Carl "Spitz" Channell. Channell's ties to North later come under scrutiny because of their involvement in contra- and election-related activities this year. It is unclear what steps North takes on Chavez's behalf. The advertisements, produced by the New York firm Blakemore and Killough, "Maryland Project Media Placement" run as planned. That Chavez contacts North raises questions later about his involvement in the domestic political activities of conservative groups such as Channell's. (AP 12/17/86; Newsweek 12/29/86)

- China denies a U.S. charge that it had sold weapons to Iran, insisting that no sides were taken in the Gulf war. "China always takes a neutral stand in the Iran-Iraq war," a Foreign ministry spokeswoman claimed. "China does not provide any weapons to either Iran or Iraq." (Reuters 8/30/87)

AUG 31 - Telephone records from the Salvadoran phone company, ANTEL, show a phone call on this date from the Hasenfus safehouse in San Salvador, to PropAir in Quebec, the company later reported to have sold two Caribou cargo planes to the contras. (ANTEL phone records, 10/8/86, p. 4752)

SEPTEMBER 1986

SEP - In fiscal year 1986, American National Management Corp. (ANMC) continues to grow thanks to its dealings with the military. The company wins more than $1.8 million in contracts from the Military Airlift Command and the Air Force. Competitors complain that ANMC's connections with Secord are helping it unduly. (WSJ 2/13/87)

- Early in the month, John Singlaub sends a memo to North to alert him of the tight control the Honduran military holds over arms shipments to the contras. According to a press account later, the Hondurans' designated chief liaison with the rebels during most of the period of the congressional ban is Col. Hector Aplicano, the head of Honduran military intelligence. Access to Aplicano, the report says, is essential to doing business with the contras. In the memo, Singlaub mentions Mario Dellamico, an independent weapons dealer with connections to several Honduran military officers, including Aplicano, and a close relationship to Felix Rodriguez, later revealed to be a key player in the contra resupply effort. Singlaub cites Dellamico's "great powers" in Honduras and also boasts of Rodriguez' "daily contact" with Bush's office. The memo warns that this information, if true, could "damage President Reagan and the Republican Party." Singlaub says later that he received word that his memo was appreciated but that it did not seem to cause great concern. (WP 2/26/87)

- Jim Steveson, an unemployed aircraft maintenance specialist, says in a later report that William J. Cooper, a pilot on the downed C-123K flight in Nicaragua, asked him in September of this year to sign an agreement swearing not to disclose classified government information he may have received "by virtue of my duties" in connection with the private aid program to the contras. Other Americans who are taking part in the rebel supply network have also apparently been asked to sign the form. (BG 2/12/87 in NYT 2/13/87)

- According to press reports, McFarlane makes a second trip to Iran with another 23 tons of weapons. (NYT 12/25/86)

- Abrams testified that in September and October the State Department sought assurances from the donating country that they were going to give the $10 million and would deposit it in the account provided by North. Documents received by the Committee confirm this statement.

Abrams testified that on several occasions after that he checked with North to see if the money had been deposited. According to Abrams, North reported to him on several occasions that the money had not reached the account. (SSIC 1/29/87)

- Arif Durrani, who has been asked to acquire spare parts for Hawk missiles that are to be shipped to Iran, cuts short a business trip to the Far East to fly to Lisbon for a meeting on the matter. Durrani, who claims to believe he was working at least with the support of the U.S. government, later describes what followed: "Upon arrival in Lisbon, I met with an individual who was said to be a staff member of the NSC. I was told at that meeting for the first time of the urgency in obtaining the parts, which I was told were part of a package for freeing American hostages being held in Lebanon." After a quick trip to the U.S. to pressure the company he is dealing with, Radio Research, Inc. of Danbury, CT, "a small dealer of surplus parts" that reconditions and resells scrap from the U.S. military, Durrani is requested to fly to London where he meets with an individual he comes to believe is Oliver North (see October 1 entry). (Affidavit of Arif Durrani, 2/4/87)

SEP 1 - Telephone records from the Salvadoran phone company, ANTEL, show three phone calls on this date to Richard Secord's home number in Virginia, (703)560-4931; and a phone call to Southern Air Transport in Miami—all from the San Salvador safehouse where Eugene Hasenfus and other contra resupply crew members were staying. (ANTEL phone records, 10/8/86, p. 4750)

SEP 2- Two phone calls are made from the Hasenfus safe-house in San Salvador to Southern Air Transport in Miami (305)871-5171. (ANTEL phone records, 10/8/86, p. 4750)

- On this date, the State Department signs a $276,186 contract, initially classified secret, with International Business Communications (IBC) for "public diplomacy efforts" and "distribution services." This contract has almost identical specifications as the unclassified $90,000 contract of Mar. 1, 1985 (see entry of that date). It is also unusual in that the contract was not signed until this date, but it was backdated to Oct. 1, 1985. IBC is later connected to private American funding of weapons for the contras. (DOS Contract 1001-602066 effective 10/1/85 but signed 9/2/86; WP 3/7/87)

- Guillermo Quant, vice chairman of Nicaragua's Chamber of Commerce, confesses to having worked for the CIA. In a news conference he says that he had sent information "requested" by the CIA to Miami and Costa Rica. Some of the information included "the location of military fuel reserves." Quant states that he spied for "political reasons" and "the mystery of it." Three U.S. officials recruited him in Managua in mid-1983, he says. (AFP 9/2/87)

SEP 2-3 - On September 2, North formally proposed trying to use the new connection with the Relative. He wrote Poindexter:

"NEXT STEPS WITH IRAN

"Ongoing Activities

"There are currently five separate activities underway which are related to resolution of the American hostage situation and a potentially broadened relationship with the Government of Iran:

"—[Third Country] Initiative: [The Foreign Minister] has been given a message for delivery to the Iranian Foreign Ministry indicating a willingness on the part of the USG to improve relations with Iran and to undertake direct, private discussions with responsible Iranian officials. No response has yet been received.

"—[Another Third Country Connection]: [Its] Ambassador in Tehran during a meeting with Rafsanjani discussed the hostage situation and further U.S.-Iranian contacts. Rafsanjani, for the first time, suggested certain material (F-14 spare parts and embargoed helicopters) as items that could

cause Iran to act on behalf of the American hostages. Per
instructions, [that government was] advised that such "barter
arrangements" were unacceptable to the U.S. and contrary to
our policy. [They] remain willing to advise Rafsanjani that
we are prepared to hold private discussions with the Iranians.

"— . . . . [redacted]

"—[The Relative]: In coordination with the CIA, Copp and
two of his associates met for two days last week with [the
Relative] indicated a full awareness of the May trip to
Tehran and the ongoing activity involving [the official in
the Prime Minister's office] and Ghorbanifar. [The Relative]
clearly indicated that he had c [sic] specific mandate from
[Rafsanjani] to meet with USG official seeking a means for
"getting beyond the hostage issue" and [the Relative] starting a dialogue with the USG. [The Relative] has returned to
Tehran and has since informed us of a pending TOW sale
through Madrid and further indicated that he is prepared to
proceed with further discussions. He has further noted that
the government in Tehran is very concerned over Soviet activities in the Gulf and is aware that a "final victory" over
Iraq will not be possible. There is considerable evidence that
[the Relative] is indeed a bonafide [sic] intermediary seeking
to establish direct contact with the USG for Rafsanjani's faction within the Government of Iran.

"—[Official in Prime Minister's Office]/Ghorbanifar:
Since the release of Father Jenco, that portion of the 240
parts which was available has been delivered. The Iranians
have advised through Nir that at least 63 (In a number of
telephone conversations taped by Cave early in September,
Cave and the Iranian official talked about the problems associated with what the Iranian official said were 65 "broken"
parts. (Transcripts of telephone calls) The confusion over the
number of spare parts to be shipped apparently results from
the fact that certain of the line items requested included multiple parts. (Army/IG Report)) of the items delivered are improper or inoperable. Further, 299 of the items promised
have not been received. They have offered to return the
damaged/incorrect parts, but have been told to return them
on a "future delivery flight." The Iranians continue to insist
on a sequential delivery process and in a meeting in London
with Nir a specific seven step delivery/release pattern was
proposed:

"—Deliver 500 TOWs and the 39 electron tubes for the HAWK system previously requested.

"—[Hostage] released.

"—Deliver 500 TOWs and one of the HAWK radars previously requested.

"—[Hostage] released.

"—Meeting in Tehran to discuss broadened relationship, Soviet intelligence, etc.

"—Deliver remaining radar and 1000 TOWs while we are in Tehran.

"—[Hostage] released and Buckley's body delivered.

"CIA concurs that the [Iranian official]/ Ghorbanifar connection is the only proven means by which we have been able to effect the release of any of the hostages. Though the sequential plan is not what we prefer, the commodities and quantities are within the framework of our original understanding. CIA believes that we should proceed expeditiously with the Ghorbanifar connection and pursue the other five alternatives as subsidiary efforts. (Tab I, "Next Steps with Iran," to North to Poindexter, 9/2/86) The copy obtained by the Board of North's Action Memorandum, to which this document is attached, shows a check mark next to the word 'Approve.'

North was impatient for Poindexter's approval of the plan. He wrote McFarlane that evening:

"We still have no response fm JMP re proceeding w/ the sequential release proposal outlined to you some time back. Have now undertaken to have Casey raise same w/ JMP tomorrow at thr weekly mtg. The things one must do to get action. Am hopeful Bill can push hard enought [sic] to move on the matter. Nir will be here next week and will raised [sic] enough hell to move it if it hasn't all fallen apart by then. The basic problem, as you know, is that we dither so long on these things that by the time we're ready to go to bat, the rules have changed again. I agree w/ yr assessment that the next mtg in Tango [Tehran] is unlikely to be for some time. My hope is that we will not be trying to adjust yr sched for next June for this mtg." (North PROF note to McFarlane, 9/3/86, 20:12:50) (Tower)

SEP 3 - Three phone calls from the Hasenfus safehouse in San Salvador to Southern Air Transport in Miami, (305)871-5171. (ANTEL phone records, 10/8/86, p. 4750)

- Costa Rican authorities seize a two-kilometer airstrip in northern Costa Rica being used by the contra resupply missions. The strip, located on an isolated hacienda called Santa Elena near a Civil Guard training center at Murcielago twenty kilometers from the Nicaraguan border, was constructed in 1985 by Udall Research Corp, ostensibly as part of a "tourism project." Udall is registered in Panama. Its president, Robert Olmsted, receives messages—(202-944-8218)—and picks up mail at Sincerely Yours Answering Service in Washington D.C. (Tico Times 9/26/86; NYT 9/29/86; interviews)

SEP 4 - Four phone calls are placed from the Hasenfus safehouse in San Salvador to Stanford Technology Trading Group International in Virginia, (703)356-4801, Secord's office; and one phone call to Southern Air Transport in Miami, (305)871-5171. (ANTEL phone records, 10/8/86, p. 4750)

SEP 5 - Four phone calls are made from the Hasenfus safehouse in San Salvador to Southern Air Transport in Miami, (305)871-5171; and two phone calls are placed to Stanford Technology in Virginia (703)356-4801. (ANTEL phone records, 10/8/86, p. 4750)

- International Business Communications sends a memo to Spitz Channell at the National Endowment for the Preservation of Liberty billing Channell for the August ($20,000) and September ($20,000) retainer for former Reagan White House aide David C. Fischer. Two NEPL checks, each for $20,000, are subsequently made out to Fischer from an NEPL account at Provident National Bank in Philadelphia and an NEPL account at the Palmer National Bank in Washington. (IBC memo 9/5/86; photocopied checks 112 and 2635 both dated 9/9/86)

SEP 6 - A phone call is placed from the Hasenfus safehouse in San Salvador to Southern Air Transport in Miami, (305)871-5171. (ANTEL phone records, 10/8/86, p. 4750)

SEP 8 - At the same time, the families of the hostages called North to complain about the "deal" being made for Daniloff, a U.S. News & World Report journalist arrested in Moscow, apparently in retaliation for the arrest in New York of a suspected KGB agent. North reported on September 8:

"Some, like Jacobsen's son Paul, accused us of being callous to the LebNap victims—and unwilling to pressure the Kuwaitis because the issue has "slipped from the public eye and that we are willing to make deals for Daniloff because it was more important to the President because of the visibility." All indicated that they are planning to hold a press conference later this week to "turn the heat on" the Administration. My rejoinder that no deal for Daniloff was in the mill was, because of earlier press coverage to the contrary, not taken seriously. Bob Oakley has made a similar effort w/ the same unfortunate results.

This afternoon, Louis Boccardi, President of the AP came to see me. He is supportive of our policy on terroprism [sic] and on the hostage issue—and notes that we are not credible in saying that a deal was not in the making. He pointedly noted that this could well have an effect on Terry Anderson's fate in that the Hizballah could not but take heart from the talk of our willingness to deal with the Soviets over Daniloff. While it was an amiable discussion, I was impressed by his concern that no matter what we do now re Daniloff, we are going to be perceived as having made a deal that will hurt chances for Anderson's release and jeopardize his other reporters elsewhere. He made cogent observation [sic] that I think is relevant: "I sure hope that you are dealing with someone regarding Terry and the others in Lebanon—and that you can keep it quiet—that's the only way that any of this will work." (North PROF note to Poindexter, 9/08/86, 19:08:10)

On the same day, North updated his paper on "Next Steps with Iran" for Poindexter to use with the President. In North's view:

"[The Relative] continues to indicate that he has a specific mandate from [Rafsanjani] to meet with USG officials seeking a means for 'getting beyond the hostage issue' and starting a dialogue with the USG.

"—[Iranian official]/Ghorbanifar: Pursuant to guidance, efforts were made over the weekend to convince [the Iranian official] to release of [sic] all three Americans simultaneously. He steadfastly rejected this proposal citing the intransigence of the captors and Iranian inability to ensure results.

"—Since last week, CIA and Army Logistics have located a significant number of HAWK parts which had previously been listed as 'unavailable.' We now believe that the total 'package' will be sufficient to entice the Iranians to proceed with the sequential release pattern proposed in the London meetings.

"—Since Sunday [September 7], [the Iranian official] has sought, in dozens of calls, to contact Abe [Hakim], Goode [North], Sam [Cave] and Copp [Secord]. This afternoon, when Sam returned call to him he told Sam that his 'boss approved of the meeting that was to take place' and referred specifically to the meetings two weeks ago with [the relative] in Brussels. CIA evaluates this information as confirmation that Rafsanjani may be moving to take control of the entire process of the U.S. relationship and the hostages.

"Other Issues

"This weekend, . . . an eleven minute address by the Shah's son [was broadcast] over Iranian T.V., by pirating the national network broadcast frequency. This broadcast reportedly sparked protests in Tehran and elsewhere by supporters of the Shah's family. [The Iranian official], in one of his calls to Sam, asked pointedly how it was that we could profess to 'accept the Iranian revolution as fact' and still sponsor such an event.

"Separate intelligence reporting indicates that a major Iranian offensive is likely to occur on/or about Monday, September 22—the anniversary of Iraq's attack against Iran in 1980. Given the urgency of calls from Iran and Rafsanjani's apparent willingness to endorse U.S./Iranian discussions, Iran may be making all possible attempts to acquire requisite arms to support this 'final offensive.'

"Director Casey conducted a review of the Iranian project today and has directed his people to initiate necessary preparations for acquiring the parts promised in earlier discussions with the Iranians. CIA continues to believe that the [Iranian official]/ Ghorbanifar connection is the only proven means by which we have been able to effect the release of any of the hostages. Though the sequential plan is not what we prefer, the commodities and quantities are within the framework of our original understanding. CIA believes that we should proceed expeditiously with arrangements to implement the sequential plan proposed by [the Iranian official]— with hopes that we could improve on it in discussions with Rafsanjani's representatives when they arrive in Europe. In this regard, our window of opportunity may be better than it will ever be again, if we are able to consummate the release of the hostages before the Iranian offensive begins." (Tab I ("Supplement Next Steps with Iran") to North to Poindexter, 9/8/86)

North also attached a report from Charles Allen about a threat to kill the hostages. Allen wrote that "we" believe that the captors were frustrated that they were no closer to freeing the Da'wa prisoners than when they captured Buckley:

"More and more, we suspect that some Hizballah leaders would be willing to settle for the release of the Americans and French in exchange for Shia prisoners held by Antoine Lahad's Southern Lebanese Army." (Allen to Poindexter, 9/8/86, Tab II to North to Poindexter, 9/8/86) (Tower)

- On September 8, Allen had written Poindexter that [n]o threat from Mughniyah should be considered idle. He is a violent extremist capable of impetuously killing the hostages. Yet he does not operate without constraints, among them:

"—Iran, which certainly has significant influence over the captors, including Mughniyah. We doubt that Iran wants the hostages disposed of without recompense,

"—other Hizballah leaders, who probably see in the hostages a valuable lever over the US and France, and an indirect means of deterring the Israeli Defense Forces from air attacks on Hizballah facilities in the Biqa', and

"—his own assessment of his self-interest, which would likely reflect that the cost of holding the hostages is minimal whereas killing them would run a serious risk US or French retaliation. As for conducting terrorist efforts against the Gulf states, Mughniyah could certainly do that without killing the hostages. (Allen to Poindexter, 9/8/86, Tab II to North to Poindexter, 9/8/86)

- North's proposal (see September 2 entry) appears to have been rejected by either Poindexter or the President, for a September 8 memorandum from North to Poindexter mentions "guidance" to seek the simultaneous release of all three hostages, rather than sequential releases. This memorandum was a supplement to the September 2 memo, and again states that it was prepared in conjunction with CIA. The memo noted that it had proved impossible to convince the first channel to consider simultaneous release of all the hostages; that DoD had located enough material to make a sequential release approach attractive to the Iranians; that the first channel may now have been acting pursuant to direction by the new channel; and that Director Casey, having conducted a review of the Iranian project that day, considered Ghorbanifar's channel "the only proven means" to get hostage releases, and so supported expeditious efforts to meet the plan proposed by Ghorbanifar, while holding out hopes that the new channel might make modifications later in September. The memo argued that "our window of opportunity may be better than it will ever be again."

After meeting with Poindexter, LTC North told a CIA official that the old channel was to be shut down and put on hold, and the new channel was to be developed instead. According to a memorandum received by the Committee, LTC North had been warned that the Ghorbanifar channel would have to be closed in a secure manner, which meant finding enough money to get Ghorbanifar out of trouble. The memo noted a figure of $4 million. Further, according to testimony received by the Committee, others were warned of the risks associated with closing down the Ghorbanifar channel at that time.

A CIA official testified that he began at this time to consider the possibility that one reason for Ghorbanifar's problems was a diversion of funds, in light of Secord and Hakim's roles in providing aid to anti-Sandinista forces. These concerns, especially the concern that Ghorbanifar's problems could lead somebody to go public, led the CIA official to raise the issue with Director Casey and Deputy Director Gates in early October, just as another source began to warn of a possible lawsuit. (SSIC 1/29/87)

- According to testimony and documents received by the Committee, during September there was a shift to the new channel. In early September, the shipment of medical supplies that Hakim had proposed in July began to move forward as the CIA took steps to purchase and pack the materials. (SSIC 1/29/87)

- Two phone calls are placed from the Hasenfus safehouse in San Salvador to Southern Air Transport in Miami, (305)871-5171. (ANTEL phone records, 10/8/86, p. 4750)

SEP - The new Iranian emissary whom Secord has developed visits Washington for a series of meetings with U.S. officials. As a result of these discussions, the envoy offers a swap in October of 500 TOW missiles for one hostage (see October 3 entry). (WP 12/31/86)

- Ghorbanifar, Khashoggi and Roy Furmark meet in Paris. Ghorbanifar voices his suspicion that $15 million from Iran arms sales have been diverted to the contras. According to Khashoggi, North had asked Ghorbanifar to get Khashoggi to raise $100 million for the rebels. (Khashoggi says he refused.) Ghorbanifar reached his conclusion concerning the diversion based on North's request and based on the 300 to 500 percent mark-up on the weapons Iran was buying at the time. Furmark reports this to Casey at a meeting with the CIA director on November 24. (WP 12/24/86 & 2/1/87)

SEP 9 - Phone calls are made from the Hasenfus safehouse in San Salvador to Lt. Col. Oliver North's listed direct line at the National Security Council, Old Executive Office Building, Washington, D.C. (202)395-3345. (ANTEL phone records, 10/8/86, p. 4750)

- On September 9, 1986, following Costa Rica's decision to close the airfield, LtCol North received word that the Costa Rican government was planning to call a press conference to announce the existence of the airfield.

The same day, LtCol North informed VADM Poindexter that he had held a conference call with then U.S. Ambassador to Costa Rica, Louis Tambs, and Assistant Secretary Elliott Abrams to discuss the potential public revelation of the airfield. All three participants confirm the conference. North said that they had decided North would call Costa Rican President Arias and tell him if the press conference went forward the U.S. would cancel $80 million promised A.I.D. assistance and Arias' upcoming visit with President Reagan. North added that both Ambassador Tambs and Assistant Secretary Abrams reinforced this message with Arias.

VADM Poindexter replied: "You did the right thing, but let's try to keep it quiet."

Assistant Secretary Abrams and Ambassador Tambs told the Board that the conference call took place, but only Tambs was instructed to call Arias and that no threat to withhold U.S. assistance was made. They each doubted that North ever called the President of Costa Rica on this matter. The Costa Rican Government later announced the discovery and closure of the airfield. (Tower)

- Frank Herbert Reed, director of the Lebanese International School in West Beirut, is kidnapped. (WP 11/26/86; NYT 12/25/86)

- On September 9, Cave informed [the official in the Prime Minister's office] by telephone. Cave informed [him] that Islamic Jihad had seized another hostage. [The Iranian office] said "I know nothing of this. I have no news." (Transcript, 9/10/86) Cave explained that the kidnapping had been undertaken by "Mugniyyah's group."

- The freighter Erria steams out of Setubal harbor, Portugal, after waiting in port for about two months with a cargo of weapons. Four days later it arrives in Cherbourg, France. (LAT 1/21/87)

- Notes taken by Mr. McDaniel indicate that the President was briefed about the second channel on September 9, 1986. (Tower)

- The President considered the new Iranian interlocutor, the prospects for a hostage release, and the possibility of a rescue operation at his morning briefing on September 9. (McDaniel log) Later that day, North and Poindexter discussed the hostage problem. (Tower)

SEP 10 - Allen reported to the Director of Central Intelligence on September 10 that he had seen North shortly after this meeting. Allen wrote:

"2. Poindexter has given Ollie new guidance on the American hostages, namely:

"—Ollie is to continue to develop links to the Iranian Government through Albert Hakim and Dick Secord of Stanford Technology Associates. (Hakim, as you are aware, has links to [the Relative]. [The Relative] apparently is attempting to arrange for Ollie and George Cave to meet with Rafsanjani; presumably with the next shipment of arms to Tehran.)

"—Ghorbanifar will be cut out as the intermediary in future shipments of cargos to Iran, if at all possible. To cut Ghorbanifar out, Ollie will have to raise a minimumm [sic] of $4 million.

"—If there is no other channel for financing future arms shipments, then Ghorbanifar will be used as a last resort.

"3. Ollie is greatly relieved by Poindexter's decisions because he feared that John and the President would shut down completely this back channel to Iran because of the kidnapping yesterday of Frank Reed. [Handwritten note]—'Reed released immediately.' (C. Allen to DCI, 9/10/86)

- Cave told [the Iranian official] that this matter (Reed) has got to be settled as soon as possible. Please look into it and settle as soon as possible because our boss is very very mad. The boss called me at seven and asked me what was going on, then about an hour ago the islamic jihad [sic] announced that they had taken him hostage. He lkthe [sic] head of a college in Beirut, his name is Reed.

"[The Iranian official]. Yes.

"[Sam O'Neil]. You look into this matter, and I will call you this afternoon at about 8 your time, okay? Will you be at home?

[The Iranian officials]. Yes, yes, yes. (very dejected). (Transcript, 9/9/86) Mughniyah's brother-in-law was one of the Da'Wa prisoners in Kuwait.)

On September 10, Nir met with Poindexter and North in Washington. To prepare Poindexter for the meeting, North wrote:

"Nir is coming to the U.S. at the urgent request of Prime Minister Peres. Incoming PM Shamir and outgoing PM Peres have agreed that Nir will remain in his current capacity after the change of government in October. You will be meeting with Nir the day before you meet with Defense Minister Rabin. It is likely that Nir has been given the task of approaching the USG on the matter of the hostages and counter-terrorism—leaving to Rabin broader security issues.

- Nir arrives in the wake of renewed terrorist attempts against Israel, the Istanbul Synagogue attack, and the seizure of another American in Beirut. The Israeli government has been anxious to consummate the hostage release plan worked out with Iran. Undoubtedly, Peres would like to achieve the release of the Israeli soldier believed to be held by Hizballah before leaving office in October. The Israelis recognize that this morning's seizure of another American in Beirut jeopardizes all previous plans in this regard.

"It is important to note that Nir has become partially aware of our contact with [the Relative]. He is not aware that we have been advised that the Iranian delegation will be headed by Rafsanjani's brother Mahmoud Rafsanjani, the former Ambassador to Damascus. The Israelis were initially concerned that the USG was moving to establish a separate channel which would not include the release of the Israeli soldier seized in February. Under instructions, Nir advised that his government's position remained as follows:

"—The Government of Israel has supported this joint effort for over a year and has not at any time acted unilaterally.

"—The Government of Israel expects that the effort to obtain the release of hostages held in Lebanon will continue to be a joint endeavor and include U.S. demands for the release of the Israeli hostage.

"Nir has been told that we will continue to support these two objectives and that the U.S. and Israel will work together to that end.

"Your talking points at Tab I provide a rationale for how contact was established with Rafsanjani and how we expect to proceed. Please note that your talking points indicate that Nir will participate in these discussions. Nir will also be meeting with Director Casey, the OSG-TIWG principals, and Father Jenco, and has asked to meet with the Vice President—who he met with in Israel. The Vice President has not yet agreed to this meeting.

"RECOMMENDATION

"That you use the points at Tab I during your meeting.

"Talking Points

"Meeting with Amiram Nir

"—Glad we could have this opportunity to talk again. Understand you have a number of important meetings during your four days here.

"—We are certainly pleased that you will be continuing in your current capacity during the political transition in October.

"—I believe our joint efforts to safely recover the hostages in Lebanon and to broaden our relationships with Iran are important to both our nations.

"—The President recognizes that were it not for your efforts that Weir and Jenco would not yet be free.

"—We are committed to continuing our joint efforts to achieve the release of all of our citizens—yours and ours.

"—In that spirit of cooperation, I want to make you aware of an opportunity that we became aware of last week.

"—In the process of investigating a possible illegal diversion of TOW missiles to Iran, Copp made contact with an agent in [country deleted] working the sale.

"—The European agent indicated that [the Relative] was involved with this purchase. Copp met with [the Relative] in Brussels on August 25, 1986 and advised him that it will not be possible to obtain TOW missiles without the help of the USG.

"—[The Relative] . . . , was clearly interested in this possibility and also raised the following points:

"—He was checking on obtaining TOWs for Moshen [sic] Rafsanjani who is Speaker Rafsanjani's brother, who suspected the $16 million deal would not be possible.

"—[The Relative] had been probed by representatives of Senator Kennedy and former Secretary of State Haig concerning the possible release of the hostages.

"—[The Relative] also knew full details of our meetings in Tehran last May to include the fact that "Miller was an Israeli."

"—Queried Copp re Iran-Iraq war and Soviet designs in the region.

"—Noted that Rafsanjani is now head of 'Supreme War Council' and wants to change perception of current military situation and establish basis for truce talks with Iraq.

"—Provided details on immediate needs re TOWs, HAWKs, technical spares, and other technical assistance.

"—Provided three scenarios for "getting beyond the hostage issue:

*"Provide us with intelligence on current locations and let us (U.S. and Israel) handle the problem.

*"Let [the official in the Prime Minister's office] project continue.

*"Rafsanjani personally intervenes to free hostages.

"—Would it be possible to set up a meeting between a personal representative of Rafsanjani and a high-level USG contact?

"—Yesterday, the Presient [sic] approved proceeding with a meeting with the Rafsanjani representative."

Poindexter approved North's talking points. (North to Poindexter, 9/9/86) (Tower)

- Poindexter noted on the memorandum received by the Committee, that he discussed it with the President. (SSIC 1/29/87)

SEP 10 - Two phone calls are made from the Hasenfus safehouse in San Salvador to Oliver North's unlisted direct line at the National Security Council, (202)395-5887; and two phone calls to Stanford Technology in Virginia, (703)356-4801. (ANTEL phone records, 10/8/86, p. 4751)

SEP 11 - North had additional news about the abduction of Reed.

"[The Relative] called Abe [Hakim] last night to advise

that Reed was not, repeat not, held by Islamic Jihad, that no Iranian "influenced" groups were responsible, and that Iran wd do whatever they could to find him and either return him or tell us where he is being held. We have not yet gotten a call from [the official in the Prime Minister's office] Back to Sam [O'Neil— Cave] on this matter, but hope the news will be the same on that front. If it is, we may well be getting somewhere w/ the highest levels of the present regieme [sic]." (North PROF note to Poindexter, 9/11/86, 07:17:56) (Tower)

- Five phone calls are placed from the Hasenfus safehouse in San Salvador to Oliver North's unlisted direct line at the NSC, (202)395-5887; and two phone calls to Stanford Technology in Virginia, (703)356-4801. (ANTEL phone records, 10/8/86, p. 4751)

SEP 12 - Two phone calls are made from the Hasenfus safehouse in San Salvador to Oliver North's unlisted direct line at the NSC, (202)395-5887; and one phone call to Stanford Technology in Virginia, (703)356-4801. (ANTEL phone records, 10/8/86, p. 4751)

- Queen Shipping, owned by Tom Parlow, who is involved in North-directed clandestine operations connected with the freighter Erria, charters a second ship, the Iceland Saga, in Flossing Roads, Netherlands and orders it to steam to Cherbourg. (LAT 2/13/87)

- Joseph James Cicippio, controller at the American University in Beirut, is kidnapped. (WP, 11/26/86; NYT 12/25/86)

- The memorandum [prepared by North for the President; see next entry] reported that on the previous Friday, September 12, Israeli Defense Minister Rabin had offered a significant quantity of captured Soviet bloc arms for use by the Nicaraguan resistance. These arms were to be picked up by a foreign flag vessel the week of September 15 and delivered to the resistance. The memorandum advised that if Peres raised this issue, the President should thank him because the Israelis held considerable stores of bloc ordnance compatible with arms used by the Nicaraguan resistance. (SSIC 1/29/87)

SEP 13 - Poindexter informed North that he had discussed "our plans on the hostages" with the Director of Central Intelligence "and he is on board. Also went over the Secord matters. Bill agrees Secord is a patriot. He will check into our suspicions. I told him he could get more detail from you." (Poindexter PROF note to North, 9/13/86, 12:01:00) (Tower)

- According to a document received by the Committee, two days before the President's meeting with Peres, Poindexter had replied by note to a message from North advising him to "go ahead and make it happen" as a "private deal between Dick and Rabin that we bless." Poindexter's note also referred to another note providing that Poindexter had talked to Casey that morning about Secord. Poindexter instructed North to keep the pressure on "Bill" to "make things right for Secord." (SSIC 1/29/87)

- The Erria docks at Cherbourg, France, where its cargo of munitions weighing 348 or 358 tons, according to various reports, and including AK-47 rifles picked up in Poland, is unloaded. (A French regional daily says the Erria docked on September 15.) The ship's agent, Thomas Parlow, says later there was no buyer in Cherbourg; "the cargo was transshipped" out of the country. (LAT 1/21/87 & 2/13/87; AFP 1/24/87)

SEP 14 - The freighter Iceland Saga arrives in Cherbourg. Six days later, it leaves with cargo weighing exactly the same as that unloaded by the Erria on September 13. (LAT 2/13/87)

SEP 15 - A phone call is placed from the Hasenfus safehouse in San Salvador to Stanford Technology in Virginia, (703)356-4801; one call to Oliver North's unlisted direct line at the NSC; one call to Secord's home number in Virginia; and one call to Southern Air Transport in Miami. (ANTEL phone records, 10/8/86, p. 4751)

MID-SEP - The Prime Minister of Israel visited Washington in the middle of September; the Iran operation constituted one of the topics addressed. Nir saw Poindexter and North. As instructed by Poindexter, North prepared briefing papers.

"You are scheduled to meet with Ami Nir again this afternoon at 1:30 p.m. for 10 minutes. Purpose of this meeting is to debrief Nir on his meeting with Peres over the weekend. You will then be able to brief the President on Peres' views regarding the several on-going and contemplated initiatives with the Israelis....

"Issues, which Prime Minister Peres may raise privately

with the President, are outlined at Tab III. Nir notes that it is unlikely that Peres will discuss any of these with anyone else in the room.

"RECOMMENDATIONS

"2. That you brief the President on the initiatives outlined at Tab III.

Approve "JP Done"

"POSSIBLE PERES DISCUSSION ITEMS WITH THE PRESIDENT

"Amiram Nir, the Special Assistant to Prime Minister Peres on Counter-Terrorism, has indicated that during the 15 minute private discussion with the President, Peres is likely to raise several sensitive issues:

"emphasizing his new role as Foreign Minister. He feels frustrated by the lack of progress and may suggest several areas wherein the U.S. could boost the image of Israeli flexibility.

"—Hostages: Several weeks ago, Peres expressed concern that the U.S. may be contemplating termination of current efforts with Iran. The Israelis view the hostage issue as a "hurdle" which must be crossed enroute [sic] to a broadened strategic relationship with the Iranian government. It is likely that Peres will seek assurances that the U.S. will indeed continue with the current "joint initiative" and ensure that we will include the two missing Israelis in the process. In that neither Weir nor Jenco would be free today without Israeli help (particularly in logistics), it would be helpful if the President would simply thank Peres for their discrete [sic] assistance.

"[Marginal note in Poindexter's handwriting: Thanks for assistance on Weir and Jenco. Will continue to work Iran with you. Include 2 missing Israelis in it.]

"—Israeli Arms: On Friday night, Defense Minister Rabin offered a significant quantity of captured Soviet bloc arms for use by the Nicaraguan democratic resistance. These arms will be picked up by a foreign flag vessel this week and delivered to the Nicaraguan resistance. If Peres raises this issue, it would be helpful if the President thanked him since the Israelis hold considerable stores of bloc ordnance, compatible with what the Nicaraguan resistance now uses.

"[Marginal note in Poindexter's handwriting: Rabin, Very tightly held.]." (North to Poindexter, 9/15/86) (Tower)

- Regan testified that he attended a briefing of the President one hour before the Peres meeting and that the Rabin offer was discussed. Regan testified that the subject was not expected to come up at the President's meeting, but that if Peres raised it, the President should "just say thanks." Regan recalled no discussion as to legality under American law.

Regan testified that the President never told him what came up in a 15 minute private meeting between the President and the Prime Minister, and the subject did not come up in the open meeting. (SSIC 1/29/87)

- Ledeen attempted to see Secretary Shultz around this time to discuss the program, as he would again in October, but Shultz testified that he declined to meet with Ledeen. (SSIC 1/29/87)

- In testimony to the Committee, the senior CIA analyst on the Iran project stated that he began a thorough analysis of the intelligence on the program in mid-September 1986 and became concerned that Iran was being overcharged and that the funding might have been diverted for other projects including support for the Nicaraguan resistance.

He testified that he had conversations with Ghorbanifar and with Nir in August and September about funding problems with the Iran arms transfers. He knew, he said, that North was active in political support of the contras and that Hakim and Secord were involved in flights to supply the contras as well as the Iran program. Because the money issue was unresolved, he suspected money was already spent or allocated. (SSIC 1/29/87)

SEP 16 - A phone call is placed from the Hasenfus safehouse in San Salvador to Oliver North's unlisted direct line at the NSC, and one call to Stanford Technology in Virginia. (ANTEL phone records, 10/8/86, p. 4751)

SEP 17 - Once past the visit of the Israeli Prime Minister, the United States entertained [the issue of the Relative]. The morning of September 17, North wrote Poindexter:

"We are planning to bring him [the Relative] into the U.S. at the end of the week, via parole papers thru Istanbul. Iranians can go to Turkey w/o visas and parole papers avoid the necessity of stamping a visa in his passport—a complication which frequently causes major problems for those living in Iran. We (Cave, Clarridge, C/NE, North) decided to honor their request to keep this first meeting private (w/o Nir/ Israelis) and to have it here so that they can confirm that they are indeed talking to the USG. We knew this when you and Nir met on Monday, but I had not yet had the chance to brief you. We will have a followup mtg with [the Relative] in Europe and we will work Nir back into this op then. In the interim, Clair [George] has put a hold on bringing [the Relative] in because he does not know whether you have 'approved the operation.' Wd you pls call Casey and tell him to get on with moving the guy in so that we don't embarrass the hell out of ourselves w/ Rafsanjani." (North PROF note to Poindexter, 9/17/86, 07:56:26)

Poindexter replied that he had already enlisted the approval of the Director of Central Intelligence on September 13. "If Clair [George] has a problem," Poindexter noted on North's memorandum on surveillance for [the Relative], "he should talk to Casey." (Poindexter note on North to Poindexter, 9/17/86)

North orchestrated preparations for the visit, which included electronic surveillance...(North to Poindexter, 9/17/86, enclosing Casey to Meese, 9/17/86, with Poindexter's concurrence, and memorandum by Odom) He reported to Poindexter:

"Casey called and told me what he wanted to do. I don't think Clair [George] will be a problem. He was actually enthusiastic about Cave's talking to Khomeini's relative...." (Poindexter PROF note North, 9/17/86, 14:35:04)

He also explicitly responded to Poindexter's note on the memorandum:

"Per your note on the surveillance package I called Casey and told him we need to get on with the parole paperwork in that you had already agreed—and had furthermore just endorsed the surveillance request. He acknowledged yr approval for the plan but said he as [sic] concerned about Shultz. He said he planned to tell Shultz in general terms that we were talking to another high level Iranian and that we would fill him in after the interview. I protested that experience showed that Shultz would then talk to...or... who would in turn talk to...and that...could well be the source of the Jack Anderson stuff we have seen periodically. Casey Agreed [sic] to proceed with the INS parole paperwork for the Relative and the visa for his escort but noted that he would still talk privately to Shultz about this.

"We are now underwaywith [sic] getting [the Relative] aboard a chartered jet out of Istanbul. CIA could not produce an aircraft on such 'short notice' so Dick has chartered the a/c thru one of Project Democracy's overseas companies. Why Dick can do something in 5 min. that the CIA cannot do in two days is beyond me—but he does. How the hell he is ever going to pay for it is also a matter of concern, but Dick is a good soldier and never even groused about it. You may want to talk to Sec Shultz about [the Relative] before Casey does. I will prepare a memo for you as soon as we talk to him." (North PROF note to Poindexter, 9/17/86, 12:59:11)

North relied on Secord to bring [the Relative] to the United States. (North PROF note to Poindexter, 9/17/86, 16:19:33)

Secord reported to North, also on September 17, that:

"[The Relative] will want intell info and a scheme for future provision of same. In the past, Casey has wanted to establish comms in Tehran and this might be the vehicle. We should give some very good OB data in narrative form so that he can take it back and make an impact. The stuff we used for [the official in the Prime Minister's office] will have changed. It is no big task for an analyst to prepare such a briefing. I know there is skepticism about this new connection, but we will fail if we do not use our senses and produce something of use. Next he will want some kind of secure voice device for use in telecoms back here to us in the next few weeks or months—there are a number of these items available commercially and I would hope that CIA could supply same in a briefcase for him to take back. Finally, [the Relative] will want to talk about war material and its relation to a long-term connection from U.S. to Iran. My opinion is that he and his group are attaching more importance to a longterm relationship than to any shortterm [sic] quick fix, such as a few thousand TOWs. He will, however, have a list of needed items and will no doubt suggest some kind of shipment to clear the hostage matter and to firmly establish direct USG to GOI transactions and to eliminate the Gorbas and [official in Prime Minister's office]. Thus, if I'm right, CIA must deliver the goods re good OB and come up with suitcase secure phone device." (Copp to Goode [North], 9/17/86, 1720) (Tower)

- Phone calls are made from the Hasenfus safehouse in San Salvador to Oliver North's unlisted direct line at the NSC and to Stanford Technology in Virginia. (ANTEL phone records, 10/8/86, p. 4751)

- North opens a channel of communications to Iran without informing the Israelis, according to the draft Senate intelligence committee report on the Iran-contra affair. Some reports say the new contact is the son of Iranian Speaker of Parliament Ali Akbar Rafsanjani. North, former CIA agent George Cave (who traveled to Iran in May with McFarlane), and others meet the new contact on October 3 in Hamburg, West Germany. (McFarlane says later that a Bible is given by North to an Iranian on a post-May 28 trip to Germany.) (NYT 1/11/87; ABC Nightline 1/20/87)

SEP 18 - Phone calls are made from the Hasenfus safehouse in San Salvador to Southern Air Transport in Miami and to Stanford Technology in Virginia. (ANTEL phone records, 10/8/86, p. 4751)

SEP 19 - Israel sends a shipload of Soviet-made weapons, presumably captured in Lebanon, to the contras, according to the draft Senate intelligence committee report leaked in early 1987. Elliott Abrams of the State Department later denies knowledge of such a shipment. (NYT 1/11/87)

- Phone calls are made from the Hasenfus safehouse in San Salvador to Secord's home in Virginia and to Stanford Technology in Virginia. (ANTEL phone records, 10/8/86, p. 4752)

SEP 19-21 - LtCol North, Mr. Cave, and a CIA official met with the second channel and two other Iranians in Washington between September 19 and 21, 1986. The two sides discussed the Soviet threat, cooperation in support of the Afghan resistance, and improved relations between the United States and Iran. The bulk of the time, however, was spent discussing the "obstacle" of the hostages and Iran's urgent need (within two months) for both intelligence and weapons to be used in offensive operations against Iraq.

LtCol North reviewed a list of military equipment and agreed "in principle" to provide that equipment, subject to the constraints of what was available within the United States or obtainable from abroad. The parties discussed the establishment of a secret eight-man U.S.-Iranian commission to work on future relations. Finally, LtCol North told the Iranians that unless contact came from North, Richard Secord, or George Cave, "there is no official message from the United States." Notes by Mr. McDaniel indicate that on

September 23, the President was briefed on recent discussions with the second channel. (Tower)

- On September 19 and 20, North, Secord, and Cave (as O'Neil) met with the Relative and the Iranian expatriate who had introduced him. The two days of negotiations were surreptitiously taped. North reported to Poindexter on September 20 that:

"Talks going extremely well. They and we want to move quickly beyond the "obstacle" of the hostages. Sincerely believe that RR can be instrumental in bringing about an end to Iran/Iraq war—a la Roosevelt w/ Russo/Japanese War in 1904. Anybody for RR getting the same prize? . . ." (North PROF note to Poindexter, 9/20/86, 12:04:15) Poindexter replied two days later: "Good on the talks. Will look forward to debrief. Ok on trip to London." (Poindexter PROF note North, 9/22/86, 8:37:02) (Tower)

SEP 20 - The Iceland Saga leaves Cherbourg with a cargo weighing exactly the same as that unloaded by the Erria there one week ago. It lists its destination as Puerto Barrios, Guatemala, but arrives instead in North Carolina eighteen days later (see October 8 entry). (LAT 2/13/87)

- Two phone calls are made from the Hasenfus safehouse in San Salvador to Stanford Technology in Virginia, and one call to Southern Air Transport in Miami. (ANTEL phone records, 10/8/86, p. 4752)

SEP 21 - A phone call is placed from the Hasenfus safehouse in San Salvador to Richard Secord's home number in Virginia. (ANTEL phone records, 10/8/86, p. 4752)

SEP 22 - North gave Poindexter a preliminary report on September 22:

"Talks with [the Relative] commenced on Friday night and proceeded almost nonstop until Sunday at 1100 when he departed for Istanbul aboard charter. George and Dick agree that things went extremely well. He is assured that the GOI is dealing directly with the USG and that the mutual interests of both parties transcend the "obstacle" of the hostages—but that this problem must be solved first. Much credit in this goes to Dick, who established the initial contact in Brussels. [The Relative] wants to set up a "joint committee" in Turkey or Portugal for resolving the issues which separate us—an idea which would then lead to putting a discrete [sic] communications team in Tehran. At one point he asked if Secord could return with him to advise on how to set this up. He asked specifically for a sign from the USG that we are indeed moving in the right direction and we agreed to a carefully constructed phrase in a VOA broadcast which would mention the nations which denied access to the hijacked PA 73 a/c—and include Iran in the list. He will be back to us later in the week after he has met with the leadership in Tehran. In discussing what we could do for them he raised the issues of 2M homeless in Iran, the collapse of the economy and the destruction of their oil industry. He complained bitterly about the French effort this spring which he said was designed only to get their hostages out and to help Chirac get elected.

"We noted that RR could not be reelected, that his motivation was to bring about an honorable end to the killing in the Iran/Iraq war, and to reestablish a positive relationship with the Iranian government that would lead to Christians, Jews and Moslems living in peace with one another. On a number of occasions he was told that RR believed deeply in the teachings of our Holy Book, a copy of which was on the table, and reference was made to a number of pertinent passages (e.g, Gen. 15:7-21; Gal. 3:7; etc.). At one point he noted to George that RR being a man of God had removed the only argument they had—that Allah was supposed to be on their side.

"He has promised prompt action on the hostages, is looking for assurances that we will not walk away once they use their influence to get them free and noted that the USG should stop other attempts to make contact w/ the GOI to prevent confusion with factions at home. He expressed several concerns about the [Ghorbanifar] channel and admitted that they believed someone close to [Ghorbanifar's Tehran contact] was working for the KGB. He expressed great concern that the Soviets could exploit confirmation of the contact by making the contact public and doing great mischief in Iran and the U.S. and by rapidly escalating their assistance to Iraq or even intervening in Iran. We did all we could to feed this anxiety. Nir has been calling regularly to exhort us to move on the next shipment. Because [the Relative] has asked us to wait to see what the result of his discussion in Tehran is, we have decided to stall by telling Nir and Gorba that we must have a meeting w/ [the official in the Prime Minister's office] before we can proceed. We have told Nir that you and RR are very concerned about the two new hostages and that we cannot proceed w/ further deliveries until such a meeting takes place. [The Relative] has asked that for the time being we leave the Israelis out of this because of the problems at home. Contrary to what Nir said here, [the Relative] did know that Nir was an Israeli. We will put together a summary of the talks by my return Wednesday. You can brief RR that we seem to be headed in a vy positive direction on this matter and have hopes that the hostage resolution will lead to a significant role in ending the Iran/Iraq war. (North PROF note to Poindexter, 9/22/86, 9:22:57)

"In the course of the meetings, [the Relative] asked that the United States 'stop other attempts to make contact [such as those through third countries] now that we were in direct discussions.' (North PROF note to Poindexter, 9/20/86, 12:06:57.)

"Geo Cave will brief Casey this afternoon on the results of the discussions w/ [the Relative]," North wrote Poindexter. "Casey has asked what we are doing abt bringing Sec State up to speed on results. I told him this was your call. Casey is urging a mtg on Weds. among you, Casey, Cave and me to discuss situation prior to discussion w/Shultz. Can we schedule same?" (North PROF note to Poindexter, 9/22/86, 12:00:49) (Tower)

Apparently, the Director of Central Intelligence discussed the Relative's visit with the Secretary of State. North wrote Poindexter the afternoon of September 22:

"FoMin Velayati is one of the few non-clerics at the top of the GOI. He is a technocrat, reportedly a conservative and relatively close to Rafsanjhani [sic]. He reportedly is a member of the "War Council" which determines the distribution of resources and funds within the Iranian government. According to [the Relative], Velayati participated in the meetings regarding our earlier diplomatic approaches to the GOI and evaluated these initiatives as sincere. [The Relative] reports, however, that Velayati was not in the final sessions they had which authorized [the Relative] trip to the U.S. In these sessions Rafsanjhani, Moshen [sic] Rafiq-Dust and Mohammad Hosein Jalalai along with Musavi-Khamenei made the decision for him to come to the U.S. and to be assured that he was indeed talking to the top of the USG.

"Re the Casey/Shultz discussions: Casey informs that he

told Shultz, alone, that the CIA was assisting in bringing [the Relative] into and out of the U.S. for talks and that he (Casey) wd get back to Shultz at some point in the future on what had transpired. According to Bill, Shultz simply said 'OK.'" (North PROF note to Poindexter, 9/22/86, 14:35:55) (Tower)

- Four phone calls are made from the Hasenfus safehouse in San Salvador to Stanford Technology in Virginia, and one call to Richard Secord's home number in Virginia. (ANTEL phone records, 10/8/86, p. 4752)

SEP 23 - Notes by Mr. McDaniel indicate that on September 23, the President was briefed on recent discussions with the second channel. (Tower)

- A phone call is placed from the Hasenfus safehouse in San Salvador to Southern Air Transport in Miami. (ANTEL phone records, 10/8/86, p. 4752)

SEP 24 - Glenn Souham, a dual U.S.-French citizen who is alleged to have worked for the NSC on the contra issue, is shot to death outside his apartment in Paris. He was the founder of Century, a security firm in France with politicians and show business figures as clients. A friend of Souham's says later that he "first learned from Glenn that he was doing something for the NSC in 1985." A newspaper account later quotes an unidentified congressional source as saying that North told the source that Souham's murder made secret arms deals to the contras "serious business." According to White House spokesman Don Mathes, "He was never a paid or unpaid consultant to the National Security Council." Michael Castine, director of the NSC's communications division and a personal friend of Souham, says Souham helped make some preliminary arrangements last year for a White House private sector initiative conference in Paris. Souham also reportedly traveled to Grenada in 1984 on a trip sponsored by the quasi-governmental Overseas Private Investment Council (OPIC) and again in February 1986 to assist on a volunteer basis a White House advance team preparing for a presidential visit to the island. (Reuter 9/25/86; WT 1/19/87; AP 1/20/87)

- A phone call is placed from the Hasenfus safehouse in San Salvador to Southern Air Transport in Miami; two calls to Richard Secord's home number in Virginia; and one call to Stanford Technology in Virginia. (ANTEL phone records, 10/8/86, p. 4752)

SEP 24-5 - North also prepared a full memorandum of conversation to Poindexter on September 25 which had additional material including the statement: "I want to tell you that unless one of the three men sitting here in the room right now (North, Secord, Sam O'neil) [sic] contact you, there is no official message." North noted that "[t]he only other copy of this memorandum of conversation has been given (by hand) to the DDO of CIA." (North to Poindexter, 9/25/86)

The Secretary of State told the Board that he heard nothing about Iran from July 2, 1986, when Under Secretary Armacost sent him a memorandum he does not recall reading and October 31, 1986, when, after making a speech in Los Angeles, someone asked him about a hostage release. "I was totally barn-sided. I had no idea what was taking place." (Shultz, SRB, 56-57)

On September 24, North provided Poindexter with materials for a meeting among Poindexter, the Director of Central Intelligence, Cave, and C/NE to discuss the September 19-20 conversations.

During the discussions, [the Relative] asked for a "discrete [sic] public sign" that he could use to support his debriefing back in Tehran. We decided that a VOA editorial, broadcast in Farsi, which mentions the Iranian Government's denial of flight clearance to the hijacked Pan Am flight, would suffice. At Tab II is a VOA editorial regarding the hijacking of Pan Am Flight #78.

"We appear to be in contact with the highest levels of the Iranian Government. There is no doubt that [the relative] is far more competent and better 'connected' than our other interlocutor, [the official in the Prime Minister's office]. It is possible that the Iranian Government may well be amenable to a U.S. role in ending the Iran-Iraq war. This, in and of itself, would be a major foreign policy success for the President. We, therefore, need to determine how we will proceed from here on with the Iranians, specifically:

"—Should we proceed with the 'joint committee' proposed by [the Relative] during our discussions.

"—Who, if anybody, at the State Department should be brought into this activity.

"RECOMMENDATION

"That you review the attachments prior to your meeting. Approve "JP" Disapprove" (North to Poindexter, 9/24/86) North attached Cave's summary of the meetings. ([Cave], "Rundown of Visitor's comments on 19/20 Sept 86," Tab I to North to Poindexter, 9/24/86)

North also attached a draft of a Voice of America editorial entitled "International Cooperation Against Terrorism," in which, as promised to the Relative, Iran among others, was thanked for its assistance in the successful resolution of the PanAm Flight 73 hijacking. (Tab II to North to Poindexter, 9/24/86)

On September 23, after Craig Coy, a member of the NSC staff and former executive assistant to Admiral Holloway, Executive Director of the Vice President's Task Force on Terrorism, spoke to Ambassador Bremer about the editorial, North sent the editorial to Bremer with instructions to broadcast it on September 26 and 27. (North to Bremer, 9/25/86 Coy 3-4, Tower)

Cave recalled that, at the meetings on September 19 and 20, "an enormous amount of progress was made." (Cave 17) Cave told the Board that "we were talking to someone at the political level, even though the gentleman was very young." (Id.)

"[W]hen we were in Tehran, at the political and strategic level, we really didn't get anywhere. But at this meeting [September 19- 20], he proposed to us that we form a joint commission of four U.S. members and four Iranian members, that we meet in secret and come up with a program for improving U.S.-Iranian relations.

"He also discussed in great detail their concerns about Afghanistan, the Soviet Union, and the Persian Gulf. He told us that they had taken our advice and in early September had sent their Oil Ministry [sic], under cover of doing OPEC business, on a trip around the Persian Gulf to talk to the Saudis, the Kuwaitis and the United Arab Emirates, and had gotten what they had considered a rather positive response, particularly from the Saudis.

"At that meeting, we also gave them a briefing on what we considered to be the Soviet threat toward Iran.

"We also agreed at that meeting that at the next meeting they had, which was going to be in early October, we would give them a briefing on our view of the war, their war with Iraq. We also gave them at the September meeting a briefing on our view of how the insurrection in Afghanistan was going against the central government and the Soviets, and they promised at the next meeting that they would give us their views." (Id. at 18-19)

To C/NE, this meeting had been remarkable for another reason. He told the Board that [the Relative] "immediately presented bona fides in the sense of saying, look, we can't get all your hostages out. It was the first time we had heard that in this channel. Always before the promise was don't worry about a thing; we can get them all. He said, we can get two out, maybe three, but we can't get them all." (C/NE (1) 38) (Tower)

According to Charles Allen, the "new channel" informed the Americans in September that Khomeini's son "briefed the father in great detail . . . [and] the Iranians had decided that it was worth talking to the Americans not just for arms but, I think, for broader reasons." (C. Allen (1) 19-20) (Tower)

SEP 25 - Two phone calls are made from the Hasenfus safehouse in San Salvador to Southern Air Transport in Miami, and one to Stanford Technology in Virginia. (ANTEL phone records, 10/8/86, p. 4752)

SEP 26 - North wrote Poindexter on September 26 that

"[t]his morning, immediately after the VOA broadcast of our PA-73 message, [the Relative] deposited $7M in the numbered Swiss Account we gave him last week. The money will be transferred by noon (EDT) to another account in another bank. In order to save time, I have told Dick to pay CIA's account for the remaining HAWK parts and the 500 TOWs so that they can be assembpled [sic], packed and moved to [location deleted]. UNODIR, CIA will commence acquisition as soon as they receive the money—though nothing will be shipped to final destination until we have had the follow-on discussion w/ [the Relative] and reached an understanding on the 'obstacle.' We believe he will want to meet on the week of October 6-10 *** . Nothing will move from . . . until you so approve. Will sit down tomorrow w/ the CIA logistics guy who is doing the ordering to see if for once they can get it right." (North PROF note to Poindexter, 9/26/86, 09:47:48) (Tower)

- One call is placed from the Hasenfus safehouse in San Salvador to Southern Air Transport in Miami, and one to

Stanford Technology in Virginia. (ANTEL phone records, 10/8/86, p. 4752)

- Costa Rican authorities seized a clandestine airstrip near the Nicaraguan border, it is reported today. Costa Ricans living near the strip tell reporters that two Americans named "Rob" and "Bill" supervised construction of the airfield on property owned by Udall Research Corp., a Panamanian registered company. (Tico Times 9/26/86)

LATE SEP - By the end of September, the stage was set for a complete switch to the new channel, and, in effect, the first channel was left to fend for itself. (SSIC 1/29/87)

- According to Roy Furmark, at the end of September 1986, Khashoggi asked Furmark to visit Casey and ask for his assistance. Khashoggi was deeply involved in financing arms deals between the U.S. and Iran, and he was owed $10 million. The funds belonged to some investors and had been deposited in an account belonging to Lake Resources, a firm connected to North, Secord & Hakim. According to Furmark, Khashoggi assumed that Lake was a U.S. Government account. The solution, he said, was for the U.S. Government either to refund the $10 million or to complete the weapons shipment. (SSIC 1/29/87)

- Furmark testified that at the end of September, Khashoggi asked him to visit Casey to get the U.S. to resolve the financial problems. Furmark testified that all those involved considered the Lake Resources account at Credit Suisse to be an American account. Furmark testified that he had known Casey for twenty years in business matters, OSS dinners, et cetera. (SSIC 1/29/87)

SEP 29- Lieutenant General Aktar Abdul Rehman, the head of Pakistan's Interservice Intelligence, skews the distribution of the arms the U.S. buys to the two resistance groups led by Gulbuddin Hekmatyar and Abdul Rasul Sayaf, it is disclosed. (Afghan Update 9/29/86)

SEP 30 - LtCol North indicated in a memorandum dated September 30, 1986, that the [Costa Rica] airfield was used for direct resupply of the Contras from July 1985 to February 1986, and thereafter as the primary abort base for damaged aircraft. (Tower)

- In a message to VADM Poindexter dated July 15, 1986, LtCol North described "Project Democracy" assets as worth over $4.5 million. They included six aircraft, warehouses, supplies, maintenance facilities, ships, boats, leased houses, vehicles, ordnance, munitions, communications equipment, and a 6520-foot runway. The runway was in fact a secret airfield in Costa Rica. (Tower)

- According to LtCol North, press reports on the existence of this airfield in September, 1986 "caused Project Democracy to permanently close Udall Corporation, and dispose of its capital assets." (North memo to Poindexter 9/30/86) (Tower)

In a memorandum North to Poindexter, North states that "the airfield at the Santa Elena has been a vital element in supporting the resistance. Built by a Project Democracy proprietary, (Udall Corporation S.A.—A Panamanian company), the field was initially used for direct resupply efforts [to the contras] (July 1985-February 1986)...the field has served as the primary abort base for aircraft damaged by Sandinista anticraft fire. (Tower)

FALL - The attorney for Thomas Clines, who is on trial for securities fraud, is told over the phone by a person representing himself as "working with the National Security Council," that Clines is on assignment with the government. The attorney, A. Hoyt Rowell, says later the person, who was not a government official, called him to explain Clines's repeated absences from the court proceedings. Asked if the caller was Richard Secord, Rowell said, "You'll have to draw your own conclusions." (WSJ 1/2/86)

- By early fall, the Drug Enforcement Administration (DEA) office in Guatemala has uncovered convincing evidence that American flight crews working with the covert arms supply operation to the contras are involved in smuggling cocaine and marijuana. One of the crew members, after DEA agents searched his house in San Salvador for drugs, warned that he and his colleagues had White House protection, and invoked North's name, although some officials later say the warning was a bluff. After the C-123K crash on October 5, the arms supply operation collapses, the crew members scatter and the drug investigation is no longer actively pursued. (NYT 1/20/87)

OCTOBER 1986

OCT - U.S.-made Stingers are deployed by Afghan rebels. (WP 1/27/87)

- The CIA buys a 358-ton shipment of ammunition and Polish automatic rifles and land mines aboard the freighter Iceland Saga, according to intelligence sources. The shipment, bound from Cherbourg after its delivery on the Erria from Poland and Portugal, was headed for Puerto Barrios, Guatemala when the Hasenfus plane is shot down October 5. Instead, it docks in Wilmington, N.C. three days later (see entry). One intelligence source says North prevailed upon Casey to authorize the purchase, which takes place just after CIA aid to the contras becomes legal again. The Erria is registered in Panama to Dolmy Business Inc., which shares offices with CSF, often retained by Secord associate Albert Hakim, who Danish shipping agent Thomas Parlow says has controlling interest in the Erria. (WSJ 2/13/87)

OCT 1 - The congressional ban on U.S. military aid to the contras expires. (LAT 2/13/87)

- The CIA analyst [Charles Allen] testified that on October 1, 1986, he brought his concerns to the Deputy Director of Central Intelligence, Robert Gates. He explained that given the individuals involved, he was concerned that funds were being diverted to Central America.

According to testimony, Gates was surprised and disturbed and told the analyst to see Director Casey. The analyst testified that he and Gates did not discuss the legality or illegality of diversion. They talked about it being an inappropriate commingling of separate activities and the risk to operational security.

Gates testified to the Committee that the analyst viewed the problems as a serious threat to the operational security of the Iran project. Gates recalled that the analyst's conclusion was that some of the money involved was being diverted to other U.S. projects, including the contras. (SSIC 1/29/87)

- Charles Allen told the Board:

" . . . I was very troubled in September that the operation was to spin out of control, and I became convinced, without any evidence, but I've been trained all my life as an intelligence officer to make assessments, that perhaps because Secord and Hakim were directly involved and were also directly involved in supplying the contras, and I could not understand this incredible price markup that we were seeing —the complaints were coming from Iran, from Ghorbanifar, from the Special Assistant to the Prime Minister of Israel, although later he didn't raise that issue again, and I think perhaps—it's just speculation—he was advised by the NSC that maybe some of the money was being diverted to the contras.

" . . . On 1 October I went to Bob Gates, the Deputy Director . . . And I added at the end of my conversation . . . [that] this first channel that has been shut down by the NSC is a running sore. The creditors are demanding payment and I said this is going to be exposed if something isn't done. I said perhaps the money has been diverted to the contras, and I said I can't prove it. Gates was deeply disturbed by that and asked me to brief the Director." (Tower)

- According to the testimony of Gates and a CIA officer (Charles Allen), in early October 1986 a CIA officer (Allen) expressed concern to DDCI Gates that abandoning the old channel altogether for the new channel might be a risk to operational security because the old channel had not been taken care of financially.

- Arif Durrani, a participant in the attempt to ship HAWK missile parts to Iran, flies to London at the request of Manuel Pires, whom he describes as "a weapons supplier for Secord for the Contra rebels in Nicaraugua," [sic]. In London, he later says, "I met with individuals who identified themselves as United States officials. One individual, who identified himself as 'Mr. White,' I have come to believe was Lt. Col. Oliver North of the NSC. I had met Mr. White two other times. Others at the meeting included a representative of the Anglican Church. At that meeting, the American officials urged me to quickly obtain the parts. I told that Radio Research [the company in Connecticut Durrani is dealing with] was delaying the shipment for lack of licenses. American officials made numberous telephone calls that night from London (see October 2 entry). (Affidavit of Arif Durrani, 2/4/87)

OCT 2 - A week later, North submitted the views of his team (Cave, Clarridge, C/NE, Secord, and North) on "Next Steps for Iran." They argued for the program discussed with [the Relative], who added pressure for acceptance. North reported on October 2:

"[The Relative] contacted Dick this morning and asked that George, Dick and I meet him on Monday in Frankfurt. He claims to have just returned to Tehran from Beirut and that he will have good news regarding the "obstacle" (hostages). I am preparing a paper for you which will include the travel approval for Goode (North) and a Bible for [the Relative]—since he is bringing a Koran for the President. We will also use the opportunity of this meeting to set Nir straight on how we are going to proceed. He is beside himself at the delay in action since he was here—and we can, I believe take care of that whole problem in the next few days. Will include our collective recommendations (from George, Dick and me) in the package. Hope to have it to you this afternoon. Warm regards, North p.s. PLEASE authorize us to be polygraphed re this Woodward mess. You, the President, WE need to find the person who is doing this. p.p.s. On the Costa Rican airstrip; it is a C-135K, not a C-130. We had to sell the C-130 last month just to keep Project Democracy afloat (actually an L-100, the commercial variant of the C-130). The airplane in the photo—and referenced in the memo is a smaller precedent to the C-130 w/ 2 reciprocating piston engines and two ram jets outboard (like the old P2V Neptunes). (North PROF note to Poindexter, 10/02/86, 15:11:48.)

- "[The Relative] called Dick this morning to advise that he had just returned from Beirut and would very much like to meet with us in Frankfurt, Germany, on Monday, October 6. He indicates that he has "good news" regarding the hostages and that he wishes to get past the "obstacle" as quickly as possible. An appropriate travel approval is attached at Tab I.

"George Cave is taking a well-deserved "mini-vacation" in Rome. We are telling all callers that he is in the hospital for tests on his back. In accord with [the Relative's] request, the U.S. side would be represented by: Sam O'Neil, Copp, and Goode.

"This meeting also affords us the opportunity to deal with the issue of Israeli cooperation. Nir has been calling daily (often several times) urging that we get on with the process in our 'joint venture.' He constantly cites his September 10 meeting with you as the basis for proceeding urgently. Because we have not told him about our intention to pursue the '[the Relative channel]' first, he continues to encourage Ghorbanifar to raise the requisite funds for another delivery. Ghorbanifar, in turn, has a frequent dialogue with [his Tehran contact] in this regard. All of this tends to create confusion among the various participants and an unnecessary OPSEC vulnerability. We need to act now to reduce the number of channels into the Iranians (at least on a temporary basis) and clarify various roles and missions. As is evident on the diagram at Tab II, the various channels of communications are, at the very least, a source of great vulnerability to KGB and other SIGINT penetration.

"We (Cave, Clarridge, C/NE, and Copp) believe that we should move promptly on both fronts as follows:

"—[The Relative]: O'Neil, Copp, and Goode meet with [the Relative] in Frankfurt on Monday, October 6. [The Relative] has indicated that he has an internal consensus on how to proceed with regard to the hostages 'obstacle.' He has said that he will bring with him to this meeting 'one of the officials we met with in Tehran' and has asked that we bring with us a definitive sample of the intelligence we had discussed when he was here. Based on this, we believe that [a Revolutionary Guard Intelligence official] may well accompany [the Relative]. You will recall that [the Relative's] request for intelligence was very specific (the details were forwarded to you via PROFs). While the sensitivity of providing this information is well-recognized, it must also be noted that intelligence was given a higher priority by [the Relative] than any other assistance we could provide. In the Casey-C/NE-Cave-North meeting we had with you after [the Relative] departed, we all agreed that it was unlikely that providing such information would change the course of the war. Further, we all recognized that the information need not be accurate and that it was highly perishable given the dynamic nature of the conflict. In short, we believe that a mix of factual and bogus information can be provided at this meeting which will satisfy their concerns about 'good faith' and that we can use the 'perishible' [sic] argument as an incentive for the Iranians to accept a CIA communications team in Tehran. As before, we would not leave any documents with the Iranians, but will provide an exposition during which they could take detailed notes. Director Casey needs to be told to prepare the intelligence for handcarry to the meeting.

"[The Relative] has said he is bringing a Koran for the President. As a reciprocal gesture, we have purchased a Bible which we would present to [the Relative] for him to take back to Tehran with him. Given our earlier discussions (see transcript), it would be very helpful if the President would inscribe a brief note citing a particular Biblical passage (Tab III) in the front of the Bible. This particular excerpt is important in that it is a New Testament reference to Abraham, who is viewed by Moslems, Jews, and Christians as the progenitor of all the world's nations. It would be most effective if the President hand wrote the inscription and initialed/signed it without addressing the note to any particular person.

"—Nir: When Amiram was here, we made a conscious decision not to apprise him of our near-term efforts with [the Relative]. We did inform him earlier of the contact and he continues to inquire regarding the status of this initiative. Meanwhile, lacking guidance to the contrary, Nir has sought to stimulate further activity between Ghorbanifar and [the official in the Prime Minister's office]. This has resulted in [this official] calling directly to George's home and office several times daily and considerable confusion regarding why we have not accepted the [Iranian official]/Ghorbanifar 'offer' to purchase the remaining HAWK spare parts and 500 TOWs.

"From an operational perspective, the current communications arrangements are a command and control/OPSEC nightmare (Tab II). Nir essentially controls our access to both [the Iranian official] and Ghorbanifar and, thus, we often find ourselves reacting to his well intentioned efforts. We believe that we now have an opportunity to change the relationship in such a way that Nir is placed in a supporting role rather than acting as a primary source of control. We also recognize that Israel's participation in this activity is both politically and operationally important. In altering Nir's status, we need to do so in such a way that he and those officials in his government who are cognizant continue to perceive that this is still a 'joint venture.'

"In order to accomplish the objectives outlined above, we propose that on Saturday, October 4, Copp would fly to Tel Aviv and meet with Nir. At the meeting, Copp would use the talking points at Tab IV. In an effort to ameliorate Nir's angst over his 'new status,' we urge that the letter at Tab V to Prime Minister Peres be signed by the President. If you agree, we need your approval of the talking points at Tab IV and a Presidential signature (real or autopen) on Tab V by 3:00 p.m. Friday, October 3.

"The steps above are designed to give us a chance to make the new relationship through [the Relative] function without destroying the Ghorbanifar/[Iranian official] channel. We would, in effect, put Ghorbanifar [the Iranian official in the Prime Minister's office] on 'hold' until we see what [the Relative] produces. Please note that when Copp briefs Nir in Tel Aviv on Saturday, he will not reveal that he is enroute to Frankfurt to meet [the Relative]. Given [the Relative's] strong antipathy toward the Israelis and our uncertainty as to whether or not he knows that Nir (aka Miller) is Israeli, we would tell Nir on Sunday night that we were going to a hastily arranged meeting with [the Relative] which he (Nir) will be unable to make due to a lack of connecting flights to Frankfurt.

"[The Relative] has already told us, that shortly after the October 6 meeting, there will be a follow-on meeting of the 'Joint committee' in which [the official in the Prime Minister's office] will be a participant. Unless we are convinced that the Iranians would recognize Nir as an Israeli, we would intend to invite Nir to this follow-on meeting. A memo from you to the President has not been prepared for obvious reasons. It is hoped that between now and 3:00 p.m. Friday you will have an opportunity to privately discuss this with the President and obtain his approvals/signatures on the steps indicated above." (North to Poindexter, 10/2/86) (Tower)

Poindexter approved North's travel request (in the name of William P. Goode); agreed to have the President inscribe a Bible with the designated passage from Galatians; approved talking points for Secord; and agreed to persuade the President to sign the letter to Peres. Poindexter neither accepted nor rejected the request to have the Director of Central Intelligence prepare an appropriate intelligence package by October 4 for the meeting on October 6. (Tower)

The President's inscription read: "And the scripture, foreseeing that God would justify the Gentiles by faith, preached the gospel beforehand to Abraham, saying, "All the nations shall be blessed in you." Galatians 3:8' Ronald Reagan Oct. 3, 1986" The President told the Board that he did inscribe the Bible because VADM Poindexter told him this was a favorite passage with one of the people with whom the U.S. was dealing in Iran. The President said he made the inscription to show the recipient that he was "getting through."

The second attachment to this memorandum was a diagram of the communications between "Tango" [Tehran]—Merchant (Ghorbanifar), [the official in the Prime Minister's office], [the Relative], [the Iranian expatriate] and [Secord's Iranian agent]—and the United States team—Goode (North), Sam (Cave), Charlie (Allen), Copp (Secord), and C/NE. Apart from Cave and [the official in the Iranian Prime Minister's office], who sporadically communicated one-on-one, and Allen and Ghorbanifar, who also communicated directly, the others talked through middlemen. Ghorbanifar generally used Nir; while those in the second channel used Hakim (Abe). (Id. at Tab II) North added the recommendation:

"Pare the U.S. communicators down to no more than two individuals (who either compare notes directly each day, or report to a common supervisor); e.g., Sam and Copp, who both report daily to North. Cut Charlie, C/NE and anybody else out. Have them stop communications cold turkey (to support cover story of [old] channel being blown, rolled up, and finished)." (Tower)

Secord's instructions for his meeting with Nir on October 4 noted:

"The objective of this discussion is to improve our control of events in this joint effort to establish a strategic relationship with Iran. The talking points below are intended to establish the parameters of your discussion and are designed to elicit further cooperation:

"—ADM Poindexter has directed that I see you regarding our current Ghorbanifar/[Iranian official] channel and discuss with you ways in which we can move together to accomplish our mutual objective—a strategic relationship with Iran.

TOP 25 CONTRIBUTORS

AS OF OCTOBER 3, 1986

CONTRIBUTOR	TOTAL	CAFP	TOYS	FOOD	SDI
GARWOOD	2,546,598	501,000	1,995,598	50,000	
NEWINGTON	1,148,471	994,471			
KING	921,500	466,500		5,000	150,000
SACHER	400,000	400,000			
WARM	355,232	335,232			
HUNT	237,500	237,500			
HOOPER	145,000	45,000	100,000		
O'BOYLE	130,000		130,000		
BECK	108,133	108,133			
DRISCOLL	106,000	46,000			60,000
BRANDON	100,000	100,000			
O'NEIL	76,125	76,125			
RAMSEY	48,000	30,000			
GIDDENS	42,500	10,000	32,500		
SALWASSER	42,000	20,000		2,000	
LYNCH	39,000	32,000		4,000	
STARNS	30,000	30,000			
MERCULSSON	22,535	22,535			
ROBERTS	22,125	16,125		1,000	5,000
CLAGGETT	20,000		20,000		
MARVIN	15,000				15,000
ADRAKIEWICZ	11,700	10,500			
ANDERSON	10,000	5,000		5,000	
FERGUSON	10,000	10,000			
PIERCE	10,000				
CHRISTIAN	7,700	2,700		5,000	

1331 Pennsylvania Ave., N.W. Suite 350 South Washington, D.C. 20004 (202) 662-8700

"—We have fairly strong evidence that [the Iranian official] was directly involved with the seizure of the second new hostage in Beirut (Cicippio).

"—We believe that the first new hostage (Reed) was taken by elements other than Hizballah—although they may have him in their hands now.

"—We think that [the official in the Iranian Prime Minister's office] may have believed that he could bring additional pressure to bear on us to commence further deliveries by seizing another hostage (or hostages).

"—Quite the contrary is true. The President is adamant that we will not move forward on this channel until we resolve the new hostage issue.

"—We are also concerned that the two new hostages (or at least Cicippio) represents a clear violation of the "understanding" we have had with the Iranians on anti-U.S. terrorism since June of last year.

"—We do not want to engage in a process that results in new hostages just to bring 'pressure to bear.' Nor will we continue this process if, when the current hostages are released, more are taken, simply to elicit further deliveries of arms.

"—Aside from this very strong policy objection to continuing, we have, as you know, had repetitive financial and communications dufficulties [sic] with Ghorbanifar. While we could debate as to whether or not Ghorbanifar had received all that was due him by the Iranians, the most important factor is potential OPSEC risk.

"—In an effort to 'keep things moving,' Ghorbanifar has made commitments in our name which are patently beyond our ability to meet. This has resulted in increased expectations on the part of the Iranians.

"—We know . . . that neither [the official in the Prime Minister's office] nor other Iranian officials in Tehran trust Ghorbanifar.

"—Finally, both of us know that [the Iranian official], himself, is not intellectually astute enough to realize the importance of our contact nor the sincerity of our desire to establish an official government-to-government relationship.

"—In short, this channel is not serving our mutual objective: the reopening of a strategic relationship with Iran.

"—The President has directed that we will not proceed with any further receipt of funds from Ghorbanifar nor deliveries to [his Tehran contact] until we resolve these issues.

"—Several months ago, I apprised you of a contact with [the relation of a powerful Iranian official]. The USG decided to pursue this contact to determine its validity.

"—We are confident that [the Relative], the man I met with in Brussels, has been franchised to act as a liaison between the U.S. and Iranian governments.

"—When Prime Minister Peres was in Washington last month, the President assured him that we are going to continue this effort as a joint project. [Poindexter penned a question mark in the margin next to this point.]

"—I have been instructed to seek out a second meeting with [the Relative] as soon as it can be set up and that I will act as the U.S. intermediary until we establish direct contact with government officials from our side.

"—Once we have established direct USG contact with [the Relative], we intend to introduce you into this process under the same conditions as obtained when you went to Tehran with us.

"—Based on my initial meeting with [the Relative] and the intelligence we have been able to collect, we believe that this contact may well prove to be the one that both your government and mine have been seeking.

(Remember Nir has been told that you "came upon" [the Relative] as a consequence of looking into the possible diversion of TOWs through Spain/Portugal during an investigation undertaken in late July/early August.)

"—While we explore the sincerity of the nephew and confirm his ability to speak for the Iranian government, we want to keep the Ghorbanifar/[Iranian official] channel on "hold."

"—To that end, we have told Sam(Cave)—who is in the hospital—he is to contact [the Iranian official] and tell him that:

"—there must be a meeting with [the Iranian official] before we proceed any further;

"—the issue of the two new hostages has become a strong, negative factor in proceeding at all;

"—this matter (the two new hostages) must be resolved before we will take any further steps for any further deliveries;

"—the problem is not the merchant and his financing, but rather the two new hostages;

"—contrary to what he [the Iranian official] may expect, there will be no further deliveries until we have met and resolved this matter;

"—we have asked [the Iranian official] to meet with us in Frankfurt on October 9—we do not yet have an answer.

"—I intend to meet with [the Relative], somewhere in Europe or Turkey, hopefully this week. I will then report back to Washington on my findings and a follow-on meeting will be set-up—in which we will attempt to have you included.

"—I want to caution you, however, that in my meeting in Brussels [the Relative] indicated that he and others in Tehran are aware that you are an Israeli—and knew it when you went to Tehran,

"—Neither of us want this contact, if it is indeed what I think it to be, to founder because of this.

"—I have been instructed to find a way to have you in the meeting in which Goode and Sam will serve as the USG representatives.

"—If the meeting with [the Relative] this week goes well, I would expect that all of us could meet with him next week.

"—In the interim, if [the Iranian official] does indeed agree to meet with us under the conditions we have established, we should proceed with that meeting."

Poindexter met with the Director of Central Intelligence and his Deputy the evening of October 2. (DCI Telephone Calls and Meetings; Gates, Memorandum for the Record, 10/3/86) In addition to discussing the proposal to provide Iran with military information . . . both North and Poindexter reported on the new channel to McFarlane. (Tower)

-In reality, the idea of the Bible and the choice of the inscription were contained in an October 2, 1986, memorandum from LtCol North to VADM Poindexter [see previous entry]. The Bible was to be exchanged for a Koran at the October 5-7 meeting. VADM Poindexter approved the idea and the President inscribed the Bible the next morning. (Tower)

- An "Ed Garay" signs a visitor's logbook at American National Management Corporation. Edward T. de Garay is president of the Pennsylvania air charter company, Corporate Air, for which Eugene Hasenfus said he was working. (WP 3/22/87)

- According to Arif Durrani (see October 1 entry), "I was told that President Reagan would sign orders the next day [October 3] to authorize shipments of arms to Iran. I was told by Mr. White not to worry about the paper work." In a court affidavit filed in 1987, Durrani says, "I returned to the United States from London on October 2, and had intended to fly to Washington after confirming that Radio Research had shipped the parts to Jetstream Freight Services, as instructed to Pires. I was to inform [Jack] Koser [who Durrani says worked for the NSC] that the parts were shipped to Jetstream, and I understood that I would have no further involvement with the parts after that point. I knew that the shipment was so small that the government would not ship them in a separate airplane, which was normal practice." Durrani goes on to say, "It is my understanding that the arms shipments made by the United States government to Iran were made to the National Iranian Oil Company, generally shipped in individual airplanes in boxes labelled 'oil drilling equipment,' those being the arrangements set by the United States government." (Affidavit of Arif Durrani, 2/4/87)

OCT 3 - According to Durrani (see October 2 entry), "I have come to learn that on October 3 the President did execute such an order, and that he sent a message to Iran saying he would honor the American commitments to ship arms in exchange for the hostages." (Affidavit of Arif Durrani, 2/4/87)

- A list labeled "Top 25 Contributors" as of this date on National Endowment for the Preservation of Liberty stationery shows that two wealthy widows provided more than half of NEPL's total budget. Ellen Garwood of Austin, Texas, gave $2,546,598, of which almost $2 million went into the "Toys" account later reported to be a direct funnel of funds for Contra weapons. Barbara Newington of Greenwich, Connecticut, gave $1,148,471, almost all of which went to the Central American Freedom Program account which paid for TV ads and the services of International Business Communications. (NEPL list 10/3/86; ABC News 2/12/87)

- On October 3, North invited McFarlane to review the transcripts of the September 19-20 meeting. (North PROF note to McFarlane, 10/03/86, 22:08:16)

Poindexter expressed enthusiasm about the meetings:

"We have made contact with [the Relative of a powerful Iranian official (the "Relative")]. Two meetings so far. One here in US. Ollie, Cave and Secord meet with him this weekend in Frankfort [sic]. Your trip to Tehran paid off. You did get through to the top. They are playing our lines back to us. They are worried about Soviets, Afghanistan and their economoy [sic]. They realize the hostages are obstacle to any productive relationship with us. They want to remove the obstacle. [The Relative] has been in Beirut, says he has good news for Frankfort. We shall see. Still insisting on group release. If this comes off may ask you to do second round after hostages are back. Keep your fingers crossed." (Poindexter PROF note to McFarlane, 10/03/86, 20:35:35)

OCT 4- McFarlane responded:

"Roger; anytime John.

"By the way, I watched the news tonight and saw Peggy Say [Terry Anderson's sister] beating up on the Administration for not getting the Beirut hostages out. I haven't heard anything on that score for a while. But I get [sic] the sense that we are pretty much at the mercy of the Iranians.

"If you think it would be of any value, I might be able to take a couple of months off and work on the problem. No guarantees and no need for any sponsorship (except for airfares and hotels) but I might be able to turn something up. Think about it." (McFarlane PROF note to Poindexter, (10/04/86) (Tower)

- An airplane operated by Southern Air Transport crashes 35 seconds after takeoff from Kelly Air Force Base in San Antonio, Texas. Rep. Henry Gonzalez (D-Tex.) charges the plane was transporting arms to the contras. Human error is listed as the accident's cause. (MH 12/16/86)

OCT 5 - At 9:50 a.m., a C-123K cargo aircraft leaves El Salvador's Ilopango airbase loaded with military supplies including 70 AKAM rifles, 100,000 rounds of ammunition and seven RPG grenade launchers. It is scheduled to make an air drop to the contras but is shot down over southern Nicaragua. Three crewmen are killed and a fourth, Eugene Hasenfus of Marinette, Wisconsin, is captured and eventually tried on charges of terrorism in Managua. It is later reported that Richard Secord helped arrange the flight. (WP 12/7/86; NYT 12/25/86)

- Felix Rodriguez telephones Bush aide Samuel Watson to inform him that the plane is missing and possibly downed. (Bush Chronology in WP 12/16/86; NYT 12/16/86)

- The day North left (for Frankfurt), an aircraft with Eugene Hasenfus aboard crashed in Nicaragua. (Footnote from the Tower Commission report)

TRANSACTION SIX: OCTOBER 1986 SALE OF 500 U.S. TOW MISSILES AND VARIOUS HAWK MISSILE SYSTEM SPARE PARTS

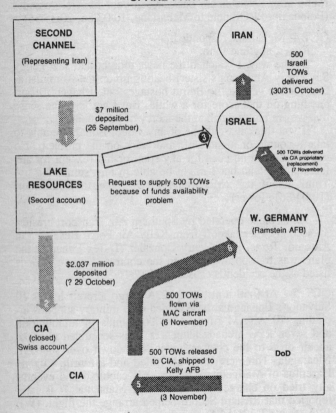

- According to documents received by the Committee, during this same time frame a meeting was scheduled in Europe with the new Iranian channel. In preparation for this meeting, North drafted a memorandum for Poindexter to send to Casey, stating that the President had authorized the delivery of intelligence information to the Iranians. The January 6, 1986, Presidential Finding was cited as the authority.

The CIA assembled an intelligence package in preparation for a meeting in Europe with the new Iranian channel. The CIA author of the memorandum transmitting the package cautioned, however, that "such information, if it were to come into Iranian possession, would likely help Iran plan and execute military operations against Iraq." (SSIC 1/29/87)

OCT 5-7 - LtCol North, Mr. Cave, and Mr. Secord met with the second channel in Frankfurt, Germany. They carried a Bible for the Iranians inscribed by the President on October 3.

LtCol North misrepresented his access to the President. He told Mr. Ghorbanifar stories of conversations with the President which were wholly fanciful. He suggested without authority a shift in U.S. policy adverse to Iraq in general and Saddam Husain in particular. (Tower)

In presenting the Bible, LtCol North related the following story to the Iranians:

"We inside our Government had an enormous debate, a very angry debate inside our government over whether or not my president should authorize me to say 'We accept the Islamic Revolution of Iran as a fact . . .' He [the President] went off one whole weekend and prayed about what th [sic] answer should be and he came back almost a year ago with that passage I gave you that he wrote in front of the Bible I gave you. And he said to me, 'This is a promise that God gave to Abraham. Who am I to say that we should not do this?' (Tower)

- North, former CIA agent George Cave and other Americans meet in Hamburg, West Germany, with a new Iranian contact set up by Secord and said in some reports to be the son of Speaker of Parliament Ali Akbar Rafsanjani. At the meeting, the Iranian offers to help with the release of an American hostage if the U.S. will ship 500 TOW missiles to Iran. He also offers to pay for the weapons in advance and work on freeing a second hostage. Cave apparently provides the Iranians with data on the Soviet threat to their country (see Mid-February 1986 entry also). According to published reports, some information the U.S. gave Iran during this period deliberately distorted the danger of a Soviet intervention. (See January 12, 1987 entry.) (NYT 1/11/87 & 1/12/87; WP 12/31/86 & 1/29/87)

OCT 5-8 - The Erria waits at Limosol, Cyprus, apparently in hopes of picking up hostages from Lebanon. According to Tom Parlow, the ship is supposed to pick up "seven Marine Corps people." It is later reported that North and the White House are indeed planning another delivery of arms to Iran in return for hostages at this time. A meeting to discuss the issue with Iranian officials apparently takes place in Frankfurt "a few days subsequent" to the October 3 session, according to Larry Speakes. It is at this meeting that North apparently presents his counterparts with a Bible signed by Reagan on the 3rd. As it turns out, the shipment that is being planned at this time is delayed until October 27, and no hostages are forthcoming. On the 8th, the Erria leaves its station and heads for the Israeli port of Haifa. (LAT 1/21/87; Speakes briefing 1/29/87)

OCT 6 - Robert Earl, who shared an office with North, reported to Poindexter: "[o]ne of the Democracy Inc aircraft apparently went down on a resupply mission to FDN forces in the north. It is overdue from its mission, and no radio contact was received. It is currently unknown where or why the aircraft went down, but [third country] assets are discreetly organizing a SAR effort over international waters & friendly territory portions of the route. Three Americans and one Nicaraguan national aboard. I will keep you advised of details as I get them." (Earl PROF note to Poindexter, 10/06/86, 11:49:16)

- Rodriguez calls Watson again. Watson follows established practice and notifies the White House Situation Room and the NSC staff of the missing plane. North immediately flies to El Salvador to prevent publicity over the event and to arrange death benefits for families of the crew. (Bush Chronology in WP 12/16/86; NYT 12/16/86 & 12/17/86 & 12/25/86; WSJ 12/19/86 & 12/24/86)

- After the crash, the Pentagon's top Central America expert, Nestor Sanchez, participates with Elliott Abrams, assistant secretary of state for inter-American affairs and North in putting together a cover story about the Hasenfus flight that is reported widely by the American media. The story attributes the mission to purely private efforts, specifically those of retired General John Singlaub. Abrams tries to get Singlaub to claim responsibility for the mission, but Singlaub is in the Philippines at the time and cannot be reached before news reports mention his alleged role. Singlaub, who has organized several overt shipments to the contras, angrily denies any responsibility for the operation in a news conference after returning to the U.S. Abrams later denies this entire account of the affair. (Singlaub press conference transcript 10/9/86; NYT 1/15/87)

- Robert Dutton, an associate of Secord who is supervising the contra resupply operation out of the Virginia offices of Stanford Technology Trading Group International, complains to operatives in El Salvador that Rodriguez has been passing inaccurate information about the downed Hasenfus C-123K cargo plane "directly to high-ranking officials." The reference is apparently to Bush aide Samuel Watson. (WP 12/16/86)

- William Perry, an NSC staff member who worked on Latin America, wrote Poindexter on October 7: "Plane down in Nicaragua and survivor of crash had no USG connection according to CIA and DIA. This tracks with Elliott's denial and has been passed on to Dan Howard. FYI, and not for release. The flight originated in El Salvador and is probably tied in with private U.S. assistance to the Contras. Survivor could testify to this type of connection. . . . "(Perry PROF note to Poindexter. 10/7/86. 12:42) (Tower)

- Furmark told the Board that, on October 7, he met the Director of Central Intelligence in Washington, and explained that "the Canadians were putting lots of pressure on Adnan [Khashoggi], and that they were going to sue him and he would have to then bring in [sic] the U.S. into the transaction." (Furmark 10) (Tower)

- According to Khashoggi, he invented the Canadian investors who reportedly had threatened to disclose the U.S.'s secret arms sales to Iran unless they were reimbursed for a $10 million loan used to finance a $15 million arms sale to Iran in May 1986. The money used in the deal, the Saudi businessman says, came from an unnamed Saudi business associate, and not from Ernest Miller and Donald Fraser, the two Khashoggi associates presumed to have been the Canadian investors described by Khashoggi. (NYT 3/10/87)

- Furmark [Casey's former client] and Casey met on October 7, 1986 and, according to Furmark's testimony, he told Casey about the financial problems with the Iran project and that Casey seemed unaware of details. Furmark testified that Casey tried to call Poindexter who was in and that Casey said he would look into it.

At this meeting, Casey claims, Furmark informs him for the first time of the possible diversion of Iran arms profits to the rebels. However, Furmark claims not to have raised the diversion issue until November 24. Casey testifies that he initiates an internal CIA inquiry at this time. (SSIC 1/29/87; WP 12/11/86 & 12/24/86; WSJ 1/9/87)

- CIA Deputy Director Robert Gates and Charles Allen, national intelligence officer for counterterrorism, inform Casey of their suspicion concerning the channeling of funds to the contras. CIA memoranda dated this month describe meetings attended by Allen, former Agency official George Cave and Furmark, at which Furmark discussed Ghorbanifar's claims to him that the prices of weapons to Iran were inflated in order to transfer the profits to the rebels. (WSJ 1/9/87; NYT 1/19/87)

- A CIA officer testified that he met with Casey on October 7 and repeated what he had told Gates (see October 1 entries). At this meeting, Casey told the CIA officer that he had received a call that day from Roy Furmark, a former legal client and long-time acquaintance. Casey said that Furmark had told him that Khashoggi had put up the money to finance the purchase of arms by Iran, but that the money was not actually Khashoggi's; that Khashoggi had borrowed the money from two Canadians for a 20 percent return on investment after 30 days; and that the Canadians had not been repaid and were threatening to go public with the details of the operation. According to the CIA officer, Casey called Poindexter that same day and told him of Furmark's call. (It should be noted that Furmark testified that he had met with, not called, Casey that day.) (SSIC 1/29/87)

- [Charles Allen to the Tower Board] For one reason or the other, I did not talk to the Director of Central Intelligence until 7 October. I raised that issue at that time about the operational security of the problem. I also raised the issue of diversion to the contras, and Mr. Casey at that stage said Mr. Furmark has just talked to me, and he didn't talk about the contras, but he talked about the problems of the Canadian investors, and that they are threatening to take law suits to try to take some action.

"I said to Mr. Casey, I think I should put all my troubles down in a memorandum, and he said that would be good . . ." (Tower)

- Also on October 7, a meeting was held between a senior CIA analyst [Charles Allen, National Intelligence Officer for Counterterrorism], the Deputy Director of CIA, Bob Gates, and Casey. This senior CIA analyst testified he believed Furmark did not mention to Casey on October 7 the possibility that Iran arms proceeds had gone to the Nicaraguan resistance.

Casey later told the analyst that he, Casey, called Poindexter on October 7 and that Poindexter knew of the problems raised by Furmark.

Gates testified that it was *possible* that during the October 7 meeting Furmark may have raised with Casey the possible diversion of money to the contras.

At the meeting with Casey on October 7, Gates told Casey of the senior analyst's concerns about the possible diversion of funds to Central America. Casey directed the analyst to put all his concerns in writing. Gates testified that Casey was startled by the information. (SSIC 1/29/87)

- Rep. Henry B. Gonzalez, D-Texas calls for a House investigation into two recent air crashes in Texas and Nicaragua to determine if they were part of an alleged covert CIA operation aimed at toppling the Sandinista government. He also claims that the CIA is recruiting Spanish-speaking Texans for duty in Central America. Gonzalez claims that a Southern Air Transport plane that crashed during a predawn takeoff from Kelly Air Force Base was on a secret CIA mission carrying weapons to the contras. Three civilians were killed in the crash. (AP 10/8/86)

- Hassan Kangarloo, an Iranian businessman who tried to purchase millions of dollars worth of embargoed U.S. military equipment for his country, is jailed. Kangarloo, at a hearing in September, was convicted on five counts including conspiracy, violating arms export control laws and filing falsified shipping documents. The court heard that he had bought equipment ranging from rockets to battlefield radios. According to an assistant U.S. Attorney, Kangarloo posed as the head of a British firm when he approached U.S. manufacturers. (DPA 10/7/87)

- The guilty verdicts on the Americans and the Argentinian captain of the Nobistor are overturned in a Brazilian court of appeals. While the captain goes free, the eight Americans are held pending extradition to Argentina to face charges of smuggling. (In These Times 2/18/87)

OCT 8 - FBI agents visit the Miami headquarters of Southern Air Transport for about 45 minutes as part of an investigation into alleged shipments of arms to the contras by the air carrier. Attorney General Meese later in the month asks the FBI to put the investigation on hold temporarily due to "national security concerns," according to a Justice Department spokesman. (MH 12/13/86)

- Oliver North calls Oliver "Buck" Revell, executive assistant director of the FBI. Webster says during the Senate Select Committee on Intelligence hearings on his confirmation as Director of Central Intelligence that North was afraid FBI agents probing Southern Air Transport would discover the airline's links to the Iran arms deals. Revell contacts the Miami field office and gets a report on the progress of the investigation. (Later, Revell is taken off the inquiry.) On the same day, FBI officials contact Southern Air and ask for a name of someone to talk to about the crashed Hasenfus plane. When a company executive suggests Richard B. Gadd the next day, an FBI agent says he isn't interested. (Webster testimony 4/8/87; WP 4/8/87 & 4/9/87)

- Casey informs Poindexter of his conversations with Furmark. According to Casey's testimony, Poindexter is surprised and upset that the Iran operation might be jeopardized at a moment when he hopes one or two more hostages might be released. (WP 12/11/86)

- Casey advised the Attorney General [in a letter dated November 25] that he and Gates had passed Furmark's information on to Poindexter a day or so after the October 7 meeting. (SSIC 1/29/87)

- After waiting in vain to pick up American hostages from Lebanon, the Erria departs the area and docks at Haifa,

Israel, to take on a container loaded with machine guns, apparently American-made. Still in October, the ship leaves Haifa and anchors weeks later off the coast of Oman. There it awaits word that a deal has been struck with Iran to swap the weapons for one or possibly two captured Soviet T-72 tanks. However, the deal falls through for unknown reasons and the ship steams through the Red Sea and Suez Canal to the Israeli port of Eilat to unload the machine guns. (LAT 1/21/87)

- The Danish freighter Iceland Saga docks at the U.S. Army's Sunny Point munitions depot where, according to Tom Parlow, it unloads 268 tons of arms. It also delivers 90.3 tons of supplies, including ammunition, landmines, and Soviet AK-47 rifles, according to various reports, into the custody of the Defense Department at Wilmington, N.C. According to a French report, the arms are ultimately intended for the contras as part of the Oliver North's Project Democracy. The expiration on October 1 of Congress' ban on aid to the rebels makes it legal for the Defense Department to accept the arms on the contras' behalf. Both DOD and CIA reportedly maintain warehouses for Soviet-bloc arms. Pentagon officials concede that Wilmington is often used as a drop-off point for such weapons, which they say Poland and other East European countries sell for hard currency, without concern for their ultimate destination. One report says the CIA bought a 358-ton shipment of ammunition and Polish automatic rifles and land mines, which were bound from Cherbourg after its delivery on the Erria from Poland and Portugal and was headed for Puerto Barrios, Guatemala, when the Hasenfus plane was shot down October 5. One intelligence source says North prevailed upon Casey to authorize the purchase, which takes place just after CIA aid to the contras becomes legal again. (AFP 1/24/87; LAT 2/13/87; WSJ 2/13/87)

- International Business Communications sends a memo to Spitz Channell at the National Endowment for the Preservation of Liberty billing Channell for the October retainer ($20,000) of former Reagan White House aide David C. Fischer. The memo pointedly notes that the check should be made payable to IBC, since the last two checks were directly to Fischer. The next day, NEPL makes out the check to IBC on its Provident National Bank account in Philadelphia. (IBC memo 10/8/86; photocopied check 10/9/86)

OCT 9- It is reported that the pilot of the plane shot down on October 5 over Nicaragua once was employed by Southern Air Transport. A Southern Air identification card belonging to William J. Cooper was found among the plane's wreckage. A Southern Air spokesman acknowledges that Wallace B. Sawyer, Jr., the plane's copilot, had worked for Southern Air as a pilot but had quit in 1985. (MH 10/9/86)

- Casey telephones North shortly after the C-123K cargo plane was shot down over Nicaragua. North assures him during the call that no CIA resources were used in the unofficial contra resupply effort. Casey denies having any advance knowledge of the diversion of funds to the covert program. Casey and Deputy CIA Director Gates have lunch with North where, according to press reports, they discuss the possible channeling of profits from Iran arms sales to the Nicaraguan resistance. North denies diverting any funds to the rebels, but for reasons not yet clear does mention a Swiss bank account, according to a leaked Senate report on the affair. During testimony at his confirmation hearings for the Agency directorship, Gates provides a slightly different version of the meeting, saying only, "I recall that toward the end of the lunch Lt. Col. North made a cryptic remark about Swiss accounts and the contras . . . Neither [Casey] nor I pursued the comment." Asked why not, Gates says he was prevented by a congressional ban on CIA involvement with the contras. However, as pointed out by Sen. Bradley (D-NJ) at the hearing, the ban had expired as of October 1. Gates then refers to another U.S. law prohibiting CIA investigations of Americans, but fails to explain how this prevented him from questioning North further. He adds that he did consult with Casey after the lunch as to whether "we should be concerned" about North's remark but Casey, he says, "either hadn't heard or picked up on the remark at all, or seemed unconcerned, so I did not pursue it further." (NYT 12/17/86, 12/25/86; WSJ 12/19/86, 12/24/86 & 1/9/87; LAT 2/18/87; WP 2/19/87)

- Gates further testified that on October 9, 1986, Casey, Gates, and North met for lunch to give North an opportunity to debrief Casey and Gates on a meeting on the Iran project that had recently taken place in Europe [between the U.S. team of North, Secord and a CIA officer, and the new Iranian channel]. Gates testified that problems with the Iran program were discussed and that during lunch North made a very cryptic reference to a Swiss account and money for the contras. Gates recalled that he and Casey did not pursue it but instead asked North whether there was any direct or indirect CIA involvement in any funding efforts for the contras. North's response reportedly was that CIA was "completely clean" and that he had worked to keep them separate. Gates testified that he and Casey discussed after lunch the fact that they did not understand North's comments. After the lunch, Gates noted for the record that North had "confirmed" that the CIA "is completely clean on the question of any contact with those organizing the funding and operation," and that a clear separation between all CIA assets and the private funding effort had been maintained. A senior CIA analyst testified that Gates later told him that there had been a discussion with North of integration of the private effort to support the contras and CIA activities, and that North had told Gate there was no commingling and CIA was clear. (SSIC 1/29/87)

According to testimony received by the Committee, the European meeting took place between the U.S. team, which consisted of North, Secord and a CIA officer, and the new Iranian channel, and, subsequently, on October 9, North visited CIA headquarters and briefed Casey and Gates on the meeting. (SSIC 1/29/87)

- On October 9, North visited CIA headquarters and briefed Casey and Gates on the meeting. According to testimony by Gates, during the course of this briefing, he asked North if there was any CIA involvement in North's efforts on behalf of private funding for the Contras. Gates testified that North responded that there was no CIA involvement. Gates further testified that at this same meeting, he urged Casey to insist on getting a copy of the Iran Finding, a document which the CIA did not have. North said that he would assist in this effort, and a few days later the CIA received the Finding. (SSIC 1/29/87)

- The C-123K downed over Nicaragua is reported to have been carrying supplies to contras associated with the FDN, according to one of the group's directors. Aristides Sanchez, a top official of the FDN says the plane's cargo was destined for a group of 1,400 fighters in southeastern Nicaragua. Sanchez also says that the third unidentified victim in the crash was an FDN rebel on board to kick supplies out of the plane. (MH 10/9/86)

- Corporate Air Service, the company for which Eugene Hasenfus says he was hired, is revealed to be a phantom company. According to the Federal Aviation Administration, a C-123K identical to the one that crashed in Nicaragua is registered to a firm called Corporate Air Service, supposedly based at Southern Air Transport's address at Miami International Airport: The Drug Enforcement Agency in Washington confirms that the C-123K shot down over Nicaragua was the same plane used by Barry Seal on one occasion in June 1984 in connection with a DEA investigation. In June 1985, Seal sold the plane, which he called the "Fat Lady," back to Doan Helicopter of New Smyrna Beach, Florida, the company from which Seal had originally obtained the plane in a swap for a Merlin 3B. (MH 10/10/86)

OCT 10 - North to Poindexter:

"Copp has just returned from Frankfurt. According to both he [sic] and Sam, my donkey act with the Relative and [a Revolutionary Guard Intelligence Official] had quite an effect. [The Revolutionary Guard Intelligence Official] told Dick that if he returned home without the hope of further help that he "would be sent back to the front." [The Revolutionary Guard Intelligence Official] gave Dick a proposal closer to the line in my original seven points and asked Dick if there was any way that he could get us to meet before the 3 Nov. meeting I had suggested. Dick told him that he would pass the points on but could not guarantee anything. Points as follows:

"1. They pay $3.6M next week.

"2. We deliver 500 TOWs (no HAWK parts) 9 daysafter [sic] payment.

"3 . . .

"4. Two hostages (if possible, but no less than one) released w/in 4 days of TOW delivery. If only one hostage released, whole process stops and we meet again.

"5. Repeat funding and Delivery [sic] cycle as in steps 1 & 2 above.

"6. We send Tech support for HAWKs, update on intel and secure comm team to Tehran and provide location/availability or artillery items noted on the original list provided by [the Relative] in Washington mtg.

"7. Iran does utmost to secure release of remaining hostages. [The Revolutionary Guard Intelligence Official] told both Sam and Copp that the group holding Reed and Cicippio is not, repeat not, responsive to Iran. Further, that only

[Hostage 1] and [Hostage 2] are "immediately available." [The Revolutionary Guard Intelligence Official] begged Dick to let them find out exactly where [Hostage 3] is and "you can rescue him and not ruin us (Iran) with the Hizballah."

"Both Sam and Copp believe we should let them stew in Tehran for a few more days and then accept the proposal indicated above. [The Revolutionary Guard Intelligence Official] and [the Relative] both said that Pattis was not now available, but that they were sure they could work it out once things were moving. Only changes from my proposal is sequential nature of their plan and lack of mention of Buckley body & transcript of interrogation. We do not believe that they can be sure of getting all three—all available info indicates [Hostage 3] is held elsewhere. Dick and Sam believe that we will, however, get two back for nothing more than the two sets of 500 TOWs. They point out that the rest of what the Iranians want (a plan for approaching the Kuwaitis, the location/availability of the artillery, and the intel) all can be managed w/o any great complications. [C/NE], Cave and Casey all seem to be convinced that this is best/fastest way to get two more out—probably w/in next 14 days. [C/NE] also notes that the situation in Leb is getting much worse and that we may be getting close to the end of the line for any further movement. Finally, all here now believe that these guys do not have Reed/Cicippio, who are probably in hands of Libyan controlled group which earlier bought/killed Kilburn. [C/NE] and Sam believe that these guys may be the only way we can ever get our hands on Reed/Cicippio since their access and info in Lebanon are so much better than ours.

"BOTTOM LINE: Recommend that we wait for their call on Tuesday, if their position is same as above or better, we shd push them to include Buckley remains and transcript and then get on with it. Pls advise. (North PROF note to Poindexter, 10/10/86, 21:55:31) (Tower)

- Cave told the Board that the most important part of the Frankfurt meeting was the Iranian's statement that he could obtain the release of one hostage. In addition, Cave said, the participants discussed Iran's weapons requirements, the Afghan war, and the Iraq war. Cave recalled that he gave them a briefing on our view of their war with Iraq. This briefing was structured so that we told them basically the truth, but the stress we placed on the briefing was such that it would give them considerable pause about launching this final offensive that they had been talking about for the last six months. (Cave 19-20)

Cave recalled that the Iranians wanted to end the war in a way they could present as a victory. (Id. at 20) The negotiators agreed to meet again toward the end of the month. During that meeting, Cave said, "we caused the 500 TOWs to be shipped. . . . That's when we got Jacobson [sic] out." (Jd.[sic] at 21)

As it happened the Israelis shipped the TOWs because Secord tried to deposit the Iranians' payment for the weapons into a CIA account that had already been closed. (Tower)

OCT 12 - Vice President Bush denies reports that he was involved in the secret air drops of arms and equipment to the Contras. He specifically denies allegations that he or his staff are linked to a gun-running operation that led to the downing of a C-123 supply plane by Sandinista troops in Nicaragua last Sunday. Bush, a former CIA director, acknowledges that he has talked to one of the men that survivor Hasenfus and U.S. news reports have implicated in that flight—Max Gomez. Bush says he spoke only about Gomez' operations against Marxist guerrillas fighting the U.S. backed government in El Salvador. Sources close to Bush are quoted saying Gomez had got from Bush "approval of his efforts to help the Contras." Several sources report that Gomez coordinated the drops after being recommended for a position at Ilopango Air Base in El Salvador by Bush or his national security advisor Donald Gregg. It is also reported that Gomez had told associates that he reported to Bush about his activities leading the air drop operation. (Reuters 10/12/86; WP 12/16/86; MH 11/30/86)

- North wrote McFarlane on October 12:

We urgently need to find a high powered lawyer and benefactor who can raise a legal defense for Hassenfus [sic] in Managua. If we can find such persons we can not only hold Gene and Sally Hassenfus together (i.e., on our side, not pawns of the Sandinista propaganda machine) but can make some significant headway of our own in counterattacking in the media. Obviously, there is the added benefit of being able to do something substantive in the legal system to defend this young man. I know that this is a tall order and that many U.S. lawyers will not want to step up to this task, but for the man (or woman) who does, there will be a fair bite of history made in the next few weeks. There will, no doubt, be a show trial of some kind launched and unless we have an overt, competent legal defense, Hassenfus will become nothing but a tool in their hands—none of which is in our interests, or his.

By Tuesday, a Swiss lawyer, retained by Corporate Air Services, should be in Managua. We should not rely on this person to represent the whole case since he is supported by covert means. We would be far better off if we had an overt mechanism here in the states which represented USG/Hassenfus' interests, and who would not have to respond to questions regarding the origins of Corporate Air Services, Inc. (CASI), or its other ongoing activities. The CASI lawyer is being instructed to cooperate fully w/ this U.S. Attorney, whoever he/she may be.

Have also located approx. $100K from a donor who does not care if this contribution becomes known (though the donor has done things in the past to keep CASI in operation —a fact which need not become known). Can you help? If need be, I can meet w/ you/ others tomorrow or Tues. [October 13 or 14] Believe this to be a matter of great urgency to hold things together. Unfortunately RR was b;efed [sic] that this plan was being contemplated before he left for Iceland and am concerned that along about Wednesday when people begin to think of things other than meetings in cold places, he will remember this and nothing will have been done. Any thoughts wd be much appreciated. Elliott Abrams willing to sit-in any time after Yom Kippur fast is finished tomorrow night. Pls Advise. (North PROF note to McFarlane, 10/12/86, 16:33:11) (Tower)

- On Columbus Day, October 13, I [Allen] laid out a comprehensive memorandum which laid out what I thought were the original objectives of the NSC initiative—to open up a geostrategic relationship in the long term with Iran, to get the hostage situation out of the way as a stumbling block to any further relations with Iran, and to discourage Iran from conducting terrorism.

"And throughout this initiative Colonel North constantly reiterated to the Iranians no more terrorism against Americans. And in fact terrorism against Western targets and against Americans have been substantially reduced since 1984. (Tower)

OCT 14 - CIA Deputy Director Gates, according to the Senate intelligence committee's draft report, orders an internal investigation into the possible siphoning of funds from the Iran arms sales to the Nicaraguan resistance. The order follows another meeting with Casey and counterterrorism official Charles Allen. (WSJ 1/9/87)

- "I [Allen] presented this memorandum to Mr. Gates on the 14th because I wasn't certain what he wanted. I gave three recommendations—that we immediately set up a planning cell in the NSC headed by an individual like Henry Kissinger, Hal Saunders, Dick Helms—I forgot who else— to really take a hard program review of this whole Initiative. What are we trying to achieve? What are our short-term objectives? What are our long-term objectives? What are our options? A critical review of everything. And I said this is the first recommendation.

"The second recommendation was to get ready for exposure of this initiative. We don't even have press guidance. We ought to start preparing some. And to get together a group that's familiar with the Ghorbanifar channel and decide how best we can shut it down in an orderly system-like fashion.

"The Director was taken by this memorandum, and he took the original, called Poindexter and said I must see you right away. (Tower)

- On October 14, 1986, Gates and the senior CIA analyst met with Casey and gave him the memorandum prepared by the analyst pursuant to the October 7 meeting. A cover memorandum from the analyst to Casey and Gates said the analyst had not consulted with North or other individuals involved on the U.S. side in drafting the memorandum. The attached 7-page memorandum discussed the risk that Ghorbanifar might disclose to the press an account, charging that the U.S. and Israeli governments had acquired substantial profit from the Iran arms transactions, some of which was redistributed to "other projects of the U.S. and Israel." The analyst testified that the reference in his memo to "other projects" related only to speculation about possible allegations of improper diversions of money to Central America, misappropriation of funds by arms dealers, and indications of funds needed for some unknown purpose by an Israeli official. (SSIC 1/29/87)

- According to documents received by the Committee [shortly after North briefed Casey and Gates about the October 9 meeting in Europe] a CIA officer drafted a memorandum analyzing the NSC arms to Iran initiative which, in part, proposed certain damage control procedures in the event the initiative became public and speculated that creditors might assert that money from the arms sales was being "distributed to other projects of the U.S. and Israel." Upon seeing the memo, Casey called Poindexter and set up an appointment for the next day. (SSIC 1/29/87)

- Southern Air chairman James Bastian responds to recent publicity with a three-page letter to the company's 200-odd employees. "First," he writes, "Southern Air is not owned by the CIA and is not performing any services with any company connected with the CIA. Any statement to the contrary is simply not true. Second, the C-123K aircraft which crashed in Central America, and any other aircraft identified with that operation were not and are not owned by Southern Air Transport, and were not and are not being operated by Southern Air Transport, nor were the operators of those aircraft controlled or directed by Southern Air through any other entity." (Southern Air letter 10/14/86; VV 12/16/86)

OCT 15 - Casey and Gates saw Poindexter on October 15 and gave him a copy of the memorandum (see October 14 entries). Gates testified that he and Casey recommended to Poindexter that the President ought to reveal the initiative to the public, to avoid having it "leak out in dribs and drabs." Meanwhile, according to Gates, he directed the CIA's General Counsel to review all aspects of the Iran project to insure that the CIA was not doing anything illegal. The General Counsel subsequently reported to Gates that he had looked into the situation and that there was "nothing amiss from the CIA standpoint." (SSIC 1/29/87)

-[Allen told the Board] "And he and Gates jointly met with Poindexter on the 15th. They presented the memorandum. They talked in considerable detail about it. Poindexter read it carefully in their presence, asked who wrote it. I have known John Poindexter for several years and I admire him greatly. And they said Charlie Allen wrote it, and Admiral Poindexter promised to look into it. And Bill Casey told me that he advised Admiral Poindexter to get a White House counsel involved right away because it contained in the memorandum that there would be allegations of impropriety and shabby conduct by U.S. officials, regardless of how this comes out, if this was publicly exposed.

"And at this meeting the Director and Bob Gates called me in after they had returned from seeing Admiral Poindexter and Director Casey asked me to see Roy Furmark again." (Tower)

- Chairman Tower: What occurs to me is that anything that critical, that important, he would have discussed with Admiral Poindexter.

Mr. Allen: He did, and he discussed this whole problem on the 7th. He discussed it in depth with Admiral Poindexter on the 15th, when he said you better get your White House counsel involved immediately.

Chairman Tower: And he was never aware that Poindexter had not gotten the memo? (See Oct 16–22 entry below)

Mr. Allen: Not until the 25th of November, when Mr. Casey asked me to pull all the memos together, and he said I sent that memo down and I also talked to him on the 24th of October is actually the date it finally got into his in box. But he found out he had not sent it. He was deeply disturbed and upset. As a matter of fact, on the 7th of October he had called Admiral Poindexter. He had met with Admiral Poindexter, along with Mr. Gates, on the 15th. He had also talked to Admiral Poindexter on the 24th about this.

He had given a lot of warning to Admiral Poindexter that this operation was spinning out of control. (Tower)

- Gates testified that he did ask CIA General Counsel Dave Doherty to review all aspects of the project and to ensure that the Agency was not involved in any illegalities. According to Gates, Doherty later told him that he had looked into things and not found anything wrong. Doherty testified that Gates mentioned that Southern Air Transport was involved, linking the whole thing to Central America, because Southern Air transport was also shipping material to the Nicaraguan resistance. According to Doherty, the FBI was looking at the issue of humanitarian funds to see if any were being spent unlawfully.

According to testimony by Doherty, Gates also mentioned to the General Counsel speculation and rumors that Iran funds could have been sent to Central America as part of private funding efforts. Doherty testified that Gates told him he was concerned that CIA did not know how funding transfers were being handled by the NSC and middlemen.

Doherty further testified that he undertook no review other than to evaluate the activities as described to him by Gates. He testified that he did not interview other CIA employees, nor did he suspect NSC involvement in diversion to the contras. According to other testimony received by the Committee, Doherty did, however, direct in late October or early November that nothing relating to the Iran program be destroyed. Two CIA employees, concerned, subsequently put all notes, documents et cetera in a box. (SSIC 1/29/87)

- Casey advised the Attorney General in his November 25, 1986 letter that he had this memorandum prepared and believed it was delivered to the NSC to review the state of play on the channel to the Iranian government. (SSIC 1/29/87)

- Assistant Secretary of State for Inter-American Affairs Elliott Abrams says the U.S. had nothing to do with the C-123K flight that crashed in Nicaragua ten days ago. Testifying before the House subcommittee on Western Hemisphere Affairs, he says, "I can tell you that there was no government role in this flight." Later, when evidence of government involvement surfaces, Abrams declines comment. (WP 1/13/87)

OCT 16 - On October 16, Earl reported a call from chief of the Iran desk at the Agency:

"The fool's [sic] want to get Nir to grease the skids in advance on their request for flight clearance to Tel Aviv before they submit the paperwork. I've got the info when you're ready to let Nir know. . . . I recommend you DON't [sic] tell him the flight plan data when you first tell him the thing is approved, however; it's so detailed he'll know we held out on him. Suggest you tell him I'm working w/ the fool's now to develop that info and we'll pass it to him as soon as we have it. Then we can call him again later tonight or tomorrow. New subject: The fool's are leaning forward as far as they can—e.g. the toes [sic] are apparently being palletized in Alabama already—but they can't get everything going until they have the money ($2.037m) in hand. They've asked for a heads up when Copp/Abe deposit it in their Berne account. I've codedup [sic] this request for a heads up/confirmation and sent it to Bob M. [J. Robert McBrien (wrong I.D. by Tower Commission, they later admit)] and [encryption device]. (Earl PROF note to North. 10/16/86, 17:42:53)

McFarlane again expressed concern about North. He wrote Poindexter on October 10: "At some point I would like to raise Ollie's situation with you. I really think he has become every Democrat's best target and as hard as it would be to lose him, it will serve your and his long term interest to send him back to the Corps." (McFarlane PROF note to Poindexter, 10/10/86, 15:10:42) (Tower footnote)

- At Casey's direction, a CIA officer met with Furmark to discuss the Iran initiative and Khashoggi's involvement in financing the arms sales. Subsequent to the meeting, a memo to Casey was drafted recounting the conversation with Furmark, which provided in part that Furmark had recommended an Iranian arms shipment "to maintain some credibility with the Iranians . . . and to provide Ghorbanifar with some capital so that the investors can be repaid partially and so that Ghorbanifar can borrow money to finance additional shipments." This, according to Furmark, would keep the process rolling and could result in release of additional hostages. (SSIC 1/29/87)

- Furmark testified that he next talked to Casey on October 16, 1986, and again asked for Casey's help in getting the U.S. government to resolve his clients' financial claims. According to his letter to the Attorney General of November 25, Casey had a senior CIA analyst and a CIA contract employee go up to New York to discuss the whole thing at length with Furmark. Memoranda dated October 17 and November 7 discussed their meetings with Furmark.

The memorandum dated October 17 recounted a brief conversation between the senior CIA analyst and Furmark on October 16. It did not mention use of arms sale profits for "other projects," but did relate Furmark's allegation that $3 million of the $8 million paid by the Iranians for the May 1985 transaction had been used "to cover expenses and for other matters" and that $10 million was still owed to the Canadian investors who financed the May transaction. (SSIC 1/29/87)

OCT 16-22 - [Charles Allen told the Tower Board] "I saw Roy Furmark on the 16th. I got additional information. I wrote another memorandum on October 17 which I laid out how deeply troubled I was because I could see this thing blowing up and we were going to have an incredible mess on our hands.

"I told Mr. Furmark I needed to sit a long time with him and debrief him fully, and I was to see him early—I guess it was about the week of the 20th of October—but it was the 22nd before we could get together in New York.

"I took George Cave with me, and at that stage Mr. Furmark made an allegation that he had been told by Ghorbanifar that the bulk of the $15 million that had been raised by the Canadian investors and the Arab investor, which Khashoggi had guaranteed, would be repaid within 30 days at 20 percent interest and that the bulk of that money had gone to the contras in Central America.

"I recorded all this in a memorandum. Mr. Cave and I jointly prepared the memorandum. It went to Mr. Casey. Mr. Casey again was deeply disturbed. He talked to Admiral Poindexter on secure [telephone]. For some reason, the memorandum from Casey to Poindexter was never sent. It fell into the wrong out box." (Tower)

MID-OCT - The CIA reportedly makes a delivery of arms to the guerrillas in Angola via an air base in Zaire. Using C-130 and Boeing 707 cargo jets with the markings "Santa Lucia Airways," diplomatic and business sources say, the Agency twice before has brought arms to the rebels through this route (see March 20 and May 15-30, 1986 entries). U.S. officials have refused to reveal how American aid to Angola, set at $15 million in 1986, makes its way there. (NYT 2/1/87)

OCT 17 - Congress passes the Continuing Appropriations resolution on the 1987 budget, which contains the previously approved $100 million in aid for the contras. Reagan signs it into law (P.L. 99-500) the next day. (CSM 11/5/86; CRS "U.S. Assistance to Nicaraguan Guerrillas" 12/4/86)

- Assistant Secretary of State for Inter-American Affairs Elliott Abrams writes Spitz Channell at the National Endowment for the Preservation of Liberty. "Dear Spitz," the letter says, ". . . your tireless efforts in telling the story of Nicaraguan suffering at the hands of the Sandinistas were crucial elements in developing the public and political awareness that resulted in Congressional victory." The letter is signed "Elliott." (Abrams letter 10/17/86)

- Eugene Hasenfus claims in an interview that Bush knew about the covert arms supply operation for the contras. "They had his knowledge," Hasenfus says. (CBS "60 Minutes" in MH 11/30/86)

- A Danish freighter delivers a shipload of Israeli-made military equipment to Iran, according to a news report. Another report says a Danish ship unloads arms and ammunition there on October 21 (see entry). It is unclear if the two reports refer to the same shipment. (PI 11/26/86)

OCT 19 - It is reported that the American-manned cargo plane shot down over Nicaragua was following a flight pattern that was intended to be used to transport new congressional aid from El Salvador to the contras in the southern part of the country. The air route, it was hoped, would replace the land route from Costa Rica, according to officials close to the program. According to these officials, the U.S. was planning to use the same facility in El Salvador, Ilopango Air Base, that the C-123K cargo plane had used before it crashed. (WP 10/18/86)

OCT 20 - Coy reports to Earl on the 20th that the chief of the Iran desk had relayed information about 12 pallets, each carrying 44 TOWs. "Material [TOWs and medicine] is put together and will be shipped from AL when money is avail. Planning delivery to Adam [Nir] in T.A. [Tel Aviv] on Oct 29." (Coy PROF note to Earl, 10/20/86, 11:59:29) (Tower)

OCT 21 - American author Edward Austin Tracy is kidnapped in Beirut, according to the Revolutionary Justice Organization, a group with pro-Iranian connections. (WP 12/7/86)

- A Danish freighter delivers 26 containers full of arms and ammunition to Iran, according to a news report. (Another report cites a delivery by a Danish ship on October 17—see entry.) According to a crewman quoted in the Danish newspaper Politiken, the ship, originally named the Morsoe, entered the Israeli port of Eilat under the name Solar where it was then loaded with arms. Upon reaching the

Iranian port of Bandar Abbas, the cargo was unloaded and the freighter reassumed the name Morsoe. (AFP 11/6/86)

OCT 22 - A follow-up meeting with Furmark in New York with two CIA officers occurred on October 22. According to documents and testimony received by the Committee, in addition to discussing the sources of financing for the various shipments of arms to Iran, Furmark said that Ghorbanifar "firmly believed" that "the bulk of the $15 million (for the HAWK spare parts) had been diverted to the Contras." The CIA officer testified that it was his impression that Furmark shared Ghorbanifar's belief. The two CIA officers briefed Casey upon their return, including the subject of possible diversion of funds to the Contras. A summary memorandum was drafted for Casey to send to Poindexter, but it was never signed by the DCI and was apparently never sent to Poindexter.

. . . . The memorandum continued that in this regard, Ghorbanifar told Furmark that he was relieved when the $100 million aid to the contras was passed by Congress.

According to the memorandum, Furmark also presumed that $2 million of the $8 million paid by the Iranians to Ghorbanifar went to Nir, as agreed to at a meeting among the financiers, Ghorbanifar, and Nir in May.

A signed copy of this memorandum has not been received by the Committee. In his November 25, 1986 letter to the Attorney General, Casey said he had not read it "until this morning" and did not recall ever having read it before. In this letter Casey further said that he had been told the memorandum was prepared but apparently never went forward.

The senior CIA analyst testified that he was not looking at the question of improprieties but rather as an intelligence officer was focusing on damage control.

The analyst testified that Furmark felt Ghorbanifar firmly believed money was diverted to the contras, and the analyst had the impression Furmark also believed the money was diverted.

According to testimony by the analyst, the October 22 meeting with Furmark was the first time he had heard a direct allegation that Ghorbanifar suspected the bulk of funds raised for HAWK spare parts had gone to the contras. He testified that the quick briefing he and the CIA contract employee gave Casey after their October 22 meeting with

Furmark included mention of diversion. The contract employee who drafted the memo to Poindexter, testified that Casey may have conveyed its substance to Poindexter by phone and that Casey remembers seeing the memo. (SSIC 1/29/87)

- In other testimony, the executive assistant to Deputy Director for Operations at CIA testified that although there is a record in the DO registry of a memo from the senior CIA analyst on the analyst's third meeting with Furmark, he had only a vague recollection of the DDO having viewed the memo. The executive assistant said he had helped draft Casey's testimony for November 21, but in none of the drafts was there ever any mention of diversion of funds. (SSIC 1/29/87)

- Senator John Kerry (D-MA) writes a letter to the Justice Department concerning an FBI informant who has given his staff "significant information" regarding the involvement of U.S. government officials and Southern Air Transport in international weapons and narcotics trafficking (see October 1983 and October 1985 entries). Kerry writes that he intends to seek congressional immunity for the informant, if the Justice Department or FBI decline to provide protection, in order to induce the informant to testify before the Senate Foreign Relations Committee. (MN 10/30/86)

OCT 23 - I [Allen] came back and Mr. Cave and I briefed Casey at 9:00 on the 23rd. We told him the whole thing. Mr Casey was deeply upset and said immediately prepare that memo. For some reason, the memo was never sent, but he talked to Admiral Poindexter again. (Tower)

- Rep. Barbara Boxer (D-CA) writes to Weinberger about the Blazing Trails exercise, citing information from a whistleblower which shows that Reservists "have been used and currently are being used without authorization to perform controversial work in a status which does not have specific funding or authorization from Congress." When Reserve tours go over 180 days, they must be classified as active duty, for which there are congressionally mandated ceilings and separate authorization and funding accounts. By extending Reserve tours in Central America, the Defense Department diverts training funds for active duty purposes. Boxer subsequently (on October 31) releases the letter to the press, with supporting material detailing 47 Reserve tour abuses in

FY86 and at least eight more scheduled for Exercise Blazing Trails during FY87. (Boxer letter to Weinberger, 10/23/86; Boxer press release, 10/31/86; Tour Log for FY86, 8/8/86)

OCT 24 - [Charles Allen to the Tower Board: "Gates] had also talked to Admiral Poindexter on the 24th about this.

"He had given a lot of warning to Admiral Poindexter that this operation was spinning out of control. (Tower)

LATE OCT - According to other testimony received by the Committee, [CIA Counsel] Doherty did . . . direct in late October or early November that nothing relating to the Iran program be destroyed. Two CIA employees, concerned, subsequently put all notes, documents et cetera in a box. (SSIC 1/29/87)

- Casey calls North again to ask if any funds from Iran arms sales have been funneled to the rebels, according to testimony cited by a House member. North reportedly replies in the negative. Casey may have been prompted to call by information later included in a five-page memo, dated November 23. The memo, prepared for him by two aides, is the result of an inquiry he ordered into the diversion of Iran arms profits to the contras after his conversations with Furmark on October 7 and 8. (NYT 12/16/86 & 12/17/86)

- At a meeting in Mainz, West Germany, an Iranian emissary reportedly hands over a check for $4 million for 500 TOW missiles to American officials. News reports later suggest that the Iranian may have been that country's foreign minister, Ali Akbar Velayati, who arrived in Damascus around the end of the month, apparently to help with the hostage situation. (WP 12/31/86)

- The next arms shipments to Iran continued during this period. At a meeting in late October, the Iranians produced a check for $4 million to pay for 500 TOWs. (SSIC 1/29/87)

OCT 26 - While preparations for another shipment of TOWs continued, North and his team went to Frankfurt for another meeting with the Relative. North left Washington on October 26. (North Calendar) (Tower)

- During the October 26, 1986 meeting in Frankfurt, Germany, the U.S. side, as in the past, insisted that the release of the hostages was a prerequisite to any progress. [The Relative] urged that we take a more active role in support for the Afghan resistance ... The Iranians also proffered, and the U.S. accepted, the offer of a Soviet T-72 tank captured from Iraq. [The Iranians have also offered to provide a copy of the 400-page interrogation of William Buckley.] At this meeting, [the Relative] stated that there was a "very good chance that another American or two would be [f]reed soon." (Maximum Version 9; Historical Chronology 13-14.) (Tower)

OCT 26-27 - Another shipment of arms is sent via Israel to Iran. According to Adnan Khashoggi, in the latest phase of negotiations, marked by North's meeting with a new Iranian contact, the U.S. put up $5 million to help cement a deal. As of mid-December 1986, this delivery is thought to be the fourth and final one, but it is later reported that seven shipments take place, the seventh arriving October 31, 1986. (WP 12/7/86, 12/21/86 & 2/1/87; NYT 12/25/86)

OCT 26-28 - In the nine-point agenda discussed on October 26-28, he [North] committed the United States, without authorization, to a position contrary to well established U.S. policy on the prisoners held by Kuwait. (Tower)

LATE OCT - From the first hint in late-October, 1986 that the McFarlane trip would soon become public, information on the Iran initiative and contra activity cascaded into the press. The veiled hints of secret activities, random and indiscriminate disclosures of information from a variety of sources, both knowledgeable and otherwise, and conflicting statements by high-level officials presented a confusing picture to the American public. (Tower)

OCT 27 - Three workers at the U.S. Embassy in San Salvador claim the embassy paid for repairs on the house of Felix Rodriguez, and loaned him a radio that linked him to an embassy communications network. (UPI 10/27/86)

- The Republican Senatorial candidate in Nevada, Rep. Jim Santini, sends a mailgram to Spitz Channell to "protest vehemently" the American Conservative Trust media campaign attacking Santini's opponent. "Nevadans ... do not welcome outside influences," Santini's mailgram states, and goes on to demand that the campaign be stopped. (Mailgram 10/27/86)

OCT 28 - Of this amount [the $4 million paid by the Iranians], the CIA received $2.037 million on October 28. (SSIC 1/29/87)

OCT 29 - 500 TOW missiles were shipped from Israel to Iran. On that same day, North sent a message to Poindexter providing a status report on the meeting with the Iranians. According to that document, the United States was assured of getting two hostages back "in the next few days." On November 2, Peter [sic] Jacobsen was released.

According to testimony received by the Committee, the October 29 shipment of arms from Israel to Iran—for which the Israelis received 500 TOWs in reimbursement on November 6—marked the end of U.S.-Iranian arms deals. (SSIC 1/29/87)

- On October 29, with U.S. acquiescence, Israel provided Iran with an additional increment (500 TOW missiles) of these defensive weapons. (Maximum Version 9; Historical Chronology 13-14.) (Tower)

- Earl relayed a report from North to Poindexter:

Gist of following message already given to you by phone on the plane, but thought you may need some of the details:

"For JMP from North. Iranian rep [the Relative] assures us we will get 2 of the 3 US hostages held by Hizballah in next few days—probably Fri or Sat but NLT Sunday. To ensure good coordination w/ all concerned, propose North, [and] Secord . . . proceed ASAP to Beirut to coordinate release of two hostages. If approved, we wd proceed from Frankfurt to Larnaca via charter jet then to Beirut via US military helo to brief our ambassador. . . . Neither Secord nor North wd be visible but wd brief Amb Kelly on details. Secord wd attend because he will have to brief Amb on third hostage as well as remaining three (ie total of 4 Americans) when we get info from Rafsanjani on locations, shd we decide to proceed on a rescue msn when Iranians give us locational info. Press guidance for a Presidential announcement of the release before if becomes known will be developed along lines of quote The USG is grateful to all those who have assisted in this effort—and that two more AMCITS have been released unquote. Our effort is to have RR make the announcement before CNN knows it has happened, but after the AMCITS are in USG hands, so that RR is seen to have influenced the action and Syrians are not. . . . " (Earl PROF note to Poindexter, 10/29/86, 22:23:43)

North's account to Poindexter omitted the extensive discussion about the third American hostage and what could be done to secure his freedom. North told the Relative that he had already found a technician to work with the Iranians on their HAWK systems, but Secord added that it would be "highly unlikely that we would be allowed to send technicians into Iran, to Isfahan, until we get that guy out." The Relative replied that Rafsanjani "has been taken with the subject of the Phoenix [air to air missile]," and that if the Iranians "could just get a couple of these things working, and if it would hit an . . . Iraqi plane . . . it would be a terrible blow to [Iraqi] morale. . . . " The Relative promised that, if the U.S. would send a technician to help with the Phoenix missiles Iran already had, he would "personally get the third guy out, and . . . could tell [the U.S.] where the rest of the guys [three most recent U.S. hostages] are." North promised the technician, planning to send him in at the same time as the additional HAWK parts. Responding to the Iranian's question on the next delivery of 500 TOW missiles, North answered: "If you get the hostages out, we'll send you a million of them. All you have to do is pay for them. And if you guys get your act together, we'd open up an FMS account and you'd get a better price on them." (Tower)

- North had written Poindexter: "This is the damndest operation I have ever seen. Pls let me go on to other things. Wd very much like to give RR two hostages that he can take credit for and stop worrying about these other things." (North to Poindexter, through Earl, 10/29/86). (Footnote: North also expressed frustration over the investigation of Southern Air Transport. (See Oct. 30 entry) (Tower)

- France and Iran reach an agreement on a financial dispute over a loan of $1 billion to France during the time of the Shah's regime. The issue is already twelve years old. The breakthrough on negotiations was a central condition laid down by the Iranians for an improvement in relations with France. The French Foreign Ministry says that the agreement will be signed later at the "political level." (DPA 10/29/86)

OCT 30 - On behalf of Meese, who in turn has been asked to intercede by Poindexter, Associate Attorney General Stephen S. Trott requests a delay in the investigation of Southern Air Transport's role in ferrying arms to the contras on the grounds that "delicate hostage negotiations" in the Middle East might be jeopardized. FBI Director William Webster agrees to the 10-day delay. On the same day, a memo originating in the Department of Justice with Mary Lawton, chief of intelligence policy and review, is sent to Webster requesting that certain information relating to FBI "sources and methods" not be forwarded to North on the grounds that he may later be subject to prosecution by an independent counsel. Webster reads and initials the memo. (Webster testimony 4/8/87; WP 4/8/87 & 4/9/87)

- The disclosure of Poindexter's request raises new questions about what and when Meese and other Justice Department officials knew of the Iran-Contra operation. The Justice Department later acknowledges that the investigation does not actually resume until November 26, almost one month later, due to what spokesmen describe as purely bureaucratic delays. (LAT 12/19/86; WSJ 12/12/86 & 12/29/86; WP 12/16/86 & 12/19/86)

- Reagan signs continuing appropriations legislation (P.L. 99-591), which prohibits American personnel from providing assistance in Honduras and Costa Rica within twenty miles of the Nicaraguan border, and also forbids any member or component of the U.S. armed forces or government to provide military advice, training, or logistical support to paramilitary groups operating in Nicaragua. (CRS "War Powers Resolution: Presidential Compliance" 12/22/86)

- Pursuant to the October 27 Executive Order implementing Congressional sanctions on South Africa, particularly prohibiting U.S. aircraft from taking off or landing in South Africa, Southern Air Transport files comments with the Department of Transportation asking for an exemption from this prohibition. Southern Air states that SAFAIR (Safair Freighters Pty. Ltd. of Kempton Park, South Africa, listed by the FAA as a "certificated repair station") is "the only qualified facility on the African continent for the maintenance of Lockheed L-100 Hercules equipment. . . . The nearest other facility which can perform maintenance on these aircraft is Marshall located in Cambridge, England." Southern Air requests an exemption to land and takeoff from SAFAIR "to the limited extent necessary to maintain the airworthiness of SAT's Lockheed L-100 Hercules aircraft when operating in Africa. Under no circumstances would such flights be conducted as part of any commercial, revenue generating operation." (DOT Docket 44454 10/30/86)

OCT 30-NOV 4 - U.S. Ambassador John H. Kelly conducts "numerous conversations with . . . North and Secord, relating to the hostage negotiations with Iran," according to a cable Kelly sends to Shultz over the weekend of December 6-7, 1986. Kelly uses a CIA "privacy channel" to communicate with the White House. (Kelly says later Poindexter told him by cable that Shultz concurred with the plan to bypass State.) (Shultz testimony 12/8/86)

OCT 31 - International Business Communications sends a memo to Spitz Channell at the National Endowment for the Preservation of Liberty billing Channell for the November retainer ($20,000) of former Reagan White House aide David C. Fischer. The memo pointedly notes that the check should be made payable to IBC, since two previous checks were directly to Fischer. The memo includes a handwritten notation at the bottom that funds were wired Nov. 13. (IBC memo 10/31/86)

- The seventh and final shipment of arms, consisting of 500 TOW antitank missiles, are flown from Israel to Iran, apparently to be exchanged for American hostage David Jacobsen. (WP 12/21/86; CBS News 12/31/86)

- Notes taken at the [November 23 Meese-North] meeting indicated North said there was no money for the contras in the October shipment of 500 TOWs to avoid a perception of private profit and because the resumption of U.S. funding made it unnecessary. According to North, Nir was upset because the October price was not the same as charged earlier. (SSIC 1/29/87)

- Using the code name "Mr. Goode," North flies with Secord from Cyprus to Beirut to cement arrangements for the release of three remaining American hostages. After negotiations from the U.S. Embassy compound, the two return that night to Cyprus where they hope to meet the freed Americans. North has reportedly been dealing with a new Iranian contact, developed by Secord and known as the "doctor," since the fifth shipment of arms was delivered in August; the previous contact, Manuchehr Ghorbanifar, was dropped after the August delivery failed to bring about the release of more hostages. The White House is so certain that this mission will succeed that on November 1 Reagan's assistant for congressional affairs, William L. Ball III, telephones House Democratic leader Jim Wright to alert him. (WP 12/20/86 & 12/31/86; MH 12/21/86)

- Late on October 31, [the Relative] called the U.S. citizen (Hakim) tasked to maintain contact and advised that Iran had "exercised its influence with the Lebanese" in order to obtain the release of American—David Jacobsen—and an uncertain number of French hostages. He further noted that this was part of the purpose of the Iranian Foreign Minister's visit to Syria. [The Relative] stated that the situation in Tehran, as well as Iranian influence over Hizballah were both deteriorating; ... (Maximum Version 9; Historical Chronology 13-14.) (Tower)

NOVEMBER 1986

NOV - Sometime this month, the freighter Erria anchors off the coast of Oman where it waits in vain for approximately one month to consummate a deal with Iran to swap arms for one or more advanced Soviet T-72 tanks. (See December entry also.) (LAT 2/13/87)

- Early in the month, Poindexter reportedly convinces Casey not to consult the White House counsel on the legality of diverting funds to the contras. Poindexter says he is concerned the counsel may not be able to keep the matter secret. (NYT 1/12/87)

- The CIA Inspector General testified before the Committee and described as "fairly significant" the evidence that had begun to develop in the CIA by early November that some diversion might be taking place . . . (SSIC 1/29/87)

NOV 2 - Early in the morning, American Ambassador to Beirut John Kelly is told to go to the embassy's west annex where he finds hostage David Jacobsen. Secord and his deputy, Robert Dutton, go back to Beirut to debrief Jacobsen. When North hears that only one hostage has been freed, he reportedly tells a colleague there has been "a mistake." He reportedly stays on in Cyprus November 3 and eventually flies to West Germany while Cave attempts to locate the Iranian intermediary. (WP 12/7/86, 12/20/86, 12/21/86 & 12/31/86; MH 12/7/86; CBS News 12/31/86)

- Jacobsen was released November 2. North kept hoping others would be released if the story could be kept quiet for a few days. (Coy PROF note to Poindexter, 11/02/86, 4:25:06) It was not to be. (Tower)

- Reagan announces Jacobsen's release, saying it came about "through a number of sensitive channels for a very long time." (WP 12/20/86)

- Donald Regan reveals on a television news program that negotiations for hostages have been going on "over the past several months" and that "we are still negotiating for the other hostages." This is the first public acknowledgment by a senior Administration official that the U.S. has been negotiating with the kidnappers. (WP 12/20/86)

NOV 2-4 - On November 2, hostage David Jacobsen was released. The next day, a pro-Syrian Beirut magazine published the story of the McFarlane mission. On November 4, Majlis Speaker Rafsanjani publicly announced the mission. (Tower)

NOV 3 - President expresses his personal appreciation of the release of kidnapped American David Jacobsen in Beirut. "No political goals will be achieved by resorting to extortion and terrorism," Reagan says in a written statement. Larry Speakes conveys the President's personal appreciation "to the various parties and intermediaries who have been helpful in arranging this release." Crediting Anglican Church envoy Terry Waite, Speakes declined to name any of the others involved. He says the U.S. has not altered its policy of refusing to make concessions to secure the release of the hostages. In announcing the release of Jacobsen, the Jihad

Islami claims that it was responding to "overtures" by the U.S. government. Speakes will not respond to that. In Damascus, diplomats suspect that Syria had something to do with the release. (Reuters 11/3/86)

- On November 3, the Lebanese magazine, *Al Shiraa*, reported that the United States had been supplying arms to Iran and stated that McFarlane had visited Tehran earlier in the year to meet with Iranian officials. (SSIC 1/29/87)

- The Lebanese magazine, *Al-Shiraa*, prints the first account of McFarlane's visit to Iran in late May. The report surfaces in the American press two days later, sparking the initial furor over arms shipments to Iran and the diversion of funds to the contras. (FBIS 11/5/86; PI 11/26/86; WP 12/10/86)

- According to documents and testimony received by the Committee, Secretary of State Shultz, upon learning of the revelations, sent a cable to Poindexter in which he expressed his concern over possible press attempts to portray the arms deal as a violation of U.S. counterterrorism policy. Shultz suggested that the best course of action would be to go public on the NSC initiative in an attempt to make it "clear that this was a special one time operation based on humanitarian grounds and decided by the President within his Constitutional responsibility to act in the service of the national interest." Shultz testified that he did not know at this time about the January 17 presidential Finding authorizing the arms transfers to Iran and that neither he nor Secretary Weinberger learned of the Finding until it was revealed at a White House meeting on November 10. (SSIC 1/29/87)

- (From McFarlane's testimony before the Board February 21, 1987) "On the day that the story was leaked or published in the Beirut magazine, Admiral Poindexter called and stated that because of the continuing hope of being able to release or secure the release of other hostages that the White House was going to take a position of essentially not commenting on the story, that he hoped that I would honor that, too, and I assured him that I would.

"He stated as well that he was going to begin, at the President's direction, putting together a narrative of events of how the entire policy initiative had been conducted, conceived, approved and so forth. And he stated then in the call that he recalled the meeting in July or August of 1985 in which the President had discussed with his Cabinet officers the pros and cons, the President then reaching a decision later on.

"But he said I cannot document that and can you help out. And I said that I would, and I added in the same call that, John, you have very little time on this and I recommend that the President not have a long period of forelorned hopes that I think are unlikely to be fulfilled about further hostages, just based upon past performance.

"It seemed to me, first of all, just thinking about why would I write the memo, well, I was inspired to write the memo because I was being told that a version was coming from the White House to the effect that I had taken this on basically and it wasn't until after the fact that the President had approved this.

General Scowcroft: How did you know that? You didn't have a draft at that point?

Mr. McFarlane: No. I had nothing from the White House on this, but I was receiving word from people indirectly, journalists, that were saying this is what we are being briefed by the White House and I just want you to learn about it.

"Well, I had to say that I could fully accept that as a policy advisor to the President and out of loyalty to him I wanted to take full responsibility for all of my own actions, to assure that the President was placed in the best position possible. But one must not avoid the truth. Consequently, I was upset to hear that possibly—this was through hearsay —that possibly the White House might be taking a position which was fundamentally untrue."

Chairman Tower: When you say "the White House," Bud, can you be more specific?

General Scowcroft: Who is in charge of putting all this stuff together?

Mr. McFarlane: Well, the briefings that were being given to magazines referred to here were originally by Mr. Regan, and five days or four days prior, when Admiral Poindexter had called me, he said that he had been asked, through Mr. Regan, to prepare an account, but already an account was being put out, or so I was told.

"At any rate, my point is in saying that there would have been no reason to write a memo on my part, the point of writing a memo at all is to alter what I was hearing was the

White House version, and that was that the President had not approved the Iranian arms sale or provided authority for it by us or anyone else until after it took place. And that's false.

"So I sat down and I wrote down the memo. But again having returned from out of town and still not looking at records or calendars, because I was relying upon recollections, I put together a series of events from primarily July spread out until a decision by the President in early September, which in truth occurred in a shorter span of time, a span of time from about early July until the first ten days of August.

....."I think it is accurate and useful to point out that the motives behind Admiral Poindexter's actions right after the release of the story on November 3 were inspired by concern for hoped-for still getting out more hostages and that was, I think, rather too ambitiously pursued even by the President, who went to the point of denying that anything at all had occurred.

Mr. McFarlane: [Poindexter's] original call to me on November 3 had, and he recalled it the way that I have, and I have testified to that—that the President met in his pajamas in the residence and then subsequently approved it. (McFarlane testimony, February 21, 1987) (Tower)

- North reportedly remains in Cyprus and keeps in contact with Ambassador Kelly about the possible release of Terry Anderson and David Sutherland. (WP 12/20/86)

NOV 4 - An Administration statement read by Larry Speakes declares: "As long as Iran advocates the use of terrorism, the U.S. arms embargo will continue." The statement, written by Poindexter, adds there has been "no manifestation of a definitive change in Iran's policy on terrorism." (NYT 12/4/86)

- According to documents received by the Committee, Poindexter, by cable, rejected the Secretary's advice, [Shultz's recommendation to go public on the Iran initiative] citing a need to get the hostages out and a desire to brief the Congressional Intelligence Committees. According to the cable, Poindexter had spoken with Vice President Bush, Weinberger and Casey and they had all agreed with the necessity for remaining "absolutely close-mouthed while stressing that basic policy toward Iran, the Gulf War and dealing with terrorists had not changed." (SSIC 1/29/87)

- The day after a Beirut magazine published an account of the May trip to Tehran, Teicher wrote Poindexter:

"The reports of Bud's trip in pro-Syrian Lebanese newspapers coming on the heels of high-level Iranian visits to Damascus, are the clearest possible signals we could receive that the succession struggle is underway and U.S.-Iranian relations are likely to play an important role in the struggle. Obviously there are many possible interpretations of the story; maybe it was put out by Mugniyas to embarrass Iran for putting so much pressure on him. We may never know the exact reason, but we must not let this opportunity to assess the consequences in Iran of these revelations from slipping through our fingers. I think it would be useful to produce an assessment of the range of possible interpretation, and possible U.S. options. To be fair, I also think it would be appropriate to involve Dennis Ross. He is unaware of the compartment or our activities. Once we finish the analysis, I strongly urge you to discuss our options with Shultz and Casey. At a minimum, we need to determine how best, other than parts, etc., to signal the Iranians in a productive manner." (Teicher PROF note to Poindexter, 11/04/86, 09:35, through Pearson (lower case in original)) (Tower)

- Former and current aides to Reagan meet at the White House to put together a chronology of events in connection with the Administration's Iran policy over the past 18 months. They are reportedly unable to agree on what happened. (WP 12/28/86)

- Ali Akbar Rafsanjani, speaker of Iran's Parliament, says that a five-man delegation headed by a person who identified himself as Robert McFarlane secretly and illegally came to Iran, but says the men were detained and no officials spoke with them. (Translation in FBIS 11/5/86; WP 11/5/86)

- North presents conservative activist Carl R. Channell with a "Freedom Fighter" award at a dinner Channell sponsors at Washington's Willard Hotel. North and Channel are later tied to a multimillion-dollar campaign in the U.S. in support of the contras. (MH 12/11/86)

- In today's elections, conservative political action committees are reported to have used $5 million siphoned from sales of arms to Iran to help defeat Senate candidates opposed to contra aid, according to The Lowell (Mass.) Sun of

12/14/86. If true, these activities would be in violation of the Hatch Act. ("Face the Nation" 12/14/86)

NOV 5-20 - Within several days of the leak in Beirut, VADM Poindexter and LtCol North along with Mr. McFarlane, LtCol Robert Earl and Commander Craig Coy, both of whom worked for LtCol North, and others began to prepare a chronology of the initiative. In a 15-day period from November 5 to November 20, they produced at least a dozen versions of the chronology. The earliest versions were merely lists of events; the later versions, called "Maximum Versions" mixed events with rationale.

The last edit, on November 20, also changed the title from "Maximum Version" to "Historical Chronology." The effort, hamstrung by poor record-keeping, produced a series of documents which are often conflicting and occasionally far from what we believe transpired. In short, the NSC chronologies provide more questions than answers.

At best, these chronologies suggest a sense of confusion about both the facts and what to say about them. At worst, they suggest an attempt to limit the information that got to the President, the Cabinet, and the American public. The following represents how the description of some of the events contained in the chronologies changed over time.

How the idea began.—The chronologies variously trace the beginning of the operation to 1984, 1985, and the spring of 1985. They state that an American citizen sometimes referred to by name, Michael Ledeen, was either approached by or learned from the Israelis that an Iranian expatriate sometimes referred to by name, Mr. Ghorbanifar, could either be useful or wanted to establish a contact with the U.S. government for Iran. In the November 17 maximum version, we learn that the Israelis "analyzed this intermediary's background exhaustively in order to validate his legitimacy" and that the U.S. "established an indirect contact with the Iranian intermediary, through the private U.S. citizen and a senior Israeli official." The version continued that this contact was established through the NSC staff with the "full knowledge of appropriate Cabinet officers." This section does not exist in the November 20 historical chronolgy.

 . . . The November 20 historical chronology added that "(t)he Israelis told us that they undertook the action, despite our objections, because they believed it to be in their strategic interests. * * * After discussing this matter with the President, it was decided not to expose this Israeli delivery because we wanted to retain the option of exploiting the existing Israeli channel with Tehran in our own effort to establish a strategic dialogue with the Iranian government."

November, 1985 HAWK shipment. The early versions of the November shipment offered little commentary; by November 20 the following story emerged: "In mid-November, the Israelis, through a senior officer in the Foreign Minister's office (Kimche), indicated that the Government of Israel was convinced that they were nearing a breakthrough with Iran on a high-level dialogue. The Israeli contacted a U.S. official (North) and asked for the name of a European-based airline which could discreetly transit to Iran for the purpose of delivering passengers and cargo. He specifically noted that neither a U.S. carrier nor an Israeli affiliated carrier could be used. We were assured, at the time, that the Israelis were going to 'try oil drilling parts as an incentive,' since we had expressed so much displeasure over the earlier TOW shipment." Apparently Kimche was given the name of a proprietary and Israel "subsequently chartered through normal commercial contract for a flight from Tel Aviv to Tabriz, Iran on November 25, 1985."

"In January, we learned that the Israelis, responding to urgent entreaties from the Iranians, had used the proprietary aircraft to transport 18 HAWK missiles to Iran in an effort to improve the static air defenses around Tehran. Our belated awareness that the Israelis had delivered HAWK missiles raised serious U.S. concerns that these deliveries were jeopardizing our objectives of meeting with high-level Iranian officials. As a consequence of U.S. initiative and by mutual agreement of all three parties, these missiles were returned to Israel in February 1986."

This version also states that, in a conversation in January, 1986 with Mr. Nir, VADM Poindexter "noted our stringent objections to the HAWK missile shipments in November and noted that the U.S. would have to act to have them returned."

The January Finding. The date is variously listed as the 6th, 9th, and 17th.

February, 1986 shipment. Outside a brief mention on an II/7 chronology, the early versions contained nothing of the shipment of 1000 TOWs in February. The November 17 maximum version described a "mechanism for transfer of the weapons" with the Iranian intermediary depositing funds through an Israeli account into a "sterile U.S.-controlled account." Using these funds, "the CIA would covertly obtain materiel authorized for transfer from U.S. military stocks and transport this to Israel for onward movement to Iran."

Through this mechanism, "funds were deposited in the CIA account in Geneva on February 11, 1986 and on February 14 1,000 TOWs were transported to Israel for pre-positioning. The TOWs were off-loaded and placed in a covert Israeli facility.

"On February 19-21, U.S. and Iranian officials * * * met again in Germany to discuss problems in arranging a meeting among highlevel officials. At this meeting, the U.S. side agreed to provide 1,000 TOWs to Iran as a clear signal of U.S. sincerity. This delivery was commenced on the morning of February 20 and completed in two transits to Tehran on February 21."

May through October, 1986. The presentation of the facts of the May trip to Tehran and the use of a second channel is comparatively accurate, though far from complete.

There is little pattern to the inaccuracies of these documents, though it is clear that the authors tried to portray the initiative as an orderly operation and in the best light. (Tower)

NOV 5 - Larry Speakes says that a U.S. embargo against Iran remains in place. Lack of denial of the charge by Iranian official that had flown to Tehran with gifts for the Iranians in an attempt to bargain for the release of the hostages keeps speculation alive. (Reuters 11/5/86)

- In a speech reported by Iranian radio, Ayatollah Hussein Ali Montazeri, referring to Iran's policy toward the U.S., declares "it would be correct to establish humanitarian relations between two independent countries, if the United States comes to its senses." (FBIS 11/7/86)

- The White House confirms that the U.S. is working with other countries for the release of hostages in Lebanon. It refuses to rule out the possibility that Iran may be one of them. Israeli radio reports that Israelis may have helped provide military spare parts to Iran in a deal to free American hostages. (NYT 12/4/86)

NOV 6 - Rafsanjani denies that Iran received arms through Israel. Israeli Prime Minister Yitzhak Shamir refuses to comment on the matter. (FBIS 11/7/86)

- The Israelis received 500 TOWs in reimbursement on November 6. (SSIC 1/29/87)

- Poindexter, McFarlane and deputy national security adviser Alton Keel meet over lunch concerning the burgeoning Iran affair. According to McFarlane, Poindexter says at the meeting, "We've got to put together a full chronology." McFarlane agrees, saying it is necessary to "Get it all out" and to have the President follow up by proposing a series of foreign policy initiatives to show that the affair is behind him. However, according to McFarlane, Poindexter resists the suggestion to go public, hoping it will still be possible to free the hostages, and reminds McFarlane of the difficulties involved in putting together foreign policy offensives. According to sources, Poindexter also complains about Shultz's lack of support for the Iran program. (WP 2/19/87)

- On either the same day as the luncheon meeting or the following day, McFarlane draws up a one-page summary of the Iran program on the secure computer terminal in his home. He mentions that Reagan approved the 1985 Israeli shipment of arms. Poindexter writes back to McFarlane that his account is correct, according to McFarlane's statements later. (WP 2/19/87)

- American intelligence sources disclose that the U.S. has secretly sent military spare parts to Iran for more than 18 months in an attempt to bring about the release of American hostages, and that Washington persuaded Israel to help. Reagan declines comment. (NYT 12/4/86)

- A debate in the Irish parliament on the misuse of Irish passports by U.S. envoys on the May 28 trip to Iran is overruled by the Dublin government. (FBIS 11/10/86)

- Reagan declares that reports of McFarlane's trip to Iran have "no foundation." He further denies that the U.S. reached a secret agreement with Tehran on the release of American hostages in return for arms. Reagan says : "May I suggest and appeal to all of you with regard to this, that the speculation, the commenting on a story that came out of the Middle East and that to us, has no foundation—all of that is making it more difficult to get the other hostages out." No officials issue outright denials, including the President. Abolhassan Bani Sadr, former Iranian president now in exile in Paris, says in an interview that an unmarked American plane delivered spare parts to Iran early in September and that there had been "other shipments long before." Tass news agency reports that McFarlane recently made a secret visit to Iran. Washington refuses to comment. (Reuters 11/6/86; NYT 12/4/86; FBIS 11/10/86)

- Felix Rodriguez delivers a speech at the National War College on low-intensity conflict in El Salvador. That night Rodriguez has dinner with Bush aide Samuel Watson in McLean, Virginia. (WP 12/16/86)

- North, McFarlane, Poindexter and a representative of Casey meet to try to work out an agreed-upon version of what happened regarding U.S. Iran policy. North eventually produces a chronology, but its accuracy on certain counts is questioned. (WP 12/28/86)

- According to testimony by Gates, on November 6, Casey and Gates met with Poindexter at the White House. Casey recommended that Poindexter bring in the White House counsel, but Poindexter replied that he did not trust the White House counsel and would talk instead to Paul Thompson (a lawyer and military assistant to Poindexter). Gates also said he learned at that meeting that Casey had a prior discussion with Poindexter in which he may have recommended that North obtain legal counsel. A similar rendition of this conversation was later contained in Casey's November letter to the Attorney General. (SSIC 1/29/87)

- According to his letter to the Attorney General of November 25, Casey had a senior CIA analyst and a CIA contract employee go up to New York to discuss the whole thing at length with Furmark. Memoranda dated October 17 and November 7 discuss their meetings with Furmark.

The senior CIA analyst's memorandum dated November 7 describe a meeting between Furmark and the senior CIA analyst on the afternoon of November 6 in Washington in which Furmark warns that the Canadian investors intended to expose fully the U.S. government's role in the Iran arms transactions. Furmark, according to the memorandum, says that the Canadians knew that Secord was heavily involved in managing the Iran arms transactions for North, and that Secord was also involved in assisting North in support of the contras in Nicaragua. Furmark also said the Canadians believed they had been swindled and the money paid by Iran for the arms may have been siphoned off to support the contras in Nicaragua. (SSIC 1/29/87)

NOV 6-7 - In the first days after the disclosure, the President stood firmly with VADM Poindexter in support of protecting the channel and the operation. Mr. McDaniel noted that during VADM Poindexter's morning briefings the issue was discussed on November 6 and 7; in both discussions, the President apparently agreed to make no comment in hope that additional hostages would be freed and out of fear for the safety of the second channel. (Tower)

NOV 7 - Furmark tells the CIA officer with whom he had been meeting that the Canadian investors who had not received their funds from Khashoggi were planning to sue the Saudi arms dealer and a private firm into which they paid the $11 million to cover the cost of the HAWK missile parts. According to documents received by the Committee, Furmark said that he had persuaded the Canadians to delay their lawsuit. Furmark indicated he was unimpressed with the new Iranian channel and expressed support for the ability of Ghorbanifar, who "coordinated his initiatives...with all significant factions in Iran." (SSIC 1/29/87)

- Charles Allen told the Board: ....
"I later met with Mr. Furmark on the 7th of November, but at that stage the operation was starting to be exposed in a major way, so the fact that the Canadian investors were threatening a law suit didn't seem to be as significant to me at that stage." (Tower)

- A St. Lucia Airways 707 cargo plane leaves Belgium for Israel, according to Belgian flight records. Its cargo is unknown. (WP 2/24/87)

- Administration officials say Reagan approved a plan by McFarlane 18 months ago to establish secret contacts with Iran in order to improve relations with that country, end its support for terrorism and help gain the release of hostages. Officials say that the plan did not mention supplying arms and spare parts, but that the White House accepted an Israeli offer to deliver older American-made spare parts and weapons to Iran. It is unclear at this point if the President approved the arms shipments. (NYT 12/4/86)

- Rodriguez meets with Gregg and Watson in Gregg's office, where Rodriguez describes his role in El Salvador as having been primarily directed towards counterinsurgency in that country. He also indicates that he, himself, had been able to assist the contra resupply effort. (WP 12/16/86)

- . . . Below is the portion of the memo sent [by McFarlane] as a PROF note to VADM Poindexter dated November 7, 1986, time log 20:30:32:

"It might be useful to review just what the truth is.

"You will recall that when the Israelis first approached us in June '85, I presented the idea of engaging in a dialogue with the Iranians—no mention at all of any arms exchange at all—and he [Reagan] approved it.

"We then heard nothing until August when the Israelis introduced the requirement for TOWs. I told Kimche no.

"They went ahead on their own but then asked that we replace the TOWs and after checking with the President, we agreed. Weir was released as a consequence of their action.

"My next involvement was to go to London where I presented our willingness to open a political dialogue but that we could not participate in an arms transfer for hostages. Gorbanifar ranted and raved but we did not change our position.

"I returned to the States and debriefed the President (with Cap present, and Regan) that we had taken the position of being open to a political dialogue once our hostages were released but not before and ruled out an arms transfer. I also said that Gorbanifar was not to be trusted and recommended that we no longer carry on business with him. You were present John. I then left the government.

"Some dialogue must have continued with Gorbanifar between New Year's and April, notwithstanding my recommendation. In April you contacted me to go to Iran to open the political dialogue. I did so. Once there, faced with bad faith on their part (not having released our people and without meetings with the decision makers) I aborted the mission. Ollie can verify all this.

"Upon my return, I debriefed the trip and once more recommended against carrying on the arms connection but waiting them out on the political dialogue.

[Returning to Mr. McFarlane's testimony:]

"Now as one reads the memo, if you refer to it, that series of decisions, first of all to say yes to a political dialogue, secondly, when confronted by an insistence on selling TOWs by us to say no, and then, thirdly, when the Israelis decide that they will take it on their own to sell arms if we agree, and that they can buy replacements from us instead of spreading out in time from the early July until early September, those events take place in about a month's period of time." (pp. 5-6).

"On November 7 I could not have documented it for you, and it wasn't until about three weeks later—actually until I got my record of schedule out of storage. Another point I would make, however, about this cross-note that I'm talking about is that there's no question here in that cross-note about prior approval prior to Mr. Weir's release.

"I said it then. I've said it since, and it is true today: The decision process had three milestones on it—early July, political without any arms of any kind; mid-July, the Israelis saying political dialogue, but if the United States will sell arms and we responded no; and then early August, in which the Israelis said, well, if we do, and my meeting with Mr. Kimche resulted in our discussion on the pros and cons and so forth, and my going to the President and once more his discussion of it with his advisors, and the decision, yes, that we will replace the sale replacements for any Israeli arms that they may ship." (pp. 6-7) (Tower)

"I have felt since last November—and that is where we started—that it has been, I think, misleading, at least, and wrong, at worst, for me to overly gild the President's motives for his decision in this, to portray them as mostly directed toward political outcomes.

"The President acknowledged those and recognized that those were clearly important. However, by the tenor of his questioning, which was oriented toward the hostages and timing of the hostages, from his recurrent virtually daily questioning just about welfare and do we have anything new and so forth, it is very clear that his concerns here were for the return of the hostages." (McFarlane testimony p. 11) (Tower)

- Because of a delay in the transfer of funds the TOWs actually delivered to Iran on October 29, 1986, were Israeli TOWs. The 500 U.S. TOWs were provided to Israel as replacements on November 7.

" . . . The President, VADM Poindexter, and LtCol North hoped that more hostages would be released. Notes taken by the NSC Executive Secretary indicate that on November 7, 1986, the President decided not to respond to questions on this subject for fear of jeopardizing the remaining hostages. No further hostages were released.

Mr. Ghorbanifar told the Board that the switch to the second channel was a major error. He claimed that he had involved all three major lines or factions within the government of Iran in the initiative, and that the second channel involved only the Rafsanjani faction thus stimulating friction among the factions and leading to the leak of the story to embarrass Rafsanjani. In addition, the price offered to this faction was lower ($8000 per TOW) than the price charged for the earlier TOW deliveries ($10000 per TOW). (Tower)

NOV 8 - Casey briefs the chairman and vice chairman of the Senate intelligence committee on the Iran arms deal and the Administration's rationale. (NYT 1/19/87)

- Members of Congress say the House and Senate foreign relations and intelligence panels will investigate whether the Administration violated congressional restrictions on covert operations. (NYT 12/4/86)

NOV 8-10 - American and Iranian officials meet in Geneva to discuss further hostage releases. The issue is reportedly set aside temporarily because of the recent publicity surrounding the Iran dealings. At around this time, the U.S. sends Israel 500 TOW missiles to replace those shipped to Iran. (WP 12/31/86)

- In November, the U.S. team, including North, met again with the new Iranian channel. During three days of meetings with the Iranian, the topics included hostage release, Dawa prisoners being held by Kuwait, the Israeli role in the arms transfers, and Iranian intelligence requirements. The new channel admitted that Iran owed Ghorbanifar $10 million, but stated that Ghorbanifar owed Iran 1,000 TOW missiles. According to testimony received by the Committee, by this point the Executive branch had come to believe that the Senate and House Intelligence Committees would have to be briefed on the Iranian initiative. The CIA thereupon began to prepare the materials needed for Casey's presentation. The CIA officer who had dealt directly with the Iranians was asked to prepare an outline of the meetings he had attended, and the CIA Comptroller attempted to reconstruct the financial aspects of the Iran program. (SSIC 1/29/87)

NOV 9 - American officials acknowledge that U.S. involvement in arms shipments to Iran marks a policy reversal by the Reagan Administration. (NYT 12/4/86)

- According to international arms trade sources cited in a report today, U.S. diplomats and representatives of the Iranian military have met in London over the past few weeks to discuss the transfer of spare parts for Iranian tanks, and for F-4 Phantom, and F-14 Tomcat aircraft. The delivery of "moderate but useful" quantities of AIM-9 Sidewinder and AIM-7 Sparrow air-to-air missiles, Maverick air-launched anti-tank missiles and HAWK air defense missiles were also discussed. (Sunday Telegraph (London) 11/9/86)

NOV 10 - Reagan rejects demands that he disclose details of the administrations dealings with Iran, saying "no U.S. laws have been or will be violated" and that "our policy of not making concessions to terrorists remains intact." (NYT 12/4/86)

- Shultz [later] testified . . . that neither he nor Secretary Weinberger learned of the [January 17 Presidential] Finding until it was revealed at a White House meeting on November 10. (SSIC 1/29/87)

- The President met with the Vice President, Secretaries Shultz and Weinberger, Mr. Regan, Director Casey, Attorney General Meese, VADM Poindexter, and Dr. Alton Keel (Acting Deputy at NSC) on November 10 to discuss the initiative and possible government reactions. Notes of the meeting by Dr. Keel provide some insight into this meeting. The President felt a need for a statement of U.S. intentions in the initiative. VADM Poindexter offered a brief history of the initiative. Following questions by Secretaries Shultz and Weinberger, the President stated that rumors had endangered what they were doing. Dr. Keel's notes suggest that the President felt that we had not dealt with terrorists or paid ransom and that one of the purposes of government was to protect its citizens. The President felt that a basic statement had to come out but that we needed to avoid details and specifics of the operation; he urged that we could not engage in speculation because the lives of the hostages and the Iranians were at stake. (Tower)

- FBI Director Webster telephones Associate Attorney General Trott for permission to continue the inquiry into Southern Air Transport's role in ferrying arms to the contras. Trott, who requested the delay on Meese's behalf on October 30, tells Webster he will have to check, but waits until November 20 before calling FBI Assistant Director Oliver Revell to grant permission to resume the probe. Although originally reported to have been only a ten-day shutdown, the investigation does not get under way again until November 26. Justice Department spokesmen attribute the extended delays to "the way the bureaucracy works." (WP 12/25/86)

- An informed oil industry weekly reports the U.S. has withdrawn the support of its Saudi-based AWACS aircraft for Iraq in response to an Iranian promise to help free American hostages. (FBIS 11/12/86)

- Lake Resources Inc., the company into whose Credit Suisse bank account Ghorbanifar and Khashoggi deposited funds, is dissolved, according to public registry records. (MH 12/13/86; WP 12/14/86)

- A Rome newspaper, Paese Sera, reports that "five thousand tons of spares for F-104's of the Tehran Air Force were shipped from Italy" on behalf of the U.S. government. The spare parts reportedly were shipped from the central Tyrrhenian port of Talamone. The Italian government denies the story the following day, November 11. Prime Minister Bettino Craxi again denies the allegations on November 12, and on November 14, he orders members of his government's ministries to supply any information dealing with alleged Italian involvement in covert U.S-Iranian arms deals. A government official later speculates that cargo marked "Destination Iran" could be mistakenly interpreted as being bound for that country rather than simply signifying "Inspection and

Repair as Necessary." (Rome ANSA 11/11/86 & 11/14/86; Rome Domestic Service 11/12/86; Avanti! (Italy) 11/22/86)

NOV 11 - Another freighter from Israel delivers a load of U.S. military equipment to Iran. (PI 11/26/86)

- Officials say Peter J. Wallison, the White House counsel, has begun to examine the legal issues involved in the sale of arms to Iran. (NYT 12/4/86)

- At a dinner in Washington, North presents conservative lobbyist Carl "Spitz" Channell with a letter from Reagan expressing his thanks for Channell's efforts in support of the contras. Earlier in the year, Channell's National Endowment for the Preservation of Liberty (NEPL) reportedly boasted that it would spend more than $2.5 million furthering Administration policy aims toward Nicaragua. (Newsweek 12/29/86)

- Rodriguez is again in Washington, D.C., this time accompanying El Salvador air force commander Juan Rafael Bustillo. The two eat dinner that night with Col. Watson. (WP 12/16/86)

NOV 12 - At a meeting with congressional leaders attended by Bush, Reagan personally acknowledges for the first time sending military supplies to Iran. He defends the action as necessary to establish ties to moderate elements there. (NYT 12/4/86)

- Larry Speakes says repeatedly from November 12-24 that Meese "provided legal advice on U.S. dealings with Iran from the start," in mid-1985. But Patrick S. Korten, a Justice Department spokesman, says that Meese was unaware of the Iran deal until Reagan signed the January 17 finding. Today, Speakes says, "The President has been guided by the Attorney General all along in all of this." However, Meese appears to contradict this on November 25 when he says that he provided no more than "routine concurrence" in the finding. (NYT 12/4/86)

- Senate staff members visit CIA headquarters for an initial briefing on the Iran arms deal. CIA briefers discuss Reagan's January 17, 1986 finding but make no mention of the November 1985 arms shipment to Iran. (WP 2/12/87)

- Rodriguez and Bustillo eat dinner with Gregg. At both this dinner and that of the night before, Bustillo makes it clear that he would welcome Rodriguez back to El Salvador to continue his assistance in the counterinsurgency operation. (WP 12/16/86)

NOV 13 - In Tehran, Iranian Prime Minister Mousavi says the U.S. is the "Great Satan" and it is unlikely that his government would intercede with the groups in Lebanon as long as the U.S. refused to release the arms purchases, frozen since the Shah fell. Iran's U.N. representative denies that his country has been involved with any deal with the U.S. to supply arms in exchange for the hostages. But he does not deny that Iran might have received U.S. weapons in a deal unrelated to the hostages. (Reuters 11/13/86)

- VADM Poindexter briefed reporters on background the same day [as the president gave his televised address]. The following interchange between VADM Poindexter and reporters officially exposed a connection between Israel and the United States in the 1985 shipments.

Q. "—a few things on the shipments, just to clarify this. Any shipments that were made prior to January of 1986 you're saying the U.S. had no role in, either condoning, winking, encouraging, or anything of that nature? Is that correct?

VADM Poindexter: "That's correct."

Q. "Could you say then what prompted the release of Benjamin Weir then in September of '85? What event do you think was related to his release?

VADM Poindexter: "Well, I think that it was a matter of our talking to the contacts through our channel, making the case as to what our long-range objectives were, demonstrating our good faith——

Q. "How was that done?"

VADM Poindexter: "Well, that was one of the motivations behind the small amount of stuff that we transferred to them."

Q. "But that was done later?"

VADM Poindexter: "The problem is—and don't draw any inferences from this—but there are other countries involved, but I don't want to confirm what countries those are and—because I think that it is still important that that be protected. And going back to the question you asked me earlier, there was one shipment that was made not by us, but by a third country prior to the signing of that document."

Q. "This shipment to Israel?'

VADM Poindexter: "I'm not confirming that, George."

Q. "Was that on our behalf?"

VADM Poindexter: "It was done in our interests."

Q. "Was that before Weir was released?"

VADM Poindexter: "I honestly don't know. And if I knew, I don't think I would tell you precisely."

Q. "You just said previously that you did not condone any shipments?"

VADM Poindexter: "I went back and corrected—there was one exception and that was the one I just described." (Tower)

- A senior Administration official, later identified as Poindexter, tells reporters that a shipment of arms was sent to Iran before Reagan's January 17 finding around the same time that Benjamin Weir was released. (WP 12/18/86)

- On November 13, Mr. McDaniel noted that the President decided to address the nation that evening. There appear to have been several drafts of the President's speech and a hectic struggle to produce the final product. That night, the President addressed the nation. (Tower)

- Reagan in a televised address to the nation defends his "secret diplomatic initiative to Iran" which he says included only "small amounts of defensive weapons and spare parts" that could fit into a single cargo plane. Before the address, a senior Administration official says the transfer amounted to no more than one cargo planeload, or about 260,000 pounds of materiel. Reagan expresses satisfaction that "there's been no evidence of Iranian Government complicity in acts of terrorism against the United States" in 18 months. He insists "we did not, repeat did not, trade weapons or anything else for hostages, nor will we." (NYT 12/4/86; Transcript in WP 11/14/86; WP 12/28/86)

-The President told the American people that they were "going to hear the facts from a White House source and you know my name."

The President stated that a diplomatic initiative had been underway for 18 months, for the following reasons:

—to renew relationship with Iran;

—to bring an honorable end to Iran-Iraq war;

—to eliminate state-sponsored terrorism;

—to attain the safe return of the hostages.

The President said, "The United States has not swapped boatloads or planeloads of American weapons for the return of the American hostages."

"I authorized the transfer of small amounts of defensive weapons and spare parts for defensive systems to Iran. . . . These modest deliveries, taken together, could easily fit into a single cargo plane. They could not, taken together, affect the outcome of the . . . war . . . nor . . . the military balance."

The President noted that various countries had tried to broker a relationship between Iran and the United States since 1983. "With this history in mind, we were receptive last year when we were alerted to the possibility of establishing a direct dialogue with Iranian officials."

"It's because of Iran's strategic importance and its influence in the Islamic world that we chose to probe for a better relationship between our countries."

"Our discussions continued into the spring of this year. Based upon the progress we felt we had made, we sought to raise the diplomatic level of contacts. A meeting was arranged in Tehran. I then asked my former National Security Adviser, Robert McFarlane, to undertake a secret mission and gave him explicit instructions."

"There is ample precedent in our histroy for this kind of secret diplomacy. In 1971, then President Nixon sent his national security adviser on a secret mission to China."

"Although the efforts we undertook were highly sensitive and involvement of government officials was limited to those with a strict need to know, all appropriate Cabinet Officers were fully consulted. The actions I authorized were and continue to be in full compliance with federal law. And the relevant committees of Congress are being and will be fully informed."

"We did not—repeat—did not trade weapons or anything else for hostages—nor will we."(Tower)

- The CIA Inspector General testified before the Committee and described as "fairly significant" the evidence that had begun to develop in the CIA by early November that some diversion might be taking place. The IG testified that he asked for the senior CIA analyst memos about suspected diversion of money to Central America on November 13 and that Casey and Gates saw Poindexter the next day to discuss the issue again. (SSIC 1/29/87)

- A shipment of arms leaves Setubal harbor, Portugal, for Iran aboard the Panamian-registered freighter Angelique, according to reports from Portuguese shipping sources. The ship is owned by a company named the Wyvern Navigation Corp. It is reportedly the last shipment of "large quantities" of Portuguese arms sent to Iran over the past week. A week earlier, a shipment of mortars and heavy artillery ammunition was reportedly flown from Lisbon to Iran. According to Arab diplomats, Iran has spent $132 million on arms from Portugal in the past three years. Last year, Portugal is said to have sold $79 million of weapons to Iran and $5 million to Iraq. (AFP 11/15/86)

NOV 14 - The CIA Inspector General testified . . . that Casey and Gates saw Poindexter the next day [November 14] to discuss the . . . suspected diversion of money to Central America . . . again. (SSIC 1/29/87)

- The White House acknowledges that the CIA was directly involved in the shipment of arms to Iran in an operation run by the NSC. Reagan says he had the right to delay briefing Congress, but congressional officials say they will research the laws. Meanwhile, a high-level Israeli official discloses that Israel has been shipping arms to Iran with American knowledge since 1982 and that the American Ambassador to Israel was notified of each shipment. (NYT 12/4/86)

- North discusses the Iran arms sales with antiterrorism specialist Neil C. Livingstone, telling him they are part of an attempt to strengthen pragmatic elements within Iran against a Soviet intervention being prepared at the time. Senior Administration officials later say that no reliable evidence exists to suggest a possible Soviet invasion. (NYT 1/12/87)

- On or around this date, Fawn Hall, North's secretary at the NSC, alters four documents concerning North's role in the Iran affair with the intent of substituting the revised versions for the originals in NSC files. Investigators later discover the altered papers on Hall's desk along with carbons of the originals. The changes are apparently intended to obscure the role of North's superiors in the affair. (WP 2/24/87; NYT 2/24/87)

- Regan and Poindexter separately give a total of eight interviews on television shows and to reporters as part of the Administration's policy of "damage control," supervised by Regan. However, their statements only add to the confusion. Regan at a breakfast meeting with reporters first characterizes the Iran arms deal as a "trade" for the hostages, contradicting earlier Administration claims, then immediately says that word is inappropriate. He then remarks that it was the Iranians who "came up with the idea" of providing arms as a show of good faith. But Poindexter in a separate interview denies this, hinting that the notion originated with a third country, later identified as Israel. Regan himself says later in the interview, "In the summer of '85 . . . there was a request that a third country be allowed to sell [the Iranians] some weapons." He then adds, "we agreed [to this]. We were asked if we would object and we said no." Poindexter backs this up, saying that the arms shipment "was authorized verbally . . . by the President." (Regan appears to contradict both these statements in testimony on December 18 when he says that the President approved the August shipment only after the fact.) At the same breakfast, and at other times, Regan declares that the arms deal has been justified because Iran has modified its support for terrorism since the operation began. He insists that the three Americans seized in Beirut in September and October were not taken by groups supported by Tehran. However, Poindexter, Shultz and Deputy Secretary of State John Whitehead all state subsequently that the terrorists in each case had ties with Iran. (NYT 12/4/86; WP 12/18/86 & 12/27/86 & 12/28/86; LAT 12/19/86)

- Both Speakes and Poindexter say Shultz, Weinberger and other Cabinet officers helped prepare Reagan's January 17 finding, contradicting initial State Department claims that Shultz was not "directly involved" in the decision to permit sales to Iran. On November 21, Shultz admits taking part in two "full-scale discussions" of the issue in December 1985 and January 1986. In December, he testifies before Congress that he was not present when Reagan decided to proceed with the January 17 finding and did not learn of it until November when it became public. (NYT 12/4/86; WP 12/28/86)

- A spokesman for the Spanish government denies reports the country is being used as a transit point for U.S. arms bound for Iran. At the same time, the vice director general of customs control has ordered stiffer controls on the entry and exit of goods at all Spanish ports, and the Danish Seamen's Association says that a Danish shipping company is storing weapons headed for the Middle East in the terminal at Alicante, Spain. (FBIS 11/17/86)

- The President was quite clearly concerned about the hostages. Mr. McFarlane told the board that the President inquired almost daily about the welfare of the hostages. Chief of Staff Regan is reported to have told reporters on November 14, 1986, that "the President brings up the hostages at about 90 percent of his briefings." Mr Regan is reported to have said that at the daily intelligence briefing, the President asked VADM Poindexter: "John, anything new on the hostages?" (Tower)

NOV 15 - At a meeting at Camp David, Reagan and his advisers cannot agree on how to handle the Iran problem. Shultz, at odds with the others, asks Reagan for a promise not to provide more military equipment to Iran and an assurance that the State Department will take part in future diplomatic contacts with Tehran. (NYT 12/4/86)

- Mehdi Bahremani, Ali Akbar Rafsanjani's eldest son and a close associate of Manucher Ghorbanifar, flees to Canada after apparently receiving at least $6 million in commissions from U.S. arms deals with Iran. Bahremani, reportedly concerned that his involvement in the deal would embarrass his father, left his home in Brussels for Toronto closely pursued by an Iranian investigator. (MH 12/22/86)

- The Nicaraguan Anti-Somocista Popular Tribunal convicts U.S. citizen Eugene Hasenfus, sentencing him to 30 years in prison. He is found guilty of violating a public security law prohibiting "actions aimed at subjecting the nation totally or partially to foreign domination," and of "illicit association." No finding is delivered on the charge of terrorism. After the charges are read, Hasenfus is asked if he wants to appeal the court decision. Denied consultation with his attorney, Hasenfus says yes. (WP 11/16/86; NYT 11/16/86)

NOV 16 - Shultz publicly says he opposes sending any more military equipment to Iran. Poindexter says the Joint Chiefs of Staff were not informed of the Iran operation in advance. Shultz also contradicts Reagan's statement three days ago concerning Iran's alleged suspension of terrorist acts in recent months; Shultz maintains that "Iran has and continues to pursue a policy of terrorism." The Secretary of State appears on television to air his views on the Iran affair after he is unable to convince Reagan to declare that there will be no more arms sales to Tehran and to put the State Department in charge of Iran policy. (NYT 12/4/86; WP 2/12/87)

- Poindexter says that no covert operations other than the sale of arms to Iran has been kept secret from Congress. On November 25, Meese informs the public of the diversion of funds to the contras. (NYT 12/4/86)

- Regan, responding to criticism, says: "Some of us are like a shovel brigade that follows a parade down Main Street cleaning up. We took Reykjavik and turned what was really a sour situation into something that turned out pretty well. Who was it that took this disinformation thing and managed to turn it? Who was it [that] took on this loss in the Senate and pointed out a few facts and managed to pull that? I don't say we'll be able to do it four times in a row. But here we go again, and we're trying." (Foreign Affairs)

- McFarlane in a television interview says "No American nut, bolt or any other item from anywhere in the United States" went to Iran in 1985. (NYT 12/4/86)

NOV 17 - Reagan says he has "absolutely no plans" to send more arms to Iran. (NYT 12/4/86)

- Judge Leonard B. Sand of the Federal District Court in New York asks prosecutors to determine if American arms shipments to Iran have changed the Government's position about prosecuting defendants Evans, Bar-Am, et. al. in the $2 billion Iran arms shipments case. (NYT 12/4/86)

- Poindexter asked North in mid-November to compile a history of the Iran program. North reportedly told Meese that he went to the files and also talked to McFarlane, Poindexter, and others in compiling the chronology. None of the materials prepared in the White House during this period and received by the Committee referred to the use of Iran arms sales proceeds for the Nicaraguan resistance, although one chronology dated November 17 and labeled "maximum version" has handwriting at the end of a list of Iran program accomplishments the notation "nicargua" [sic]. (Attorney General's Inquiry Notes: North 11/23/86) (SIRP)

NSC Executive Secretary Rod McDaniel testified that sometime during October or November, North commented to the effect that "one of the great ironies was how the Iranians were helping the contras." McDaniel testified that he did not give much thought to the comment at the time because North was given to hyperbole. (SSIC 1/29/87)

- In the November 17 maximum version [of the chronology prepared by North, Poindexter, McFarlane, Earl and Coy(see Nov 5-20, 1986 entry)] we learn that the Israelis "analyzed this intermediary's background exhaustively in order to validate his legitimacy" and that the U.S. "established an indirect contact with the Iranian intermediary, through the private U.S. citizen and a senior Israeli official." The version continued that this contact was established through the NSC staff with the "full knowledge of appropriate Cabinet officers." This section does not exist in the November 20 historical chronology.

...By November 17, the story was as follows: "On August 22, 1985, the U.S., through the U.S. citizen intermediary, acquiesced in an Israeli delivery of military supplies (508 TOWs) to Tehran. We were subsequently informed that the delivery had taken place at the end of August, though we were not aware of the shipment at the time it was made." Again, the U.S. decision was made at "the highest level."

... February, 1986 shipment. Outside a brief mention on an II/7 chronology, the early versions contained nothing of the shipment of 1000 TOWs in February. The November 17 maximum version described a "mechanism for transfer of the weapons" with the Iranian intermediary depositing funds through an Israeli account into a "sterile U.S.-controlled account." Using these funds, "the CIA would covertly obtain materiel authorized for transfer from U.S. military stocks and transport this to Israel for onward movement to Iran."

Through this mechanism, "funds were deposited in the CIA account in Geneva on February 11, 1986 and on February 14 1,000 TOWs were transported to Israel for pre-positioning. The TOWs were off-loaded and placed in a covert Israeli facility. (Tower)

NOV 18 - Larry Speakes says Reagan does not want Shultz to resign. (NYT 12/4/86)

- The Justice Department begins an investigation into the financial disclosure statements filed by the Washington spokesman for the FDN, Bosco Matamoros. Matamoros said the department had begun the "routine verification procedures" to be certain he was complying with the Foreign Agents Registration Act, which requires disclosure of the sources of financing for lobbyists representing foreign groups. (NYT 11/18/86)

- Poindexter briefs Undersecretary of State Michael Armacost and legal adviser Abraham Sofaer on Casey's prepared testimony for his upcoming November 21 appearance before Congress. Later in the day, the two State officials are permitted to view a copy of the draft of Casey's proposed testimony. The draft includes the statement that all U.S. officials believed that the November 1985 shipment of arms to Iran was actually oil drilling equipment. Upon hearing this from his aides, Shultz, who knows this statement is untrue, becomes "very much concerned" and on November 20 has an angry confrontation with Reagan and the chief of staff about the accuracy of the information Poindexter is giving White House officials. (WP 2/12/87)

- At about 8:00 pm, McFarlane goes to the White House to help prepare Reagan for his news conference the following day. According to McFarlane's version of events, Poindexter asks him to look over a draft statement on Iran that Reagan intends to read at the conference. McFarlane reportedly spends about an hour editing the statement, providing it with "a more global theme," in the words of an associate, including a description of the program as being aimed at "bringing Iran back into the community of responsible nations." After he finishes editing the statement, he transmits the changes via computer to Poindexter, who has gone home by this time, and confers with him over the phone. Poindexter approves the new version. At this point, according to sources, McFarlane begins to look through a CIA master chronology and notices a number of errors, which he tries to correct. He is also given a sheet of paper with two paragraphs written on it, one saying that Reagan did not approve the 1985 Israeli shipment, the other that he was upset upon learning it had taken place and that he wanted McFarlane to convey his reaction to Israel. According to sources, McFarlane tells his associates at the session, including Howard Teicher, North and two of North's assistants, Marine Lt. Col. Robert L. Earl and Craig Coy, that neither statement is true. At this point, North remarks that "The President must absolutely not be hurt by this." Apparently acquiescing to what he says is the overall strategy of putting distance between Reagan and the operation, McFarlane later admits, "I acceded to a portrayal of events that minimized the role of the President and was not technically wrong." (WP 2/19/87)

- According to one account of the practice session for Reagan's news conference the following day, Reagan is corrected by Poindexter when he denies approving any Israeli shipments to Iran. Ignoring his usual practice, Reagan does not try to answer the question a second time after being corrected, according to this account. At the conference, he denies three times that he authorized shipments by Israel in 1985. Another report on the session, however, says that Poindexter makes no mention to the President of several important details concerning the Iran deals, including the fact of Israeli participation. Immediately after the news conference, according to this version, several aides, including North, approach the President and inform him of his misstatements. (WP 12/28/86; NYT 2/24/87)

- On November 18, the chronology [prepared by North, Poindexter, McFarlane, Earl and Coy(see Nov 5-20, 1986 entry)] read, "On August 22, 1985, a senior Israeli official (David Kimche) visited Washington and met with the National Security Advisor. The Israeli asked us to acquiesce in a single Israeli delivery of defensive military materiel to Tehran. . . . Mr. McFarlane stated that the U.S. could in no way be construed as an 'arms for hostages' deal [sic] and that there could be no guarantee that whatever items of U.S. origin Israel sent, could be replaced. We were subsequently informed that the Israelis had delivered 508 TOWs at the end of August."

After a PROF note from Mr. McFarlane to VADM Poindexter on November 18, this section changed drastically. At Mr. McFarlane's suggestion, the arms and hostages were handled as distinct and unrelated examples of bona fides for a broader relationship. The chronology now read that Mr. McFarlane "elevated this proposition to the President within days at a meeting that included the Secretaries of State and

Defense and the Director of Central Intelligence." The President, according to this account, could not authorize any transfers of material. Within days, the Israeli offered the option to have Israel ship "modest quantities of material" and would the United States resupply. Mr. McFarlane reportedly elevated the issue again and, once again, the President said that he could not do so. "We subsequently learned that in late August the Israelis had transferred 508 TOW missiles to Iran." (See the November 18, 1986 PROF note from Mr. McFarlane to Mr. Poindexter). (Tower)

. . . The Board reviewed the different histories offered by Mr. McFarlane in three PROF notes on the 7th, 18th, and 21st of November and in his several testimonies on the Hill and before the Board.

" . . . It seems to me that by the time the President had made his speech on this [see February 21, 1987 entry] which had not had the intended effect of explaining satisfactorily what had happened that his wish to say something more and at the same time minimize his own role grew to the point that on November 18, by the time that group convened, a principal objective, probably the primary objective, was to describe a sequence of events that would distance the President from the initial approval of the Iran arms sale, distance him from it to blur his association with it. The November 18 chronology, which I indeed helped prepare, was not a full and completely accurate account of those events, but rather this effort to blur and leave ambiguous the President's role. The language was intended, I would say, to convey the impression that the United States had not expressly authorized the sale of arms either directly from the United States or by the Israelis on behalf of the United States, but, second, to preserve the ability to say that if Israel were to make such sales that they could expect to purchase replacement items from the United States. (pp. 42-43) (Tower)

"I think it was . . . the 18th . . . I believe it was actually North saying the Admiral had directed that he call me and ask my help in coming over that evening to scrub and finish a chronology that would be used in helping out in the pre-brief of the President for the press conference. And he said we were under the gun to get it done, but we have it. And that was about 5:00, as I recall, or late in the day.

"And so I canceled a dinner I was supposed to go to and went over, but I didn't get there actually until about 8:00 and it was in Colonel North's office. It was kind of a feverish climate in which four or five officers—Colonel North, Mr. Teicher, Mr. Coy, Colonel Earle, a couple of secretaries, (Al Keel) periodically, but not originally. Cut and paste—some original, some typed, some handwritten documents, ones that had been prepared, I believe, in Mr. Buchanan's office to be used the next day. And separately a draft chronology, the so-called master of which had been done by the CIA, or so I was told by Colonel North.

I started by looking at the opening statement and believed that it did not fully treat the political purpose at issue here of the longer-term relationship with Iran and other points that were less important. But I sat down and drafted a three-section note that went out in three separate messages by PROFs to Admiral Poindexter.

Mr. McFarlane prepared a portion of the chronology on November 18. He sent his edit to VADM Poindexter at 23:06:20 on the 18th. Below is a complete text of that PROF note:

"I have just finished reading the chronology. Much of it is coming to me for the first time—primarily the material on what went on between Jan-May '86—and I am not really able to comment on how to deal with that.

"It seems to me that I ought to limit my input to what I recall from my involvement before Jan '86 and then from the May meeting. In that context, I would recommend deleting all material starting on the 11/17 (2000) version at page three, penultimate para (i.e. In 1985, a private . . .) down through the third para on the following page (ending with . . . strategic dialogue with the Iranian government.) and replace with the following.

" 'In July of 1985, during a visit to Washington, an Israeli diplomat advised National Security Advisor, Robert McFarlane, that Israel had established a channel of communications with authoritative elements in Iran who were interested in determining whether the United States was open to a discreet, high level dialogue with them. The Iranians were described as comprising the principal figures of the government (i.e. Speaker of the Majlis Rafsanjani and Prime Minister Musavi) and as being devoted to a reorientation of Iranian policy.

" 'At this first meeting, McFarlane went to great length to draw out the Israeli diplomat as to why he found the Iranian proposal credible, given the events of the past 6 years. He replied that their exhaustive analysis had gone beyond the surface logic deriving from the chaos and decline within Iran and the degenerative effects of the war, to more concrete tests of the willingness of the Iranians to take personal risks (i.e. by exposure of themselves in meetings with Israelis to compromise as well as by the transfer of extremely sensitive intelligence on the situation (and political lineup) within Iran; information which was proven valid).

"'The Israeli asked for our position on agreeing to open such a dialogue. No mention was made of any pre-conditions or Iranian priorities. McFarlane conveyed this proposal to the President (in the presence of the Chief of Staff). The President said that he believed such a dialogue would be worthwhile at least to the point of determining the validity of the interlocutors. This was conveyed back to the Israeli diplomat.

"'Within days the Israeli called again on McFarlane. This meeting, he stated that he had conveyed our position and that the Iranians had responded that recognizing the need for both sides to have tangible evidence of the bona fides of the other, that from their side they wanted us to know that they believed they could affect the release of the Americans held hostage in Lebanon.

"'As a separate matter the Iranians stated that they were vulnerable as a group and before having any prospect of being able to affect change within Iran they would need to be substantially strengthened. To do so, they would need to secure the cooperation of military and/or Revolutionary Guard leaders. Toward this end, they expressed the view that the most credible demonstration of their influence and abilities would be to secure limited amounts of US equipment. The Israeli asked for our position toward such actions.

"'Mr. McFarlane elevated this proposition to the President at a meeting within days that included the Secretaries of State and Defense and the Director of Central Intelligence. The President stated that while he could understand that, assuming the legitimacy of the interlocutors, they would be quite vulnerable and ultimately might deserve our support to include tangible material, that at the time, without any first hand experience in dealing with them, he could not authorize any transfers of military material. This was conveyed to the Israeli.

"'Within days (mid August) the Israeli diplomat called once more to report that the message had been conveyed and that an impasse of confidence existed. He asked what the position of the US Government would be to an Israeli transfer of modest quantities of material. McFarlane replied that to him, that would represent a distinction without a difference. The Israeli diplomat explained at great length that Israel had its own policy interests that would be served by fostering such a dialogue in behalf of the US but that a problem would arise when ultimately they needed to replace items shipped. He asked whether at that time Israel would be able to purchase replacement parts. McFarlane stated that again, the issue was not the ability of Israel to purchase military equipment from the US—they had done so for a generation and would do so in the future—but rather the issue was whether it was US policy to ship or allow others to ship military equipment to Iran. The Israeli asked for a position from our government. McFarlane elevated the question to the President (and to the Secretaries of State and Defense and the DCI). Again the President stated that while he could imagine the day coming when we might choose to support such elements with material, he could not approve any transfer of military material at that time. This position was conveyed to the Israeli diplomat.

"'On September 14, 1985, Reverend Benjamin Weir . . . (continue as written on page 4)

"'(At end of para, insert the following) We subsequently learned that in late August the Israelis had transferred 508 TOW missiles to Iran. Later in the fall, other transfers of equipment were made between Israel and Iran although some of the items were returned to Israel. McFarlane conveyed these reports to the President who directed that we insist on a direct meeting with the Iranian interlocutors while expressing our position against further arms transfers. A meeting was arranged to take place in London in early December. The President instructed McFarlane to represent the US at the meeting and to make two basic points: 1. That the US was open to a political dialogue with Iran; but that no such dialogue could make progress for as long as groups seen as dominated by Iran held US hostages, and 2. That we could under no circumstances transfer arms to Iran in exchange for hostages. These points were made to the Iranian interlocutor. He replied that unless his circle of associates were strengthened they could not risk going ahead with the exchanges. Mr. McFarlane acknowledged the position but stated we could not change our position and returned to Washington. He debriefed the President and appropriate

Cabinet officers, recommending that no further action be pursued. He then left the government.

"'(Note: Enter at the appropriate place the following account of RCM's involvement in the May meeting.)

"'In April, Mr. McFarlane was contacted and advised that further staff-level contacts had been pursued since he had left government that had led to an arrangement for the release of the remaining hostages. He was asked whether he would be prepared to meet with Iranian officials to open the political dialogue. He agreed to do so and traveled to Iran in late May to do so. (Then pick up with existing text.)'"

McFarlane's PROF note "was done as a briefing memo to be used by people who would brief the President prior to the next day's press conference, and in my judgment expected to go through a number of iterations before it reached that point. But that is my opinion of the climate in which that session occurred and the intent of its outcome." (McFarlane testimony p. 43)

(Poindexter) reacted to the first two by telephone after he got them, probably by 10:00 by this time, at night. Other people had been working on the chronology for the same two hours, while I'd been working on the opening statement. And at that point I finished and 10:30 or so turned my attention to the chronology and was given the master, which was a CIA product, and I think fairly it was understandably wrong because the officer asked to prepare it had not been involved in many of the events.

"But you could see several errors in it, and I pointed out perhaps a half dozen and got through it to about the middle of it, to where it treated the President's involvement in the original decision. The treatment that was there was ambiguous in a number of respects, but it said, for example, that he had acquiesced in the sale, as I recall, and it left out issues of timing.

"And I sat down and, after looking through a separate stack of several pieces of paper, was given one that had two paragraphs on it on this issue. The first part of it treated the basic matter of the approval itself, and the second paragraph dealt with his reaction once he had learned about it in an ex post context.

"And in looking at the first part of it it was not technically wrong. As I recall, it had words to the effect that the President did not approve, did not formally approve the September 2 shipment and then it went on in the second paragraph to say upon learning about it after Mr. Weir's release was upset and directed someone to have me—it didn't say—directed that Mr. McFarlane so advise the government of Israel.

"Well, in looking at those, those were expressive to me, first of all, of a climate in which there was an obvious effort to, as I said, distance and to blur the President's role in the initial authorization, in both timing and substance."

"General Scowcroft: 'Did you raise that point with anybody here? I mean, this is the first time you've seen this maneuvering.'

"Mr. McFarlane: 'Well, I did, and it was a little—it was very curious because in truth none of those officers there were involved at that point in time, and so they weren't in a position to say. They could have written this. No one owned up to it. Mr. Teicher said and has said since that he did not. Colonel North asked me. I said, well where does this come from? They said well, I don't know, but it's something I can't personally throw any light on.'

"And innocent shrugs from Mr. Coy and Colonel Earle. There was no one in the room that had written it." (McFarlane testimony)(Tower)

NOV 19 - Reagan in a news conference on the Iran arms sale confirms that he authorized "a waiver of our own embargo." He announces further that he has ordered an end to the arms sales. Asked repeatedly about Israel's role in the affair, he denies it, saying "We did not condone and do not condone the shipment of arms from other countries." However, 20 minutes after the news conference, the White House acknowledges that "there was a third country involved in our secret project with Iran." (WP 11/20/86 & 12/7/86; NYT 12/4/86; MH 12/14/86)

- Excerpts from the news conference follow:

"Several top advisers opposed the sale of even modest shipment of defensive weapons and spare parts to Iran. Others felt no progress could be made without this sale. I weighed their views. I considered the risks of failure and the rewards of success, and I decided to proceed, and the responsibility for the decision and the operation is mine and mine alone.

"I was convinced then and I am convinced now that while the risks were great, so, too, was the potential reward.

Bringing Iran back into the community of responsible nations, ending its participation in political terror, bringing an end to that terrible war, and bringing our hostages home—these are causes that justify taking risks."

On the Danish ships and the Danish sailor's union officials' stories the President commented, "we certainly never had any contact with anything of the kind."

On conflicts with established policy, the President responded, "I don't think it was duplicity, and as I say, the so-called 'violation' did not in any way alter the balance, military balance, between the two countries."

Q. "Mr. President you say that the equipment which was shipped didn't alter the military balance. Yet, several things —we understand that there were 1,000 TOW anti-tank missiles shipped by the U.S. The U.S. apparently condoned shipments by Israel and other nations of other quantities of arms as an ancillary part of this deal—not directly connected, but had to condone it, or the shipments could not have gone forward, sir. So, how can you say that it cannot alter the military balance, and how can you say, sir, that it didn't break the law, when the National Security Act of 1977 plainly talks about timely notification of Congress and also, sir, stipulates that if the national security required secrecy, the President is still required to advise the leadership and the chairman of the intelligence committees?

The President: "Bill, everything you've said here is based on a supposition that is false. We did not condone, and do not condone the shipment of arms from other countries."

Q. "Is it possible that the Iraqis, sir, might think that 1,000 anti-tank missiles was enough to alter the balance of that war?

The President: "This is a purely defensive weapon—it is a shoulder-carried weapon and we don't think that in this defensive thing—we didn't add to any offensive power on the part of Iran. . . . And, as I say, all of those weapons could be very easily carried in one mission.

"We, as I say, have had nothing to do with other countries or their shipment of arms or doing what they're doing."

Q. " . . . Are you telling us tonight that the only shipments with which we were involved were the one or two that followed your January 17th finding and that, whatever your aides have said on background or on the record, there are not other shipments with which the U.S. condoned?"

The President: "That's right. I'm saying nothing but the missiles that we sold—and remember, there are too many people that are saying 'gave.' They bought them."

Q. "Mr. President, to follow up on that, we've been told by the Chief of Staff Donald Regan that we condoned, this government condoned an Israeli shipment in September of 1985, shortly before the release of hostage Benjamin Weir. . . ."

The President: "No, that—I've never heard Mr. Regan say that and I'll ask him about that, because we believe in the embargo and, as I say, we waived it for a specific purpose . . .

". . .To the best of our knowledge, Iran does not own or have authority over the Hezbollah. They cannot order them to do something. It is apparent that they evidently have either some persuasion and they don't always succeed, but they can sometimes persuade or pressure the Hezbollah into doing what they did in this instance. And, as I say, the Iranian government had no hostages and they bought a shipment from us and we, in turn—I might as well tell you—that we, in turn, had said when they wanted to kind of know our position and whether we were trustworthy and all of this, we told them that we were—we did not want to do business with any nation that openly backed terrorism. And they gave us information that they did not and they said also that they had some evidence that there had been a lessening of this on the part of—Khomeini and the government and that they'd made some progress. As a matter of fact, some individuals associated with terrorist acts had been put in prison there. And so that was when we said well, there's a very easy way for you to verify that if that's the way you feel, and they're being held hostage in Lebanon."

On being corrected about a TOW missile, the President responded, ". . .if I have been misinformed, then I will yield on that, but it was my understanding that that is a man-carried weapon, and we have a number of other shoulder-borne weapons."

The President concluded, "I don't think a mistake was made. It was a high-risk gamble, and it was a gamble that, as I've said, I believe the circumstances warranted. And I don't see that it has been a fiasco or a great failure of any kind. We still have those contacts, we still have made some ground, we got our hostages back—three of them. And so I think that what we did was right, and we're going to continue on this path." (Tower)

- In the wake of the press response to the news conference, the President asked Attorney General Meese to come to the White House to straighten out what had happened over the course of the initiative. It was during these discussions on November 21-23 that the Attorney General discovered the possibility of diversion. (Tower)

- Immediately following the news conference, several advisers, including North, reportedly approach Reagan and tell him of his incorrect statements concerning Israel's involvement in arms deliveries to Iran. Also, Shultz reportedly complains angrily to chief of staff Regan that the President made at least five factual errors at the session. According to one report, it is this confrontation with Shultz that prompts Regan to schedule a meeting with the President the following day (see entry). (NYT 2/24/87)

- According to one report, Regan is informed by an aide after the conference that a chronology of events surrounding the Iran affair has been prepared by members of the White House staff. Regan reportedly demands a copy from Poindexter and refuses to return it two days later as requested. He is said to have asked the White House legal adviser to review the document. There are conflicting accounts later over whether Regan in fact authorized the preparation of the chronology in the first place, and whether he, among other officials, deliberately misrepresented certain facts to protect the President's or their own involvement. (NYT 2/24/87)

- According to testimony by Meese, he spoke with Poindexter after the President's news conference on November 19. Meese testified that he was concerned about the absence of a "factual chronology" and Casey's forthcoming testimony. Meese said he had also talked to Poindexter earlier in the day in Poindexter's office after a meeting where Casey was present. Poindexter reportedly asked Meese to come back the next day to help prepare Casey's testimony. (SSIC 1/29/87)

- According to testimony received by the Committee, on Wednesday, November 19, Casey was briefed in preparation for an appearance before the Senate Intelligence Committee set for November 21. Testimony received by the Committee indicated that in this briefing Casey may have been made aware that there might be a problem in the area of diversion of Iran project funds to the contras. The CIA task force chief recalled being totally flabbergasted upon learning of the possible interconnection between Nicaragua and the Iran program from Casey's aide. (SSIC 1/29/87)

- The CIA Comptroller testified that he learned of the possible diversion of funds to the contras on November 18-19. The Comptroller recalled that a CIA operations officer speculated about the diversion as they were preparing Casey's testimony for November 21.

The Comptroller's testimony that he shared this information with the CIA Director and learned that Casey and Gates had made their concerns known to Poindexter after learning of the subject in October. (SSIC 1/29/87)

NOV 20 - House Majority Leader Jim Wright (D-Tex.) discloses that Israel, with U.S. approval, shipped Iran 2,008 TOW antitank missiles and at least 235 Hawk anti-aircraft missiles, a quantity much greater than previously acknowledged by the Administration. He says at least three statutes may have been violated. (NYT 12/4/86)

- McFarlane contradicts State Department statements that Shultz was only "sporadically informed" of the Iran arms deal, saying he told Shultz "repeatedly and often of every item" in the operation. Shultz admits to a fuller role the following day. (NYT 12/4/86)

The November 20 historical chronology [Prepared by North, Poindexter, McFarlane, Earl and Coy(see Nov 5-20 entry)] added that "(t)he Israelis told us that they undertook the action, despite our objections, because they believed it to be in their strategic interests. * * * After discussing this matter with the President, it was decided not to expose this Israeli delivery because we wanted to retain the option of exploiting the existing Israeli channel with Tehran in our own effort to establish a strategic dialogue with the Iranian government." (Tower)

- Mr. McFarlane described for the Board the process used by the NSC staff to create a chronology that obscured essential facts. Mr. McFarlane contributed to the creation of this chronology which did not, he said, present "a full and completely accurate account" of the events and left ambiguous the President's role. This was, according to Mr. McFarlane, done to distance the President from the timing and nature of the President's authorization. He told the Board that he wrote a memorandum on November 18, which tried to, in his own words, "gild the President's motives." This version was incorporated into the chronology. Mr. McFarlane told the Board that he knew the account was "misleading, at least, and wrong, at worst." Mr. McFarlane told the Board that he did provide the Attorney General an accurate account of the President's role.

. . . The chronology he [North] produced has many inaccuracies. These "histories" were to be the basis of the "full" story of the Iran initiative. These inaccuracies lend some evidence to the proposition that LtCol North, either on his own or at the behest of others, actively sought to conceal important information. (Tower)

- Late in the afternoon, Meese, Casey, Poindexter, North and Assistant Attorney General Charles J. Cooper meet in Poindexter's office to discuss Casey's intended testimony to Congress. (WP 2/12/87)

- The NSC staff had prepared a 17-page historical summary of the Iran program dated November 20 which appears to contain numerous important omissions and misstatements of fact about the program (the White House chronology). According to testimony by Meese, on November 20 he and Assistant Attorney General Charles Cooper went to a meeting at the White House where Casey, Poindexter, and others from the NSC staff reviewed Casey's testimony and a chronology to see if they squared with Meese's recollection of the legal discussions and the facts. Meese testified that he left before the meeting was over, but that Cooper stayed. (SSIC 1/29/87)

- After this meeting, State Department legal adviser Abraham Sofaer talks by telephone with Cooper about Casey's testimony. Shultz authorized Sofaer to speak directly with Meese about the secretary's concerns, but Meese is at West Point delivering a speech. According to an Administration official, Cooper immediately agrees with Sofaer that the proposed testimony is "a very serious matter . . . a matter to be disturbed about." (WP 2/12/87)

- Following his conversation with Sofaer, Cooper telephones Meese at West Point and passes along Shultz's concerns. Meese reportedly agrees at this point that government attorneys should make a much more serious inquiry into the conflicting information circulating within the Administration. (WP 2/12/87)

- Poindexter, North, Casey, Regan, Meese, Shultz and Weinberger review the prepared testimony of key administration officials who have been called before Congress regarding the Iran-contra affair. (It is not clear from news reports whether all the officials meet together or in separate groups, as above, for example, during the day and evening.) Meese says later that "troubling gaps" in the prepared statements and disagreements over what occurred led him to request authority from Reagan to investigate the matter. (WP 12/5/86, 1/20/87 & 2/12/87)

- In the evening, Meese received a secure call advising him that other Justice Department officials working on the Iran matter were concerned about gaps in information and inconsistent recollections.

On the same night of November 20, according to notes of the Attorney General's inquiry, Secretary Shultz went to the White House residence to see the President and told him that some of the statements would not stand up to scrutiny. (SSIC 1/29/87)

- Shultz has an angry confrontation with Reagan in the President's living quarters, with Regan present, about the accuracy of the information Poindexter is giving the president and others. Poindexter is coordinating the preparation of Casey's testimony which Shultz says does not tell the truth about the Administration's knowledge of arms shipments to Iran in November 1985. Casey's testimony is altered to reflect the concerns of Shultz and other officials but according to congressional sources, Casey's written remarks are still far from candid. (WP 12/5/86, 1/20/87 & 2/12/87; NYT 2/24/87)

- According to the Attorney General's inquiry, prior to [Casey's?] appearing before the Senate Intelligence Committee, Shultz went to the White House and informed the President that some of the statements being made about the Iran arms affair would not stand up to scrutiny. Shultz also informed Meese of his feelings on this matter. A Justice Department staff member then obtained information from the State Department about the November 1985 HAWK missile shipments that did not fit with other information gathered by the Attorney General. At that point, Meese decided to go see the President. (SSIC 1/29/87)

- Secord's [alias] passport [provided by the CIA on March 3] was returned on November 20, 1986. (CIA/IG Chronology 20). (Tower)

- Adolfo Calero speaks at a World Anti-Communist League (WACL) meeting in Toronto, urging support for the contras. The chairman of the North American branch of WACL, former Member of Parliament John Gamble, is later reported to be linked to the Iran-contra deal. (See December 20, 1986 entry). ACL is headed by retired U.S. general John Singlaub, who is also vice-chairman of the North American branch. (VV 12/30/86)

NOV 21 - . . . The senior CIA analyst testified that he helped prepare the DCI's testimony which focused on what CIA knew and what support they gave the NSC. He said there was no discussion in his presence of the possibility of diversion of funds. (SSIC 1/29/87)

- Casey appears before Congress in the morning. His prepared testimony has been altered after discussion the previous day by senior officials to omit certain untrue statements (see November 20 entries). However, Casey's written and oral remarks are still reported by congressional sources to be incomplete and misleading. In the course of his testimony he states that Iran bought 2,000 TOW missiles and paid more than $12 million into a Swiss bank account. He says he does not know who arranged the transaction or where the money was transferred. He does not mention the roles of North or Richard Secord. He also assures lawmakers that no other covert operations have been withheld from Congress. (On November 25, Meese informs the public of the diversion of funds to the contras.) Casey also makes no reference to the unusual manner in which the President's January 17, 1986 finding was drafted. North prepared the document himself, rather than in concert with the NSC inter-agency working group; the draft was not circulated among the national security planning group as required; and several key Administration officials were not informed that Reagan had signed it. Casey's prepared (and spoken) testimony refers only to standard drafting procedures. Later, medical experts say Casey's brain tumor (he suffers a seizure on December 15) may have affected his testimony. (NYT 12/4/86 & 2/13/87 WP 12/5/86, 12/7/86, 1/14/87, 1/20/87 & 2/12/87)

- Casey testified before the Senate Intelligence Committee on November 21, 1986. He did not mention any possibility that there had been a diversion of funds from the arms sales to Iran. When asked about this omission, Gates later testi-fied that the reason for the omission was that "the informa-tion was based on analytical judgments of bits and pieces of information by one intelligence officer, and that they [Casey and Gates] didn't consider that very much to go on, although it was enough to raise our concerns to the point where we expressed them to the White House." (SSIC 1/29/87)

- Reagan meets at 11:30 a.m. with Meese, Regan and Poindexter to discuss the need for a "complete, comprehen-sive overview." Meese is assigned the task and told to report to the NSC on November 24 at 2 p.m. However, he is un-able to meet the deadline and does not meet with the Presi-dent until early the following morning. (Reagan Briefing, 11/25/86; WP 12/5/86)

The morning of Friday, November 21, when Casey was testifying on the Hill, after learning from his staff of more discrepancies with State Department information, he met with the President and Regan. Meese testified that he re-ported his concerns about the need for an accurate account, particularly in view of upcoming testimony to Congressional committees. The President reportedly asked Meese to review the facts to get an accurate portrayal by the different agen-cies involved. Meese testified that he "didn't smell some-thing was wrong," but was bothered "that there were things we didn't know." According to Meese, the President did not request an investigation but asked Meese to pull the facts together so they could have a coherent account. Regan re-portedly suggested that Meese's review be completed by

2:00 p.m. on Monday, November 24, when an NSC meeting on Iran was scheduled. (Meese testimony) (SSIC 1/29/87)

- According to testimony received by the Committee, in this same time period, on November 21 Poindexter briefed the leadership of the SSCI in the White House in the morning. (SSIC 1/29/87)

- Poindexter briefs members of the Senate and House intelligence panels about the Iran initiative as part of what the Administration claims is an effort to bring out the facts on the affair. Poindexter and other officials tell Congressional leaders that one previously unstated purpose of the secret Iran operation was to open a new supply route to the hard-pressed Afghan rebels. Specifically, intelligence sources said, Iranian officials agreed to pass some 100 of the 2,008 TOW anti-tank missiles they received from the U.S. along to the neighboring Afghans. Another source said some of the arms shipped to Iran from Israel also were intended for the Afghan rebels. Two months later, after other aspects of the matter have come to light, one legislator characterizes Poindexter's presentation as "stonewalling . . . compared to what we now know." (WP 1/20/87; WSJ 1/24/86)

- Meese turns down FBI Director William Webster's offer of assistance in the Iran arms investigation. Meese later says that both he and Webster "agreed there was no legal basis" for involving the FBI "because there was no even [sic] suggesting of anything criminal which would justify legally their entrance into the matter." However, law enforcement officials acknowledge that no evidence of a federal crime is required before the FBI can join an investigation. (WP 12/5/86)

- Meese then discussed his mission with FBI Director Webster, and the two of them agreed that it was not a criminal matter and it would not be appropriate to involve the FBI. (Meese testimony) (SSIC 1/29/87)

- On the afternoon of November 21, Meese assembled a small team of Justice Department officials and aides, including Assistant Attorneys General Charles Cooper and Bradford Reynolds. This team did not include any senior Department officials responsible for criminal investigations. (SSIC 1/29/87)

- Meese testified that on the afternoon of November 21, he assembled a team of three lawyers "who had experience with this type of matter." Meese then made a list of people to talk with, including North, Shultz, Weinberger, Poindexter, McFarlane, and the CIA's General Counsel. (SSIC 1/29/87)

- According to the Attorney General's inquiry, one of the first persons interviewed by Meese was McFarlane, who said he had told Kimche at a December meeting in London that the United States was "disturbed about TOWs—can't approve it." By contrast, McFarlane testified that he had told Meese during this interview that the President had favored the Iran initiative from the beginning. McFarlane stated that Meese seemed glad to hear this, as an early presidential approval would legitimize subsequent acts. According to McFarlane, Meese then opined that an oral, informal presidential decision or determination was no less valid than a written Finding. McFarlane testified that when he and Attorney General Meese discussed the legality of an oral Finding November 21, 1986, Meese told him that he believed an oral, informal presidential decision or determination to be no less valid than a written Finding. (SSIC 1/29/87)

-Mr. McFarlane: "Well, the meeting was called at the Attorney General's initiative, and he called me. I was at home."

General Scowcroft: "When was this?"

Mr. McFarlane: "This was the 21st, which would have been Friday. He called and I was at home working on a speech that I had to give and he asked me—well, he said, first of all, Bud, I have been asked by the President to put together an accurate record of events in this matter and I would like to talk to you. When can you come in? I volunteered as soon as possible—driving time.

"And within about an hour—it would have been 2:00 or 3:00—I was in his office, his inner office, and it was the Attorney General and an associate, Mr.—I assume, Charles Cooper. We were seated about like this, between the Attorney General and myself, and Mr. Cooper was sitting next to us taking notes.

"And in the course of about an hour I went through my recollection really, because I hadn't referred to records still, what I remembered about the decision process and my account was essentially as I had acceded to it in the Tuesday night session. And Mr. Meese then had a number of questions about the President's involvement, other people's involvement, positions of various Cabinet officers.

"And this was a back and forth that went for perhaps another half hour and he said okay, that's fine.

"And we rose to break up. His secretary came in and gave me a message that had come in some time before and said your wife called with some urgency and you need to call her right away.

"Mr. Cooper left the room and Ed began to leave the room. And I said: Ed, wait a minute. I want to talk to you about this. Now, I wanted to talk to him because it was very apparent. I'm talking to the chief law enforcement officer of the country. It is essential that there not be any ambiguity in what he is telling the President about the truth of the actions here. And so I told him, you know, as you may have seen in this morning's papers I gave a speech last night and I have taken on responsibility for every bit of this that I can, Ed, and I shall continue to do that.

"And he interrupted and said yes, that's been noted. But I want you to know that from the very beginning of this, Ed, the President was four-square behind it, that he never had any reservations about approving anything that the Israelis wanted to do here. Ed said, Bud, I know that, and I can understand why. And, as a practical matter, I'm glad you told me this because his legal position is far better the earlier that he made the decision.

"And I said well, I don't have any knowledge of that, but there was no question about it, Ed. He said, okay. I may have to get back to you. Thanks a lot. And that was that.

"And then, on Sunday night—no, Monday afternoon he called and asked me to come by again, and I went down to his office again, and by that time he had learned, I suppose from his associates turning up the evidence of the diversion of funds to the Contra business, about it and he asked me to come down and began to ask questions about that. I told him when I learned about it and my lack of knowledge on the antecedents to it and so forth.

"And he said fine. And I said, Ed, you know, I think this has gone well beyond timewise what it should have and the President ought to get out the facts right away, and I think also that there are a number of other policy initiatives that ought to be taken if he's going to be able to show leadership in foreign policy at all. And if you think that it's of value I'd be glad to jot some of these down and send them to you.

"And he said, yes, I'd appreciate that very much. So I went home—this is Monday afternoon—and in the space of about an hour put down about three or four pages of ideas." (McFarlane testimony, pp. 53-57)(Tower)

- From approximately 6:30-7:30 pm, North and his secretary, Fawn Hall, destroy a "mammoth" amount of NSC documents and computer messages, hours before the Justice Department is scheduled to review NSC materials relating to the Iran deals. Administration officials claim in subsequent weeks either that they have copies of "all national security documents" in "a central file," or that they are unaware of any shredding of documents. (WP 2/22/87; NYT 2/24/87; WSJ 2/25/87)

- Shultz admits he participated in two "full-scale discussions" of the Iran arms deal in December 1985 and January 1986, contradicting earlier State Department statements that he was only "sporadically informed" of the operation. However, he insists his information on the deal itself was "fragmentary." (NYT 12/4/86)

- Mr. McFarlane sent another PROF note to VADM Poindexter at 21:01 on the 21st of November. A portion of this note follows.

"I spent a couple of hours with Ed Meese today going over the record with him. The only blind spot on my part concerned a shipment in November '85 which still doesn't ring a bell with me. But it appears that the matter of not notifying the Israeli transfers can be covered if the President made a "mental finding" before the transfers took place. Well on that score we ought to be ok because he was all for letting the Israelis do anything they wanted at the very first briefing in the hospital. Ed seemed relieved at that." (Tower)

NOV 21-23 - In the wake of the press response to the news conference, the President asked Attorney General Meese to come to the White House to straighten out what had happened over the course of the initiative. It was during these discussions on November 21-23 that the Attorney General discovered the possibility of diversion. (Tower)

NOV 22 - At 8:00 a.m. Saturday, Meese spoke with Shultz to discuss the Secretary of State's recollection of certain events. Meese testified that he was not shocked to learn that Shultz had not known of the January 17 presidential Finding and stated that he himself had heard nothing of it after it had been signed. (SSIC 1/29/87)

- Assistant Attorney General William Bradford Reynolds and other Justice Department officials discover an unsigned, undated memo in North's office at the NSC concerning a possible plan to divert $12 million to the Nicaraguan rebels. However, Meese does not call in the FBI until November 25. By then North and Poindexter are reported to have destroyed key documents from their files. In addition, North is interviewed today at length. According to a Justice Department source, some advisers to the Attorney General who are present at the questioning take notes, transcripts of which Meese later uses in testimony before Congress. (WP 12/7/86; NYT 12/4/86 & 1/1/87; VV 12/30/86; LAT 12/31/86)

- The next morning, Saturday, November 22, while Meese was meeting with Shultz, members of the Attorney General's staff including Reynolds, examined documents in NSC files at the White House. Meese later testified that Poindexter had given permission for this file review and that NSC staff including North and Paul Thompson were present in the NSC offices when it was conducted. Meese testified that he received no information that North shredded documents in his office.

Meese's staff went through the documents presented to them and had copies made of those they thought important. . . . According to testimony by Meese, on the morning of November 22, the Meese team discovered the early April NSC memo which referred explicitly to the diversion of arms profits to the contras. Assistant Attorney General William Bradford Reynolds told Meese about the document at lunch on Saturday. Meese testified that this was the first time that he felt as if something was "not in accord with the President's plan.". . . . Meese testified that following a meeting with former CIA General Counsel Sporkin in the afternoon, Meese made an appointment with North to meet the following day. Meese testified that he had planned to interview North in the morning, but agreed to a delay until 2:00 p.m. because North wanted to have time to go to church and be with his family.

According to testimony received by the Committee, North arranged to consult with an attorney after meeting with lawyers from the Justice Department on Saturday, November 22, to obtain legal counsel. (SSIC 1/29/87)

- (An) Undated Memorandum (i)s discovered in the files of the NSC on November 22, 1986 by members of the Attorney General's staff. Meese (makes) an appointment to meet with North the next day, at which time North (i)s questioned at some length about the Iran program and then confronted with the Undated Memorandum. (SSIC 1/29/87)

- According to testimony by Meese, that Saturday evening Meese met with Casey at Casey's home. They had talked on the phone earlier in the day. At their meeting Casey discussed Furmark and the Canadian investors. Meese recalled no mention of the contras, Nicaragua, anti-Sandinistas, Democratic Resistance, Freedom Fighters or Central America. At one point he said it was possible that Casey may have mentioned something similar, but he subsequently said he was sure Casey did not mention the possible diversion of funds. (SSIC 1/29/87)

- Reagan reportedly sends Shultz a message through Bush saying, in effect, "support me or get off the team." Bush aides later deny the report but officials say relations between Shultz and the White House are extremely tense over this weekend. There are questions whether Reagan wants Shultz to remain in his post, and whether Shultz himself, described as "very discouraged and angry," is willing to stay on. (WP 2/12/87)

NOV 23 - McFarlane testified that on Sunday morning, November 23, North called him and asked to meet him in McFarlane's office. According to McFarlane, North arrived at 12:30 p.m. and the two had a private discussion for about fifteen minutes. North said he would have to lay the facts out for the Justice Department later that day on the diversion of Iran to the contras. McFarlane testified that North also stated it was a matter of record in a memorandum North had done for Poindexter. McFarlane asked if it was an approved matter, and was told that it was.

According to McFarlane, North stated that McFarlane knew North wouldn't do anything that was not approved.

McFarlane testified that after their private meeting, an attorney named Tom Green arrived; as the meeting ended, Secord arrived. McFarlane testified that he learned later that Green was Secord's lawyer. (SSIC 1/29/87)

- North is interviewed a second time for three to four hours by Meese aides. (WP 11/29/86 & WP 12/5/86; NYT 12/4/86 & 12/25/86)

Notes taken at the November 23 meeting indicate that North confirmed the accuracy of the Undated Memorandum as reflecting the plan for use of residual funds from the Iran arms sale for the Nicaraguan resistance. Notes of the meeting recount North saying the $12 million figure in the memo was based on what he was told by the Israelis and that he did not know how much was moved to the Nicaraguan—the Israeli (Nir) decided the amount given to the resistance, with no involvement by the CIA or NSC.

According to the notes of the Attorney General inquiry, North stated that he had not discussed the matter with the President. According to documents received by the Committee, North was in 17 meetings with the President over the two-year period, 1985-1986, and none alone, and had one phone conversation with the President on December 4, 1986.

According to testimony by Meese, North said that he did not know the amount of money involved. North said the CIA did not know about the handling of the money, although some might suspect.

Notes taken at the meeting further reflect that North said presidential approval of something would be reflected in the working files. Asked whether he would have a record if the President approved in this case, the notes reflect that North replied affirmatively, and said he didn't think it was approved.

Notes taken at the meeting further reflect that North described the money that the Israelis were to get to the Nicaraguans as Iranian money for profits of the arms deals and saying he understood this part of the deal. The notes further reflect that North said he had told McFarlane in April or May 1986 about the deals and that the only three people who could know in the U.S. were McFarlane, Poindexter and North.

According to testimony by McFarlane, during their return trip from Tehran, North told McFarlane that part of the profit from the arms transaction was going to the Nicaraguan resistance. McFarlane testified that he took it from the summary reference that this was a matter of policy sanctioned by higher authority.

When Attorney General Meese testified before the Committee, he said that North was surprised and visibly shaken when shown the Undated Memorandum. According to testimony by Meese, North said that he did not recall the account numbers which were given to the Israelis [see January 2, 1986 entries] and that the Israelis arranged for the money to be deposited. Meese testified that North was very definite that the money got to the Nicaraguan resistance forces, but could not remember or did not know the amount apart from an estimate of $3-4 million on one occasion.

Meese testified that he got the impression that the three bank accounts were set up by somebody representing the Nicaraguan resistance forces, that the numbers were given to North, and that North gave them to the Israelis. (SSIC 1/29/87)

- At 2:00 that afternoon North met with Meese, Reynolds and Cooper, and another Justice Department official names Richardson, who took extensive notes. According to the notes, Meese began by explaining that he wanted to get all the facts from everyone involved and flesh out different recollections. Meese said he had talked to the President and Poindexter. He stated that the worst thing that could happen was if someone tried to conceal something to protect themselves or the President or put a good "spin" on it. (SSIC 1/29/87)

.... In response to Meese's question about whether McFarlane's problem was the perception or the fact of arms to Iran for hostages, North stated that he believed the President himself authorized the deal. North said that when he spoke with the President it was in terms of a strategic linkage. With the President, said North, it always came back to hostages. According to Meese, North said it was a terrible mistake to say that the President wanted a strategic relationship, because the President wanted the hostages. . . . (SSIC 1/29/87)

Meese further testified that he was not positive that North told him the Undated Memorandum was not used or sent for approval. Meese testified that North did not mention any problem in his mind that, by some interpretations, U.S. money was being used for the Nicaraguan resistance. Meese testified that he did not go into that with North and that there was no discussion of the Congressional restrictions on soliciting funds.

Meese testified that he did not advise North of his right to counsel because he did not consider his inquiry to be a criminal investigation. (SSIC 1/29/87)

- Meese testified that he did not know North well on a personal basis, but did have considerable contact with him in and out of the White House on a casual basis. Based on his discussion with North and what he read subsequently, Meese was convinced North was "zealous about the mission he felt he had." Meese concluded that North had let Poindexter know what he was doing and had not been forbidden from doing it. Meese testified that it never occurred to him that there would be any collusion of an untoward nature and that it was at the time still not a criminal matter. North was questioned at some length about the Iran program before being confronted with the Undated Memorandum with the passage on use of residual arms sale funds for the Nicaraguan resistance.

Meese testified that he recalled being disturbed and troubled, but not apprehensive. Steps were taken, however, to get McFarlane in right away, the next morning—North had said he told McFarlane during the Tehran trip about use of arms proceeds for the Nicaraguan resistance.

Meese was asked by the Committee if he sought out Poindexter immediately so as to prevent any communications between Poindexter and North on what North had just told Meese and the other Justice Department officials. Meese testified that he did not. (SSIC 1/29/87)

- Attorney General Meese told the Board that during his interview with LtCol North on November 23, 1986, North indicated that the idea [of diversion] surfaced during a discussion with Mr. Nir in January, 1986, about ways Israel could help the contras.

- Attorney General Meese told the Board that during his interview with LtCol North on November 23, 1986, North said that $3 to $4 million was diverted to the support of the contras after the February shipment of TOW missiles and that more (though how much LtCol North was not sure) was diverted after the May shipment of HAWK parts. Contemporaneous Justice Department staff notes of that interview indicate that LtCol North said that the Israelis handled the money and that he gave them the numbers of three accounts opened in Switzerland by Adolpho Calero, a contra leader. The notes also indicate that LtCol North said there was no money for the contras as a result of the shipment in October, 1986. By then Congressional funding had resumed. (Tower)

- Justice Department staff notes of North's interview with the Attorney General on November 23, 1986, show North telling the Attorney General that only he, McFarlane, and Poindexter were aware of the diversion. (Tower)

- Aides to Casey produce a five-page memo on the diversion of Iran arms profits to the contras, following up on Casey's earlier conversations with Furmark. The director later falls ill and is unable to provide the memo to the Senate intelligence committee as anticipated on December 16. (NYT 12/16/86)

NOV 24 - Meese met with his staff and went over what they had found. Meese recalled asking his attorneys to look over what criminal laws or other laws might be applicable. Meese was not sure whether he talked to the FBI Director on Monday. (SSIC 1/29/87)

Later that morning Meese also talked to McFarlane to find out what he knew about money being available to the Nicaraguan resistance. According to Meese, McFarlane said he knew nothing until his trip to Tehran, and that was the only thing he knew about it. Meese's conversation with McFarlane was brief; he said he was only trying to verify certain facts. Meese also talked briefly to Weinberger by phone; Weinberger did not have much to add. (SSIC 1/29/87)

- Meese reports his preliminary findings to Reagan and Chief of Staff Regan. Meese's inquiry has included interviews with Reagan, Casey, Shultz, Weinberger and Poindexter. Reagan, who in the coming weeks repeatedly claims that this is the first time he has been told of the diversion of funds to the contras, calls for a Justice Department review of events and a special panel to examine the role of the NSC in foreign and national security policy. (Reagan Briefing 11/25/86; WP 12/7/86)

- Meese testified that at 11 a.m. that morning he met with President and Regan telling them that during his review, Meese had come across indications that money from Iranian arms transactions may have gone to the Nicaraguan resistance. Meese testified he told them he had talked to North who had acknowledged that in fact that had happened.

Meese told the President he had not completed his review and would get back to him later that afternoon after talking to other people, including Poindexter. Meese said the President looked shocked and very surprised, as did Regan, who uttered an expletive.

Meese recalled that at this meeting or at one later in the day, the President said it was important "to get this out as soon as possible." Regan recalled a discussion with Meese in the morning at which Meese told him he needed to arrange a meeting with the President about what he had found out on Monday afternoon. (SSIC 1/29/87)

- Meese testified that he talked to Poindexter in the latter's office very briefly on Monday afternoon. No notes were taken and Meese was alone. Meese recalled telling Poindexter what had been learned from North and asking if he knew about the matter. According to Meese, Poindexter said yes, he knew about it generally. According to Meese, Poindexter said North had given him "enough hints" that he knew there was money going to the contras, but he "didn't inquire further." Meese further testified that Poindexter said he had already decided he would probably have to resign because of it.

Meese testified that he asked Poindexter if he had told anyone about the money going to the contras, and Poindexter said he had not. Their conversation lasted about ten minutes, because Meese needed to get back to see the President. Meese testified that he did not consider his talk with

Poindexter an "investigation" or a "criminal investigation," and Meese said he did not consider the matter a law violation "on its fact." He was trying, he said, to find out what happened from a respected member of the Administration. (SSIC 1/29/87)

- Reagan meets for two hours at the White House with Shultz, Poindexter, Regan, Bush, Weinberger, Casey and Meese to discuss future Middle East policy. (Speakes 11/25/86; PI 11/25/86)

- Meese testified that he met with the President and Regan at 4:30 p.m. that afternoon and related what he had learned, including Poindexter's acknowledgement that he had knowledge of the contra funds. Meese said he discussed looking at what applicable criminal laws there might be. They arranged to meet again the next morning at 9:00 after sorting things out because it was "a tremendous surprise and shock to everybody." Meese testified that he knew that "neither Don Regan nor Ronald Reagan knew anything about this." Regan recalled the President's dismay and surprise at the discovery, and his decision to go public with it. Regan testified that the President had made clear to his staff that while he strongly supported the Nicaraguan resistance, such support should be provided by lawful means. (SSIC 1/29/87)

- Meese testified that he talked with the Vice President that Monday and told him what had been learned. Meese "asked him if he had known anything about it, and the Vice President said no, he had not." Meese also recalled that the possibility of Poindexter's resignation was discussed Monday evening, possibly between Regan and the President. Meese learned that Regan talked to Casey on Monday night. (SSIC 1/29/87)

- On November 24, 1986, the day after Meese met with North, an attorney, Tom Green, met with Assistant Attorney General Charles Cooper. According to Cooper's notes, Green said he represented North and Secord and described the role played by Secord and Hakim in the Iran project. Green reportedly said that at a meeting on the arms sales in Europe in early 1986, where Hakim served as interpreter for the Americans, Hakim told the Iranians that in order to foster the relationship and show their bona fides, the Iranians should make a contribution over the purchase price for use of the contras or "of us." Green added that Hakim probably said the U.S. government was desirous of this. Green said that was the basis upon which the February shipment of TOWs was priced.

According to Cooper's notes, Green said the money from that sale was routed through Israelis into Hakim's financial network. Hakim, in his private capacity, routed money into other accounts belonging to foreigners. The same thing happened again in May. Green reportedly said none of this violated the law because no U.S. money was involved—only Iranians making a contribution. (SSIC 1/29/87)

- After discussing Hakim's role in proposing use of Iran arms proceeds to the Nicaraguan resistance, Green said Hakim and Secord felt like they were doing the Lord's work. They believed they were not violating any laws. Cooper's notes say Green warned that if the matter blew up, Iran would kill one or more of the hostages and two other individuals would also probably be killed. (SSIC 1/29/87)

- Casey meets for the third time with Furmark, who reveals Ghorbanifar's suspicions that up to $15 million may have been diverted to the contras. Furmark repeats his earlier complaint to Casey that Khashoggi is owed $10 million from the Iran deal. Casey telephones several top administration officials but is unable to reach anyone. He ultimately calls North, who replies, "Tell him the Iranians or the Israelis owe him the money." (WP 12/24/86)

- According to testimony by Furmark, also on Monday, he met again with Casey at CIA headquarters. According to Furmark, Casey told him there was $30,000 in the account. Furmark assumed he meant the Lake Resources account. Furmark testified that Casey called North. Then Casey stated repeated [sic] that he did not know where the money was. Casey also called Assistant Attorney General Cooper. Furmark testified that Casey's staff told him the only way they knew about the Lake Resources account was because Furmark had told them about it. According to Furmark, North apparently told Casey that the Iranians or the Israelis owed Ghorbanifar and Khashoggi the money. Furmark said Casey tried and failed to reach Regan and Meese. (SSIC 1/29/87)

- Deputy Secretary of State John Whitehead testifies on Capitol Hill concerning U.S.-Iran policy. He contradicts Reagan's November 13 contention that Iran is no longer involved with terrorism, and calls for an investigation of the role of the NSC in the Reagan White House. Whitehead's remarks greatly increase the tension between Shultz and White House officials who believe the secretary has instigated his deputy's comments. According to White House sources, Regan slams a wire service account of the testimony on Reagan's desk and declares, "This is what your Secretary of State is up to." (Speakes 11/25/86; PI 11/25/86; WP 2/12/87)

- Whitehead discusses his testimony with the White House later in the day and manages to convince some officials that he was speaking for himself and did not intend to undermine presidential policy. Regan reportedly is not mollified, however, and continues to bear a grudge against Shultz for this and other episodes. (WP 2/12/87)

- As a general matter, LtCol North kept VADM Poindexter exhaustively informed about his activities with respect to the Iran initiative. Although the Board did not find a specific communication from Lt. Col North to VADM Poindexter on the diversion question, VADM Poindexter said that he knew that a diversion had occurred. Mr. Regan told the Board that he asked VADM Poindexter on November 24, 1986, if he knew of LtCol North's role in a diversion of funds to support the contras. VADM Poindexter replied that, "I had a feeling that something bad was going on, but I didn't investigate it and I didn't do a thing about it. . . . I really didn't want to know. I was so damned mad at Tip O'Neill for the way he was dragging the contras around·I didn't want to know what, if anything, was going on. I should have, but I didn't." Attorney General Meese told the Board that after talking to LtCol North, he asked VADM Poindexter what he knew about the diversion. "He said that he did know about it . . . Ollie North had given him enough hints that he knew what was going on, but he didn't want to look further into it. But that he in fact did generally know that money had gone to the contras as a result of the Iran shipment." (Tower)

NOV 25 - Meese testified that he met with Casey at Casey's home the next morning at 7 a.m., Tuesday, November 25. Casey had called Meese at 6:30 to ask him to stop by. Meese could not recall the conversation, except that it was generally about the situation and what Meese had learned. Casey told Meese that Regan had talked to him the night before about the money-to-the-contras situation. While with Casey, Meese received a call from Regan who said he was going to talk with Poindexter. Regan verified that Meese would be at the White House at 9:00. Casey also apparently told Meese he would send him the Furmark memoranda, which he did by letter. At 8:00, according to his testimony, Regan talked with Poindexter and indicated he felt Poindexter should be ready to resign when he saw the President at 9:30. Regan testified that when he questioned Poindexter about his negligence, Poindexter responded that he had felt sorry for the contras and wanted them to get help. He had, therefore, not questioned where the money came from. (SSIC 1/29/87)

- In a letter to Attorney General Edwin Meese dated late November 25, 1986, Casey described Furmark as a friend and former client—someone he had not seen in six or seven years. . . . Casey said Furmark had provided him with more information than Casey had ever heard about the Ghorbanifar-Israeli channel to the Iranians. The letter quotes Furmark as saying that he had been involved in a Ghorbanifar-Israeli channel to the Iranians from its inception. Casey advised the Attorney General that he and Gates had passed Furmark's information on to Poindexter a day or so after the October 7 meeting.

Casey advised the Attorney General in his November 25, 1986 letter that he had this memorandum prepared and believed it was delivered to the NSC to review the state of play on the channel to the Iranian government. Gates testified that the next day, October 15, 1986, he and Casey met with Poindexter and delivered a copy of the analyst's memorandum. Gates testified that they advised Poindexter, in view of the people who knew about it, to think seriously about having the President lay the project before the American public to avoid having it leak in dribs and drabs.

According to his November letter to Meese, Casey said that he and Gates urged Poindexter to get all the facts together and have a comprehensive statement prepared because it seemed likely that the litigation which Furmark said his clients were contemplating would require it.

In the same letter, Casey stated that Gates had said he would apprise the CIA General Counsel of the matter and get his advice. Gates testified that he did ask CIA General Counsel Dave Doherty to review all aspects of the project and to ensure that the Agency was not involved in any illegalities. According to Gates, Doherty later told him that he had looked into things and not found anything wrong.

In his November 25, 1986 letter to the Attorney General, Casey said he had not read it [a memorandum prepared by aides after an October 22 meeting with Furmark at which the New York businessman discussed Ghorbanifar's suspicion that Iran arms money had been diverted to the contras] "until this morning" and did not recall ever having read it before. In this letter Casey further said that he had been told the memorandum was prepared but apparently never went forward. (SSIC 1/29/87)

- Meese testified that at 9:00 he met with the President and Regan. He testified that he told them more of what he had found out and that a criminal investigation would probably be convened. According to Meese, they realized this was "a very momentous occasion" and that the worst thing for the President would be the appearance of covering up. The emphasis was on getting it out to the Congressional leadership and the public and, in parallel with that, commencing a criminal investigation. (SSIC 1/29/87)

- Charles Allen told the Board: . . . .
"Casey, when this whole thing erupted on the 25th of November, he was deeply upset to find out he had not signed it [a memorandum regarding allegations by Roy Furmark; see October 23 entry]. He thought it had gone to Admiral Poindexter. But it laid it out starkly that there would be allegations, that Ghorbanifar had made allegations of diversion of funds to the contras." (Tower)

- Reagan calls North to thank him for his service, according to sources close to North. (WP 12/7/86)

- Fawn Hall, North's secretary, removes about a half-inch thick stack of documents from the NSC and gives them to North. The materials reportedly concern the Iran affair. (WP 2/24/87; NYT 2/24/87)

- Reagan meets in the morning with Shultz and, at the secretary of state's initiative, Regan. Relations between Shultz and Regan are reported to be very strained as a result of the Administration's handling of the Iran affair. At this meeting, the President reportedly asks Shultz to remain in his post until the end of the Administration and tells him the State Department is in charge of Iran policy from this point forward. (WP 2/12/87)

- Following his meeting with Reagan, Shultz immediately authorizes his spokesman to announce that the State Department will assume the lead role in U.S. policy toward Iran. (WP 2/12/87)

- Reagan meets in the morning with national security advisers and congressional leaders to inform them of the actions he intends to take. (Reagan Briefing 11/25/86)

- Reagan declares at a noon press conference that he "was not fully informed of the nature of one of the activities undertaken in connection" with the Iran affair. He announces that Poindexter has resigned and North has been relieved of his duties. Meese then announces that $10 million to $30 million of Iran's payments for U.S. arms were diverted to Swiss bank accounts financing the contras. He says North, who organized the operation, was the only individual who "knew precisely" about the diversion, although Poindexter "did know that something of this nature was occurring." He confirms that the U.S. "condoned" at least one Israeli shipment in August or September 1985. (WP 11/26/86 & 12/7/86; NYT 12/3/86 & 12/4/86)

- Meese disclosed his findings at a noon press conference. Meese testified that he arrived at the $10-30 million figure he used at the press conference by taking North's statement that $3-4 million went to the Nicaraguan resistance on one occasion and the April 4 document which referred to $12 million. North had said two or three shipments were involved. Multiplying the sums for one transaction by three gave $10-30 million as an approximation. (SSIC 1/29/87)

- Meese told the Committee that after his press conference and a luncheon with the Supreme Court, Meese walked back to the Oval Office with the President. He told the President that he was going back to the Justice Department because they were pursuing a criminal investigation. (SSIC 1/29/87)

- Meese recalled that, at the press conference, he did not know if any criminal violations were possibly involved. According to his testimony, Meese commenced a criminal investigation that afternoon.

He directed the Deputy Attorney General to notify the

White House Counsel to be sure that security precautions were taken on all documents, and he directed the Assistant Attorney General for Criminal Division to meet with the Assistant Attorney General for the Office of Legal Counsel (Mr. Cooper) to discuss possible laws that might apply, including criminal laws. Meese testified he also met with FBI Director Webster and told him he was turning the matter over to the Criminal Division and would "probably" need FBI resources. According to Meese, FBI resources were requested the next day, November 26. (SSIC 1/29/87)

- Combinations on the locks of North's office are changed. (PI 11/28/86)

- According to an NSC staff member who shared North's office suite, a security officer came to the office on the evening of November 25 for the purpose of sealing the office. The staff member said he had no knowledge that any papers were destroyed. (SSIC 1/29/87)

- Israel, in its first offical comment, says it transferred arms to Iran "upon the request of the United States" and did not know of the diversion of money to the contras. (NYT 12/4/86)

- Meese testified that Israeli Foreign Minister Peres called him on the afternoon of November 25. According to Meese, Peres said they had heard what had happened and that all they had done was tell the Iranians where to put the money. They had not handled the money. They had told the Iranians what bank accounts to put the money into, and how much. (SSIC 1/29/87)

- Assistant Secretary of State Elliott Abrams testifies before the Senate intelligence panel that he played no part in soliciting assistance from third countries for the contras. In a December appearance before the committee, however, Abrams says that in June or July 1986, he discussed a contribution from Brunei, which he referred to as "Country X," with Oliver North. (MH 1/8/87)

- On November 25, 1986, Assistant Secretary Abrams and the CIA task force chief [Alan Fiers] appeared before the Committee at a regular hearing to review implementation of U.S. Nicaragua programs. In response to questions about third-country support for anti-Sandinista forces, neither witness revealed the solicitation of $10 million in August. In testimony on December 8, 1986, under oath, Mr. Abrams apologized to the Committee for withholding this information. He said he did not feel he had been asked a direct question and did not realize until shown the transcript that his statements clearly left a misleading impression. (SSIC 1/29/87)

- FBI Director William Webster is not informed until today of Meese's November 22 discovery of a key NSC document relating to the diversion of funds. (WP 12/5/86)

- The President said he had no knowledge of the diversion prior to his conversation with Attorney General Meese on November 25, 1986. No evidence has come to light to suggest otherwise. Contemporaneous Justice Department staff notes of LtCol North's interview with Attorney General Meese on November 23, 1986, show North telling the Attorney General that only he, Mr. McFarlane, and VADM Poindexter were aware of the diversion. (Tower)

NOV 26 - The NSC hosts a morning meeting of an interagency group, including Undersecretary of State for Political Affairs Michael Armacost, on Iran policy. (State Dept. Briefing 11/26/86)

- The Justice Department authorizes the FBI to conduct a full-scale criminal investigation of Iran weapons shipments. (WP 12/7/86)

- Reagan appoints a three-member panel consisting of former Senator John G. Tower (R-TX.), former Secretary of State and Senator Edmund S. Muskie (D-ME), and former national security adviser Brent Scowcroft to review the "role and procedures of the National Security Council staff in the conduct of foreign and national security policy." (NYT 12/4/86; Reagan Briefing 11/25/86)

- Contra leaders deny knowledge of receiving up to $30 million from arms sales to Iran. Adolfo Calero, leader of the Nicaraguan Democratic Front (FDN), says that in 1986 the contras received only a "trickle of money" amounting to no more than $300,000 to $500,000 beyond the humanitarian aid approved by Congress. He also denies ever discussing money with North. (PI 11/26/86)

- State Department spokesman Charles E. Redman denies the Department had any knowledge of the diversion of Iran arms profits to the contras. He claims the Department was unaware of the contras' funding sources when U.S. government funding was not available. Finally, he declares that Operation Staunch, a three-year drive by the Department to prevent other countries from shipping weapons to Iran, "continues to be pursued vigorously," despite recent disclosure of the Iran arms deal. (State Dept. Briefing 11/26/86; WP 12/10/86)

- Regan tells reporters that Poindexter reported directly to the President, not to him, about national security matters. However, White House officials have stated that Regan routinely attended almost all of Poindexter's briefings of Regan. (PI 11/28/86)

- North's papers are transferred to NSC vaults. One official terms "incredible" the Justice Department's failure to secure the documents as soon as the Iran-contra connection is discovered, over the weekend of November 22-23. According to a source, North "was shredding over the weekend. They closed the barn door after the horses were gone." (PI 11/28/86; NYT 12/4/86)

- Michael Ledeen ends his service as a consultant to the NSC. He says his involvement in the Iran affair, which he insists was was strictly that of a messenger, came to an end in November 1985 when Poindexter replaced him. Ledeen says the reason for his removal from operation was his opposition to trading arms for hostages. He later acknowledges, however, that he kept in contact with Ghorbanifar while the Iranian remained a key middleman with Iran and that the two eventually became close friends. (CSM 3/4/87)

NOV 27 - North is denied entry to his White House office. (WP 12/7/86)

- The first diversion of money to the contras is reported to have taken place in 1985, months earlier than acknowledged by the White House. Oregon businessman Richard J. Brenneke says he was told by U.S. Government intelligence sources early this year that the Defense Department planned to buy weapons for Nicaraguan rebels with profits from the Iran arms sales. He says he told an aide to Bush, Lt. Col. E. Douglas Menarchik, who told him, "We will look into it." Menarchik says in an interview later that he does not have "any specific recollection of telephone conversations with" Brenneke. (NYT 12/4/86; NYT 11/30/86)

- The Saudi government denies Khashoggi acted on behalf of Riyadh in arranging financing for Iran's purchase of U.S. arms. (PI 11/28/86)

- A White House official says Regan knew about and approved details of the funneling of money from Iran arms sales to the contras. According to the official, Regan was aware of the plan from the beginning and was briefed regularly by Poindexter on its progress. Associated Press also quotes a "well-placed" official as saying "Regan . . . would know everything Poindexter knew," apparently contradicting Meese's statement on November 25 that North was "the only person in the United States government that knew precisely about this" except for Poindexter, who had rough knowledge of the affair. Regan flatly denies any prior knowledge of the operation, saying he was "never briefed thoroughly on all of this. . . . I never heard of it until the news came out on Monday [November 24] about what was happening with the Iranian money and the contras." Other White House sources disagree as to the likelihood Poindexter or North would not have informed Regan of their activities. (PI 11/28/86; WP 11/30/86)

- Regan appears to contradict Meese again by saying neither he nor the President have been talked to by the Justice Department, and that "the President wouldn't be talked to in any event." Meese on November 27 remarked that "we have pretty clearly established at this point" that no top administration officials, including Reagan and Regan, were involved in the operation. Judiciary Committee Chairman Peter W. Rodino, Jr. (D-N.J.) later questions how Meese could make this assertion before completing his investigation. (PI 11/28/86; WP 1/6/86)

NOV 28 - The Senate Select Committee on Intelligence announces it has initiated an investigation into the sale of weapons to Iran and the funneling of profits to the contras. (WP 11/29/86)

- A Defense Department memo directs Pentagon officials to find all documents pertaining to the activities of McFarlane, Poindexter, Calero, Secord, North, NSC staff counsel

Paul B. Thompson, and the late Donald Fortier who was North's boss and Poindexter's deputy. (Newsweek 12/15/86)

- The Union Bank of Switzerland denies that an account held there by Wallace B. Sawyer, the co-pilot of the C-123K cargo plane downed in Nicaragua on October 5, had anything to do with recent arms shipments to Iran. A business card belonging to Jean Paul Cuche, an assistant vice president of the bank's Cornavin branch in Geneva, was found in the wreckage. Bank investigators apparently found that Cuche had opened the account for Sawyer in 1981. (NYT 11/29/86)

- Letters from Oregon businessman Richard Brenneke to Vice President Bush suggest that the U.S. may have approved arms sales to Iran as early as the Summer of 1985, and that Poindexter may have orally approved the sale of 10,000 TOW missiles to Tehran, five times the number stated by the Administration. (NYT 11/28/86; WP 11/29/86)

- Iranian parliament speaker Rafsanjani denies Iran received any arms through Israel, but offers to help try to win the release of hostages held in Lebanon in exchange for weapons. He says that recently the U.S. attempted to offer arms through the Gulf Cooperation Council and through Japan, but the Iranian government did not believe the offer. (WP 11/29/86)

NOV 29 - Dimokratikos Logos, an Athens newspaper, says tapes of McFarlane's talks with Iranians in Tehran in 1985 and 1986 show that the U.S. shipped Iran as much as $1.3 billion in military equipment and sent an additional $2 million to a group holding Americans in Lebanon. The paper says Washington agreed to supply Iran with equipment worth $5 billion. In addition, the Saudis are reported to have played a larger role, the Israelis a less central role in the Iran-contra affair. (NYT 12/4/86)

- Top NSC officials reportedly gave $12 million from January to September 1986 to a Swiss company to purchase military supplies for Iran, including spare parts for F-14 jet fighters and several thousand missiles. The equipment was then shipped to Iran on three flights and sold for $30 million, it is reported. Profits from the deal are said to have been deposited in the account of Credit Services Fiduciaires (as printed in the London Times), a Geneva-based investment banking house operated by former CIA officials. Eventually, the funds were transferred to CSF's account in the Cayman Islands, according to the Times. (WP 11/29/86)

- Secretary of State Alexander Haig is reported to have given Israel permission in 1981 to sell U.S.-made military spare parts to Iran, after discussing the matter with McFarlane, then counselor at the State Department, and David Kimche, director general of Israel's foreign ministry. Both Haig and McFarlane deny the allegations. (WP 11/29/86)

NOV 30 - Congressional leaders from both parties urge a special committee like the one used during the Watergate scandal to investigate the arms deals with Iran and the diversion of funds to the contras. In an interview today, Reagan calls North "a national hero." (NYT 12/4/86)

- French Prime Minister Jacques Chirac discloses that Iran approached France with a request for arms as a gesture to help improve relations between the two countries. Chirac says France refused. France is Iraq's second largest supplier of weapons. (WP 12/1/86)

- Vice President Bush is reported to have been briefed regularly throughout 1984, 1985 and 1986 by North, contra leaders and others about the situation in Nicaragua and efforts to fund the contras. To date, no sources have been able to confirm that Bush knew of North's plan to divert Iran arms sales profits to the rebels, however. Bush denied participating in the scheme. (MH 11/30/86)

- It is reported that Vice President Bush knew about, and was prepared to approve, a covert plan proposed in January by private arms dealers to sell $2 billion worth of weapons to Iran. The information comes from transcripts of telephone conversations between a participant in a U.S. Customs Service sting operation and alleged arms dealers. The transcriptions are part of a New York court case against 18 individuals. (See January 31, 1986 entry, for example). (MH 11/30/86)

LATE NOV - Reagan meets with Regan and counselor Peter J. Wallison about the Iran-contra affair. (WP 1/21/87)

DECEMBER 1986

DEC - Sometime this month, the freighter Erria leaves its station off the Omani coast and steams to the Israeli port of Eilat. For several weeks the ship has been waiting for word that a trade would be made of its cargo of apparently U.S.-made machine guns for one or possibly more Soviet T-72 tanks captured by Iran. (A later report says the planned swap, arranged by Hakim, involved $20,000 of Soviet-made AK-47 rifles and ammunition in return for as many as five tanks, which would then be dropped off at the U.S. Navy base at Diego Garcia. Secord, apparently astounded at the low value of the U.S. side of the exchange, reportedly orders photographs of the weapons to prove that Hakim has not stowed anything aboard that is of greater value to the Iranians.) After the deal falls through, the freighter, according to one report, returns the weapons to Israel and sets off for Denmark, arriving in mid-January. (LAT 1/21/87)

- In December 1985 Congress approved classified amounts of funds to the contras for "communications" and "advice." The authorization was subject, however, to a classified annex negotiated by the Senate and House intelligence committees. An exchange of letters, initiated the day the law passed, evidences the extreme difficulty even the Chairmen of the two committees had in deciding what the annex permitted or proscribed.

The support for the contras differs from the Iranian initiative in some other important respects. First, the activities undertaken by LtCol North with respect to the contras, unlike in the Iranian case, were in support of the declared policy of at least the Executive. Second, the President may never have authorized or, indeed, even been apprised of what the NSC staff was doing. The President never issued a Covert Action Finding or any other formal decision authorizing NSC staff activities in support of the contras. Third, the NSC staff's role in support of the contras was not in derogation of the CIA's role because, [sic] CIA involvement was expressly barred by statute.

The Board had neither the time nor the resources to conduct a full inquiry into the role of the NSC staff in the support of the contras that was commensurate with its work on the Iran arms sales. As a consequence, the evidence assembled by the Board was somewhat anecdotal and disconnected. (Tower)

DEC 1 - The Committee initiated its preliminary inquiry on December 1, 1986 after the Attorney General disclosed evidence of the possible resistance. According to documents and testimony received by the Committee, several individuals played key roles in both the arms sales to Iran and the possible diversion of funds to the Nicaraguan resistance, including Lt. Colonel North, retired Major General Richard Secord, and Secord's business associate, Albert Hakim. North was assigned NSC responsibility for the Nicaragua-Central America account. (SSIC 1/29/87)

- North invokes his Fifth Amendment right against self-incrimination and refuses to testify before the Senate Select Committee on Intelligence about arms shipments to Iran and the diversion of profits to aid the contras. (WP 12/7/86)

- McFarlane testifies before the Senate intelligence committee that Reagan authorized Israel's shipments of U.S. arms to Iran after a meeting with top aides on August 6, 1985. McFarlane says that in a private meeting he had with the President, Reagan approved the idea and said he would replenish any weapons Israel shipped. (WP 12/28/86)

- McFarlane testified that in preparing his response to press reports and Congressional inquiries in the summer of 1985, he went to considerable length in interviews with North and looking at files to determine the nature of North's activities in connection with the Nicaraguan resistance. He further testified that North assured him categorically at that time that his role was nothing more than encouraging the contras and advising people who volunteered support that they should contact the contras. McFarlane further testified that he had learned nothing since that time to contradict this view of North's activities. (SSIC 1/29/87)

- Reagan says he will welcome the appointment of a special prosecutor if the Justice Department recommends one.

He denies "flat out" any prior knowledge that Iran arms profits were diverted to the contras. His public approval rating in a NYT/CBS News poll plunges to 46 percent, a 21-point decline, the sharpest one-month drop ever recorded by such a poll. (NYT 12/4/86)

- Israeli Prime Minister Shamir publicly rejects Reagan's apparent assertion in an interview with Time magazine that Israel helped funnel money to the contras. Israeli diplomats ascertained that Reagan had Israel in mind when he referred to an unnamed third country involved in the deal. Israeli officials late last night sent a formal request for clarification from Washington. (NYT 12/3/86)

- Assistant Secretary of State Elliott Abrams suggests that the money diverted from the Iran arms deals may never have reached the contras. He notes that the rebels were "clearly broke...they had no cash and had substantial debts." (Newsweek 12/15/86)

- Honduran President Jose Azcona summons U.S. Ambassador Everett Briggs to a meeting also attended by Foreign Minister Carlos Lopez Contreras and several high-ranking officers of the Honduran military. The Hondurans stress their desire that contra forces based in their country leave as soon as possible. (WP 12/10/86)

DEC 2 - In a televised statement, Reagan says he has urged Meese to apply for the appointment of an independent counsel, and announces Frank C. Carlucci will be his new national security adviser. (WP 12/7/86)

- Congressional leaders meet with Reagan and express approval of his plan to call for a special counsel. Still, they say they will push for inquiries on the Hill about arms to Iran and aid to the contras. (NYT 12/3/86)

- Administration officials are quoted as saying the contras have received less aid than the $10 million to $30 million indicated publicly by Meese. (NYT 12/2/86)

DEC 3 - Poindexter repeatedly invokes the Fifth Amendment before the Senate Select Committee on Intelligence. His appearance comes the day after Reagan pledges to "cooperate fully" with congressional investigations. Meese has identified Poindexter and North as the only two administration officials with knowledge of the diversion of funds. (WP 12/7/86; NYT 12/4/86)

- Bush, in his first detailed public statement on the controversy, denies that he had prior personal knowledge of the diversion of money. But he acknowledges that "mistakes were made" and that the Administration's "credibility has been damaged." (NYT 12/4/86)

- Congressional investigators are reported to have traced proceeds from the sale of U.S. arms to Iran to a Swiss bank account run by the CIA. The same account has been used, the report says, to provide military support to the contras and to rebels in Afghanistan. This revelation appears to contradict statements by Meese on November 25 that profits from the Iran sales were "deposited in bank accounts which were under the control of representatives of the forces of Central America." (WP 12/3/86)

- The CIA, in an unusual public statement, denies a report that its bank accounts were used for diverting funds from the Iran arms sales to the contras "or any other covert action programs." The only money related to the Iran program that the Agency handled, according to the statement, was the "$12 million owed to the Pentagon for the arms," which the Agency "passed on to the Pentagon promptly." (NYT 12/4/86)

- Senior State Department officials are quoted as saying "[f]rom the moment that the President agreed to supply arms to Iran it was always apparent to us that the driving motivation was to free hostages" and that seeking an opening to Iranian moderates was only a secondary aim. (NYT 12/3/86)

- An "unconfirmed report" in the Israeli newspaper, Yediot Aharonot, says that "millions of dollars that the Khomeini regime paid for arms that it received from the United States and Israel were transferred to private accounts of some of the central religious leaders in Iran," apparently in the form of kickbacks. (NYT 12/3/86)

- Further allegations surface concerning activities of the Geneva-based Compagnie de Services Fiduciaires, S.A. (CSF), which relate to the company's connections with Stanford Technology Corporation, and to its role in hiring the aircraft McFarlane reportedly used to travel to Tehran on May 28 this year. (NYT 12/3/86)

- Press reports note a rash of break-ins at offices run by groups opposed to U.S. policy in Central America. In the past two years, over two dozen such incidents have taken place all over the country. Rep. Don Edwards (D-CA) says, "quite obviously, there is a pattern to these burglaries and there very likely is a foreign connection." (CBS News 12/3/86)

- Nicaraguan President Ortega says U.S. and Honduran troops are massing on his country's northern border. (MH 12/5/86)

- It is revealed that Belgian arms manufacturers, principally Fabrique Nationale (FN), have been supplying arms, missiles and spare parts to Iran for the past six years. According to Danish seamen's union leader Henrik Berlau, Danish vessels have carried major shipments of weapons, often at a rate of two a week, from the Belgian ports of Antwerp and Zeebrugge to Iran. The Belgian Foreign Minister, Leo Tinderman, who had earlier claimed that the supplies of weapons by Belgium to Iran had been limited to two hunting rifles, announces that an inquiry will begin on the matter. (Brussels Domestic Service 11/27/86; Le Soir (France) in AFP 12/3/86)

- Bofors, a Swedish company, is reported to the police by the Swedish Peace and Arbitration Association for having smuggled Robot-70 (RBS 70) missiles to Iran. (Stockholm International Service 12/3/86)

DEC 4 - House and Senate leaders agree to form separate Watergate-style select committees to investigate the scandal, with work expected to begin in January. (WP 12/7/86)

- CIA Deputy Director Robert Gates testifies before the Senate Select Committee on Intelligence. (MH 12/5/86)

- The Justice Dept. formally applies to a federal court panel for the appointment of an independent counsel to investigate North and anyone else who might have been involved in the Iran arms sales and the diversion of the proceeds from January 1985 on. The petition is made public Dec. 8. (WP 12/9/86)

- Weinberger says it would have been "clearly the exception" for Reagan not to have been fully informed of the Iran-contra operation. "The President has to know what is being done in his name," he said. Yesterday, Weinberger told reporters he believed Reagan acted on "very bad advice" in pursuing the initiative toward Iran. (MH 12/5/86)

- Reagan greets Costa Rican President Oscar Arias with the declaration that "[t]here has been no deterioration of our commitment, no weakening of our resolve" toward Central America. (MH 12/5/86)

- Sources who participated in the covert contra supply program describe in an article how planes used to ferry "humanitarian assistance" from the U.S. to El Salvador and Honduras were then used to ship weapons transferred from Europe to the contras. They say the operation was closely monitored by American diplomatic, military and intelligence officials. (NYT 12/4/86)

- Nicaragua sends protests to the U.S. and Honduras concerning their alleged massing of U.S. troops within 15 miles of Nicaragua's northern border. American officials have said the 100 Florida National Guardsmen are training in Honduras but will not come within 30 miles of the border. (MH 12/5/86)

- The Carter administration's top Iran specialist, former NSC official Gary Sick says in a speech that he estimates Iran received $500 million to $1 billion in arms from Israel and the U.S. Sick, now with the Ford Foundation, said 9 to 12 arms shipments from the two countries have "made a difference" in the Iran-Iraq war and accuses the Reagan administration of reporting an artificially low $12 million arms figure to avoid the appearance of a violation of laws requiring Congressional approval for arms deals of $14 million or more. (WP 12/5/86)

DEC 5 - Following up on the government's denials concerning Cyprus' role in the U.S.-Iran arms deals, a Nicosia news report reiterates its statement of yesterday that the "agreement to sell U.S. arms to Iran was finalized in Cyprus, and the port of Limassol was used to ship these weapons." The report goes on to allege that the principals were Oliver North, the brother of Parliament Speaker Rafsanjani, and an Israeli official. The meeting reportedly took place at the Four Lanterns Hotel in Larnaca, as confirmed, the report says, by the hotel staff who said the U.S. official was there, along with "certain others." The discussions reportedly lasted for "many hours." The reported agreement (for which no date is given) included the shipment of large amounts of arms from Israel, on board Israeli ships, to Limassol. There the weapons were transported onto German ships and sent to Turkey, from where they headed to Iran. The report adds, "In an apparent attempt at deception, a different destination was put down on paper." (Ta Nea (Cyprus) 12/4/86)

- Republican congressional leaders confront Reagan at a White House meeting and insist that he divulge all the facts concerning the Iran-contra affair. Told of widespread public skepticism that he was unaware of the operation, Reagan replies, "I could put my hand on the Bible and swear I didn't know it and I wouldn't jeopardize my ticket up there." (MH 12/6/86)

- The Justice Department delivers a formal request to the Swiss Embassy in Washington asking the Swiss government to cooperate in a criminal investigation of North, Secord, and a third, unnamed American involving the possible use of Swiss bank accounts to transfer Iran arms profits to the contras. Sources say at least three and possibly more accounts may be involved and name the Credit Suisse Bank branch in Geneva as the location of at least one of the accounts. (WP 12/8/86 & 12/9/86)

- White House spokesman Dan Howard reveals that North is now believed to have "lied" to White House officials concerning Iran weapons deliveries. (MH 12/6/86)

- The senior U.S. military adviser in El Salvador, Army Col. James Steele, is reported to have been under orders from Ambassador Edwin Corr to "keep track" of the covert arms resupply network to the contras since the operation's inception in early 1986. Embassy officials have repeatedly denied any direct knowledge of, or participation in, the weapons drops. Corr denies he "supervised" the network. (WP 12/5/86; NYT 12/13/86)

- The United Nations General Assembly votes 83-2 with 44 abstentions to approve a resolution demanding that the U.S. revoke its trade embargo against Nicaragua. Israel casts the only other negative vote. (MH 12/6/86)

- In a memorandum dated December 5, 1986 to the Deputy Director for Operations, CIA Associate General Counsel Jameson stated that "contacts with the benefactors, although contrary to policy, were not contrary to law." Flight vectors, Sandinista antiaircraft positions, and other similar information needed to carry out safe aerial deliveries fell within the terms of the "advice" authorized in December, 1983 by the Intelligence Authorization Act. (Tower)

DEC 6 - Reagan in his weekly radio address acknowledges for the first time that "mistakes were made" in the plan to sell weapons to Iran and funnel profits to the contras. He says the errors occurred only in the execution of policy, not in "the policies themselves." He insists that "it was not my intent to do business with Khomeini, to trade weapons for hostages, nor to undercut our policy of antiterrorism." The president promises that the initiative has been "broken off" but on the same day, American officials meet with Iranians in Europe to discuss the matter further. (WP 12/7/86; NYT 1/23/87)

- Former CIA agent George Cave and an official from the State Department meet in London with Iranian representatives to continue discussions on arms and hostages, according to testimony by Shultz, as reported later. One Administration official says that Cave is the only American at the time who is involved in the negotiations. Shultz says that one new point raised at the meeting was an Iranian demand that seventeen Shiites being held in Kuwait on terrorism charges be released as part of a bargain to free American hostages. Shultz testifies that after learning that the U.S. may have forwarded the demand on to Kuwait he sent a cable to that country's foreign minister assuring him that the U.S. remained opposed to dealing with terrorists. He is said to have been angered by such incidents and by Cave's activities generally, which he believed reflected a lack of State Department control over Iran policy. Cave reportedly stays on in London after the meeting to explore a new channel to Iranian leaders provided by Albert Hakim. On December 13, according to Shultz, Cave and State analyst Charles Dunbar meet with Iranian representatives in Frankfurt. Shultz claims the purpose of that gathering was to impress upon the Iranians the Unted States' intention not to ship any more arms to them. (NYT 1/23/87; Shultz testimony 1/27/87)

- It is reported that the Sultan of Brunei made a severall-million-dollar contribution to the contras after an unusually lengthy visit from Shultz (see June 24, 1986 entry), and that the U.S. provided the sultan with the number of a Swiss bank account into which to deposit the funds. It is thought at first that Elliott Abrams came up with the idea, but newspaper reports later say that North passed it on to Abrams, along with the number of the Swiss account, after contra supporters suggested it to him in December 1984. An Administration official later reveals that approximately $10 million was deposited, significantly more than congressional investigators initially suspect. (LAT 12/6/86; MH 12/14/86; NYT 12/25/86)

DEC 7 - Newspaper accounts reveal that American diplomats have solicited aid for the contras from several foreign governments over the past two years, in addition to the Sultanate of Brunei. (WP 12/7/86)

- President and Nancy Reagan met this week with former Deputy White House Chief of Staff Michael K. Deaver, former Secretary of State William Rogers and former Democratic National Chairman Robert Strauss about the Iran-contra affair. The meeting took place without the knowledge of Donald Regan. Sources say Deaver is attempting to convince the president to oust the current chief of staff for the sake of the country and Reagan's presidency. Among other evidence cited that Regan may be forced out is the disclosure by a close aide that the chief of staff will not be spending the New Year's holiday with the Reagans in California. (MH 12/13/86)

- North is reported to have told a United Methodist Church group on February 10, 1986 that he briefs Reagan twice a week, half of the briefings on terrorism and half on Central America. According to White House officials, Reagan's meeting records indicate only 19 meetings with North in attendance, none with North alone, since January 1985. The officials say Reagan rarely meets alone with any of his top advisers. (WP 12/7/86)

DEC 8 - Shultz testifies before the House Foreign Affairs Committee, distancing himself again from the Administration's actions concerning arms sales to Iran and the channeling of funds to the contras. He reveals that U.S. Ambassador to Lebanon John H. Kelly dealt secretly with Poindexter, North and Richard Secord on the arms and hostage issues, bypassing the State Department. This is the first time an administration official links Secord with the Iran operation. Shultz also refers to the apparent transfer of money as "illegal," but later retracts that characterization. (Shultz testimony; WP 12/9/86)

- McFarlane testifies before the House Foreign Affairs Committee that North informed him in May that "the U.S. Government had applied part of the proceeds" from the sale of arms to Iran "to support the contras." His testimony contradicts statements by Reagan and Meese that the U.S. was not involved in any transfer of funds to the rebels. (McFarlane testimony; WP 12/9/86)

- Elliott Abrams, Assistant Secretary of State for Inter-American affairs, testifies before a closed session of the Senate Select Committee on Intelligence. Committee Chairman Durenberger later says in an interview that Abrams told the panel that in June or July 1986 he discussed with North a contribution of aid to the contras from Brunei. Durenberger notes the discrepancy between this statement and Abrams' testimony on November 25, 1986, in which he claimed not to have played a role in soliciting third-country aid for the rebels. Durenberger adds in the interview, "I wouldn't trust Elliott Abrams any further than I could throw Oliver North." (MH 6/8/86, 12/11/86 & 1/8/87; WP 12/9/86)

- On November 25, 1986, Assistant Secretary Abrams and the CIA task force chief [Allan Fiers] appeared before the Committee at a regular hearing to review implementation of U.S. Nicaragua programs. In response to questions about third-country support for anti-Sandinista forces, neither witness revealed the solicitation of $10 million in August. [See August 8, 1986 entries.] In testimony on December 8, 1986, under oath, Mr. Abrams apologized to the Committee for withholding this information. He said he did not feel he had been asked a direct question and did not realize until shown the transcript that his statements clearly left a misleading impression. (SSIC 1/29/87)

- Robert Owen, a former consultant to the State Department's now-defunct Nicaraguan Humanitarian Assistance Office (NHAO), and liaison between North and the contras, appears before a closed session of the Senate Select Committee on Intelligence. He invokes the Fifth Amendment and refuses to testify. (MH 6/8/86, 12/11/86; WP 12/9/86)

- The Justice Department announces it is seeking the appointment of an independent counsel to investigate North and anyone else who might have been involved in the Iran-contra operations beginning in January 1985. The scope of the investigation will not include other allegedly illegal efforts to supply arms to the Nicaraguan rebels. (WP 12/9/86)

- Switzerland rejects the U.S. request to freeze two accounts thought to have been used by North and others to divert funds from Iran arms sales to the contras, advising the Justice Department that more detailed information is needed. (NYT 12/16/86)

- Israeli Prime Minister Shamir tells visiting members of the Senate Armed Services Committee that part of "our agreement with the Americans" included the possible release of Israeli soldiers by Shiites in Lebanon. (WP 12/9/86)

- David Kimche, in an interview with Israeli radio, acknowledges that he played a role in the Iran arms deal but insists he "was asked to come in," without saying by whom. The Foreign Ministry last night released a report denying that Kimche "was the initiator for the transfer by Israel of U.S. arms to Iran." (WP 12/9/86)

- Saudi Arabia denies any role in the transfer of arms to Iran. (WP 12/9/86)

- Reagan and his top advisers are reported to have bypassed their own secret interagency counter-terrorism group on the sale of arms to Iran. The group meets weekly at the White House, but North, the NSC's representative, never informed his colleagues of the arms deal. (WP 12/8/86)

- One of Iran's demands before freeing American hostages was reportedly the release of 17 persons held in Kuwaiti prisons on charges of terrorism in that country. The Administration has said it has never pressured the Emir of Kuwait to release any of the 17, "and will not," according to a high Reagan official. (WP 12/8/86)

- Pat Buchanan, White House communications director, strongly defends North and Poindexter in a speech in Miami. Speaking to a mostly Cuban-American audience, he says, "if Colonel North ripped off the Ayatollah and took some $30 million to give to the contras, then God bless Colonel North." Larry Speakes says later that Buchanan's comparisons of North to Americans who have broken the law for a good cause do not reflect White House views. Buchanan's attacks on the press and the Republican congressional leadership in the wake of the Iran-contra affair are considered politically damaging by Donald Regan and other senior members of the White House staff. (WP 12/10/86; NYT 12/10/86)

- The White House sends political director Mitchell Daniels to meet with GOP governors in New Jersey. He assures them the Iran-contra scandal is not another Watergate and insists "[t]here will not be a cover-up" by the Administration. (WP 12/9/86)

- The U.S. Army announces that it has suspended TOW missile firings after two "ruptures" during training exercises at two separate locations September 11 and 13. At least 2,000 TOW missiles have been sent to Iran as part of the Administration's secret arms deal. (WP 12/9/86)

DEC 9 - Poindexter and North, in separate appearances before the House Foreign Affairs Committee, invoke the Fifth Amendment. Secord, appearing before the Senate intelligence committee, also refuses to testify. (CSM 1/2/87)

- Shultz meets privately in London with foreign ministers from Great Britain, West Germany and France. The trip has been scheduled prior to the disclosure of the Iran-contra deal, but one of his goals is to convince his counterparts that he remains a trusted and influential Reagan adviser. At the same time, Assistant Secretary of State Richard Murphy is meeting in London with senior American diplomats from selected Middle East countries to discuss regional developments. Tomorrow, Shultz travels to Brussels to prepare for a meeting of NATO foreign ministers. (WP 12/10/86)

- Meese tells reporters in London that Reagan's Iran policy made "considerable progress" in identifying and encouraging moderate elements in that country, despite acknowledgements that there were "mistakes made." He repeats the Administration's contention that the aims of the policy have been to develop relations with moderates, to end the Iran-Iraq war and to decrease "Iran's participation in and support for subversion and terrorism." Responding to a question, Meese adds that freeing the hostages was also "one of the objectives" but suggests that their release "was one of the things that was indicated that they would provide as a sign of their good faith and commitment to this process." U.S. officials have said previously that it was the Iranians who required a show of American good faith in the form of arms shipments before agreeing to address the hostage issue. (WP 12/10/86)

- The State Department and FBI begin interviewing U.S. Ambassador to Lebanon John Kelly about his role in connection with the White House effort to gain release of the hostages. Kelly has been ambassador in Beirut since August. (WP 12/9/86 & 12/10/86; MH 12/11/86)

- A Brunei official confirms that his country transferred several million dollars via the National Bank of Brunei, which is no longer operating, to the contras. (WP 12/10/86)

- Iran and the Soviet Union hold their first high level economic talks since the 1979 revolution, setting the stage for a series of trade and economic agreements. Iranian Speaker of Parliament, Ali Akbar Rafsanjani, meeting with the visiting head of the USSR's State Committee for Foreign Economic Relations, Konstantin Katushev, declares Tehran is "fully prepared to improve relations" with Moscow. (WP 12/10/86)

- The Soviet Union warns the U.S. not to take a direct military role in Nicaragua following reports American helicopters ferried Honduran troops to an area near the border where Sandinista troops had crossed over. (WP 12/10/86)

DEC 10 - William Casey testifies before the House Foreign Affairs Committee that on October 7 he was told by New York businessman Roy Furmark, a former legal client, about "the whole operation" involving arms to Iran and the possibility that "some of the money may have been diverted for other purposes." However, Casey claims he has no knowledge of the diversion of funds to the contras and repeatedly professes ignorance about CIA cash transactions involving Swiss bank accounts. He says the first official information he received came from Meese on or shortly before November 25, the date Meese disclosed the operation to the public. Later, medical experts say Casey's brain tumor (he suffers a seizure on December 15) may have affected his testimony. (WP 12/11/86 & 1/14/87)

- Members of Congress are reported to object to the Justice Department's insistence on continuing its investigation into U.S.-based activities for the contras. Sources say Democrats on the Senate Judiciary Committee have forwarded a secret petition to the U.S. Court of Appeals complaining that the independent counsel should have broader authority. In addition, Democrats on the House Judiciary Committee have stated that all allegations of illegal contra aid, not just those pertaining to North and Iran, should be dealt with by the independent counsel. According to Rep. John Conyers, Jr. (D-MI), "The Justice Department has the same conflict of interest in investigating [U.S.-based activities] as it does in investigating the Iran arms transfers." (WP 12/11/86)

- Rep. Stephen Solarz (D-NY) says it is "absolutely clear" that Reagan knew of the diversion of funds to the contras. "Now that we've completed our hearings for the week, I'm convinced of it," he says. However, Rep. Michael DeWine, (R-OH) called Solarz' remarks an "outrage," saying "[t]here is absolutely no evidence of linkage" to Reagan. (USA Today 12/11/86)

- Robert Dutton, a business associate of Secord, invokes the Fifth Amendment and refuses to testify before the Senate Select Committee on Intelligence, according to Chairman Durenberger. (WP 12/11/86)

- The State Department recalls its senior officer in Syria, David Ransom, to try to determine what he may have known of Administration efforts to swap arms for hostages. (WP 12/11/86)

- Poindexter refuses to testify during a 10-minute appearance before the House Permanent Select Committee on Intelligence. CIA Deputy Director Robert Gates and McFarlane spoke before the committee. (WP 12/11/86)

- Swiss officials report the U.S. has failed to provide documentation to back up its request to freeze two bank accounts. As a result, one account effectively remains open to further transactions. Legal experts have expressed surprise at the U.S. delay, one Swiss official hypothesizing that perhaps "the Americans don't really want us to block the accounts at all." (WP 12/11/86)

- Gen. Fabian Ver, the former chief of staff of the Philippine armed forces, signed false arms resale certificates in an effort to deceive certain Reagan administration officials concerning the sale of weapons to Iran via Israel. The San Francisco Examiner reports today that Ver signed the "end-user certificates," which are required by the Pentagon and State Department before U.S. weapons can be shipped or resold to a third nation, from the fall of 1985 to February 1986, in order to hide the Iran deal from Shultz and Weinberger. (WP 12/11/86)

- Mehdi Hashemi, ex-chief of Iran's office for exporting revolution, confesses to murder and collaboration with SAVAK, the Shah's secret police. Hashemi is the brother of the son-in-law of Khomeini's designated successor, Ayatollah Hussein Ali Montazeri. His arrest along with some of his supporters last October is seen as part of a power struggle within the leadership. Hashemi is a hard-liner who opposed Speaker of the Parliament Rafsanjani's recent dealings with the U.S. (WP 12/11/86)

- Sears, Roebuck & Co. acknowledges that the subsidiary headed by Reagan's designated national security adviser, Frank Carlucci, has engaged in international arms sales since 1983. Carlucci maintains that a consulting group named International Planning and Analysis Inc., which has operated under Sears World Trade for the past three years, has not been "in the arms business." It has done "nothing other than give advice in the defense contracting area." (WP 12/11/86)

- U.S. District Judge Robert Vining writes to the U.S. Parole Commission in Dallas to recommend the immediate release of Lemuel M. Stevens III, of Marietta, Georgia, whom Vining sentenced to prison in September 1985 for conspiring to export military equipment to Iran. Vining reportedly makes the recommendation in light of reports that the current Administration has been engaged in the same activities. (MH 12/16/86)

DEC 11 - Ghorbanifar reveals that North and Secord were his American contacts in the Iran arms deal and that they told him to deposit funds totaling approximately $30-35 million in the Credit Suisse account of Lake Resources Inc. Ghorbanifar says he believes nobody in the Administration higher than McFarlane, with whom he discussed the deal, was involved. According to public registry records, Lake Resources was dissolved November 10 of this year. (ABC "Nightline" 12/11/86; MH 12/13/86)

- Special reports broadcast by Israeli television today and tomorrow disclose that in the early phases of the arms deal with Iran, Shimon Peres, who was then Prime Minister, asked a former chief of military intelligence, Shlomo Gazit, to help coordinate plans. Gazit allegedly was upset to learn that McFarlane had told Kimche "that if the arms deal were revealed, the United States would deny its involvement and throw all the responsibility onto Israel." Both Kimche and Gazit decline comment on the report. (NYT 12/13/86)

- Graham Fuller, vice chairman of the National Intelligence Council, warns at a conference in Philadelphia that "immense chaos" might result from Khomeini's death. Fuller says that pro-Soviet radicals may try to seize power and invite Moscow to intervene on their behalf. He expressed similar concerns in an internal CIA memo early in 1985 that reportedly was a catalyst for the Iran arms deal. (WP 12/21/86)

- McFarlane in a speech repeats assertions that an opening to Iranian moderates was justified. He says a Soviet invasion of Iran is "more than conceivable if you have examined Soviet exercises conducted in recent years." On December 15, a story describing a "top secret" 1980 Pentagon report on a Soviet exercise near Iran appears in the press. (NYT 12/15/86)

- North is reported to have worked with conservative activist Carl R. Channell on a multimillion-dollar public relations and congressional lobbying campaign this year on behalf of the contras. Federal law prohibits government employees from participating in partisan politics. (MH 12/11/86)

- A news report reveals connections between Richard Gadd, a retired Air Force officer, and the covert contra resupply effort. Gadd is said to specialize in chartering commercial aircraft for the Pentagon and CIA in a way that cannot be traced back to the government. Early this year he was reported to be using Southern Air Transport to carry nonlethal aid to Central America (see January 1986 entry). (NYT 12/4/86; WP 12/7/86; CBS News 12/11/86)

- The President's Special Review Board conducts the first of three interviews with Robert McFarlane. (Report of the Board 2/26/87)

DEC 12 - American mercenary Sam Nesley Hall is arrested at the Punta Huete Air Base in northern Nicaragua on suspicion of intelligence gathering. Hall claims to be a member of the "Phoenix Battalion," which he describes as a private paramilitary organization that works for the U.S. armed forces. He later claims that his mission to Nicaragua was "strictly recon, information": he was to scout out what he called Cuban assembly crews said to be building Soviet Bloc Hind-D Mi24 helicopter gunships and other military aircraft, as well as "fuel storage tanks." (WP 12/14/86 & 12/23/86; Speakes Briefing 12/15/86)

- North's aide, Marine Lt. Col. Robert L. Earl, cites the Sixth Amendment right to counsel in refusing to testify before the Senate Select Committee on Intelligence. NSC senior director for political-military affairs, Howard Teicher, also asks for more time to find private counsel and is dismissed until December 16 by committee chairman Durenberger. (WP 12/13/86)

- Bush is interviewed for 25 minutes by FBI agents concerning the Iran-contra controversy. (WSJ 1/23/87)

- The President's Special Review Board interviews former NSC Executive Secretary and Counsel Robert Kimmitt. (Report of the Board 2/26/87)

- Incoming Senate Judiciary Committee Chairman Joseph Biden (D-Del.) writes to the Justice Department's internal inspector concerning the possible improper or unethical 10-day delay in the FBI's investigation of the covert contra resupply operation. On the basis of the letter, Michael Shaheen, head of the department's Office of Professional Responsibility, opens an inquiry into the incident. According to sources, the probe may also include Meese's initial investigation into the Iran-contra affair. (WP 12/16/86)

- The Justice Department releases a statement on the FBI's suspension in October of its investigation into the private contra resupply effort. It reads in part, "Legitimate national security concerns required a brief delay in portions of inquiries involving Southern Air Transport several weeks ago . . . This brief delay did not adversely affect the conduct of these inquiries." (VV 12/30/86)

- Two Federal court officials, John Mattes and Rafael Maestri, allege that Assistant U.S. Attorney Jeffrey Feldman ordered them on March 14, 1986 to stop investigating reports of an illegal arms shipment from Florida to the contras that purportedly originated in the NSC. Mattes states that American and British gunrunners in Costa Rica had told him that an American farmer, John Hull, ran an operation in Costa Rica to resupply the contras and that Hull had bragged of a "liaison with the NSC"—Robert Owen (see January 9, 1985 entry). Mattes says that he and Maestri reported this information to the FBI on March 12. Ana Barnett of the U.S. attorney's office, upon reviewing memos of the March 14 meeting, denies that any effort was made to impede the investigation. (NYT 12/13/86)

- Patrick Buchanan says the State Department has vetoed his bid to become U.S. ambassador to the North Atlantic Treaty Organization, citing certain opposition from within NATO and the U.S. Congress. Buchanan says the "national security leadership" had backed him. (MH 12/13/86)

- The Canadian government denies any involvement in the sale of arms to Iran and orders the Royal Canadian Mounted Police to investigate reported statements by Casey that Canadian business executives were involved in financing the sales. A top American customs investigator estimates that there has been a "Canadian connection" in roughly half of the American arms and technology smuggling cases to Iran since 1981. (NYT 12/13/86)

- Two French hostages who were held in Beirut, Philippe Rochet and Georges Hansen, were released in June reportedly after a $2.2 million ransom was paid to their kidnappers, according to a French newspaper report. French officials deny the story. (NYT 12/13/86)

- An Italian parliamentary watchdog committee finds that the Italian government was not involved in the U.S. arms deals with Iran. (Rome ANSA 12/12/86)

- In a letter to Poindexter, Senator Tower, as Chairman of the President's Special Review Board, requests that Poindexter appear before the Board to answer questions "regarding the manner in which foreign and national security policies established by the President have been implemented by the NSC staff." (From the Tower Commission Report, December 12, 1987, Tower to Poindexter)

- In a letter to North, Senator Tower, as Chairman of the President's Special Review Board, requests that North appear before the Board to answer questions "regarding the manner in which foreign and national security policies established by the President have been implemented by the NSC staff." (From the Tower Commission Report, December 12, 1987, Tower to North)

DEC 13 - Retired CIA official George Cave and State Department analyst Charles Dunbar meet with an unnamed Iranian representative in Frankfurt, West Germany, according to testimony by Shultz. Dunbar's orders from Shultz are to present "set talking points" reflecting the U.S. position that no further sales of American weapons, "directly or through any third party," will take place, according to Shultz. The Iranian refers to a nine-point agenda of arms sales and steps to free seventeen Shiite terrorists held by Kuwait. A news report says later the broad outlines of the agenda have apparently been agreed to already by Poindexter. (Reports following Shultz's January 21 appearance before Congress indicate that American and Iranian representatives first raised these issues at a December 6 meeting in London.) After the encounter, Cave remains on in West Germany, reportedly for personal reasons, and is contacted by the "Iranian interlocutor." The two meet again to discuss the Iranian's response to today's meeting. (Shultz testimony 1/27/87; NYT 1/28/87)

- As recently as mid-December, State Department (Charles Dunbar) and CIA (George Cave) officials met with an Iranian representative to discuss U.S. policy toward Iran. The State Department official relayed the message that there would be no more arms to Iran unless Iran stopped supporting terrorism and agreed to negotiate an end to the war with Iraq. U.S. hostages, said the official, must be released unconditionally. The Iranians, in turn, cited a previously-agreed upon nine-point agenda which included the report of PHOENIX missiles, an approach toward Kuwait about releasing Dawa prisoners, and shipment of 1,000 TOWs to Iran. Following this unsuccessful session, the CIA officer met privately with the Iranian, without the State Department's knowledge or approval. (SSIC 1/29/87)

- At a meeting between representatives of the State Department and the second channel on December 13, 1986, the Iranian said that both sides had agreed to this nine-point agenda. The Board found no evidence that LtCol North had authority to agree to such an agenda. Of particular concern was the point that the United States had consistently given strong support to Kuwait in resisting terrorist demands for the release of the Da'Wa prisoners. (Tower)

- Swiss officials lift a freeze on transactions involving the two bank accounts controlled by North and others involved in the Iran arms operation. (CBS News 12/12/86; MH 12/13/86; WP 12/14/86)

- Faith Ryan Whittlesey, the U.S. ambassador to Switzerland, says in a statement that "[p]rior to reading news accounts of the Iran arms contra incident I had no knowledge of it." Members of the House Foreign Affairs subcommittee on international operations intend to investigate telephone calls made to Whittlesey by North, and plan to ask her at a January hearing why she allegedly withheld embassy telephone records from investigators. (MH 12/14/86)

- The offices of Horace Dunbar, a California attorney representing Albert Hakim, Richard Secord's business associate, are apparently burglarized, the only missing item a file on Hakim. Dunbar gives police several different accounts of what was stolen and what specifically the file contained. First he says that it pertained to "the sale of weapons and nuclear devices to Iran. These sales involved Albert Hakim, the Stanford Technology Corp. and an involved party in Korea." Later he says the file had nothing to do with the Iran arms deal. Still later, he tells police the file dealt with a Stanford Technology contract to install a security system in a nuclear plant in Korea. (WP 12/17/86 & 12/19/86)

- Steven Paul Carr, an American who took part in military missions with the contras in 1985, dies of an apparent overdose of cocaine. Carr, who also claimed to have accompanied a secret contra arms resupply flight from Florida to Ilopango air base in El Salvador in March 1985, was involved in federal investigations concerning American support for the contras at the time of his death. (LAT 12/21/86)

DEC 14 - Shultz meets with Reagan to discuss the points raised by an Iranian representative at a meeting the day before with two U.S. officials in West Germany. The Iranian, Shultz says later, presented a nine-point agenda dealing with arms sales and the release of Shiite terrorists from Kuwait. Secretary Shultz told the Board that he informed the President the next day. He said that the President was "stricken" and could not believe anything like this had been discussed. (Shultz testimony 1/27/87; NYT 1/28/87)

- Senate Intelligence Committee Chairman David Durenberger (R-Minn.) and House Foreign Affairs Committee Chairman Dante Fascell (D-Fla.) refuse to grant immunity to North and Poindexter in exchange for their testimony. (MH 12/15/86)

- Weinberger is reported to have authorized the transfer of TOW antitank missiles and Hawk antiaircraft components from Department of Defense stocks to the CIA four times this year, following Reagan's decision to ship arms to Iran. He was not obliged to notify Congress, Defense officials claim, because Reagan's finding obviated the notification procedure and because the burden of notification rested with recipient, the CIA. (WP 12/14/86)

DEC 15 - Bush's office releases a chronology of dealings between his aides and people working with the contras. The chronology contradicts certain statements made by the aides. For example, Donald Gregg insists early today that Felix Rodriguez did not contact him or anyone working for him about the C-123K cargo plane that crashed in Nicaragua. Twelve hours later, the chronology is released and Gregg acknowledges Rodriguez' call to his deputy, Samuel Watson, within hours of the crash. (WP 12/16/86; CBS News 12/16/86)

- Senate intelligence panel chairman Durenberger tells reporters that his committee has discovered Reagan signed "multiple findings" last December and January without Congress' knowledge. In addition, several findings have been uncovered that relate to Iran but were not signed by the President. "[I]n each case there is an instruction not to inform the Congress," Durenberger says. Portions of the committee's staff report on the Iran-contra affair, including details of some of the findings, are later leaked to the press. (See January 5, 1987 entry.) (WP 12/16/86; 1/5/87)

- Administration officials confirm a newspaper report that the U.S. has been providing Iraq with aerial reconnaissance photographs of Iranian targets since 1984. (MH 12/16/86)

- CIA Director Casey suffers arm and leg seizures and is admitted to Georgetown University Hospital where he is diagnosed as having a lymphoma, a rare form of brain cancer. He is scheduled to testify before Congress the next day. (NYT 12/16/86; LAT 12/19/86)

- State Department spokesman Redman says U.S. policy toward Iran and Iraq remains essentially unchanged. Redman declares, "We don't sell arms to either side, nor do we allow transfers by others of U.S.-sourced or licensed arms to either side" and adds that the U.S. will continue to "actively discourage shipments of arms from any source to Iran." (NYT 12/16/86)

- Swiss officials say they have received an expanded request, 12 pages in length, from the U.S. government requesting that all accounts associated with North and two others be frozen. On the basis of this request the Swiss government asked the Credit Suisse bank to block the appropriate accounts, and Credit Suisse today announces that at least two accounts have been frozen. The officials appear to have taken the action despite the fact that the request arrived in English and therefore will not become formal until translated into one of Switzerland's three official languages, later this week. (WP 12/16/86; NYT 12/16/86)

- The FBI interviews Linda Chavez, unsuccessful Republican candidate for the Senate from Maryland this year, about her call to North in August asking him to help get a pro-Chavez campaign commercial off the air. The advertisement was independently paid for by the Anti-Terrorism American Committee (ATAC), headed by Carl "Spitz" Channell. Chavez says she went through North because she was told he knew Channell and "had some influence with him." She also says in a four-page statement issued through her lawyer, "I had no knowledge at that time, nor do I have any basis now, to believe that Col. North was at all involved in any political campaigns or in the political organization which Mr. Channell operated." (AP 12/17/86; WP 12/20/86; Newsweek 12/29/86)

DEC 16 - Reagan urges the Senate intelligence committee to grant limited immunity from prosecution to North and Poindexter. (NYT 12/17/86)

- Regan testifies in closed session before the Senate intelligence committee. He says neither he nor Reagan had any prior knowledge of funds being diverted to the contras, and that the President authorized the Israeli arms shipments only after the fact. Durenberger has said beforehand: "I can't believe Don Regan would come up here if he knew anything." (MH 12/16/86; CSM 1/2/87)

- Regan testified that he never saw the Undated Memorandum until shown it by White House counsel several days before his testimony and that his reaction on seeing it was he could not believe it. Mr. Regan further testified that the President was never in his presence briefed on anything of that nature and that he is confident the President would not have approved it if he had been told by Poindexter or North. Regan testified that he had not shown the document to the President. (SSIC 1/29/87)

- Due to his hospitalization yesterday, Casey does not testify before the Senate intelligence committee as scheduled. He was expected to provide the committee with a five-page memo on the diversion of Iran arms profits to the contras. The memo, dated November 23, is the result of an internal CIA inquiry Casey ordered after his conversations with Furmark. (NYT 12/16/86)

- Reagan urges congressional committees to grant immunity to Poindexter and North to compel them to testify as soon as possible. (CSM 1/2/87)

- An 11-member Senate select committee, to be chaired by Daniel K. Inouye (D-HI), is named to investigate the Iran-contra affair. (CSM 1/2/87)

- Terry Waite issues a statement denying any involvement in U.S. dealings with Iran. Sources in Washington had claimed that Waite and North had met at least six times over a period of two years and that Waite had used U.S. aircraft and American diplomatic missions in London and the Middle East in his attempt to free hostages being held in Beirut. (Press Association (London) 12/16/86)

DEC 17 - Weinberger testifies before the Senate intelligence panel that he had no knowledge of arms shipments to Iran until early this year, and was unaware of the diversion of funds to the contras until Meese's public statement in November. He also tells the panel he has ordered an Army inspector general's report on how the pricing of the 2,008 TOW missiles the Pentagon transferred to the CIA, and which were reportedly sold to Iran at inflated prices, was determined. The report is due in early January (see January 26, 1987 entry). (WP 12/18/86)

- According to Justice Department officials, in late October Meese put off an FBI probe of Southern Air Transport's role in shipping arms to the contras, after Poindexter told him the investigation might jeopardize efforts to free the hostages in the Middle East. Meese testifies before the Senate intelligence committee panel and says afterward that he has seen nothing to contradict his earlier finding that only McFarlane, Poindexter and North knew of the secret plan to channel funds to the contras. Meese tells the committee that he discussed his November 21 inquiry with FBI director Webster, and the two of them agreed that it was not a criminal matter and it would not be appropriate to involve the FBI. (CSM 1/2/87; LAT 12/19/86, 12/12/86, 12/16/86)

- The FBI begins to investigate the delay of the bureau's Southern Air Transport probe ordered by Meese last October. (CSM 1/2/87)

- A 15-member House investigatory committee is selected to look into the private contra supply operation. Rep. Lee H. Hamilton (D-Ind.) will chair. (CSM 1/2/87)

- Larry Speakes confirms that North told NSC colleagues of an apparently fictitious plan to kidnap and hold in cages relatives of Iranian leaders, in order to trade them for American hostages in Lebanon. (WP 12/18/86)

- Eugene Hasenfus, who has already begun serving a 30-year sentence for transporting arms to Nicaragua, is pardoned by Daniel Ortega and released to visiting Senator Christopher Dodd. (WP 12/18/86)

- Furmark and Khashoggi meet to review their financial transactions in the Iran deal, one day before Furmark testifies before the House intelligence committee. (WP 12/24/86)

- Casey telephoned North shortly after the C-123K cargo plane was shot down over Nicaragua. North assured him during the call that no CIA resources were used in the unofficial contra resupply effort. Casey has denied having any advance knowledge of the diversion of funds to the covert program. (NYT 12/17/86)

DEC 18 - Justice Department officials reveal that Meese, in late October, put off an FBI probe of Southern Air Transport's role in shipping arms to the contras after Poindexter told him the investigation might jeopardize efforts to free hostages in the Middle East. Meese related this in testimony to Congress yesterday. (LAT 12/19/86, 12/12/86, 12/16/86)

- McFarlane and Regan, repeating statements they have made previously, continue to contradict each other over when Reagan authorized shipments of arms to Israel. Testifying before the Senate intelligence committee, McFarlane says Reagan orally approved the operation in a meeting in August 1985. Regan, speaking before the House intelligence panel, says the President initially opposed the plan and did not sanction it until October or November, two months after it occurred. (WSJ 12/19/86; LAT 12/19/86 & 12/21/86)

- Associates of Bush say he believes Regan should resign, but he has not broached the issue with the President. White House political director Mitchell E. Daniels, Jr. has reportedly suggested to the chief of staff in the past two weeks that he quit in order to give the President a "fresh start." Regan insists to reporters he has no intention of quitting. (WP 12/18/86; WSJ 12/19/86)

- Doctors remove a cancerous tumor from Casey's brain. (WP 12/19/86)

DEC 19 - Meese testifies before the House Select Committee on Intelligence that Reagan may have given McFarlane oral approval for the first Israeli arms shipment to Iran in August 1985 while ill or under sedation, and therefore may not have remembered making the decision. Reagan was hospitalized for polyp surgery July 12-20. This is the first time an Administration official has distanced himself from the White House claim that Reagan did not authorize the first Israeli shipment. Meese also testifies that North claimed not to know how much money was in the Swiss bank accounts being used to fund the contras, or who controlled the accounts. (LAT 12/20/86, 12/21/86)

- Meese tells reporters that North assured him Reagan was unaware of the funneling of profits to the contras. (LAT 12/20/86)

- Lawrence E. Walsh is named independent counsel with authority to investigate the Iran arms sales, the diversion of funds to "any foreign country, including, but not limited to Nicaragua," and "[t]he provision or coordination of support for persons or entities engaged as military insurgents in armed conflict with the Government of Nicaragua since 1984." Walsh's mandate is somewhat broader than that requested by Meese in his December 4 application. Meese requested that the probe concentrate on the Iran arms sales and what happened to the profits. (LAT 12/20/86)

- According to testimony received by the Committee, on December 19 Senator Dave Durenberger, Chairman of the Intelligence Committee, and Bernard McMahon, the Committee's staff director, met with the President, Peter Wallison, Don Regan, and Alton Keel, at the request of the White House to discuss matters relating to the sale of arms to Iran and possible diversion of funds to the contras. The Committee was not informed of this meeting until January 20, 1987. (SSIC 1/29/87) Durenberger briefs Reagan for approximately 20 minutes on the contents of the committee's draft report on the Iran-contra affair. (WP 1/21/87; WSJ 1/21/87)

- Intelligence sources reveal that profits from only the first arms shipment to Iran were diverted to the contras, indicating that the figure was probably well below the $30 million maximum originally estimated by Meese. (LAT 12/20/86)

- Administration sources say the contras received more than $10 million in military equipment during the last year, much of it via arms sales to Iran. The figure is a rough estimate arrived at by CIA and other intelligence agencies, according to the sources, which still leaves millions of dollars from the Iran sales unaccounted for. Contra leader Alfonso Robelo has said the contras received no more than around $7.5 million of the $30 million reportedly gained from the sales. (LAT 12/19/86)

- In a speech to the Iowa Law Enforcement Academy, Bush urges Poindexter and North to "step forward and tell us the whole truth." He says "only they know all the facts and all the details. Well, you have a right to know them, too. We all do. The country cannot wait any longer." (WP 12/20/86)

- Swiss authorities disclose that the U.S. Justice Department has requested that they freeze the accounts of a total of ten persons and two companies. In addition to North, Secord and Albert Hakim, the individuals are: Adnan Khashoggi; Roy M. Furmark; Canadian businessmen Donald Fraser and Walter (Ernest) Miller; Manuchehr Ghorbanifar; Swiss attorney Jean de Senarclens; and American attorney Willard I. Zucker. The two companies named are Audifi, a fiduciary firm, one of whose officers, Suzanne Hefti, was president of Lake Resources Inc.; and Hyde Park Square Corp. (LAT 12/20/86)

- According to testimony received by the Committee, on December 20 Senator Dave Durenberger and Bernard McMahon met (for ninety minutes) with the Vice President, Craig Fuller and a second member of his staff to discuss matters relating to the sale of arms to Iran and possible diversion of funds to the Contras. The Committee was not informed of this meeting until January 20, 1987. (SSIC 1/29/87; WP 1/21/87; WSJ 1/21/87)

- Canadian and congressional investigators are said to be inquiring into former Canadian Member of Parliament John Gamble's alleged ties to the Iran-contra deal. Gamble is chairman of the North American branch of the World Anti-Communist League (WACL). (The Los Angeles Times describes Gamble as chairman of the Canadian Freedom Foundation, an affiliate of WACL, while Canadian Television refers to him as the head of North American WACL, or NARWACL.) John Singlaub is the head of WACL and vice-chairman of its North American branch. Canadian Television reports that Gamble is also a director and treasurer of Vertex Investments, Ltd. (referred to in the Times as Vertex Financial Corp.), two of whose directors, Donald Fraser and Ernest Miller, have reportedly invested millions of dollars in the Iran arms deal through Adnan Khashoggi. Both Vertex and WACL's North American branch are located in Gamble's Toronto law offices. (LAT 12/20/86; VV 12/30/86)

DEC 21 - The Reagan Administration is reported to have sent new messages to Iran through intermediary countries including Switzerland in a continued effort to improve relations. Arms deals, according to the State Department, will not be a part of the policy. (WP 12/21/86)

- Captured American mercenary Sam Nesley Hall, interviewed on television, describes himself as one of the last remaining members of a paramilitary, counterterrorist group he calls the Phoenix Battalion. (See November 28, 1984 entry). He says he has met in the past with a "courier" of North's, Robert Owen (a consultant with the State Department's NHAO, and North's intermediary with the contras), and with retired general John Singlaub. (MH 6/8/86; CBS "60 Minutes" 12/21/86)

DEC 22 - John Bolton, assistant attorney general for congressional affairs, refuses a request by Peter W. Rodino (D-NJ), chairman of the House Judiciary Committee, that the Justice Department provide a variety of documents related to the Iran-contra controversy and that Meese respond to questions about his involvement in the affair. Rodino is "astounded" by the refusal, which is made on the basis that no staff member of the Judiciary Committee has the necessary security clearances to review the requested materials. (WP 12/24/86)

DEC 23 - Secord again refuses to testify before a closed session of the House Select Committee on Intelligence, citing the Fifth Amemdment. (NYT 12/24/86)

- Reagan and the Senate intelligence committee disagree over who should release the committee's findings on the Iran-contra affair. The issue revolves around whether congressional oversight or the President is responsible for informing the public. (NYT 12/24/86)

- It is revealed that North was hospitalized at the Bethesda Naval Medical Center for 10 days in December 1974 for emotional distress. He told Marine Corps officials in the past week that the late Gen. Richard C. Schulze removed the record of his stay from his files. Richard Allen, who hired North to the NSC in the summer of 1981, says that he was unaware of North's hospitalization and probably would not have offered him the post had he known. (NYT 12/24/86).

DEC 24 - French hostage Aurel Cornea is released in Lebanon following mediation by Iran, Syria and Algeria. French sources say the release may be connected to the arrest in

France of six Arabs thought to be fundamentalists opposed to the Syrian regime. (NYT 12/25/86)

DEC 26 - David M. Abshire, outgoing NATO ambassador, is appointed by Reagan to "coordinate White House activities in all aspects of the Iran matter," effective January 5. (WP 12/27/86)

- Tambs unexpectedly announced his retirement, effective January 1987, shortly after the Iran-contra affair became public. Tambs and other embassy officials reportedly maintained close contact with the private supply network set up by North. Udall Research was reported closely tied to other companies that held secret Swiss bank accounts funneling profits from the Iran arms sales to the covert supply operation. (NYT 12/26/86)

DEC 30 - Administration officials do not intend to block the return to Iran of over $500 million held in escrow at the Federal Reserve Bank of New York, it is reported. The money is what remains of a sum Iran deposited in 1981 to settle claims by American banks prior to the Iranian revolution. While the State Department sees "no link whatsoever" between the U.S. decision and the possible release of hostages in Lebanon, an Iranian spokesman has indicated the recovery of assets would "positively affect" the hostage situation. (WSJ 12/30/86; NYT 1/1/87)

DEC 31 - Sources close to Mitchell Daniels, Reagan's chief political adviser, say that his position at the White House has become increasingly untenable and that he plans to resign soon. In a meeting in Regan's office on December 5, Daniels told the chief of staff he agreed with Republican congressional leaders who viewed Regan as a liability, and said he believed Regan should resign. Daniels and his deputy, Haley Barbour, had also urged the President to name an independent counsel much earlier than he did. (LAT 12/31/86)

JANUARY 1987

JAN 3 - Reagan holds a "lengthy meeting" with Regan and counselor Peter J. Wallison on the Iran controversy. The subject is primarily the Senate intelligence panel's draft report. (WP 1/21/87)

JAN 5 - The outgoing 99th Congress' Senate Select Committee on Intelligence votes 7-6 not to release a 160-page staff report on the Iran-contra scandal that says Reagan was unlikely to have known of the diversion of profits from Iran arms sales to the contras. The report, entitled "The U.S.-Iran Initiative, 1984-1986: A Covert Action Case Study," includes new information on the process by which the Administration sought in late 1985 and early 1986 to provide a legal basis for covert arms shipments to Iran. The Administration had previously acknowledged that Reagan signed an intelligence finding authorizing the shipment; however, the report discloses that this was the third legal document drafted for this purpose. The first version was drafted November 25, 1985 to pacify then-Deputy CIA Director John McMahon, who had learned that North had obtained CIA assistance (without proper reports to Congress) in acquiring an airplane to deliver arms to Iran earlier that month. The second, January 6, 1986, version referred to the Israeli role as an intermediary in the arms transfers to Iran. After it was signed, the White House apparently became distressed with the Israeli middlemen in the deal because of the discovery that they had shipped the Iranians malfunctioning parts for HAWK antiaircraft missiles. As a result, a third intelligence finding was drafted omitting any reference to Israel. It was signed by Reagan on January 17, 1986. (WP 1/6/87)

- According to a draft set of conclusions to the Senate intelligence committee's report that was deleted by the full panel, the White House and CIA violated the Intelligence Oversight Act of 1980 by not fully informing the House and

Senate Select Committees "in a timely fashion" of foreign intelligence operations, and did not comply with Executive Order 12333 of December 4, 1981 governing intelligence operations, by not formally designating the NSC as the responsible agency for the Iran operation. The Iran program was not based on sufficient prior intelligence assessments, especially with regard to Israel's motivations in the arms sales and the reliability of Manuchehr Ghorbanifar and the program was not adequately monitored, as in the case of CIA officials waiting more than a year to investigate the possible flow of money from the arms sales into non-American Swiss bank accounts, according to the report. (Draft conclusions, 1/5/87)

- Lawyers for Samuel Evans, one of 18 defendants accused of conspiring to ship $2 billion worth of military equipment to Iran and Khashoggi's former general counsel, assert in a court filing that Casey told Furmark in January 1985 that the U.S. had "supplied and permitted the supply of arms to Iran." (NYT 1/6/87)

- The State Department advises the sultan of Brunei to ask for a refund of the $10 million he gave to the contras because "we don't know whether the contras ever saw a dime," says one State Department official. Some of the $10 million may have gone to reimburse Adnan Khashoggi for money he and others advanced to finance the Administration's secret arms sales to Iran. (LAT 1/7/86)

- Larry Speakes says news reports have "grossly misrepresented" possible shredding of documents by North before he was fired on November 25. Speakes says, "If there was shredding, it was very limited, and we have not uncovered any missing documents," adding that only a small amount of destroyed material was found in a machine in North's office after he left. Later the Tower Commission reveals an attempt to destroy massive amounts of computer messages. (WP 1/7/87)

JAN 7 - Regan did not recall the [January 6 meeting at which Regan signed the draft finding]. Mr. Regan told the Board that the draft finding may have been signed in error. He wondered if Poindexter had not simply placed the document in the President's daily briefing book for signature during the morning intelligence briefing. (Regan 20, 41-42) (Tower)

JAN 9 - A Navy official meets with a young Iranian engineer—an emissary from Rafsanjani—to discuss the purchase by the U.S. of at least five diagnostic F-14 "test benches" (see summer 1985). Despite earlier failures to complete the deal because of Iranian demands for weapons, Iran set up the meeting last November after the arms scandal broke. (Anderson and Van Atta in WP 3/15/87)

JAN 14 - Medical experts are quoted as saying Casey's brain tumor may have affected his testimony before Congress on November 21 and December 10 last year. (WP 1/14/87)

JAN 15 - Nestor Sanchez, deputy assistant secretary of defense for inter-American affairs, will leave office on January 31. Administration and congressional sources say he is being investigated in connection with the Iran-contra controversy. Officials say also that he played a role in developing a cover story following the October 5 crash of a C-123K cargo plane in Nicaragua, saying the aircraft was on a private mission that had nothing to do with official government activities. (NYT 1/15/87)

- Some congressmen are now reported to believe that legislation restricting aid to the contras last year was written so loosely that it created a number of loopholes for the Reagan Administration to exploit, although they insist the laws' intent should have been clear to the Administration. According to Senator Durenberger, "In retrospect, when we shut down the United States involvement in the contra thing, we should have nailed it down." He adds, "I'm sorry about not dotting the i's or crossing the t's, but at some point you trust the Administration to get the message. We said no lethal aid, and we meant it." (NYT 1/15/87)

JAN 16 - McFarlane testifies before the Senate Foreign Relations Committee that Shultz and Weinberger were informed in the summer of 1985 of Reagan's approval of Israeli sales of arms to Iran. Shultz and Weinberger both maintain that they were unaware that the President had authorized the shipments until January 1986. (WP 1/17/87)

JAN 17 - It is reported that the CIA has recently recalled its station chief in Costa Rica for allegedly overstepping his authority in providing aid to the unofficial contra resupply network. The station chief, who is known by the pseudonym Tomas Castillo, reportedly relayed messages between contra groups in Costa Rica and the private air force operated by Richard Secord, and is said by one source to have passed messages on the operation directly to North as well. The CIA has consistently denied any role in the airlift, but news reports indicate that Congress is probing the possible encouragement of the station chief by high Agency officials. (WP 1/17/87)

MID-JAN - Tomas Castillo (see previous entry) testifies before the Tower Commission that he had authorization for the contra resupply missions from the CIA's covert operations chief Clair George and the head of the Agency's Central America Task Force, Alan Fiers. (See, however, February 17 entry.) (MH 3/1/87)

JAN 21 - Shultz testifies before the House Foreign Affairs Committee on the Iran arms deals. He reveals information about meetings between American representatives and Iranians in Europe (see December 6 & 13 entries), the first of which took place the same day the President declared that such contacts had been "broken off." He also testifies that he went to Reagan himself to demand a halt to arms shipments to Tehran after he learned the CIA was ignoring an order to stop. Shultz told the committee the Agency continued to conduct an arms-for-hostages effort after Reagan's November 19 public announcement of an end to U.S. arms sales to Iran. (Reuters 1/22/87; NYT 1/23/87)

JAN 22 - By memorandum to the CIA General Counsel of January 22, 1987, the CIA Inspector General's office questioned Jameson's interpretation that "contacts with the benefactors [of the contras], although contrary to policy, were not contrary to law." Flight vectors, Sandinista anti-aircraft positions, and other similar information needed to carry out safe aerial deliveries fell within the terms of the "advice" authorized in December, 1983 by the Intelligence Authorization Act. The Inspector General maintained, among other things, that the field officer's activities could be characterized as planning for a paramilitary operation, expressly barred in the joint Explanatory Statement accompanying the Conference Committee Report to H.R. 2419. (Tower)

- Arthur L. Liman, a New York City criminal lawyer, is appointed chief counsel of the special Senate committee probing the Iran-contra connection. (NYT 1/23/87)

JAN 23 - Administration sources reveal that North dealt regularly with a number of high Administration officials in connection with the contra aid program and efforts to free hostages in Lebanon. North began discussing the private aid network with Meese shortly after Reagan approved its establishment in the fall of 1984, according to the sources. Meese later acknowledges meeting or speaking on the telephone with North at least twelve times over the past two years, but does not recall ever discussing the contras. However, some officials say that North told them of meetings attended by the Attorney General at which contra-related issues were raised. North also kept Bush and his aide, Donald Gregg, apprised of certain aspects of the aid program, according to officials, and worked closely with Elliott Abrams of the State Department. Moreover, he was in contact with high CIA officials, the sources said, including Clair George, the Director of Operations, with whom he often spoke twice a day. Agency officials who asked were told by superiors that North was acting under the authority of Casey and Poindexter. According to one official, "It was clear that Ollie had someone's hand on his shoulder. He was never perceived as an unauthorized loner." (WSJ 1/23/87; 1/26/87)

JAN 24 - The Army admits it undercharged the CIA $2.5 million for 2,008 TOW antitank missiles and HAWK missile parts sent to Iran last year. According to the Army inspector general's report, ordered by Weinberger (see December 17, 1986 entry), $11.7 million was listed as the price for the weapons and parts, rather than $14.2 million. The discrepancy was "an honest mistake," according to the report, arising from the fact that two categories of TOW missiles were included in the delivery. The Army charged the price of the less expensive missiles for the entire batch, then failed to add on the standard packing and handling fees. As a consequence, the Administration did not have to report the sale to Congress because it fell below the $14 million cut-off for notification. (Reuters 1/24/87; WSJ 1/26/87)

JAN 26 - Reagan meets for 76 minutes with members of the Tower Commission. This is the first discussion of the controversy the President has held with any group other than his staff. Reagan takes with him a copy of testimony by McFarlane and tells the panel that the former national security adviser had accurately characterized his Iran policy. In other words, he acknowledged authorizing arms shipments to Iran in August 1985. (WSJ 1/27/87; WP 2/19/87)

- The President told the Board on January 26, 1987, that he did not know that the NSC staff was engaged in helping the Contras. The Board is aware of no evidence to suggest that the President was aware of LtCol North's activities.

At his meeting with the Board on January 26, 1987, the President said he approved a convoluted plan whereby Israel would free 20 Hizballah prisoners, Israel would sell TOW missiles to Iran, the five U.S. citizens in Beirut would be freed, and the kidnappings would stop. A draft Covert Action Finding had already been signed by the President the day before the meeting on January 6, 1986. . . . The President did not recall signing the January 6 draft.

The President told the Board that he had several times asked for assurances that shipments to Iran would not alter the military balance with Iraq. He did not indicate when this occurred but stated that he received such assurances. The President also said he was warned by Secretary Shultz that the arms sales would undercut U.S. efforts to discourage arms sales by its allies to Iran. (Tower)

- [Reagan] told the Board on January 26, 1987, that the Finding was presented to him under cover of a memorandum from Poindexter of the same date. The President said he was briefed on the contents of the memorandum but stated that he did not read it. This is reflected in Poindexter's handwritten note on the memorandum. That note also indicates that the Vice President, Regan, and Fortier were present for the briefing. (Tower)

- After the session, Chief of Staff Regan spends considerable time with the President, after which Reagan decides to return to talk to the panel. In the second round, he openly acknowledges discussing with Regan the issue of when he approved the arms sales and says that in fact he did not give advance approval for the shipments. (WSJ 1/27/87; WP 2/19/87)

JAN 27 - In his State of the Union address, Reagan acknowledges that "serious mistakes were made" in the program of selling arms to Iran, but does not disavow the policy itself. He also stands firmly behind the policy of aid to the contras. (WP 1/28/87)

- Swiss officials disclose that at least eight parties have appealed Switzerland's decision to waive bank secrecy rules in order to assist the U.S. Justice Department's investigation of the Iran-contra affair. Six of the parties are individuals named by the Justice Department in its request for help, the officials say, while two are companies not named by the U.S. The officials would not reveal the identities of any parties. The appeals are expected to take months to resolve and cause lengthy delays in the investigation. (NYT 1/28/87)

JAN 28 - Iranian Speaker of Parliament Rafsanjani holds a press conference at which he displays a Bible signed by Reagan and a false Irish passport he says McFarlane used to travel to Tehran last year. The Bible was presented to Iranian officials at an October 3, 1986 meeting in Hamburg, West Germany attended by North, retired CIA official George Cave, and others, including possibly Rafsanjani's son. The passport bears McFarlane's picture but uses the name Sean Devlin. (WP 1/29/87)

JAN 29 - The Senate Select Committee on Intelligence releases its Report on Preliminary Inquiry into the Iran-contra affair. (Sens. Boren and Cohen press conference transcript 1/29/87)

JAN 30 - Moslem militia officials report that Terry Waite has been taken hostage. The Anglican church envoy has been in Beirut since January 12 to negotiate the release of American hostages. (WP 1/31/87)

FEBRUARY 1987

FEB 1 - It is revealed that Tomas Castillo, the CIA's former station chief in Costa Rica, facilitated the flow of weapons to the contras by sending secret messages to Oliver North and to private Americans involved in the contra aid network. Castillo reportedly used encoding devices obtained by North from the National Security Agency to pass along seven messages to the aid network after he received authorization from the CIA Central American task force chief on Nicaragua, Alan Fiers, and from Clair George, the CIA's deputy director for clandestine operations. George reportedly was in close contact with North, often speaking with him once or twice a day. Two internal CIA investigations of Castillo's conduct initially concluded that he had broken no laws in sending the messages. However, after investigators found documents belonging to North which indicated that Castillo was more deeply involved in private contra aid efforts than he had previously disclosed, CIA officials suspended Castillo and forced him to accept early retirement. (WP 2/2/87)

FEB 2 - Casey resigns as Director of Central Intelligence. Reagan asks him to become counselor to the President. (Fitzwater briefing 2/2/87)

FEB 3 - Daniel Inouye, chairman of the Senate investigating panel, says the State Department is finalizing a procedure for submitting written questions to Israeli officials. (MH 2/4/87)

- A Miami federal grand jury investigating private aid to the contras subpoenas Tom Posey, an associate of Sam Nesley Hall and Alabama grocer who heads the paramilitary Civilian Military Assistance (CMA). (MH 2/5/87)

FEB 4 - John Tower, in a letter to President Reagan, requests on behalf of the Special Review Board that, as Commander-in-Chief, he order Poindexter and North to appear before the Board and to cooperate with its inquiry. (Letter from Tower to Reagan, 2/4/87, From the Tower Commission Report)

FEB 5 - In a memorandum from H. Lawrence Garrett III, Office of the General Counsel of the Department of Defense, to Peter Wallison, counsel to the President, referring to the Tower request regarding former NSC personnel, Garrett recommends that the President may not lawfully order Poindexter and North to answer the Commission's questions, according to their constitutional rights. (From Tower Commission Report, February 5, 1987, memorandum from Garrett to Wallison)

FEB 6 - Gerald Seib, the journalist detained in Iran for reasons that remain unclear, is released and expelled from the country. (WP 2/7/87)

- A February 6, 1987 letter from Peter J. Wallison, Counsel to the President, to Senator Tower, states that the President, while desiring that Poindexter and North "cooperate fully with all on-going inquiries," recognizes their constitutional right not to testify. Wallison points out that under Article 31 of the Uniform Code of Military Justice and according to their constitutional rights, they cannot be ordered by the President to appear and cooperate before the Board. (Tower)

FEB 9 - McFarlane takes an overdose of 20-30 Valium pills. Police officials, calling it a suicide attempt, say he wrote a note relating to the incident. Friends attribute his action to failing to live up to his own standards rather than fear of pending investigations. McFarlane was to testify before the Tower Commission the next day. He says later he tried to kill himself because he felt that he "failed the country." (NYT 3/2/87, 2/10/87 & 2/12/87; MH 2/10/87)

FEB 10 - After Reagan and White House Counsel Peter Wallison review the President's handwritten notes, a White House courier delivers typed excerpts to the Special Review Board, then stands by to take back the material. The panel is not allowed keep the notes or make copies. (NYT 2/12/87)

FEB 11 - The Administration, acknowledging the unlikelihood of a sympathetic Congress, announces it will postpone its formal request for $105 million in aid to the contras until around September. The Administration is expected to get the $40 million final installment of the $100 million Congress voted last year. (NYT 2/12/87)

- Reagan spends 70 minutes with the Special Review Board discussing, according to spokesman Fitzwater, "the National Security Council process and the development and execution of the Iran policy and the president's role." On this occasion, Reagan reportedly changes his earlier statement to the panel that he approved the sale of arms to Iran in August 1985. After lengthy discussions with his chief of staff following the January 26 interview, the President now tells the board that in fact he did not authorize the sale in advance. The President reportedly acknowledges openly the fact that he and Regan talked at length about the issue following the first interview with the panel. (NYT 2/12/87; WP 2/19/87)

- The President did not amplify those remarks [concerning the effects of furnishing arms to Iran (see January 26, 1987 entry)] in his meeting with the Board on February 11. He did add, however, that no one ever discussed with him the provision of intelligence to Iran. (Tower)

FEB 12 - A former fundraiser for The National Endowment for the Preservation of Liberty, Jane McLaughlin, says that President Reagan has hosted briefings for people who made donations of $30,000 to the contras. These meetings were arranged by her former employer, "Spitz" Channell, she says. Channell raised $5 million for the contras after Congress cut off government aid, according to McLaughlin. Internal records and former employees say that Texas resident Ellen Garwood gave $2.5 million to the contras through Channell, and that $2 million of that sum went to military assistance. (ABC News 2/12/87; AFP 2/13/87)

- The contras deploy 30 surface-to-air missiles inside Nicaragua. The missiles were bought with part of the $60 million in U.S. aid that was given to them this year. (AFP 2/13/87)

- At a press breakfast in Washington, Chairman of the Joint Chiefs Adm. William Crowe warns the contras that if they do not overcome unity problems and improve their performance on the battlefield, they will lose American support. Meanwhile, speaking to the American Bar Association in New Orleans, Shultz pleads for continued aid to the rebels, stating that if it is not forthcoming, U.S. military intervention in the region may become inevitable. (NYT 2/13/87)

- Bush, seeking to avoid further damage from the Iran arms affair, declares in a speech to Republicans in Michigan that he expressed "certain reservations" about the deals as they were developing. However, he does not identify what his concerns were, indicate when they arose, or reveal whether he discussed them with Reagan. (NYT 2/13/87)

- Tom Parlow, a Danish businessman who cooperated with North, Secord and Hakim in a number of deals involving the freighter Erria and the Iran-contra affair, wins a Danish court order seizing the ship. Parlow claims that Hakim owes his company, Queen Shipping, more than $200,000 in expenses incurred during the eight months the ship was used in clandestine operations ordered by North. Dolmy Business Inc., a Panamanian front company, is legal owner of the ship, which was bought by Compagnie de Services Fiduciaires (CSF) through Hakim and CSF's attorney, Willard Zucker last April. (LAT 2/13/87)

MID-FEB - The Sandinista army claims to recover almost 4 tons of mortars, grenades, TNT, jungle boots, AK-47 rifle ammunition and Yugoslavian-made rockets from a parachute drop intended for the contras, the first such interception since the Hasenfus crash Oct. 5. The flight was CIA-directed and originated in El Salvador or Honduras, Sandinista army officials say. Western diplomats estimate that there have been about six successful drops to the contras so far this year. The U.S. stopped supervising flights after Hasenfus' capture but resumed around the end of January as the first $60 million of the $100 million in contra funding approved by Congress late last year was disbursed. (LAT 2/23/87)

FEB 16 - Adolfo Calero resigns under pressure from the UNO leadership in the midst of a power struggle with Arturo Cruz. The leadership's evident lack of unity leaves the organization in an especially difficult position in terms of winning congressional support this year. Calero nominates former editor of La Prensa, Pedro Joaquin Chamorro, to succeed him. (WP 2/17/87)

FEB 17 - Robert Gates, the Administration's nominee to take over as director of the CIA, appears for confirmation hearings before the Senate Select Committee on Intelligence. He tells the panel he did not inform Congress of the possible diversion of funds to aid the contras because, while the evidence he had was "worrisome" it was also "extraordinarily flimsy." Gates says that, knowing what he does now, he "probably would have" opposed Reagan's decision to provide arms to Iran. His testimony draws criticism from committee members who repeatedly question his performance during the Iran affair. He is asked specifically why he did not request a briefing on the matter when he was promoted to Deputy Director last April; and, why he and Casey did not press North on October 9 when North mentioned in passing the existence of Swiss bank accounts and the funneling of money to the rebels. Gates says Tomas Castillo, the former CIA station chief in Costa Rica, was a renegade who acted on his own (see January 17 entry). (MH 3/1/87; WP 2/18/87)

FEB 18 - Robert Gates ends the second day of his confirmation hearings before the Senate intelligence panel. Asking to be judged on the basis of his performance as acting director rather than on the basis of his record during the Iran-contra affair, Gates continues to draw fire from some quarters, particularly with regard to the question of whether a presidential Finding was necessary in the case of the November 1985 arms delivery to Iran (the CIA general counsel told him it was not), and the issue of why he and Casey did not pursue North's references to Swiss bank accounts and funds to the contras during their October 9, 1986 discussions. (WP 2/19/87)

- The Senate Foreign Relations Committee is reported to be investigating allegations that the contras and their American supporters helped smuggle drugs into the U.S., but Drug Enforcement Administration officials say that DEA agents have found no proof of the dozens of allegations. The committee's special counsel, Jack Blum, says the first hearings will concern the Bahamas and allegations of payoffs to government officials there. Also included in the committee's investigation are: 1) allegations by convicted smugglers in Miami that they took guns down to the contras and brought cocaine back; 2) the connection between former contra leader Eden Pastora and drug pilot Gerardo Duran, who donated a C-47 plane to the contras; 3) a FBI informant's claims to have witnessed Southern Air Transport planes loading cocaine in Barranquilla, Colombia, in 1983 and 1985; 4) allegations that members of the El Salvador-based contra resupply operation brought drugs back into the U.S.; 5) allegations of drug smuggling through the Costa Rican farm of John Hull, a defendant in the Tony Avirgan/Martha Honey lawsuit against the contras; 6) allegations that contra military commander Enrique Bermudez narrowly escaped a drug sting arrest in Honduras; and 7) the Nicaraguan drug smuggler arrested in San Francisco in 1984 who claimed to be working for the FDN, the largest contra group, which denied the claim. (LAT 2/18/87)

Office of the Attorney General
Washington, D.C. 20530

18 February 1987

The Honorable John Tower
President's Special Review Board
New Executive Office Building, Room 5221
Washington, D.C. 20506

Dear Senator Tower:

In my appearance before the President's Special Review Board I was asked whether a finding under the Hughes-Ryan Amendment would have been necessary if it were found that the Central Intelligence Agency rendered certain kinds of assistance to a covert arms transfer to Iran prior to the President's authorizing such a transfer. The purpose of this letter is to respond to the Board's request for a considered, written answer to this question.

The Board's question assumed that the CIA, without prior presidential authorization, assisted in the November 1985 arms shipment to Iran by attempting to obtain flight clearances at a foreign airport and by arranging for a proprietary airline to carry the arms from Israel to Iran. The question further assumed that the objective of the transfer was to influence the policy and actions of a foreign government while not publicly disclosing the American role in exerting that influence. Under these assumed facts, I believe that a finding under the Hughes-Ryan Amendment would be required.

The so-called Hughes-Ryan Amendment, section 662 of the Foreign Assistance Act, (codified as amended at 22 U.S.C. 2422), provides in its present form:

> No funds appropriated under the authority of this chapter or any other Act may be expended by or on behalf of the Central Intelligence Agency for operations in foreign countries, other than activities intended solely for obtaining necessary intelligence, unless and until the President finds that each such operation is important to the national security of the United States. Each such operation shall be considered a significant anticipated intelligence activity for the purpose of section 413 of title 50 [i.e. section 501 of the National Security Act].

The arms transfer you describe would constitute an "operation in a foreign country," the kind of situation at which the Hughes-Ryan Amendment was apparently aimed. Assuming the accuracy of the facts outlined above, and assuming further that intelligence gathering was not the sole objective of the operation, I believe that such CIA assistance in transferring the arms would require a prior finding by the President that the operation was "important to the national security of the United States."

I am aware of statements that CIA personnel did not fully understand or did not have full information concerning the nature of the operation at the time the agency was asked for its assistance. If the operation was described to CIA personnel in terms that made Hughes-Ryan seem inapplicable, that would have a bearing on whether the CIA could be held responsible for the lack of a presidential finding. Moreover, nothing in this letter should be read as implying that a Hughes-Ryan finding would be required for every single foreign operation that is not strictly intended solely for obtaining necessary intelligence. Nor do I intend to imply that every form of CIA assistance to another agency, no matter how peripheral or indirect, would require a Hughes-Ryan finding merely because the other agency was engaged in a covert operation.

Please let me know if I can be of further assistance.

Sincerely yours,

Edwin Meese III

EDWIN MEESE III
Attorney General

- A lawsuit has been filed by fifty-one plaintiffs against the conservative Western Goals Foundation charging that the data base it maintains on terrorism and subversion contains material that was obtained in violation of certain individuals' right to privacy. One of the principal officers of Western Goals is Carl "Spitz" Channell, who acknowledges he worked closely with North on fundraising and political campaigns in support of Administration policy in Central America. (CSM 2/18/87)

- Nancy Reagan is reportedly no longer talking to chief of staff Regan, who, it is said, may leave voluntarily within the next few weeks. The First Lady has apparently been seeking Regan's replacement since December on the grounds that his managerial practices and style are poorly serving the President. (WP 2/18/87)

- In a February 18, 1987 letter to Senator Tower, Attorney General Meese responds to the Board's question of "whether a finding under the Hughes-Ryan Amendment would have been necessary if it were found that the CIA rendered certain kinds of assistance to a covert arms transfer to Iran prior to the President's authorizing such a transfer." Meese states that a finding would be required. (Tower).

FEB 19 - In an interview with members of the Special Review Board in his hospital room, McFarlane acknowledges writing a memorandum on November 18, 1986 at Poindexter's request describing a way in which Reagan could plausibly deny authorizing the August 1985 Israeli arms shipment in advance. McFarlane knew, however, that Reagan had given his private approval of the project before it occurred, according to sources. (NYT 2/20/87)

FEB 20 - Fitzwater responds to reports in today's press of a coverup of Reagan's approval of Israeli arms shipments in August 1985. "As far as the President is concerned," Fitzwater says, "there is no coverup. He certainly was not aware of any." On the question of whether White House officials devised a plan for a joint U.S.-Egyptian invasion of Libya, as reported today, Fitzwater replies, "There was no policy or plan to do that that was put in motion." (NYT 2/21/87)

FEB 21 - The Board reviewed the different histories offered by Mr. McFarlane in three PROF notes on the 7th, 18th, and 21st of November and in his several testimonies on the Hill and before the Board. His various positions on the question of Presidential authorization in August and September, 1985 have made this question very difficult to resolve. This issue was discussed extensively in Mr. McFarlane's final interview with the Board. What follows are excerpts from that discussion.

(McFarlane tells the account which appears as the November 3 entry above.)

"It seemed to me, first of all, just thinking about why would I write the memo, well, I was inspired to write the memo because I was being told that a version was coming from the White House to the effect that I had taken this on basically and it wasn't until after the fact that the President had approved this.

"I had nothing from the White House on this, but I was receiving word from people indirectly, journalists, that were saying this is what we are being briefed by the White House and I just want you to learn about it.

"I could fully accept that as a policy advisor to the President and out of loyalty to him I wanted to take full responsibility for all of my own actions, to assure that the President was placed in the best position possible. But one must not avoid the truth. Consequently, I was upset to hear that possibly—this was through hearsay—that possibly the White House might be taking a position which was fundamentally untrue."

" . . . [T]he briefings that were being given to magazines referred to here were originally by Mr. Regan, and five days or four days prior, when Admiral Poindexter had called me, he said that he had been asked, through Mr. Regan, to prepare an account, but already an account was being put out, or so I was told.

"At any rate, my point is in saying that there would have been no reason to write a memo on my part, the point of writing a memo at all is to alter what I was hearing was the White House version, and that was that the President had not approved the Iranian arms sale or provided authority for it by us or anyone else until after it took place. And that's false.

"So I sat down and I wrote down the memo. But again having returned from out of town and still not looking at records or calendars, because I was relying upon recollections, I put together a series of events from primarily July spread out until a decision by the President in early September, which in truth occurred in a shorter span of time, a span of time from about early July until the first ten days of August.

"On November 7 I could not have documented it for you, and it wasn't until about three weeks later—actually until I got my record of schedule out of storage. Another point I would make, however, about this cross-note that I'm talking about is that there's no question here in that cross-note about prior approval prior to Mr. Weir's release.

"I said it then. I've said it since, and it is true today: The decision process had three milestones on it—early July, political without any arms of any kind; mid-July, the Israelis saying political dialogue, but if the United States will sell arms and we responded no; and then early August, in which the Israelis said, well, if we do, and my meeting with Mr. Kimche resulted in our discussion on the pros and cons and so forth, and my going to the President and once more his discussion of it with his advisors, and the decision, yes, that we will replace the sale replacements for any Israeli arms that they may ship."

"I have felt since last November—and that is where we started—that it has been, I think, misleading, at least, and wrong, at worst, for me to overly gild the President's motives for his decision in this, to portray them as mostly directed toward political outcomes.

"The President acknowledged those and recognized that those were clearly important. However, by the tenor of his questioning, which was oriented toward the hostages and timing of the hostages, from his recurrent virtually daily questioning just about welfare and do we have anything new and so forth, it is very clear that his concerns here were for the return of the hostages."

"I think it is accurate and useful to point out that the motives behind Admiral Poindexter's actions right after the release of the story on November 3 were inspired by concern for hoped-for still getting out more hostages and that was, I think, rather too ambitiously pursued even by the President, who went to the point of denying that anything at all had occurred. And I take it that attitude persisted even into the third week of November, although becoming ever more frail.

"It seems to me that by the time the President had made his speech on this, which had not had the intended effect of explaining satisfactorily what had happened that his wish to say something more and at the same time minimize his own role grew to the point that on November 18, by the time that group convened, a principal objective, probably the primary objective, was to describe a sequence of events that would distance the President from the initial approval of the Iran arms sale, distance him from it to blur his association with it.

"The November 18 chronology, which I indeed helped prepare, was not a full and completely accurate account of those events, but rather this effort to blur and leave ambiguous the President's role. The language was intended, I would say, to convey the impression that the United States had not expressly authorized the sale of arms either directly from the United States or by the Israelis on behalf of the United States, but, second, to preserve the ability to say that if Israel were to make such sales that they could expect to purchase replacement items from the United States." (McFarlane Testimony) (Tower)

Mr. McFarlane prepared a portion of the chronology on November 18. He sent his edit to VADM Poindexter at 23:06:20 on the 18th. (The text appears at the November 18 entry above)

Returning to Mr. McFarlane's testimony:

"I think that is an accurate reflection of how that is cast. Now it was done as a briefing memo to be used by people who would brief the President prior to the next day's press conference, and in my judgment expected to go through a number of iterations before it reached that point. But that is my opinion of the climate in which that session occurred and the intent of its outcome."

"I think it was . . . the 18th . . . I believe it was actually North saying the Admiral had directed that he call me and ask my help in coming over that evening to scrub and finish a chronology that would be used in helping out in the pre-brief of the President for the press conference. . . . It was kind of a feverish climate in which four or five officers— Colonel North, Mr. Teicher, Mr. Coy, Colonel Earle, a couple of secretaries, ... (and Al Keel) periodically, but not originally (were doing) cut and paste—some original, some typed, some handwritten documents, ones that had been prepared, I believe, in Mr. Buchanan's office to be used the next day. And separately a draft chronology, the so-called master of which had been done by the CIA, or so I was told by Colonel North.

"I started by looking at the opening statement and be-that it did not fully treat the political purpose at issue here of the longer-term relationship with Iran and other points that were less important. But I sat down and drafted a three-section note that went out in three separate messages by PROFs to Admiral Poindexter. He reacted to the first two by telephone after he got them, probably by 10:00 by this time, at night. Other people had been working on the chronology for the same two hours, while I'd been working on the opening statement. And at that point I finished and 10:30 or so turned my attention to the chronology and was given the master, which was a CIA product, and I think fairly it was understandably wrong because the officer asked to prepare it had not been involved in many of the events.

"But you could see several errors in it, and I pointed out perhaps a half dozen and got through it to about the middle of it, to where it treated the President's involvement in the original decision. The treatment that was there was ambiguous in a number of respects, but it said, for example, that he had acquiesced in the sale, as I recall, and it left out issues of timing.

"And I sat down and, after looking through a separate stack of several pieces of paper, was given one that had two paragraphs on it on this issue. The first part of it treated the basic matter of the approval itself, and the second paragraph dealt with his reaction once he had learned about it in an ex post context.

"And in looking at the first part of it it was not technically wrong. As I recall, it had words to the effect that the President did not approve, did not formally approve the September 2 shipment and then it went on in the second paragraph to say upon learning about it after Mr. Weir's release was upset and directed someone to have me—it didn't say—directed that Mr. McFarlane so advise the government of Israel.

"Well, in looking at those, those were expressive to me, first of all, of a climate in which there was an obvious effort to, as I said, distance and to blur the President's role in the initial authorization, in both timing and substance."

General Scowcroft: Did you raise that point with anybody here? I mean, this is the first time you've seen this maneuvering.

Mr. McFarlane: "Well, I did, and it was a little—it was very curious because in truth none of those officers there were involved at that point in time, and so they weren't in a position to say. They could have written this. No one owned up to it. Mr. Teicher said and has said since that he did not. Colonel North asked me. I said, well where does this come from? They said well, I don't know, but it's something I can't personally throw any light on.

"And innocent shrugs from Mr. Coy and Colonel Earle. There was no one in the room that had written it."

Mr. Dawson: But these two conversations that you had with Admiral Poindexter, did they concern the President's involvement and his authorization?. . . .

"I recall having talked to Admiral Poindexter that evening when I sent him the first two sections on the opening statement, and then later on when he came back on the third one and said yes, it is good too. Now I do remember very clearly talking to him after I had finished all work that evening, and it is only unclear in my mind whether it was that night or the following day.

"But I wrapped up what I had done for him and I said: 'John, there are at least a half dozen or more serious problems with this chronology. I have noted them. Colonel North believes that he can straighten out the ones that I have pointed out to him. And the portrayal of the President's role in this is directed toward, apparently, putting some distance and ambiguity around the timing and the substance of his approval—that is, was it before or after.'

"Now it isn't technically wrong the way somebody has written it down here, but we know that the President approved this before the Israelis did it. And I tend to think that that was exchanged with him in a stand-up conversation the next day—that is, the day of the press conference, Wednesday. And he acknowledged what I had said, and he said, yes, we are working on it still. Or we will continue to work on it after you have finished and thanks for your help.

"I say that because just the memory of saying that I had pointed out the several mistakes is pretty vivid in my mind as a stand-up exchange between myself and him and Mr. Keel present as a witness, and his acknowledging, okay, we will get this straightened out.

"But I said, and I had participated the night before in preparing it, I said: You know, it is technically not inaccurate to say that the President didn't formally approve the September 2 shipment discretely. But, of course, he approved it as an authority for it to be done. And, secondly, the part that I accepted and sent you in my note about his being upset about it, I can imagine maybe he was and so I can't disprove it, but he didn't say that to me."

"I remember speaking to him that night at least once, and perhaps twice, again after that session before the press conference, to make it emphatic that it was not an accurate chronology."

Mr. Garment: "Rhett, do you intend to get into the business of the meeting with the Attorney General and that sequence of events? If not, I think it would be helpful for him to continue with that in the same vein."

Mr. Dawson: "I think that's a good idea."

Mr. Garment: "Discussing matters which he has now had an opportunity to refresh his recollection with documents on."

(McFarlane's account appears at the November 21 entry.)

Regarding the President's Approval in August 1985, McFarlane testified:

Chairman Tower: "Now, did you communicate the President's approval and inform anybody on your staff about it? Did you tell Poindexter? Who did you tell? Who did you contact to tell them the President had approved this on our side?"

Mr. McFarlane: "Admiral Poindexter is the short answer. In my recurring memory of how it took place—and I've asked my wife to try to recall this image—is that it occurred at home, and he called me from Camp David and that I then called Mr. Kimche and not until the next day, however, did I tell Admiral Poindexter."

"There ought to be a record, although not on my record because I was at home, probably in the Camp David operators that a call took place."

General Scowcroft: "Did you tell Mike Ledeen about the approval? Did you tell him to convey it?"

Mr. McFarlane: "I don't have any mental image of a meeting, but I expect that I did convey it to him, not for him to further carry it out but to inform him that that was the decision. [I've called that.] He came out to make a speech in Los Angeles at a moment when the Presidential party was there . . . And, if not before, surely then I would have told him about it."

Chairman Tower: "Understanding that this was on a pretty closely held basis, was there anybody beside Poindexter that you would have told that the President communicated to you his approval?"

Mr. McFarlane: "Not on the NSC staff, no, sir."

Chairman Tower: "And you did not inform the other NSC principals?"

Mr. McFarlane: "Within a day or so I did."

Chairman Tower: "Which ones?"

Mr. McFarlane: "It would have been the Secretary of State, Defense, Mr. Regan and the Vice President."

Chairman Tower: "That the President had given you the go-ahead on this?"

Mr. McFarlane: "That is correct."

Mr. McFadden: "How about Mr. Casey?"

Mr. McFarlane: "And Mr. Casey, yes."

Chairman Tower: "Bud, were you aware if there was ever a contingency plan to deal with this issue, a planned public diplomacy campaign of any kind to deal with it once it became public knowledge, whether by official release or by just simply being exposed?"

Mr. McFarlane: "I know of no such plan." (Tower)

FEB 22 - It is reported that Fawn Hall, North's secretary for four years, has been given immunity in the Iran-contra affair by Independent Counsel Lawrence Walsh. (WP 2/22/87)

FEB 24 - North files suit against Meese and Independent Counsel Lawrence Walsh claiming that the law governing the selection of a special prosecutor is unconstitutional. The Ethics in Government Act, enacted in 1978, requires the Attorney General to apply to a special federal court to select an independent prosecutor, a process which North's attorneys argue violates the constitutional principle of separation of powers between the executive and judiciary branches of government. The suit is seen by some observers as an attempt to delay the investigation into North's activities in the NSC. (NYT 2/25/87)

FEB 26 - The President's Special Review Board releases its report.

FEB 27 - Reagan meets with Howard Baker to discuss Baker's taking over as White House chief of staff. After the 20-minute session, Baker accepts. Later in the afternoon, Carlucci is reported to rush into Donald Regan's office to inform him of Baker's appointment. Unaware of the news, Regan immediately has a one-sentence letter of resignation typed out and "storm[s] out" of the White House. (WP 2/28/87)

FEB 28 - It is reported that the Thatcher government has given preliminary approval to the sale of British-made "Blowpipe" antiaircraft missiles for use by the contras. The sale reportedly stems from an earlier deal negotiated by North and McFarlane. The British government denied selling Blowpipes to North or Secord but would not comment on the report that it was prepared to sell them to the CIA for the contras' use. At least 150 of the four foot long missiles and shoulder launchers would be included in the sale, which must still be approved by the CIA. Sources say the agency would pay for the missiles from the $100 million U.S. aid fund for the contras. Contra leader Adolfo Calero says that his army has not received the Blowpipes yet, but hopes that the deal will be concluded. (LAT 2/28/87)

MARCH - APRIL 1987

MAR 1 - The Rev. Lawrence Martin Jenco, a Lebanon hostage who was released in July 1986, tells reporters he questions President Reagan's credibility after the Tower report found that the priest's freedom was the result of a weapons deal. Jenco says he would rather have remained a hostage than be a bargaining chip in a weapons deal. "I had to accept his word that I was not exchanged for arms. Now . . . I have a deep question mark." (AP 3/1/87; WP 3/2/87)

MAR 2 - It is reported that Carl "Spitz" Channell has hired an accounting firm to examine the finances of his various lobbying and non-profit organizations in an effort to clear his name, according to two associates. J. Curtis Herge, general counsel for the National Endowment for the Preservation of Liberty (NEPL), and former Representative Dan H. Kuykendall, a paid consultant to Channell since August 1986, say Channell is determined to achieve "absolute vindication" of his role in the Iran-contra affair. According to Kuykendall, Channell is worried about "a level of concern among some of his contributors that he has to repair." Kuykendall adds that "Spitz Channell is absolutely convinced of his own innocence and up to this point he's convinced me of his innocence." (NYT 3/2/87)

- Bowing to congressional opposition, Reagan withdraws Robert Gates' nomination to replace William Casey as Director of Central Intelligence. It is reported that former Senator John Tower has refused Reagan's offer of the position and that a search for a replacement is continuing. (WP 3/3/87)

- Retired Gen. Richard Secord writes a three and a half page single-spaced letter to the counsel of Random House, the company which published Peter Maas's account of the renegade former CIA officer Edwin P. Wilson's case. Secord's letter disputes the book's references to his involvement in selling arms to the Iranian secret police under the Shah and in other activities, and denies that the Wilson episodes are related to the current investigations. Secord confirms that he and Albert Hakim own Stanford Technology Trading Group International in Virginia, and that he had talked with Thomas Clines, a former CIA officer identified as helping supply the contras. Legal authorities question whether Secord should have sent the letter while asserting his Fifth Amendment rights against testifying before Congress. (NYT 3/14/87)

MAR 3 - Contra leader Adolfo Calero testifies before a federal grand jury looking into the Iran-contra affair. He also makes available financial records of the FDN to Independent Counsel Lawrence Walsh. (NYT 3/6/87)

- Reagan nominates FBI head William Webster to succeed Casey as Director of Central Intelligence. Howard Baker and John Tower already turned down the job after Gates withdrew under fire. (WSJ 3/4/87)

MAR 4 - In a televised speech to the nation, Reagan responds to the report of the Special Review Board, admitting for the first time that selling arms to Iran in exchange for the freeing of American captives "was a mistake." He says his original intention was to establish an opening to new Iranian leaders but that the effort "deteriorated in its implementation into trading arms for hostages." Reagan acknowledges criticism of the Tower board, saying that his management of national security policy was inadequate. "When it came to managing the NSC staff . . . my style didn't match its previous track record," he says, accepting "full responsibility for my own actions and for those of my Administration" in the Iran-contra affair. He states that he is adopting all of the Tower report's recommendations and outlines a number of specific steps he will take, including undertaking a review of all government covert activities, directing that the NSC will be prohibited from such operations, and reforming national security policy-making procedures. He says he will report to Congress by the end of March on the progress of these measures. (Transcript of Reagan address in LAT 3/5/87)

- Poindexter receives an automatic demotion from a three-star vice admiral to a two-star rear admiral. He is assigned to the long-range planning staff of the Chief of Naval Operations. He received his third star when he began working at the White House in 1985. After leaving the NSC for his current post, which is of lower stature, he would require specific approval from the White House within 90 days of his transfer in order to retain the third star. (LAT 3/4/87)

MAR 5 - Adolfo Calero says that during the period of the congressional ban on aid to the rebels, Richard Secord was one of three intermediaries who provided a total of around $18 million in arms. The other two, according to Calero, were John Singlaub and James L. McCoy, who was a defense attache at the U.S. embassy in Managua when the Sandinistas took power. Calero says the contras obtained about $8 million or $9 million from Secord himself. (WP 3/7/87; NYT 3/6/87)

MAR 8 - Adnan Khashoggi, in an interview in Paris, says that he has "played games within games"—including the invention of the two Canadian investors—in his dealings with CIA director and other U.S. officials. In addition, the Saudi claims he paid Manucehr Ghorbanifar throughout his participation in the arms deals and that he was responsible for introducing the Iranian middleman to the Israelis, who in turn brought him together with American officials. In the interview, Khashoggi also states that investigators have only been able to find and freeze six of his bank accounts totaling $60 million in assets. FBI investigators were hampered by

Khashoggi's "games," which included telling them that his financial records were buried in the sand under seven hills in the Saudi Arabian desert. Further, records of Khashoggi's dealings reviewed during the interview suggest that previously unreported Khashoggi firms, such as Trivet and Garnet, were used to transfer funds to both Lake Resources and Ghorbanifar.

Khashoggi also says that he spoke recently with Ghorbanifar, Roy Furmark, and Amiram Nir, and the four agreed that the Tower Commission and Senate intelligence committee reports had erred in stating that millions of dollars of proceeds from the Iran arms deals had moved through Ghorbanifar and Khashoggi. He also criticized the Tower Commission report for suggesting that creditors who were the beneficiaries of a life insurance policy on Ghorbanifar had threatened to kill Ghorbanifar, although he disclosed that he had taken out a short term life insurance policy on the Iranian for $22 million. (NYT 3/10/87)

MAR 9 - The White House renews Reagan's request of December 16, 1986 that Congress grant limited immunity to Poindexter and North. (NYT 3/10/87)

MAR 10 - United Nicaraguan Opposition leader Arturo Cruz turns in his resignation letter to two newspapers in San Jose, Costa Rica without warning U.S. officials or other members of the UNO directorate. Other contra officials concede that the resignation dims their prospects for winning additional U.S. aid, since Cruz was seen by Congress as the most politically moderate member of the contra leadership. (LAT 3/11/87)

MAR 11 - The House and Senate select investigating committees vote to grant immunity to Hakim, who is believed to have extensive knowledge of the complex financial networks involved in the Iran/contra affair. He is also believed to be out of the country. Two days later, it is reported that Walsh has decided to exercise his right to delay the immunity for up to 30 days. (LAT 3/12/87; WP 3/12/87 & 3/13/87)

- The House of Representatives votes 230-196 to suspend further aid to the contras until President Reagan accounts for the money previously provided. Secretary of State George Shultz tells a Congressional committee that the State Department still cannot account for $10 million solicited from the Sultan of Brunei for the contras. The House vote, largely symbolic since it does not actually cut off money to the contras, still indicates the extent to which the House has turned against Reagan policy on Nicaragua. Nine months ago the House voted 221-209 in favor of aid to the contras. (NYT 3/12/87)

MAR 12 - A U.S. District Court judge dismisses Oliver North's two lawsuits challenging the constitutionality of the independent counsel. Judge Barrington Parker holds that North has no grounds for complaint as yet, and, if he did, would probably lose his case on the merits. (WP 3/13/87; WSJ 3/13/87)

MAR 14 - In President Reagan's weekly radio address, he says he should have listened to Secretary of State Shultz and Secretary of Defense Weinberger when they told him to stop selling arms to Iran. "As we now know, it turned out they were right and I was wrong," Reagan says. (NYT 3/15/87)

- It is reported that the private, federally funded National Endowment for Democracy (NED) has decided to cease funding the Institute for North-South Issues, a company active in the Carribean founded in 1983 and whose director for operations is International Business Communications president Richard Miller. Both INSI and IBC show up on North's chart of companies in the private contra supply network, and NED president Carl Gershman says NED hasn't found any wrongdoing by INSI but wishes to distance itself from the controversy. INSI has received $444,000 from NED.(AP in WP 3/14/87)

MAR 15 - Bush, in an interview on the CBS News show "60 Minutes," repeatedly denies having any knowledge of North's activities in support of the contras. He states that he did not know that his national security advisor, Donald Gregg, met frequently with CIA operative Felix Rodriguez, who helped direct arms deliveries from El Salvador to the contras. (MH 3/15/87 & 3/16/87; WP 3/16/87)

MAR 18 - House and Senate committees investigating the Iran-contra affair vote to grant immunity to six more witnesses, including Robert Earl, Robert Owen, and Richard Gadd. Under an agreement reached with Independent Counsel Lawrence Walsh, the panels also agree to vote in April to grant limited immunity to John Poindexter and to wait until

June 15, at the earliest, on voting on immunity for Oliver North. (WSJ 3/19/87; WP 3/18/87; FT 3/19/87)

MAR 19 - Reagan renounces his Iran policy in his first news conference in four months, stating that "I would not go down that road again" if given the opportunity. He says, however, "I will keep my eyes open for any opportunity for improving relations, and we will continue every legitimate means of getting our hostages back..." Reagan also again emphatically denies that he had any knowledge of the diversion of funds to the rebels in Nicaragua from the secret sale of U.S. arms to Iran. (NYT 3/20/87)

- Saudi financier Adnan Khashoggi says in an interview with the Washington Times that he had sent Vice President George Bush a $1,000 contribution for the contras after Bush invited him to a fundraising lunch during a period when Congress had prohibited U.S. government aid to the contras. "My No. 2, Bob Shaheen, called me and said the vice president had asked me to lunch. I asked Bob what was the occasion, and he said Mr. Bush was raising funds for Nicaragua. So I told Bob: 'Send him $1,000.' And I received a very nice letter from the vice president thanking me for my contribution." Bush denies the claim. (LAT 3/20/87; WP 3/20/8; WSJ 3/20/87)

- After telling Israeli officials only that he was taking a two-week vacation in London, Nir flies to London and then on to Switzerland, where he meets Ghorbanifar. Nir claims he accidentally ran into the Iranian at the airport. (NYT 3/30/87)

MAR 23-25 - Republican Senators filibuster in order to prevent passage of a bill to block further military funding to the contras. Votes to halt the filibuster fail, 46-45, 50-50 and 54-46 to muster the three-fifths majority needed. (NYT 3/25/87; WP 3/25/87; LAT 3/26/87)

MAR 28 - A press report indicates that Casey personally oversaw North's efforts to supply and train the contras, and sources say he tried to act largely outside of his role as director of the CIA. Casey lent CIA staff and equipment to the campaign, and intelligence sources concede that while personnel tried desperately to stay within the letter of the law, slip-ups were not infrequent. (LAT 3/28/87)

MAR 29 - Independent Counsel Lawrence Walsh has begun to survey the complete history of U.S. assistance to the Nicaraguan opposition, rather than just the specifics of the arms deals with Iran and the funneling of profits to the contras. The inquiry now includes the CIA's role in supporting the guerrillas, its involvement in the mining of Nicaraguan harbors in 1984, and the distribution of a handbook for the rebels advocating the "neutralization" of Nicaraguan officials. (NYT 3/30/87)

MAR 30 - The GAO reports that President Reagan is responsible for failing to inform Congress about the covert arms sales to Iran that "ordinarily" would have been "subject to Congressional notification requirements." The GAO also confirmed the findings of a Pentagon investigation in January that the CIA, which served as a middleman in the deals, was undercharged by the Army for the weapons, although the amount of the undercharge is found to be $2.1 million, $500,000 less than previously thought. (WP 3/31/87; NYT 3/31/87)

MAR 31 - Reagan issues a directive prohibiting NSC members from engaging in covert activities. He also orders that his National Security Advisor, Frank Carlucci, review all covert operations and propose changes in procedures for approving and coordinating such operations by April 30. (WP 4/1/87)

APR 1 - The Reagan Administration has rejected a request from Iraq for C-130 aircraft and artillery radar, U.S. officials report. The U.S., however, continues to provide the Iraqis with intelligence data on Iranian deployments gathered by American reconnaissance satellites. (NYT 4/2/87)

APR 7 - The FBI and Office of the Independent Counsel are examining the activities of Attorney General Edwin Meese during the "non-criminal" inquiry he conducted in November 1986 to determine if they constitute an obstruction of justice. (WP 4/8/87)

APR 8 - FBI Director William Webster testifies at confirmation hearings before the Senate intelligence panel on his nomination to become Director of Central Intelligence. He admits for the first time that the day after Attorney General Meese asked on behalf of Poindexter that the FBI suspend its investigation of Southern Air Transport's contra aid activities (said to be managed by Oliver North), Department of Justice intelligence policy chief Mary Lawton requested that routine FBI information not be passed to the NSC staff member. Lawton informed Webster she felt North could come under investigation by a special prosecutor for his involvement with contra support. Webster claims he did not associate the two requests. (Webster testimony 4/8/87 & 4/9/87)

- The contras received between $83 and $97 million in support between 1984 and 1986, more than $20 million of which cannot be accounted for and nearly twice what they needed for the war effort, according to a review of their finances. Oliver North's repeated assertions in memos that the contras were desperately lacking in funds raises suspicions that North funneled money to Project Democracy companies for the contras. The $10 million donation from the Sultan of Brunei to Secord's Lake Resources, Inc. may have gone to pay off debts, bribe Honduran officials and aid anticommunist rebels in Afghanistan and Angola it is reported. (NYT 4/8/87)

THE CONGRESSIONAL COMMITTEES

U.S. Senate Select Committee on Secret Military Assistance to Iran and the Nicaraguan Opposition

Democrats

Inouye, Daniel K. (HI),
   Chair
Boren, David L. (OK)
Heflin, Howell (AL)
Mitchell, George J. (ME)
Nunn, Sam (GA)
Sarbanes, Paul S. (MD)

Republicans

Rudman, Warren B. (NH),
   Vice-Chair
Cohen, William S. (ME)
Hatch, Orrin G. (UT)
McClure, James A. (ID)
Trible, Paul S., Jr. (VA)

U.S. House of Representatives Select Committee to Investigate Covert Arms Transactions with Iran

Democrats

Hamilton, Lee H. (IN),
   Chair
Fascell, Dante B. (FL),
   Vice-Chair
Foley, Thomas S. (WA)
Rodino, Peter W., Jr. (NJ)
Brooks, Jack (TX)
Stokes, Louis (OH)
Aspin, Les (WI)
Boland, Edward P. (MA)
Jenkins, Ed (GA)

Republicans

Cheney, Dick (WY)
Broomfield, William S. (MI)
Hyde, Henry J. (IL)
Courter, Jim (NJ)
McCollum, Bill (FL)
DeWine, Michael (OH)

Glossary

a/c: Aircraft

ACE: Amalgamated Commercial Enterprises

AID: Agency for International Development

AMC: Army Materiel Command

AMCITS: American citizens

AIPAC: American-Israel Public Affairs Committee

ANTEL: The El Salvadoran telephone company

ARDE: Alianza Revolucionaria Democratica, a Costa Rican-based contra group formerly headed by Eden Pastora

Arms Export Control Act: Legislation governing the export of arms from the United States, including reporting requirements to the Congress

AWACS: Airborne Warning and Control System

Big Pine I/II: Joint U.S.-Honduras military maneuvers, 1983

Blowpipe: Portable British-made anti-aircraft missile system

Boland Amendment: Legislation forbidding the CIA and DOD from dispensing funds for the purposes of "overthrowing the Government of Nicaragua or provoking a military exchange between Nicaragua and Honduras"

Burn Notice: CIA bulletin identifying subject as unreliable and to be avoided

CANAC: Nicaraguan Anti-Communist Aid Committee, a Miami-based, Cuban exile group

CATF: Central American Task Force, CIA

CASI: Corporate Air Services, Inc.

CIA: Central Intelligence Agency

CIA/IG: Central Intelligence Agency, Inspector General

CINC/SOUTHCOM: Commander-in-Chief, U.S. Southern Command

CJCS: Chairman of the Joint Chiefs of Staff

CMA: Civilian Military Assistance

C/NE: Chief of Near East Division, Directorate of Operations, CIA

C/NE (I): Iran Branch, Directorate of Operations, Central Intelligence Agency

CNN: Cable News Network

Col Q: Colonel Khaddafi

CONDOR: Nicaraguan Coalition of Opposition to the Regime

Contadora Process: Attempt to negotiate a settlement to the Central American conflict led by Mexico, Colombia, Venezuela and Panama

Core Group: An NSC interagency group also known as the Thursday Afternoon Club and the Restricted Interagency Group

CP: Command post

CPPG: Crisis Pre-Planning Group, an inter-agency group set up under the auspices of NSC

CRS: Catholic Relief Services

CSF: Compagnie de Services Fiduciares, SA

DCI: Director of Central Intelligence

DCM: Deputy Chief of Mission

DC/NE: Deputy Chief, Near East Division, Directorate of Operations, CIA

DDCI: Deputy Director of Central Intelligence

DDI: Deputy Director of Intelligence, CIA

DDO: Deputy Director for Operations, CIA

DEA: Drug Enforcement Agency

Demavand project: Effort to channel American arms to Iran through private individuals

Democracy Inc.: Corporation/effort tied to Oliver North and the Iran-contra operations. See also Project Democracy.

DIA: Defense Intelligence Agency

DO: Directorate of Operations, CIA

DOD: Department of Defense

DRB: Defense Resources Board

DRF: Democratic resistance forces, contras

DSAA: Defense Security Assistance Agency

DT: Data transmission

EATSCO: Egyptian American Transport and Services Corporation

EDA: European Defense Associates

El Op: Israel Electric Optical Industry

EUC: End-user certificate

EUCOM: U.S. European Command

FAA: Federal Aviation Administration

FARN: Nicaraguan Revolutionary Armed Forces, a Nicaraguan rebel force based in Costa Rica

FBI: Federal Bureau of Investigation

FDN: Nicaraguan Democratic Force, the largest Nicaraguan rebel group, Honduras-based

FOMIN: Foreign Ministry

FM: Foreign Minister

FMS: Foreign Military Sales, U.S. military assistance credit program

GAO: Government Accounting Office

GOI: Government of Israel, Government of Iran, depending on context

Gorba: Manuchehr Ghorbanifar

Halcon Vista: Joint U.S.-Honduras military exercise

HARPOON: cruise missile capable of being launched from a variety of platforms

HAWK: Homing-All-the-Way Killer missile, a ground-launched, anti-aircraft missile

H/CATF: Head, Central American Task Force, CIA

HLTF: Hostage Location Task Force, CIA

IAD: Dulles International Airport

IAF: Israeli Air Force

IAW: In accordance with

IBC: International Business Communications, Inc.

I.C., Inc.: Intel Co-Operation, Inc.

ICRC: International Committee of the Red Cross

IDEA, Inc.: Institute for Democracy, Education and Assistance, Inc.

IDF: Israeli Defense Force

IG: Interagency Group

IHIPIR: Radar system

IJO: Islamic Jihad Organization

INS: Immigration and Naturalization Service

IPAC: International Planning and Analysis Center, Inc.

IRG: Iranian Revolutionary Guard

IRGC: Iranian Revolutionary Guard Corps

ISA: Intelligence Support Activity

JCS: Joint Chiefs of Staff

JMP: John M. Poindexter

JSOC: Joint Special Operations Command, Fort Bragg

KGB: Komitet Gosudarstvennoi Bezopasnosti (Committee for State Security), Soviet intelligence and security agency

Kisan: Miskito Indian faction, one of three associated with the contras and a recipient of NHAO funding

LAF: Lebanese Armed Forces

LebNap: U.S. citizens kidnapped in Lebanon

LOA: Letter of Offer and Acceptance, contract between United States government and foreign countries purchasing U.S. arms financed through security assistance

LTC: Lieutenant Colonel

MAC: U.S. Military Airlift Command

Majlis: Iranian Parliament

MEMCON: Memorandum of conversation

MGEN: Major General

MOD: Israeli Ministry of Defense

Mod HAWKS: Modified HAWK missiles

MOU: Memorandum of Understanding

NARWACL: North American World Anti-Communist League

NATO: North Atlantic Treaty Organization

NED: National Endowment for Democracy

NEPL: National Endowment for the Preservation of Liberty

NESA: Bureau of Near Eastern and South Asian Affairs, CIA

Neutrality Act: Legislation prohibiting persons in the U.S. from knowingly financing, organizing, or carrying out hostile acts against foreign powers with which the U.S. is at peace

NHAO: Nicaraguan Humanitarian Assistance Office, Department of State

NIACT: National Intelligence Agency Communications Terminal

nlt: No later than

NSA: National Security Agency

NSC: National Security Council

NSDD: National Security Decision Directive

NSPG: National Security Planning Group

OB: Order of battle

O/DDO: Office of the Deputy Director for Operations, CIA

OEOB: Old Executive Office Building

OLN: Oliver L. North

OPEC: Organization of Petroleum Exporting Countries

Operation Elephant Herd: Secret, joint CIA-military plan to bypass congressional restrictions to aid the contras

Operation Staunch: U.S. State Department program to discourage countries from selling arms to Iran, regarded as a terrorist state

OPIC: Overseas Private Investment Corporation

OPSEC: Operations security

OSD: Office of the Secretary of Defense

OSG: Operations Sub-Group, inter-agency group to coordinate counterterrorism activities, headed by Oliver North

PHOENIX: Air-to-air missile

Phoenix Battalion: Alleged covert paramilitary group organized by Sam Nesley Hall at the direction of the Pentagon

PIP: Product Improvement Package

PLO: Palestine Liberation Organization

PM: Prime Minister

Project Democracy (a.k.a. PRODEM, PD, Democracy Inc.): Series of undercover operations run by Lt. Col. Oliver North, including the hostage deals with Iran. Democracy Inc. is sometimes referred to as a corporation tied to the Iran-contra effort.

PROF: Professional Office System, an interoffice computer mail system managed by the White House Communications Agency and the NSC

Project Recovery: Covert dealings with Iran designed to rescue Americans held hostage in Lebanon

PRT-250: Sophisticated multi-channel radio communications system capable of transmitting voice and text in code via satellite

p/u: pick up

PWR: Prepositioned war reserves

RCM: Robert C. McFarlane

RDVU: Rendezvous

RIG: Restricted Interagency Group, also known as the Core Group, the Thursday Afternoon Club, and occasionally as a SIG

RR: President Ronald W. Reagan

SAR: Search-and-rescue

SAT: Southern Air Transport

SATCOM: Satellite communications

SAVAK: Iranian secret police force during the period of Shah Mohammed Reza Pahlavi

SIG: Senior Interagency Group, see also RIG

SIGINT: Signals intelligence

SNIE: Special National Intelligence Estimate

SOUTHCOM: United States Southern Command, located in Panama

SRB: President's Special Review Board, the Tower Commission

SSIC: Senate Select Committee on Intelligence

STOL: Short takeoff and landing aircraft

TAYACAN: Pseudonymous author of the CIA's "Psychological Operations in Guerrilla Warfare" drafted for the contras in 1983

TIWG: Terrorist Incident Working Group (NSC)

TOR: Terms of reference

TOW: Tube-launched, Optically-tracked, Wire-guided missile

UCLA: Unilaterally controlled Latino assets

UNO: United Nicaraguan Opposition, the Nicaraguan rebel umbrella group

UNODIR: Unless Otherwise Directed

USAF: United States Air Force

USG: United States Government

USIA: United States Information Agency

VADM: Vice Admiral

VOA: Voice of America

VP: Vice President George Bush

WACL: World Anti-Communist League

Index